Converging Media

An Introduction to Mass Communication

Converging Media

An Introduction to Mass Communication

John Pavlik
Rutgers University

Shawn McIntosh
Iona College

PEARSON

Boston · New York · San Francisco · Mexico City · Montreal
Toronto · London · Madrid · Munich · Paris · Hong Kong
Singapore · Tokyo · Cape Town · Sydney

To my wife, Jackie, and
my daughters, Tristan and Orianna.
—J.V.P.

To my parents, Dennis and Kathie.
—S.M.

Series Editor: Molly Taylor
Senior Development Editor: Carol Alper
Editorial Assistant: Michael Kish
Production Supervisor: Joe Sweeney
Marketing Manager: Mandee Eckersley
Editorial–Production Service: Heckman & Pinette
Composition and Prepress Buyer: Linda Cox
Manufacturing Buyer: Megan Cochran
Cover Administrator: Linda Knowles
Text Designer: Joyce C. Weston
Photo Researcher: Sarah Evertson, ImageQuest
Electronic Composition: Monotype Composition

For related titles and support materials, visit our online catalog at www.ablongman.com

Between the time Web site information is gathered and published, some sites may have closed. The publisher would appreciate notification where these occur so that they may be corrected in subsequent editions.

ISBN: 0-205-30803-1

Printed in the United States of America
10 9 8 7 6 5 4 3 2 1 VHP 09 08 07 06 05 04 03

Contents

PART 1   THE CHANGING MEDIA LANDSCAPE

Chapter 2   Media Literacy and Ethics   34

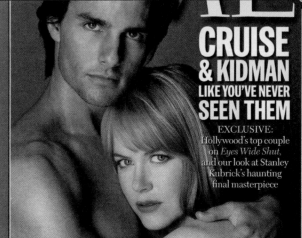

PART 2 MASS COMMUNICATION FORMATS

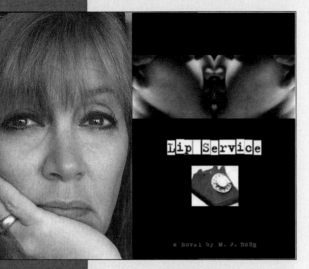

Chapter 3 Books, Newspapers, and Magazines 64

Chapter 4   Photography and Movies   102

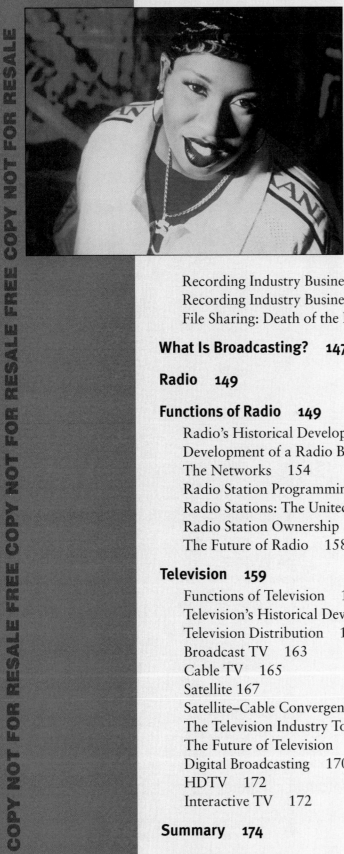

Chapter 5 Music Recordings, Radio, and Television 136

Chapter 6 Digital Media: Online and Ubiquitous 176

PART
3   HOW DIGITAL MEDIA ARE CHANGING OUR WORLD

Chapter 8 User Interface: Interacting with Digital Content 246

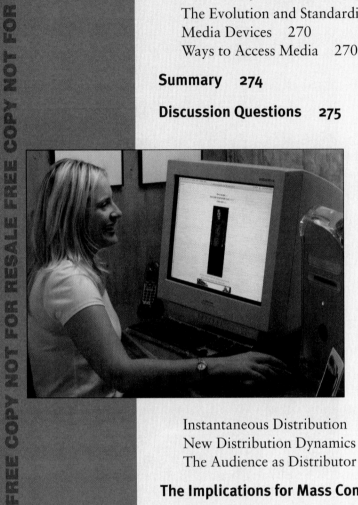

Chapter 9 Bringing the Masses to Mass Communication: Distribution of Digital Content 276

PART 4 MEDIA PERSPECTIVES

Chapter 10 Journalism 306

PART 5 MEDIA: THE LARGER VIEW

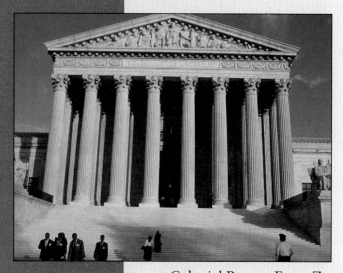

Chapter 14 Communication Law and Regulation in the Digital Age 452

Chapter 16 Media and Convergence: International Perspectives   510

Preface

Today we live in two media worlds. There is the traditional media world of newspapers, magazines, books, film, music, radio, and TV that we are all familiar with, and there is the digital media world that is absorbing and transforming all these media types and changing the ways we use them.

Digital media are not simply new chapters to be added in a book on mass communication—they constitute a major revision in how we perceive, understand, and work with the media of mass communication. *Converging Media: An Introduction to Mass Communication* reflects the dramatic changes that are taking place yet puts them within the context of mass communication theories, industries, issues, and practices. In order to understand the future of media and mass communication, we must understand how they developed and how they are being used today—and changed—by digitization and the Internet.

There are three basic approaches to teaching media and mass communication in the early 21st century. One approach is to ignore the changes digital media have brought and simply teach the subject as it has been taught. However, this is becoming increasingly hard to do, as digital media become more important and prevalent. Another approach is to reject traditional media practices and principles and declare a new digital utopia. This too is hard to justify while newsstands brim with newspapers, magazines, and books and while people still spend several hours a day watching plain, old-fashioned TV.

Converging Media represents a third way to teach modern mass communication. It integrates existing elements of the old with the new terms and principles of digital media and the Internet. For young people who live comfortably in the digital media world, the book explains the principles and trends behind the media they are using. For people still apprehensive about what digital media and the Internet seem to bring, it puts them within their proper contexts within the world of mass communication.

This book is a bridge between old media practices and new media practices, many of which are rapidly changing. That is why a companion Web site provides some of the latest information on important developments in the digital media world. Students will be able to learn the principles discussed in the book and then visit the Web site to see how those principles were applied (or not applied) by real-world companies they see and hear about in the news every day.

How This Book Is Organized

To meet the needs of teaching a course from our unique perspective, we wrote a book with a unique organization.

Part 1: The Changing Media Landscape provides some of the basic theories of mass communication and introduces basic concepts of digital communication, showing how the two areas interrelate. Media literacy is more important than ever in helping students learn to think critically about the media, and examples of ethical issues raised by media industry practices are raised. **Chapter 1: Mass Communication and Its Digital Transformation** explains underlying basic theories of mass communication, such as transmission models, as well as basic elements of digitization of media content, showing how convergence of media, computers, and telecommunications is transforming mass communication. **Chapter 2: Media Literacy and Ethics,** explains the importance of media literacy not only in terms of using traditional media but also considering how it becomes crucial in a changing media world. Students can apply critical thinking and media literacy to some examples of media ethics issues and ethical principles used in media.

Part 2: Mass Communication Formats covers the traditional media formats, their historical development, and their various transformations in the digital age. It puts digital media in perspective of traditional media and their evolution. **Chapter 3: Books, Newspapers, and Magazines** presents a historical review of the development of print media and how that development fits into larger current trends of mass communication and technology. By seeing how printing technology had much of the same effect that the Internet does, it puts the development of this oldest of mass media in a historical and current context. How books, newspapers, and magazines may further evolve and the challenges they face in an online, digital environment are examined. **Chapter 4: Photography and Movies** presents a historical review of the development of photography and movies and how their development fits into larger current trends of mass communication and technology. In many ways, the earliest days of movies can be compared to the early days of the World Wide Web, in which technological constraints limit the medium but are also a driving force in its development. **Chapter 5: Music Recordings, Radio, and Television** is a historical review of the development of music recording, radio, and television and how their development fits into larger current trends of mass communication and technology. It explains how these are tied together not only in production and promotional aspects, but how digitization is affecting them all, although the music industry currently faces the brunt of transformative changes and is most threatened by digitization. **Chapter 6: Digital Media: Online and Ubiquitous** reinforces that digital media are not simply "new types" of media but that they encompass all types of media before them and have media properties that analog media simply do not have. It covers a brief historical review of certain aspects of technology that have not been covered in earlier chapters and looks at potential problems digital media have as well as promises they hold for the future.

The topics covered in this section are not typically covered in a course in mass communication, but **Part 3: How Digital Media Are Changing Our**

World provides the intellectual foundation to understand how digital media work in mass communication and society. **Chapter 7: Storing, Representing, and Retrieving Digital Content** explains the importance of storage technology throughout the history of media, not just with digital media, and puts the advances made with computerized and optical storage technologies into a historical perspective of mass communication. Storage, representation, and retrieval of digital content will continue to play an important role in the evolution of digital media in a mass communication context. **Chapter 8: User Interface: Interacting with Digital Content** explains the difference between passive media consumers in the analog media world and active media users on the Internet and how the user interface plays an important role in encouraging new patterns of media use. It explores new types of user interfaces with media content and the many weaknesses media users still face when interacting with digital content, many of which hinder the development of the field. **Chapter 9: Bringing the Masses to Mass Communication: Distribution of Digital Content** explains a crucial element of digital content using Napster and file sharing services as real-world examples—the fact that anyone can now become a distributor of digital content at low cost online. This threatens traditional media business models and raises issues of privacy, First Amendment rights, and copyright, among other legal and business issues. Various online communities are explained and the role they play in moving the public from a centralized mass media system to a largely decentralized one.

Part 4: Media Perspectives examines the three main mass communication fields from a historical context and explains how digital media are changing each field. Ethical issues within each area are examined, in addition to workplace issues such as the problems of diversity. **Chapter 10: Journalism** explains the role journalism plays in a larger mass communication context, its historical development, ethical issues, and the changes digital media are bringing to the profession. Different styles of journalism are examined, as well as how new technologies can be applied by working journalists in order to better report the news. **Chapter 11: Entertainment** explains how entertainment is an important part of a larger mass communication context and looks at various types of entertainment, such as sports, arts, and video games, and the roles they play for the public. It looks at how digitization is changing many aspects of the entertainment industry, from production to its basic business models, as well as the changing relationships between different entertainment industries. **Chapter 12: Advertising and Public Relations** explains the roles and historical development of advertising and public relations as well as basic persuasive communication theories. Advertising and PR agencies and the business aspect of these types of mass communication are discussed, as well as changes digitization is bringing to them and ethical issues that arise from advertising and PR.

Media and society have long had powerful effects on each other, and this section, **Part 5: Media: The Larger View,** discusses some of the past research on media effects, political communications, and regulations and legal issues. How digital media and the Internet are fundamentally changing some of these issues is examined, with information on likely important issues to watch for the future. **Chapter 13: Media Research and Effects: From Film to the Internet** explains basic principles of media research and effects on society, especially with 20th-century media from film, radio, TV, and the Internet. It examines specific famous studies and what they tell us about media effects, looking at implications these might have in the digital media world, such as playing video games or spending time on the Internet. **Chapter 14: Communication Law and Regulation in the Digital Age** explains basics about communication law and regulation, starting with an overview of various First Amendment issues and going through to the regulatory development during the early days of radio and creation of the FCC and into television regulation and new initiatives toward regulating the Internet. It examines privacy, security, and copyright issues in light of recent court cases involving digital media. **Chapter 15: Mass Communication and Politics in the Digital Age** examines the role the media play in the American political process and general theories about how media affect that process. It explains how the Internet is starting to change the traditional media and political patterns not only by allowing politicians to speak directly with constituents, but also allowing activists to better organize and distribute their messages without using centralized or traditional media channels. **Chapter 16: Media and Convergence: International Perspectives** is a brief look at other political theories of communication in other government systems. It also provides a general overview of the international arena and specific countries in terms of what types of media they have, their level of Internet use, and what practices they follow that U.S. media consumers could possibly learn from.

■ Opening vignette

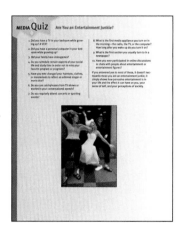

■ Media Quiz

Special Features

The boxed feature program in *Converging Media* offers examples and applications of key media issues from the digital perspective and helps students retain knowledge.

- **Opening vignettes** with related photos connect the new-media theme to the chapter content in a student-friendly way.

- **Media Quizzes** provide light-hearted quiz questions to measure students' media or tech savviness and spark their interest in digital media.

- **Media Inventors and Innovators** boxes tell the stories of real people whose inventions and innovations have had an important impact on some aspect of the media or mass communication.

- **Real World Media Ethics Dilemma** boxes present ethical issues and questions for students to consider or serve as springboards for class discussion.

- **Media Future** boxes anticipate trends expected to affect media in the (not so distant) future.

■ Inventors and Innovations

■ **Real World Media Ethics Dilemma**

■ **Media Future**

■ **Media Technology**

- **Media Technology** boxes look at how technology works and define technological concepts in media. Important but complex technological discussions are taken out of the main text for closer examination.

- **Media Spotlight** boxes discuss media organizations, anecdotes, or technology, as well as social issues involving media.

- **Weblinks** lead the student to related Internet sites for additional information on selected topics.

Many tools in *Converging Media* are specifically designed to help the student learn the material.

- **Chapter objectives** provide students a framework within which to read and organize the chapter material.

- **Key terms** are set in boldface type, and their definitions in the margins act as a glossary that familiarizes students with important concepts in the chapter.

- **Media Timelines** outline a list of dates and media events to help students put the events into a historical context.

- End-of-chapter **Summaries** provide students with a helpful study tool that reinforces their understanding of the material. This tool relates directly back to the objectives found at the beginning of the chapter.

- **Discussion Questions** equip students with the opportunity to think critically about the material they just read and to deepen their understanding of that material.

Resources for Instructors

An integrated package of supplemental materials is designed to help demystify teaching with *Converging Media*. Some instructors who find themselves in a classroom full of media-savvy students may feel uneasy about teaching the new media. The *Converging Media* package of resources for instructors is designed to allay these fears.

- The **Instructor's Manual** offers a wealth of resources, including lecture launchers, learning objectives, lecture outlines, discussion topics, and suggested activities.

- The **Test Bank** contains multiple choice, true–false, and essay questions to help the instructors accurately assess their students' mastery of the material.

- The **Computerized Test Bank** provides the test questions electronically through our computerized testing system, TestGen EQ. The fully networkable test-generating software is now available in a multiplatform CD-ROM. The user-friendly interface enables instructors to view, edit, and add questions, transfer questions to tests, and print tests in a variety of fonts. Search and sort features allow instructors to locate questions quickly and arrange them in a preferred order.

- The **PowerPoint**™ **package**, which is available on the Web site at http://suppscentral.ablongman.com, is designed to help organize lectures. It can be personalized to meet the needs of a particular class or used as is. The package is compatible with Windows and Macintosh systems.

- The **Allyn & Bacon Interactive Video** brings media issues to life in your classroom. Encompassing a wide range of media issues and problems, this supplement features specially selected news segments complete with commentary and on-screen critical thinking questions. A printed guide will help you integrate the video program into your curriculum effectively. Some restrictions apply.

- The **Allyn & Bacon Communication Studies Digital Media Archive, Version 2.0** is available on CD-ROM and offers more than 200 still images, video excerpts, and PowerPoint slides that can be used to enliven classroom presentations.

- **Blockbuster Video Guide for Introductory Mass Communication Classes,** prepared by Deborah Petersen-Perlman, University of Minnesota, Duluth, assists teachers in reaching today's students through film and video to convey basic media concepts, illustrate complex interrelationships, and present historical facts.

■ Media Spotlight

- Cartridges for **CourseCompass for Mass Communication** are available as course management tools. CourseCompass is powered by Blackboard and is hosted nationally as Allyn & Bacon's own course management system. CourseCompass helps you manage all aspects of teaching your course. The mass communication course features preloaded content such as quiz questions, video clips, instructor's manuals, PowerPoint presentations, still images, course preparation and instruction materials, weblinks and much more! This course provides an abundance of resources to help you effectively teach and manage your class in the CourseCompass environment. Go to www.coursecompass.com for more information.

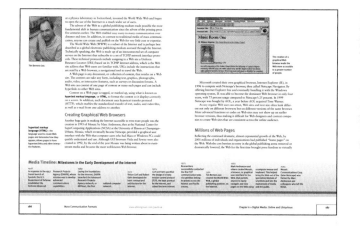

■ Media Timelines

- The **A&B Mass Communication Video Library** and the **Movie Library** offer adopters of this text access to two rich libraries: (1) a set of videos about the media, created through Insight Media and Films for the Humanities; and (2) the *Movie Library,* featuring popular entertainment movies that can be used to illustrate key media topics and issues. Some restrictions apply.

Resources for Students

- Because the media are ever-changing, no book can possibly stay up to date. The **Companion Web Site with Online Practice Tests,** available at www.ablongman.com/pavlik1e, contains periodic updates of content, weblinks for the URLs included in the text, and interactive activities, plus multiple choice and true–false practice tests.

- The entire book is also available as an **e-book** in PDF format in the Course-Compass course management system, online at www.coursecompass.com. Access codes are required and can be packaged with the text for no additional charge. Your instructor will provide the information you need to log on, register, and begin using the system.

- **Research Navigator Guide for Mass Communication,** by Ronald Roat of Southern Indiana University, includes tips, resources, activities, and URLs to help students. The first part introduces students to the basics of the Internet and the World Wide Web. Part two includes over 30 Net activities that tie into the content of the text. Part three lists hundreds of WWW resources for mass communication. The guide also includes information on how to correctly cite research and a guide to building an online glossary. In addition, the Reasearch Navigation Guide booklet contains a student access code for the Research Navigator database, offering students free, unlimited access to a collection of 25,000+ discipline-specific articles from top-tier academic publications and peer-reviewed journals, as well as popular news publications and the *New York Times*. This is available packaged with new copies of the text.

- The **Media Literacy Guide,** prepared by Ralph Carmode, Jacksonville State University, helps students use critical thinking skills to develop an awareness and understanding of how and why the media and their messages affect us.

Acknowledgments

Writing a textbook on mass communication while keeping abreast of rapidly changing technology, media regulations, and changes in ownership can often feel a bit like trying to go up a down escalator. It is easy to get lost in the details and forget the larger picture, yet difficult to give enough detail to make examples meaningful. We are especially grateful to the many reviewers who made detailed comments on early drafts of the chapters, pointed out weak areas or points that needed clarifying or correcting, and offered encouragement that we were at least heading in the right direction with this book: Jerome Aumente, Rutgers University; Robert Bellamy, Duquesne University;

Gerald Boyer, Maryville University; Mark Braun, Gustavus Adolphus College; Margaret Cassidy, Adelphi University; Steven Chappell, Truman State University; Joseph R. Chuk, Kutztown University; Vic Costello, Gardner-Webb University; David Gordon, University of Wisconsin–Eau Claire; Charlotte Kwok Glasser, College of Notre Dame; Colin Gromatzky, New Mexico State University; Steven Keeler, Cayuga College (SUNY); Yasue Kuwahara, Northern Kentucky University; Dianne Lamb, Georgia Southern University; Mitchell Land, University of North Texas; Jeremy Harris Lipschultz, University of Nebraska–Omaha; Arthur Lizie, Bridgewater State College; John Lule, Lehigh University; Thomas McPhail, University of Missouri; Anthony A. Olorunnisola, Penn State University; Kathleen K. Olson, Lehigh University; Ronald C. Roat, University of Southern Indiana; Marshel D. Rossow, Mankato State University; Andris Straumanis, University of Wisconsin–Eau Claire; L. Lee Thomas, Doane College; and Max Utsler, University of Kansas.

We would like to thank the editors at Allyn & Bacon for their support, advice, and encouragement. Executive editor Karon Bowers, who first persuaded us to write this book, helped us focus a vision for the project. Development editor Carol Alper's excellent eye for organizational weaknesses and perfectly timed sending of homemade cookies helped us get through finishing the chapters. We are also grateful for the encouragement series editor Molly Taylor gave us throughout the process and the excellent marketing efforts by marketing manager Mandee Eckersley. Photo researcher Sarah Evertson was a joy to work with and often was able to find much better photos than what the authors had originally imagined. Margaret Pinette's careful copyediting and eye for detail and consistency were also very much appreciated even if she, like the authors, often worried about dating herself when deciding that it probably was necessary to clarify that yes, Paul McCartney was once a member of a band called the Beatles.

Finally, the authors would like to thank their families for putting up with odd hours and loved ones spending far more time in front of the computer than is probably healthy for a good family life. John Pavlik would like to thank his wife Jackie and daughters Tristan and Orianna. Shawn McIntosh would like to thank his wife Naren, whose patience and support were always appreciated, even though he didn't tell her that nearly as much as he should have.

Comments and feedback on this book are very welcome. Please email Shawn McIntosh at shawn@netgraf.org.

John Pavlik

Shawn McIntosh

Foreword

For hundreds of thousands of years our ancestors lived in small tribal groups. Their ways of living varied greatly, but mostly their lives were short and hard, and they shared what they had. Tribes fought tribes to the death. Then, a few thousand years ago, clever people learned how to keep livestock and grow food, and people generally ate better and lived longer, but some people tended to run things while others did the work: class society.

Plato is supposed to have said somewhere, "It is important not to allow the wrong kind of music in the Republic." And an ancient Arab proverb says, "When the king puts the poet on his payroll, he cuts off the tongue of the poet." In the 20th century the way was to flood the new media so that troublesome information would be drowned out. President Hoover is said to have told popular singer Rudy Vallee around 1930, "Mr. Vallee, if you can sing a song that will make the American people forget the depression, I'll give you a medal." Bing Crosby had a hit song: "Wrap your troubles in dreams, and dream your troubles away."

Now the twin towers have fallen, watched by hundreds of millions. A friend of mine was working on the 102nd floor. He leaves a wife and five-year-old son behind. People are talking with each other as never before. The whole world is asking, who, how, and, most important: WHY? And I'm glad to see more community activism among a wide range of citizens. Maybe we will all realize finally the danger the entire world is in, if it is governed by selfishness and shortsightedness.

Everywhere I go these days I hand out a short piece of paper with these words:

> The ultimate weakness of violence is that it is a descending spiral, begetting the very thing it seeks to destroy. Instead of diminishing evil, it multiplies it. Through violence you may murder the liar, but you cannot murder the lie, nor establish the truth. Through violence you may murder the hater, but you do not murder hate. In fact, violence merely increases hate. So it goes. Returning to violence for violence multiplies violence, adding deeper darkness to a night already devoid of stars. Darkness cannot drive out darkness: only light can do that. Hate cannot drive out hate: only love can do that.
>
> —Martin Luther King, Jr.

If we do our job, people will learn to smile at our differences, instead of frown. But we should learn from the mistakes of others. We can't live long enough to make 'em all ourselves. Censors. We need 6 billion censors—all of us thinking about how best to use our powers of tongue and pen—I mean, of tongue and computer. And the pros and cons of every word.

Here's to all you young folks. Don't let your studies interfere with your education.

Pete Seeger
October 21, 2001

Pete Seeger is best known as a folk musician, song writer, and banjo player. He has issued over a hundred records, written many songs (including

"If I Had a Hammer" and "Where Have All the Flowers Gone?"), and supported labor, civil rights, environmental, and peace causes through song. Among his many accomplishments he marched in support of civil rights in the 1960s and sailed the sloop Clearwater *up and down the Hudson River in support of the environment in the 1970s. In 1994 he was given the nation's highest artistic honors at the Kennedy Center. In 1996 he was inducted into the Rock and Roll Hall of Fame.*

Mass Communication and Its Digital Transformation

Lovesick teenagers in countries

such as Pakistan and Iran sit in crowded cyber-cafes to socialize, flirt, and explore fantasies that could get them arrested if acted upon. But it all takes place online, largely anonymously, and is considered harmless if titillating fun by the teens and young adults.

The Internet may have opened up new communication channels for teens in socially restrictive cultures, but it has also opened the floodgates to mass communication from around the world. China had been battling the proliferation of unlicensed cybercafes and the subversion of state control of the information its citizens receive until the summer of 2002, when a fire in one cybercafe that killed 24 people gave the government the excuse to temporarily close down 2400 cybercafes in Beijing—92 percent of which were unlicensed.

Just as the Internet can be a socially liberating tool for interpersonal communications and a politically liberating tool of mass communication, it can also be used to rapidly spread rumors and hate. "At its best, the Internet can educate more people faster than any media tool we've ever had," wrote journalist Thomas Friedman. "At its worst, it can make people dumber faster than any media tool we've ever had."[1] He cited the lie circulated over the Internet and widely believed in the Muslim world that 4000 Jews were warned not to go into the World Trade Center on September 11. The Internet's aura of "technology" gives it unquestioned authority for many people while it provides a forum to meet others who share their views. "You can scrap the BBC and just get your news from those Web sites that reinforce your own stereotypes," said Friedman.

Understanding how the convergence of mass media, computers, and telecommunications can be liberating and threatening at the same time is what this book is about.

OBJECTIVES

In this chapter we will:
- Define mass communication.
- Review basic theories of mass communication.
- Identify the basic components and functions of the mass communication process.
- Outline key concepts of digital media.
- Examine convergence and its consequences.
- Describe the essential differences between the traditional, analog model of mass communication and the emerging digital media system.

Afghan President Hamid Karzai transmits his message to a wide audience through mediated communication.

Prologue

The media of mass communication have long played a fundamental role in people's lives. The media inform, persuade, entertain, and even sell. Media can provide companionship. They can shape perception. They are fundamental to an informed and educated public.

We will examine the nature of mass communication and how it is changing in the so-called digital age, the age of computerization of the media. Far more than just a technical change, this change is cultural, social, and economic. Journalists, public relations professionals, advertising practitioners, programmers, and content creators, as well as media consumers, are facing a new world of media symbols, processes, and effects.

Before we can examine digital media in more depth, however, it is necessary to understand the concept of mediation and differentiate some fundamental types of communication and how they change in their unmediated versus mediated forms, as well as developing an understanding of the elements of mass communication.

Mediation

Because we are surrounded by **mediated communication** in our daily lives it is easy to confuse mediated communication with "real-world," or unmediated, communication. Simply put, mediation is the process by which a message, or communication, is transmitted via some form, or medium. If you whisper something to your neighbor in class, that is unmediated communication. He or she is receiving the message directly from you (air could be considered the medium of transmission in

mediated communication— communication that involves a process by which a message, or communication, is transmitted via some form, or medium.

this case, but that is getting too technical for our purposes). If you write a note and give it to the person next to you, that is mediated communication.

If you are saying exactly the same thing by whispering or passing the note, then what is the difference between the two forms of communication? The note exists as a type of media, in this case text on paper, and therefore has some characteristics very different than unmediated communication. For one, the note can be left, and someone can come later and read the same message, whereas this is obviously impossible if you spoke the message. Mediated communication also creates a greater chance for misinterpretation by the receiver. Think of when you have had to apologize or clarify your intentions after writing an ironic comment in an email that the receiver misunderstood and became angry or upset about. Because you can convey additional meanings through your tone of voice, facial expressions, or gestures, unmediated communication is less likely to be misunderstood.

Anything you directly encounter during your waking hours—talking to friends, listening to a lecture, smelling food from the cafeteria, feeling rain on your skin—is unmediated communication, although the information value of these experiences varies. Anytime you listen to the radio, see an advertisement on a bus, browse through a magazine or newspaper, watch the television weather forecast, or go online, those are examples of mediated communication. They too have different levels of information value.

Personal versus Mass Communication

The traditional mass communication model differs from other forms of communication, which often are not mediated and include **interpersonal** (between two or more persons, such as chatting with a friend) and **intrapersonal** (within an individual) communication. Interpersonal and intrapersonal communication often interact with and intersect **mass communication**, which is always mediated.

Interpersonal Communication

Interpersonal communication usually flows two ways, is generally one-to-one, and tends not to be anonymous. Think of chatting with a friend or talking with a small group of friends. Responses are generally immediate, and the speaker or speakers will often adjust their messages based on the responses they receive.

These same principles apply to live public speaking, even though this is a one-to-many model, and opportunities for audience feedback will be more limited than in a casual small group setting. The speaker and audience can communicate through a variety of nonverbal cues, such as facial expressions, physical contact, or body language. If speakers see looks of boredom or audience members yawning, they can react to that information and try to make their presentation more interesting.

Examples of mediated interpersonal communication would be talking on the telephone or writing back and forth online using instant messaging or in a chat room. Note how the mediation limits some aspects of interpersonal communication. There are no visual cues either on the telephone or online (unless using a

interpersonal communication—communication between two or more individuals, usually in a small group, although it can involve communication between a live speaker and an audience.

intrapersonal communication—communication within an individual.

mass communication—communication to a large group or groups of people that remain largely unknown to the sender of the message.

webcam), and meanings can be misconstrued by text messages. The online medium also blurs the line between interpersonal and mass communication, as a chat room can have hundreds or thousands of participants.

Intrapersonal Communication

Intrapersonal communication involves largely one's own internal communications, where individuals come to perceive or understand themselves and their relationship to external stimuli. Writing in a personal diary or otherwise recording one's thoughts and feelings are examples of mediated intrapersonal communication.

Intrapersonal communication can be closely intertwined with interpersonal communication, which in turn can be influenced by the media. For example, there is a long-standing view that many audience members regard family members and close personal friends as major influences in their decision-making processes. These opinion leaders often pass on information received from the media to other people in society. Developed by researchers Elihu Katz and Paul Lazarsfeld, this notion has been dubbed the **two-step flow.** With digital, **networked** media, the connections between or among interpersonal, intrapersonal, and mass communication are beginning to grow even stronger. **Weblogs,** or blogs, which are journal-like entries written by individuals and posted on the Internet that sometimes can generate many online discussions, are an example of this phenomenon.

Interpersonal communication takes place between two people or a small group and can be unmediated or mediated.

Mass Communication

The term **media of mass communication** refers to any technologically based means of communicating between or among large groups of people distributed widely over space or time.

Since Johannes Gutenberg invented the Western world's first mechanical printing press in Germany in 1455, the media of mass communication have been characterized by a single, overarching model. This model has had the following four main characteristics:

1. Communication flow is largely one-way, from sender or source to receiver or audience.

2. Communication is from one or a few to many (i.e., one or a few sources generate and distribute content to large, heterogeneous audiences).

3. Communication is anonymous (sources generally do not know their audiences and audiences do not know the sources, except at a general level).

4. Audiences are largely passive recipients of the messages distributed by the media, with little opportunity for feedback and practically no opportunity for immediate feedback.

In other words, media companies create content they believe the audience will want and distribute that content to an audience that has very few ways to provide immediate feedback on whether that's what they do indeed want. This model has characterized all media of mass communication, whether books, magazines, newspapers, broadcast television or radio, cable or satellite TV, recorded

two-step flow hypothesis—a theory about how mass communication affects the public that states that information flows from print or electronic media to opinion leaders and then to less active members of the population.

networked media—media that exist in an interconnected series of communication nodes or points.

weblog—a type of Web site in which a person posts regular journal or diary entries with the posts arranged chronologically.

media of mass communication—any technologically based means of communicating between or among large groups of people distributed widely over space or time.

Claude Elwood Shannon

Claude Elwood Shannon was one of the leading media pioneers of the twentieth century. Trained as a mathematician and engineer at Michigan State University and the Massachusetts Institute of Technology, he started working for Bell Telephone Laboratories in 1941.

His work laid the foundation for the digital age of media by proposing a system of electronic communication that was based on Shannon's earlier work with information processing machines that used either a "yes" or "no," or "on" or "off," format, which is represented by a 1 or 0 in computer code. It was this work in which the basic computing information unit **bit** was first used, which is short for binary digit. He believed that information was no different than any other quantity and therefore could be manipulated by a machine. He presented his research in the late 1940s in *The Mathematical Theory of Communications,* which he coauthored with Warren Weaver.[2]

In the 1950s Shannon worked on creating intelligent machines. Shannon created Theseus, an electromechanical mouse that could be taught to work its way through a maze, one of the earliest experiments in artificial intelligence.

Claude Shannon and his electromechanical mouse.

bit—short for binary digit, it is the smallest unit of digital information. A bit has a single binary value, either 0 or 1.

synchronous media—media that take place in real time, such as live television or radio and that require the audience to be present when the media is being broadcast or performed.

asynchronous media—media that do not require the audience to assemble at a given time in order to use that media. Examples of asynchronous media are printed materials or recorded audio or video.

time shift—the recording of an audio or video event, usually by the audience, so they can watch the event at a time other than when it was originally broadcast. Setting a VCR to record a favorite program while out is an example of time-shifting.

music, or motion pictures. Digital media, however, are radically changing that model, as we will see later and throughout this book.

In the traditional mass communication model, content creators play a fundamental role in society by representing and defining reality (as done by journalists or other communication professionals), or by authoring fictional narratives to explain, interpret or entertain (as done by artists, authors, and film auteurs). Authors and artists create stories about issues and events, they write books and articles, they create music or motion pictures, and then they publish, broadcast, or present those stories at set dates or times and in set locations.

Some, such as live television or radio, are **synchronous media.** Synchronous media require the audience to be assembled simultaneously with the broadcast or transmission. Others are asynchronous. **Asynchronous media,** such as newspapers or magazines, do not require the audience to assemble at any given time. Note that audio and video recording devices let people **time shift** and record a live concert or performance so it can be watched anytime, thereby becoming asynchronous media.

Theories of Mass Communication

Researchers and scholars have proposed a variety of theoretical perspectives on mass communication, including technological determinism, structural functionalism, and mass society. One of the earliest communication theorists was Aristotle, who 300 years before the common era called the study of communication "rhetoric" and spoke of three elements within the process: the speaker, the subject, and the person addressed. His basic ideas laid an enduring foundation for communication research, even today.

Transmission Models

In 1949, Bell Telephone Laboratories scientist Claude E. Shannon, who later wrote the first computer chess program in 1952, and Warren Weaver formulated an influential model of communication. It is known as a transmission model of communication and is closely related to communication theorist Harold Lasswell's famous question about media effects, which he posed in 1948. Lasswell asked, "Who says what in which channel to whom with what effect?" This model has allowed for many general applications in mass communication.

The Shannon and Weaver mathematical theory of communication, as they described it, is based on a linear system of electronic communication. The original formulation of the model included five main elements:

- Information source
- Transmitter
- Channel
- Receiver
- Destination

In this model, an information source formulates a message. A transmitter encodes the message into signals. The signals are delivered via a channel. A receiver decodes the signals, "reconstructing" the original message, which reaches its destination. The communication flow in this model is decidedly one-directional, from the sender to the receiver. The system has a limited capacity to provide feedback from the receiver back to the information source to acknowledge receipt of the message and to indicate whether the message has been understood and how she or he might react. The communication process can be adversely affected by noise, or interference, from the environment, possibly by way of competing, or distracting, messages, or even electrical interference. The original Shannon and Weaver mathematical theory of communication, or model, is depicted in the diagram in Figure 1-1.

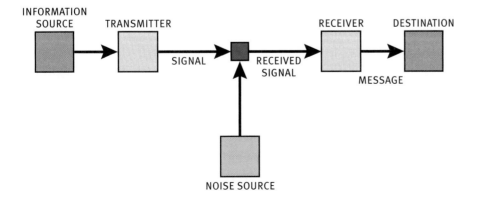

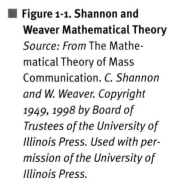

■ **Figure 1-1. Shannon and Weaver Mathematical Theory**
Source: From The Mathematical Theory of Mass Communication. *C. Shannon and W. Weaver. Copyright 1949, 1998 by Board of Trustees of the University of Illinois Press. Used with permission of the University of Illinois Press.*

The model clearly explains how a telephone works. The information source speaks (encoding a message), the phone (transmitter) transforms the sound waves into electrical impulses (the signal), which are sent over the channel (the tiny box in the center); and those electrical impulses are turned back into sound waves by the phone (receiver) at the other end of the line where they are heard and (one hopes) understood (decoded) by another person (destination). Noise is any interference anywhere along the way.

The Shannon and Weaver model is especially technological in its orientation and therefore limited in its utility for understanding traditional mass communication, because it does not fully reflect the role of humans in the process of mass communication. Moreover, the advent of digital, networked communication media is greatly expanding the interactive nature of communication, making the limited feedback capacity of the model even more problematic.

Looking at the application of the Shannon and Weaver model to a single mass medium, radio, is helpful in understanding how it might explain the process of mass communication. In radio, the source might be a news anchor. She or he formulates, or encodes, a message, perhaps an invitation to participate in a contest. In other words, the news anchor has an idea and expresses it in words. That message is transmitted via radio waves where the audience, or receiver, decodes, or understands it. Interference might cause static on the radio, or there may be loud talking taking place in the room with the radio, both of which might affect the listener's ability to hear the message correctly.

Adapting the Shannon and Weaver model and integrating concepts from Aristotle, pioneering communication scholar Wilbur Schramm in 1954 developed a **simplified communications model** in the book *The Process and Effects of Mass Communications.*[3]

In the Schramm model, communication requires three main elements:

1. a source, who encodes
2. a message, or signal, which is transmitted (via the media or directly via interpersonal communication) to
3. a destination, where the receiver decodes it.

Importantly, Schramm envisioned the importance of understanding as part of human communication. This had been largely ignored in the Shannon and Weaver model. Schramm suggested that people have fields of experience, or common culture, such as a shared language. To the extent to which any two people's experiences overlapped, their shared culture would affect their ability to communicate or understand each other. The same is true in mediated communication, or mass communication, where the degree of understanding between a source and a receiver, or audience, depends in large part on the extent of common culture or shared fields of experience. This model can be seen in Figure 1-2.

Schramm realized that another important aspect of the traditional communication model needed correcting. In human communication, mediated or not, communication is not a one-way process. Schramm wrote, "In fact, it is misleading to think of the communication process as starting somewhere and ending somewhere. It is really endless. We are little switchboard centers handling and rerouting the great endless current of information." As a result, Schramm and Charles Osgood developed a circular model of communication. The participants exchange roles of source/encoder and receiver/decoder. This model is depicted in Figure 1-3.

simplified communications model—developed by Wilbur Schramm in 1954 and based on the mathematical theory of communication. It includes a source, who encodes a message, or signal, which is transmitted (via the media or directly via interpersonal communication) to a destination, where the receiver decodes it.

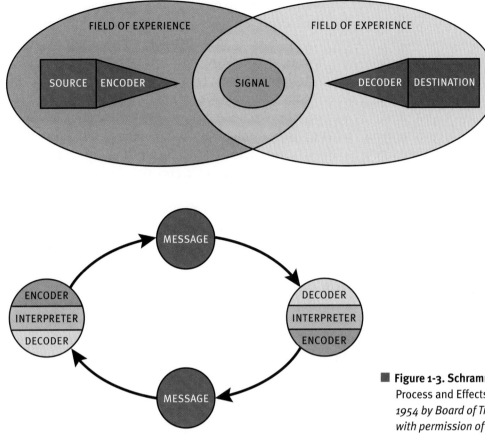

Evolving a New Approach

In 1957, the basic transmission model was expanded to recognize the importance of social interaction as a part of the mass communication process. The research of Westley and MacLean suggested that the electronic transmission model's direct path from media to the audience was supplemented by an interpersonal network of friends, family, and coworkers.[4]

The Westley-MacLean Model was the basis for the development of media **gatekeeping** models in which experts, or editors, serve as gatekeepers, or filters, of mediated content for others, deciding what is more or less important, what should be featured more or less prominently or included or excluded entirely. This notion had been introduced in the context of journalism a decade earlier by D. H. White, who in 1950 wrote that journalists operate as gatekeepers of news and information for society.[5]

Many scholars have criticized this electronic transmission model approach as being too technological in its orientation. Sociologists John W. and Matilda White Riley proposed in 1965 that communication must be understood with the broader social structure and process.[6] The Rileys' model of communication emphasized the role of each person's primary group affiliation as well as the broader societal context in influencing communication.

Since these early theorists, a number of communication scholars have moved away from empirical approaches and used critical or **cultural studies** approaches to mass communication theory. Critical theorists primarily research the role of ownership and control in media and criticize empirical researchers for inappropriately

gatekeeping—an aspect of communication theory in which experts, or editors, serve as content filters of mass mediated communication for others in deciding what is more or less important and what an audience sees.

cultural studies approach—a framework in studying theories of communication that shuns the scientific approach used by scholars in the empirical school and that tries to examine the symbolic environment created by mass media and the role it plays in culture and society.

Media scholar James Carey.

applying physical science research methods to humans and society and focusing their research too narrowly. Empirical researchers criticize the critical theorists for presenting conclusions without evidence and for substituting argumentation for scholarship. Cultural studies researchers join critical theorists in rejecting the scientific approach taken by empirical researchers. They try to examine the symbolic environment created by mass media and study the role that the mass media play in culture and society. Communications scholar James Carey is a leading cultural studies theorist and uses what he calls a ritual view of communication. From this view, the act of reading a newspaper has less to do with receiving information than it does with participating in a shared cultural experience that portrays and confirms the world in a certain way.[7]

One notable proposition was offered in 1993 by Oxford's Anthony Smith, who observed that developments in information technology are redefining not just media, but all of society by reshaping notions of nationhood.[8]

The Nature and Function of Mass Communication

Defining mass communication was once a relatively straightforward matter. The media were relatively stable and well known. Print media included books, newspapers, and magazines. Electronic media included television, radio, the recording arts, and cinema, although the latter two were usually created and originally distributed on chemical-based media, such as albums or film.

The functions of mass communication in society were also relatively well understood and thoroughly researched. Studies by Harold D. Lasswell, Charles Wright, and others suggest that these functions have tended to fall largely into four broad categories.[9]

Surveillance

Surveillance refers primarily to the journalism function, which provides information about the processes, issues, events, and other developments in society. This can include news on the latest military developments to weather alerts to political scandals. Surveillance can also include aspects of advertising and public relations, as well as educational aspects of mediated communication.

One weakness in the surveillance function is that too much news about disasters, murders, or other unusual events can skew the audience's perception of what is normal in society. Another weakness is that too much information can make the audience apathetic.

Correlation

Correlation refers to the interpretation of aspects of society, and the individual to society, including how journalism, advertising, and public relations shape public opinion through comments or criticism or through propaganda. Through the

surveillance—primarily the journalism function of mass communication, which provides information about the processes, issues, events, and other developments in society.

correlation—primarily the interpretation of aspects of society as a function of mass communication, and the individual to society, including how journalism, advertising, and public relations shape public opinion through comments or criticism or through propaganda.

Journalists like CNN's chief international reporter Christiane Amanpour play an especially important role in surveillance, or informing the public of news and events of importance.

correlation function, the media can shape and form public opinion and help maintain social stability, although this function can be taken too far and the media can thwart social change or block minority views from being disseminated to a mass audience.

Cultural Transmission

Cultural transmission refers to the transference of the dominant culture, as well as its subcultures, from one generation to the next, or to immigrants. This function includes socialization, which the media perform in helping persons learn society's rules or how to fit into society. This function is especially important for children but also is performed for adults who may have recently immigrated to a new country with a different culture.

The other side of the coin regarding the cultural transmission function is a criticism that it creates a homogenized, stagnant culture in which people learn to think, dress, and speak the same way through countless hours of exposure to the media.

Entertainment

The entertainment function is performed in part by all three of these activities but also involves the generation of content designed specifically and exclusively to entertain. Although some say that this function helps raise artistic and cultural taste among the general populace, critics argue that mass media encourages lowbrow entertainment at the expense of fine art, encourages escapism, and does not help raise the cultural level of society.

The U.S. Office of War Information used propaganda posters during World War II to help shape public opinion about the war.

cultural transmission—primarily refers to the transference of the dominant culture as a function of mass communication, as well as its subcultures, from one generation to the next or to immigrants. This function includes socialization, which the media perform in helping persons learn society's rules or how to fit into society.

One of the functions of media is to transmit the dominant culture's values.

Key Concepts in Analog to Digital Media

Digital media are those that have been created in or transformed into machine-language, or computer-readable form. Computers can only understand "on" or "off" states, or the presence or absence of information, which are represented by either a 1 or 0, called bits. Each "bit" of information (the term "bit" is a shortening of "*b*inary dig*it*") in a computer is stored in what is called binary code. Eight bits make a byte (pronounced BITE). A series of bits, a byte, or a series of bytes can represent any information. For example, the number five in binary code is "000101" or "101" for short. Each letter of the alphabet is one byte, so capital A is represented in computer-readable code as "01000001." Every digital word, image, song, or movie is represented by nothing but a string of 0s and 1s. This may seem like an inefficient system to process information—and it is—but computers simply process all these 0s and 1s extremely quickly. A computer

Media can entertain simply for its own sake, but critics charge that most entertainment encourages escapism and does not elevate the cultural level of society.

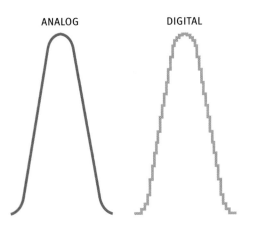

ANALOG   DIGITAL

■ **Figure 1-4.** A digital sample can never exactly match its analog counterpart because digital media only has two states, "on" or "off," which are represented in the steplike pattern. The reason a digital recording can sound as good as an analog recording is that the digital sampling can be done at small enough intervals that the human ear cannot detect the gaps between the steps.

makes no distinction between a digital video clip and a digital text document, except for the differing amount of memory each takes up in the computer. The process in which media is made into computer-readable form is called **digitization.**

Although it may be extremely useful to have a computer that can solve complex calculations or make it easier to write and edit a novel, its use is greatly diminished if the computer user cannot share information with other computer users. If other computer users are nearby, then using some kind of physical media such as tape or a diskette to transfer information between computers can work, but that does not solve the problem of distant computer users wanting to share information or what to do when multiple users are working on the same information and need to share with each other. The solution to this problem is to put the computers on a network.

The digitization of media and networking of communication are transforming not just journalism. The traditional entertainment, educational, advertising, and public relations functions of mass communication are also undergoing a metamorphosis. All media of communication or information, including telephony, broadcasting, motion pictures, recorded music, books, newspapers, and magazines, are converting from their traditional analog, or noncomputerized form, to digital, computerized form, even if the end product we are most familiar with is not digital.

The term **analog media** derives from the world of audio recording, in which the modulation of the sound carrier wave is analogous to the fluctuations of the sound itself. Because of the on–off nature of digitization, it can never exactly capture a sound in the way analog media can; the best it can do is sample the original data and get as close to the original as possible. Figure 1-4 shows the difference between an analog sound wave and a digital sample of the same wave.

Analog media works differently. Consider, for example, how Thomas Edison's original phonograph, created in 1877, worked. Edison's phonograph, an analog media device, required the user to speak into a sound horn while rotating an attached tin cylinder. A needle, attached to a diaphragm that vibrated in corresponding fashion to the sounds of the speaker's voice, "recorded" or scratched onto the tin cylinder a pattern analogous to the sounds emitted by the speaker. Playing back the sound required the needle to move over the groove etched during the recording. The needle would vibrate as it moved over the groove, which caused the diaphragm to vibrate and emit via the sound horn a replica of the original voice. Modern phonographs use essentially the same principles, although

Weblink
How Stuff Works: Analog-to-Digital Conversion
[www.howstuffworks.com /analog-digital.htm]

digitization—the process in which media is made into computer-readable form.

analog media—originally used in audio recording for media that was analogous to the sound it was recreating. It now refers to all nondigitized media, such as print media, audio and video recordings, photography, and film.

helped greatly by improvements in materials, design, and the use of electronic rather than mechanical amplifiers.

In the case of digital audio and video, an **analog-to-digital converter** (ADC) samples at a very high rate from the continuous wave pattern of the audio or video and represents each sample numerically in bits and bytes.

Multimedia

When all information consists of bits, it becomes easy to juxtapose various media types that could not coexist in the media world. There will never be an option to watch a video clip in the newspaper or listen to the interview of the story; the inherent character of print media and physical laws of nature simply will not allow it. The best that can be done is to read and perhaps look at a photograph or use other media such as a radio or television to supplement the reading. Likewise, it is impossible to read a brief biography on a historical figure while watching a film, just as it is impossible to retrieve the lyrics of a song from the radio.

The idea of **multimedia,** or combining various media "types" into one package, is not new. Putting photographs with text is a type of multimedia, but a better example is the combination of moving pictures and sound, as in film and video. In the digital world, however, there are more opportunities for multimedia. Video can sit side-by-side with a text transcript, and audio can play while the media consumer reads the lyrics of a song or reads information about the artist or even watches a concert of the artist.

Interactivity

Interactivity is a crucial aspect of digital media but is, ironically, extremely hard to define to everyone's satisfaction. There is no doubt that the term is misunderstood, misused, and abused. According to WhatIs? online encyclopedia, it is defined as:

> In computers, interactivity is the dialog that occurs between a human being (or possibly another live creature) and a computer program. . . . In addition to hypertext, the Web (and many non-Web applications in any computer system) offer other possibilities for interactivity. Any kind of user input, including typing commands or clicking the mouse, is a form of input. Displayed images and text, printouts, motion video sequences, and sounds are output forms of interactivity.[10]

Sheizav Rafaeli states that interactivity is "the condition of communication in which simultaneous and continuous exchanges occur."[11] In other words, interaction involves two or more parties to a communication engaging in an ongoing give-and-take of messages.

Some scholars claim that because the human–computer interface is by its nature interactive; the necessity of using some form of input such as a mouse or keyboard to even use a computer makes the term "interactivity" meaningless.[12]

Even critics of the term *interactivity* acknowledge that there are qualitative interactive differences between clicking to open a browser and typing in a ZIP code to obtain specific crime data on a town, for example. The first case is equivalent to using a television remote control in which pushing a button for channel

analog-to-digital converter (ADC)—a device that electronically changes the continuously variable analog signal into a multilevel digital signal without changing its content.

multimedia—a combination of different types of media in one package; thus film or video with sound is a type of multimedia because it combines visual and audio elements. Web pages that combine text, video, animation, audio, or graphics are another type of multimedia.

interactivity—for digital media purposes, interactivity can be defined as a dialog (verbal, via text, or clicking a mouse) that occurs between a human and a computer program that occurs simultaneously or nearly so.

Computer-drawn 3D objects have applications in media as well as a host of other fields.

two, is expected to take the viewer to channel two rather than increase the volume. The second case involves the user seeking information he or she wants and may not know.

For digital media purposes, we will define interactivity as having the following elements:

1. A dialog that occurs between a human and a computer program (this includes e-mails, online chats, and discussion groups, as at either end of the communication flow it is a human interacting with a computer program, with the Internet simply the channel).

2. The dialog occurs simultaneously or nearly so (i.e., response time should not be more than a few seconds).

3. The audience has some measure of control over what media content they see and in what order they see it (getting personalized information, magnifying an image, clicking on a hyperlink, and so on).

Automation

Computers can be programmed to automate many complex and time-consuming tasks, which are made easier because all data exist in essentially the same format. Search engines and other elements that make computers and the Web relatively easy to use are all possible through automation. Automation enables computers to draw 3D objects, makes computer games engaging, and is changing the way journalists and other media professionals do their work. But automation also makes it much easier for companies to find and track individuals and makes media use no longer anonymous.

Automation plays a crucial role in the ability of online media to be **personalized,** or to provide user-specific information. Users can specify what kinds of news or information they want to receive based on any number of factors such as geography, interests, or specific topics. With automation, computer programs can even select media content that is more likely to be of interest to a specific user simply based on tracking the Web sites or type of content the user has visited.

personalization—the ability of media content producers to provide content that is of interest to a specific user based either on criteria the user has selected, such as a ZIP code, or on automated tracking of their Web-viewing habits.

Bits, Not Pieces

It has already been mentioned that digital media is made up of representations of 1s and 0s. CDs and DVDs are examples of digital media transplanted onto real-world objects, but digital information itself can exist just as easily in the ether—or Ethernet—as on a physical medium. In fact, in some ways digital information is better without a physical presence.

The "unreal" quality of digital information has far-reaching consequences in terms of audience, media companies, the law, and society. Digital libraries will not need time limits for books that are checked out, as online visitors simply download a perfect copy to their own computer and leave the original for others. In fact, the concept of "checking out" a book becomes meaningless. Likewise for the concept of watching a show broadcast at 8 P.M. on a certain night of the week. The shows are available, all the time, and can be accessed and watched whenever is convenient. Endless copies of media content can be made and easily distributed, as Napster and other file-sharing services have shown.

Benefits of Digitization

Nicholas Negroponte, a well-known media futurist, has proclaimed that the World Wide Web is, above all else, an engine of public relations, for better or worse. One of the most fundamental shifts in the world of mass communication is that organizations of all types now have direct access to individuals they once could reach effectively only through traditional media. Organizations of all types can create their own Web sites and present their messages directly to the public, without the traditional media editing or otherwise filtering their communications. As a result, corporate, nonprofit, and government Web sites are flourishing with information and services aimed directly at their publics.

Advertising, which in a traditional analog media system served largely as a means to an end (i.e., goods and services are promoted in order to sell them), is changing in the digital, networked world. For the first time, products and services can be not only promoted via the media, but they can be sold and delivered directly and in real time to the consumer, as in the case of downloadable music, books, and many other information products such as software. This is much different than shipping a product to the consumer, a process that could take days or weeks. Now the product can be delivered digitally and in real time to the consumer anywhere in the world and for theoretically much lower costs, as there are no shipping, storage, manufacturing, or middleman retail charges to pay.

Reproduction and distribution costs are generally cheaper with digital media than analog media, giving many more people the tools to create, produce, and distribute media content to a worldwide audience. This kind of audience-centered mass communication can lead to a flowering of diverse ideas, art, and creativity that is not dependent on a handful of large media companies to distribute the content. The general public can become more involved in political and social issues as they organize online—and sometimes offline—using digital communication in a networked environment.

Problems with Digitization

All is not better in the networked, digital world, however. The digital world of media brings a variety of problems to mass communication. Among these problems are the erosion of privacy (witness the rise of corporate big brother, "spam," and online marketing), uneven access to news and information across social groups and societies, easy access to online hatred and pornography, and threats to national security from terrorists who might use the Internet to hack into and vandalize media and military Web sites.

The "addressability" of the networked, digital media system is fundamentally altering the entire mass-communication enterprise. The digital network, a term that here refers to the telecommunications network, permits media organizations to address, or target, messages to the individual yet do so on a mass scale, thanks in part to automation. This results in audiences being marketed to in new ways that extend far beyond the traditional realm of advertising in the analog world.

Media now can monitor a variety of personal data about their audience members, including not only their names, but their addresses (both in the physical and electronic worlds), genders, ages, media and shopping preferences, and much more. Much of this information is sold to advertisers and others seeking to market goods and services. What are the ethical guidelines that should and will shape privacy in the digital age? What rules should media organizations follow with regard to protecting the privacy of their audience members? Should they collect, use, and redistribute or even resell personal information they might collect automatically when audience members visit a media Web site? Should this information be made available to advertisers? Many of these questions will be addressed in later chapters.

Web sites are sometimes shut down for business, security, or legal reasons that have nothing to do with the media, thereby depriving many people of sources of news and information. An example of this happened with all U.S. Department of Interior Web sites in early December 2001 when a judge ordered the sites shut down until security holes could be fixed that made it easy to access a system that handles $500 million annually in royalties from Indian lands held in a trust fund.[13] Although only a part of long-standing legal battles between Native Americans and the U.S. government, the result was that a number of government Web sites remained offline even as late as March 2002, and for a short time after the shutdown 11,000 Geological Survey workers could not even access their e-mails in order to receive urgent alerts on a 6.1 magnitude earthquake that had hit New Zealand a few days before. Likewise, in the aftermath of the September 11 terrorist attacks, many government agencies took down previously accessible and public information from their Web sites, citing security concerns.

Convergence and Its Consequences

The coming together of computing, telecommunications, and media in a digital environment is known as **convergence,** although scholars still do not agree on an exact and complete definition of the word. Convergence can also be used to

convergence—the coming together of computing, telecommunications, and media in a digital environment. Convergence and the changes it is bringing are fundamentally changing many aspects of mass media and communication.

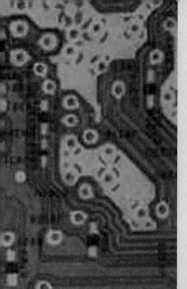

3D Faxes

A technology known as the **3D fax**—also known as 3D printing or stereolithography—may soon extend online product distribution to other physical products beyond the realm of informational products. The 3D fax can print copies of physical, or three-dimensional, products on demand. Today, the 3D fax prints with layers of plastic, gradually building a 3D copy of an object originally scanned by a laser. In the future, other materials will be printable, as well. Consumers with a 3D printer at home might go on the Internet, buy a toy for a child, and have it instantly "printed" at home.

mean the merging of Internet companies with traditional media companies, such as AOL with Time Warner. It can also be used in talking about specific types of media, such as print, audio, and video all converging into one digital media.

Even if a specific definition is still not agreed upon, convergence is transforming the very nature of mass communication, which of course has dramatic implications. These implications fall into four areas:

1. The content of communication.
2. The relationships between media organizations and their publics.
3. The structure of communication organizations.
4. How communications professionals do their work.

These four implications are recurrent themes throughout this book.

Convergence is leading to a complete reexamination of the term "mass" communication. This will be a major theme of this book, with a central premise being that although there will continue to be "mass" communication, in the sense that media companies and others will continue to produce messages for large audiences, frequently the members of those audiences may receive messages tailored to each individual, and audiences will become much more active in their engagement with mediated communication than they have been.

Fundamentally, convergence is transforming the kinds of media audiences have grown up with. In the preconverged world of media, the process of mass communication consisted largely of a system of messages communicated through words, images, and sound. The converged media world still features these elements but brings with it new paradigms that are possible with digital, networked media.

Convergence and Communication Content

Stories told in a digital, online medium can make connections with other types of content much more easily than in any other medium. This is done primarily through the use of **hyperlinks,** or clickable pointers to other online content. This is just as true for news content as it is for other forms of mass communication, including advertising, public relations, and entertainment. For example, advertisements in a digital, online environment permit visitors to click on interactive ads or even images of products in which they can be purchased directly online. Or, in entertainment programming, hyperlinked content allows a viewer to explore a story in a nonlinear narrative, where the outcome of a story may be unchanged, but the path one takes to get there is unpredictable.

Content is much more fluid, dynamic, rapid, and global in an online environment, which enables better representation of events and processes in real life. Moreover, it is increasingly possible to obtain communications and content on demand. In the traditional media world, news, entertainment, or marketing information was broadcast or published on a schedule solely determined by the publisher or broadcaster. Technology exists currently that would allow the audience to even choose from which camera angles they wish to watch a sporting event, for example, and switch between angles or watch their own replays during the game. This is not to say that everyone will want to—or should be—a television director whenever they watch television. Sometimes passively consuming media is all a person wants. But that is not to say that simply being able to be a more active

3D fax—a fax that sprays fine plastic particles in layers onto a surface that allows for the construction of a three-dimensional model of the object being faxed.

hyperlink—a word, graphic, or image that is linked through HTML code to another Web page or media element either within the same Web site or in a different Web site on the World Wide Web.

Digital media is changing many aspects of media, from the way film-makers like Steven Soderbergh shoot movies to how they are distributed.

participant in the kind of content one is watching won't alter how mass communication content and media in general are perceived.

Digitization is transforming both how and when media organizations distribute their content. They are no longer distributing content solely through traditional channels and instead are delivering digital content via the Internet, satellite, and a host of other digital technologies. They are increasingly making that content available 24 hours a day, with news organizations updating the news almost continuously, and to a worldwide audience, leading to a reexamination of the tiered approach to distribution.

The production cycle and process is similarly being transformed by digital technology. In fact, the transformation may be even deeper in terms of media content production. Whether Hollywood motion pictures, television shows, news, books, magazines, newspapers, or online, the process of producing media content is rapidly becoming almost entirely digital. Movies are shot using digital cameras and edited on computers. Reporters working for television, radio, newspapers, or any other news operation capture their raw material with digital devices as well, editing their stories digitally. Even book authors typically write on a computer, with words increasingly remaining digital throughout the entire production process.

Convergence and Media Organizations' Relationships with Their Audience

As already mentioned, the process of analog mass communication was largely one-way, from the source of a message to the receiver, or audience. The audience was relatively large, heterogeneous, and anonymous. Audience members had relatively few means by which to communicate either with each other on a mass scale or with the creators and publishers of mass communication content. Audiences in the age of convergence can communicate via e-mail, online forums, and other interactive media more easily and quickly with those who create and publish mass communication content. In addition, they can also create mass communication content themselves and reach far larger audiences for much lower costs than they could have with traditional media. They are generally not anonymous, although it is easy to create an online persona that bears little resemblance to one's real life.

Automation in digital media allows for mass communication organizations to keep detailed and automatically updated records on their audiences as they track their paths within their Web sites through intelligent software agents and programs known as **cookies,** which allow a Web site to recognize when a previous user comes to the Web site and gives them personalized content. This is invaluable information for media organizations to better understand an audience's media behaviors, preferences, and habits.

Increased Media Consumption

As the media system continues to evolve toward a digital future, audience demand for media is growing. The "15th Annual Communications Industry Forecast," prepared by Veronis Suhler, shows that audiences are consuming more and more media as part of their daily lives.[14] The report indicates that the average person in the United States will spend 10.3 hours per day with various forms of information and entertainment media by the end of 2004, an increase of an hour since 1999. Notably, U.S. media consumers are shifting away from the use of traditional news and entertainment sources, including newspapers, magazines, broadcast television, and radio—media traditionally supported primarily by advertising. Audiences are shifting their media consumption toward digital media and consumer-supported media, such as cable and satellite television, books, and the Internet. Advertiser-supported media made up 69.1 percent of total media consumption in 1995 and just 60.9 percent in 1999; and the percentage is expected to fall to 54.7 percent by the end of 2004.

Active Media Production and Distribution

Digital media make it easier than ever for the public to create and distribute media content, whether it is an original drawing done using illustration software, an animation or video, or a song sampled and mixed from current hits by famous recording artists.

Writing and music have led the way in media consumers creating content, although in music especially remixes of previously recorded (and copyrighted) music are more common than an amateur copying passages from a number of famous books and claiming it as his or her own work. Even before it became possible to download songs and send music files over the Internet, music fans were rerecording their favorite artists onto blank audio cassettes and making "garage band" recordings. Although by today's standards it was a laborious process, individuals could create music remixes of songs from their favorite band, for example, or certain songs from a variety of favorite artists. Distributing numerous copies of these tapes was usually too expensive and labor intensive to be worthwhile, and making subsequent copies from the copies noticeably reduced the sound quality, which is not the case in the digital world.

Distribution Alters the Balance of Power

Audiences are increasingly active in their communication both with each other and with the creators of mass communication content. This gives them much greater control over what media they consume and shifts some of the power

cookie—information that a Web site puts on a user's local hard drive so that it can recognize when that computer accesses the Web site again. Cookies allow for conveniences like password recognition and personalization.

away from media organizations providing content and toward the audience. Through **viral marketing,** the online equivalent of word-of-mouth advertising, a popular Web site, product, or piece of content can potentially reach millions of online users in a very short time, all without corporate promotion or advertising. The success of **peer-to-peer** file-sharing programs such as Morpheus and KaZaA are examples of how an Internet audience shifts the balance of power away from media organizations, even though those organizations are the ones that created and provided that content in the first place.

Audiences aren't willing to wait for the evening news or the next day's paper for developments in a breaking story. "When you don't have access to radio or TV, the Internet is the best news source," said Jarvis Mak, a senior Internet analyst for NetRatings. "It can become, in a way, your immediately updated newspaper."[15]

Audiences can get their information and entertainment from literally thousands of sources around the world. Audiences aren't content to sit back and listen in silence to what the media report. They want their own voices to be heard. The Internet enables audiences around the world to participate in a global dialog about the world's events and issues and can bring individuals into direct contact with each other though separated by thousands of miles and political and cultural boundaries. It is not clear what the net effect of this sea change in communication will be, but it is clear the foundation is being laid for a more connected and engaged global public.

Fragmentation and "The Daily Me"

These changes are not without some dangers, however. Actively choosing the media you want to see, hear, or read can narrow the scope of news items or entertainment that may be encountered by accident that unintentionally engage or entertain. Former MIT Media Lab director, the late Michael Dertouzos, called the specialization of news to one's specific interests "The Daily Me." This phenomenon could fragment audiences into small groups of like-minded individuals who do not interact with other groups or with society as a whole and choose to receive only the news and information that reinforces their beliefs and values. Media fragmentation has already been a trend in analog media, and digital

viral marketing—spreading news and information about media content through word-of-mouth, usually via online discussion groups, chats, and e-mails, without utilizing traditional advertising and marketing methods.

peer-to-peer (P2P)—a computer communications model in which all users have equal abilities to store, send, and accept communications from other users.

media can easily accelerate that trend. Cass Sunstein, law scholar and author of *Republic.com*, voices similar concerns over the social effects in a democratic society when media audiences become increasingly fragmented and stop discussing broad social and political issues.

However, personalization and localization of news does have benefits in potentially getting the public to become more engaged in news and in helping them become better informed about current events. Making better connections between news analysis and primary source materials is one of the most important developments in online journalism. It is important because it helps to place stories in better context and can hold journalists accountable for their reporting by enabling the audience to compare a journalist's report with the actual primary source material about which he or she is reporting. This may help slow or even reverse the steady decline in credibility suffered by U.S. news organizations during the past quarter century.

Consider how MSNBC on the Web incorporated customization capability into its reporting. On its cable channel, MSNBC transmitted a report about the five most dangerous roads in America. On its Web site, not only did MSNBC provide the text of this report, but producers linked to a federal traffic database that permitted visitors to the site to enter a ZIP code and obtain traffic fatality data for that community and see which roads are the most dangerous in their town. Within 24 hours, the site had logged 68,000 visitors interested in learning about the most dangerous roads in their own communities.

Weblink
MSNBC
[www.msnbc.com]

Table 1-1 summarizes the qualities of mass communication in the preconverged (analog) and postconverged (online, digital) media worlds.

Convergence and Communications Organizations

In the preconverged world, centralized media organizations created and published or broadcast content on predetermined schedules. A newspaper was printed and distributed within a certain period of time; a television broadcast appeared within a given time slot. Centralized means media organizations where content production and distribution, as well as marketing and other functions, are controlled by a central unit or individual. Internet-based media can be less centralized. Many divisions may determine the design or content of individual Web pages of an overall Web site. Web-based media are certainly not exempt from the economic consolidation of all mass media, but the nature of the Web permits more flexibility and adaptability in publishing or webcasting content.

Social, Political, and Economic Pressures

The digital media system is a product of more than simply technological change. Economic, cultural, and political influences also are reshaping media, just as they have ever since Gutenberg printed his first Bible in 1455.

Governments, both domestic and international, regulate most media in an attempt to shape or control them or their content. This is true whether in the analog or digital worlds of media. Broadcast media have traditionally been subject to extensive government regulation, whereas U.S. print media have been relatively free of government regulation, with strong legal independence established in the First Amendment to the Constitution of the United States.

Table 1-1 Analog versus Digital Mass Communication

	Analog Mass Communication	Digital Mass Communication
Audience	Large, heterogeneous, anonymous, private. Bounded by geographic, cultural, and political boundaries. Passively read, watch, and listen to media to gratify needs.	Fragmented, homogenous, known and addressable, erosion of privacy. Geographic, political, and cultural boundaries less important. Increasingly active in consumption, creation, and participation of media.
Feedback	Few mechanisms for audience feedback and generally slow.	Instant, increasingly extensive through e-mail, online discussion forums.
Functions	Surveillance, correlation, cultural transmission, entertainment, marketing/advertising, mobilization.	Surveillance, correlation, cultural transmission, entertainment, and e-commerce, mobilization.
Program/Content Availability	Centrally controlled schedule. One-way, dominated by centralized content providers.	Decreasingly centrally controlled schedule. Increasingly on-demand from a diverse array of voices. Less dominated by centralized content providers, often times many-to-many and audience-created.
Government regulation	Extensive for electronic, audio-visual media, little for print.	Little for print, reduced for traditional electronic media but uncertain and still evolving.
Storytelling	Stories are linear and static (i.e., they are fixed in print, on film or magnetic tape) and designed for mass audience; modalities of expression are limited to those possible in each analog medium.	Linear and nonlinear, multimedia, interactive, exploratory, customizable, and dynamic. Content creator is more like a guide to knowledge, information, entertainment, and discovery.
Distribution channels	Separate, analog, one-to-many. Usually physical products.	Increasingly convergent, digital, many-to-many. Often not physical products.

Yet, in the digital, online realm, even "print" media organizations become subject to greater government regulation, whether in the United States or internationally. As newspapers move from the analog to the digital world and their products reach an increasingly global audience transmitted via satellite, telephone, or cable lines, they are finding themselves increasingly subject to international rules, regulations, and restrictions foreign governments may place upon the Internet. Libel and obscenity laws differ widely between countries, raising the question of whose version of libel should be used when an article published on the Internet libels someone according to his or her local laws. Likewise, should Internet communication be considered under telephone regulations, because many people access it through telephone lines, or regulated according to the cable industry, because it is also available through cable modems? These are just some examples in which digital technology and convergence have sped ahead of our current legal framework.

Concentration of Media Ownership

Although there are many public service media, most media companies throughout the world try to make a profit. Many media companies are among the most profitable private enterprises in the world, with average profit margins often in excess of 20 percent a year—double the average for other industries.

Vivendi Universal, one of the world's largest media companies, suffered setbacks in 2002. Convergence temporarily stalled as stock prices plunged and chairman Jean-Marie Messier was replaced in an attempt to regain investor confidence.

Concentration of media ownership has been a growing trend in the analog world, and the same process is taking place in the digital media world. Convergence is in some ways fuelling media concentration, by leading traditional media giants such as Time Warner to join with an online colossus such as America Online, giving way in 2001 to AOL Time Warner. Although by mid-2002, with plummeting stock prices and executive shake-ups at a number of media giants such as AOL Time Warner and Vivendi, some media analysts were saying that they moved too rapidly toward convergence without first figuring out a good business model. However, the trend is clear: Analog and digital media are rapidly being consolidated into the hands of a few, very large, very powerful and very rich owners, an economic structure referred to as an **oligopoly**. These media enterprises today are increasingly likely to be part of large, global media organizations publicly owned and accountable to shareholders whose main interest is the financial bottom line.

This centralized control over the signs and symbols of mediated communication can threaten the numbers and types of different voices heard on the Web. Inclusivity, diversity, and plurality of voices, both mainstream and marginal, have felt the increasing squeeze of global corporate owners eager to turn a double-digit profit in the online digital world. The trend is especially worrisome when a company can also control the means of distribution, such as AOL Time Warner with its control of online access through America Online, the largest Internet Service Provider (ISP) in the United States, and through their Time Warner cable system with Time Warner's large amount of media content.

Convergence and Communications Professionals

With all the changes brought to mass communication because of convergence, it is obvious that the way communications professionals do their jobs will also change. Just as the differences between print, video, and audio largely disappear in a digital media world, so will the divisions between print and electronic journalists, advertising and public relations professionals. Although it is likely journalists will still emphasize one or another field, print journalists will need to learn aspects of electronic journalism, and electronic journalists will have to learn more about

oligopoly—an economic structure in which a few very large, very powerful, and very rich owners control an industry or series of related industries.

Media **Inventors and Innovators**

The Drudge Report

Internet gossip reporter Matt Drudge used his Web site, The Drudge Report, to break the story of the affair between White House intern Monica Lewinsky and President Bill Clinton. *Newsweek,* whose reporters had gathered much of the story, felt the allegations of the affair needed further fact checking before it would publish the story and refused to compromise its ethical standards and publish the story before thoroughly checking it out. Drudge felt he had enough information to publish the story, and he did.

Notably, much of what makes up the controversial Drudge Report is links to other, credible news and information sites, such as columnist Jack Anderson, humorist Dave Barry, and international news wire, Agence France-Presse.

Drudge's quickness to publish unsubstantiated gossip has gotten him into trouble, however. In 1997 he was sued for $30 million by former Clinton aide Sidney Blumenthal when Drudge published an item saying that Blumenthal had a history of domestic violence. Although Drudge says he received the information from two sources, he retracted the piece the next day and apologized to the Blumenthals. In May 2001 the libel suit was dropped.[16]

Matt Drudge.

Weblink

Drudge Report
[www.drudgereport.com]

aspects of print journalism in order to fully utilize the digital media environment. Advertising and public relations professionals will have to learn how to best attract the attention of a public that encounters ever more media and in which the public is more active than in the past.

Just what constitutes a television or radio receiver, or TV or radio programming, is in a state of flux. Once it was simple. Radio programming was what a listener heard on a radio. Today, however, there are radio stations that transmit their programming via the Internet and listeners tune in via their computers. Moreover, these radio stations can include images, graphics, text, and video. For example, some Voice of America radio reporters have been trained in digital video shooting and editing and can now be "VJs," or videojournalists, webcasting their stories visually as well as through audio. With little more than a small digital video camera and a laptop computer with video editing software, journalists can now shoot, edit, and produce a professional-quality news video segment.

But in order to take advantage of digital media, new skills will have to be learned, and it will be more important than ever that the fundamental principles and ethics of each profession are not abandoned in the march toward the digital environment.

We will take a brief look at journalism here to provide a specific example of new factors the digital media professional must face. Advertising and public relations, as well as journalism, are covered in separate chapters later in the book.

What Makes a Journalist?

The distinctions between professional journalists and the their audience are getting fuzzy. It's not always clear who is a journalist or content provider in today's online world, where anyone with a computer and Internet access can publish to a global audience. This highlights the need for journalists and content providers to distinguish themselves by accurate reporting and thoughtful analysis if they want to regain credibility as a trusted source of news. It also emphasizes the point that media consumers need to be able to distinguish better than ever between trusted and questionable news sources, a point that is discussed in the next chapter.

Just because a person is not a professional journalist does not make her or him a questionable source of information. In fact, the more voices there are, the harder it will be for governments or large organizations to hide the truth.

One of the most compelling voices on the Internet in the late 1990s was that of an Orthodox Christian priest named Father Sava Janjic, whose words have been read by millions around the world via the **listservs** on San Francisco–based Yahoo Groups. During the war in Serbia, Janjic sent daily dispatches via Yahoo Groups (then called eGroups), frequently contradicting NATO claims that only military sites had been targeted and that civilian casualties had been minimal.

In the aftermath of the September 11 terrorist attacks, many people around the world created Web sites where they told their own accounts of what happened to them or people they knew. One example was the Web site (now no longer online) of Bob Mintz, a Wall Street accountant who lived near the World Trade Center and was home when the first plane crashed into the Tower. He published a series of photos he took of the crash and its aftermath and wrote narratives telling the "story behind the photos."

Here's how he started his account: "I was always curious how it would be to attend my own funeral. You would get to see who would attend, be a fly on the wall and listen to all of the kind (and perhaps not too kind) words, etc. I suppose this past week's 'event' was probably the closest that I would ever like to come to actually getting my fantasy fulfilled."

Such first-person Web sites (first-person means it is told from the point of view of the individual who experienced the event) were viewed extensively by audiences around the world.[17] Without any marketing, Mintz's site received more than 25,000 unique visitors in the few weeks following the attack. Another first-person site, which combined images from ABCNews.com and Ray Charles singing *God Bless America,* garnered 2.6 million unique visitors during the same period.

Nontraditional news sources can provide needed background information and alternate views that current online news stories might not have and that analog media could not have because of space or time constraints. Consider the Kosovo primer assembled by Pennsylvania State University political science professor Zachary Irwin in response to numerous requests for information about the Kosovo conflict. Irwin has assembled a wide-ranging and comprehensive list of online and other resources and put them on a Penn State Web site.[18] Included are a list of Internet sources on the conflict, a chronology of events in Kosovo and the surrounding region, background material from United Nations humanitarian agencies, and details on ways to help Kosovo.

Weblink

Yahoo!groups
[groups.yahoo.com]

Doubtless Designs
[www.doubtlessdesigns.net
/godblessamerica.html]

Weblink

Kosovo Primer
[www.psu.edu/ur/NEWS/news
/kosovohelp.html]

listserv—an automated mailing list for e-mail that allows a user to send a message to multiple users on the list and that allows list members to automatically subscribe, unsubscribe, or post messages to all other members in the list, depending on the listserv settings.

MEDIA Quiz

What's the nature of your media world? Is it analog or digital?

1. Do you have a compact disc (CD) player?

2. Have you ever listened to music on a CD?

3. Do you have a computer?

4. Does your computer have access to the Internet?

5. Have you ever downloaded digital music, such as an MP3 file, perhaps off KaZaA or another file-sharing service?

6. Do you use e-mail?

7. Have you ever received spam (unsolicited e-mail advertising messages)?

8. Have you ever watched streaming video (such as Real Player or Windows Media Player) or listened to streaming audio via the Internet?

9. Do you (or does your family/home) have a cable modem or do you have digital cable television?

10. Do you (or does your family/home) have DirecTV or DISHnetwork direct broadcast satellite television?

If you're like most college students, you probably answered yes to at least seven or eight of these questions. That means your media world is very much a digital one.

Online News Credibility

Gallup and Roper data show that Internet news sources have as high or higher levels of credibility than traditional sources, such as newspapers, news magazines, network news, or 24-hour cable news operations. A November 1998 survey by Jupiter Communications found that 80 percent of Web surfers trust online news as much as they do news provided by more traditional media like newspapers and television (not everyone surfs the Web—NielsenNetRatings reports that 60 percent of the U.S. population surfs the Web).[19] A small percent, 7.3, actually trust online sources more than offline.

Of course, much of the news online is provided by the same firms that provide off-line news (such as the *New York Times* or CNN), so it's not entirely surprising that the public might find online news as credible as offline sources.

Online news sites saw record numbers of visitors in the wake of the September 11, 2001, terrorist attacks on the World Trade Center and Pentagon.

CNN.com received double its usual average number of weekly visitors from work in the weeks following September 11. They got an average of 6.2 million weekly visitors logging on from work and 5 million from home, overtaking MSNBC.com as the most visited online news source. MSNBC.com also saw an increase, although not as great as CNN.com's, and got 5.4 million per week on average logging on from work and 4.2 million from home during the same period, as reported by NielsenNetRatings.[20]

Audiences are finding diverse reporting voices by also going to Internet-only sites such as Slate.com or Salon.com, as well as accessing foreign online newspapers that often provide different perspectives from mainstream U.S. media. The public is finding many of these previously unavailable or new sources as reliable—or more reliable—than the traditional sources of news.

Looking Back and Moving Forward

This book begins with the premise that we cannot go back to the world of analog media that existed for most of the twentieth century and earlier. That world is either already gone or is fast disappearing, even though the end products we often see, such as printed newspapers, books, and magazines, are still often analog. However, what we normally do not see is how much—if not all—of the creation, production, and even distribution of that end product is done digitally.

The transformation from an analog to a digital system should not be viewed as a threat to merely the traditional values and role of media in society, although many communication professionals may view it as such, because it represents a deep level of change to the way they have understood mass communication.

It is true there are dangers, but these fundamental changes should be viewed as an opportunity, perhaps an unprecedented opportunity, for the media to increase their contribution to contemporary society by providing not just more information and more entertainment, but better, higher-quality, information and entertainment.

Moreover, the leaders of the industry known collectively as the media business have a unique opportunity to transform their media enterprises into institutions that better serve society. Rather than follow the familiar path of the commercially dominated media industry, journalists and other communication professionals can take this opportunity to reinvent the media enterprise and help lead a troubled industry into a renaissance. But doing that takes money, and media companies for the most part have still not figured out new business models that work with digital media, at least none that would still leave them with the same kind of control they have enjoyed over media content.

Will the Internet and other digital media flourish and lead to a rich blend of eclectic voices, or will the emerging global media system become a homogenous blend of commercial banality where news and entertainment are little more than commodities? No one knows the answer to this question or to matters of privacy and other ethical considerations (such as access to digital media), but these issues will not go away. Dealing with them responsibly is the moral mandate of mass communication in the digital age. This books hopes to give you the tools to understand and address these issues.

SUMMARY

It is important to understand the differences between interpersonal, intrapersonal, and mass communication, and the role that mediation has on these types of communication. From 1455 until the late twentieth century, mass communication followed four basic principles that did not change even with the invention of new forms of media, such as film, radio, and television. The four principles are that communication flow is largely one-way, communication is from one or a few to many, communication is anonymous, and audiences are largely passive recipients of the messages distributed by the media. Digital networked media, however, are turning many of these rules on their head.

Modern theories of communication, such as transmission models, seemed to explain how communication works but were criticized by later scholars who felt that the models were too technically inclined and did not accurately reflect the role of people and society in a theory of mass communication.

The four basic functions of mass communication—surveillance, correlation, cultural transmission, and entertainment—are undergoing drastic transformations with digital media. Digital media have some key concepts that explain what makes them so different from new types of media that came before them. These elements of digital media are ease of creating multimedia, interactivity, automation, and the fact that digital media are simply made up of bits, or electrons, rather than anything physical.

The coming together of computers, the telecommunication industry, and content in digital form is called convergence. Convergence is fundamentally changing aspects of mass communication in four main areas, which are expanded on throughout this book. These areas are how communications professionals do their work, the content of communication, the structure of communication organizations, and the relationships between media organizations and their publics.

Some trends found in the analog media world, such as audience fragmentation and concentration of media ownership, are being accelerated with digital, networked media. Other aspects of digital media are changing the media industry and society. One example is the new power the media audience has to obtain content from a variety of sources, including from other members of the audience, and their ability to widely distribute their own created content for relatively little cost.

Discussion Questions

1. If you were asked to create a time capsule that would be opened in the year 3000, what would you put in it to help a future society understand the nature of the media of mass communication of the twenty-first century?

2. What are the key functions of mass communication identified by Harold Lasswell, Charles Wright, and others?

3. How does the Shannon and Weaver mathematical theory of communication differ from the Schramm and Osgood circular model?

4. Based on your own communication experiences, develop your own model of communication. Is it an empirical model or a cultural model?

5. Convergence has many implications for the mass communication process. What are some of the ways the convergence of media in the digital age affects the relationship between the media and their many publics, including the audience?

6. How much fact-checking do you feel is needed before publishing a story such as the Clinton–Lewinsky affair? Traditional standards dictate that a story must be substantiated by at least two sources before publishing, broadcasting, or webcasting it. Do you think this standard is applicable in an online news environment?

7. What are the key differences between the traditional, analog world of mass communication and mass communication in the digital age?

8. Do you think there is any difference in interactivity when clicking a mouse to close a window and clicking on a mouse to open a pop-up window that provides more in-depth information on a topic? If not, why are they the same? If so, what makes them different?

9. In which direction do you think digital media is more likely to go—toward a more open, diversified and democratic medium, or toward a more corporate, commercialized, and centrally controlled medium? Why?

10. List some changes you have seen in the past few years on the Internet and explain why you think these changes came about and whether you feel they are for better or for worse.

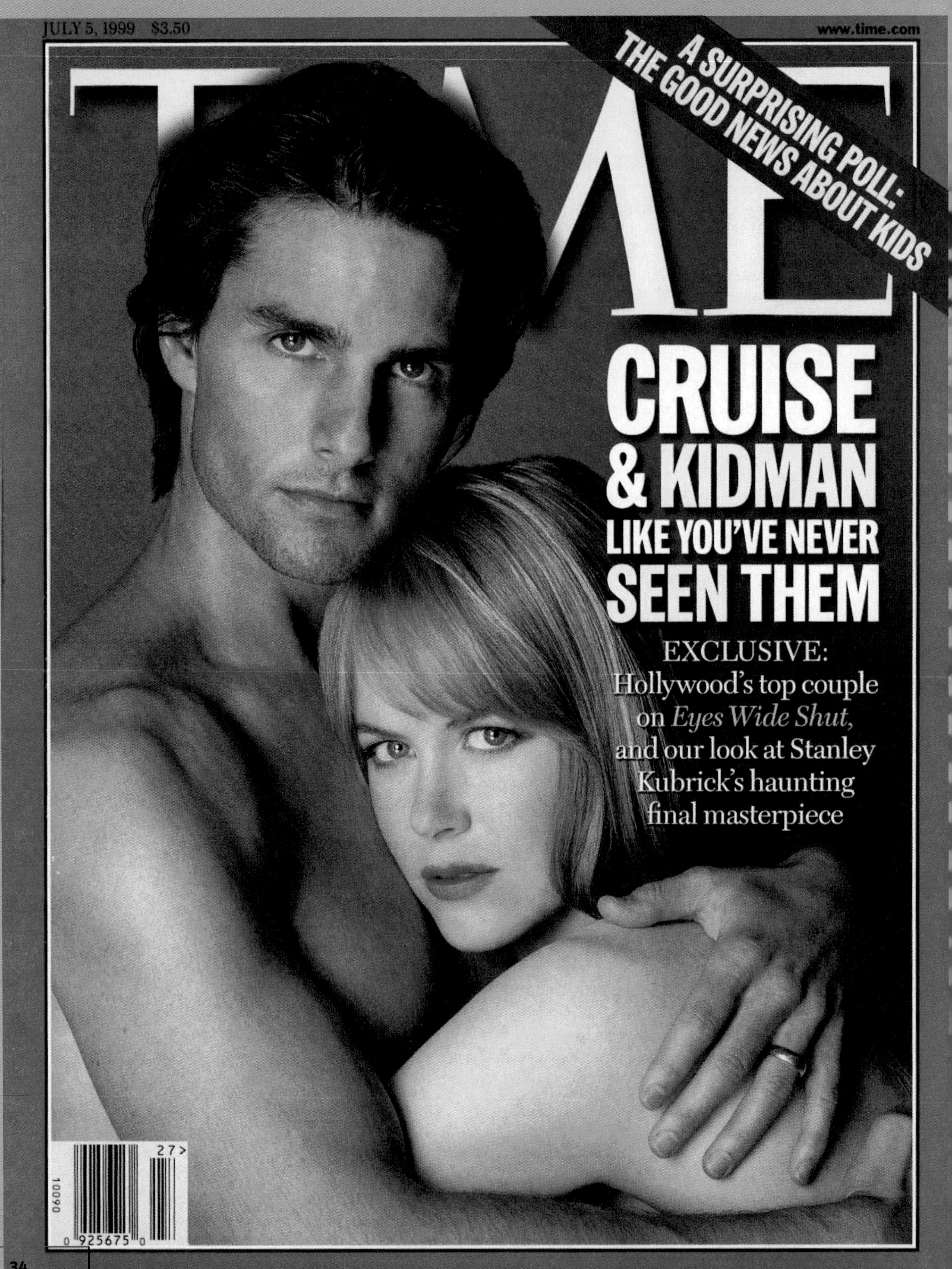

JULY 5, 1999 $3.50

www.time.com

TIME

A SURPRISING POLL:
THE GOOD NEWS ABOUT KIDS

CRUISE & KIDMAN

LIKE YOU'VE NEVER SEEN THEM

EXCLUSIVE:
Hollywood's top couple
on *Eyes Wide Shut*,
and our look at Stanley
Kubrick's haunting
final masterpiece

27>

10090

0 925675 0

34

Media Literacy and Ethics

Noted director Stanley Kubrick

had worked in seclusion for a year with stars Tom Cruise and Nicole Kidman in making *Eyes Wide Shut.* When Kubrick, director of *Dr. Strangelove, A Clockwork Orange,* and *2001: A Space Odyssey,* died in March 1999 shortly after filming was completed, interest in seeing his last film was heightened.

But was the release of the film news that was important enough to appear on the July 5, 1999, cover of *Time* magazine, two weeks before the movie was going to open in theaters? Other major news outlets during that week did not think so, as they covered news of fighting in Sierra Leone and Kosovo.

Could the fact that the Warner Bros. movie studio made the film, a division of Time Warner (now AOL Time Warner), have had anything to do with the editorial decision to feature *Eyes Wide Shut* so prominently in the magazine, as well have the film's two sexy stars on the cover? Despite mediocre reviews from most critics, the film was number one at the box office its first weekend, bringing in $22 million, although it fell rapidly after that as the public apparently agreed with the critics that despite the hype nothing much happens in the movie.

How many people read the glowing preview of the film in *Time,* were enticed by the exclusive interview with Cruise and Kidman or the photos of the stars and the movie, and decided to go see it? We'll never know.

However, this case illustrates how media concentration of ownership can bring pressures on news organizations to use their credibility with the public for purposes other than pure news, even if no orders are explicitly given. It also demonstrates why it is more important than ever for the public to be media literate.

OBJECTIVES

In this chapter we will:

- Define media literacy and provide some basic skills to improve critical thinking ability when consuming mass communication content.
- Explain three elements of media literacy: media grammar, fragmentation of media channels, and the commercial forces that shape media content.
- Provide tips on how to recognize reliable online information and evaluate online sources.
- Define some basic elements in media ethics.
- Describe the consequences and societal repercussions when ethical principles are not followed in media.

Prologue

We live in a media society. Mass communications surround us and influence our world in a variety of ways. They entertain us, they inform us, and they sell us everything from household products to political candidates. In 2001, for example, New York City's mayoral election was won by billionaire media tycoon Michael Bloomberg, who spent roughly $50 million of his own money on his campaign, most of it for television advertising. That's about $70 a vote (he got roughly 50.4 percent of the vote, or 718,488 votes).

With the pervasiveness of media in modern life, it is more important than ever to understand when and how we are being manipulated by media messages. We must look critically at all media we receive and understand something about how media organizations work as businesses and how they fit into other aspects of society.

This chapter explains some basic principles behind media literacy while teaching you to critically analyze the media messages you receive. Finally, it explores some important issues in media ethics, especially in relation to the concentration of media ownership.

What Is Media Literacy?

Being able to read, understanding how to navigate a Web site or send an e-mail attachment, and realizing a scary part of a movie is coming up when the background music changes are all types of literacy that involve media. Some are what we would consider as the traditional meaning of the term *literacy*, and others can be classified as visual literacy or computer literacy. Knowing all the movies a director has ever made, how much he or she made them for, and how much they grossed is also a type of literacy involving media, albeit a limited one. **Media literacy** encompasses all these skills and much more.

Media literacy can be defined as the process of interacting with media content and critically analyzing it by considering its particular presentation, its underlying political or social messages, and ownership and regulation issues that may affect what media is presented in what form. In the age of digital media, additional issues when interacting with media must also be considered, such as erosion of media–consumer privacy and tracking of consumer behavior.

In other words, media consumers should question what they see, hear, or otherwise experience when receiving or interacting with mediated communication. Is a news story biased? Why might it be biased? Why is it even news? Does a popular television show or video game have too much violence, or does it encourage gender or racial stereotypes? What is an advertiser really trying to sell and to whom? Does the placement of articles and photos on a newspaper fairly represent the relative importance of those items as news? These are just a sample of the kinds of questions critical media consumers should ask.

Developing media literacy is an ongoing process, not a goal. There is no qualification test in media literacy to differentiate the media literate from the media illiterate. You will never receive a certificate in "media literacy." If you do,

media literacy—the process of interacting with media content and critically analyzing it by considering its particular presentation, its underlying political or social messages, and ownership and regulation issues that may affect what media is presented in what form.

Because of widespread media exposure, most young people have a relatively high level of media literacy in some areas. Although you may have seen every movie your favorite actor has ever been in and can swap MP3 music files with friends over the Internet, you don't necessarily have an adequate level of media literacy in today's world.

Get a general idea of how media literate you are by taking the following quiz. Answers are at the end of the chapter. Be sure to try this quiz again at the end of the semester to see if your media literacy has improved.

1. Can you name the number-one song in the pop chart right now by title and artist?
2. Name other hit songs the group or artist may have had.
3. Name the recording company this artist or group is signed to.
4. Name the titles of at least three books by best-selling author Stephen King.
5. Name at least three movies made from Stephen King's books.
6. Describe the last time you saw product placement in a movie.
7. Have you ever downloaded a song via the Internet via a file-swapping service such as Morpheus or KaZaA?
8. Have you ever "burned" a CD?
9. Have you ever created a Web site?
10. Is your local newspaper independently owned or owned by a national newspaper chain? If the former, who is the owner and what other businesses in town, if any, does he or she own? If the latter, which chain?
11. Match the following corporations with this partial list of what they own.

Corporations:
Disney,
AOL Time Warner,
Viacom,
News Corp.,
Bertelsmann,
Sony

Media entity:
People, Sports Illustrated, Fortune, CNN, HBO, Random House, RCA, Arista Records, ESPN, Miramax Films, ABC, NFL.com, Fox TV, *New York Post, The Times* (UK), L.A. Dodgers, Columbia Tri-Star, Epic Records, E! Latin America, UPN, MTV, Paramount Pictures, CBS, Simon & Schuster Books.

12. True or false: Personal information about yourself from registering on a Web site can be sold to another company without your knowledge.

you should apply your newfound media literacy skills and ask whether it is worth the paper it is printed on.

If it is impossible to establish perfect media literacy, then why even bother trying to reach the unattainable? The answer is because it is always possible to improve your level of media literacy and thus be a wiser media consumer. The importance of media in contemporary society makes it imperative that audience members exercise critical thinking in their consumption of media content so they can better control their actions and not be controlled by media messages.

Media literacy scholar W. James Potter talks about building "knowledge structures" to improve one's level of media literacy.[1] A knowledge structure is simply a way to visualize building one's level of knowledge on a given topic or topics. For example, if you have a basic understanding of the history of television and someone tells you he or she remembers watching *I Love Lucy* in the 1920s, you can be confident that that person is incorrect because television as a mass medium did not yet exist in the 1920s.

It might seem like an impossible task to learn about all the issues surrounding media, especially in the rapidly changing world of digital media that relies so heavily on complex technology. However, three basic categories represent the foundation for critical media consumption. These are:

1. media grammar;
2. fragmentation of media channels; and
3. commercial forces that shape media content.

Media Grammar

Being a critical consumer of media messages begins with understanding the grammar of the media, or how that media presents itself and is used and understood by the audience. Each medium of mass communication presents its messages uniquely. With media that we are familiar with through widespread use or exposure, we often do not think about the role media grammar plays in what we see, how we see it, and what our perceptions are. In many ways, it becomes "background," but it nevertheless can have profound implications for our understanding of media. We become more aware of media grammar when we encounter a new media type that we do not know the "rules" for yet, such as online media.

Subtext Messages

Common to the grammar of all media, however, is **subtext.** Subtext is the message beneath the message—the underlying, or implicit, message that is being conveyed by media content. A situation comedy such as Warner Brothers' popular television show *Friends* (aired on NBC) may be explicitly about the humorous lives of a group of friends living in Manhattan, but the subtext may be that friends should be of the same race. In *Friends*, all six friends are white. Viewers, especially children and adolescents, may watch the show to be amused, but they may be subtly learning that they, too, should choose best friends of the same race.

subtext—the message beneath the message; the underlying, or implicit, message that is being conveyed by media content.

Being aware of subtext messages does not mean becoming a conspiracy theorist and assuming all television producers or book authors have a hidden agenda that they are trying to spread to the public. The creators of content may not be aware that they are propagating subtext messages; they feel they are simply telling an interesting or amusing story or writing about what they are familiar with. But that doesn't mean that the audience should not be on guard of possible implicit messages in media that reinforce stereotypes or influence one's opinions in the real world.

Print Media

The print media, partly due to their long history compared to other types of mass communication, have developed a very sophisticated media grammar. Everything, including the physical dimensions of a book, whether it contains pictures or not, the size and style of the type, whether it is hardcover or paperback, and the artwork on the book jacket, conveys important messages to the potential book buyer beyond the actual content of the book. Within a book itself, there are several aspects of media grammar that have evolved over the years. Spacing between words to help aid reading comprehension is an early example, as are page numbering, tables of contents, an index, and chapter headings as we know them today. We take many of these elements for granted, but some took years to develop.

Newspapers have their own types of media grammar that have also evolved over time and that continue to change. An obvious example is the amount of color photos and graphics used in newspapers today compared to 30 or 40 years ago. Since space is limited in a newspaper in terms of page size and number of pages, more graphics means there is less room for text. Although many media critics and journalists have complained that this "packaging" of news into relatively short, easy-to-read units accompanied by splashy pictures or graphics does readers a disservice by not providing them with the depth of information they need in today's world, U.S. newspapers have continued to add color and graphics to their pages to make them more visually appealing. Proponents of the trend say that newspapers must compete with television and other visual media for audience attention and so must present news in a way that suits peoples' busy lifestyles.

Most newspapers are organized into sections such as sports, business, and local news. These not only act to help organize information so readers can quickly find stories that interest them, but they create subconscious parameters for readers on what types of stories to expect in those sections. The editorial page and op-ed pages are where newspaper readers expect to hear opinions on events, either from the newspaper staff or publisher itself (editorials) or from guest columnists in the op-ed page.

In terms of size, newspapers conform largely to the rules of either tabloid (typically more sensational in tone) or broadsheet (more serious). They use headlines to capture attention and "teasers" on the front page or front section pages to entice readers to see articles inside the paper. They use a variety of graphic techniques to attract and guide the reader's eye. More important stories usually appear "above the fold," or on the upper half of the broadsheet paper, so when the papers are stacked in a newsstand, those stories and graphics are what people first see.

Media Spotlight: From *Gilligan's Island* to *Survivor*: A Three-Decade Cruise in Media Literacy

Gilligan's Island, a 1960s sitcom about seven ship-wrecked characters on a deserted Pacific island, is still often seen in reruns. After the first few episodes aired in 1964, Sherwood Schwartz, the show's producer, said in a 1984 interview that he had been contacted by the Coast Guard, who told him they had received several dozen serious complaints from people saying that the military should send a ship to find and rescue the people. Schwartz asked, "Who did these viewers think was filming the castaways on that island? There was even a laugh track on the show. Who was laughing at the survivors of the wreck of the *S.S. Minnow?* It boggled the mind."[2]

In June 2000 CBS aired the first of a series of "reality-based TV" shows called *Survivor,* in which 16 people were sent to a remote island and largely left to fend for themselves and undergo a series of trials and contests even as they voted a member off the island each week. The sole "survivor" would win $1 million. The show became a huge hit. It is estimated that 52 million people watched the finale of the first season. The show was copied from a popular 1997 Swedish show called *Expedition Robinson.* As of this writing, there were no reports that the Coast Guard received any complaints that the people should be rescued, although in February 2001 one of the former contestants, a 27-year-old San Francisco attorney named Stacey Stillman, sued the show claiming that producers had rigged the selection process to bolster the show's demographic appeal.[3]

Newspapers present hard news using an inverted pyramid organization (most important items first) in the body of the text report. Sources, or people interviewed, are quoted to establish the credibility of what is being reported, enliven the report, and to show that it's not just the reporter offering his or her views. Photos and illustrations are accompanied by a brief tag line that explains what the artwork is about. Features, such as human-interest stories or profiles, are written in a different style, sometimes starting with a vignette that helps humanize the story and hook the reader.

Even if you can't read the language, you can probably make an educated guess as to what type of news these Mideast newspapers cover. Why? Because their formats are similar to newspapers you are already familiar with.

Magazines similarly use sophisticated graphic and design techniques and feature more long-form writing, often with just one or two articles per page and multipage articles. Advertising in magazines often takes up a full page, and in some magazines it is hard to immediately tell if something is an ad or graphics for the beginning of a feature. In some ways magazines combine elements of books and newspapers in their media grammar. Because of their length, they usually have a table of contents (many also have an advertiser index), which helps readers find specific articles quickly. Like newspapers, they are often divided into subject-related sections within their topic area, which usually contain short, newsy items on the subject.

Radio and Recorded Music

Radio and recorded music similarly have their own grammar, that of sound. Radio uses a combination of audio techniques to achieve different ends. Among these techniques are volume changes, multiple audio tracks, **actualities** (i.e., edited audio clips from people interviewed), sound effects, and **voice-overs,** all of which can be used to convey information, capture attention or achieve some other purpose.

Recorded music typically conforms to particular stylistic conventions, especially with regards to length (less than five minutes a song) and music format. Popular music genres, such as hip hop, rock, country, or swing, have certain rhythms, lyrical styles, and sounds that make them clearly distinguishable. This underlying media grammar facilitates easier marketing and promotion.

Even a format as apparently chaotic as talk radio has a well-defined media grammar. Many talk radio shows include call-ins from comic imitators of famous people and a "sidekick" in the studio who supports or provides counterpoints to the main host.

Film and Television

Although film and television have much shorter histories as mass media than does print, they have already developed a sophisticated media grammar that is based on editing, camera angles, lighting, movement, and sound.

actualities—used in radio and television to denote edited audio or video clips of people interviewed.

voice-over—an unseen announcer or narrator talking while other activity takes place either on radio or while a scene is being shown on television.

In a scene from the movie *Natural Born Killers,* filmmaker Oliver Stone addressed serious societal issues by turning the media grammar of the sitcom on its head. He used garish colors; strong, abusive language that referred to wife battering and incest; and a laugh track at intentionally inappropriate times.

For example, in the early history of film, most movies were only a few minutes long and either simply recorded daily activities or were essentially uncut filmed short stage plays. Although the short length of movies was more a function of the limited technology at the time, audiences soon tired of the novelty of watching silent filmed plays and wanted something more interesting.

Filmmakers started producing more sophisticated storylines for their short films and introduced a technique that was unique to film at the time—crosscut scenes. By crosscutting different scenes to simulate simultaneous events happening in two different locations, filmmakers were able to tell much more complex and dramatic stories. Further, by increasing the speed between crosscut scenes, it helped increase dramatic tension in the audience.

Today's filmmakers have many more such tools at their disposal and are able to give audiences a lot of information, all with visual or audio techniques. Think of the combination of low music and strong shadows in many horror movies, or how we understand an on-screen dream sequence or flashback, or how we differentiate "good" from "bad" characters even before they have spoken or revealed their characters through the narrative plot.

The media grammar of television fiction uses many of the same techniques seen in movies, although of course television production budgets are much smaller than movie budgets. Think of the media grammar of your average sitcom—it is usually shot on a set, with perhaps less than half a dozen "locations" generally used, and the actors come and go as if on a stage. The camera is usually stationary, although multiple camera angles are used, and a **laugh track** is used with the various punch lines, which in some sitcoms can almost be timed with clockwork precision (even if the line isn't particularly funny).

laugh track—a device used in television sitcoms that generates prerecorded laughter, timed to coincide with punch lines of jokes.

Bringing History to Life Online

An intriguing example of what's possible in the new media environment comes in the form of a Web site called "Race and Place: African American Community Histories." The site focuses on the history of Charlottesville, Virginia, and presents its story through a rich blend of digital media, interactivity, and diversity. The site was developed by students as part of a course introducing them to archival research at the University of Virginia, a university known for its innovative use of educational technology. The site is a component in a larger online archive called "Race and Place: African American Community Histories."

The site features more than 9500 pictures of African Americans from the late 1800s, taken by Rufus W. Holsinger, a commercial photographer who operated a studio in Charlottesville. More than 500 of the photos are of people who lived in the Charlottesville area. Holsinger provided scant information about his subjects, so the students faced the challenge of placing names to faces.

The students' persistence paid off. Having no more than a few scraps of information to accompany a set of photographs of African Americans at the turn of the century, students at the university set up a table at a local festival in search of anyone who could put names to the faces. At the festival, one woman alone recognized 15 of her family members and acquaintances.

The students built an online data base incorporating records from the 1910 census and the Charlottesville business and city directories from the period. Now, visitors to the site can quickly identify local enterprises, places of worship, social clubs and organizations, or schools by sorting or searching the database, as well as identifying people. If they do, they can provide information about anyone they might recognize.

W

Weblink
Race and Place: African American
Community Histories
http://www.vcdh.virginia.edu/afam
/home.html

Other types of television shows have their own types of media grammar, such as game shows, soap operas, talk shows, and news. Although we tend to think of the news as objective—or at least the media grammar used in news shows tries to encourage that kind of thinking by the audience—it is important to understand how camera angles, lighting, distance from the subject and interviewer, sound, and intercut scenes all affect our perceptions of the news.

The "objective point of view" used in television news reporting interviews treats the viewer as an observer. Typically, the camera is kept still, with shots over the shoulder of the journalist interviewing a subject. Prior to the interview, the subject is instructed by the journalist never to look directly into the camera. Rather, only the news anchor or field reporter in his or her stand-up, often used as a means to summarize or conclude the report, is allowed to look directly into the camera and thereby establish eye contact with the audience. This grammar establishes the authoritativeness and objectivity of the journalist and helps the viewer recognize the difference between the subject and the reporter.

It has been interesting to see how television news especially has borrowed some elements from the online world in its media grammar—which originally had borrowed heavily from television when graphical user interfaces such as windows and digital video started appearing online. Multiple windows on the television screen showing different kinds of information, scrolling news across the bottom of the screen giving news updates, and icons such as blinking cursors are just some examples of how television news is borrowing from the online world and thus adding new types of media grammar.

Online Media

Online media are still so new that their grammar is still developing. Imagine a media world in which not all the audience members know how to turn pages in a book; where they try to use a remote control on a magazine; where they are afraid to use their remote control lest they break the television, or where they see a different kind of image on the TV than their neighbors because their television was made by a different company or their television is last year's model. That is roughly the state of online media in the early twenty-first century, and it is unlikely to change anytime in the near future.

However, some media grammar elements are starting to form. **Hypertext,** for example, is generally either underlined or otherwise set apart typographically or graphically from nonlinked text. An unwritten rule to have a Web site logo in the upper left corner of the screen linked to return to the Web site's homepage is being followed by more and more Web developers. The increased use of icons to create a visual, interactive "language" that transverses Web sites allows computer users to quickly learn how to use new types of programs or utilize interactivity on a Web site. Examples include more or less standardized icons for functions such as printing, opening a document, sending a file, e-mailing a document, on-screen drawing, painting, or image editing tools, and icons to allow for image manipulation such as zooming in or out, where applicable.

Mass communication in an online digital environment increasingly exploits a full range of storytelling and communication tools, including text, audio, video, graphics, and animation. This broadened set of tools enables the journalist or other communication professional to tell each story in a way uniquely suited to that story. Because of the lack of experience of many users of online media and the ever-changing state of technological improvements, it still can be a challenge to guide users in accessing that information easily as an online media grammar develops.

The value of enriched storytelling capabilities has been demonstrated in a variety of publishing enterprises. One early example is Voyager, a company founded by Bob Stein, whose electronic publishing produced a series of highly acclaimed digital products, such as "Poetry in Motion," featuring a rich multimedia presentation of poet Amiri Baraka (formerly known as LeRoi Jones), "Starry Night," which explores Van Gogh's remarkable painting, and "First Person: Mumia Abu-Jamal," the black journalist convicted of murder and sentenced to life in prison in a sensational case involving racial and political crosscurrents in Philadelphia, Pennsylvania.

Weblink
Voyager
[voyager.learntech.com/cdrom/]

How to Recognize Reliable Information and Evaluate Resources

With the increased availability of media channels, especially online, it has become increasingly difficult for audiences to recognize which channels offer reliable information and how to evaluate the information they encounter.

hypertext—text online that is linked to another Web page, Web site, or different part of the same Web page by HTML coding.

There are at least three principal ways to evaluate media in the digital age. First is brand name. Some brands are well-established and have proven their reliability over time. Among these are leading news publishers, such as The New York Times Company, which publishes news and information in print, online, and also on television. News consumers who see this brand, regardless of medium, can probably count on it to be a good source of information.

The second way is to examine the new or unfamiliar source's own internal standards, practices, organization, and personnel. Most Web sites include a section called "about us," and it usually provides useful information about who operates the site, how it is run, and what procedures it follows in creating content. This information should lay out a compelling case as to why readers should trust the site. More and more Web sites offering news are also posting their mission statements online in order to help establish their credibility.

Or, it might be worth looking at a Web site called "Who Is?" Who Is? provides a comprehensive and up-to-date database on all Web sites. They provide a wealth of useful information, including who owns each site's domain name, to whom it is registered, and their contact information. Such information can be useful in establishing the legitimacy of a Web site. Web sites that do not have accurate or complete contact information should not be as trusted as those that do.

The third way to evaluate media is to compare the new or unfamiliar source of information with other trusted or independent sources. For example, if one encounters a new Web site on financial information and is unsure of its veracity, it may be useful to compare its reports with an established or trusted brand, such as *The Wall Street Journal,* which has spent more than a century establishing its reliability. Another option when looking at online news sources is to look at the original source material as well to see if the article accurately portrayed what was important.

Dos and *Don'ts* when Evaluating Online Information

The Internet is full of hoaxes, cranks, scams, and cons. The up-to-the-minute, 24/7 nature of news on the Web and low-cost distribution make it an ideal place for misinformation to be spread, because facts cannot always be quickly verified. How do you know when you are being fed a line when online?

- Do check the "About Us" section of a Web site to find out background information on who runs it. Do they clearly state their mission, what they stand for, and who any sponsors are, or do they seem evasive and unclear? If they fall in the latter category, that could be a warning sign that they are not being on the level as to their real purpose.
- Do check what other sites they link to in a "Useful Links" page and scan what those sites stand for. Most Web sites link to others who share their views or at least will have more similar-minded links than links to opposing Web sites.
- Do compare the information in the Web site with similar stories in other Web sites, both from branded news names and from smaller sites. If you receive information that a well-known or respected group has made an important announcement, check the organization's Web site, as they should have that information posted as well.

- Don't trust the name of the organization who owns the Web site. Lobbying groups and other organizations that are trying to push a specific agenda will often adopt names that mask their true goals or at least put them in a euphemistic light.
- Don't trust information that has no date somewhere on the page. Information that may have been accurate when it was first posted may well be out of date when you come to the site.
- Don't trust information you read from discussion groups, online chat rooms, or Usenet, even if the person posting claims to be an expert or authority on the subject. As the old newsroom saying goes: If your mother says she loves you, check it out.

The Fragmentation of Media Channels

Today's media system is increasingly fragmented. The number of media channels has exploded since the mid-1970s, when most people in the United States had access to four national television networks (three commercial, one public), one or two national news magazines, a local daily newspaper, and a handful of local radio stations. Today, the typical media consumer has hundreds of national channels of television and radio content to choose from, as well as dozens of international channels. Online, media consumers have thousands of media Web sites from around the United States and the world to explore.

The Multichannel Universe

The explosion in the number of channels has enormous implications for media literacy. In the past, one needed only to turn the television dial a few times to see the entire spectrum of television programming. Today, it can take half an hour to navigate through the **electronic program guide** listings of just the current program offerings. Making sense of all the media available on the Internet is even more daunting.

The consequences of fragmentation are potentially significant in terms of the impact of media on society. Rarely do national audiences come together for common, simultaneous media experiences. The effects of this fragmentation have been hard to document, but many people have asserted that fragmentation leads to less social cohesion. This fragmentation can be amplified by many of the personalization features on the Web. Internet users can choose what kinds of news and entertainment content they see when they get online and thus filter out views and news that they would otherwise be exposed to in traditional media. As mentioned in the previous chapter, a concern is that people will become so focused on some narrow aspect of a particular topic or subject with other like-minded individuals that they will ignore larger societal issues that do not directly affect or interest them.

Before television, national magazines were said to help the young American nation define itself and give people a common platform to look at and discuss issues. A sometimes-heard lament is that when the three networks dominated

electronic program guide (EPG) — guide available on television that provides program listings and some simple interactivity, such as ordering pay-per-view programs through the television or buying CDs or DVDs of music or shows that are listed.

American television viewing, television played a vital role in establishing or reinforcing a common culture or a common agenda for the nation. Television, for example, provided live coverage of our first step on the moon, and this helped foster great national pride.

One also needs to consider other programming commonly seen during the era when three commercial networks dominated. Although there were some great programs to be sure, such as Edward Murrow's *See It Now* or *Playhouse 90,* among the most widely seen programs were situation comedies such as *The Beverly Hillbillies* and *Gilligan's Island.* Entertaining though these programs may have been, it is hard to argue they provided the glue that held our nation together. Even more, it was during the 1960s when the networks were at their peak in terms of viewing dominance that the nation was embroiled in its greatest social upheaval since the Civil War, a century before.

A Diversity of Voices

The flip side of fragmentation is increased diversity of voices in programming. When the three long-standing commercial networks dominated, their programming was almost devoid of cultural diversity. It was an almost entirely white world, frequently suburban in nature. Despite an occasional program featuring black, Latino, or other minority group lead characters, it was not until the development of Fox, WB, and UPN that commercial network television began to show significantly more inclusive programming during prime time—although it is still highly skewed in terms of the portrayal of many social, cultural, and ethnic groups. Moreover, the growth of cable and direct broadcast satellite (DBS) has ushered in even more cultural diversity and diversity of voices on television. Although it may be hard to get the nation gathered around the television set watching a single program anymore, it is also true that television of the early twenty-first century provides a window of greater cultural diversity of the nation and the world. Of course, it is still far from a perfect social or cultural mirror.

The proliferation of online media has also led to a huge growth in the diversity or plurality of media voices available to consumers. Although many media consumers may still be most comfortable with a relatively small number of

The creation of TV networks Fox, UPN, and WB has helped increase the diversity of characters seen on broadcast television with shows like *The Hughleys.*

media channels, they now at least have access to a diverse set of voices and perspectives online. Research from the Pew Center indicates that frequent users of the Internet appreciate and value this variety of media voices.

Mass Audiences

Despite media fragmentation, certain programs still draw record audiences. An excellent example was CBS's coverage of the 1994 Winter Olympics. The coverage set a ratings record, making it the most-watched event in TV history, with 204 million U.S. viewers, or 83 percent of the country, seeing at least a portion of CBS's coverage. International viewership was even higher, with estimates of more than 1 billion viewers worldwide.

More recently, when the terrorist attack on the World Trade Center occurred on September 11, 2001, almost all media turned their attention to the attack and its aftermath. For days, weeks, and even months following the attack, it was hard to find any media channel—print, broadcast, cable, or online—that didn't focus in large part on terrorism and the U.S. response to it. In this case, fragmentation of channels probably helped in the depth of coverage, as more media outlets covered various angles of the tragedy and thus gave the public more information than they would have had if the media outlets were confined to only a few.

Commercial Forces That Shape Media Content

Even in an open and democratic society with a free press such as in the United States, economic factors and corporate decisions often influence what is and is not covered in the news and what kind of entertainment is created and shown to the general public. Rarely does the average media consumer think of how commercial forces are shaping the content we see everyday, but these forces affect everything from what types of shows are produced to whether a news report critical of an important advertiser is downplayed or even pulled by the media corporation.

These activities happen at the local level and national or international level. At the local level, a cutback in the number of reporters to help save money can result in a noticeable drop of local coverage, such as coverage of area schools. The newspaper company may save money, but the public is poorer for the lessened coverage of local issues that they should be informed about. A company that advertises heavily in a local newspaper may have undue influence on decisions whether articles critical of it are published or not by threatening to withdraw its advertising.

But this kind of manipulation of media content is not confined to small-town media outlets. In 1998, Chris Patten, former British governor of Hong Kong, had his book contract cancelled by HarperCollins, which is a subsidiary of Rupert Murdoch's News Corporation. Patten's book, *East and West,* was reportedly going to be highly critical of China's policies, and Murdoch at the time was trying to get China to accept Murdoch's Star TV satellite and cable programs.

Chris Patten, former British governor of Hong Kong.

Similarly, a few years prior to that he removed the BBC from Star TV when Chinese leaders expressed displeasure at the BBC's reports on the killings in Tiananmen Square in June 1989.

These incidents are not meant to show that Rupert Murdoch and News Corporation are particularly greedy or selfish; similar stories of corporate decisions influencing what we see or do not see can be told about all of the major media corporations and will be covered in more detail later in this chapter when discussing media ethics.

Profit and Nonprofit Media

Basic to all media is the underlying commercial nature of mass communication. As such, there are two main systems for funding media in the United States. One system relies on the commercial marketplace where print and electronic media are run to make money. The other system is not for profit and relies on a combination of public funding, or support from government or other public institutions, corporate gifts and sponsorships, and audience contributions. This system is used especially for electronic media. There are a variety of other funding models used around the world for nonprofit media, including systems where the public pays a tax on television or radio receivers, which then is used to fund media programming.

In the for-profit model, ownership plays a key role in determining the nature of the media enterprise. For-profit media companies are either publicly held companies or privately held, often family-owned, operations. For publicly held media companies, shares are bought and sold on the stock market, just like any other company. The people who run these companies are responsible to their shareholders, who, by and large, expect their investments to return a profit.

In recent history, media businesses have been among the most profitable of any industry, with profit margins typically in double digits, or 10 percent or higher, on an annual basis. Sometimes, profit pressures lead media companies, especially publicly traded companies, to focus on the short term—cutting costs, laying off staff, or making decisions that can increase near-term profits—but that negatively influence the quality of a product, such as a news enterprise. The result can be an immediate increase in profitability, but that profitability is not sustainable.

Conversely, making money can also be an incentive for media companies to produce a better-quality product. The Disney Company, for example, is among the most profitable of major publicly owned media companies in the United States, and it is recognized for its quality products, including award-winning motion pictures, recorded music, and television (it owns the ABC television network, one of the most highly regarded and watched).

The influence of this commercial foundation is especially evident in entertainment media, such as in much television programming and many motion pictures. Most of the television schedule is organized with commercial breaks on the hour and throughout each program so advertisers can insert their commercial messages. Broadcast television, although thought of as "free" television, is still essentially paid for by the consumer in the form of higher prices for products as companies have to recoup their expenses for advertising and marketing budgets. But in addition to commercials, advertisers can influence the content of shows and motion pictures directly.

Product Placement and Corporate Sponsorship

Influencing the content of shows and motion pictures can happen in at least two ways. The first is product placement, where advertisers pay to have their product displayed in a movie or show with the brand name highly visible to the audience. Second, advertisers or marketers sometimes work directly with media organizations to sponsor specific programs on television or special sections in newspapers. A brand of beer or soft drink sponsoring a concert tour that is televised on MTV is an example of this.

Even entire channels of content are based on corporate sponsorship. An example is the Hallmark Channel. Launched in August 2001 by Hallmark Cards and Crown Media Holdings, the Hallmark Channel features dozens of series, specials, movies, and miniseries, ranging from *Gulliver's Travels* to *Animal Farm*. The Hallmark Channel is widely distributed through 1700 cable systems, DirecTV and EchoStar direct-to-home satellite services, and C-Band dish owners across the United States and worldwide to 100 international markets; the channel is seen by more than 80 million subscribers globally.[4] It's worth noting that simply because a program or channel is advertiser-sponsored, it isn't necessarily flawed. In fact, advertising sponsorship has produced some of the best programming on television, including the Hallmark Channel, which features a library of 4500 hours of programming that has won nearly 200 Emmy Awards.

Shaping Public Service Media

Although the U.S. media system includes public service broadcasting, even that is increasingly influenced or shaped by commercial forces. In the United States, a large portion of the funding for public service broadcasting comes from corporate sponsors, and those sponsors tend to be most interested in programming that is consistent with the image they want to cultivate among public broadcasting's generally upscale audiences. The Public Broadcasting Service (PBS), which produces and distributes public programming, received 17 percent of its funding from businesses in 2000, the second highest source of funding for public television. The largest portion, 26 percent, comes from member donations. Less than a third of PBS's funding comes from government sources.[5]

As a result of the relatively large portion of corporate sponsorship and the relaxing of rules that do not allow corporations to advertise on public television, even public service broadcasters sometimes shape their programming in accordance with commercial forces. PBS has also faced especially tough competition with some of the specialized cable channels, which produce targeted or niche educational programming on sciences, nature, or history much like that shown by PBS.

Concentration of Media Ownership

Regardless of ownership, there are incentives for media companies to seek economies of scale. Strictly speaking, economies of scale refer to the decrease in unit manufacturing cost that results from mass production. In the context of media, it means essentially that media enterprises can reduce costs and increase profit by getting larger and reaching a larger market with their content. Of course, just getting bigger doesn't necessarily translate into greater economies of scale, but it is the basic reason behind a fundamental trend in media over the past half century. Successful media enterprises have acquired other media enterprises, either through purchase or merger, and thereby become larger in size and scope. Newspaper companies have bought other newspaper companies; radio station groups have bought other radio station groups. Cross-media enterprises have acquired other media enterprises, sometimes extending internationally as well. The result is a media system that is increasingly large, multifaceted, and international in ownership. These companies compete with other large media enterprises and across international borders.

Some critics have argued that despite the possible economies of scale, there is a significant downside to media conglomerates or media monopolies (i.e., when in a community there is just one media organization serving the public). Greater concentration of ownership, or fewer owners owning more media, results in less diversity of media voices, and the public is thus poorly served. Minority voices and nonmainstream views are silenced.

One of the most vocal critics of concentrated media ownership is Ben H. Bagdikian. In his book *Media Monopoly,* Bagdikian presents evidence that during the 1990s a small number of the country's largest corporations purchased more public communications power than ever before. In 1983, the biggest media merger in history was a $340 million deal involving the Gannett Company, a newspaper chain, which bought Combined Communications Corporation, whose assets included billboards, newspapers, and broadcast stations. In 1996, Disney's acquisition of ABC/Capital Cities was a $19 billion deal—56 times larger. In 2001, AOL's acquisition of Time Warner dwarfed even this deal at $160 billion, or nearly ten times the price of the 1996 Disney deal.

These companies, Bagdikian contends, have built a communications cartel within the United States. A cartel is a group of independent businesses that collaborate to regulate production, pricing, and marketing of goods by the members of the group. In this case, the group is controlling not just industrial products such as gasoline, refrigerators, or clothing. At stake are the words and images that define and shape the culture and political agenda of the country. "Aided by the digital revolution and the acquisition of subsidiaries that operate at every step in the mass communications process, from the creation of content to its delivery into the home, the communications cartel has exercised stunning influence over national legislation and government agencies, an influence whose scope and power would have been considered scandalous or illegal twenty years ago," writes Bagdikian.

Bagdikian further notes that 99 percent of the 1500 daily newspapers in the country are the only daily in their cities. All but a few of the nation's 11,800 cable systems are monopolies in their cities. Most of the country's 11,000 commercial radio stations are part of national ownership groups and just a half dozen formats (e.g., all-talk, all-news, rock, rap, adult contemporary) dominate programming in every city. The major commercial television networks and their local affiliates carry programs of essentially the same type all across the country. This system is a **media oligopoly.** The term *media oligopoly* refers to a marketplace in which media ownership and diversity are severely limited and the actions of any single media group substantially affect its competitors, including the content and price of media products for both consumers and advertisers.

The Globalization of Media

Dominating the media worldwide are diversified global media giants (see Table 2-1). These corporations are international conglomerates, many of whom are either financially dominated themselves by nonmedia business interests or at least contain in their financial portfolio significant nonmedia commercial properties and investments. They include a wide range of media or channels of distribution, especially video.

AOL Time Warner

As shown in Table 2-1, the largest media company in the world is AOL Time Warner. Notably, this company has existed only since 2001. The parent companies, America Online and Time Warner, had existed for many years, but in January 2000 they announced their plans to merge and create the new, largest media enterprise in the world. In January 2001, the merger (technically, AOL acquired Time Warner) became official as federal regulators gave their approval. By the time the merger was complete, however, the bottom had fallen out of the dot-com financial sector, the economy had weakened in general, AOL Time Warner's stock had dropped substantially in 2001 and 2002, and there were several executive shake-ups during 2002.

AOL Time Warner has more than 200 subsidiaries, including Time Inc. (the largest magazine publisher in the United States); Warner Bros. (producer and distributor of movies, TV programs, and videos); Warner Music Group; Home Box Office (the largest pay TV service in the United States); Cinemax (another pay TV service); Time Warner Cable (the largest cable system in the United States); Warner Books (a major book publisher); cable TV networks, including CNN, TBS, TNT, and Comedy Central (50 percent owned with Viacom); the WB television network; and various other properties ranging from *Mad* magazine to the Atlanta Braves baseball team and a number of other professional sports teams. It employs more than 90,000 people and has its headquarters in New York City's Rockefeller Center, although a new headquarters is being built for $1.7 billion near Columbus Circle, on the southwest corner of Central Park. Its chairman is Stephen M. Case, the founder of AOL and now sole representative from the

media oligopoly—a marketplace in which media ownership and diversity are severely limited and the actions of any single media group substantially affect its competitors, including the content and price of media products for both consumers and advertisers.

Table 2-1 Global Media Corporations, Ranked by 2000 Revenues in Billions of Dollars

Company	Revenues in billions of dollars	Head-quarters	News-papers/ Magazines	TV, Movies	Radio	Cable	Book	Music	Internet
1. AOL Time Warner*	$36.4	United States	*Time,* many other magazines	Warner Communications, HBO, WB	None	TWC	Warner Books	Warner Music	AOL, many online publications, Road Runner cable modem
2. Disney	$25.4	United States	None	ABC, Buena Vista, Miramax	ABC	ESPN	Hyperion	Walt Disney Records	ESPN.com, Infoseek
3. Viacom CBS	$20	United States	None	Paramount, UPN, CBS	Infinity	MTV, Showtime, Nickel-odeon	Simon & Schuster	Famous Music Pub.	MTV.com, CBS MarketWatch.com, Sports-line
4. Sony	$16 (only media portion, not including consumer electronics; total revenues are $58)	Japan	None	Columbia Pictures, Sony	None	Game Show Network	None	Columbia, Epic, Nashville	Limited, but big in electronics, games, and devices, which are increasingly online
5. Bertels-mann	$15.8	Germany	Gruner+ Jahr	CLT-UFA	CLT-UFA	None	Random House	Bertels-mann Music Group	Bn.com

(continued)

AOL side of the business among upper-level executives, and CEO is Richard D. Parsons, a long-time executive at Time Warner.

The Walt Disney Company

Second in size to AOL Time Warner is the Walt Disney Company. The legendary Walt Disney founded the company, which still maintains its unique flavor of family-oriented media entertainment. Its properties include ABC Television Network; Buena Vista Motion Pictures Group; Miramax Films; various theme parks, such as the Animal Kingdom, Disneyland, Disneyland Paris, Tokyo Disneyland, Disney-MGM Studios, Epcot Center, and the Magic Kingdom in Orlando, Florida (the most-visited theme park in North America); a cruise line; Internet companies; and the professional NHL hockey team the Anaheim Mighty Ducks. The ABC TV network includes a dozen owned and operated TV stations

Table 2-1 Global Media Corporations, Ranked by 2000 Revenues in Billions of Dollars (continued)

Company	Revenues in billions of dollars	Head-quarters	News-papers/ Magazines	TV, Movies	Radio	Cable	Book	Music	Internet
6. Vivendi Universal	$14.6 (only media portion, not including water-services; total revenues are $40)	France	Many magazines	42% of USA Networks, Universal Studios, CANAL+ (French pay-TV service)	None	None	Houghton Mifflin	Universal Music Group	Cegetel
7. News Corp	$13.8	Australia	*New York Post, Times* (London)	20th Century Fox, Fox net-work, Star TV	None	Fox News, Sports, Family Channel	Harper Collins	Mush-room Records	Fox.com
8. AT&T Broad-band & Internet Services	$8.2	United States	None	Liberty Media	None	Former TCI and MediaOne	None	None	Digital cable
9. Comcast	$8.2	United States	None	QVC, and E! Entertainment TV	None	Comcast	None	None	High-speed cable. digital cable
10. Cox Media	$7.8	United States	Cox NPs	Cox TV stations	Cox radio stations	Cox Cable	None	None	With 28 city-specific Internet sites, cable modem

Sources: Hoovers.com, Fortune.com, company reports.

*Note: AOL announced its acquisition of Time Warner in January 2000, but the official merger of the two companies was not completed until January 2001.

as well as shares in nine cable channels, including premier sportscaster ESPN. Disney employs 117,000 people worldwide. The company is headquartered in Burbank, California. Chairman and CEO is Michael D. Eisner, and the vice chairman is Roy E. Disney.

Viacom CBS

Third on the list of media giants is Viacom CBS. Viacom was founded as a cable channel spin-off from CBS in 1971, following an FCC order forcing the networks to divest their programming syndication and cable TV businesses, and it is ironic that 29 years later the spin-off had grown to such proportions that it was large enough to buy its parent.

Cable pioneer Ralph Baruch headed Viacom during many of its early years after the CBS spin-off and helped the company grow through a series of smart business

Pamela Thomas-Graham

On Sept. 1, 1999, NBC Chairman and CEO Robert Wright named Pamela Thomas-Graham the president and CEO of CNBC.com and executive vice president, NBC. Thomas-Graham, a graduate of the Harvard Law School and the Harvard Business School, was the first black woman partner at McKinsey & Company, the world's largest management consulting firm, where she specialized in new media. In her NBC posts, she is among the most influential executives in television, online, and overall media businesses. In 2001, *Black Enterprise* magazine named Thomas-Graham the African American executive of the year.

Pamela Thomas-Graham.

moves, tempered by a strong commitment to public service. During the Baruch years, Viacom was pronounced reflecting its Latin roots, as "Vee-ah," but with Sumner Redstone's acquisition in 1987 and a shift of corporate culture, the pronunciation was changed to a more Anglo flavor, with a long "i" sound (as in "high").

The reunited behemoth has wide-ranging interests, including Blockbuster, the number-one video chain with 4200 stores that represent 25 percent of videotape rentals (Viacom CBS owns 80 percent of the chain); MTV Networks (MTV, VH-1, Nickelodeon); Showtime Networks; the United Paramount Network (UPN, 50 percent); the CBS Television Network; the Nashville Network; Country Music Television; and 82 percent of Infinity Broadcasting, which owns 160 radio stations in 34 U.S. markets. Also in its empire are book publisher Simon & Schuster, Paramount Pictures, 34 TV stations, and more than 100 theaters in Canada. The merged operation also has a strong online presence in CBS MarketWatch.com (37 percent ownership) and SportsLine USA (a 21 percent stake). With its MTV Internet division, MTVi, including both MTV and VH-1, as well as SonicNet (a premiere provider of online music), Viacom CBS is positioned well to provide not only online music but also online music video. Its Nickelodeon channel, already one of the most popular children's destinations on the Web with 2.4 million registered users, also is well positioned to bring more online video.

Sumner Redstone, CEO of Viacom CBS, controls 67 percent of Viacom voting stock. The company is headquartered in New York.

Of the remaining seven largest media companies worldwide, four are based outside the United States, although each has various U.S. media business interests. These four international media companies are Japan's Sony Corporation, Germany's Bertelsmann AG, France's Vivendi Universal, and Australia's News Corporation.

Media Executive Diversity

One noteworthy aspect of these ten media giants is that in every case but two, the chief executive (either the chairman or the CEO) is a white male of western European descent. The exceptions are Richard Parsons, CEO of AOL Time Warner, who is African American, and the Japanese chairman of Sony. Not until one travels far down the media hierarchy does one find significant diversity in media ownership at firms such as $577 million Spanish-language television network Univision, Yahoo!, or the $1.5 billion Black Entertainment Television, whose founder Robert Johnson in 2000 launched a major black-oriented Web presence.

One notable attempt at greater diversity or inclusivity at the top of the networks failed with a resounding thud in 1999 when Jamie Tarses resigned from her position as head of ABC Entertainment. In 1996, at age 32, Tarses became not only the youngest but the first woman to head a network entertainment division. She had achieved considerable success in programming at NBC, where she helped create prime-time hits such as *Friends*. At ABC she introduced a series of sophisticated urban comedies such as *Dharma and Greg*. In response to a restructuring at the network, Tarses resigned her post as the president of ABC Entertainment. In leaving she said, "I definitely never want to be an executive again."[6]

Media Ethics

It is important to understand the difference between ethics and laws. Although many of our most basic laws are based on ethical precepts, many unethical actions are not illegal. Ethics are moral codes that we live by, and philosophers have struggled with understanding principles of ethics for thousands of years. As societal and cultural mores change over time, ideas of what constitutes ethical practices also shift. Ethics can also differ between cultures. For example, lying to someone to save them or someone else from embarrassment may be perfectly acceptable, even expected, in some cultures, whereas people in other cultures would believe lying under any circumstances is unethical.

There is no single, underlying unified ethical principle that all people can follow for complete justice and peace. A useful approach to applying ethical principles in life and in the practice of mass communication is outlined by three prominent ethics scholars in their book *Media Ethics.* Clifford G. Christians, Kim B. Rotzoll, and Mark Fackler outline five theoretical approaches to ethics that can be used as philosophical principles from which to frame ethical issues that arise:

1. *The Golden Rule.* A basic ethical principle in Judeo-Christian belief, which dominates most Western societies, the Golden Rule is often cited as "Do unto others as you would have them do unto you." Another way to phrase the same belief is "Love thy neighbor as thyself." In other words, we should help other people not simply when we perceive some future benefit for us in helping them, but simply because it is the right thing to do.

   This principle could be applied by a journalist who is interviewing the grieving relative of an accident or crime victim, for example. By treating the person with respect and dignity and asking him- or herself if he or she would want to be treated in the same way if in the subject's situation, the journalist can perhaps avoid some of the charges of invasion of privacy or tastelessness in coverage that the media are often accused of. Some journalists who have been on the receiving end of news stories have often mentioned their shock when they realize how insensitive and intrusive the news media can be.

2. *The Golden Mean.* One of the oldest ethical principles, the Golden Mean was espoused in different forms by Aristotle and Confucius, each of whom said that finding a balance between two extremes is the most ethical way. This "middle way" may well shift as the extremes shift, of course, and even this principle has to be taken in moderation. It would not be ethical to steal only half the money from a cash register rather than all of it, for example, because stealing is wrong in the first place.

   Applying the Golden Mean to news stories would involve trying to find balance and fairness among all sides of an issue. It does not mean automatically giving each side the same amount of coverage or space in the newspaper, however, as the relative importance of the groups must be judged.

3. *The Categorical Imperative.* Immanuel Kant was an influential German philosopher in the eighteenth century who stated that actions should be decided on moral laws that would apply to everyone. In other words, if someone was going to be punished for lying, then every person who lied should be punished, even if the lie was told to save a life or protect someone else.

   For media organizations, examples of applying Kant's categorical imperative would be in their decisions to publish names of crime victims or to cover all crimes of a certain seriousness, for example. In this case, if a newspaper published all names of drivers arrested for drunk driving, then even the mayor (or newspaper publisher) would have his or her name published if arrested.

4. *The Principle of Utility.* This theoretical approach states that what is most ethical is what does the most good for the greatest number of people, a concept called utilitarianism. This means that even if a decision or act severely hurts someone or a small group, if it helps a much greater number of people, then it is right. Scientific research on animals and humans operates under a utilitarian principle, although there are many safeguards to minimize potential suffering and harm of test subjects.

Utilitarianism can often be used to justify media coverage of sensitive or painful events for a small number of people, because the coverage can help many others. Examples include investigative reports of government wrongdoing in which a few individuals may go to jail or lose their jobs while society as a whole is better for exposing the wrongdoers.

5. *Veil of Ignorance.* Twentieth-century philosopher John Rawls argued in his 1971 book *A Theory of Justice* that fairness is the fundamental idea in the concept of justice. However, in complex modern society it is often difficult to establish what is fair because some groups have greater wealth, power, and advantages than others. In order to better understand fairness, Rawls advocates the parties step behind a "veil of ignorance" in which they are no longer the owner or the employee. They must stake out a basic position on the issue not knowing what role they would have after it is decided. From this framework Rawls says the parties would be able to better establish fair practices.

Immanuel Kant.

Using the technique of applying a veil of ignorance to an issue helps those involved see the issue from a different perspective. The journalist may realize that if he were the politician, then he could do his job better or communicate more effectively if a journalist was not always so cynical and abrasive in dealing with him. This may lead to a change in that journalist's behavior.

It should be obvious that one theoretical approach will not work for all situations, and that conflicts between ethical precepts are at the crux of ethical dilemmas in life and in media. The Golden Rule may often conflict with the categorical imperative, as an editor may well imagine she wouldn't want her own name to appear in an embarrassing front-page story although the newspaper's policy is to always print crime victims' names. Media organizations often do not show the same vigor in reporting about their own business practices and mistakes—even giving "no comment" responses to questions—as they do about other businesses—a clear violation of the categorical imperative. The principle of utilitarianism can be used to run roughshod over people's rights of privacy, as editors justify heavy coverage of tragic stories involving famous people as "the public's right to know." But what good does such intrusive coverage actually serve? On the other hand, should a story that could close a polluting factory that employs many people in the town not be published because it would break the principle of utilitarianism?

Media professionals must deal with a number of ethical problems throughout the course of their daily work, some of which are discussed briefly later in this book in the chapters dealing with each of those professions. Because of the nature of the work in mass communication, ethical lapses can have repercussions far beyond the unethical media professional, potentially ruining others' careers, affecting the public's perception and trust of media in general, and even in some cases ending lives.

However, sometimes corporate decisions made in executive boardrooms far above the journalist's level can also have ethical repercussions. Sometimes journalists or media professionals may be willing pawns in unethical practices and at other times they simply try to do their jobs as best they can within the larger organizational environment.

We will concentrate here on media ethics issues that arise from commercial forces shaping media content and the concentration and globalization of media ownership. Two examples of ethical issues raised have already been mentioned in this chapter: the case of *Time Magazine's* cover and extensive coverage of the film *Eyes Wide Shut* and Chris Patten's cancelled HarperCollins book contract as parent company owner Rupert Murdoch tried to get his Star TV cable and satellite service into the Chinese market. Would either of these instances have happened if the movie studio and the book publisher were not owned by larger media companies with substantial business interests in other areas?

Public Interests vs. Business Interests

Businesses in a capitalistic society are expected to make money for their owners, whether the companies are privately held or traded publicly on the stock market. Members of the public invest in companies that are or are expected to be successful, which means making profits. Media companies are no different than other types of corporations in that regard.

However, media organizations are in a uniquely powerful position to influence the public compared to other types of companies because of the "product"—media content—they create. In fact, a shoe manufacturer or cereal maker who wants to influence public opinion has to go through the media to do so. Because of the power of media to shape and influence the public, some aspects of the media industry such as journalism are given special protection under the Constitution. Partly as a result of these protections and partly through historical traditions, media—and journalists in particular—have had a strong public service mission. Many questions arise on how seriously the public service mission of news is kept in mind when news organizations become divisions of larger entertainment media companies or corporations that do not have any background in media at all.

At the heart of many media ethics dilemmas are the conflicting goals of serving the public with information and maximizing profit for the business. These issues can arise in a number of ways.

Commercial interests can take precedence over what is covered when powerful advertisers cancel or threaten to cancel their advertising in a media outlet. A blatant example may be when an unflattering story on a large local advertiser is going to run in a local newspaper and is either altered or pulled when the advertiser complains. A far more common case involves advertisers pulling their ads when there is coverage of unpopular issues or unpopular editorial stands taken by a media organization. Examples of this include Southern newspapers that supported the civil rights movement in the 1950s and 1960s, losing local advertisers. Although news coverage was not about the advertisers directly, the newspaper became associated with an opinion that the advertisers either did not agree with or thought might hurt their businesses if they were seen as advocating that position by advertising in the newspapers.

Another way that commercial interests may interfere with the public interest is when media outlets do not adequately cover certain groups or portions of the population because of a lack of audience and advertiser interest. For example, the *Los Angeles Times* had expanded its coverage and spent tens of millions of dollars on creating zoned editions that covered the growing, largely middle-class and affluent surrounding areas even as it largely ignored coverage of the urban, largely poor, central city. A special section of the paper concentrating on complex urban issues of the south central area was created in 1992, with the *Times* emphasizing

Southern papers that supported the Civil Rights movement in the 1950s and 1960s often lost local advertisers, an example of the types of commercial influences that can affect news coverage.

its public service mission, but it was closed three years later despite greater than expected advertising because of costs associated with the special section.[7]

Related to the case cited above are the costs associated with running a modern newsroom. Cutting staff is one of the surest ways to drastically reduce operating costs, but at what expense in terms of news coverage? Fewer staff means less coverage of certain subject areas and neighborhoods, which can end up giving the public an incomplete picture of what is happening in their town or region. Similarly, investigative reports are often time consuming and expensive and are less likely to be conducted in a media organization intensely aware of maximizing profits.

Professional training and development are other areas that often suffer. Many journalists interested in learning how to use computer-assisted reporting tools or digital media in order to help make them better reporters must pay their own way to conferences or workshops and use their personal vacation time in order to attend.

Media Types Influencing Content

Just as the type of media used to present content influences how that content is created and how it is received and perceived by the public, various business pressures arise with the various media types. The expense of producing feature-length films, for example, is an important factor for large media companies that want to maximize their profits. A film could have a greater likelihood of getting produced if the media company already owns the rights to the character to be used in the film, for example, and if there is good potential for other media content from within the company, such as music and television shows, to be tied in with the movie to help in marketing it.

The individual divisions of a large media company must deal with the demands of the corporate parent to maximize profits, which can affect decisions within a particular branch such as a book publisher to emphasize publishing books from established authors in a popular genre in order to generate sales at the expense of new authors or types of books that don't fall within established categories.

The need for exciting visual elements has even affected news coverage. *Dateline NBC*'s 15-minute segment "Waiting to Explode," which ran on November 17, 1992, was meant to demonstrate the danger of the gas tanks exploding on certain models of General Motors' pickups. The only trouble was that the trucks shown exploding on the segment had been rigged by the production team to ensure a fiery explosion and that several elements of the information they presented were misleading or inaccurate. It wasn't until later independent investigations and information given by sources who were at the initial filming that the truth behind the segment came out, forcing NBC to make a public apology and settle the lawsuit that GM had brought against NBC.[8] In this case, the need to have an exciting visual element helped make the ethical breaches that took place in this television news segment more likely.

Not every dramatic photograph on the front page of a newspaper is an example of a breach in media ethics, but it is important to have a critical eye and good media literacy when looking at visual media to ask how much of the decision to put that element in the news segment or on the page was driven by the need to capture the public's attention rather than its news value.

SUMMARY

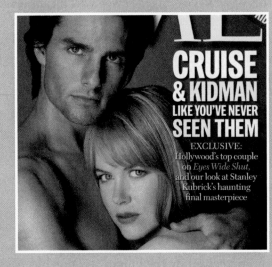

Media literacy is not a goal to reach, but an ongoing process in which one can always improve in order to become a better mass media consumer. Media literacy involves critically thinking of the media and understanding the subtext of messages that mass media may be sending. By developing a better understanding in four key areas—media grammar, commercial forces that shape media content, fragmentation of media audiences, and changes in media use because of digital technology—today's audience member can be aware of when mass media are trying to manipulate them and can act accordingly.

Each type of media has its own unique grammar that has developed over time and that helps set the stage for how we perceive certain types of content. Online media, because they are so new, are still developing their media grammar and will continue to do so for several years.

Commercial forces shape the kinds of media content we see because the vast majority of media companies are for-profit and thus must make money to stay in business. Concentration of media ownership has affected how media companies are run, as more and more media outlets become concentrated in fewer and fewer companies.

Because of advances in broadcasting and digital technologies, including the Internet, there is an increasing fragmentation in media audiences. Although this gives a wider diversity of voices, it also threatens to weaken a common sense of community and society as individuals focus on narrow and specific interests.

Media ethics has many facets, ranging from decisions journalists and other media professionals must make every day to ethical repercussions in news coverage and entertainment content that originate at the corporate level and are largely motivated by business interests. Especially for news organizations, the historic mission of serving the public interest can be threatened by corporate parent interests in maximizing profits. This becomes of special concern when companies with media entertainment backgrounds or nonmedia backgrounds take over news organizations.

MEDIA ? Quiz Answers

If you are like most people, you probably answered questions 1, 2, 4, and 5 correct or mostly correct. Question 3, however, might have been more difficult, even if you were familiar with the artist or group. Depending on how much of these questions you got correct, you have showed a normal to above-average media literacy in terms of "fan knowledge."

If you knew the answers to questions 3, 10, and 11, then you demonstrated a fairly high level of media literacy in terms of media ownership. If you knew what product placement is in question 6 and could quickly think of when you last saw it, then you show an above-average knowledge of how advertising can creep into media content where we wouldn't normally be looking for it.

If you answered yes to two out of the three questions of 7 to 9, then you have a pretty good media literacy in terms of producing media and digital technology.

If you knew the answers to questions 12 to 14, then you show a fairly advanced media literacy in terms of some of the important business, legal, and privacy issues facing media consumers of digital media.

Question 4. Some titles by Stephen King include *Carrie, The Shining, Cujo, It, The Tommyknockers,* and *Pet Sematary.*

Question 5. Movies based on King titles include *Carrie, The Shining, and Pet Sematary,* among others.

Question 11. AOL Time Warner: *People, Sports Illustrated, Fortune,* CNN, HBO; Bertelsmann: Random House, RCA, Arista Records; Disney: ESPN, Miramax Films, ABC, NFL.com; News Corp.: Fox TV, *New York Post, The Times* (UK), L.A. Dodgers; Sony: Columbia Tri-Star, Epic Records, E! Latin America; Viacom: UPN, MTV, Paramount Pictures, CBS, Simon & Schuster Publishing.

Question 12. True. Web sites sometimes change their privacy policies without informing users, and when Web sites go bankrupt and are sold, the companies buying them out often purchase their registered user lists so they can use them for their own marketing.

Discussion Questions

1. Go to the library and look at a newspaper from 30 years ago (probably available only on microfilm now) and compare the front page with the same paper today. What differences do you notice? What is your first impression of each one? Which one informed you better about matters you need to know?

2. Think about your favorite television program and create a list of at least three subtext messages the show may be sending. Explain what effect you think these messages may have on viewers.

3. Over 30 years ago, at least some television viewers could not distinguish that a sitcom like *Gilligan's Island* was pure fantasy. Now we have "reality TV," which has as its main selling point that the situations and environments are "real," even though a camera crew is also taping. What do you think this change says about U.S. society and media literacy? Is it a change for the better or for the worse?

4. Discuss four ways in which online media could develop or standardize a grammar that would either help people use the Web or help people understand what kind of Web site they are looking at.

5. Would you be willing to pay a mandatory annual television licensing fee if television networks and cable companies promised to show fewer commercials in their shows? If so, how much would you be willing to pay? What advantages or disadvantages could there be to a stronger public-supported media presence in the United States?

6. Discuss the moral and ethical implications of using someone else's artistic creation as the basis of a new creation. What steps can be taken to ensure that artists continue to have incentive to create original works even though they can easily be copied, altered, and distributed on the Web?

7. What social or human barriers are there to the public fully utilizing all the capabilities of broadband cable if it was widely accessible? How could these barriers be overcome or minimized?

64

Books, Newspapers, and Magazines

3

M. J. Rose had a problem common to many first-time authors—no publisher was willing to buy her manuscript. However, Rose's case was perhaps unique in that editors said they liked *Lip Service* but could not decide what genre it fit in; this would make marketing the book difficult, thus they couldn't publish the book.

So Rose turned to a unique solution: the Internet. For $9.95, people could download her book from her Web site, mjrose.com; and she submitted *Lip Service* to Amazon.com's Advantage program, which allows individual authors to sell printed copies of their books through Amazon. She self-published 3000 copies and sent out books for review to every appropriate Web site she could find.

Feedback was so positive that *Lip Service* became the highest-ranked small press novel on Amazon. The Doubleday Book Club and

Literary Guild selected *Lip Service* as a featured alternate selection in their print catalogue, the first self-published novel to ever be chosen. With numerous reviews, her sales figures, and the book club selection in hand, Rose saw *Lip Service* start an active bidding war between the very same publishers who had rejected the manuscript months before. Pocket Books signed to publish *Lip Service,* and Rose has since published two more novels through traditional publishing methods.

Rose's unorthodox methods for publishing and marketing her novel may not seem so strange in the years to come, and her experience showcases some of the dramatic changes taking place in the publishing industry because of digital technology.

OBJECTIVES

In this chapter we will:

■ Identify print media: books, newspapers, magazines.

■ Describe functions of print media.

■ Review the historical foundation and evolution of print media.

■ Outline readership and distribution patterns of print media, including book sales and newspaper and magazine circulation.

■ Identify forces—including political, cultural, economic, and technological—that have shaped development of print media.

■ Describe content characteristics of print media.

Prologue

Shelves full of books, racks brimming with magazines, and newsstands overflowing with newspapers are familiar to generations of Americans. America is a society steeped in the traditions of reading. Publishing, or print media, represents a $750 billion worldwide industry. Yet print media are undergoing momentous changes, as they move from analog to digital form, emerging transformed in the online world of the Internet and World Wide Web. This chapter examines the history, traditions, and business of print media and touches on some of the changes brought by the digital age.

Readership Patterns: Unconventional Wisdom

A 1999 study shows that among adults in the United States reading of all types—offline and online, books, newspapers, magazines, and digital text included—is rising.[1] The report says that the average time spent reading among young people is 24 minutes a day, while people over 50 spend double that amount of time reading. The data were obtained from 24,000 men and women who kept daily diaries of all media activities for one week during March or April 1992 through 1999. These data suggest that reading is alive and well in the digital age.

Print media represent the foundation, the beginning of the system of mass communication. Their origins lie in the "typographical era" of the Middle Ages. The rise of mass forms of mechanical printing and typography led to sweeping social change, including mass literacy and the Renaissance. The advent of print media challenged society in its ability to adapt to technological change, just as modern society is struggling to adapt to the change brought about by digital media today. What noted communication scholar **Marshall McLuhan** wrote about electronic media in 1962 in *The Gutenberg Galaxy* could equally be applied to the effect of digital media: "We are today as far into the electric age as the Elizabethans had advanced into the typographical and mechanical age. And we are experiencing the same confusions and indecisions which they had felt when living simultaneously in two contrasted forms of society and experience."

Books and Their Functions

Although young people may spend more time watching television, listening to recorded music, or playing computer games than reading books, books still hold a special place in the lives of many people. Reading is the basic building block for literacy, whether analog or digital. By age five or six, most children can already read beginner books. Books play a central role in the lives of vast numbers of Americans, whether for entertainment, education, or escape.

McLuhan, Marshall—A communication scholar who wrote *Understanding Media* and *The Gutenberg Galaxy*, among other books. He is perhaps most famous for creating the "global village" metaphor regarding electronic media and his often-misunderstood phrase "the medium is the message."

Books serve many functions in society. Among the most important are the transmission of culture from generation to generation, the diffusion of ideas and knowledge, and entertainment.

Transmission of Culture

From childhood on, people learn the language, values, and traditions of a culture from all types of media. Although not the sole means of transmitting culture, books teach what is considered right or wrong in a society, what is socially acceptable and unacceptable. Immigrants often learn about the rules and norms of a society from reading books. In learning how to read, children absorb from books the basic principles and practices of a culture. On a grander scale, consider the lasting impact of ancient religious texts such as the *Bible, Koran,* or *Torah* in imparting cultural mores and values.

Diffusion of Ideas and Knowledge

An important part of the transmission of culture is education. Books lay the foundation for formal education and are central to many people's lifelong continuing education, formal and informal. Textbooks and other works of nonfiction impart everything from scientific knowledge to psychological self-help. Books not only teach how to do things but explain what is known about the arts, literature, history, contemporary society, and social and natural sciences.

It's worth noting that books can teach both knowledge and values, and often the two are intertwined. Even textbooks, which are designed primarily to impart knowledge, can also transfer values, as much by what they omit as what they contain. Witness the ongoing debate in the state of Kansas, where the state board of education has struggled over the relative merits of including in high school textbooks either evolution or creationism, two subjects that may symbolize knowledge as much as they do value systems. Or consider the effect

Rachel Carson's 1962 book *Silent Spring,* which highlighted the harmful side effects of DDT, had in inspiring environmental awareness and action to ban the pesticide.

Entertainment

Whether you find reading this book a pleasure or not, many books are read purely for the joy they provide. Books can offer escape or diversion, and millions of readers thereby travel to exotic places, fantastic worlds, or far-away planets without ever leaving their living room. Some books offer humor, others a glimpse into lifestyles of the rich and powerful.

Just because a book is read primarily for entertainment does not mean that it also cannot impart knowledge to the reader at the same time. Readers who may not otherwise know or care how our legal system works, or what it is like to be in military intelligence, nevertheless can learn a lot when they read legal thrillers such as *The Firm* by John Grisham or military action stories such as *The Hunt for Red October* by Tom Clancy.

Even books written for entertainment can cause controversy because of cultural values they supposedly do or do not impart. Some have criticized the Harry Potter children's book series, written by J. K. Rowling, for not featuring stronger female characters in central roles, and others have said the books promote witchcraft. Despite these criticisms, Rowling's Potter books have won many awards, including the National Book Award and the Children's Book Award. For much of 2000 the top three books in the *New York Times* best-sellers list were all Harry Potter tales: *Harry Potter and the Prisoner of Azkaban, Harry Potter and the Sorcerer's Stone,* and *Harry Potter and the Chamber of Secrets.*

The Historical Development of Books

Since the Sumerians of 3500 BC pressed marks into wet clay tablets to create what some scholars consider the first form of books, authors have been writing long-form text narratives to record and convey their ideas in packages more

J. K. Rowling's series of Harry Potter books were best-sellers in 2000 and have spawned popular movies based on the novels.

Paper and woodblock printing were invented in China in 600 AD.

portable than clay tablets. By 2500 BC writers in western Asia were using animal skins to publish books in scroll form. The ancient Egyptians wrote the *Book of the Dead* in 1800 BC on papyrus. Between the first century BC and the sixth century AD the **codex,** or manuscript made of bound individual pages, began replacing the scroll-form book and established the modern book form. Book publishing continued to evolve, with paper and block printing being invented in China by 600 AD; movable type, a copper-alloy type, invented in Korea in 1234; and the Western world's first mechanical printing press in Germany in 1455. The portability of books and their wider distribution after the development of printing gave rise to the earliest form of mass media. They have had profound effects on culture and society in disseminating new ideas and building a common body of knowledge that can be shared across generations.

Monastic Scribes

Until the invention of printing, books had to be laboriously hand copied. In the Middle Ages, this work was done by specially trained monks called scribes, who worked in monastic scriptoria, or writing rooms. Scribes copied religious and classical works, and work in a scriptorium was considered an important task dedicated to promoting the ideas of the Christian church. Many of the books published in the Middle Ages were written in beautiful calligraphy and are richly illustrated.

Early books were published in scroll format, but eventually the codex, or bound manuscript, replaced scrolls. Until paper arrived from China via the Middle East in the later Middle Ages, scribes wrote on parchment or vellum, which were specially treated hides of either goats, sheep, or calves, respectively. Copying and illustrating books by hand was extremely time consuming, and creating parchment was expensive, so books were generally not widespread up to and throughout the Middle Ages.

codex—a book with individually bound pages; the form that replaced the scroll in the early centuries AD.

Gutenberg, Johannes— German printer credited with creating the first mechanical printing press in Europe in 1455.

Johannes Gutenberg

As the Christian church grew in Europe, the need for religious texts grew as well. It was out of this need that **Johannes Gutenberg** found his inspiration for the

Bringing medieval publishing into the digital age, Microsoft founder and billionaire **Bill Gates** in 1994 bought the Codex Leicester, Leonardo da Vinci's 500-year-old scientific bound manuscript, for $30.8 million. Gates plans to make the codex a centerpiece of a Seattle art museum. An annotated version of the Codex Leicester is online.

The British Library has a collection of digitized medieval manuscripts and early printed books on their Web site, including copies of the Gutenberg Bible; one of only two complete surviving copies of the Tyndale New Testament, the first New Testament printed in English; and the Lindisfarne Gospels, an illuminated manuscript written and created around 698.

Weblink
Codex Leicester
[www.amnh.org/exhibitions/codex/index.html]

Gutenberg Bible
[prodigi.bl.uk/gutenbg/default.asp]

Tyndale New Testament
[www.bl.uk/collections/treasures/tyndale.html]

Lindisfarne Gospels
[www.bl.uk/collections/treasures/lindis.html]

---

invention of printing with lead, using movable type in 1455 AD in Mainz, Germany. Gutenberg's invention employed oil-based ink on paper using a converted wine press.

Johannes Gutenberg was born to one of the region's patrician families about 1400 and died in either 1467 or 1468 in Mainz, Germany. Gutenberg met the silversmith Waldvogel in Avignon in 1444, who taught the craft of "artificial writing," as early printmaking was called. In 1450, Gutenberg formed a partnership with the wealthy Mainz burgher Johann Fust in order to complete his own printing invention and to print the famous Gutenberg "42-line Bible." The publication of the **Gutenberg Bible** in 1455 is considered the beginning of mechanical printing.[2]

In the early years of printing, illustrators would embellish printed pages with drawings and artistic flourishes in order to more accurately represent handwritten manuscripts. By combining a printing press with existing technology such as

Gates, Bill—founder, chairman, and chief software architect of Microsoft Corporation, which produces the Windows operating system and popular software such as Word, Excel, PowerPoint, and Access.

Gutenberg Bible—one of a handful of surviving Bibles printed by Johannes Gutenberg, considered the first mechanically printed works in Europe.

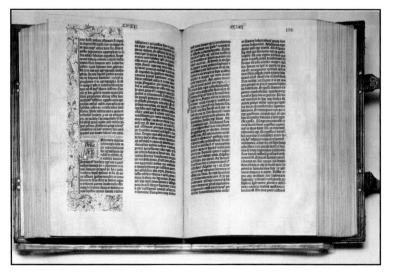

An examination of one of Gutenberg's early Bibles reveals the true beauty of his genius.

book binding, it was possible to begin the mass production of books at a fraction of the time and cost it took to produce an equal number of hand-copied books. The printing press spread rapidly after the conquest of the city of Mainz by Adolf of Nassau in 1462 and was initially met with enthusiastic reception by the Church and in the centers of culture throughout Europe.

The Beginnings of Mass Communication and Mass Literacy

The printing press had an important role in the growth of Renaissance culture, the sharing of scientific discoveries, and the spread of religious beliefs—some of which challenged the authority of the Catholic Church. Greater numbers of books and other printed materials helped increase literacy among the populace and laid the foundation for the rise of mass communication in the Western world. Many books, especially scientific works, were printed in Latin, which effectively reduced readership to elites educated in the classics. Books and other material such as broadsheets printed in the local vernacular usually found a much wider audience. Books had left the quiet monastic scriptoria and entered the bustling commercial world of printmakers and the average person.

Despite a greater number of books and printed materials from the Renaissance onward, large numbers of Europeans and Americans remained illiterate until the nineteenth century. In the American colonies and early years of the United States, education was largely available only to the wealthy, who could afford to hire and house private tutors for their children. Increased public education in the early 1800s helped reduce illiteracy among the general populace, and textbooks played a crucial role in the public education system.

One of the first textbooks published in America was the *New England Primer,* published initially in about 1690 by Benjamin Harris. The textbook introduced children to the English alphabet, the rudiments of reading, and basic Christian religious values.

Noah Webster, known today for his *Webster's Dictionary,* wrote his 1783 textbook, *A Grammatical Institute of the English Language,* as a reaction to the textbooks imported from England that were commonly used and that taught English cultural values. Known popularly as the "Blueback Speller," Webster's textbook provided tutorials on language, religion, morals, and domestic economy. *McGuffey Readers,* first published in 1836, became standard reading books for schoolchildren throughout the nineteenth century.

Textbooks of the 1800s often reflected the power structure of contemporary society, just as modern textbooks do. In order to appeal to the widest cross-section of society, textbooks generally avoid controversial subjects and embrace perspectives and bodies of knowledge in which there is general agreement among members of the dominant group.

Books Become Cheaper and Smaller

Changes in technology since Gutenberg's time have radically altered the production and printing of books. However, the very same forces that helped drive the invention of the printing press—wider distribution of printed materials and

Noah Webster wrote a widely used textbook as well as the popular dictionary that bears his name.

lower cost to produce books—have continued to play major roles in successful publishing ever since 1455. To some extent, books entering the digital realm can be seen as a continuation of these same historical forces on publishing.

One way to make money publishing is to publish a book that many people want to buy and read, which usually means publishing books that entertain people. Another way is to make the book affordable enough for many people to buy. The invention of the dime novel and later the creation of mass-market paperbacks satisfied both these criteria.

Dime Novels

The **dime novel** was the first paperback book form and, as its name suggests, sold for ten cents. This made it accessible even to the poor. Introduced in 1860 by Irwin P. Beadle & Company, the dime novel initially featured stories of Indians and pioneer tales that were often nationalistic in tone. Ann S. Stephens wrote the first dime novel, *Malaeska: The Indian Wife of the White Hunter*. Within a year of publication, *Malaeska* sold more than 300,000 copies. The 1870s saw an expansion of dime novels to include melodramatic fiction, adventures, detective stories, romances, and rags-to-riches tales.

Mass-Market Paperbacks

Mass-market paperbacks were introduced in the United States in 1939 by Robert de Graff's company, Pocket Books. Pocket Books, with its familiar kangaroo mascot, Gertrude, published a line of plastic-laminated books priced at 25 cents each that were small enough to be carried in a back pocket. It ushered in the paperback revolution by offering the public an alternative mass distribution network, as the books were sold in places like drugstores and supermarkets. Among Pocket Books' early successes were paperback editions of *The Good Earth* and Emily Bronte's classic, *Wuthering Heights*.

The post–World War II baby boomers who became the students of the 1950s and '60s were dubbed "the paperback generation." They were raised on Dr. Benjamin Spock's popular best-selling paperback, *Dr. Spock's Baby and Child Care*, and influenced by paperback copies of J. D. Salinger's *Catcher in the Rye* and Kurt Vonnegut's *Slaughterhouse Five*.

The dime novels of the late 19th century were widely read and were the precursors to today's mass-market paperbacks.

Three Major Trends in Today's Book Industry

Books are part of a global publishing industry. In 2001, the book publishing industry's annual U.S. sales volume was $25 billion and $80 billion worldwide. As a result of this enormous market, there has been tremendous consolidation in the ownership in the book publishing industry worldwide, which has significant repercussions for the diversity of book titles and perspectives that are published.

There are at least three significant trends affecting the business of book publishing. First, mergers and consolidation in the industry enable publishers to reduce operating costs, including the costs associated with warehousing titles

dime novel—the first paperback book form, which cost ten cents. This made it accessible even to the poor.

mass-market paperbacks—introduced in 1939 by Pocket Books, these books were small enough to fit in a back pocket, had laminated covers, and cost 25 cents, ushering in the paperback book revolution.

Media Future: Print on Demand

One interesting development of note in the late 1990s is **print on demand (POD)**. POD employs low-cost technology to enable writers to publish using low-cost publishers and have their paperback books available through sellers such as Amazon.com or bn.com—all for as little as $400 a book. High-quality laser printing and binding machines can print a book in less than a minute (800 pages a minute), obviating the need for expensive offset presses that are used in traditional publishing and which require expensive set-up and relatively large press runs to achieve economies of scale. This traditional model of printing has made access to book publication very limited.

The combination of low-cost, digital, online technologies may release a flood of POD authors publishing their own books in the twenty-first century. 1stBooks, a leading POD publisher, released Howard Olsen's *Diplomatic Immunity* in May 1999—after he paid a fee of less than $400.

Even more significantly, the publication of digital books, or e-books as they are sometimes called, may completely transform book publishing, with self-publishing becoming a viable option, and even spurring a re-examination of just what it is that constitutes a book, or long-form text narrative. Digital, or e-books, are those in which the text and other content of a book-length treatment of a subject or story is produced, kept, and distributed entirely in electronic, computerized form.

One possibility that exists with print on demand is that kiosks or shops can also become on-the-spot bookstores. Travelers could decide what book they want from an almost limitless selection or even combine parts of various books into one book and have it printed out within minutes.

The Perfect Book Machine can accept individual orders for books electronically, print the pages and cover, and bind the book, all within minutes.

and marketing and sales, and thus increase profit margins. Size also gives the book publishing giants more leverage in negotiations on terms with retail giants such as Barnes & Noble and Amazon.com, who dominate the industry. Such negotiations include obtaining good display locations in bookstores and on the Web.

Second, the book publishing industry is intertwined with the global media and the entertainment industry. Many books are published and subsequently produced as motion pictures or made-for-television movies or miniseries, from Mary Wollstonecraft Shelley's *Frankenstein* (written in 1818 and made into a movie in 1910 and many times since then) to Stephen King's *Bag of Bones* (written in 1999 and made into a movie in 2002).

Third, book sales and distribution are being transformed by the emergence of online booksellers, electronic books, and on-demand printing. Online booksellers such as Amazon.com, bn.com, and others are capturing an increasing portion of total book sales. Moreover, these and other online booksellers are distributing electronic books. As electronic books and online book sales grow, the future of traditional brick-and-mortar bookstores is uncertain. Another big shift has been toward megabookstores and the sale of discounted books at warehouse shopping outlets. These venues offer brick-and-mortar booksellers the needed economies of scale to compete with online enterprises. Independent bookstores are gradually on the decline.

Mergers and Consolidation

Today, the world's largest trade-book publisher is Random House, whose sales totaled nearly $4.2 billion in 2000. The publishing division of Bertelsmann, Random House is nearly twice the size of its two nearest competitors, HarperCollins, owned by Rupert Murdoch's News Corporation, and Time Warner Books, owned by AOL Time Warner. Random House publishes hardbacks and trade and mass-market paperbacks, as well as multimedia products. Its operations include Random House Trade Publishing, Knopf, Ballantine, Bantam Dell (formerly Bantam Doubleday Dell), Random House Children's Publishing, and Fodor's Travel Publications.

Publishing, Entertainment, and Other Media

In 1998, an important historic shift occurred in the relative position of book sales and video sales and rentals. That was the first time ever that consumers spent more on home videos ($88.79) than on books ($88.09). People are also spending an increasing amount of time online, reading and exploring the Internet and other digital media content. They also simply have less leisure time, spending more time working and involved in other less discretionary activities, such as caring for their children or elderly parents.

Where Books Are Sold

Figure 3-1 presents data on where books of all types are sold and how things have changed since 1992. In 1992, the leading place for book sales was independent bookstores and small chains. By 2000, independents and small chains

print on demand (POD)—a technology developed in the late 1990s that allows for high-speed printing and binding of a book requested by a customer.

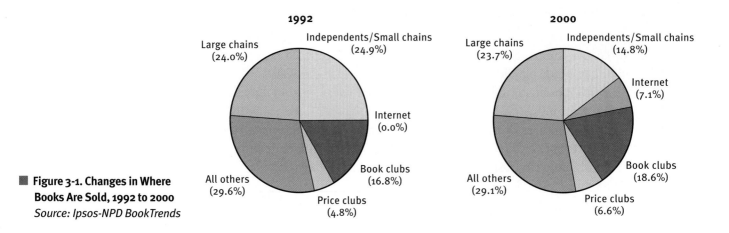

1992

Large chains (24.0%)

Independents/Small chains (24.9%)

Internet (0.0%)

Book clubs (16.8%)

Price clubs (4.8%)

All others (29.6%)

2000

Large chains (23.7%)

Independents/Small chains (14.8%)

Internet (7.1%)

Book clubs (18.6%)

Price clubs (6.6%)

All others (29.1%)

■ **Figure 3-1. Changes in Where Books Are Sold, 1992 to 2000**
Source: Ipsos-NPD BookTrends

had been supplanted by large chains as the leading seller of books. Book clubs increased slightly, and a nonexistent seller in 1992—Internet sales—outsold price clubs by 2000.

Book Sales and Readership

Book sales have been in a mixed pattern since 1990, with revenues increasing a percent or two some years and then dropping a few percent in other years. Categories of book sales include trade books, professional and scholarly publishing, elementary and high school textbooks, higher education or college texts, mass-market paperbacks, book clubs, religious publishing (perhaps the oldest category), and now electronic or digital books (although numbers here are scarce).

Trade book publishing, or books intended for general readership, has the greatest revenues worldwide. As shown in Figure 3-2, trade books generated

■ **Figure 3-2. Book Publishing Annual Sales, 2001** *Source: Association of American Publishers*

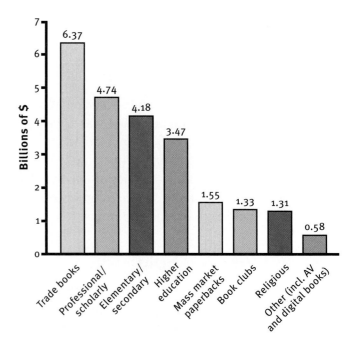

Billions of $

Trade books	6.37
Professional/scholarly	4.74
Elementary/secondary	4.18
Higher education	3.47
Mass market paperbacks	1.55
Book clubs	1.33
Religious	1.31
Other (incl. AV and digital books)	0.58

$6.37 billion in the United States in 2001, roughly 26 percent of the total U. S. market. Revenue from trade books in the United States dropped 3.7 percent from 1999 to 2000 and 2.6 percent from 2000 to 2001. Within the category, juvenile hardbound books dropped 22.7 percent from 2000 to 2001, while juvenile paperbound books rose 17.9 percent, indicating important shifts within these categories.

Paperbacks are less expensive to produce, ship, and market than hardcover books and are less expensive to buy, making them more accessible to the public. They have been one of the mainstays of mass commercial trade book publishing for more than half a century, making up $1.55 billion in annual sales in 2001, although they are not as important to the industry as they once were. Mass-market paperback book sales in the United States have remained almost steady since 1992. Paperbacks, which once sold eight to ten times their hardcover counterparts, now sell at a rate of just two to one, despite their lower price. Although the market remains profitable, it does so largely by increasing the price. The average price of a paperback has now reached $7.

Book clubs, along with mail-order books, faced steep competition for sales from the large bookstore chains and price clubs. Despite this, they have continued to grow since 1998, with a 3.3 percent increase in sales over 2000.

Religious books can be divided into two main categories: Bibles, testaments, and so on; and other religious publications such as inspirational works, biographies, autobiographies, and histories. Sales in the "other" category make up 76 percent of religious category sales and grew 7.2 percent from 2000, while Bibles, testaments, prayer books, and hymnals saw their sales decrease 2.6 percent during the same time period.

Despite limited growth, and even some decline in overall book sales, the number of book titles published each year in the United States continues to rise in dramatic fashion. In fact, the growth in book titles has been steady since the earliest available statistics have been compiled, dating to the 1880s. The number of book titles published annually in the United States has increased more than tenfold since the 1880s, when 37,896 titles were published.[3] One hundred years later, between 1980 and 1989, the number of book titles published in the United States was 510,286.

Newspapers and Their Functions

Newspapers, as almost everyone knows, consist largely of words, pictures, and graphics printed on lightweight, inexpensive paper stock. They are very portable and inexpensive. They are typically printed either daily or weekly. Although they are called "news" papers, most newspapers consist mostly of advertising. The typical daily newspaper in the United States, for example, is roughly 60 percent advertising and about 40 percent editorial content. Similarly, about two-thirds (65 percent) of the cost of producing a newspaper goes into printing and distribution, and only about a third (35 percent) goes into the actual creation of the news (reporters' salaries and the like).

U.S. newspaper publishing is a $50 billion industry with about 5 percent annual growth. Newspapers are the biggest segment of the publishing world, accounting for 40 percent of the industry's revenue. The percentage of population that subscribes to newspapers has been in a long downward decline, but the industry slowly continues to grow, largely because of population growth.

The most important function served by newspapers in modern society is **surveillance,** or to inform the public of important events taking place. However, they also play a role in the **correlation** and **entertainment** functions. Typically, the front page of a newspaper is all "news," with section front pages similarly constructed, and most news placed "above the fold," or the top half of the page, on other pages.

In the late nineteenth century, newspapers developed the independent press model that came to characterize journalism of the twentieth century, where a wall between editorial and business (i.e., advertising) was built.

Regardless of their business model, newspapers have tended to serve communities bounded by geographic, political, cultural, and economic borders. Correspondingly, newspapers are generally organized into sections often defined by geography, including local, national, and international news; and topic, including business, culture, health, science, sports, and technology.

Local Newspapers

The vast majority of U.S. newspapers serve local geographic communities (usually city-based, with suburban, zoned editions). Local newspapers tend to provide coverage of the local communities they serve, monitoring the activities of local government, law enforcement, business, religion, education, the arts, and other area institutions. In addition to local news, they also carry some regional, national, and international news, although most of this tends to be gathered from other news-gathering organizations better equipped to cover these broader areas of coverage, including the news services, which are discussed in more detail later in this chapter. Local papers also tend to serve as the legal record of public communications in their communities, running obituaries and various legal announcements. They also provide an important part of the community's economic infrastructure by carrying extensive advertising for products, services, and businesses with local interests and markets.

National Newspapers

A few newspapers have emerged as truly national newspapers, with readership throughout the country. These include *The New York Times, USA Today,* and *The Wall Street Journal.* Each of these papers offers its own distinctive brand of news. *The New York Times,* known as the U.S. paper of record, as well as the Old Gray Lady, offers especially strong coverage of international events and issues.

USA Today offers a strong mix of general interest news packaged in well-designed, colorful, easy-to-read news packages. Launched in 1982, *USA Today* was the brainchild of newspaper mogul Al Neuharth and ushered in a new age of newspaper design. The paper took ten years to become profitable, but in the meantime transformed the look and feel of most U.S. newspapers and many around the world.

Prior to *USA Today*'s launch, many twentieth-century newspapers were dull in appearance and filled with long columns of text. *USA Today* introduced color-

surveillance—primarily the journalism function of mass communication, which provides information about the processes, issues, events, and other developments in society.

correlation—primarily the interpretation of aspects of society as a function of mass communication, and the individual to society, including how journalism, advertising, and public relations shape public opinion through comments or criticism or through propaganda.

entertainment—a function of mass communication that is performed in part by all three of the other four main functions (surveillance, correlation, cultural transmission) but also involves the generation of content designed specifically and exclusively to entertain.

USA Today revolutionized newspaper design by using colorful graphics and short news packages within its pages.

ful graphics and an overall design that was inspired by television and easy to read. Even the newsstand boxes first used by *USA Today* were designed to look like a television set. *USA Today* was also made possible as a national newspaper because of a new age of satellite communications that made it technically and economically feasible to distribute the content of the paper electronically via satellite to printing and distribution centers around the country and the world for local distribution in a timely, cost-effective, and inexpensive manner. Prior to this, it was possible and practical to distribute papers nationally or internationally only via postal service, which meant papers didn't arrive at distant outposts until, at best, days after their printing.

The Wall Street Journal is the nation's leading newspaper covering business and finance. With a circulation of more than 1.7 million, the *Journal* is also the largest-circulation newspaper of any type in the United States.[4] It is published Monday through Friday, with an online edition that provides expanded coverage and updates. The online edition is a leading example of a subscription online news product and has more than 620,000 paid subscribers. Many in the world of business or finance consider the *Journal* a must-read for their work. The *Journal* faces its stiffest competition from other electronic business and financial publications, such as Bloomberg, as well as international organizations, including Reuters and the *Financial Times,* both of which have strong online publications. *The Wall Street Journal* is also one of the oldest U.S. newspapers, having been launched in 1882 by Charles Dow and Edward Jones (famous as well for creating the Dow Jones financial index) as a handwritten news service offering up-to-the-minute information for people working in New York's financial district.

The Historical Development of Newspapers

The first English-language newspaper published in what is today the United States was *Publick Occurrences, Both Foreign and Domestick*. It was launched

Early colonial newspapers usually focused on either commercial or political news.

on September 25, 1690, in Boston, printed by Richard Pierce and edited by Benjamin Harris.

The U.S. colonial press took two forms: political papers and commercial papers. This duality was reflected in the names of the papers of the day, such as *The Boston Daily Advertiser*, the *Daily Mercantile Advertiser*, *Federal Gazette*, or *Federal Republican and Daily Gazette*. Theses papers were physically quite small, usually no more than four pages and 10 × 15 inches in size.

The broadsheet format common to most daily newspapers today is partly a result of British tax law—which the colonies were subject to—that in the eighteenth century placed a tax on the number of pages contained in a newspaper. As a result, newspaper publishers created papers with larger sheets and smaller text in order to reduce the amount of tax they paid.

The Commercial Press

The commercial papers were published by merchants who printed reports on the arrivals and departures of ships, contents of their cargo, weather reports, and

Weblink
Comprehensive Media Chronology
[mediahistory.umn.edu/]

Media Timeline: History (and Prehistory) of Newspapers

200 BC: *Tipao* gazettes distributed among Chinese officials.

59 BC: Julius Caesar orders publication of first daily news sheet, *Acta Diurna* (Daily Events) in Rome.

748 AD: The first printed newspaper—Beijing, China.

1502: *Zeitung* ("newspaper") published in Germany.

1513: The earliest known English-language news sheet and first illustration in a news sheet—*Trewe Encountre*.

1609: The first regularly published newspaper in Europe, Germany—*Avisa Relation oder Zeitung*.

1620: The first English-language newspaper—*The new tydings out of Italie*, published in Amsterdam.

1621: The first English-language newspaper printed in England—

Coranto or news from Italy, Germany, Hungarie, Spaine and France.

1638: The first printing press arrives in what later became the U. S.—Cambridge, Mass.

1665: The first issue of the *Oxford Gazette* published at Oxford, England, offering first use of double columns in a news publication; considered the first true newspaper.

Mass Communication Formats   www.ablongman.com/pavlik1e

other information useful to commercial enterprises. Both types of papers were sold by subscription at a cost of $8 to $10 per year, or about six cents an issue. Because the average worker made just 85 cents a day, the subscription price of most newspapers put them out of reach of the masses. By 1750 most American colonists who could read had access to a newspaper, although literacy was generally limited to the elite.

The Partisan Press

Prior to the 1830s in North America most newspapers were affiliated with a political party or platform. Political papers were sponsored by political parties, and the articles were often written by political figures, usually anonymously. The partisan press, as it was called, did not subscribe to the modern notions of good journalism, free of bias and impartial in its coverage of the day's events and processes. The newspapers of the eighteenth and early nineteenth centuries were decidedly opinionated and took a position not only on their editorial pages but throughout the entire papers. Readership was also limited in at least two ways. First, readership was largely limited to those who supported or agreed with the political position of the paper. Second, readership was largely limited to society's elite, well-educated, land-owning, and economically advantaged groups.

The Golden Age of Newspapers

Technology has always shaped the newspaper. A series of changes beginning in the 1830s, brought about by technological developments, brought about a transformation of newspapers and the emergence of a "golden age" for newspapers in America. This golden age lasted until about 1930 and the arrival of electronic mass communication, first in the form of radio and later television and other media. For 100 years, however, newspapers exerted their greatest influence on American society. In many ways, the rise of newspapers was born in response to an appetite for news in large eastern cities such as New York, Boston, and Philadelphia. Between 1870 and 1900, the U.S. population doubled, the city population tripled, and the number of daily newspapers quadrupled. In fact, the 1880 U.S. Census counted 11,314 newspapers, compared to 2397 newspapers in 2000. Papers sprouted in growing metropolitan areas throughout the nation,

1666: The *Oxford Gazette* becomes the *London Gazette;* will be published continuously for more than 300 years.
1690: The first newspaper published in what is now the U. S., in Boston— *Publick Occurrences Both Foreign and Domestick.*

1702: The first daily newspaper—the *Daily Courant*—is published in London.
1704: North America's first regular newspaper— *The Boston News-Letter.*
1721: The first independent newspaper in North America, *New*

England Courant, is published by James Franklin, Benjamin Franklin's brother.
1764: *The Hartford Courant* is established; is now the oldest continuously published newspaper in the U. S.

1784: The first daily newspaper in the U. S.— *Pennsylvania Packet.*
1800: The first iron hand press—The Stanhope, England.
1830s: The first steam-powered rotary press makes mass distribution possible; prints on both

sides of paper, 4000 sheets per hour. Prior to this, hand presses printed just 200 sheets per hour.
1971: Newspapers switch from hot-metal letterpress to offset printing.

1977: Toronto *Globe and Mail* offers public access to newspaper text database.
1982: *USA Today* founded; typeset in regional plants by satellite commands.

The *New York Sun* was an example of the penny press—news written for the masses.

lead by press innovators such as James Gordon Bennett, Horace Greeley, Joseph Pulitzer, William Randolph Hearst, and E. W. Scripps.

Prior to the 1830s, printing technology was largely powered by hand, and briefly by horses, and could print from 200 to 600 sheets per hour. This severely limited the circulation of the papers of the day. But in the 1830s steam-powered printing presses were developed. These could print up to 4000 sheets per hour, on both sides. This made mass-scale printing possible. Seizing upon this opportunity, publisher **Benjamin Day** ushered in this new era, offering on September 3, 1833, a mass-medium daily newspaper, the *New York Sun,* for one cent, sold by newsboys in the streets each day rather than by subscription. Unlike the partisan press or commercial papers, this **penny press** offered news for the masses. News was written to appeal to the lowest common denominator, and sensationalized news frequently appeared in the paper. Day's paper quickly reached a circulation of 8000, and within three years its circulation had reached 30,000, astounding other contemporary publishers.

The penny press denoted newspapers for the mass public and exerted important social effects. These metropolitan dailies developed large circulations aimed at expanding audiences that included, even focused on, the middle class. In many ways, it was analogous to the social shift that accompanied Gutenberg's printing press some four centuries earlier. News was no longer for the political or commercial elite; it was for everyone.

The penny press changed the nature of news by employing reporters to seek out the news, not just publishing items that came into the office. The penny press also brought a new marketing function to newspapers. The price for a newspaper did not cover printing and distribution costs; but, because the penny press brought large audiences, businesses seeking to sell their products to mass markets saw potential in advertising their wares in those newspapers. The penny press began advertising medicines, entertainment, and jobs, as well as items the commercial and partisan press frowned upon, such ads for theaters, lotteries, or abortionists. Advertising emerged as the primary revenue source in the modern newspaper business model. Today, about 70 percent of newspaper revenue typically comes from advertising.

Day, Benjamin—publisher of the *New York Sun,* he ushered in the era of the penny press when he began offering his paper on the streets for a penny on September 3, 1833.

penny press—newspapers that sold for a penny, making them accessible to everyone. They differed from older newspaper forms in that they tried to attract as large an audience as possible and were supported by advertising rather than subscriptions.

Newspapers Today

Just as improvements in technology helped in driving the rise of newspapers as a mass medium, technology has also played a role in the decline and transformation of newspapers in the last half of the twentieth century. A combination of sociological forces in post–World War II America, including a change to a largely suburban society and increased use of automobiles, along with electronic media such as radio and later television, helped draw audiences away from newspapers as their primary sources of news.

Television's ease of use and entertainment value contributed to the continuing decrease of American newspapers, especially afternoon papers, in the second half of the twentieth century. Where previously cities usually had two or more competing daily newspapers, now many cities have only one newspaper or a morning and evening paper, which are ostensibly competitors operating under a joint operating arrangement that leaves virtually monopolistic control over the circulation area.

Modern newspapers are still undergoing significant changes, including marked change in their news and advertising content. As newspaper circulation numbers become more important in an increasingly competitive market, even leading newspapers are more likely to pander to popular taste. Departing from the established editorial tradition of selecting newsworthy topics regardless of general appeal, many newspapers are deferring to marketing polls and focus groups when setting standards for content, tone, and layout.

Brightly colored photos and graphics like those pioneered in *USA Today,* created to emulate TV viewing, can actually help readers digest the news more easily when they are done properly. However, when done poorly they can trivialize the news and at worst be confusing or misleading.

How newspapers reach the reader is changing dramatically, especially with the rise of the Internet. Although the Internet and its impact on media delivery are examined in detail in a later chapter, it is worth noting here that newspapers have been in the forefront of experimenting with the electronic delivery of news to news consumers since the late 1970s, when newspapers like the Toronto *Globe and Mail* allowed public access to their news database. Most of these early efforts were not very successful, however, as many people at the time did not have computers or Internet access and the state of technology with screens made reading text on the computer tiring.

As the Internet has grown as a medium of public communication, most daily newspapers have launched online news operations and have increasingly used this new medium as a vehicle for serving an audience no longer limited to or defined by geography, political, or even cultural or linguistic boundaries.

One of the most interesting developments occurred on October 24, 2001, when *The New York Times* began delivering its electronic edition. *The New York Times* electronic edition is an exact digital replica of the printed paper, but it is delivered to readers via the Internet and downloaded onto their computers. It uses what is called the NewsStand Reader, which includes keyword searching of the full text, zooming in for closer views of photos, one-click jumping on article continuations, and saving of past issues for easy reference. Importantly for the business of *The New York Times*, the electronic edition costs 65 cents a copy, raising revenue to support the enterprise.

Weblink
NewsStand Reader
[nytimes.com/ee]

Media Technology
Telephone Newspapers (1876–1912)

Online newspapers in the 1990s have drawn large audiences as more and more people dial up and go online to get their news. But the practice of getting your newspaper over a telephone line is more than 100 years old, with trials of **telephone newspapers** taking place as early as the 1870s. Although the telephone, invented in 1876, was initially meant to help the hearing impaired, several trials from the 1870s to 1890s, especially in Europe, demonstrated the potential for delivering news via the telephone. The *Telefon Hírmondó* in Budapest, Hungary, debuted in 1893 as a telephone-delivered newspaper. In 1911–1912 the *Telephone Herald* operated in Newark, New Jersey.

The way a telephone newspaper worked was simple. A person in the editorial office of the newspaper read the news into a telephone handset. Subscribers to the service, including persons at home, at the office, or often in department stores, had a dedicated phone line connected to the newspaper office. They could pick up the phone at any time of the day when news was being read and listen in to the stream of news. A typical news schedule began at 8 AM with the time, weather, and top news headlines. Then, throughout the day at various set times, different news sections were read, such as news from New York at 11:30 AM, sports at 2:45 PM, the New York Stock Exchange at 3:45 PM, and vaudeville entertainment at 8 PM. As many as 1000 subscribers paid a nickel a day for the service. Compared to a penny a day for a newspaper, this was relatively expensive.

Although telephone-based news and entertainment proved economically unviable in the United States at the time, in the 1980s U.S. newspapers successfully delivered audiotext, or audionews and information via the phone. Early newspaper attempts to deliver news via the telephone set a benchmark for radio news, and then television news, in the decades to follow.

Newspaper Readership and Circulation

Newspaper readership, circulation, and the number of daily newspapers have all been in decline for more than five decades. Daily newspaper circulation has been decreasing for at least a decade, and there are fewer and fewer cities served by competing dailies.

Newspaper readership refers to the number or percentage of people who read a newspaper, which is larger than the circulation number (number of copies sold or distributed) because some copies are read by more than one person. This is called pass-along readership. Because of the growth of the U.S. population, the actual number of persons reading newspapers has declined less dramatically. But the percentage of the U.S. population that reads a daily paper has been declining, and the amount of time people spend reading newspapers has been slipping as well.

Readership among the young is lower than for people between 35 and 65. A 1990 *Times Mirror* survey shows that just 24 percent of those under 35 years of age reported reading "yesterday's" paper, compared to 67 percent in 1965. Another survey shows that newspaper readership among the 18 to 24 age group dropped by 20 percent between 1967 and 1987, from 77 to 57 percent.

By 1997, less than two-thirds (approximately 60 percent) of people aged 16 to 29 in the United States read both a weekday and a Sunday paper, although another 15 percent read only a Sunday paper. The rise of the Internet has further eroded young people's readership of printed newspapers, with young people increasingly turning to online sources for breaking news rather than daily newspapers. Of course, many of these online sources are published by daily newspaper parent organizations.

The Declining Number of Daily Newspapers

In 1940, there were 1878 daily newspapers in the United States, with 380 morning and 1498 evening papers. By 1950, there were 549 papers printed on Sunday and 1772 daily newspapers, with 81.8 percent still being evening papers—1450, to 322 morning papers. The long-term shifts were already starting to occur.

Since 1940, the total number of daily newspapers has dropped 21 percent (398) to just 1480 in 2000. Most of the decline has been in evening papers, which in 2000 totaled 727, a decrease of 51 percent (771) since 1940. In 2000, for the first time the number of morning dailies exceeded the number of evening papers. Since 1940, the number of morning papers has increased 101 percent (386) to 766. The number of Sunday papers increased 65 percent (356) to 905 in 2000. There are approximately 9180 daily newspapers throughout the world.[5]

Table 3-1 lists the top circulation newspapers in the United States for 1990 and 2000. With the exception of *USA Today*, each of these newspapers lost circulation from 1990 to 2000, and the overall circulation for the top ten papers and the number of newspapers overall also decreased. If these patterns continue for the next decade, newspapers are likely to have even lower total circulation (despite a growing U.S. population), and *USA Today* will be the leading circulation paper in the country. Actual readership is about double these circulation

telephone newspapers—a type of news delivery tried between 1876 and 1912. News stories were read on telephone lines at certain times during the day, and subscribers would call in to hear the news.

Table 3-1 Top Circulation Papers in the United States; 1990, 2000

1990	Newspaper	Circulation	2000	Newspaper	Circulation
1	*The Wall Street Journal*	1,857,131	1	*The Wall Street Journal*	1,762,751
2	*USA Today*	1,347,450	2	*USA Today*	1,692,666
3	*Los Angeles Times*	1,196,323	3	*The New York Times*	1,097,180
4	*The New York Times*	1,108,447	4	*Los Angeles Times*	1,033,399
5	(New York) *Daily News*	1,097,693	5	*The Washington Post*	762,009
6	*The Washington Post*	780,582	6	(New York) *Daily News*	704,463
7	*Chicago Tribune*	721,067	7	*Chicago Tribune*	661,699
8	(New York) *Newsday*	714,128	8	(New York) *Newsday*	576,345
9	*Detroit Free Press*	636,182	9	*Houston Chronicle*	495,597
10	*San Francisco Chronicle*	562,887	10	*The Dallas Morning News*	495,597
	Total for Top Ten	10,021,890		Total for Top Ten	9,332,908
	Total for all newspapers	62,324,156		Total for all newspapers	55,772,847

Sources: *Editor & Publisher,* Newspaper Association of America.

numbers, because each weekday newspaper is read by an average of 2.2 persons. Each Sunday paper is read by an average of 2.39 persons.

Joint Operating Arrangements

It is apparent from the circulation numbers over the past 50 years that more and more Americans have had less time or interest in reading an afternoon or evening paper. As a result, most afternoon papers have seen their readership plummet, causing declining advertising and falling revenues. Consequently, most afternoon papers have ceased publication, merged with morning papers, or formed legally permitted **joint operating arrangements (JOAs).**

JOAs refer to the legal agreements that permit newspapers in the same market or city to merge their business operations for reasons of economics (to exploit simplified and advantageous systems for circulation, advertising, and the like), yet maintain independent editorial operations.

In 2001, fewer than a dozen U.S. cities are served by two or more major daily newspapers not operating under a JOA. JOAs are permitted under the **Newspaper Preservation Act of 1970,** which is intended to preserve a diversity of editorial opinion in communities where only two competing, or independently owned, daily newspapers exist.[6] They are permitted despite their creation of a virtual newspaper monopoly in many local communities. Permission for a new

joint operating arrangements (JOAs)—legal agreements that permit newspapers in the same market or city to merge their business operations for reasons of economics while maintaining independent editorial operations.

Newspaper Preservation Act—created in 1970, it is intended to preserve a diversity of editorial opinion in communities where only two competing, or independently owned, daily newspapers exist.

Table 3.2 Newspaper Joint Operating Arrangements (JOAs)	
Newspaper JOAs	**Year of Expiration**
The Albuquerque Journal and *Albuquerque Tribune*	2022
The Birmingham News and *Birmingham Post-Herald*	2015
The Charleston (WV) *Gazette* and *Charleston* (WV) *Daily Mail*	2036
Chattanooga Free Press and *The Chattanooga Times*	2015
Cincinnati Enquirer and *Cincinnati Post*	2007
Detroit Free Press and *The Detroit News*	2086
Journal-Gazette (Fort Wayne, IN) and *News-Sentinel* (Fort Wayne, IN)	2020
The Honolulu Advertiser and *Honolulu Star-Bulletin*	2012
Las Vegas Review-Journal and *Las Vegas Sun*	2049
Salt Lake City Desert News and *Salt Lake Tribune*	2012
San Francisco Chronicle and *San Francisco Examiner* (now being merged)	2005
Seattle Post-Intelligencer and *The Seattle Times*	2033
The Arizona Star (Tucson) and *Tucson Citizen*	2015
The York (PA) *Dispatch* and *The York* (PA) *Daily Record*	2090

Source: Newspaper Association of America.

JOA requires the approval of the Federal Trade Commission (FTC). Table 3-2 presents the 14 newspaper JOAs that now are permitted and their date of expiration.

The Newspaper Industry Today

Newspapers are the oldest U.S. media business, yet the newspaper business continues to evolve in significant and sometimes unpredictable ways. No longer is the newspaper industry the largest portion of the media business overall, and trends suggest that its presence on the media landscape will continue to decline, at least from an economic perspective.

Increasing concentration of ownership, which was discussed in the previous chapter and which will be seen elsewhere when looking at electronic and digital media, has also taken place in the newspaper industry.

Newspaper Chains; Newspapers Change

In the early days of the republic, most newspapers were owned by families, individuals, or in some cases political parties. These owners lived in the communities their newspapers served. The twentieth century brought new patterns of owner-ship to newspapers, both in the United States and around the world. The most fundamental shift has been toward increasing concentration of ownership. In other words, most newspapers today are now part of newspaper groups or chains, often owned by families or individuals but more often owned by stock-holders. The increasing concentration of newspaper ownership is the result of many forces, primarily economic. The newspaper business has traditionally been highly profitable, with profit margins often in the range of 20 percent of gross revenues. This placed the newspaper industry among the most profitable in any sector of the economy at double the average profit margin for all industry sectors.

The high profit margin of many newspapers has made them a desirable target for investors, and there are certain economies of scale that newspapers can enjoy through chain ownership. Consequently, facing declining audiences and new threats for advertising revenue from television and other media, as well as rising costs for newsprint and other necessary resources, larger newspapers and news-paper groups have acquired other smaller newspapers and newspaper groups. Newspaper chains bring both benefits and problems to formerly independent local or regional papers.

Benefits of Chains

One of the benefits to the chains is that smaller, struggling newspapers can gain access to the resources of the entire chain. This can be especially important in communities where a single advertiser or industry controls an especially large share of the advertising revenues in that community. As a result, a single adver-tiser can pose a strong economic threat to the commercial viability of the local newspaper by threatening to reduce or remove advertising. Subject to this influ-ence, the newspaper can find itself in the compromising position of not reporting as rigorously on an advertiser as may be warranted.

Chains also offer newspapers advantages involved in sharing of resources for news gathering, especially when covering regional or national or international stories, much as newspapers have benefited from the shared news-gathering resources made possible through the Associated Press news service.

Problems with Chains

Chain-owned newspapers also bring certain problems to the communities they serve. Among these problems are an increasing disconnection between the local media and the local communities. As original, local reporting gets squeezed out by wire service or chain-produced content, local communities are being forced to look elsewhere for local news and information.

Among the most significant considerations are the potential for chains, espe-cially those that are publicly owned and traded on the stock market, to place increasing pressure on those newspapers to bring greater levels of profitability. This pressure can mean many things, including cutting editorial costs. One com-mon strategy is to cut costs by reducing the size of the reporting staff and filling the news hole with wire service copy or material from the chain's other papers. Thus, the amount of local news is reduced, but the overall newspaper does not shrink in size—just expenses. Newspapers often also raise advertiser rates to increase overall profitability, but this approach is difficult, especially as circula-tions decline.

Leading Newspaper Chains

In general, the trend is toward more concentration of ownership and control of circulation. Most chains are publicly traded, with some still under family control, but increasing pressure is being felt to provide greater attention to the bottom line.

For the top 25 newspaper chains in the country, the combined circulation is an estimated 39,119,728, an increase of 1.4 percent since 1992. The top 25 chains have also increased their number of dailies owned from 566 in 1992 to 659, an increase of 93 papers, or 16 percent.[7]

Gannett

The Gannett Company, a publicly controlled chain, publishes 74 daily newspapers in 41 states and the United Kingdom with a combined daily paid circulation of more than 6.7 million in 1999. It also owns *USA Today*, several magazines, and 22 television stations nationwide.

Weblink
Gannett
(www.gannett.com)

Knight-Ridder

Knight-Ridder is a publicly controlled company with founding family members on board. It publishes 31 daily newspapers in 28 U.S. markets, with a readership of 9.2 million daily (circulation about 4 million) and 13.1 million (circulation about 5 million) Sunday.

Weblink
Knight-Ridder
(www.kri.com)

Advance Publications

Advance Publications is a private family-controlled company, lead by Chairman and CEO Samuel I. "Si" Newhouse, Jr. Advance owns newspapers in 22 cities as well as Condé Nast magazines. Overall circulation at the papers has dropped 2.4 percent to 2 million since 1992.

Weblink
Advance Publications
(www.advance.net)

Times Mirror

The Times Mirror Company is a publicly traded company based in Los Angeles but is family-controlled by descendants of cofounder Harry Chandler, with five metropolitan papers, the *Los Angeles Times*, (Long Island, NY) *Newsday, The Baltimore Sun,* the *Hartford Courant, The Morning Call,* (Allentown, Pennsylvania) and two suburban dailies, *The* (Stamford) *Advocate* and *Greenwich* (Connecticut) *Time.* Circulation is 2.5 million, roughly a 10 percent drop since 1992.

Weblink
Times Mirror
(www.tm.com)

Dow Jones

Dow Jones & Company trades shares publicly but is owned by the Bancroft family, which owns 42 percent of the company and controls 68 percent of its voting power. Its flagship paper is the *Wall Street Journal,* the largest circulation paper in the United States. Overall circulation is up roughly 10 percent since 1992, to 2.7 million. Dow Jones is also very strong online, with more than 1.3 million subscribers to the Dow Jones Newswires, Dow Jones Interactive, and The Wall Street Journal Interactive Edition. The Wall Street Journal Interactive Edition has more than 620,000 paid subscribers to the online newspaper.

Weblink
Dow Jones
(www.dj.com)

The New York Times Company

The New York Times Company also is publicly traded but controlled by the Sulzberger family. It owns 20 daily newspapers, including *The New York Times,* the *Boston Globe,* half of the *International Herald Tribune,* 18 other regional dailies newspapers, and three regional weeklies, as well as eight network-affiliated television stations, two New York radio stations, and three golf magazines. Circulation is up 15 percent to 2.5 million from 1992. Chairman Emeritus is Arthur Ochs Sulzberger, and chairman of the company and publisher of *The New York Times* is Arthur Sulzberger, Jr.

Cox Enterprises

Cox Enterprises is a global media giant whose interests include 15 newspapers. Cox's flagship newspaper is the *Atlanta Journal-Constitution.* The number of dailies in the chain has decreased by four since 1992, and circulation has dropped by more than 4 percent, to 1.3 million.

The Tribune Company

The Tribune Company a publicly traded company with founding family members on the board, includes Tribune Publishing, whose holdings include four market-leading newspapers: the *Chicago Tribune,* the south Florida–based *Sun-Sentinel, The Orlando Sentinel,* and the Hampton Roads (VA)–based *Daily Press.* Daily circulation is down about 9 percent, to 1,360,568, from 1992.

E. W. Scripps

The E. W. Scripps Company is a publicly traded company under family control. Family trusts own 60 percent of the company and control 90 percent of the votes. The Cincinnati-based chain owns 18 daily papers, down 15 percent since 1992, with circulation dropping 19 percent as well, to 1.3 million.

The Hearst Corporation

The Hearst Corporation's diverse media properties include television, radio, cable network programming, online services, and 12 daily newspapers, including the *San Francisco Chronicle,* the *Houston Chronicle,* 18 weeklies, and 16 consumer magazines.

Newspaper Economics

The cost of the printing press, the newsprint or paper, the ink, the press operators, the delivery trucks and drivers, maintaining subscriber databases, as well as various other non–news-related production and distribution costs, make up roughly two-thirds of the overall cost of publishing a newspaper.

It is the ironic fact that most of the cost of a newspaper goes to a function other than producing news that represents an interesting opportunity for newspapers in the digital age. Today, it makes far more economic and environmental sense to distribute a newspaper electronically than to print it on paper. But so far the *Utah County Journal* is the only daily U.S. newspaper to stop printing a product on paper and publish exclusively online. After nine months of printing on paper, Publisher Levor Oldham announced the shift in July 1999. "Clearly, the future of newspapers is on the Web," he said.

Although printing and delivery costs would of course be greatly reduced, there are other economic and customer issues to consider for online newspapers. One is the cost of maintaining Web servers and other computer equipment, especially for sites that receive lots of traffic. Although still cheaper than printing a physical product, the costs can be substantial for large sites. Whether a paper can maintain its advertising base online or find a successful subscription-based model like The Wall Street Journal Interactive Edition will also largely determine its profitability. And online publication assumes that readers have ready access to Internet-connected computers, which is still not the case for many Americans, since Internet penetration varies greatly by region and income level.

Weblink
Utah County Journal
[www.ucjournal.com/]

The Future of Newspapers

"The rumors of my death have been greatly exaggerated," once quipped American novelist and humorist Mark Twain, a former journalist himself, after reading his own obituary in a local newspaper. This may have been true for Twain, but can the same be said for newspapers?

With only three exceptions (Cox Enterprises, Bertelsmann, News Corp.), the world's largest media companies do not own newspapers. It is likely that the unique newspaper culture that places a premium on public service is not well understood by the ownership and leadership of media firms, which are largely entertainment companies. But some of the readership and circulation factors discussed earlier, as well as the economic pressures associated with the printing and publishing business, declining circulation, and reduced advertising make publishing on dead trees look like a dead end. Most of the world's media giants don't want to be part of this disaster waiting to happen.

In general, the only media giants who have serious newspaper holdings have holdings outside the United States, where the penetration of the Internet is generally less and the future for newspapers is not yet quite as bleak. As newspapers, at least in their current printed form, become less important as primary sources of news for people, serious questions for society must be asked. Foremost, will these giant media corporations fill the journalistic void left by the possible extinction of most local daily newspapers? Weeklies and nationals may survive, but many local dailies face a very questionable future unless they adapt to the digital, online world. The top ten media giants are all publicly owned and tend to have a business-oriented bottom line, with their mainstays in entertainment, music, movies, television, books, and magazines. Where might the public interest fit into the bottom line?

Magazines and Their Functions

What differentiates magazines from newspapers? In addition to their name, there are three factors that most clearly distinguish magazines and newspapers.

First, magazines tend to feature more long-form writing, whether in the form of news and analysis or features and human-interest articles. Historically, many journalists and other writers who are today most famous for their books or novels often introduced their subjects in serial form in contemporary magazines. The great English writer Charles Dickens, author of *A Tale of Two Cities, A Christmas Carol,* and *Oliver Twist,* had many of his classics first published in this fashion, typically one chapter at a time. American writer and sometime journalist Edgar Allan Poe, whose dark tales are still popular today, also had many of his stories first published in magazines. His *The Murders in the Rue Morgue,* said to be the first modern detective story, was published in the April 1841 issue of George Rex Graham's *Lady's and Gentleman's Magazine,* whose circulation jumped from 5000 to 25,000 the year Poe started writing for it. Many contemporary writers also use magazines, both in print and online, to introduce their books, often featuring chapters and other excerpts to new readers.

Second, magazines are published at regular intervals but tend to be published less frequently than newspapers, most typically on a monthly basis, although weeklies and quarterlies are also common. This contributed to the alternative writing format of the content of magazines, typically less time sensitive, often more analytical or interpretative, creative, or fictional.

Finally, magazines often have been published on different, higher quality paper stock than newspapers and are often designed to be kept considerably longer than dailies. In addition, magazines have tended to be printed in a certain size, namely 8.5 by 11 inches. However, certain clever magazine publishers have sometimes reduced the size of their magazines, what is known as the trim size, by a quarter or a half inch, in order to save money on printing costs, yet maintain the same cost to advertisers and subscribers. On the other hand, some magazines such as *Rolling Stone* and *ESPN Magazine* print on larger stock, which helps make their magazines stand out on shelves crowded with other magazines.

Charles P. Daly, Patrick Henry, and Ellen Ryder outline in their definitive book on magazine publishing, *The Magazine Publishing Industry,* several additional qualities that define magazines. Perhaps the most important of these is that magazines have a defined audience. Although this is true today in a generally descriptive sense, it is not necessary conceptually speaking and has not always been true historically, with general interest magazines of the mid-twentieth century such as *Look* and *Life* being two exceptions. Magazine historian Frank Luther Mott, winner of a Pulitzer Prize in 1939, argued in 1943 that a true magazine must also be bound, but today that contention seems obsolete as more and more magazines go online.

Magazines serve several important functions in society. Among the most important functions are surveillance, correlation, entertainment, and marketing of goods and services. Surveillance is the most basic function magazines perform. However, unlike most newspapers, most magazines tend not to specialize by reporting on local geographic communities. Rather, most magazines specialize by subject matter. They cover relatively narrow topics, such as science, health, or sports. Some concentrate on extremely specialized topics, such as doll collecting, harness racing, or scuba diving.

Many magazines have national, regional, or even international readership and distribution. A few major weekly news magazines such as *Time, Newsweek,* and *U.S. News & World Report* take a broader approach to their reporting on the goings-on of the world. Magazines can provide information in relatively great detail compared to newspapers, because they tend to feature longer stories. Because magazines are typically printed on higher quality paper, they can provide exceptionally effective photography and illustration, making them well suited to covering fashion, nature, and science.

Many magazines are either exclusively or largely designed to provide entertainment for their readers and are largely read as leisure activities. Magazines such as *People* or *Entertainment Weekly,* with their coverage of celebrities and Hollywood, are illustrative of magazines that emphasize the entertainment function.

Almost all magazines serve a vital marketing function for a broad cross-section of goods and services. It often happens that readers spend more time looking at ads than reading editorial content as they browse a magazine. This is especially true of fashion magazines, such as *Vogue, Glamour,* or *GQ,* which often feature not just the latest news on designer clothes but the hottest advertising.

Benjamin Franklin, publisher of *Poor Richard's Almanack.*

The Historical Development of Magazines

In some ways, the early history of magazines and newspapers is interwoven, with technological, business (i.e., advertising), and journalistic/entertainment functions overlapping between the two. It was not until 1731 that the first English-language periodical used the word magazine in its title, *The Gentleman's Magazine,*

The New York Ledger was one of the late 19th-century magazines featuring literary works by some of the period's leading writers.

Media Future: Electronic Paper

A number of researchers have made great strides toward creating electronic paper. Some examples include "Gyricon" from Xerox PARC and E Ink from MIT. These products are lightweight tablets that are flexible and will be inexpensive and capable of producing the resolution of ink on paper. No more dead trees, no more printing presses, trucks, and delays. Veteran journalist Roger Fidler, who has been pioneering work in the flat-panel newspaper for more than a decade, may finally get his wish. Fidler is the author of *Mediamorphosis* and director of the Information Design Laboratory at Kent State University's School of Journalism and Mass Communication, where he is collaborating with the Liquid Crystal Institute and ALCOM, the National Science Foundation Science and Technology Center for Advanced Liquid Crystalline Optical Materials.

published in London. Benjamin Franklin published *Poor Richard's Almanack* in 1732, a predecessor of the modern-day magazine. The first magazine published in North America was the *American Magazine, or A Monthly View of the Political State of the British Colonies*, published in 1741 in Philadelphia. The first news weekly magazine was *Niles' Weekly Register*, first published in 1811.

In the nineteenth century, magazines helped a young United States define itself as they reached a nationwide audience. This is in contrast to newspapers, which were primarily metropolitan or local in scope.

Also important in this period were Frank Leslie and Miriam Florence Folline Leslie. Frank founded a variety of periodicals, including one of the first influential newsweeklies, *Frank Leslie's Illustrated Newspaper*, launched in 1855. In 1871 Leslie hired Miriam as editor of *Frank Leslie's Lady's Journal;* the two married in 1874. Frank's business went bankrupt in 1877, but Miriam took over upon his death in 1880 and skillfully restored the enterprise to financial health. She become one of the wealthiest and most powerful women in journalism and bequeathed some $2 million to the cause of suffrage.

Important magazine developments in the late 1800s and early 1900s include the 1888 debut of *National Geographic*, founded by the National Geographic Society. *National Geographic* introduced color plates in 1906. Time, Inc., founded by Henry Luce, launched *Life* magazine in 1936, a large-format, general interest magazine with excellent photography.

Specialization of Magazines

A series of major sociological and media shifts in the 1940s and 1950s brought major change to the magazine industry. These complex changes included not only a dramatic decline in public appetites for general interest magazines and afternoon newspapers but a marked shift in advertising dollars from these media to television. Television quickly became the dominant medium of mass communication and drew national advertisers seeking large audience reach. As a result, general interest magazines such as *Life* and *Look* saw their business base dissolve.

Magazine publishers had to adapt in order to survive. Overall, they stopped publishing general interest magazines in favor of specialized magazines on almost every conceivable topic with highly targeted audiences. Advertising returned, as well, with advertisers finding appeal in the target marketing possible in specialized publications. This is a trend that has continued in the online arena. There are nearly 18,000 largely specialized magazines available in print and online.

Circulation Patterns and Titles

Today, U.S. magazine publishing is a $9 billion industry based on subscriptions and newsstand sales for 1998 but a $13.8 billion industry based on advertising expenditures in 1998.[8] Contemporary magazines, like all media, are increasingly subject to ownership consolidation, although in contrast to newspapers, many magazines are seeing their circulations increase, and the number of magazines is also gradually increasing. The number of magazine titles has increased from 13,541 in 1988 to 17,694 in 2001, with only five years during that time when there were decreases in the number of titles.

Despite overall increases in the number of magazine titles, many magazines go out of business every year, including some well-established titles. In 2002, for example, just some of the magazines that ceased publication or were suspended included *New Choices* (established 1960), *Teen* (established 1957), *Internet Week* (established 1983), *Talk* (established 1999), and *Style 24/7* (established 2001). The odds are generally against new magazines becoming successful, even those with strong corporate backing.

The leading circulation magazines are reflective of the general trends in magazine publishing. The top magazines target specific audiences. They cover specialized subjects in depth, and they do so with quality. Those with the largest circulation appeal to the audience segments that are relatively large and, in many cases, growing, such as older adults.

Table 3-3 shows the top ten paid circulation magazines in the United States in 2000. Both *Modern Maturity* and *NRTA/AARP Bulletin* are publications of the American Association of Retired Persons (AARP). NRTA, The National Retired Teachers Association, was founded in 1947 by Dr. Ethel Percy Andrus, herself a teacher. Moreover, among these top circulation magazines, most are either targeted toward senior citizens and retired persons (the fastest growing demographic segment of the U.S. population), and women, with five of the seven major women's magazines—dubbed the "seven sisters"—among the top ten circulation magazines. The other major women's magazines are also in the top 50. All these magazines also maintain Web sites, with at least a portion of their magazine content available online, plus additional content and interactive features.

There has been a significant shift in the top ten circulation magazines during the past quarter century. As detailed in Table 3-3, although the women's magazines, *Reader's Digest,* and *TV Guide* were on the list in 1972, the AARP publications, which were not even in the top 10 then, have since swept past all the others to the top spots. *McCall's,* ranked sixth in 1972 with a circulation of 7.5 million, stopped publication and was relaunched as the Rosie O'Donnell star vehicle *Rosie* in April 2001. However, despite strong sales and good advertising revenues, disagreements between O'Donnell and the publisher over the editorial direction of *Rosie* have caused them to sue each other as O'Donnell was forced to leave the magazine.

Playboy has seen its ranking and circulation drop substantially. It is now out of the top 10 and has a circulation of less than 4 million, a decrease of a third. Notably, its online readership has soared to millions of pageviews a month. Perhaps as a result, *Playboy* is planning to expand its online presence into a men's lifestyle portal, offering a range of men's content, from sex to sports. Competition is likely to be intense, although scant at the time of this writing, with the newly created but rapidly growing *Maxim* men's magazine also planning a men's lifestyle portal and spending more than $1 million in the site's 2000 relaunch.

Table 3-3 Top 10 Circulation Magazines, 1972 vs. 2000, Ranked by Paid Circulation				
	1972		**2000**	
Rank	**Title**	**Circulation**	**Title**	**Circulation**
1	*Reader's Digest*	17,828,000	*NRTA/AARP Bulletin*	20,826,000
2	*TV Guide*	16,411,000	*Modern Maturity*	20,824,000
3	*Woman's Day*	8,192,000	*Reader's Digest*	12,590,000
4	*Better Homes and Gardens*	7,996,000	*TV Guide*	10,388,000
5	*Family Circle*	7,890,000	*National Geographic*	7,892,000
6	*McCall's*	7,517,000	*Better Homes and Gardens*	7,622,000
7	*National Geographic*	7,260,000	*Family Circle*	5,002,000
8	*Ladies' Home Journal*	7,014,000	*Good Housekeeping*	4,532,000
9	*Playboy*	6,401,000	*Woman's Day*	4,195,000
10	*Good Housekeeping*	5,801,000	*Ladies' Home Journal*	4,137,000

Sources: Audit Bureau of Circulation, the organization that audits print publication circulation in the United States and internationally, and the Magazine Publishers of America.

Content Specialization

Specialization in the magazine industry breaks out into several major topical areas. In fact, Bacon's, the publisher of an annual directory of magazines, list 225 "market classifications," and The *National Directory of Magazines* identifies 279. Ten of the most important, at least in terms of circulation, are news, fashion, women (with at least three major subgroups: middle-age and older women, women under 35, and teenage girls), families (especially aimed at parents of children under age 12), sports (with some general interest, but many specialized by type of sport), ethnic, medical/health, political, farm (*Farm Journal* alone has a circulation of 815,000), and lifestyles (many by type of home, region, or cooking).

Notably, most of the new titles introduced each year tend to be in relatively new or smaller, less-established niche specialties where growth potential may be greater. For instance, of the more than 500 new titles introduced in 1998, the largest number was in the interest category of "media personalities," with 39 new titles. The next largest number of new titles in 1998, 34, was introduced in the interest category of "sex." Crafts and games had 33 new titles, while rounding out the top five interest categories for new titles were sports and computers, each with 32. None of these interest categories are in the top ten for overall circulation.

John H. Johnson, founder of *Ebony* and a Multimillion-Dollar Media Empire

One entrepreneur who decided to do something to serve the media needs of African Americans in the mid-1900s was John H. Johnson, then a young African American whose hometown high school in Arkansas City, Arkansas, was "whites only." As a result, Johnson's family moved to Chicago, where Johnson got his formal high school education. His mother funded his business undertaking by pawning her household furniture and giving her son $500 to start *Ebony* magazine. *Ebony* has become one of the leading magazines targeting the interests of African Americans, with a circulation of more than 1.5 million. Johnson has become one of the leading cross-media owners in the United States, with a book publishing company, a nationally syndicated television program, and two radio stations.[9]

John H. Johnson, chairman and CEO of Johnson Publishing Co., with his daughter Linda Johnson Rice, president of the company.

Magazines and the Internet

Weblink
Zines by Title
[www.meer.net/~johnl/e-zine-list/zines/]

The rise of the Internet has not only given new life to existing magazines that have found a welcoming home online but rejuvenated what was a largely underground and self-publishing subculture of "zines" (taking their name from the last part of "magazine"). One online source lists more than 4000 zines.

Before the Internet, zines were often low-budget productions of photocopied sheets distributed, often for free or requesting donations, to a small but dedicated readership on the topic the zine covered, whether it was the local music scene, art, or politics. However, being able to distribute on the Internet for a lower cost to a much wider audience has helped push zines to professional levels of journalism and production.

Some online magazines have tried to establish themselves, such as Salon.com, which specializes in original reporting and analysis; Slate.com, a Microsoft content entrant edited by Michael Kinsley; and Hot Wired, the online companion to *Wired* magazine. These online magazines often have first-class writers and journalists contributing to them, although they generally have still not found successful business models, as online users generally seem unwilling to pay for subscriptions to online content and online advertising revenues do not cover production costs.

The tendency online for young users especially to get their information in small chunks and from various sources would seem not to lend itself well to a long-form, noninteractive text format that magazines specialize in. Whether improvements in screen clarity and mobile devices will make people more inclined to read text online or if online magazines will be forced to adapt their styles in radical ways remains to be seen.

W

Weblink
Salon
[www.salon.com]

Hot Wired
[hotwired.lycos.com/]

SUMMARY

This chapter has examined the media of books, newspapers, and magazines. For each of these media, much has changed historically. Although the basic functions of each have not changed, their form, scope, and role in society have evolved as technology has advanced and as our society changes.

When introduced, printed books exerted a profound influence on society as the pre-eminent medium of knowledge dissemination. Books tend to take the longest-term view and provide the greatest depth of all analog media. They include works of fiction and nonfiction and can be entertaining as well as educational.

Newspapers have gone through a series of significant changes, each time adapting to both technological and societal changes. Nevertheless, both daily and weekly newspapers have maintained a leading role as a medium of surveillance in society. Most U.S. newspapers have tended to serve individual cities or metropolitan areas, although the rise of online publishing is widening the potential newspaper audience. Internationally, newspapers are more often national in coverage than are those in the United States.

Magazines have complemented other print media, tending to take a longer-term view than newspapers but being more timely than and not as in-depth as books. They too are adapting to technological and social change by becoming very specialized in subjects and audience demographics. As a result, there are almost 18,000 magazines published in print and online on virtually every subject imaginable.

Discussion Questions

1. Do you think that with the Internet and digital media we are in the midst of a media revolution as far-reaching as that brought on by the printing press? Why or why not? What are some societal and technological similarities or differences between now and the mid-1400s that will support your argument?

2. If you were to travel into the future to a post-apocalyptic world to build a new civilization, what three books might you bring and why?

3. If you had to make a choice today for the rest of your life to receive your textual news and knowledge about the world only from printed materials or only from online sources, which would you choose? What are your reasons?

4. How did the development of the penny press change the nature of mediated communication in the 19th century?

5. Why have magazines seemed to adjust better than newspapers to societal and technological changes brought on since World War II? Create a brief outline business plan that a 21st century newspaper could follow in order to survive, including its target audience and type of content.

6. What forces led to the specialization of magazines in the years following World War II? What factors will shape the future of magazines in the 21st century?

7. Local advertisers can exert undue control over small, independently owned papers by threatening to reduce or stop advertising. What factors could hurt public service journalism in an age of media concentration by companies whose primary business interests are not journalism?

Photography and Movies

Filmmaker George Lucas apparently knows how to harness the power of the Force. Two of the top ten all-time grossing movies are from his Star Wars saga, while all are within the top twenty. *Attack of the Clones* reached the top twenty within a few weeks of its release.

Lucas has consistently pushed the technological limits of film, now shooting them digitally and creating ever-higher standards for digital filmmaking. He is also in the vanguard of promoting digital exhibition as well, which will give movie audiences better sound, better picture quality, and even more digital effects. Although some theaters are switching to digital projection systems, the process has been slow, as the costs to switch are high, even though studios will save millions on film distribution costs.

But Lucas has also been ahead of the Hollywood studios in another arena: letting Star Wars fans have access to plans and

developments in upcoming movies through an entirely
volunteer fan Web site called TheForce.Net. The Web site

sees up to 50,000 visitors a day and has more
than 9000 pages of material compiled by
52 staffers from the United States, Canada,
Europe, and Australia.

Through a network of information gatherers—
including some Lucasfilm employees—the site
often releases upcoming tidbits on newly developed characters, images, and even audio clips
from the upcoming Star Wars movie. The fans,
already some of the most dedicated among
entertainment entities, help generate the all-important
"buzz" as they spread the news among themselves and
create excitement for the upcoming movie.

Occasionally there are rumblings from the Lucasfilm
legal department when they feel the fans encroach too

OBJECTIVES

In this chapter we will:

- Explore the origins of photography and how its development mirrors developments in other media technologies.
- Examine issues surrounding the power of still images in storytelling.
- Review the history of movies and film and how technological constraints limited
  the evolution of content.
- Outline the control Hollywood had and has over creating movies and making
  movies successful.
- Discuss the important ways in which digital media are changing the nature of
  the movie industry and how movies are made.

strongly on the Star Wars brand or obtain items like a prerelease version of the script for Episode II, but in general Lucasfilm is uniquely relaxed among major entertainment companies about allowing fans to use and build on the Star Wars brand. With plans in the works for a massively multiplayer online Star Wars game, they will have to learn to be even more relaxed about where the fans want to take Star Wars.

Prologue

Photographs and film have played a fundamental role in framing our world through journalism, entertainment, and art. Even as digitization dramatically alters some aspects of photography and film, in other ways these media continue to shape our perceptions of what we create in a digital environment. Photojournalists, cinematographers, and videographers have used the frame of the photographic lens to place a defining structure on the linear narrative of visual storytelling. The media grammar that filmmakers have created in the past hundred years of filmmaking provides the foundation for digital videographers as they explore the limits of the new medium with more portable equipment and more sophisticated editing tools.

Photography

Still images, or photographs, have long been important to mass media. Still images have performed—and continue to perform—at least three significant functions in mediated communication.

First, photographs can tell a story or convey information quickly. At a glance, a reader can scan the photos or images in a newspaper or magazine. These photos might tell the story of a daring rescue in a fire, provide a glimpse of a reclusive celebrity, or show the latest fashions on the runways of Paris or Milan.

Second, photos and other images can provide verification of factual claims. While words might provide the narrative, photos confirm the truth of what those words say, whether it is a plane crash, an alleged extramarital affair, or a mass grave in a war-torn part of the world.

Finally, photos can engage, entertain, or elicit emotion in a way that words alone might not. Seeing photos of the devastation left from the September 11, 2001, terrorist attacks on the World Trade Center and Pentagon can stir feelings that mere verbal descriptions might never produce.

Historical Development of Photography

The principles involved in creating photographs had been known and used for hundreds of years before photography was invented, so in one respect it was unusual that photography had not been developed earlier. The earliest recorded use of a **camera obscura,** or dark box or room with a small hole in it that allowed an inverted image of an outside scene to be shown on the opposite inner wall, are in the writings of Leonardo da Vinci. He explained how a camera obscura can be an aid to drawing scenery, as one simply moves a sheet of paper around until the scene comes into sharp focus and then traces the scene.

The other important element in photography is understanding how light can affect certain chemicals, which was also known for hundreds of years before the first photograph was developed. Although some scientists could produce photographs by using various light-sensitive chemicals, they had no way to make the image permanent. In June 1827, Joseph Niepce created a picture using an asphaltlike material that hardened after being exposed to light. However, the picture was very unclear and required an exposure time of eight hours.[1]

In 1829 Niepce agreed to go into partnership with fellow Frenchman **Jacques Louis Daguerre.** Although Niepce died in 1833, Daguerre continued to experiment and in January 1839 unveiled the **daguerreotype,** a method of creating a positive

Photographs can often evoke powerful emotions in ways words alone can never do.

camera obscura—a dark box or room with a small hole in it that allowed an inverted image of an outside scene to be shown on the opposite inner wall.

Daguerre, Jacques Louis—a French scene painter and inventor of the daguerreotype, an early type of photography.

daguerreotype—an early type of photography that used a silver-coated copper plate coated with iodine vapor to create a positive image. Although image clarity was extremely good, daguerreotypes did not allow for copies of photographs to be made, unlike another early photography type, the calotype.

Media Timeline: Early Photography

1839	1850s	1860s	1878	1884	
Building on his earlier work with Joseph Niepce, Jacques Louis Daguerre develops the daguerreotype.	"Pictorial" newpapers begin widely publishing photographs and other illustrations of news events and subjects.	Mathew Brady uses photographs to document the Civil War, helping bring more visual news coverage of war to the public.	Eadweard Muybridge's innovative use of serial photographs sees what the human eye cannot: the rapid movement of a running horse.	George Eastman invents roll film, which allows photographers to take multiple pictures in succession more easily and to work	closer to deadline, making it more practic for newspapers to publish timely news photos.

image on a metal plate. He had reduced the exposure time from eight hours to thirty minutes or so.[2]

How does a daguerreotype work? Here's an explanation from an online Smithsonian exhibition:

Samuel F. B. Morse.

> A daguerreotype is made on a sheet of silver-plated copper. The surface is polished to a mirrorlike brilliance and made light-sensitive by coating with iodine fumes. The plate is then exposed to an image sharply focused by the camera's well-ground, optically correct lens. Removed by the camera, the plate is treated with mercury vapors in order to develop the latent image. Finally, the image is "fixed" by removing the remaining photosensitive salts in a bath of "hypo" (sodium thiosulfate) and toned with gold chloride to improve contrast and durability. Color, made of powdered pigment, was applied directly to the metal surface with a finely-pointed brush.

Daguerreotypes Come to the United States

The story of how the daguerreotype came to America and its fundamental influence on mass communication begins with a meeting of **Samuel F. B. Morse,** a noted painter and the inventor of the Morse code and the telegraph, and Louis Daguerre in Paris in 1839.

While in Paris to secure a French patent for the telegraph, Samuel Morse heard about Daguerre and his wonderful pictures.[3] Morse wrote a letter to his brothers, who were newspaper publishers in New York, describing Daguerre's technology. The brothers published the letter in their newspaper, the *New York Observer.* When back in New York, Morse also introduced Daguerre's technology to a young man who would be a major figure in early photography, Mathew Brady.[4]

Further Developments in Photography Technology

Not only did Morse's brothers at the *New York Observer* find promise in the daguerreotype; other newspapers quickly started using the technology as well. The daguerreotype suffered from an important flaw, however, and that was the inability to make copies of a photograph. A competing but initially inferior photographic technology, the **calotype,** solved that problem by creating a negative photograph from which positive copies could be made, the basis for photography today.

The calotype was invented by William Henry Fox Talbot around the same time the daguerreotype was announced and used a paper negative as the medium

Morse, Samuel F. B.—inventor of the telegraph and the system of clicks used to communicate on it called Morse code. He was also a noted painter and inventor.

calotype—the first type of photography that created a negative photograph from which positive copies could be made, although it was inferior in picture quality to the daguerreotype.

Photographs are valuable in capturing moments and events that can be used by later journalists and historians to help them better understand the past.

to affix the image. Image quality was greatly inferior to the daguerreotype, however, and imperfections in the paper were transferred to subsequent generations of copies, making them even poorer quality. A method for using glass plates as negatives was developed, but exposure times were too long for portraiture.

In 1851 Frederick Scott Archer introduced a new photographic process called the **wet collodion process,** which reduced exposure times down to several seconds using glass plates covered in a syrupy chemical called collodion and dipped in a silver nitrate solution to make them light sensitive. The process still required bulky equipment and specialized knowledge, however, as the plates could only be used when the collodion was still wet. After the image was fixed on the glass plate and the plate was then washed in a bath of salts to remove excess silver nitrate, paper was applied to the plate and left in the sun for a period of time, which copied the image onto the paper as a positive. In 1871 Dr. Richard Maddox discovered a way to use gelatin instead of the wet plates used in the collodion process, which led the way to dry plates that could be developed and was an important step in making photography easier without specialized knowledge.

Civil War Photography

Mathew B. Brady took many Civil War photos using the wet collodion process. Brady photographed many of the most important leaders of the Union, such as President Lincoln, and of the Confederacy, including General R. E. Lee. He also photographed abolitionist Frederick Douglass. Ironically, Brady suffered from a lifelong chronic eye condition that hindered his eyesight. He was a passionate photographer who put his own life (and the personal fortune he had accumulated from two decades of successful photographic work) at risk photographing the Civil War, despite the objections of friends and family. Brady's response to their admonitions to stay away from the conflict, "A spirit in my feet said 'Go', and I went."[5]

Brady was highly acclaimed for his work, which included photographing many of the day's greatest and most popular figures, including Zachary Taylor,

wet collodion process—a type of photography invented in 1851 that used glass plates covered in a syrupy chemical called collodion and dipped in silver nitrate solution to make them light sensitive.

Brady, Mathew B.—a famous photographer of the nineteenth century who took portraits of many famous people of his day as well as Civil War battlefield photographs.

Mathew Brady photographed thousands of Civil War scenes such as this one.

John C. Calhoun, Daniel Webster, John James Audubon, Tom Thumb, Walt Whitman, and Millard Fillmore. It is through Brady's work that many of these figures are best known to us today. His work was published in many local newspapers and some national magazines, such as *Harper's Weekly*.

Brady did not always subscribe to the standards of impartial photojournalism expected of photojournalists today. Historians have criticized Brady for sometimes "arranging" his subjects, including battlefield corpses, for dramatic photocomposition purposes. Such a practice is considered unethical in modern journalism.

Brady was not alone in sometimes arranging his photographs. Historian John Osborn explains, "Many photographers, it is said, would position the bodies in the fashion that they saw would fit the need of capturing the realistic qualities of death. Alex Gardener is said to have carried a dead soldier over a course of forty yards so he could prop his body against a specific spot at the Devil's Den, presumably to capture the essence of a single, dead sharpshooter. In response to the allegation that Gardener had manipulated the scene to help portray the sadness, he responded, "the artist, in passing over the scene of the previous days' engagements, found in a lonely place the covert of a rebel sharpshooter, and photographed the scene presented. . . ."[6]

Nevertheless, the photography of Brady and others during the Civil War, the first war to have been documented by photography, played an important role in helping the public understand the conflict, which saw the war through the window of the press.

Seeing beyond the Human Eye

Early applications of photography were not limited to journalism, of course. One of the most notable was Eadweard Muybridge's use of photography for scientific documentation. Muybridge first gained recognition in 1867 for his prize-winning series of dramatic photos of Yosemite. In 1878, Muybridge took another famous photo series through which he was able to document, for the first time, how a horse runs. The photos show that at top speed, a trotting horse has all four hooves simultaneously off the ground, in a different arrangement

Weblink
Mathew Brady's Portraits [www.npg.si.edu/exh/brady/index2.htm]

Sudan, Starvation, and Suicide

On March 23, 1993, the *New York Times* ran a photo taken by South African photojournalist Kevin Carter that seemed to epitomize the human suffering and anguish in Africa. A small, starving Sudanese girl tried to crawl to a feeding station in a remote area while a vulture stood nearby, waiting for her to die. Carter said he waited for about 20 minutes, positioning himself for the best shot and careful not to disturb the bird, hoping it would spread its wings. When it did not, he snapped some pictures, chased the bird away, and watched as the little girl resumed her struggle. A friend and colleague of Carter's said that afterward Carter was depressed and kept saying he wanted to hug his own young daughter. The photo touched many who saw it, and hundreds of people had asked the *Times* if the girl had survived, but there was no way the *Times* could learn of the girl's fate.

Kevin Carter's Pulitzer–winning photo touched many people but also raised important ethical issues.

On April 12, 1994, the *New York Times* phoned to tell Carter that he had won the Pulitzer Prize for photography. Carter was delighted to receive the prize, even though there was strong criticism about him from colleagues and other media outlets. The *St. Petersburg* (Florida) *Times* said, "The man adjusting his lens to take just the right frame of her suffering might just as well be a predator, another vulture on the scene."

Carter was painfully aware of the photojournalist's dilemma but said in describing photographing a gunfight that one simply had to think visually and think about the other issues later. American photojournalist James Nachtwey, who often worked with Carter and his photojournalist friends, says, "Every photographer who has been involved in these stories has been affected. You become changed forever. Nobody does this kind of work to make themselves feel good. It is very hard to continue."

This was apparently the case for Carter, who committed suicide by carbon monoxide poisoning in his truck on July 27, 1994, near a park where he used to play as a child. He was 33.[7]

What responsibility, if any, do photojournalists have to help the subjects they take photographs of? What implications could there be if photojournalists regularly helped people during conflicts or in times of tragedy?

Eadweard Muybridge used multiple cameras to capture the motion of a horse running.

from that of a galloping horse. Such applications of photography are of great importance in mass communication, especially where they can help us see things that human eyes, unassisted, would be unable to see. This is an opportunity taken to new heights in the digital age and is discussed in more detail later.

The Advent of Roll Film

The next important development in photography that significantly affected journalism was the development of the roll film made of celluloid in 1884 by George Eastman, who cofounded the Eastman Kodak Company. The roll film allowed photographers to take multiple pictures of an event and develop them far more easily than earlier types of photography, making roll film especially useful when on deadline for printing in a newspaper. It was after this invention that the use of photographs in newspapers began to grow dramatically. The development of roll film also revolutionized the photography industry.

The Development of Color Film

Photographers and scientists started experimenting with ways to take color photographs within 30 years of the invention of photography. The principles of how we perceive light and the color spectrum were already known, and in 1861 a British physicist created the first true color photograph using collodion plates. The process, however, could not capture the full range of colors, especially red, and it took many more experiments using colored filters and dyes and about 40 more years before a commercially viable color film was made available by **Auguste** and **Louis Lumiere.** The process they invented still had several weaknesses, however, and it wasn't until 1912 that the modern process of developing color film in which the color dyes are within the film emulsion was created by Dr. Rudolf Fischer. Kodak introduced the first, modern three-emulsion color film, called Kodachrome, in 1935. German company Agfa introduced a different technique for color film and introduced Agfacolor in 1936, which is what virtually all color films today are based on with the exception of Kodachrome.[8]

Lumiere brothers—Auguste and Louis Lumiere used Edison's Kinetoscope to create the Cinematographe, which was not only portable but allowed projection of movies as well so they could be shown to an audience.

Media Technology

Satellite Imagery

Although most media imagery and video is recorded from a perspective on or near the earth, recent years have seen the growth of imagery and video of the earth but observed from hundreds of miles above the ground. Remote-sensing satellite imagery has since the end of the Cold War grown dramatically to become an almost daily part of media content.[9] On the Web, members of the public can type in their address and see a satellite image taken of their neighborhood. Some companies even sell satellite imagery as art.

Satellite imagery not only plays an important role in military operations, it can also be invaluable for journalists covering stories on the environment or the influence of development on farmland, for example. Looking at weather patterns over time can also provide vital information to help people to prepare for severe weather.

Weblink

Aerial views of any address [www.globexplorer.com /mapquest/]

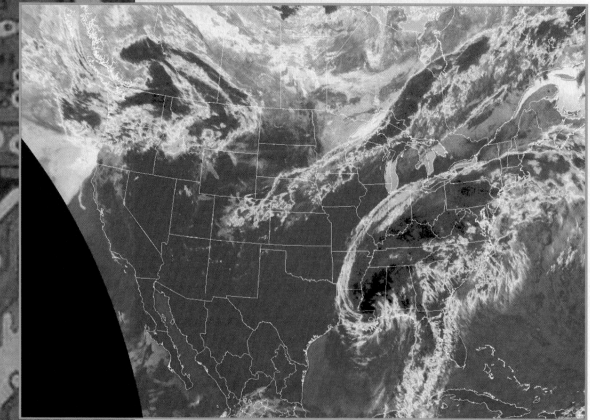

Early model Kodak camera with roll of film, circa 1884.

The Rise of Digital Photography

Digital photography differs markedly from analog photography, because the pictures are not stored on film at all but rather images are captured by sensors called charge-coupled devices (CCDs) and stored on a typical digital storage medium such as a floppy diskette or CD-ROM. Images are stored as pixels, or squares representing parts of the image, and the higher number of pixels that can be seen the better quality the image. However, because images take up much more digital storage space than text, it has taken improvements in technology such as increased computer processor power and smaller storage devices to make digital photography a viable alternative to traditional photography in terms of picture quality.

Digital photography does have several advantages over traditional film photography. Because images are digital, they can easily be transferred to a computer and manipulated via standard photo editing software, as well as easily distributed via a computer network. This means that development costs are virtually nil compared to traditional film. Photographers can also preview their photos immediately and retake photos they do not like, which gives amateur photographers much more flexibility and control over the pictures they take. Digital cameras are generally much smaller than their analog counterparts and can take good pictures in low-light conditions or other adverse circumstances.

Digital photography is becoming more popular among general users, and some professionals are starting to switch to digital cameras as well, although not entirely so. Digital photography does still have some drawbacks, however, due to current limitations in technology, picture quality, and storage.

Declining Picture Quality

Unlike the evolution of other types of media, the history of photography has been in at least one way a history of declining quality.[10] Early photography using silver halide technology recorded images with extremely high resolution and even sometimes incorporated depth information using stereoscopic imaging systems. Today's cameras, though smaller and often digital, are of considerably poorer quality, although they do have color and certain other advantages. As the twenty-first century begins, digital cameras are only now approaching the resolution of chemical-based analog photography of the 1880s. It will still be many years, if ever, before digital photography attains the image resolution of the photography of the 1860s through the 1880s. Of course, there are other advantages to today's photography, especially digital: It is much easier and cheaper to create, process (it processes instantly), and distribute. In Brady's day, the photographer needed to carry a considerable amount of photographic and chemical processing equipment that significantly restricted mobility and speed, two critically important factors for photojournalists.

Movies

Even before the invention of daguerreotype photography, inventors had tried to recreate the perception of motion through a variety of devices that were often as awkwardly named as they were to use. Most were never more than novelties. If still images proved important to mass media of the mid-nineteenth century, then the development of motion pictures at the end of the nineteenth century dramatically transformed the nature of mass communication in the twentieth century. The introduction of motion pictures meant media could, for the first time, record activity. More importantly for the movie industry, the technology could recreate reality and *create* "realities" that never could exist in the real world.

The Functions of the Movie Industry

The motion picture, or movie, industry dates back to the 1890s when Thomas Edison and the Lumiere brothers developed motion picture cameras and projection

Spike Lee's 1999 film *Summer of Sam* caused controversy because of its depiction of real-life events during the summer of 1977, when David Berkowitz, the so-called "Son of Sam killer," murdered several people.

Mass Communication Formats

devices. The primary function of motion pictures is to entertain, with many millions of movie-watchers enjoying the sweeping epics, slapstick comedies, romances, and adventure stories they see in feature-length films. Yet, many fans and critics alike consider the cinema to be more than simple entertainment and appraise its value and function as a serious visual art form comparable to painting, sculpture, or architecture, with a history of important social influence. As such, motion pictures hold a special place among other forms of mass communication, with perhaps the exception of literary books and some recorded music. Nevertheless, it would be an oversimplification to imply that movies are primarily a medium of the arts. Most commercially produced motion pictures in the United States are made to make money, and it is the exception that rises to serious art form.

Film pioneers the Lumiere brothers.

Historical Development of Movies: The Early Years

In 1891, **Thomas Alva Edison** created his **Kinetoscope,** a "peep-show" precursor to the motion picture viewer. Edison's failure to patent this technology allowed two Frenchmen, Louis and Auguste Lumiere, to manufacture a more portable camera, film processing unit, and projector, which they patented in 1895. Their invention was suitcase-sized and enabled the Lumieres through a single device to shoot footage in the morning, process it in the afternoon, and project it for an audience in the evening. It soon became the rage all over France. They called their invention the **Cinematographe,** and it was clearly based on Thomas Edison's peep-show machine. The critical difference between Edison's Kinetoscope and the Lumieres' Cinematographe was the Cinematographe's ability to display motion pictures to an audience of more than one person at a time.[11]

On December 28, 1895, the Lumieres debuted their process to a paying audience in a Paris cafe, showing a series of ten 15- to 60-second glimpses of real scenes recorded outdoors.

Perhaps this was the first form of the documentary. Louis Lumiere did not visualize the Cinematographe as a medium for news or entertainment; he typically documented some aspect of ordinary, daily life, almost like an anthropologist with a camera. Louis Lumiere's first film was the arrival of the express train from Ciotat. His other films included workers leaving the factory gates, people enjoying a picnic along a river, and parents feeding their child.

The Lumiere brothers failed to recognize the value of their invention. Their approach to filmmaking attempted to reproduce reality rather than tell a story, and Louis Lumiere felt that the novelty of watching moving images on a screen that could just as easily be seen by walking outside would eventually wear off. This mindset was distinctly different from that of other early film pioneers such as Thomas Edison and George Méliès, who saw that film could change reality as well as reproduce it.

Early Cinema Pioneers

Early cinema history began with silent films. Silent films had an advantage in that they could more easily cross language barriers than their talkie descendants because the few words that the silent movies did include, usually presented as placards to read on the screen, could easily be translated into the local language and inserted to replace the original placard scene.

Edison, Thomas Alva—inventor whose inventions include the electric light, the phonograph, and the Kinetoscope. Edison's lab in Menlo Park, New Jersey, had over 60 scientists and produced as many as 400 patent applications a year.

Kinetoscope—a peephole movie viewer invented by Thomas Edison that allowed one viewer at a time to watch a short film.

Cinematographe—an early movie projector and camera technology that allowed for projection of films to a small audience.

The storytelling aspects of the earliest films were quite limited, because the films were short in duration (a few minutes in length) and often depicted little more than people in their everyday lives. Nevertheless, Cinematographes were soon in the hands of filmmakers around the world, and the motion picture age began. It did not take long for early moviemakers to experiment with new ways of visual storytelling, many of which are still used today and taken for granted in movies.[12]

Georges Méliès   One filmmaker who pioneered the early use of film as a medium of the imagination was the Frenchman **Georges Méliès** (1861–1938). In contrast to the Lumière brothers, who saw the cinema as a device for recording reality, Méliès used the medium almost as a vehicle for magic, to conjure and create illusions. Méliès, who earlier experimented with magic lantern techniques in theatrical stage effects, was the first to use film to create special effects, such as to make objects suddenly appear or disappear or to transform them into other objects. Among his most memorable examples was the celluloid transformation of a carriage into a hearse. Méliès pioneered a variety of innovative special effects, including the first double exposure (*La Caverne maudite*, 1898), the first split-screen shot (*Un Homme de tête*, 1898) and the first dissolve (*Cendrillon*, 1899).

D. W. Griffith   Méliès notwithstanding, many silent films were little more than novelties. Early movie audiences would thrill to the scene of a train rushing toward them, for example. But by the 1910s, the medium began to evolve as an important storytelling vehicle. One of the most important silent films of this era was David Wark "D. W." Griffith's 1915 American classic, *Birth of a Nation*.[13] *Birth of a Nation* was the first major full-length film and introduced many innovative cinematic techniques. Griffith used crosscutting (parallel editing) and other techniques to portray battle scenes highly effectively. He often depicted the action in one set of shots moving from right to left, while another set of shots showed action moving from left right. Griffith's classic, however, does contain overt racism in the film; it is a screen adaptation of the racist novel, *The Clansmen*, a book glorifying the Ku Klux Klan (KKK).

Other Early Pioneers   Innovation in filming, lighting, editing and storytelling techniques continued throughout the silent era. In 1922, two silent film classics

Méliès, Georges—an early French filmmaker who pioneered the use of special effects in film in order to show imaginative stories.

Media Timeline: Early Selected Milestones in Storytelling in Motion Pictures

| 1898 Georges Méliès, director First double exposure (*La Caverne maudite*), an advance in special effects | 1915 D. W. Griffith, director *Birth of a Nation*, the first major full-length film | 1919 Oscar Micheaux, director *Birth of Race*, African American response to the racial stereotypes in *Birth of a Nation* | 1922 Robert Flaherty, director *Nanook of the North*, the first great documentary | 1925 Sergei Eisenstein, director *Potemkin*, a silent film particularly known for its editing sequence, "the Odessa Steps" |

This scene is from the classic Odessa Steps sequence in Sergei Eisenstein's film *Potemkin*.

were released. German director F. W. Murnau created *Nosferatu*, an unforgettable adaptation of the Dracula tale, penned by Bram Stoker. Through *Nosferatu*, Murnau helped to develop the language of film. Also in 1922, American Robert Flaherty directed *Nanook of the North*, the first great documentary film, which depicted the life of an Eskimo whaler. It is a film still often shown in college anthropology courses. Flaherty lived among the Eskimos for six months filming his classic, subsequently editing the film upon his return to New York.

Russian filmmaker **Sergei Eisenstein** pioneered the use of fast cuts between scenes in film, similar to the type of editing we commonly see in music videos. Prior to Eisenstein, most filmmakers kept the camera stationary and had scenes take place within the confines of the picture frame. In 1925 he released *Potemkin*, a silent film that depicts the 1905 revolt in Odessa by Russian sailors on the battleship *Potemkin* and their subsequent defeat by Czarist troops. The movie is particularly known for an editing sequence, "the Odessa Steps." In this sequence, shots of townspeople trapped by Czarist troops are intercut with shots of the troops firing upon the crowd. A mother who then picks up her dead child and

Eisenstein, Sergei—a Russian filmmaking pioneer who was the first to use quick edits and cross-cutting to help tell stories visually. He also experimented with combining music with scenes for maximum audience effect.

Al Jolson in *The Jazz Singer*.

confronts the troops is shot. A woman prays for her life but is killed by a soldier who slashes her with his saber. A woman holding her baby carriage is then killed, and the carriage, with baby inside, plummets down the steps. Shots of the baby crying are intercut with the woman as she falls to the steps. The highly charged Odessa Steps sequence was imitated in the 1987 Brian De Palma film, *The Untouchables*.

Sound and Color Come to Movies

Although movie technology was a revolutionary step in capturing daily activity and in creating imagined realities, it still didn't fully recreate what people saw and heard because of the lack of sound and the fact that film wasn't color. Making film more accurately reflect what we see and hear needed advances in technology and is a process that continues today.

Color Film

The idea of having color in films was not new when movies were created. By the turn of the century, several alternative methods for producing color motion pictures had been developed, but each was complex and cumbersome, such as hand-tinting or hand-coloring scenes. Lee and Turner used a three-color process, combining a camera and revolving filters. The system was unwieldy and expensive and was replaced by about 1920 with systems that used a beam splitter with a prism to divide light entering the lens, capturing the different color on alternating frames. Using this technology produced the first successful feature-length color films in the 1920s.

Technicolor Motion Picture Corporation was founded in 1922 and became the standard for color motion pictures for the next three decades. Among the earliest Technicolor films were *The Black Pirate* with Douglas Fairbanks in 1925, and *Gone with the Wind* and *The Wizard of Oz,* both released in 1939. It was not until the 1950s that the motion picture cameras capable of capturing color without prisms, beam splitters, or alternating frames were developed, and thus color films became more common.

Talkies

Even in the earliest days of movies, "silent" movies were not actually silent. Live pianists, actors speaking out parts, and even whole orchestras were used during shows to add sound to the movies. Actors in the films sometimes accompanied shows as well, talking about their roles and answering audience questions before or after the showing of the film. The first sound film short was shown before a paying audience in Berlin in 1896.

In 1927, Al Jolson starred in *The Jazz Singer,* the first commercially successful motion picture with sound. This popular "talkie" was not a sound movie by contemporary standards. Rather, like other early talkies, *The Jazz Singer* contained little dialogue. It had subtitles and recorded music played back via the Warner Vitaphone disc sound system. This technology was soon replaced by the superior sound-on-film systems (i.e., an optical sound track). The first motion picture to synchronize sound using Bell Labs "high-fi" Vitaphone was produced in 1925, but this film was not as much a commercial endeavor as a technical experimentation.

By 1929 it had become more practical to record and play back sound synchronously with the recorded image. Very few silent films were made after this time, the most notable exceptions being those by Charlie Chaplin in the 1930s. His character "The Tramp," whom he had invented in the 1910s and 1920s, was still popular among the viewing public.

But the silent era had ended, bringing many changes to the movie industry. Some silent era stars could not adjust to sound, either because of heavy foreign accents or unappealing voices. Screenwriting and filming techniques changed dramatically as well, as stories were written increasingly for the spoken word rather than visual effect. Slapstick comedy was out, and witty one-liners and joke-telling were in. Because of cumbersome microphones, cameras also became more stationary and experimentation with moving cameras, innovative editing, and interesting camera angles became less common. Although there were winners and losers with the development of sound in motion pictures, the industry itself was unfazed by the changes in technology. In the words of Al Jolson, "You ain't heard nothin' yet."

Weblink
Al Jolson Web site
[www.jolson.org/]

Introduction to the Movie Industry

The U.S. motion picture industry began on the eastern seaboard, especially New York and Boston, but soon moved to Los Angeles, where the powerful movie moguls of the early 1900s created Hollywood. There were many reasons for this move, not the least of which was better weather. Actors, producers, and directors all found their way to the growing movie-making center. They utilized the warm, dry weather to produce films 52 weeks a year and fed the hungry distribution chains a nonstop flow of movies. Success bred more success, and today the movie industry is securely based in Hollywood, although there are a number of regional centers for movie production across North America, including New York City and Wilmington, North Carolina, in the United States and Toronto and Vancouver, Canada.

Since its birth, the industry has grown to a multibillion dollar giant that, with a distinctly American influence, not only provides global entertainment but also shapes global culture, commerce, and imagination. As of 2000, some 1.5 billion movie tickets were sold each year in the United States, more than five tickets per citizen, across some 34,000 movie screens nationwide. The motion picture industry generates roughly $18.9 billion annually from theater ticket sales, videocassette rentals, and video sales. In addition, about $6.8 billion was made in overseas sales. Another $32.2 billion is generated annually from motion picture showings on cable television (from pay-per-view and premium channels). Most of the commercial revenue generated from the cinema industry is from the production and distribution of motion pictures that are primarily intended as entertainment.

Hollywood's Legendary Movie Moguls

To understand the development of the movie industry requires a close look at the people who created Hollywood, the motion picture capital of the world. Film critic, historian, and author Neal Gabler argues that as such, Hollywood is an invention of the Jewish media moguls of the early twentieth century. Although there are those who would disagree with Gabler, citing the important contributions of men and women of other ethnic backgrounds to the early shaping of Hollywood, in particular the contributions of early black filmmakers, there is no question that the men who ran the major studios and the movie theater chains played a vital role in the creation of the movie empire known as Hollywood.

These men were primarily Jewish, as Gabler notes, and much of their motivation for creating Hollywood lay in their Jewish cultural heritage, their embracing of the American dream (they typically came from poor, immigrant families haunted by memories of persecution), and in the creative and business talents they brought to this new, technologically driven, cultural industry. In contrast to a sometimes racist and elitist establishment cinema on the East Coast, Jewish Hollywood introduced themes of equal opportunity into its cinema. Those who were not Jewish were in fact also often motivated and enabled by these same backgrounds and talents.

Something else they all shared was an understanding of the role of technology in the motion picture business, and a willingness, even a passion, for innovative uses of technology in storytelling on film. These movie-making pioneers all were early adopters of new technology and championed its effective use in creating ever more powerful stories on film. The following discussion examines some of the most important Hollywood movie moguls from the period of Hollywood's invention as the motion-picture, or entertainment, capital of the world in the first half of the 20th century.

The Warner Brothers

Four brothers left a lasting mark on the movie industry in America and on the creative epicenter known as Hollywood. The Warner brothers, Albert, Harry, Jack, and Sam, founded their movie studio in 1923. The brothers, born in the 1880s and 1890s to a Yiddish-speaking Jewish family in Krasnashiltz, Poland (then in czarist Russia), learned to work together for survival.

In 1904 in Youngstown, Ohio, Harry hocked his family's delivery horse to buy a used Edison Kinetoscope projector, and it launched the Warner brothers' entry into the movie business. The brothers used the projector to create a traveling movie show in Ohio and Pennsylvania. Then they opened a small theater in 1905 dubbed "Cascade Theater" with seats loaned from a nearby funeral parlor.

The brothers found that they could make more money from distributing than exhibiting films, so they sold the "Cascade" for $40,000 and entered the film distribution business. Thomas Edison's Edison Trust Patents Company, however, blocked access to films among distributors who did not pay royalties for the film distribution rights, and by 1912 the brothers had to leave the distribution business in favor of the film production business. They launched "Warner Features" in a former St. Louis, Missouri, steel foundry, where their studio produced two low-budget films, neither of which proved marketable. Soon, the brothers headed west to California, where they opened the Warner Brothers studio.

Despite Harry Warner's misgivings, in 1927 Warner Brothers released *The Jazz Singer* and launched the new era of motion pictures with sound. It was an implementation of Sam Warner's concept of using film as a means to create "canned vaudeville." It also propelled the studio to a leadership position in Hollywood and was the first of many classic films produced by Warner Brothers. Other cinema classics produced by the studio during the days of the powerful studio system include *Captain Blood* (1935) and *Casablanca* (1942). Other critically acclaimed Warner Brothers' films include *Mister Roberts* (1955), *Giant* (1956), and *Who's Afraid of Virginia Woolf?* (1966).

Jack Warner emerged as the leader of the studio and one of Hollywood's great movie moguls. He had, like many of his contemporaries, a ruthless style—oftentimes running over stars and directors in the process of running the studio. Jack was the last brother to leave the company, departing in 1967 to become an independent producer.

Seven Arts Productions Ltd. of Canada took over Warner Brothers in 1967 and represented the beginning of the studio's transformation into a corporate film company, later subsumed under the corporate umbrella of Warner Communications Inc. (WCI), with much vaster entertainment and media holdings. The 1989 merger of Time, Inc., and WCI created one of the world's largest media conglomerates at the time, Time Warner, which later merged with AOL to become AOL Time Warner.

Walt Disney

Named after the Reverend Walter Parr, **Walter Elias Disney** was born on Dec. 5, 1901, in Chicago. His mother, Flora Call, was of German-American descent, and his father, Elias Disney, was of Irish descent. Expressing an early interest in drawing, in 1915 Walt enrolled in the Kansas City Art Institute. In 1917, he started taking night courses at the Chicago Institute of Art and also got a job for the Van Noyes Interstate News Company, where he sold news items on the Pacific Railroad running between Kansas City and Jefferson.

With $40 in his pocket, Walt left Missouri in August 1923 and went to Los Angeles, where his older brother Roy lived. Combining their meager resources and borrowing $500, the brothers set up shop in their uncle's garage and soon began making animated films. They received an order from New York for an *Alice in Cartoonland* animated film, their first production.

Disney, Walter Elias—creator of animated cartoon characters such as Mickey Mouse, Goofy, and Donald Duck and classic cartoons such as *Bambi, Snow White and the Seven Dwarfs,* and *Fantasia.* Founded the Disney media empire.

Walt Disney.

Their first hit was released on Sept. 19, 1928. *Steamboat Willie* introduced Mickey Mouse, a mouse (some would say it looked more like a rat) that talked and sang, featuring Walt's own voice, but very little of his own animation, although he was a talented animator. Mickey Mouse quickly became a star and made Disney a household name. Disney's first full-length feature animation, *Snow White and the Seven Dwarfs*, hit movie screens in 1937 and broke all box office records. In the next five years, Disney also produced various full-length animated classics including *Pinocchio, Fantasia, Dumbo,* and *Bambi.* During World War II, most of the Disney facilities produced special government work, including the production of propaganda films for the armed services. Walt opened Disneyland in 1955 outside Los Angeles and in 1971 opened Walt Disney World in Orlando, Florida.

Disney was always on the cutting edge of new technology. He introduced Technicolor with the 1932 animation *Flowers and Trees,* part of the Silly Symphonies series, which was the first color cartoon and won Disney his first Oscar. Disney was also a pioneer in television programming, producing his first programs in 1954, including the popular *Mickey Mouse Club.* He was among the first to offer color television programming, with the launch of the *Wonderful World of Color* in 1961. Disney won more Academy Awards, 47, than anyone else. He also won seven Emmy Awards, television's highest award, for television programming.

Some have said Disney's greatest gift was his ability to develop a concept and have others implement it, sometimes allegedly running his company with an iron fist. But he was also a genius in his innovative use of technology in creating stories and entertainment. One can only imagine what Disney would have been able to create with digital technology. Walt Disney died on December 15, 1966, leaving behind one of the best-known media and entertainment empires in the world.

Samuel Goldwyn

Shmuel Gelbfisz was born in Warsaw, Poland, in the late 1800s and died Samuel Goldwyn, in Los Angeles, January 31, 1974. He described his life in Poland as, "poor, poor, poor." His name was anglicized to Goldfish when he moved to England, and in 1899 he came to the United States. After a brief stint as a glove salesman, he embarked on a career as a motion picture producer and industry pioneer. He produced *The Squaw Man* in 1914, directed by Cecil B. DeMille, and his company became the foundation for what later emerged as Paramount Pictures, eventually built by Adolph Zukor. In 1916 he joined forces with the Selwyn brothers and cofounded the Goldwyn Pictures Corporation. Three years later he changed his name to Goldwyn.

In 1924 his company merged with Louis B. Mayer and Metro Pictures to become Metro-Goldwyn-Mayer, but Goldwyn himself was jettisoned from the new company. Although his "Leo the Lion" trademark continued, Goldwyn was ousted and forced to create an independent film company.

His new company's commitment was to the creation of quality films with high production values. United Artists and RKO distributed the films. Among the classic films his independent company produced were *Wuthering Heights* (1939), *The Pride of the Yankees* (1942), *The Best Years of Our Lives* (1946), *Guys and Dolls* (1955), and *Porgy and Bess* (1959). Like former New York Yankee great Yogi

Berra, Goldwyn was known for his colorful approach to language, speaking in what are known as "Goldwynisms." Among his most memorable: "A verbal contract isn't worth the paper it's written on," "A hospital is no place to be sick," and "Anyone who goes to a psychiatrist ought to have his head examined."

Marcus Loew: Mogul of the East

In the early 1910s and 1920s the most powerful movie mogul of all did not live in Hollywood. Marcus Loew, a financier, theater chain owner, and owner of the Metro movie studio, lived 3000 miles east, in New York City. In 1924 he merged his studio with Louis B. Mayer Productions and the Samuel Goldwyn Company to form Metro-Goldwyn-Mayer, or MGM. In a move typical of movie mogul's of the day, Loew ousted Goldwyn from the team but kept his name in the company, because "M & M" was already taken by another company.

Louis B. Mayer

Perhaps the most famous and feared movie mogul was Louis Bert Mayer, born on July 4, 1885. He died on October 29, 1957, in Los Angeles. Like his other movie mogul contemporaries, Mayer had modest immigrant beginnings. His father, Lazar Mayer, was a laborer who sought a better life in America and moved his family there when Louis was a boy. Lazar entered the junk business, and Louis joined the family business. He dropped out of school after the sixth grade.

In 1907, he bought a rundown movie theater in Boston and renovated it. He exhibited exclusively quality films and built the largest theater chain in New England. In 1915 he made a great profit showing D.W. Griffith's *Birth of a Nation* and laid the foundation for his future Hollywood success.

With the fortune he'd made in exhibiting movies, Mayer entered the movie production business in 1917, funding his own production company, Louis B. Mayer Pictures, in the former studio of "Colonel" William N. Selig, an earlier film pioneer. Mayer shared the space with another film pioneer, B. P. Schulberg, formerly of Paramount, who would eventually go on to form his own film company, Preferred Pictures. Anita Stewart was Mayer's leading lady and was featured in his first production, *Virtuous Wives*. Stewart became an immediate star.

Marcus Loew named Mayer vice president of MGM, and Mayer rose in power over the years. Mayer's name became synonymous with movie mogul power and manipulation. Although the studio's directors such as Erich von Stroheim and King Vidor, or powerful producer Irving Thalberg, shaped the creative direction of the studio, it was Mayer who pulled the strings and became patriarch to the "studio children," or actors, themselves. Mayer's influence stretched well beyond the studio gates, and in 1927 Mayer teamed with Douglas Fairbanks, Sr., to form the Academy of Motion Pictures Arts and Sciences—the foundation of movie industry artists.

The studio employed thousands of artists, and Mayer, known as Louis the Conqueror, ruled with an iron fist. He ridded the studio of talent he disliked, and when Thalberg died in 1936, Mayer took complete control of the studio.

Ephraim Katz, film scholar and author of *The Film Encyclopedia*, remembers Mayer:

> A ruthless, quick-tempered, paternalistically tyrannical executive, Mayer
> ruled MGM as one big family, rewarding obedience, punishing

insubordination, and regarding opposition as personal betrayal. He made many enemies during his reign, but also many admirers of his indefatigable capacity for work and his total devotion to his studio. He wasn't well-read and abhorred intellectualism, but he had an uncanny intuitive sense of mass taste and a knack for selecting and handling personnel.[14]

The Hays Code and Film Industry Self-Censorship

Some early films, particularly some of the black-and-white films prior to 1920, contained considerable nudity or near nudity, especially some of the biblical films, such as those created by D.W. Griffith (e.g., the 1919 *The Fall of Babylon*). Hollywood's original vamp, actress Theda Bara, was often shown in revealing costumes.[15] Although the nudity and sexuality were popular with many early filmgoers, some conservative groups were outspoken in their criticism of cinematic nudity, especially bare-breasted women or women dressed in revealing clothing, and the movie moguls feared the possibility of government censorship. As a result, they joined forces to create their own industry self-censorship in the form of the Hays office, named after its first director, Will Hays. The office produced what was called the **Hays Code** in 1930, outlining many do's and don'ts for the film industry. In some ways, the Hays Code was little more than a public relations stunt to deflect criticism, and some moviemakers treated the code as little more than a joke. Some films even continued to contain nudity or nude bodies thinly veiled. For example, Dwain Esper's *Maniac* (1934) featured rape, nudity, and women fighting.[16]

Following the 1934 box office hit *Ecstasy*, a Czech film directed by Gustav Machaty starring Heddy Lamar with an explicit nude scene, the makers of MGM's *Tarzan and His Mate* depicted actress Maureen O'Sullivan as a very scantily clad Jane with a prolonged nude underwater scene with Johnny Weissmuller, with the actress also seen nude in silhouette while dressing in a well-lit tent.[17] The film contributed to a backlash, which helped lead to the removal of Hays and the installation of a new head of the office who would prove much tighter in his reign, Joseph I. Breen. Breen strictly enforced the Hays Code and redefined Hollywood fashion. Nudity, the navel, and lingerie were no longer permitted on screen. Filmmakers had to become much more creative in their depiction of sexuality. The backless dress became popular.

If a movie did not have the stamp of approval from the Hays office, its chances for mass distribution by a major studio were greatly reduced, a chance most producers were not willing to take. In the mid-1960s, after a series of Supreme Court cases involving obscenity and a general change in public mores regarding depictions of sexuality, the Hays Code underwent a major revision and was not enforced as stringently as it had been. By 1968 the movie rating system had essentially replaced the Hays Code.

Hays Code—a code established in 1930 by the movie industry to censor itself regarding showing of nudity or glorifying antisocial acts in movies. Officials for the Hays office had to approve each film that was distributed to a mass audience.

The Hollywood Star System

For the first several years of movies, actors' and actresses' names did not even appear in the movie credits. However, it was not long before audiences showed an interest in learning not only the names, but also the personalities and histories

It Happened One Night (1934) is a classic comedy of the era and the first film to win all five major Oscars: Best Picture, Director, Actor, Actress, and Screenplay. It was directed by Frank Capra and starred Clark Gable and Claudette Colbert, who were both "loaned" to Columbia Pictures from the studios with which they had long-term contracts.

of the people they were watching on screen. Fan magazines helped stoke interest in stars, and shrewd studio heads created and cultivated personas for their popular stars, even giving them false histories in order to better market them.

In the early 1930s a new era began in American film that lasted until 1949. This was the era of the Hollywood studio-star system. Paramount Pictures (1912), Columbia Pictures (1920), Metro-Goldwyn-Mayer (1924), Warner Brothers (1923), and Twentieth Century Fox (1935) all held long-term contracts on star directors and actors and built their success on the stars they held under contract. Many of these stars are still familiar today, more than a half century after the era ended.

During this era, stars were unable to seek their own contracts for individual films, but they could be loaned from one studio to another, often in exchange for other stars. Stars were also expected to be highly productive, often starring in five or six films a year. Warner Brothers' Humphrey Bogart starred in forty films

Table 4-1 Hollywood Star System: Talent under Long-Term Contracts			
Paramount Pictures	**MGM**	**Warner Brothers**	**Twentieth Century Fox**
Gary Cooper	Joan Crawford	Humphrey Bogart	Don Ameche
Bing Crosby	Clark Gable	Jimmy Cagney	Henry Fonda
Kirk Douglas	Greta Garbo	Bette Davis	Betty Grable
W. C. Fields	Judy Garland	Errol Flynn	Marilyn Monroe
Bob Hope	Mickey Rooney	Peter Lorre	Gregory Peck
Alan Ladd	James Stewart	Edward G. Robinson	Tyrone Power
Burt Lancaster	Elizabeth Taylor		Shirley Temple
Mary Pickford	Spencer Tracy		
Mae West			

In 1941 RKO Pictures released the film some consider the greatest motion picture of all time, *Citizen Kane,* directed by Orson Welles. The film's release was fiercely opposed by William Randolph Hearst, the publishing titan whose life is unflatteringly depicted in the film.

between 1934 and 1943 and perhaps his most famous, *Casablanca,* was just one of four films he made in 1943.

Many of the films of this era, including *Casablanca,* were not made as great works of cinematic art. Rather, they were commercial enterprises made as popular entertainment. These films made a great deal of money for the studios, which also typically owned large theater chains where these films were shown. People often went to see these films for the stars they had come to know and for the characters they often represented. Gary Cooper, star of *Mr. Deeds Goes to Town* (1936) and *Meet John Doe* (1941), was known as a tall, clumsy, and humble man who may have been naïve but was also a man of integrity. He was the quintessential American, the strong silent type. Jimmy Stewart was in many ways the same type of character, immortalized in Frank Capra's *It's a Wonderful Life* (1945), now a holiday classic on American television.

The studios also imported much of their talent from abroad, including not only the star of *Gone with the Wind,* Vivien Leigh, from the U.K., but also the great English director, Alfred Hitchcock. Hitchcock became Hollywood's master of the thriller genre, but began his career in the U.K. in 1919 working on silent films at Paramount's Famous Players–Lasky studio in London.

The studio-star system came to an end in the late 1940s, when several forces converged. First, in 1948 the U.S. Supreme Court forced the studios to divest themselves from their theater empires because of monopolistic practices brought to light in *United States* v. *Paramount Pictures*. This drastically cut into the power of the studios to control the means of production and distribution of motion pictures in America. It meant that **independent films,** or films produced outside the major studios, could be shown in large numbers of theaters, thereby giving independent films financial viability. Second, the rise of television as a medium of popular entertainment drew audiences away from theaters. Third, the emergence of the director as author of his or her films reshaped the formulaic pattern for making Hollywood films. Partly because of these changes, it was no longer as profitable for studios to keep actors under long-term contracts. The high labor costs associated with studios also gave them incentive to "rent out" their studios to smaller, independent producers who worked with large studios on a per-project basis and allowed studios to still use their extensive distribution networks to earn income.

The Motion Picture Industry Today

Today's motion picture industry contrasts significantly from the days of the star system half a century ago when the movie companies were vertically integrated entertainment companies, owning not only the means of production but also the distribution system, i.e., the movie theaters. The Supreme Court's antitrust decision of 1948 forced the studios to sell their theaters, and today much more power rests in the hands of the artists making the films, especially directors and high-paid actors and actresses, than in the past.

That is not to say that the major studios are not powerful. They have found ways to adapt to changing conditions and still maintain an inordinate amount of power when it comes to deciding which movies to make and promote. With the

independent films—films made by production companies outside the main Hollywood studios.

high costs in making a movie, including several million dollars spent in marketing, and the specialized knowledge required to make one with the high production standards that U.S. moviegoers expect, it still requires large organizations like the movie studios to bring everything together. The average cost of making a motion picture is $50 million, although movies with extensive special effects often top $100 million.

Today's Major Film Companies

Much of the industry is still based in Hollywood, but there is also a strong cinema presence around the world. The leading film companies, based on U.S. domestic ticket sales—Sony Pictures Entertainment, Walt Disney Studio Entertainment, Warner Bros. Pictures, Paramount Pictures, Twentieth Century Fox, and Universal Studios—are all parts of larger media companies. DreamWorks SKG, the first new major motion picture studio created in 50 years, founded by Steven Spielberg, Jeffrey Katzenberg, and David Geffen, has had some important hits in *Antz* (1998) and *Saving Private Ryan* (1998), the latter of which has grossed an estimated $216 million domestically. Pixar Animation Studios, whose CEO is Steve Jobs, cofounder of Apple Computers, is another important new motion picture production company, with *Toy Story,* the computer-animated 1995 hit it made for Disney that has grossed an estimated $192 million. The sequel, *Toy Story 2* (1999), did even better, grossing $256 million domestically.[18]

Spider-Man (2002) was one of several hit movies produced by Sony Entertainment.

Sony Pictures Entertainment

Sony Pictures Entertainment has the Columbia TriStar Motion Picture Group, which produced the record-breaking *Spider-Man* (2002) as well as hits such as *Men in Black 2* (2002) and *XXX* (2002). Sony Pictures Entertainment had six number-one hits by midyear 2002 and brought in 21 percent of box office revenues, or $1.29 billion—surpassing their total annual revenues of $1.27 billion in 1997 in only eight months.[19] Sony Pictures Entertainment is part of the Sony Broadband unit of Japanese electronics company Sony. Within Sony Pictures Entertainment is a television production and distribution unit called Columbia TriStar Domestic Television, which produces and distributes popular shows such as *Dawson's Creek* and the game show *Jeopardy*. Sony sold its stake in movie theater firm Loews Cineplex Entertainment in 2002.[20]

Walt Disney Studio Entertainment

Walt Disney Studio Entertainment is the film production and distribution division of The Walt Disney Company, which is second in size only to AOL Time Warner, and it produces films through Walt Disney Pictures, Touchstone, and Hollywood Pictures as well as Miramax. Its Buena Vista distribution unit is the world's top movie distributor. Disney is well known for its animated films, which are extremely popular with children, and of course its recognizable classic animated cartoon characters. It was the first movie studio to strike a deal with a television network, in 1954, to produce an original television series. The program, *Disneyland,* alone accounted for almost one-half of ABC's billing that year. Disney continued to pioneer ways to recycle its film content for television

Media Future: The American Film Institute

> We will create an American Film Institute that will bring together leading artists of the film industry, outstanding educators, and young men and women who wish to pursue this 20th century art form as their life's work. —*President Lyndon Johnson, September 26, 1965.*

When President Johnson signed the National Foundation on the Arts and the Humanities Act of 1965, he not only created the National Endowment for the Arts but also established The American Film Institute (AFI). AFI is unique among American institutions, offering an independent, nonprofit organization whose mission is to:

- preserve the heritage of film and television;
- identify and train new talent for those industries; and
- increase public recognition and understanding of the moving image as an art form.

As part of its mission, AFI conducts the Directing Workshop for Women every year; organizes the Harold Lloyd Master Seminars, in which accomplished filmmakers come speak to AFI Fellows; and holds the annual AFI Awards to honor the year's best films, actors, writers, and filmmakers. In addition, AFI's film preservation efforts include an online database on silent films and the growing number of rare early films collected by AFI's National Center for Film and Video Preservation (NCFVP). Among its collection is the 1912 film *A Fool and His Money,* directed by Alice Guy, the first woman director, and believed to be the first film using an entirely African American cast.

The AFI Conservatory offers an MFA degree in six film-related subjects: cinematography, directing, editing, producing, production design, and screenwriting. Professionals from the industry are often guest lecturers, and students receive a great deal of hands-on experience in filmmmaking.

Not only is AFI the only national arts organization devoted to film, television, and video, but it also provides a national focus for the various individuals and institutions concerned with the moving image as art. AFI's headquarters are located in Los Angeles, although the AFI Theater is in the John F. Kennedy Center in Washington, DC. [21]

Producer and director Ron Howard and producer Brian Grazer were recognized by the American Film Institute for their film, *A Beautiful Mind.*

audiences. Walt Disney Studios also produces Broadway shows through Buena Vista Theatrical Group.[22]

Warner Brothers Pictures

Warner Brothers Pictures was part of Warner Communications, which included Warner Studios, Warner Brothers Television, and Lorimar Television. In 1989, Time, Inc., bought out Warner Communications for $14 billion and became Time Warner, which eventually merged with AOL to form AOL Time Warner. Warner Brothers had a range of popular cartoon characters ranging from *Bugs Bunny* to *Superman*, as well as many classic films. In 2001 Warner Brothers films included *Harry Potter and the Sorcerer's Stone* (eighth on the all-time box office list) and the Steven Spielberg film *A.I. Artificial Intelligence*. Warner Brothers has excellent video and DVD distribution capabilities through its Warner Home Video division, and Warner Bros. Television produces such hit shows as *Friends, ER,* and *The West Wing*.[23]

Paramount Pictures

Paramount Pictures is part of media giant Viacom, and it produces and distributes films through Paramount Pictures and Paramount Classics. It also has a library of 1000 films and releases about a dozen new films annually, including such movies as *Mission: Impossible 2* (2000), *Enemy at the Gates* (2001), *We Were Soldiers* (2002), and *Orange County* (2002). The company also produces and distributes television programming such as *Frasier* and owns complete or partial rights to more than 100,000 music works through its division Famous Music.[24]

Twentieth Century Fox

Twentieth Century Fox, along with Fox Searchlight Pictures, is a division of Fox Filmed Entertainment, which in turn is a part of Fox Entertainment Group, a unit of Rupert Murdoch's News Corp. Fox Filmed Entertainment makes up about a quarter of News Corp.'s sales. Twentieth Century Fox, which produces movies for mainstream audiences, has had such hits as *Cast Away* (2000), made with Dreamworks; *Planet of the Apes* (2001); and *Moulin Rouge* (2002).[25]

Universal Studios

Universal Studios is part of Vivendi Universal Entertainment, created in 2002 when French utility company Vivendi Universal, which had bought former Universal parent Seagram in 2000, acquired the assets of USA Interactive. Vivendi's board of directors fired the flamboyant chief executive Jean-Marie Messier in July 2002 and started restructuring the company to stem their financial losses, although their stock continued to sink during the summer of 2002. It is unclear what direction the new executive will take with Vivendi Universal, but it does seem unlikely that he will show the same drive to acquire and integrate various media properties in the company. Nevertheless, Universal Pictures produces and distributes a range of serious and teen movies, including *A Beautiful Mind* (2001), *Erin Brockovich* (2000), and *American Pie* (1999).[26]

Film Audiences

Audiences for film grew rapidly in the early part of the century, although reliable data are available only from 1922. In that year, the average weekly attendance at

U.S. movie theaters was 40,000 persons. Attendance grew to some 90,000 a week by 1930.[27] Audiences leveled off after WWII, however, with the rise of television. Still, audiences for films shown in movie theaters in the United States and around the world have grown markedly since then, with today's weekly film audience attendance in excess of 1 million. Around the world the numbers are similarly significant.

The Blockbuster

Emerging during the past quarter century has been the American **blockbuster** film. These are films typically made in Hollywood that capture not only enormous audiences in the U.S. but around the world. Award-winning director Steven Spielberg has directed perhaps more blockbusters than any other filmmaker. *E.T. The Extraterrestrial* (as of 2002 number three on the all-time list with more than $430 million in U.S. box office receipts since its 1982 release), *Jaws*, and *Jurassic Park* are some of his most successful films. His commercial success has also permitted Spielberg to venture into more dramatic experiments, including his acclaimed *Schindler's List* (1993), the story of a German gentile who helped Jews escape Nazi persecution during WWII.

blockbuster—a big-budget, high-production quality film, often with famous stars, that is very successful at the box office and that is usually produced by one of the large Hollywood studios.

Table 4-2 Top Ten Grossing Films of All Time, by Earnings and Director

Rank	Movie	Year released	Gross in U.S. Dollars Since Opening	MPAA Rating USA	Est. Budget (US M)	Est. Worldwide Gross (US M)	Director
1	*Titanic*	1997	$600,787,052	PG-13	$200	$1835	J. Cameron
2	*Star Wars*	1977	$460,935,665	PG	$11	$784	G. Lucas
3	*E.T.*	1982	$434,949,459	PG	NA	$757	S. Spielberg
4	*Star Wars: The Phantom Menace*	1999	$431,065,444	PG	$110	$922	G. Lucas
5	*Spider-Man*	2002	$403,620,726	PG-13	$139	$750	S. Raimi
6	*Jurassic Park*	1993	$357,067,947	PG-13	$63	$920	S. Spielberg
7	*Forrest Gump*	1994	$329,690,974	PG-13	$55	$680	R. Zemeckis
8	*Harry Potter and the Sorcerer's Stone*	2001	$317,557,891	PG	$130	$962	Chris Columbus
9	*The Lord of the Rings: The Fellowship of the Ring*	2001	$313,322,223	PG-13	$109	$855	Peter Jackson
10	*The Lion King*	1994	$312,855,561	G	NA	$767	R. Allers/ R. Minkoff

Table adapted from www.the-movie-times.com.

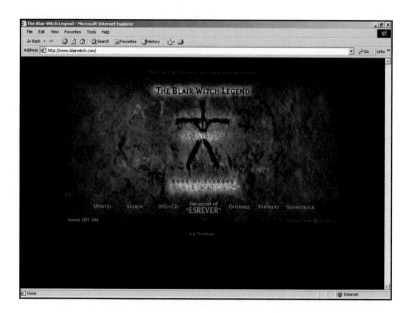

The makers of *The Blair Witch Project* used clever marketing on the Web to help build interest in the movie.

Two films released in 1999 reveal the varying approaches to blockbuster status. George Lucas, who directed the 1977 blockbuster *Star Wars*, spent an estimated $110 million to create the *Star Wars* prequel, *Episode One: The Phantom Menace*. Released in 1999, *The Phantom Menace* has grossed as of 2002 more than $430 million domestically and an additional $490 million internationally, placing it in the number-four position all time.[28] It has grossed more than $100 million in Japan alone, placing it just a bit behind the all-time box office hit in Japan (and just about everywhere else), *Titanic*, which has grossed $225 million there.

The second movie in the prequel, *Star Wars: Episode II—Attack of the Clones* (2002), shattered midweek box-office records (which had been set by *The Phantom Menace* almost exactly two years earlier) in grossing $30.1 million in its first day in theaters, despite generally lackluster reviews. Less than two weeks earlier, on May 3, *Spider-Man* (2002) set records for the biggest movie opening of all time and the biggest single day at the box office, bringing in $43.6 million. It also became the fastest movie to bring in $100 million and $200 million, respectively, and four months later, while still in movie theaters, was the fifth highest-grossing movie of all time.

In contrast to the big-budget blockbusters from the major Hollywood studios, the surprise hit of the summer of 1999 was *The Blair Witch Project*, directed and edited by Eduardo Sanchez and Daniel Myrick. Having cost just $35,000 to produce, the film grossed (so to speak) more than $100 million domestically as of 2001. Although it's not in the top ten—or even top one hundred—films based on box office receipts, it is among the most profitable in terms of return on investment. The producers used the Internet and a Web site to generate great word-of-mouth interest in the movie rather than spending millions on the usual movie marketing channels.

Not even the *Star Wars* films are likely to unseat the greatest blockbuster of all time, however. Released in December 1997, *Titanic* grossed $600 million domestically by mid-2002 and $1.8 billion worldwide. Having cost an estimated $200 million to create, however, director James Cameron's greatest blockbuster's return rate does not come close to that of *The Blair Witch Project*.

Exhibition Windows for Movies

Movies have a regular pattern of exhibition "windows," or places where they are shown, that help increase revenues. When studios were at their strongest, they could control theatrical releases to what were deemed "first-run" theaters; then, after the movies lost their appeal at those, they were placed in second-run theaters. Movie studios determined which theaters were first-run and second-run and had agreements with theater owners that ensured theaters would have exclusive showing privileges within a certain geographic area for a certain amount of time. However, studios also often forced theaters to buy package deals of movies that included a few hits but also many lower-quality films that would not be as popular. This is one of the practices that was forbidden in the landmark 1948 *Paramount* antitrust case.

The movie industry boycotted television when it first arrived, refusing to provide movies that could be shown on television and even blacklisting actors who acted on television. Studios felt that television would draw audiences away from theaters and thus ruin the movie industry. This resistance to new technological change has become a common pattern among entrenched media entertainment industries.

However, it was not long before the movie industry realized that television could be used to give new life to movies that had run through their life cycle in theatrical release, and they started selling their previously released movies to the television networks. A similar pattern can be seen of resistance, then acceptance, by the studios as they saw more revenue opportunities when cable television, and then VCRs, each were developed. Currently movie studios are insisting that digital media have guaranteed security measures to avoid illegal copying of their movies and are hampering development of digitally delivered video-on-demand or movies-on-demand.

The usual windows for a movie start with domestic theatrical release, then international release, video, pay-per-view on cable, pay cable, network TV, then syndicated TV. Each of these windows has a specified time for its showing, and they generally do not overlap. However, depending on the success of the movie, it may get released to video earlier than usual in order to take advantage of residual popularity of the theatrical release. In fact, video rentals and sales are usually the biggest money-generator for movies, long since surpassing box-office revenues. When video-on-demand becomes feasible, it will likely become the first window after theatrical release as the first nontheatrical venue for a movie.[29]

Going Digital

Digitization promises to have profound effects on the movie industry, some of which are already being seen both in the industry itself and in the theater. Amazing special effects can be created using digital technology, such as in George Lucas's *Attack of the Clones*, that far surpass special effects efforts previously done. Computer-created characters have become increasingly lifelike, and computer artists and programmers continue to improve their skills to render surfaces like snow and fur more realistically as computer power increases.

Digital distribution of films also promises huge cost savings for movie studios. It costs up to $2000 to produce, duplicate, and ship one 40-pound celluloid film print to a movie theater, and most studios ship prints to 3000 theaters nationwide if they hope the movie can be a blockbuster. That means a cost of $6 million just in distribution costs for a major film.[30] A digital film, on the other hand, would simply be sent over satellite or through high-speed wires to a movie theater, thereby avoiding all the costs associated with shipping a bulky physical product. In addition, endless perfect copies could be made, just as with other digital media, eliminating the need to receive even more prints when film breaks or loses its quality after repeated showings.

The movie industry has been relatively slow to wholly embrace digital technology, however, for a number of reasons. One reason is the high cost of converting theaters with digital projector systems, computer servers, and satellite dishes or high-speed wiring. It is estimated that theater owners will have to pay up to $150,000 to have their theaters converted.[31] In the 1990s many theaters spent a lot upgrading aspects of their theaters, and some went bankrupt as a result of spending too much, so they are unwilling to leave themselves open again to the same situation. In addition, theater owners argue that because it is the movie studios that will be getting the greatest savings through digital distribution, they should be the ones to pay at least part of the cost of upgrading theaters to digital systems. As of May 2002, there were only 23 all-digital theaters throughout the United States, although more were being converted.

Another reason the movie industry has been slow in moving to digital technology, despite potential cost savings, is their concern over piracy and subsequent loss of revenues. The studios have watched the music industry's battles with file-swapping services such as Napster and realize that they are prime targets for similar practices because of the popularity of movies. So far, the main reason movies have not become more popular with the file-swapping public is because of their huge file sizes and the slow connection speeds for most Internet users, making downloading a full-length feature film impractical for the majority of computer users. But more powerful PCs and high-speed connections will change that within a few years. Disney's Michael Eisner has spoken to Congress arguing for government control of PC technology that would block PCs from displaying movies or TV shows without the copyright owner's approval, an idea endorsed by some politicians, such as Sen. Ernest Hollings.[32]

Assuming that the movie industry does eventually adopt digital technology at all levels of movie production, it is likely that the moviegoer will see great changes, not only in digital effects such as improved picture quality and better sound but in the ways movie theaters are used as well. Once they are working in a digital format, theater owners would have more flexibility in what they show as well. There could be the possibility of showing sporting events or other performances on their screens, including film shorts or films made by local filmmakers who have created digital films.

SUMMARY

Photography helped alter how we literally and figuratively look at media by letting us see images of people as they actually were, rather than an artist's interpretation through a drawing or painting. This power to show "reality" has had a profound effect on media, especially news media, as powerful or shocking images can bring out reactions in people that even the most compelling written stories cannot.

The development of photography is one of continued innovation to make the photographic development process easier, to have shorter exposure times to better catch fast action, and to make cameras and equipment more portable. However, unlike most other media technologies, which by and large improved over time, photographic quality has actually deteriorated as cameras became smaller and easier to use, a trade-off most people seem willing to accept.

Despite the appearance of motion, a movie is simply a role of still images taken at relatively fast intervals and run through a projector so our eyes trick us into seeing motion. Early filmmakers concentrated on the novelty of simply filming short daily scenes, but it wasn't long before other filmmakers such as George Méliès and D. W. Griffith started experimenting with new narrative techniques with film, such as cross-cutting scenes to show parallel action occurring simultaneously.

It was also not long before a relatively small handful of powerful Hollywood movie moguls controlled most of what the U.S. and worldwide audience saw in the movie theaters. Although the studio–star system and vertical integration of the Hollywood studios formally ended after the Supreme Court Paramount antitrust decision in 1948, Hollywood still has an inordinate amount of power in deciding which movies get made and which become successful. Rather than detract from the powerful hold movies have over entertainment, such venues as network television, videos, and cable television have provided extra revenue streams to the movie studios, despite the studios' strong initial resistance to these new technologies.

Digitization is changing the movie industry in two important ways. For filmmakers such as George Lucas, digital effects can help enhance their artistic vision in a way that was previously unavailable to them. It is also lowering the entry cost for young filmmakers, who can film, edit, and produce a digital movie much more cheaply than a film shot on celluloid. Digital projection and distribution systems promise to be the final link in the digitization of movies, where a movie can be shot, edited, and shown all without a single reel of film changing hands.

Discussion Questions

1. With film and television, do you think still photography is still as relevant as it used to be? Why or why not?

2. The ability of the earliest filmmakers to tell stories was hampered by technological limitations that kept film reels short so that only a few minutes of filmed footage could be shown at a time. In what ways could current technological limitations hamper our ability to tell stories through film?

3. Although there are many exceptions to point to, self-censorship has long been practiced in cinema. What are some of the motivations of filmmakers to employ self-censorship of their works?

4. Recent movies such as *Spider-Man, Lord of the Rings,* and the latest *Star Wars* episodes seem to consistently break box-office records. Why do you think this is so?

5. Using the table of the top ten all-time grossing films, count how many of the movies you've seen and rank them according to your idea of their quality. Do the rankings match their income? Compare your rankings with a classmate and discuss why you may differ on some movies.

6. Could there be a group of young digital filmmakers who could revolutionize the industry and dominate movie production and distribution like the early Hollywood movie moguls did? Why or why not?

7. As motion pictures enter the digital age, what are some of the greatest concerns to be addressed? Are they justified?

8. Discuss ways that movie theaters might be able to find new ways of using their large screens and space to show digital film by not only big-name movies but by local artists as well. Consider transformational social aspects as well as economic factors that movie theater owners would have to take into account.

Music Recordings, Radio, and Television

The rap lyrics may be familiar, but the decidedly 1980s dance mix rhythms of the Cure behind it are not. And was that a whiff of a Nirvana guitar lick from "Smells Like Teen Spirit" in that song, along with strains of Dolly Parton?

The type of song is called a mash-up, or bootleg, and is created entirely from existing songs, usually illegally. There are so many bootlegs of Missy Elliott songs that making a bootleg is sometimes referred to as "doing a Missy."

There is of course nothing new about creating bootleg copies of music or creating new songs from samples of existing songs, but what is new is the professional quality of such remixes, the complexity of the remixes—sometimes using more than 100 songs in a single song—and the ability for these songs to be distributed widely through file-sharing programs on the Internet. Some are even made into CDs and sold in underground music

retailers. The CD "The Best Bootlegs in the World Ever" was made entirely from downloaded mash-ups and sold. "It is a case of bootleggers bootlegging bootlegs," said David Dewaele, one of the brothers in 2 Many D.J.s, one of the longest-standing mash-up groups.

In 2001, the Dewaele brothers created a legal mash-up album, "2 Many D.J.s: As Heard on Radio Soulwax Pt. 2," which some music critics called not only the best remix album of the year, but the best album of the year. It took them two weeks to make the album and nine months to license the music, and even then they have only been able to clear the CD release in Belgium, Luxembourg, and Holland.

Mash-ups touch on many issues involved not only with the music industry in the digital age, but the traditional role of radio and the changing behavior—and power—of media audiences to alter and redistribute the media they receive.

OBJECTIVES

In this chapter we will:

- Define the nature and functions of the recording arts (i.e., music).
- Review the history of the recording arts.
- Identify the changes digitization, the Internet, and file-sharing services have brought to the recording industry business model.
- Review the history of radio and television.
- Outline the basic structure of the radio and television industry, including the development of cable and satellite media.
- Identify three main elements that will likely play roles in the future of television.

Prologue

The recording industry has been at the vanguard of where established media interests and changes in media usage brought by digital media clash, and the recording industry has not been shy about voicing their concerns or protecting their interests. From the demise of file-sharing services such as Napster to demanding royalty payments for so-called Internet radio, the recording industry exemplifies issues that established entertainment and content companies in film, radio, and television (TV) are just starting to come to terms with or soon will in the age of digital media.

Radio and television are the most familiar and far-reaching media of mass communication in the world. Just about everyone listens to radio, or watches TV. Unlike computers, radio and TV don't require any particular technical skill of the listener or viewer. Unlike print media, radio and TV don't even require literacy; all you have to do is watch or listen (although the listener does need to know the language spoken). As a result, even preschool children can listen to radio or watch TV.

One principle in particular has guided the development of radio and other wireless communication media in the twentieth century: that the airwaves belong to the public, that they are a public good, and that those who use them have a responsibility to serve in the public interest. This concept, in tandem with the notion that the airwaves are a limited commodity, laid the foundation for the regulation of radio and other electronic wireless media. Important changes to this principle are happening in the twenty-first century, however, as digitization transforms the potential use of the broadcasting spectrum and commercial interests increasingly dominate the character of radio and other wireless communications. Moreover, the rise of cable television in the latter half of the twentieth century, first in analog form and now in digital, is challenging these long-held principles as well.

The Recording Industry

The history and development of the recording industry can be looked at as combining aspects of other types of media. In terms of the recording process, in its earliest years it was done mechanically or on some type of chemical medium but then changed to electronic forms of recording as that technology developed. In terms of distribution, the industry can be compared to the book publishing industry, in which physical items (albums, eight-track tapes, audio cassettes, and now CDs) are sent through a variety of distribution methods to consumers. In terms of marketing and promotion of music, the industry has relied heavily on radio and, to some extent, music videos such as those on MTV. And now, with digital media and the relatively small file sizes of audio, music has been at the forefront of online file-sharing and copying of songs to play on a variety of devices.

The recorded music industry also has similarities to other large media entertainment companies. It is a business controlled mostly by a few very large firms (which are often subsidiaries of even larger media corporations) and has been

Media Technology

Capturing Sound: The Microphone

In order to record sound, it first has to be accurately captured. A microphone is a collector of sound that gathers sound energy and converts it to electrical energy. A microphone is a device for converting acoustic power into electric power, which has essentially similar wave characteristics.

History has obscured the exact origins of the invention of the microphone. Although the term was coined in 1827 by Sir Charles Wheatstone, some evidence indicates that Emile Berliner first invented the microphone for Scottish inventor Alexander Graham Bell to use for what eventually became the telephone. The carbon microphone, invented by D.E. Hughes of England in 1878, was essential for the development of telephony, as it transmitted sounds more clearly because the carbon atoms were good conductors of electricity.

Microphones are transducers, or items that transform one form of communication into another form. In this case, they take sound waves, convert the sound waves to electrical energy, and then reconvert them back to sound waves again so they can be heard. They do this by using a thin diaphragm that vibrates as it is exposed to sound waves (which displace air). Depending on the type of microphone, the vibrating diaphragm either generates electricity and conducts it through attached wires or generates electricity based on its proximity and displacement to a backplate, which then generates the necessary electricity. This latter type is called a condenser microphone. Because the resulting signal is very weak, an amplifier is needed to make the electrical signal stronger and maintain coherence of the signal.

There are many types of microphones in use now, often with very specialized functions. Omnidirectional microphones gather sound from all directions and are often used to record background or ambient noise in media productions. Bi-directional, or "figure eight" microphones were often used for stereo recordings, but now duet songs done in studios usually have each singer using a separate microphone. Lavolier microphones are the small clip-on type used for television interviews and for recording some musical instruments. Wireless microphones can be convenient, because there are no cables to get tangled up, but they need new batteries frequently and are susceptible to interference from other electronic equipment, causing the high-pitched shrill sound of feedback.

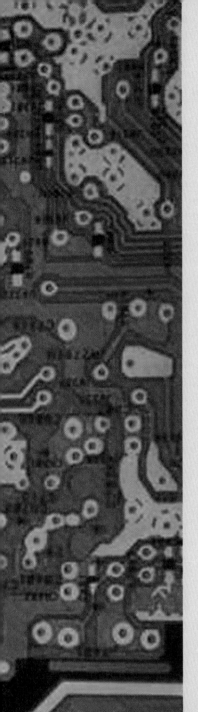

primarily promoted through radio, television, and movies. Because of this strong mass-market emphasis, the diversity of promoted music styles has been heavily restricted to ones most amenable to commercial exploitation. This situation is beginning to change with the emergence of online music distribution and the ability of fans to find music styles and artists that would not be commercially viable and therefore unavailable in the traditional marketing and distribution structure. Today's U.S. recorded music industry generates $18 billion in annual revenues.[1]

An early phonograph.

Functions of the Recorded Music Industry

Recorded music serves a variety of functions, primarily entertainment, art, and education. The principal service to the audience is to provide musical entertainment. From children to senior citizens, just about everyone in contemporary society finds at least some recorded music to their liking. Although largely a commercial enterprise driven by profit motive, the recording industry has helped produce media art, as well. Whether recordings of jazz, opera, or even hip-hop, many recorded musical performances and studio productions have achieved a cultural impact or enduring quality that critics have praised or acknowledged. Recorded music provides another important function: to educate. Children especially listen to recorded music, sometimes the same songs over and over, learning vocabulary and much more.

Taken from a turn-of-the-last-century painting, this famous logo for Victor Talking Machine Co., which later became RCA, depicted a dog named Nipper sitting attentively before a Victor "talking machine" as it plays "his master's voice."

Historical Development: From Edison to CDs

The recorded music industry, or the recording arts, is the oldest of the electronic media of mass communication. Having begun to develop as a mass medium in the 1870s, the recording arts predate even the development of cinema, which did not develop as a mass medium until the turn of the last century. Radio, which was invented in the 1890s, did not develop as a mass medium until the 1920s.

Audio recording was born of nineteenth-century technological inventions, when Thomas Edison patented his first "talking machine" in 1877, the **phonograph,** using a tinfoil cylinder as a way to record telephone messages. Edison held a monopoly in the recording industry for nine years until telephone pioneer Alexander Graham Bell and inventor Charles Tainter developed an improved audio recording device called the **graphophone** that used beeswax rather than tinfoil cylinders. Based on their invention, the American Graphophone Company was launched in 1887.

The Columbia Phonograph Company soon entered the scene, launching its own technology to sell recordings on wax cylinders that could be played on coin-operated machines. The Victor Talking Machine Company was also launched, employing technology developed by inventor Emile Berliner called the **gramophone,** which used a flat disc to record sound rather than a cylinder, as proposed by Edison.

There were very few dramatic changes in recording arts technology over the first 100 years of its existence. Even the creation of vinyl long-play (lp) albums at 33-1/3 rpms, or revolutions per minute, in the mid 1950s, which allowed playing times of 40 to 45 minutes rather than two and a half minutes as with the shellac 78 rpm albums, were simply improvements in existing production processes and sound quality rather than radical new technologies.

phonograph—first patented by Thomas Edison in 1877 as a "talking machine," it used a tinfoil cylinder to record voices from telephone conversations. Successive technological improvements in electronics and the type of material the sounds were recorded on made sound quality better.

graphophone—an improvement on Thomas Edison's phonograph in recording audio, it used beeswax to record sound rather than tinfoil. Developed by Alexander Graham Bell and inventor Charles Tainter.

gramophone—developed by inventor Emil Berliner, it used a flat disc to record sound rather than a cylinder that was used up to that time.

Electromagnetic tapes such as eight-track tapes, and later cassettes, created in 1965, actually provided poorer sound quality than lps, but consumers were willing to trade audio quality for portability.

Compact discs, developed in 1980, were the first items to have songs digitally recorded and the first real technological breakthrough in the recording arts since Edison's time. Digital technology not only can improve the sound quality on older recordings by removing the unwanted noise such as pops and hisses, but it has also allowed for easy creation of "duets" by live and dead singers, such as the song "Unforgettable" by Nat King Cole and his daughter Natalie.

Industry Growth and Development

By 1909 a handful of companies controlled the recording arts industry. Recording arts scholar Geoffrey P. Hull notes that although the companies went through major changes, a three-way corporate oligarchy dominated the music industry until the 1950s, when a variety of industry-wide changes set in. The growth of rock-and-roll music introduced much greater competition into the recording industry, with the emergence of various new recording labels such as Detroit's Motown, although it was relatively short-lived diversity.

Through extensive merger and acquisition activity, the 1990s saw the reemergence of tight oligarchy control in the recording arts. The Internet and online music distribution have triggered a titanic struggle to redefine this structure, however.

The Recorded Music Industry Today

major labels—the five biggest recording arts companies that control much of the music industry, partly through their powerful distribution channels and ability to market music to mass audiences. They are Universal Music Group, BMG Entertainment, Sony Music, EMI, and the Warner Music Group.

independent labels—small record production and distribution companies that are not part of the five major label companies. They can include companies producing only one or two albums a year to larger independents such as Disney. The independent labels produce 66 percent of the albums each year but only 20 percent of the sales.

Today, the recording arts industry is perhaps best thought of as the world of musical recording and distribution for profit. It is more than a $25 billion business worldwide. The industry is dominated globally by five companies, the **major labels.** They are Universal Music Group, BMG Entertainment, Sony Music, EMI, and the Warner Music Group. Each of the big five recording industry giants is either a subsidiary of a larger media empire or has other media and entertainment interests that stretch beyond music. Combined, these companies control much of the recording and entertainment industries. Universal Music Group alone controls 23 percent of the worldwide market for recorded music.

Independent labels, whether the small local companies producing and distributing music from even a single artist or two, or the large labels such as Disney, produce the majority of music titles, estimated at about 66 percent by SoundScan and the Recording Industry Association of America (RIAA), yet only about 20 percent of the sales. Hull elaborates: "Of more than 17,000 titles released in 1995, 11,000 were by independent labels—almost a two-to-one ratio of independent releases to major label releases. The vast majority (90.5 percent) of current releases (not just new, but catalog as well) sell less than 5,000 copies per year. The number of recordings selling more than 250,000 per year was just 148 in 1995, but those recordings accounted for over half the total sales volume. Most of those were released by the major labels."[2]

Table 5-1 The Major Record Labels

Major Label	Owned by	Holdings
Universal Group (UMG)	The industry's 800-pound gorilla, a subsidiary of French utility and media firm, Vivendi Universal	A&M, Decca, Def Jam, Deutsche Grammophon, DreamWorks, Geffen, Island, Mercury, MCA, Motown, Philips classics, Polydor, PolyGram, and Verve
BMG	German subsidiary of multimedia conglomerate Bertelsmann AG	Arista, Arista Latin, Arista Nashville, BMG Classics, Jive, LaFace, Loud, RCA, and Windham Hill
Sony Music	U.S. music arm of the Japanese media giant	Columbia, Epic, 550 Music, Legacy, Razor Sharp, Refugee Camp, Relativity, Ruffhouse, Sony/ATV, Sony Wonder, So So Def, and Untertainment
EMI	British music leader with holdings and interests in dozens of international divisions	Blue Note, Capitol, Priority, Virgin, and EMI Classics
Warner	The music division of American media titan AOL Time Warner	Atlantic, Elektra, Maverick, Reprise, Rhino, Sub Pop, and Warner Bros.

The relative portion and absolute numbers of songs released by independent labels is rising dramatically, largely due to new technology, such as inexpensive do-it-yourself home-recording studios, computer CD-burners (for recording your own CDs) and online music distribution. As a result, the number of total albums released annually has increased from 2500 to 3000 a year in the 1960s and 1970s, when most of the albums were produced by major labels, to 30,000 in 2000. Because there are so many albums being produced, getting noticed and selling albums to cover costs, especially for the independent or amateur recording artists, becomes harder than ever without the marketing might of a major label behind them. Online distribution can counter this to some extent. For example, the Web site cdbaby.com sells CDs of independent artists exclusively.

How do the major labels manage to produce so many of the big hits? There are at least two answers, and no one knows for sure which is correct. One is that they produce the best music from the best artists, market it the best, and reap the rewards. Although there is no doubt at least some truth to this, answer number two also rings at least partly true. The major labels so dominate the entire production and distribution process that even if they produce collectively only marginal-quality recorded music, they will also dominate music sales because of their ability to market what they do produce.

Weblink
CD Baby
[www.cdbaby.com]

Recording Industry Business Model

Throughout much of the twentieth century and into the twenty-first, the basic business model in the recorded music industry can be divided into three main parts: creation, promotion, and distribution.

Creation

The major record labels sign artists and financially back those artists in the creation and recording of the music. Because of their financial investment in this and other parts of the process, the recording labels have historically received the majority of the financial rewards, with most artists receiving royalty payments of approximately 10 percent of gross, or overall, sales for their endeavors. Because recording labels obviously want to sign artists whose music will sell well, they can be seen as a gatekeeper or filter of talent, although not necessarily a perfect one, much like book publishers can be filters of writing talent.

Promotion

Promoting artists and their music is crucial to an album's success. There are several venues for promoting music to fans and the public. Artists perform in concerts, for which additional royalties are received, but radio is a primary promotional vehicle for music. In the past two decades, music videos have also become an important promotional vehicle as well.

The record labels traditionally provide the radio stations and television programmers with free copies of the recorded music and music videos in exchange for their playing them on their stations and channels. Sometimes certain unscrupulous programmers or disk jockeys in major markets have demanded illegal cash, gifts, or other payments under the table—known as **payola**—from the labels in exchange for promoting a song by playing it more frequently than other songs. The labels have sometimes paid this fee because of the importance of radio, especially certain major stations, as a promotional vehicle. Payola was very big in the 1950s, until the FTC ruled it was unfairly stifling competition. Payola favors the major labels over small labels, because small labels lack the financial resources to make these payments. Moreover, payola reduces the potential for diversity on the air and also increases the likelihood that quality music, or music that the public may like, won't make it on the air.

Perhaps the most famous case of radio payola involved rock radio DJ Alan Freed. Freed is credited with naming the emerging rhythm and blues-type music "rock and roll" while working for WJW-AM in Cleveland in the early 1950s. His career in radio was ruined in 1964 when he was convicted in New York on commercial bribery charges for accepting payoffs, or payola, to play certain records. After a series of radio jobs in various cities and a worsening drinking problem, Freed died in Palm Springs, California, in 1965. In 1986, Freed was inducted into the Rock and Roll Hall of Fame.[3] Today, payola, or what is now called "pay for play" (and some suspect still done extensively) is punishable with a fine or even imprisonment, and the regulations against it are enforced by the FCC.

payola—cash or gifts given to radio disc jockeys by record labels in exchange for greater air play given to the label's artists or most recent songs. The practice is now illegal after several scandals involving payola in the 1950s.

Distribution

Although the material that music has been recorded on has changed over the years—first on tin or beeswax cylinders, then on grooved plastic as albums, then on magnetic tape as eight-tracks and audio cassettes, then in optical form on compact discs—the method of distribution has essentially remained unchanged. The record labels make copies of the music from a master copy and send the albums, tapes, or CDs to local retail outlets that sell them to consumers. Online stores, such as Amazon, act much like their real-world counterparts except consumers receive the CDs at their homes.

However, another aspect of digital media and the Internet has been changing distribution much more radically—the ability of consumers to download songs in compact file formats such as MP3. Not only can songs be copied and distributed easily by the general public, but flawless copies can be created with no loss in sound quality such as happens when recording second- or third-generation audio cassettes. This is having profound effects on the control the recording industry has had on distributing music.

Pricing Structure

A major source of debate in the industry is the pricing structure for recorded music. Price, of course, is a major determining factor in both sales and profitability for the label and royalties for the artist, as well as income for all others in the distribution chain. In the 1970s, when vinyl lps were the standard means of distributing recorded music, list prices (what the consumer paid) were about $6. In the 1980s, the compact disc was introduced as the new means of distributing music, and the percentage of recorded music album sales on CDs gradually increased from just 22 percent in 1988 to 91 percent in 2001. List prices for CDs were about $19 in the early 1980s, with wholesale prices about $12. Over time, with increases in production volume, the cost of producing CDs has fallen; and, as a result, wholesale prices have fallen to about $10, with list prices at about $17. Inside the labels, manufacturing costs are today about $1 per CD, with artist and producer royalties about $2 per album (roughly 10 to 20 percent of the list price), and distributor charges about $1.50. Marketing costs (roughly $.50) tend to be quite low, because most of the promotion is provided free by radio stations and music television. Thus, a label typically has a gross profit of $5.00 per CD sold. This is a simplified model, but it illustrates the immense profitability in the recorded music industry.

Recording Industry Business Model for the Digital Age

The recording industry has yet to find a successful new business model that accepts the changing realities that digitization has brought to the industry. Instead, they have written letters to universities and Internet Service Providers (ISPs) demanding that they block access to file-sharing services or sue some of their users, sued various companies and individuals, and lobbied politicians to change laws on royalty payments and copyright to better protect the status quo.

Their efforts in creating secure forms of digital music have largely not been successful either. Sometimes the technology created restricts consumers more than they previously had been, such as Warner Music and Sony creating music CDs that cannot play on a computer CD player, and consumers protest these types of restrictions. Other times decidedly low-tech solutions are found to subvert the new restrictions, such as using a marker pen to block out the digital encoding on the restrictive CDs that thus lets them be played on any device. Some entertainment companies are pressuring lawmakers to create new laws that would require

CDs replaced audio cassettes and lps as the most popular format to play popular music.

electronic equipment manufacturers to install digital security devices in their products, a move manufacturers are resisting because of added production costs and the fact that every security system tried so far has eventually failed.

Theoretically, in a world of digital music, consumers would pay much less for music than they do now because there would be no physical products that the labels must produce, store, and distribute. There would be no need for CD cases, album artwork, or other material items that add costs to the price of a CD, which is then transferred to the consumer, although these materials could be created and made available for those who wanted them. Recording artists would also gain more control over their copyrights and see more revenues from sales, rather than the 10 to 15 percent royalty they currently see.

Also in a digital music world, there would be no need for a preselected music selection from a particular artist, as in the case of CDs or any packaged physical media, as consumers could mix and match songs and artists and download songs individually and create their own CDs—or just leave their music on their computers in digital form or transfer it to other portable devices to play.

This is precisely what has been happening among music-loving consumers, although the impetus for this type of change in getting and listening to music has not come from the record labels. It has come from consumers and file-sharing services such as Morpheus, KaZaA, Grokster, and the now-defunct Napster, which originally made this possible.

File Sharing: Death of the Recording Industry or a New Beginning?

File-sharing services, which will be discussed in more detail in Chapter 9, have made every consumer online a potential music distributor, regardless of whether that person owns the rights to the music he or she is distributing. This not only threatens the distribution channels the record labels have traditionally controlled but can also result in lost royalties to artists and the labels as consumers download, listen to, and copy songs for free.

Labels eventually responded to this phenomenon by offering downloadable music by subscription or on a per-download basis, although the services have not been hugely popular. One reason could be the relatively high costs for downloads, which turn out to be about as much as if a CD was purchased, and the other reason could be that many of the songs are available for free online. Technology and computer companies such as Gateway, seeing an opportunity to make music subscription services easier for consumers and to get involved in online music distribution, are partnering with companies such as Emusic. This means the recording industry is likely to be facing greater competition in its traditional distribution role on a number of fronts.

Hilary Rosen, president and CEO of the Recording Industry Association of America (RIAA), the main recording industry trade group, has primarily blamed file-sharing for a 6.4 percent drop in CD sales in 2001. A survey commissioned by the RIAA showed that 23 percent of consumers who downloaded music reduced their spending on CDs. A study by Jupiter Research released in May 2002 contradicted these findings, however, reporting that 34 percent of the people who regularly used file-sharing services said they increased their spending on CDs, with 14 percent saying their spending decreased.

The recording industry has also sued various file-sharing services and ISPs, successfully shutting down and eventually bankrupting music file-sharing pioneer Napster. Many ISPs have blocked access to file-sharing services both because of threatened lawsuits and because of the heavy load that such swapping can place on networks, thus slowing it down even for users not sharing files. Other lawsuits against file-sharing services are still pending at the time of this writing, and new bills are being proposed by some politicians that would further strengthen the legal positions of the recording industry.

Weblink
RIAA
[www.riaa.com/index.cfm]

What Is Broadcasting?

The term **broadcast** was used much earlier than the development of radio or television broadcasting as we know them today, as far back as 1883. Even the term broadcasting was borrowed from agriculture, where "broadcast" referred to a form of planting seeds by casting them widely in a field, rather than depositing them one at a time.

In its early days, wireless communications, which was initially only radio, provided point-to-point communication where telegraph lines were impractical or unreliable. The main purpose first seen among early wireless inventors was ship-to-ship communications or ship-to-shore communications, which would allow ships to communicate emergencies quickly to others. Subsequently, radio technology was developed to permit the broadcasting of messages through wireless means to multiple locations to distribute information widely. The subsequent development of television broadcasting several years later offered the opportunity to transmit moving pictures as well as audio via wireless technology.

Whether it is radio or television, however, broadcasting works essentially the same way. A transmitter sends messages over a part of the electromagnetic spectrum to a receiver, or antenna, which translates the message to a device such as a radio or television. The electromagnetic waves, whether they are audio or images, are then decoded by the receiving device so they can be heard or seen.

broadcast—originally used in terms of widely spreading numerous seeds in a field as opposed to planting them one by one, it came to be the term used for radio and later transmissions from which a single source sent messages over the airwaves to a wide number of people.

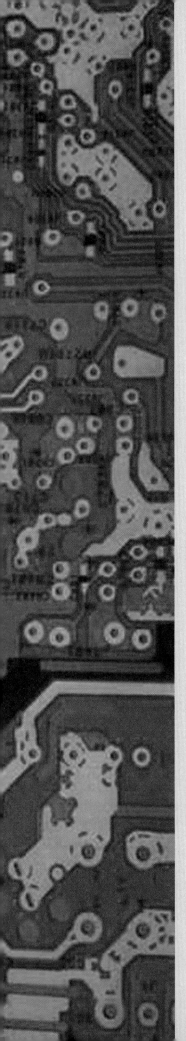

Media Technology

Spectrum Allocation: AM, FM, and Other Wireless Communication

Because the electromagnetic spectrum used for wireless communications is a limited resource, the FCC allocates various portions of the spectrum to different uses so these applications do not interfere with each other. Electromagnetic waves are divided into cycles per second, or hertz. A cycle is measured as the points between one peak and the next peak in a wave, which is how electromagnetic energy travels. If a radio station is at 99.5 on the radio tuner, this means its transmitter is oscillating at 99,500,000 cycles per second, or 99.5 megahertz (MHz).

AM stands for **amplitude modulation,** and refers to how the audio signal is encoded on the carrier frequency. In layperson's terms, it refers to a process that involves the variation of the height of the wave. In the United States, AM stations are also sometimes called "standard broadcast stations," a historical reference to the first radio signals available to the public. AM radio broadcasts between 535 kilohertz (KHz) and 1700 KHz (1.7 MHz).

FM stands for **frequency modulation;** this refers to the modulation of the length of the wave. FM radio broadcasts in the 88 to 108 megahertz (MHz) portion of the radio spectrum. This band is used exclusively for FM radio.

Other portions of the wireless bandwidth spectrum are used for other applications:

- shortwave radio (5.9 to 26.1 MHz)
- citizens band (CB, 26.96 to 27.41 MHz)
- television broadcast stations (54 to 88 MHz for channels 2 through 6 and 174 to 220 MHz for channels 7 through 13)
- cell phones (824 to 849 MHz)
- **global positioning system** (GPS is a system of satellites that provide location information anywhere in the world; 1227 to 1575 MHz)
- other bandwidths are reserved for the military, police, air traffic controllers, and other specialized uses

Weblink

How Stuff Works
[www.howstuffworks.com/]

U.S. Frequency Allocation Chart
[www.ntia.doc.gov/osmhome
/allochrt.html]

An early radio.

Radio

Radio is the most widely available medium of mass communication around the world. It is also the most heavily used medium in the United States, with people listening to radio 967 hours per person on average in 1999, or 2.65 hours a day.[4] At least 99 percent of all U.S. households have at least one radio receiver, and there are similar levels of penetration in most information societies. Even developing nations have a relatively high radio penetration. Radio is less expensive to produce, transmit, and receive than television; radio receivers are highly portable—even wearable—and radio doesn't require literacy to understand. There are basically two types of radio broadcasting, AM and FM. So-called Internet radio is an entirely different method of delivering audio programming, and is not a form of broadcasting, even though some in the industry call it "radio." Its method of delivery makes it more akin to audio programming like that in an airplane than true broadcasting, although it is "broadcast" in the sense that it reaches a mass audience.

Functions of Radio

Around the world, radio is a medium of entertainment as well as news and information, or surveillance, and marketing. The U.S. radio industry generates $14 billion in annual revenues.[5] Even in remote rural areas, radio is used to disseminate important news and information, where instructions for farming and agriculture are distributed easily, cheaply, and rapidly. Radio is also used as an emergency broadcast medium in all parts of the world, such as for severe weather events, natural disasters, or military conflict, largely because of its portability and flexible power source. Radio is especially well suited to emergency uses because in times of emergency electrical power may be lost, but radio receivers can easily operate for extended periods on battery power alone.

amplitude modulation (AM)—the original method of radio broadcasting; it refers to the height of the electromagnetic wave being adjusted. AM is generally not as clear as FM and has a shorter range, usually about 100 miles maximum.

frequency modulation (FM)—the length of the wave is modulated with FM. It generally has better sound but relies on line-of-sight transmission, meaning that mountains, tall buildings, or other obstructions can block reception.

global positioning system (GPS)—a system of satellites that provide location information anywhere in the world, operating at frequencies between 1227 MHz and 1575 MHz.

In American society, radio offers a diverse array of functions, perhaps more diverse than any other of the traditional analog media. Talk radio provides information, debate, and even limited audience interactivity with call-in shows. News programming offers breaking news reports as well as traffic and weather reports, school closings, and more. The mainstay of commercial radio has been the broadcasting of recorded music for entertainment. This latter function also serves as promotion of music for the artists and recording industry that want to get the listeners to buy their music.

Radio's Historical Development

Radio is a medium with a remarkable history. Technically, economically, and programmatically, radio has evolved considerably since its early development, and it continues to evolve as we enter the digital age. The following discussion reviews the development of radio, from its early days in the late nineteenth century to the dawn of the twenty-first century.

Hertz, Heinrich—German scientist who experimented with electromagnetic waves and demonstrated the existence of radio waves. His work set the stage for the development of modern wireless communications.

Wireless Telegraphy

Many inventors and scientists around the world were experimenting with radio technology at almost the same time. In 1884, German **Heinrich Hertz** began exper-

Media Timeline: Milestones in Early Radio Technology Development

1839	1864		1885	1887	1892
Karl Friedrich Gauss proposes that the earth's atmosphere contains a conducting layer.	James Clerk Maxwell predicts the existence of electromagnetic or radio waves using the conducting layer in	earth's atmosphere (i.e., that electric waves could travel through space).	Heinrich Rudolf Hertz demonstrates the existence of radio waves, based on Maxwell's prediction.	Granville T. Woods invents railway telegraphy, which allowed messages to be sent between moving trains.	Nathan B. Stubblefield creates and demonstrates a wireless communications device that could transmit voice and music.

imenting with electromagnetic waves, and in 1885 he demonstrated the existence of radio waves. His discovery was based on earlier theoretical notions proposed by Karl Friedrich Gauss and James Clerk Maxwell. Hertz's work set the stage for the development of modern wireless communications, both fixed and mobile, a portion of which Americans have come to know as radio. In much of the rest of the English-speaking world, radio has been known as the wireless. The measurement unit of electromagnetic frequencies was named for Hertz.

Another scientist experimenting with radio technology was African American **Granville T. Woods,** who in 1887 invented what is known as railway telegraphy. His invention allowed messages to be sent between moving trains, and between moving trains and a railroad station, reducing the frequency of railway collisions.[7]

At the twilight of the nineteenth century, in 1899, Italian **Guglielmo Marconi** invented radio telegraphy, what he called the wireless. Marconi's invention made possible real-time transmission of audio, although in the form of dots and dashes of Morse code, over distance without a wired connection, what might be called the first real radio transmission.

Guglielmo Marconi.

Exploring Radio's Early Potential

In the United States, the Department of Agriculture saw radio's potential and in 1900 financed Canadian Reginald A. Fessenden's early research for gathering reports and then distributing them over a broad area. The USDA started using radio broadcasting to transmit weather reports in 1912, although its initial transmissions were in telegraphic code, not in human voice. Fessenden in 1901 obtained a U.S. patent for his new radio transmitter, engineered to use a high-speed electrical alternator to produce "continuous waves." His design is the basis for today's AM radio.

Voice Transmission

Swedish-born inventor Ernst Alexanderson was among the first to build a working high-frequency, continuous-wave machine capable of transmitting a radio broadcast of the human voice and other sounds. Working for the General Electric Company, Alexanderson constructed a two-kilowatt, 100,000-cycle machine that was installed at Fessenden's station at Brant Rock, Massachusetts, on Christmas Eve, 1906. His invention permitted the station to transmit a radio broadcast featuring a human voice and a violin solo.

Woods, Granville T.—inventor of railway telegraphy in 1887, a type of wireless communication that allowed moving trains to communicate with each other and with stations, greatly reducing the number of railway collisions.

Marconi, Guglielmo—Italian inventor and creator of radio telegraphy, or wireless transmission, in 1899.

1893
Nicola Tesla demonstrates a wireless communications device.

1899
Marchese Guglielmo Marconi invents radio telegraphy, which he called the wireless.

1901
Reginald A. Fessenden obtains a U.S. patent for his new radio transmitter engineered to use a high-speed electrical alternator to produce "continuous waves," which is the basis for today's amplitude modulation, or AM (medium-wave) radio.

1906
Ernst Alexanderson builds a working high-frequency, continuous-wave machine capable of transmitting a radio broadcast of the human voice and other sounds.

1907
Lee de Forest develops a reliable technology for broadcasting of human voice, both for communication and for broadcasting entertainment and news.

Lee de Forest, one of the three "fathers" of radio.

Although much of the early work on radio was done by Italian Marconi and Canadian Fessenden, a U.S. pioneer in radio was **Lee de Forest,** who developed a unique transmission technology for radio broadcasting of human voice. His arc-transmitter for voice transmissions proved reliable for both point-to-point communication and for broadcasting entertainment and news, and by 1907 de Forest's company supplied the U.S. Navy's Great White Fleet with arc radiotelephones for its pioneering around-the-world voyage. This helped establish de Forest as the "father" of radio, although in reality, radio had at least three "fathers."

Radio before, during, and after WWI

Despite practical uses seen for radio, radio technology still needed to improve before it could become a mass medium. With considerable financial support from and direction by the U.S. military, research on the vacuum tube helped produce a reliable radio transmitter and receiver by about 1915. Using the perfected vacuum-tube radio transmitter, de Forest's Highbridge Station, 2XG, introduced nightly broadcasts, which offered listeners a so-called wireless newspaper for amateur radio operators.

All this activity ended with the entrance of the United States into World War I in April 1917. At this point, all radio stations were either taken over by the U.S. government or shut down completely. For the duration of the war it was illegal for private citizens to own or operate either a radio transmitter or receiver without special permission. The military continued to conduct research on radio technology, and with the end of the war in late 1918 radio restrictions were lifted and the industry took off.

Commercial broadcasting in the United States began in 1920, as well as the first election-night coverage. Regular commercial radio broadcasts began when AM station KDKA of Pittsburgh, Pennsylvania, reported results of the Harding–Cox presidential election.

Widespread Public Adoption of Radio

In the early 1920s in the United States there were roughly 6000 licenses for amateur radio stations and 4600 commercial stations, or stations run for profit. Up to this point, general public interest in radio had been slow to develop. There were amateur enthusiasts, who could be compared to the computer geeks in the early days of the Internet, but to the mass audience radio was a bit of a novelty whose application to their lives was limited.

However, a sporting event on July 2, 1921, would help establish radio as a major medium of mass communication. People across the country were keenly interested in the heavyweight boxing title fight between champion Jack Dempsey and challenger Georges Carpentier.[8] Radio networks did not yet exist, however, so only one station, a temporary long-wave station, WJY, broadcast the bout live, with technical help from The Radio Corporation of America (RCA). RCA, of course, had a financial incentive to see the success of the event. As a manufacturer of radio receivers, it wanted to see a radio set (or two) in every American household.

Organizers of the broadcast telegraphed a transcript of the commentary to pioneering station KDKA in Pittsburgh, which then broadcast the fight to its listeners on a slightly delayed basis. Because most people did not have their own

de Forest, Lee—considered the "father" of radio broadcasting technology because of his invention that permitted reliable voice transmissions for both point-to-point and broadcasting.

Mass Communication Formats

radio receivers at this time, most listeners were in halls where local organizers, including volunteer amateur radio operators, set up receivers and charged admission to offset costs. Because of the sensational nature of the event, much subsequent media commentary was given to the technical breakthrough and promise of the new medium of radio, helping propel radio as a medium of greater mass communication.

A broadcasting boom began after the Dempsey–Carpentier fight, with hundreds of radio stations springing up across the country, just as Web servers became widespread in the mid- to late 1990s. Radio receivers were selling as fast as RCA and others could manufacture them. American Telephone and Telegraph Company (AT&T) drafted a plan to create a national radio network. AT&T began implementing the programming for its national network in 1922 with flagship station WEAF in New York City and quickly set the standard for the entire industry.

Edwin Howard Armstrong, on the beach with a six-bulb suitcase radio receiver.

FM Radio, Edwin Howard Armstrong, and David Sarnoff

In 1934, an important breakthrough in radio transmission technology occurred when Columbia University engineering professor **Edwin Howard Armstrong** (1890–1954) invented FM (frequency modulation) radio, and later stereo FM radio, with his colleague, John Bose.

Armstrong completed his first field test on June 9, 1934, sending an organ recital, via both AM and FM, from an RCA tower on top of the Empire State Building to the home of a trusted old friend on Long Island. The FM organ came through loud and clear. The AM version had much more static.

Armstrong and **David Sarnoff,** head of RCA, had started out as friends, both seeing the great potential of radio broadcasting. But RCA had made much of its fortune from the mass sales of AM radio sets, called "radio music boxes." FM radio threatened to destroy the RCA empire.

Once Sarnoff realized the magnitude of the invention, he blocked Armstrong by ordering RCA engineers to ask for more tests, by lobbying federal regulators to deny Armstrong a license to test his invention, and even trying to obtain Armstrong's patent. Armstrong responded as best he could, filing suit against RCA and many other radio companies who were infringing on the Armstrong FM radio patent.

Tragically, Armstrong never reaped the commercial rewards of his invention, and he ultimately committed suicide virtually penniless in 1954 over his long-running legal battles with Sarnoff and other companies, as well as the end of his marriage. Ironically, his many lawsuits were settled shortly after his death, leaving a fortune to his widow and the Armstrong Foundation.

Armstrong, Edwin Howard— inventor of FM radio transmission and Columbia University engineering professor.

Sarnoff, David— president and chief executive officer of RCA. He helped push the development of television as a mass medium, yet blocked the development of FM radio for years because its adoption would hurt AM listenership and the AM radio receivers that RCA produced and sold.

Development of a Radio Business Model

Just as with the Internet, how to make a viable business out of radio broadcasting would prove a complex and controversial subject. Many stations in the United States experimented with commercial sponsorship, but through the mid-1920s there were many outspoken critics of advertising on the public airwaves. The May 1924 issue of Radio Broadcast magazine sponsored a $500 contest for best essay on "Who Is to Pay for Broadcasting—and How?" The fact that the magazine ran this contest suggested it wasn't convinced on-air advertising was a viable solution. However, a confluence of commercial interests, government decisions (sometimes influenced by commercial interests), and lack of coordination among advocates of publicly supported broadcasting made on-air advertising with privately owned stations the standard radio broadcasting business model that continues to this day. As a result, the engine that drives profits is audience size, especially among key demographic groups that are especially attractive to the advertisers who want to reach them and who provide sponsorship for radio programming. After television was developed, it followed the radio broadcasting model.

The Networks

During the 1920s the first commercial broadcasting networks were formed, initially as radio networks, or affiliated radio stations in multiple cities all broadcasting a common core set of programming, and later as national television networks. Prior to the passage of the **Radio Act of 1927** and the creation of the **Federal Radio Commission** (FRC), the predecessor to the **Federal Communications Commission** (FCC), broadcasting was lively but haphazard and not well-organized. There were numerous stations competing with each other on the same or nearby frequencies, which often caused reception interference. There were also few regulations regarding the power of transmitters, so powerful transmitters could drown out lower-powered, local transmitters with a stronger signal. The FRC revoked thousands of radio broadcast licenses and instituted a system that favored fewer, high-power stations over smaller but more numerous local low-power stations. This policy benefited large commercial broadcasting companies over educational or small, private broadcasters.

The National Broadcasting Network, or NBC, was the first network to form, having been created in 1926 when RCA, under the leadership of Sarnoff, purchased New York station WEAF (now WNBC) from AT&T for $1 million. That same year, NBC bought WJZ, licensed to Newark, New Jersey, but transmitting in New York, which had been owned by Westinghouse, and thus created the first network.

CBS was the second network to be formed, first as the United Independent Broadcasters in 1927, and after going on the air with a partner, the Columbia Phonograph and Records Co., becoming the Columbia Broadcasting System with 22 affiliates and 16 employees. In 1928, cigarmaker Sam Paley bought CBS for $400,000 and installed his son, William, as its head, moving the network's headquarters from Philadelphia to New York. Under his long-time leadership, and later under his corporate heir Frank Stanton, CBS held to the number-one position among the networks and described itself as The Tiffany Network, although others sometimes referred to it as Black Rock, in partial reference to the black marble façade of its midtown Manhattan headquarters.

By 1935, 58 of 62 stations nationwide were part of either the NBC or CBS networks. According to media scholar Robert McChesney, 97 percent of total nighttime broadcasting, when the smaller stations were off the air, was controlled by NBC or CBS. It was not until the 1940s that a third competing commercial network emerged, in television: ABC. In 1946, Edward J. Noble, the maker of Life Savers Candy, launched ABC, which had been NBC's Blue network. An FCC ruling in 1941 had required RCA to divest itself of one of its two networks. Noble bought NBC Blue in 1943 for $8 million and renamed it.

Radio Act of 1927—an act of Congress that created the Federal Radio Commission and that was intended to help establish some sort of regulation and order over the chaos of the largely unregulated airwaves. It helped establish the principle that the airwaves were a limited public good and that companies using those airwaves had a duty to act responsibly toward the public in terms of the type of material they broadcast.

Federal Radio Commission (FRC)—formed by the Radio Act of 1927, the commission was the precursor to the FCC and created a policy that favored fewer, high-power radio broadcasting stations rather than more numerous, low-power stations. The commission revoked thousands of existing radio licenses as it implemented its policies.

Federal Communication Commission (FCC)—the principal communications regulatory body at the federal level in the United States, established in 1934.

Mass Communication Formats

Media Spotlight: National Public Radio

National Public Radio (NPR) was incorporated in 1970 and is a not-for-profit membership organization with 490 member public radio stations nationwide and a weekly audience of 17 million.[9] It produces and distributes news, cultural, and informational programs for public radio in the United States, linking the nation's noncommercial radio stations into a national network. Public Radio International (PRI) produces and distributes additional public radio programming, such as *Marketplace* and Garrison Keillor's *A Prairie Home Companion* to nearly 600 affiliate stations in the United States, Puerto Rico, and Guam, as well as international programs including the BBC World Service.[10]

NPR debuted on April 19, 1971, with live coverage of the Senate Vietnam hearings and a month later first broadcast *All Things Considered,* establishing NPR as an important provider of news and information programming. Today, NPR broadcasts 100 hours of original programming each week.

Public radio distinguishes itself from commercial radio in a number of ways, including more extensive, impartial, and original audio news, especially long-form audio reporting, as is featured on *Morning Edition* and *All Things Considered.* Also defining NPR's coverage is its in-depth coverage of the arts and commercial-free programming (although on-air sponsorships are permitted). NPR also offers extensive music programming in classical and folk music, jazz, and opera, featuring a variety of live transmissions of the performing arts in theaters and concert halls, as well as radio dramas such as *NPR Playhouse, Selected Shorts,* and *Beyond 2000.*

Weblink

NPR
[www.npr.org]

PRI
[www.pri.org]

Radio Station Programming

Perhaps the most fundamental development in commercial radio in the twentieth century was its eventual specialization. Radio grew in its early years to become a dominant medium of mass communication. Large audiences assembled to listen to individual programs during much of the first half of the twentieth century. But with the rise of television as a medium of mass communication in the years following World War II, radio fell from a position of media dominance and, like magazines, adapted to the new media landscape by specialization.

This specialization takes a number of forms, including program formats, time of day for certain formats, and especially audience demographics. In radio, a day is broken up into different time segments called dayparts. The 6 A.M. to 10 A.M. **daypart,** for example, is a time when most people listen to the radio as they get ready for work or school or are commuting. Therefore, the programming emphasizes frequent news, traffic, and weather reports as well as some of the more outspoken talk radio shows such as *Imus in the Morning.*

Radio stations are organized according to the type of programming they air. There are dozens of radio programming formats.[11] Formats vary widely in terms of the audience they draw. Contemporary Hit Radio, for example, featuring music in 2001 from performers such as The Back Street Boys, Britney Spears, and Jennifer Lopez, draws a much different audience than the Country format, for example.

Recording star Gwen Stefani draws a much different radio audience than a country singer would.

daypart—a segment of time used by radio and television program planners to decide who the primary audience is during that time of day or night.

Table 5-2 Most Popular Radio Programming

Programming Type	Percentage of Audience (out of population)
News/Talk/Information	16.2
Adult Contemporary	15.8
Contemporary Hit Radio	10.9
Rock	9.7
Country	9.3
Urban	8.0
Oldies	7.5
Spanish	6.5
Alternative	5.1
Adult Standards	3.8
Jazz	2.9
Religious	2.2
Classical	1.7
Other	0.4

Source: Arbitron

Radio Stations: The United States Today

As of 2001 there were 12,932 licensed radio stations in the U.S.[12] These include 4716 AM stations, 6000 FM commercial stations, and 2216 FM noncommercial educational stations. This does not include hundreds of "radio" stations that transmit their programming via the Internet. Nor does this number include various low-power or micro-power radio stations for local broadcasts (AM or FM) or the thousands of proposals (13,000 per year) for such stations under consideration by the FCC.

All stations in the United States are assigned call letters, which designate the station and its geographic location east and west of the Mississippi River. For stations east of the Mississippi, W is the first letter call letter, and for stations west of the Mississippi, K is the call letter, although there are some exceptions that used call letters before the boundaries were determined, such as KDKA in Pittsburgh. Under an international agreement issued at the London International Radiotelegraphic Conference in 1912, different countries were awarded different letters. The United States received KDA to KZZ.

For most of the first half of the 20th century, AM radio listenership far exceeded FM listenership. But in the late 1970s this turned around, and today FM listenership is far greater than AM listenership, just as the number of FM stations exceeds AM stations. The ascendancy of FM radio in the 1970s was due

Weblink
FCC web site
[www.fcc.gov]

to a number of factors, including the inclusion of an FM dial in most automobile radio receivers, changes in programming, and regulatory changes, combined with the fact that FM is less subject to static.

Radio is widely available in American society and much of the world. Radio industry expert Albert N. Greco reports that 99 percent of U.S. households had at least one radio receiver in 1999, with many having more than one. This is a higher level of household penetration than other major electronic media, including television (98 percent), telephone (93.9 percent), VCR (81 percent), and cable television (63.4 percent).

Radio Station Ownership

In its early days, radio in the U.S. was a largely uncontrolled medium of public communications, not unlike the early days of the Internet. But the free-for-all quickly gave way to largely commercial interests and government regulation of the airwaves. Throughout most of the twentieth century, ownership of radio was relatively diverse. Partly this was a result of federal laws that prohibited any one person or organization from owning more than 20 FM stations and 20 AM stations nationwide.

Regulatory changes in 1992 as well as the passage of the Telecommunications Act of 1996 resulted in new FCC radio ownership rules. These new rules put no limit on the number of radio stations that can be owned or controlled by a single entity nationwide, although it is still required that the owner be a U.S. citizen. Since the passage of the Act, more than 4400 radio stations have changed ownership; and this has led to greatly increased concentration of ownership in the radio industry, or an oligopoly, in which fewer companies own a greater number of radio stations.

Recent regulatory changes also changed the FCC's so-called duopoly rules on local station ownership. Duopoly rules refer to a prohibition on any one person or group from owning, operating, or controlling more than two AM stations and two FM stations in the largest markets. The rules had also restricted the combined audience share of the co-owned stations to 25 percent, with smaller markets having even more restrictive limits. The Act ended these duopoly restrictions, and the FCC now permits a single entity to own substantially more in the same service markets than they could in the past.

This shift in regulatory policy has lead to a trend in the 1990s and early twenty-first century toward increasing consolidation of radio ownership. Throughout most of the over 50-year history of radio broadcasting, radio was a small business, with owners long-time residents of the towns in which the stations operated. Although many stations in smaller towns are still locally owned and operated, most radio stations in big cities have become corporate enterprises.

Increasingly, with the end of the duopoly rules, some groups now control eight or more stations in a single market, and most of the big, highly profitable stations are owned by the most powerful media groups. Those who support the changes in station ownership say consolidation is a good thing for many reasons, including increased efficiency; more economical, centralized production; larger budgets that permit greater programming experimentation and development; and more effective management. Critics argue that group ownership typically means less sensitivity to local concerns because owners are often remotely located.

Table 5-3 provides a breakdown of the top radio groups in the United States. As the data show, the largest radio group in the United States is Clear Channel Communications, with 1200 stations and revenues of $5.3 billion annually. Viacom CBS is a distant second in number of stations owned (164 through Infinity Broadcasting) and annual revenues of $3.8 billion.

The Future of Radio

Although the way radio is transmitted and the devices the public uses for listening to radio will change, radio itself—or more accurately, the transmission of audio content to a mass audience—will remain an important form of mass communication. A primary reason for this is that, almost alone among mass media, it allows people to easily engage in other activities while listening to audio content. No matter how advanced or portable media technology becomes, there is no way that one can watch TV or read a book or newspaper while driving safely, as they can when listening to audio content.

However, like other digital media, the public will have more control over what they listen to and when they listen to it. In that way, broadcast radio is likely to become more like audio programming delivered over the Internet, as the public could be given choices on whether they want to listen to commercial-free radio through a subscription model. Many changes will occur after digital broadcasting systems are finished early in the twenty-first century, so much so that the term "radio" may technically become obsolete or could come to mean something very different than what we think of as radio.

One of the first digital broadcasting systems to roll out commercially might be a look into what is to come. Based in New York, Satellite Radio's CD Radio con-

Table 5-3 Top Radio Groups in the United States[13]

1. Clear Channel, with 1200 stations and revenue of $5.3 billion

2. Viacom/CBS (Infinity), with 185 stations and revenue of $3.8 billion

3. ABC Inc., with 50 stations in top markets* and revenue of $500 million

4. Cox Radio, with 80 stations and revenue of $369 million

5. Entercom Communications, with 95 stations and revenue of $352 million

6. Hispanic Broadcasting Corporation (formerly Heftel), with 47 stations and revenue of $238 million

7. Emmis Broadcasting, with 20 stations in the United States, two radio networks outside the United States, and 15 network-affiliated television stations, with total revenue of $470 million

*ABC radio network also includes 2,900 affiliated stations.

XM Satellite radio's control room.

sumer service used digital satellite and terrestrial repeater towers to roll out a subscription-based radio system delivering news and music to cars and people nationwide in 2001. Its services include up to 50 channels of CD-quality music in a variety of formats and up to 50 channels of third-party news, sports, and talk-radio programs. A very small satellite dish and a "radio card" placed in a car's cassette or CD slot permit any existing car radio to receive the signal. Ford and other automobile manufacturing partners will start manufacturing cars equipped with the receivers in 2002. XM Satellite Radio is another such service.

Weblink
CD Radio
[www.cdradio.com]
XM Satellite Radio
[www.xmsatelliteradio.com
/home.html]

Television

Television, created by combining the Latin terms "distance" and "viewing," is a much-loved and much-hated medium. Unlike many other media of mass communication, television is a medium that draws as many critics as fans. Despite the rise of the Internet and other new media, people still spend more time watching television (1633 hours per person per year, or 5.4 hours a day, in 2000) than they spend with any other medium.[14] In 1999, children between the ages of 2 and 17 spent about 2 hours and 46 minutes a day in front of television on average, and about 3 hours 30 minutes a day in front of some kind of screen, which includes playing video games, watching videotapes, and computer use (see Figure 5-1). Yet many also think television watching is largely a waste of time. They see it as offering little of redeeming social value and as largely mindless entertainment. Others point to the many hours of educational television, news, and cultural programming as examples of quality content worth watching. Moreover, television is a big business.

Traditionally, terrestrial, or over-the-air broadcast, TV has been the most common way people received television programming. But in 2001 just 12 percent of

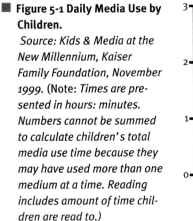

Figure 5-1 Daily Media Use by Children.
Source: Kids & Media at the New Millennium, Kaiser Family Foundation, November 1999. (Note: Times are presented in hours: minutes. Numbers cannot be summed to calculate children's total media use time because they may have used more than one medium at a time. Reading includes amount of time children are read to.)

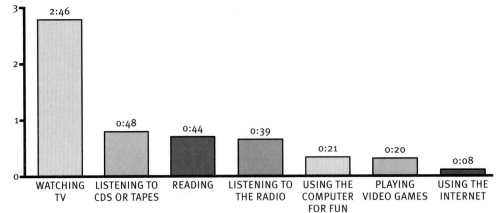

U.S. households got their television over the air on their main TV set (U.S. homes have an average of 2.41 sets). The most common way now to get analog TV is via cable, with two-thirds of homes receiving their TV this way. Many homes get satellite-delivered TV, which is actually digital, but is transferred back to analog format via a set-top converter box. Moreover, most households, at least occasionally, watch television via videocassettes or personal video recorders (PVRs). Consumer recording devices for television were an important development for a number of reasons. One reason is they allowed the audience to **time shift,** or watch a program anytime after it was originally broadcast and when it suited them, rather than be held hostage to a broadcaster's scheduling.

Time shifting was an important step in shifting the balance of power in choosing media content to the audience, a trend that will continue as TV becomes increasingly digital. Digital media in fact will complicate the very definition of television as advances such as interactive TV, video-on-demand (VOD), and Internet connectivity blur the current distinctions between personal computers, traditional broadcasting, and video programming.

Functions of Television

More U.S. households have television sets than telephones, with 98 percent of all U.S. households having at least one TV set, and it is the most influential medium of mass communication. More Americans say they get their news from television than any other source, making the surveillance function for TV preeminent.

More Americans get their entertainment from television than from any other mass medium. Americans spend more time watching television than doing any other activity, except sleeping and working. Since the advent of television as a medium of mass communication, only one development has caused TV viewership to drop—the Internet. But despite this, TV is still number one in people's media use. U.S. advertising revenues for 2000 topped $81 billion, underscoring the importance of the marketing function of television as well.[15]

Television became a mass medium much faster than did film or radio. As it became more widespread, television displaced radio—which had displaced national magazines—as the medium that provides a common set of shared experiences. Although this effect may be reduced somewhat with more channels and growing

time shift—recording an audio or video event, usually by the audience, to be watched at a time other than when it was originally broadcast. Setting a VCR to record a favorite program while out is an example of time shifting.

Being able to time shift, or record programs and watch them at a later time, is an important element in giving the public more control over the content they watch.

audience fragmentation, there is no doubt that television continues to have a profound effect on shaping people's attitudes about a variety of social and cultural issues.

Television's Historical Development

Unknowingly laying the basis for the development of television, a British telegrapher, Louis May, discovered in 1873 what some consider to be the basics of photoconductivity, a critical foundation for the electronic transmission of visual and audio information. He discovered that, when exposed to light, selenium bars conducted electricity and that the level of conduction varied in relationship to the amount of light hitting the bars. Five years later, M. Senlacq of Ardres, France, theorized that selenium could trace documents and that electrical charges could control this process. In 1881, British inventor Shelford Bidwell transmitted silhouettes using both selenium and a scanning system and called his device the scanning phototelegraph. These technologies contributed to the development of modern television by outlining an electrical method for scanning objects.

Most TV sets and computer displays today are based on the use of a **cathode ray tube (CRT)** for displaying video images. The cathode ray tube is not a modern invention. The CRT was conceived in 1859 by Julius Plucker, a German mathematician and physicist, and the first functional CRT was built in 1878 by William Crookes, a British chemist. In 1897, German physicist Karl Braun improved the cathode ray tube, which demonstrated how cathode rays could be controlled by a magnetic field.

Seeing the Light: The First Television Systems

In 1884 German inventor Paul Nipkow developed a concept for mechanical television that used a rotating disk with holes for viewing the images, a light source, and lens.

In 1923, Scottish inventor **John Logie Baird** invented Baird Television, the first mechanically scanned television device to earn any money from sending pictures through the air. Baird's 30-line TV is considered by some to be the first high-definition TV because it contained many more lines of resolution than other early TV systems and thereby displayed finer visual detail.

cathode ray tube (CRT)—a device that is still used in most television screens and computer monitors in which electrons are transmitted to a screen for viewing.

Baird, John Logie—Scottish inventor who created the first mechanically scanned television device in 1923. His 30-line TV had better resolution than the first attempts at electronic televisions.

The Dempsey/Tunney fight was one of the first television images, created by Philo T. Farnsworth.

Vladimir Zworykin.

In 1923, Russian immigrant **Vladimir Zworykin** invented a more advanced cathode ray tube he called the "iconoscope" (meaning "a viewer of icons"), which still serves as the basis of many modern television display tubes. The iconoscope was an electronic camera pickup tube and represented perhaps the first important tangible device that would eventually lead to what is now called television. In 1929, Zworykin also invented the first totally electric camera tube. The CRT is also still the basis of most computer displays, with the exception of flat panel displays.

In 1927, Philo T. Farnsworth transmitted the image of a dollar sign across his San Francisco apartment using the scanning beam and synchronization pulse technologies he invented. This was the first electronic wireless transmission of an image, the first step in the development of electronic television. Farnsworth later invented an electronic television system called the Image Dissector. His first "broadcast" transmitted images from a Jack Dempsey–Gene Tunney fight and scenes of Mary Pickford combing her hair (from *Taming of the Shrew*). Farnsworth and Zworykin became entangled in bitter legal battles over television patents, each claiming to have been the first to develop electronic television.

Modern Television Takes Shape

If television was going to become a popular mass medium for broadcasting images, then much better image resolution was needed than what the earliest attempts at television could produce. With a CRT screen, the greater number of scanned lines the clearer the picture is. In 1939, a 441-line TV technology was demonstrated by David Sarnoff at the New York World's Fair.

The 1939 demonstration brought national, even international, attention to the new medium of television. That same year, TV broadcasting began in the United States when the National Broadcasting Company (NBC) started regularly scheduled broadcasts to only 400 sets in the New York area. In 1940, Mexican Guillermo González Camarena invented the color television picture tube.

The American Federal Communications Authority (now known as the Federal Communications Commission) set the standard for television at 525 lines updated at 30 frames per second. This standard, with the addition of color in 1954 by the **National Television System Committee (NTSC),** has lasted until today, as we move toward digital, high-definition television, with 1080 active lines of resolution.

CBS announced the development of a color television system in 1948. Color television broadcasting debuted in 1951 in the United States with a live CBS telecast from Grand Central Station in New York, featuring Arthur Godfrey as host.

David Sarnoff, president of RCA and head of NBC, dedicates the RCA pavillion, in the first television news broadcast.

Unfortunately, only 25 receivers could accommodate the mechanical color technology, while viewers of the 12 million existing black and white sets saw a blank screen. In 1953, color broadcasting had its official start in the United States when the FCC approved a modified version of an RCA system that was compatible with a 525-line screen.

The government lifted its wartime ban on the construction of new TV stations and TV sets in October 1945. Commercial TV stations soon became available in New York, Chicago, Philadelphia, and Schenectady, New York. There were just 7000 receiving sets in the United States at the beginning of 1946 and only nine stations on the air. By 1949, there were 98 stations in 58 market areas. In 1950, there were 3.88 million households with television, or 9 percent of the total 43 million U.S. households.

There were four commercial television networks: NBC, CBS, ABC, and DuMont, although DuMont failed in 1955. By the end of 1955, the number of TV households grew to 30.7 million, or 64.5 percent of U.S. households, and U.S. advertisers spent more than $300 million on TV time. By 1960, 45.7 million U.S. households (87.1 percent) had at least one television set.

Television Distribution

There are three primary means of distributing television programming. These are broadcasting, cable, and direct-to-home satellite. Although some television programming is also distributed via videocassette and digital versatile disk (DVD), these methods are principally for the distribution of motion pictures, particularly after their initial theatrical release.

Broadcast TV

Broadcasting (terrestrial wireless) is the traditional means of over-the-air distribution of television programming, and includes primarily the 1678 (as of June 30, 2001) full-power VHF and UHF broadcasting stations, as shown in Table 5-4.[16] This is the way the network owned and affiliated stations and most other local stations broadcast their programming. Although in the early 1970s terrestrial TV dominated the viewing landscape, today that is far from the truth. Today, just

Media Inventors and Innovators

Rupert Murdoch and Fox Television

Australian-born Rupert Murdoch has turned his penchant for risk and media entrepreneurship into the News Corp., one of the largest media conglomerates in the world. Murdoch owned a dozen newspapers in Australia before buying his first newspaper outside his home country, the *News of the World,* in the United Kingdom. Murdoch bought this paper as he has most of his other media properties: buy cheap, cut costs, apply substantial doses of sex and violence in his media, whether news or entertainment, and watch the audiences—and profits—grow.[17]

Since his early forays, Murdoch has initiated worldwide digital satellite television initiatives, as well as a series of U.S. media acquisitions. Among his most visible U.S. media initiatives has been his acquisition of a series of television stations and the creation of the Fox Television Network, which has quickly defined itself as a popular, tabloid programming network known especially for innovative reality shows and highly successful talk shows, such as the *O' Reilly Factor.*

To accomplish his television acquisitions, however, Murdoch had to become a U.S. citizen, because federal law does not permit a foreigner to own a controlling interest in a television or radio station. In 2000, Murdoch made clear his interests in acquiring DirecTV, the leading U.S. direct broadcast satellite television system. In 2001, Murdoch found himself embroiled in a bidding war with EchoStar to purchase DirecTV. In mid-July of that year, EchoStar offered $35 billion to buy the coveted DBS system, an offer that DirecTV owner General Motors accepted. At this writing, the companies are seeking permission from the FCC to complete the deal.

Rupert Murdoch.

---

multipoint, multichannel distribution systems (MMDS)— a type of terrestrial wireless service that can transmit as many as 33 analog TV channels over the air via microwave transmission and up to 99 compressed digital channels.

15 percent of U.S. households receive terrestrial TV signals on their primary TV set.

There are also other less-used means of terrestrial wireless television distribution, of which **multipoint, multichannel distribution systems (MMDS)** are the most important. MMDS are terrestrial wireless services that can transmit as many as 33 analog TV channels over the air via microwave transmission and up to 99 com-

Table 5-4 Number of Full-Power Terrestrial Broadcast Television Stations in the United States

Type of Television Station	Number
UHF Commercial TV	734
VHF Commercial TV	570
UHF Educational TV	249
VHF Educational TV	125
Total	1678

pressed digital channels. MMDS systems are particularly effective in regions with flat terrain, especially in sparsely populated areas where wired cable systems are expensive to install and maintain, such as the rural plains areas of the Midwest. MMDS was made possible in 1983 by an FCC frequency reallocation that allowed broadcasters to use as many as 33 high-frequency 6 MHz channels for an MMDS service.

The commercial broadcasting networks dominated television programming, viewing, and the general commercial broadcasting landscape until the 1980s, when cable and satellite TV and other programming alternatives made program and audience fragmentation inevitable. These trends have continued. In 1994, the average home received 40 channels of television. In 2001, the average number of channels received had increased to 73, although people still watch about the same number of channels—10 in 1994 and 13 in 2001.

Media critic Ken Auletta deftly chronicles the shifting network landscape of the 1980s in his classic book, *Three Blind Mice: How the Television Networks Lost Their Way,* arguing persuasively that a corporate culture that put profits over program quality contributed to a decline of the networks, especially in their commitment to quality broadcast journalism. Although they have somewhat rebounded in recent years, the "big three" networks have never recaptured the leadership position they once held. NBC, CBS, and ABC are still the largest networks, each with more than 200 affiliate television stations.

In addition to competition from cable and satellite, today there are three other major commercial television networks to compete with: WB (Warner Brothers), Fox, and UPN (Universal–Paramount Network, which is owned, however, by Viacom, which also owns CBS).

Cable TV

Of the alternatives to terrestrial broadcast television, cable television and direct broadcast satellite have played the greatest role in transforming U.S. television viewing during the past quarter century. Most households' primary TV sets are connected to cable or satellite. That's not to say viewers don't see the programming carried on terrestrial broadcast stations, because those stations are carried on cable TV and many on satellite TV. In fact, the three traditional commercial networks still have a cumulative weekly audience reach of more than 81 percent.[18]

Origins of Cable TV

Many think cable TV was invented in the 1960s, when in fact the first cable television systems were created in the U.S. in 1948. The first systems, called **Community Antenna Television,** or **CATV,** were built noncommercially in Mahoney City, Pennsylvania, in June 1948 and in Astoria, Oregon, in November 1948. The main function of these early CATV systems was to bring TV signals into communities where over-the-air reception was nonexistent or poor due to hilly terrain or distance.

Although the first cable systems were built in the late 1940s, the cable system nationwide didn't begin growing rapidly until the 1970s, when the number of local cable systems grew from about 2000 in 1970 to more than 4000 in 1980.

Community Antenna Television (CATV)—also known as cable television, it was developed in 1948 so communities in hilly terrain could still have access to television broadcasts.

Cable Technology

Coaxial cable, which is an insulated and layered conducting wire typically about a half-inch thick, is the delivery medium traditionally used for delivering cable television to the home. Coaxial cable was invented in 1928, and the first use of coaxial cable was for undersea telephone transmission and later for television transmission. Most early cable TV systems were based on coaxial cable, but today increasingly consist of optical fiber. **Optical fiber** is a much faster, higher-capacity, transparent filament, usually made of glass or plastic, using light to carry media content or information, including audio and video, rather than electrical impulses that are used in coaxial cable.

Cable System Structure

The typical cable system features what is called a tree-and-branch architecture. A head-end, or main office, is the center, with fiber or coaxial cable trunk lines, feeder lines, and drops to end users. In 2001, there were 10,243 cable systems.[19] Most of these local systems are part of larger regional and national multiple system operators (MSOs).

Cable television underwent some dramatic changes in the 1980s. The government began deregulating the cable industry, permitting cable companies to buy cable television systems nationwide. Early cable giant Tele-Communications, Inc. (TCI) (now a subsidiary of AT&T Broadband) was among the most aggressive in taking advantage of this deregulation, spending $3 billion for 150 cable companies across the United States. By the end of the decade, 50 percent of U.S. households were wired for cable TV, setting the stage for the decline of network television and over-the-air broadcasting, as well as spurring audience fragmentation. During this decade, cable systems expanded their channel capacity, giving rise to a multichannel viewing environment in which most subscribers had access to more than 50 channels of television programming.

Most cable systems have been undergoing a significant transformation since the 1990s from analog to digital technology, with upgrades costing most MSOs millions or billions of dollars not only to improve and expand channel capacity (frequently upgrading to more than 100 channels) but to add interactive features, such as two-way capacity (for program ordering, for example) and cable modems and set-top box converters for high-speed Internet services. In 2001, more than two-thirds (68 percent, or 69.5 million) of American households subscribed to cable television, although cable system wires pass by more than 96 percent of all television households.[20]

Cable Services and Programming: Audience Fragmentation

Cable services are typically offered in tiers. A tier is a type of cable service offering varying program packages at varying rates. The three types of cable services, or tiers, are: basic service, cable programming service, and per-channel or per-program (or pay-per-view) service. Basic service is the minimum level of cable service. As required by the FCC, basic service must include all local over-the-air television broadcast signals and all public, educational, or government access channels mandated by the cable system's franchise agreement.

Like radio, the cable television audience has become enormously fragmented, with even leading cable channels and programs capturing relatively small ratings.

coaxial cable—an insulated and layered conducting wire typically about a half-inch thick; the delivery medium traditionally used for delivering cable television to the home. Coaxial cable provides broadband transmission capabilities for the delivery of full-motion video as well as telephony.

optical fiber—a transparent filament, usually made of glass or plastic, that uses light to carry information. This makes transmission of information much faster and with much greater capacity than twisted-pair copper wires or coaxial cable.

There are more than 150 cable program networks. Audience fragmentation has grown as the number of cable channels available on typical cable system has grown. Yet, in aggregate, cable programming captures a significant portion of the television audience.

The trend toward increased channel capacity continued into the 1990s and early twenty-first century, as most cable systems converted to digital technology that offered even greater channel capacity, in some cases up to 1000 programming channels.

Satellite

Satellite delivery of TV signals includes a variety of technical alternatives. First, television receive only (TVRO), or C-band and Ku-band, has been used traditionally by the networks to transmit their programming to owned or affiliated stations around the country or from remote trucks to main processing centers. Second, satellite master antenna TV (SMATV) is primarily a means of bringing cable TV to apartment buildings through a single shared antenna. Third, direct to home or direct broadcast satellites (DTH/DBS) are the principal home consumer satellite TV services and are received through rooftop dishes. DBS transmission in the United States is already fully digital, with MPEG-2 digital video currently the standard and companies eyeing adoption of MPEG-4 as the next standard. DBS providers are also offering high-speed Internet services.

Direct Broadcast Satellite

In 1974, the National Aeronautics and Space Administration, or NASA, began its experiments with Direct Broadcast Satellites. DBS ultimately became the first broadband digital transmission system in the United States used for video distribution to home viewers.

DBS emerged in the United States in the 1990s as a serious competitor to traditional terrestrial broadcast and cable television. Although DBS was a viable commercial television alternative in Europe, efforts made for more than a decade to launch a viable national DBS commercial TV service in the United States failed until the 1994 launch of DirecTV. Prior to that year, most of the direct-to-home satellite systems required expensive, large 3-meter dishes used to receive C and Ku band satellite transmissions.

DirecTV and other 1990s DBS entrants introduced inexpensive, compact 18-inch dishes that could be installed without professional help, with an annual subscription price that rivals cable alternatives. With its 11 million subscribers, DirecTV would rank fourth among cable MSOs.[21] Because it is all digital, however, DirecTV is the nation's leading digital television service (most of the top-ten MSOs are no more than 50 percent digital as of this writing) and has already introduced high-speed Internet services nationwide.

DBS offers more than 200 digital programming channels. The greatest problem DBS systems have faced is their inability to carry a full array of local programming. Local programming is important for delivering local news, weather, and other programming. Although the DBS systems have great channel capacity, they cannot carry every local station. Instead, they carry local channels in the largest markets and require subscribers to pay a fee to watch the local broadcasting channels available in their region. If DBS viewers opt not to pay the fee and still want local programming, they must maintain a basic cable service or another antenna to get local channels.

Satellite–Cable Convergence

The first instance in television of technological convergence, or the coming together of two or more formerly separate television media, occurred in 1978. In that year, Time Inc. beamed television programming via satellite to local cable television systems to launch Home Box Office (HBO).

Also in 1978, Ted Turner launched WTBS Atlanta as a national **superstation.** A superstation is a local TV station that reaches a national audience by beaming its programming nationwide via satellite to local cable systems, which then transmit the program to local subscribers. The concept for a satellite–cable network superstation was developed in 1973 by Bob Wormington, the president of a Kansas City UHF station, who created the idea of an independent TV station that would reach a national market if distributed via satellite to cable systems nationwide. In 1980, Turner employed the same technological combination to launch the first 24-hour TV news network, the Cable News Network (CNN).

The Television Industry Today

Ownership of television has continued to become increasingly consolidated since the passage of the 1996 Telecommunications Act, which relaxed ownership limits. Among the newly expanded limits is the 35 percent rule, which permits groups to own stations that nationwide reach up to 35 percent of television households and to own two stations in major markets.

Broadcast Station Ownership

No longer are the the three traditional networks the largest owners of terrestrial broadcast television stations. Today, as shown in Table 5-5, the greatest number of stations is owned by Paxson Communications, with 72 stations. All of these companies own other media properties, such as motion picture production companies, newspapers, and radio stations.

Cable Television Ownership

Despite the fact there are more than 10,000 local cable systems, consolidation in the cable industry has resulted in a relatively small number of companies— roughly 600 MSOs—controlling cable television for more than 90 percent of Americans who subscribe to cable TV. As Table 5-6 shows, the top six MSOs have nearly three-quarters of all cable TV subscribers.

As in other media and technology companies, changes continue to happen fairly rapidly in the cable TV industry. Prior to March 1999, TCI (Tele-Communications Inc.) had been the largest cable company in the United States. But in a $48 billion deal, AT&T acquired TCI. In the deal, AT&T will combined its consumer long distance, wireless, and & Internet services units with TCI's cable and Internet businesses to create a new subsidiary and the largest cable TV MSO in the United States—AT&T Broadband. In December 2001 AT&T Broadband and Charter Communications proposed a $72 million merger, which will make them by far the largest MSO if the merger is approved.

superstation—a local TV station that reaches a national audience by beaming its programming nationwide via satellite to local cable systems, which then transmit the program to local subscribers.

Table 5-5 The Top Ten TV Groups in the United States by Number of Stations

Rank	Owner	Number of Stations
1.	Paxson Communications	72
2.	Viacom (CBS, UPN)	34
3.	News Corp. (Fox Broadcasting)	31
4.	Sinclair Broadcast Group	28
5.	A. H. Belo	22
6.	Tribune Co.	20
7.	Gannett	20
8.	General Electric (NBC Inc.)	13
9.	Cox Communications	11
10.	Disney (ABC)	10

Table 5-6 Top Six Cable TV MSOs in the United States[22]

Rank	Company	Number of Subscribers (millions, 2001)
1.	AT&T Broadband	13.7
2.	AOL Time Warner	12.8
3.	Comcast Corp.	8.5
4.	Charter Communications	7
5.	Cox Communications, Inc.	6
6.	Adelphia Communications	5.4
Total		49.8 million (72 percent of all cable HHs)

In March 2002, Adelphia Communications, the sixth largest cable company, revealed that it had guaranteed billions in bank loans to companies controlled by family members of the founder and former chairman, John Rigas. Further investigations in the ensuing months revealed more questionable financial practices at Adelphia, causing its stock price to fall sharply and the Rigas family members on the board and in executive positions to resign and eventually declare bankruptcy in June 2002.[23] In July 2002 John Rigas, among other family members formerly at Adelphia, was arrested. As of this writing Adelphia's future, even under bankruptcy protection, is uncertain.

Telecommunications Convergence and Competition

The merger that created AT&T Broadband was made possible because of the deregulation of the cable industry and the passage of the Telecommunications Act of 1996, which, among other things, expanded competitive alternatives in the communications industries. Cable TV is now permitted to offer telephone and Internet services, which are being introduced via a number of cable modem services, such as AOL Time Warner's Road Runner cable service and Comcast. AT&T Broadband provides local, long distance, wireless, and international communications, cable television, dial-up, and high-speed Internet access services.

Many interesting questions arise in the convergence of cable TV and telephony. If a consumer uses a cable provider for their telephone service, which rules and regulations apply to them—cable TV regulations or laws created to regulate telephone companies? Why should an e-mail sent by dial-up modem over telephone wires be treated differently from a legal perspective than an e-mail sent by cable modem? Cable and DBS, both of which compete in the digital video and Internet services domains, are regulated to a less stringent standard than broadcasters. Because they do not operate a system of video delivery, the computer industry is not regulated at all with regard to these issues, although they are certainly an increasingly important player in the digital video marketplace.

Consumer issues also arise when primarily media content companies, such as Time Warner, merge with technology or Internet companies, such as AOL. After the merger, business pundits predicted a media environment in which AOL's subscribers would have ready access to the myriad of media content from Time Warner, both through AOL's dial-up service and through the broadband Road Runner service. Others worried that this type of convergence would favor one provider's content over another. However, AOL Time Warner's stock price dropped dramatically through the first half of 2002, there were several high-level executive shake-ups, and some are even wondering if the merger was a wise decision, as the reality is not living up to the promise.

The Future of Television

Regardless of ups and downs among media giants and changes in the telecommunications industry, it is possible to look at some developments in technology and see in a general sense where TV will be headed in the next several years. A look at the future can be divided into three main developments: digital broadcasting, **high-definition television (HDTV),** and **interactive television (ITV).** Some of these already exist in one form or another, and it may be a surprise to find that other "cutting-edge" developments have actually been used with varying degrees of success sometimes more than 30 years ago.

Digital Broadcasting

Digital broadcasting is the terrestrial transmission of digital video and audio to large audiences. Digital broadcasting will take a number of forms. Among the most common will be expanded hybrid systems that combine satellite transmission with terrestrial repeaters that augment signal reception in places where line-of-sight access to the satellite may be limited, such as in mountainous regions or cities with tall buildings, or even in cars where mobility may adversely affect satellite reception.

high-definition television (HDTV)—a new form of television with much higher resolution than standard television, as well as a different screen size ratio.

interactive television (ITV)—television programming that allows viewers to navigate through on-screen programming guides and set reminder times or order products, select parts of a program to view more details, choose camera angles or replays themselves, click on items in the show to purchase, or engage in online discussions with other viewers as part of the program.

Mass Communication Formats

Digital broadcasting not only enables subscription and on-demand services that can be free of advertising but new services as well, such as interactive, voice-command features, data distribution, Web access, and more. Regardless of these or other changes, the largely commercial nature of broadcasting and cable is likely to remain unchanged. Public service broadcasting will continue, but whether it grows or shrinks may depend as much on viewer contributions as government subsidies.

The Change from Analog to Digital

The passage of the 1996 Telecommunications Act served as a catalyst for the national rollout of digital television. Among its many rules and requirements, the Act mandates that all television broadcasters in the United States transmit digital television by 2006. Despite the fact that the FCC provided broadcasters with free extra spectrum, or an extra channel, to accommodate the transition of analog and digital transmission, which broadcasters would then return after the switch to digital transmission is complete, and broadcasters' promises that they would make the switch, it is still not clear that the 2006 deadline will be met. Broadcasters cite three main reasons that the switch to digital broadcasting may be delayed:

1. the expense—as much as $20 million—to convert a station to digital transmission;
2. the technical and legal difficulties in some markets of erecting digital transmission towers; and
3. the need for the public to purchase digital television sets or DTV tuners—currently less than 10 percent of TV sets sold are digital or have digital tuners.

As of April 17, 2001, just 187 commercial television stations (about 15 percent of all stations, including 29 noncommercial public television stations) in 64 U.S. markets, mostly the top or largest markets, were broadcasting in digital format terrestrially, reaching about 68 percent of the U.S. population.

The data rate of a DTV signal in the 6 MHz broadcast television channel is 19.44 Mbps (megabits per second), but whether stations will opt to use up their bandwidth quickly by broadcasting high-quality video or to multicast lower-quality bandwidth and offer more programming channels is unclear. There is a strong short-term economic incentive for broadcasters to multicast standard quality video with minimum or no interactive capabilities because they can program for niche audiences by including more channels in the same amount of spectrum (six standard-definition channels can be compressed into the bandwidth for one high-definition channel) and potentially increase revenues substantially. However, there is a compelling public interest incentive in producing high-quality video with interactive features similar to what is available on the Internet, although any financial gain from this model is seen as longer term. Some broadcasters in 2000 announced plans to use a portion of the digital spectrum to deliver Internet or Web content.

A consortium including Cox Enterprises, Inc.; Gannett Company, Inc.; Lee Enterprises; The McGraw-Hill Companies, Inc.; Media General, Inc.; Meredith Corporation; The New York Times Company; and Northwest Broadcasting formed an initiative called iBlast in March 2000 to deliver broadband and other

Internet content to potentially millions of home Internet users). As of January 2001, some 246 stations, covering 93 percent of U.S. households, had signed agreements to deliver Internet and other digital content to local audiences via the stations' local terrestrial digital spectrum.

Digital TV and the Future of Public Interest in Broadcasting

One of the major controversies that never was is the failure to auction digital spectrum or otherwise charge broadcasters for the use of the public airwaves, at least in the United States. As former NBC News President Lawrence K. Grossman writes, "To go digital, the nation's broadcasting companies persuaded Congress to give them an estimated $70 billion worth of publicly owned airwaves free of charge, pulling off one of the biggest corporate financial coups of the century."[24] The U.S. government could have raised billions of dollars through an auction of the airwaves or by the installation of a license fee, but because of the strength of the broadcasting industries lobbying and the size of its financial contributions to elected officials, this didn't happen. Moreover, the issue never was reported to any great extent in the media because of the media's inadequate ability to report about itself.

Revealing the nature of the political process in this regard, a presidentially appointed committee called the "Advisory Committee on Protecting the Financial Interest of Digital Television Broadcasters" issued at the end of 1998 a report titled "Charting the Digital Broadcasting Future." The only place "news" was mentioned in the report was in the appendix. There was a time when news was considered central to every aspect of the television landscape, business and otherwise, especially for the public interest.

Although the majority of the 22 members of the Advisory Committee were not from the broadcast industry, those from the industry "played hardball," Grossman, who was on the committee, said. "[They] threatened to walk out if we voted to recommend, as most of us wanted to, that digital TV be given major and specific public interest obligations." Even the White House was surprised by how weak the public interest recommendations of the committee turned out to be.

HDTV

In 1973, Japanese engineers at NHK began development of high-definition television (HDTV), called Hi-vision, in analog format. It is a form of television with much higher resolution than standard television, as well as other differences. There have been disagreements over the years on adopting a worldwide HDTV standard, as both the United States and Europe developed their own types of HDTV so they would not be dependent on the Japanese-developed HDTV. Although Japan has largely stood by its analog format, the development of digital HDTV formats and adoption of digital TV has made the issue of adopting a worldwide standard even more complex.

Interactive TV

The remote control notwithstanding, interactivity has been slow to develop in the TV medium, largely because the traditional broadcast medium does not allow for direct viewer input in the programs viewers receive. The first regularly scheduled

High-definition
television.

television show that encouraged interactivity was called *Winky-Dink and You*, and was produced for CBS in 1953.[25] It was interactive by inviting children to help Winky-Dink escape from situations such as being chased by wild animals by drawing things like a bridge over a yawning chasm on a piece of wax paper placed on the screen. The show was short-lived, partly because children frequently failed to put the wax paper on the screen before drawing the bridges, rope, ladder, or whatever else Winky-Dink needed and drew directly on the screen.

Weblink:
Winky-Dink and You Kit
[www.tvparty.com/requested2
.html]

QUBE

Among the most important experiments in interactive TV was Warner Amex's QUBE experiment, the first two-way cable TV system, launched in 1978 in Columbus, Ohio. The interactive video system permitted viewers in their homes to participate in public opinion polls by punching buttons on a device. Warner concluded the experiment in 1984 after winning the local cable franchise and deeming it no longer necessary to continue an expensive showcase experiment to demonstrate their superiority over competing cable companies. Although many called QUBE a failure, in fact it could be seen as a success in that it pioneered the use of true interactivity through television and demonstrated how the public could become engaged in public issues through a previously passive medium such as TV.

ITV Today

A trial of ITV in the early 1990s by Time Warner in Orlando, Florida, called the Full Service Network, collapsed under its own weight because of high costs and the creation of the World Wide Web.

After initial enthusiasm for ITV and glowing promises of how it would transform the audience experience, the cable and ITV industries have toned down their rhetoric markedly in the collapse of the dot-com boom of the early twenty-first century. Already burdened with high technology expenditures for the past several years as they try to establish themselves, many companies—including Microsoft's WebTV—have scaled back or dropped plans to develop ITV capabilities until they feel they can recoup their investments. WebTV is a product owned by Microsoft that permits a TV set to connect to the Web, browsing Web pages and sending and receiving e-mail. It is in about 800,000 U.S. households.

A related form of interactive TV known as enhanced TV (i.e., customized Web content synchronized to on-air TV programming, offered by ABC and others), which similarly links Web pages to TV content, is increasingly entering homes via the Internet, although the number of enhanced TV users is still small. ICTV is another interactive TV provider with similar, though proprietary, video-on-demand capabilities and is in about 100,000 U.S. households.

Even with setbacks in the development of ITV, there is no doubt that interactivity will enhance the television-viewing experience and give the public more control over the media they watch. The growing numbers of people who simultaneously use the Internet while they watch television, checking program Web sites, looking up information about the show, entering show contests, participating in game show quizzes, or engaging in online chats with other viewers, are all examples of what interactive TV could bring to viewers in a seamless converged media environment.

S U M M A R Y

The recording industry has long been affected by new technologies that have created ways to make better recordings and more easily distribute music to the public. Business models and large record labels built around the production, marketing, and distribution of music on items like albums or CDs are currently being threatened by online digital media. The ease of copying and distributing digital music among fans through peer-to-peer networks threatens the business model of the recording industry and has brought about several lawsuits over copyright issues and royalty payments.

Radio and television are the most ubiquitous mass media in the United States and around the world and are important vehicles for news and entertainment. Radio and television were created in a series of stages, with inventions and improvements building upon one another by a number of inventors to develop the systems we know today.

Broadcast stations in the United States are officially licensed to serve in the public interest, and the Public Broadcasting Service (PBS) offers a complement to the commercial sector. Yet, both radio and television programming forms tend to be most shaped by commercial forces and often pander to the lowest common denominator to appeal to the widest possible audience and draw the greatest number of advertising dollars.

The growth of cable and satellite media has produced channel proliferation and audience fragmentation and a corresponding increased specialization in programming, much as happened to radio and magazines a generation earlier. This has weakened the stranglehold the big three networks—CBS, NBC, and ABC—had on programming even though they still have great power. The digitization of both radio and television promises even more change ahead, primarily in the areas of digital broadcasting, high-definition television, and interactive television.

Discussion Questions

1. The public appetite for recorded music is great, but especially so among teenagers. Why is this?
2. In what ways has MTV and the music video influenced the recording arts industry and popular music?
3. What suggestions would you make to a record label executive regarding creating a successful business model for the label in the digital age?
4. If you had to choose between only public radio or television versus commercial radio or television, which would you choose, and why?
5. Many people are credited with contributing to the invention of radio. Whose contributions do you feel were most important, and why?
6. Discuss the newly created legal issues surrounding cable companies' provision of telephone services and competition with telecommunication companies. How might these issues be resolved?
7. If you had a choice of receiving high-definition TV or standard-quality TV that was interactive, which would you choose? Why?
8. The traditional commercial television networks have seen their audience share decline dramatically since the 1970s. What factors have contributed to their decline? Is the decline likely to continue?

Digital Media: Online and Ubiquitous

The still frames from an early Lumiere film, *Man Hammering Wall*, may seem an unlikely example to use when talking about digital media. However, when one considers the size and resolution of the images there is a striking parallel to early video on the Internet. With tiny video screens on computer monitors, poor resolution and the jerky motions of streaming video that too often freeze completely, many today ask why anyone would want to watch television over the Internet. They conclude that online video has no future.

But consider further parallels between early film and online video. Lumiere asked himself much the same question about films such as *Man Hammering Wall:* How long would people be willing to pay to see something they could see every day? His question was valid only as long as that was what filmmakers confined themselves to filming

and as long as the technology never improved—both of which of course turned out to be false assumptions. He did not see that technology would improve the images and that filmmakers would use human imagination to portray stories previously only dreamed of.

The same considerations can be applied to online digital media today. If technology freezes at its current level, then the naysayers are probably correct—online video and multimedia likely do not have a future. But a more important point to consider, and perhaps the most important lesson to be learned from this chapter and even from this book, is that digital media do not have to be simply the same old media delivered digitally. With creativity and imagination, they can be much, much more.

Prologue

It should be clear by now that digital media are not simply improvements on or enhancements of other forms of media in the same way that broadcast television could be thought of as "radio with moving images," for example. Changes in media brought about by digitization and the Internet are much more fundamental and transformative.

Yet ironically many of these fundamental changes will not be immediately apparent to the average media consumer. People will still watch movies and television; will still read books, magazines, and newspapers; and will still want to listen to music. For many people it will not matter that a song was created, produced, and even distributed digitally. But as we have seen in previous chapters and will see in the next section, digitization of media alters and threatens existing media business models, creates new opportunities for media content creators, and causes shifts in how media consumers access, use, and interact with media.

A useful analogy in comparing the state of digital and analog media today is to picture an iceberg floating in the ocean (see Figure 6-1). Just as only a small percentage of the whole iceberg is visible above the water, in today's media world the primarily analog media products we see, such as books or videotapes, are only a small part of the overall media creation process. Most mass media today already utilize digitization in some way, even if the final product is still predominantly analog. But this will change over time as consumers get more of their media content digitally.

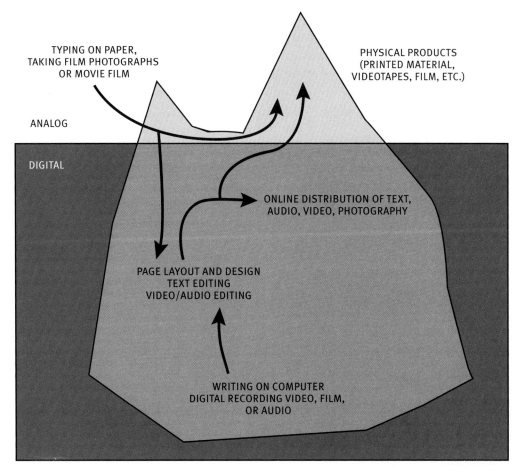

ANALOG

DIGITAL

TYPING ON PAPER, TAKING FILM PHOTOGRAPHS OR MOVIE FILM

PHYSICAL PRODUCTS (PRINTED MATERIAL, VIDEOTAPES, FILM, ETC.)

ONLINE DISTRIBUTION OF TEXT, AUDIO, VIDEO, PHOTOGRAPHY

PAGE LAYOUT AND DESIGN TEXT EDITING VIDEO/AUDIO EDITING

WRITING ON COMPUTER DIGITAL RECORDING VIDEO, FILM, OR AUDIO

■ **Figure 6-1 Media iceberg**
Digitization of media can be seen as a floating iceberg, with analog products as an increasingly small part of the media production and distribution process.

Four key concepts of digital media discussed in Chapter 1—**multimedia, interactivity, automation,** and their ethereal quality—are worth reviewing briefly here:

- *Multimedia:* Combining video, audio, and text is not unique to digital media— everyday television is just such an example of multimedia—but digital media allow for easier creation of multimedia than in analog media and provide for greater opportunities in fully integrating media types to complement each of their strengths.
- *Interactivity:* The ability to interact with media content and obtain unique, personalized, or localized information is a powerful force in changing how the public uses and perceives media. It greatly shifts the balance of power from passive media consumers to active media consumers and creators.
- *Automation:* By creating various programs and automated functions such as search tools, **collaborative filtering** (automatically determining likely interests based on previously viewed or purchased material and comparing that to what others who have purchased the same material also bought or viewed), and updating content, computers greatly reduce the amount of work humans must do and, increasingly, can supplant some human roles in the media production workflow process.
- *Ethereal quality:* Digital media are not actually physical products, like books, photographs or CDs, although they usually are eventually represented in some kind of physical product.

But even as far-reaching as these elements are in changing the media landscape, they are still incomplete without one important element: a network that connects computers or media devices to each other so they can communicate. There are many kinds of networks, but we will concentrate primarily on the Internet and the World Wide Web. Because all data that pass through the various networks—telephone, cable, or satellite—are at one or more stages digital, we will use the term "digital media" to mean not only digital but networked, or online, media as well.

Out of all modern media, the Internet/World Wide Web reached 50 percent of U.S. households faster than any other media technology. As of June 2002, Nielsen Netratings show that 58 percent of U.S. households, or 166 million persons, went onto the Web.[1] It is important to note here, however, that the Internet is more complex in its requirements for adoption than all other media. One can't simply go out and "buy an Internet" as one could for most other media, such as radio or TV. Instead, one must first have a computer and a means of connecting it to the Internet, plus a higher level of technical media literacy to use the computer than is required for a television or even VCR (see Table 6-1).

What Is Online Communication?

The broader topic of online communications, of which the Internet is a vital part, must be clarified. Although many may consider the term *online* as synonymous with the Internet, *online* is in fact a term with a larger meaning. *Online* refers to

multimedia—a combination of different types of media in one package; thus film or video with sound is a type of multimedia because it combines visual and audio elements. Web pages that combine text, video, animation, audio, or graphics are another type of multimedia.

interactivity—although an exact definition is still being debated, for digital media purposes interactivity can be defined as having three main elements: 1) a dialog that occurs between a human and a computer program, 2) a dialog that occurs simultaneously or nearly so, and 3) an audience that has some measure of control over what media content they see and in what order they see it.

automation—a process in which machines or computer programs do the work that was formerly done by humans. In mass communication terms, automation can range from spreadsheet programs that sort data in a variety of ways to Web site search engines and other such programs.

collaborative filtering—a process carried out by software that records a Web site user's viewing or buying patterns and then compares those with similar patterns by other users to determine some likely areas of common interest. Amazon.com is the most famous example of a company using collaborative filtering to help suggest books and products of interest based on previous activity on the site.

Table 6-1 Number of Years to Reach a 50 Percent Penetration of U.S. Households	
Technology/Medium	**Years**
Newspapers	100+
Telephone	70
Phonograph	55
Cable Television	39
Personal Computer	19
Color Television	15
VCR	10
Radio	9
Black & White Television	8
Internet/World Wide Web	7

Sources: John Carey[2]; Electronic Industry Association; U.S. Dept. of Commerce.

the interconnected, networked media that permit the direct, electronic exchange of information, data, and other communications. Everything from local area networks to wide area networks, such as the Internet, are part of the online world. (Local area networks allow communication in limited environments, such as inside an organization.) In other words, the Internet and the World Wide Web are part of the online communications world; they are not the entire online world. However, the Internet and the Web are among the most important parts of the online world for mass communication, because they are where much digital, online media content resides and is available to the public.

Social Implications of Digital, Online Media

Digital media of course plays a role in every communication function that analog media plays, ranging from surveillance to entertainment. Whether democracy and society ultimately will be better served by an Internet-connected society is impossible to say. However, there is no doubt digitization and online media are changing and will continue to change mass communication and the public that receives almost all of its entertainment and information from mass media. Media organizations face many challenges, as have been mentioned in previous chapters, but so do media consumers. Three general trends can be discerned with digital, online media that will affect our interactions with media.

Nonstop Media

A 24/7 media environment is quickly emerging, if not already here. Newspapers have had to create policies so their online versions do not scoop their printed morning edition the next day—as much so they do not tip off their competitors as

Twenty-four-hour news stations such as CNN have made the public used to having media access around the clock.

for not wanting to hurt their own newspaper sales. With cable TV there is of course 24-hour entertainment and news, and the always-on nature of the Internet has taught the public that they can obtain specific media content on demand as long as they are connected to the Internet. Even media that we are accustomed to thinking of as "set" once created, such as magazines or books, can easily be updated at any time if they are distributed in digital form.

A nonstop media environment, although increasing the opportunities for news, information, and entertainment, also has its negative side. With new messages being delivered all the time and a huge choice of media to interact with, it can be very easy to become distracted with flashy entertainment or essentially "drown" in information.

Pervasive Media

The pervasiveness of the media system means that wherever one goes, there is likely to be unprecedented access to mass communication. A new media pioneer who works as a civilian researcher in a naval research lab once remarked that he was leaving for a week's vacation in the Caribbean on an island where there was no Internet, no phone service, and no communication services of any kind. He had to escape. Unfortunately, with today's global satellite communications, it's not possible to truly "escape" anywhere on the planet. In May 1996, climber and guide Rob Hall was trapped high on Mt. Everest for more than a day after a sudden storm hit. Unable to descend and unable to be rescued, he did talk to his pregnant wife in New Zealand by satellite phone, the last communications he made.[3]

Increasingly portable media devices and flat-panel screen technology improvements also mean that we have a growing ability to take our media with us and access it (or have it thrust upon us) in places where we previously did not encounter media. Displays in elevators are one example of how advertisers are using technology to reach a captive audience.

Pervasive mass communication means better access to entertainment, commercial information, and news. Such access means there is at least the potential for a better-functioning democracy, because more information is available. Of course, better access may not come evenly to all or allow everyone to benefit

Portable media devices such as Web-enabled cell phones are part of a growing trend of pervasive media in our lives.

equally from that access. Simply providing more information into the media system may often result in a widening, rather than a narrowing, of the gap in knowledge between those in high and low socioeconomic groups.[4]

Personal Information Space

The convergence of digital media is leading to the development of a **personal information space.** A personal information space is a virtual location assembled and accessed online where an individual keeps data, or information. It is more than just a digital personal library, however. In a personal information space, one can process private voice, fax, and e-mail communications, and create, access, and store Web-based media content, including multimedia, all from any location around the world. No longer is one's personal information space limited by geography, time, or culture. One can access a personal information space when mobile computing and communications devices are connected to global, wired, and wireless telecommunications networks.

Increasingly, the personal information space is being integrated with public information space (i.e., the content generated by media organizations and others). Unfortunately, the personal information space is also subject to various threats and dangers, such as erosion of privacy, computer hackers, or technical failures.

Exploring the Foundations of Online Media

Is computer code protected by the First Amendment? Is a hyperlink a form of free speech, or is it simply a device to take a user elsewhere? Can an Internet Service Provider (ISP) such as Earthlink be sued if one of its members conducts illegal activities through its network, such as selling child pornography or distributing music that a member does not own the rights to? What if an article online libels a person according to his or her libel laws, but the server for the Web site is located in another country with more liberal libel laws?

personal information space— a virtual "space" online in which a user has stored information about him- or herself, contact information, and material the user may have received from the Internet.

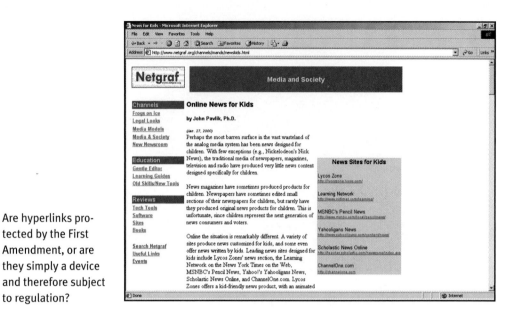

Are hyperlinks protected by the First Amendment, or are they simply a device and therefore subject to regulation?

These examples are all based on actual cases that have been in the news the past few years, and it is guaranteed that there will be more like these. These cases highlight the fact that the convergence of digital technology has blurred the lines in many legal matters that were never an issue in the analog media world. It means that if we are to understand the ripple effects that technology changes have brought to the media world and the ways we use media, then we have to understand at least some basic aspects about digital and online technology.

Why is there a need to understand media technology in order to understand how mass communication affects our lives? It was never necessary to know how a printing press worked to understand if a piece of writing was libelous or was protected by the First Amendment. It is necessary to understand the basic workings of digital and online technology for the same reasons that they are changing mass communication—they create functionalities that no other media has previously been able to do. Hyperlinks are a fairly simple, yet illustrative, example.

Until the creation of **hypertext transfer protocol (HTTP)** in 1991 by Tim Berners-Lee, there was no such thing as hyperlinks except in the imaginations of some researchers. But after it was created and started being used by large numbers of people, new issues began to arise. Although in theory hyperlinks can take the user anywhere else on the Web, in practice many organizations have protested the practice of **deep linking,** or linking to one of the Web site's inside pages, such as a particular story. This is because commercial media sites charge advertising rates based on how many visitors come to their home pages, and deep linking skirts this. On the other hand, it does little use to provide a link with a specific story in mind only to send users to another Web site's homepage and make them find it themselves. But some Web sites compiled links of other Web sites and put them under their own Web address, making it look like the content was theirs.

Another issue has arisen regarding whether a hyperlink is a form of free speech or simply a device that takes a user elsewhere. The answer, according to a federal court in *Universal City Studios* v. *Reimerdes* (2000) is that links are both expressive and functional and could be subject to regulation. The object of contention in this case was a computer program known as DeCSS, which enabled users to effectively copy DVDs. The judge ruled that it was illegal to not only

hypertext transfer protocol (HTTP)—a protocol that enables the standardized transfer of text, audio, and video files, as well as e-mail from one address to another.

deep linking—a hypertext link to another Web site's inside page or pages rather than its homepage.

publish the program on the Web but also, more extraordinarily, to link to any Web site containing the illegal computer code. However, simply writing the Web site address without actually linking to it would be protected as free speech.

In the case of hyperlinks, without an understanding of how they work and what characteristics make them different from traditional media, it is impossible to fully understand how online media are changing the overall media framework economically, legally, and in terms of media use. The same reasoning can be applied to many aspects of online and digital media.

Historical Development of the Internet and World Wide Web

Prior to the era of the Internet, institutions or organizations that had computers had no simple way for the computers to communicate with each other, even if they were connected by a wire, as computers ran machine-specific languages and programs that could not be understood by other computers.

In 1969, the foundations for the Internet were laid when the Defense Advanced Research Projects Agency (DARPA) launched the Advanced Research Projects Agency network, or ARPAnet. ARPAnet was the first national computer network, connecting many universities around the country for advanced, high-speed computing applications and research. It was not yet the Internet, but it was the beginning of online communications. But there was still no "common language," or protocol, that computers could use to easily transmit information via the network.

Creating an Internet Protocol

In 1974, Vinton Cerf, now senior vice president at Microwave Communications Inc. (MCI), and Robert Kahn, now president of the Corporation for National Research Initiatives (CNRI), published their classic article, "A Protocol for Packet Network Intercommunication." In the article, they specified the design of a **transmission control protocol (TCP)** as a part of the main protocol for the Internet and introduced the first use of the term "Internet." Also important to the creation of the Internet was the work of Jonathan Postel, who when a graduate student at UCLA outlined along with Cerf some of the key principles that underlie today's Internet protocols (IP).

Although it is difficult to pin down an exact date when the Internet officially started, in 1982 the Defense Department adopted TCP/IP as the basis for the ARPAnet. Moreover, at this time researchers began defining an "internet" (lower case *i*) as a connected set of networks using TCP/IP, and the "Internet" (upper case *I*) as a set of connected TCP/IP internets.[5]

Creating the World Wide Web

For the first decade of the Internet's existence, its usage was limited largely to researchers. Use of the Internet required knowledge of a variety of arcane commands and terminology. The limited, specialized nature of the Internet underwent a fundamental change in 1991 when Tim Berners-Lee, an MIT researcher

transmission control protocol (TCP)—a method for computers to have a common language to send messages to each other over a network and communicate.

Tim Berners-Lee.

at a physics laboratory in Switzerland, invented the World Wide Web and began to open the use of the Internet to a much wider set of users.

The advent of the Web as a global publishing medium made possible the most fundamental shift in human communication since the advent of the printing press five centuries earlier. The Web enabled easy many-to-many communication over distance and time. In addition, in contrast to traditional media of mass communication, anyone can create and publish on the Web for very little cost or expertise.

The World Wide Web (WWW) is a subset of the Internet and is perhaps best described as a global electronic publishing medium accessed through the Internet. Technically speaking, the Web is made up of an interconnected set of computer servers on the Internet that subscribe to a set of TCP/IP network interface protocols. These technical protocols include assigning to a Web site a Uniform Resource Locator (URL) based on its TCP/IP Internet address, which is the Web site address that Web users are familiar with. URLs include the instructions that are read by a Web browser, a navigational tool to travel the Web.

A Web page is any document, or collection of content, that resides on a Web site. The content can take any form, including text, graphics, photographs, audio, video, or interactive features, such as surveys or discussion forums. A Web site can consist of one page of content or many such pages and can include hyperlinks to other Web sites.

Content on a Web page is tagged, or marked up, using what is known as **hypertext markup language,** or **HTML,** to format the content so it displays correctly on a screen. In addition, each document uses hypertext transfer protocol (HTTP), which enables the standardized transfer of text, audio, and video files, as well as e-mail from one address to another.

Creating Graphical Web Browsers

hypertext markup language (HTML)—the language used to create Web pages and determine how they appear; allows pages to have hypertext links and other interactive features.

Another huge gain in making the Internet accessible to even more people was the creation in 1993 of Mosaic by Marc Andreeson, then at the National Center for SuperComputing Applications (NCSA) at the University of Illinois at Champaign–Urbana. Mosaic, which eventually became Netscape, provided a graphical user interface with the Web that computer users who had Macs or Windows PCs could quickly understand and use. Although GUI browsers Viola and Erwise were also created in 1992, by the end of the year Mosaic was being written about in mainstream media and became the most well-known Web browser.

Media Timeline: Milestones in the Early Development of the Internet

1958		1969		1973	1974
In response to the 1957 Soviet launch of Sputnik, the U.S. Department of Defense established the Defense Advanced	Research Projects Agency (DARPA), whose mission was to develop advanced communications capabilities.	Laying the foundations for the Internet, DARPA launched the Advanced Research Projects Agency network, or ARPAnet, the first	national computer network.	Vinton Cerf and Robert Kahn developed the basic concept and architecture for the Internet.	Cerf and Kahn specified the design of a transmission control protocol (TCP), the basic protocol for the Internet, and coined the term *Internet*

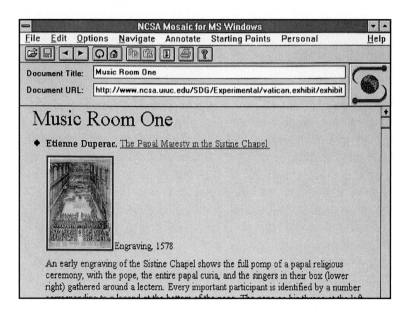

The creation of a graphical Web browser made the Web more accessible to a greater number of people.

Microsoft created their own graphical browser, Internet Explorer (IE), in 1996 to compete with Netscape's browser, then called Netscape Navigator. By offering Internet Explorer free and eventually bundling it with the Windows operating system, IE was able to become the dominant Web browser in only four years, with 75 percent usage compared to Netscape's 25 percent. In 1999 Netscape was bought by AOL, a year before AOL acquired Time Warner.

As any regular Web user can attest, Web sites and text size often look different not only on different browsers but on different versions of the same browser. More advanced functions or codes on Web sites may not show up on earlier browser versions, thus making it difficult for Web designers and content companies to create Web sites that are consistent across the online audience.

Millions of Web Pages

Reflecting the continued dramatic, almost exponential growth of the Web, by 2001 millions of individuals and organizations had published "home pages" on the Web. With the cost barriers to entry in the global publishing arena removed or dramatically lowered, the Web for the first time brought press freedom to virtually

75
searchers
successfully conducted
the first TCP
communication tests
a satellites linking
cations across the
lantic and Pacific
eans.

1991
Tim Berners-Lee
created the World Wide
Web, a global
publishing platform, on
the Internet.

1993
Mark Andreeson and
others created Mosaic,
a browser, or graphical
user interface for the
Web, that permits
anyone to easily
navigate and view
pages on the Web using

a computer mouse and
keyboard. This helped
bring the Web out of the
specialized domain of
scientists and into the
mainstream of media
and the public.

1994
Mosaic
Communications Corp.
(later Netscape) was
formed by Marc
Andreeson and
colleagues who left the
NCSA.

E-mail Is Where It's @

It is easy to forget just how much e-mail has changed the way people communicate. It is usually one of the first things people learn to do when getting on the Internet, and it doesn't take long even for computer novices to get hooked enough to check their e-mail inboxes several times a day. More messages are sent via e-mail now than through the U.S. Postal Service. E-mail combines aspects of casual conversation with the permanence of text, as well as speedy transmission of messages.

"E-mail kind of announced itself," said Ray Tomlinson, the computer engineer who invented e-mail in 1971. After debugging his program and several trials to make sure it worked properly, he sent a message to his coworkers saying they could now communicate with people on other computers. The first e-mail message? According to the *Guinness Book of Records,* it was QWERTYUIOP—the keys on the third row of the keyboard. Tomlinson said that testing and debugging his original program was a process of trial-and-error,

and he actually doesn't remember what the first message was.

Once messages could be moved from one machine to another, Tomlinson had to decide on a symbol that would separate the name of the individual from the machine he or she was working on. He said that the symbol @ ("at") was the obvious choice, as any single letter or number could cause confusion. "As it turns out, @ is the only preposition on the keyboard. I just looked at it and it was there. I didn't even try any others," Tomlinson said.[6]

---

any citizen with access to a computer and a phone line. Of course, more than half the world lack either or both of these, so we're still a long way off from realizing the dream of fully democratic communications. Still, by comparison, only some 45 percent of households in the United States subscribe to a daily newspaper, whereas almost 60 percent of U.S. adults had Internet (and thereby Web) access as of June 2002. In some Scandinavian countries Internet penetration has reached 75 percent. So even traditional mass media aren't by any means necessarily universal relative to the Internet and the Web. Yet, when one considers the fact that only a tiny fraction of the U.S. or world's population has its own printing press, television, or radio station, the Web has dramatically increased the diversity of media voices available. Of course many of these voices are lost in the global cacophony of the Web, but that is a different issue.

Weblink
Last Page of the Internet
[www.1112.net/lastpage.html]

The Internet Today

In its broadest sense, the Internet encompasses virtually all other media, as well as a broad cross-section of human culture, commerce, and creation. Virtually anything one can think of almost certainly exists in some form on the Internet, from information in the Library of Congress to deliberately misleading information created by hate groups or individuals. As distinguished communications scholar Fred Williams once observed, "Going on the Internet is like going through someone else's trash."

The Internet as we know it now is not controlled by any one person or organization. It is a medium of multimodal (i.e., it involves the various senses)

Advertisers are creating larger and more obtrusive ads on Web pages, hoping for better response rates.

content and interactive communications, in particular e-mail, where users (and organizations) send and receive text and increasingly audio, video, photos, graphics, and hyperlinks.

Although much of the content on the Internet is available free to users, there is a growing trend among media and technology companies to start charging consumers, especially after advertising dropped off sharply after the dot-com meltdown in 2000. Content or services that were previously free, such as a given amount of disk space or the ability to check remote e-mail accounts through Web e-mail accounts such as Hotmail, for example, were starting to be offered only to paying consumers. This trend of partially free services or content and payment for what is considered "premium" content can also be seen among media companies online, and it is still too early to tell whether these strategies will be successful in generating revenues. Online media companies are also experimenting with increasingly obtrusive online advertising, such as larger pop-up ad windows or automatic pop-under ads that are changing the look and experience of the Web for users. In the early 1990s there were many debates among users of online discussion groups about whether *any* advertising should even be allowed on the Internet, considering the fact that it was created by using taxpayers' money.

The Nature of Computer Networks: Key Concepts

Networks have long been a fundamental part of mass communication, especially broadcasting. Networks, or systems of interconnected communication vehicles, can take many forms. In broadcasting, networks of affiliated local stations provide a means of distributing shared programming to audiences across large geographic regions, most typically the entire country. Traditionally, these networks have been linked through analog technology. Today's networks are increasingly digital. This offers several advantages in mass communication, most importantly the ability to transmit multiple streams of information, including audio and video content, text, or other types of data.

In addition, computer-based networks permit the distribution of content to be more flexible, so if one route of the network is unavailable, the network can automatically and efficiently reassemble through a different route. Digital networks permit compression of data, which enables a mass communicator to send more information in the same amount of space on the network. Finally, a computer network easily permits downstream and upstream communications (from the source to the receiver, and vice versa), whereas traditional networks were largely one way and relatively expensive.

A **modem** (a foreshortening of **mod**ulate–**dem**odulate) is used to convert the digital information in a computer to analog signals for transmission over a phone or cable TV line and to convert analog signals to digital information for a computer. Modems can also operate wirelessly by converting data into radio signals. Modems were invented in the 1960s, before the days of the personal computer, as a means of letting "dumb terminals" (i.e., electronic machines where users typed information on keyboards) dial into a remote computer. These early modems converted the typed characters into audio tones that were sent over the telephone line and then were converted back on the other end of the line where they were received by the computer, which processed the information received.

Today's modems operate in a much more efficient and faster fashion. Whereas early modems were hard-pressed to convert and transmit 300 bits per second, today's modems can convert and send millions of bits per second. This allows them to rapidly send or receive not just text but also audio and video.

Bandwidth

Bandwidth is a crucial element for online communication to reach its full potential to be a mass medium. Without what is called high-speed, high-bandwidth, or **broadband** connections to the Internet, most people online are unable to receive audio or video in real time or at the same quality as they are used to from television or radio. **Narrowband** is the term used for low bandwidth communications, such as dial-up phone modems. Bandwidth available for Internet service has traditionally been narrowband via dial-up modems, typically delivering anywhere from 28 kilobits to 56 kilobits per second. Video at these narrowband rates is very limited, usually a small window of jerky motion, of low-resolution imagery and only marginally better sound.

In a technical sense, bandwidth refers to the electromagnetic frequency or spectrum available for delivering content. Bell Labs scientist Claude E. Shannon in 1948 provided a precise mathematical definition of bandwidth, defining the capacity of a communications channel in terms of bits per second. A voice phone call, for example, uses about 3000 hertz (Hz) bandwidth, whereas a telephone modem operating at about 33.6 kilobits per second requires a little more bandwidth, or about 3200 Hz.[7] (See Table 6-2.)

Think of bandwidth not so much as electromagnetic frequency, however, but more in terms of how large a pipe is that comes to your home delivering data rather than a physical thing like water. Someone who is able to tap the large "data pipe" directly can access the flow of data at equally high speeds. Sometimes this is called a

modem—derived from the terms **mod**ulate–**dem**odulate; a device that converts digital signals from a computer to analog signals for transmission over a phone line, as well as analog signals being transmitted to digital signals.

broadband—a network connection that allows for a large amount of bandwidth to be transmitted, which allows for more information to be sent in a shorter period of time. Although there are no agreed-upon transmission speeds that can define broadband, most experts agree it can include aDSL, DSL, ISDN, cable modem, satellite, and T1 and T3 lines, as well as fiber optic trunk lines.

narrowband—a network connection that does not provide very much bandwidth, thus receiving and sending information more slowly than broadband connections. Dial-up modems and some of the early wireless connection speeds of 56 kHz or under are considered narrowband.

Table 6-2 Connection Speeds to the Internet by Carrier Type

Carrier Technology	Speed*	Physical Medium
Dial-up Access	2400 bps to 56 Kbps	Twisted pair (regular phone lines)
ISDN	64 Kbps to 128 Kbps	Twisted pair
Cable	52 Kbps to 512 Kbps	Coaxial cable
ADSL	512 Kbps to 8 Mbps	Twisted pair (used as a digital, broadband medium)
Wireless (LMCS)	2 Mbps or more	Airwaves
Satellite	400 Kbps	Airwaves
T1	1.544 Mbps	Twisted pair, coaxial cable, or optical fiber
T3	44.736 Mbps	Optical fiber

Source: Internet Connection Speed Comparison Chart
*bps = bits per second; Kbps = kilobits per second; Mbps = megabits per second

"fat pipe." However, if the pipe that accesses the main pipes is very thin, data will come at only a trickle, no matter how fast his or her personal computer is.

As of 2002, the Internet was relatively limited in terms of available bandwidth. It varied depending on how a user connected to the Internet, such as a telephone modem or a cable modem, although a second generation of the Internet known as Internet 2 brought 45,000 times more bandwidth. At that time the Internet 2 was already providing a very high-speed connection among 170 universities. It promises in the future to bring such high-speed connectivity to a broader portion of society.

One of the great challenges that cable and telephone providers have begun to solve in the past decade is the so-called "last mile" obstacle (not always literally the last mile, but somewhere from a few hundred yards to more than a mile or so). For more than a decade, many cable and telephone companies have had considerable bandwidth available in their backbone or trunk lines but have run into a problem connecting these broadband facilities over the "last mile" to the end consumer. The cost of making these final connections has been prohibitive. But as the cost of the technology has fallen and various technological innovations have occurred, it has become increasingly feasible to provide the last-mile connections. When this is completed, it means that consumers will have the same broadband access that currently only large organizations have.

Telephone and Cable Company Broadband Services

In the world of telephony, development of the digital subscriber line (DSL) has made it possible to use standard telephone wire, the twisted-pair copper wire in most homes, to provide relatively low-cost broadband capabilities in the home. Other emerging network technologies, such as aDSL (asymmetric DSL, which means high-speed downstream, much slower upstream), are also being deployed by the phone companies.

Telephone companies have lagged somewhat behind in their delivery of high-speed Internet and broadband digital video services to the home, with DSL available in only a handful of markets. Many customers have complained bitterly about

Although most of the United States has high-speed fiber optic lines, wiring individual homes directly to the trunk lines, the so-called "last-mile" has been prohibitively expensive.

late or no installation, technical troubles with little customer support, and lack of communication between the telephone companies and the Internet Service Providers (ISPs) that have hampered easy installation of DSL services (see Table 6-3).

In the cable TV world, the cable modem and the set-top box have made it practical for many cable systems to begin rolling out digital cable services that not only provide digital TV program services to the home but also permit high-speed Internet access and telephone service. Broadband content delivery via already existing coaxial cable systems mean that cable modems are roughly 174 times faster than 56k modems.[8]

One problem of the cable modem is that the network is not switched; the network bandwidth is shared by the users within each local geographic area, or node. In other words, the more users on a given cable modem node, the slower the network becomes. Cable companies can put fewer users on nodes by increasing the number of nodes, but this of course increases their costs. TCI has already indicated that movies on demand or video on demand will be limited in its cable modem service to about 15 minutes in duration.

Bandwidth Changing Consumer Patterns

Bandwidth availability is gradually increasing as low-cost bandwidth rolls out nationwide in the first years of the twenty-first century and low-cost digital consumer access devices enter the marketplace. The importance of broadband capability to usage patterns on the Internet may be profound.[9] Research shows that Internet users with broadband access already have substantially different behaviors than when they used dial-up connections. One trend that has been noted is that they are more likely to create and distribute media content than dial-up users. Online expenditures more than double for users of broadband services. David Clark says that broadband Internet could bring "Real-time high-fidelity music, telephone, videoconferencing, television and radio programs. . . . There will be new entertainment options, such as movies-on-demand, and new features, such as the ability to call up information about a movie's director or its actors as they appear on screen. Users will be able to play online games—live—against many contestants scattered around the globe."[10] Of course, the data on

Year	Cable Modem	Digital Subscriber Line	Satellite	Fixed Wireless	Total
2001	5.5	2.5	.3	.2	8.5
2002 (estimated)	7.9	4.4	.5	.4	13.2
2005 (estimated)	13.8	11.8	1.4	1.8	28.8

Table 6-3 Broadband Internet Delivery in the United States (in millions of homes)

Source: John Carey, "The First 100 Feet for Households: Consumer Adoption Patterns," paper presented to "The First 100 Feet: Options for Internet and Broadband Access" conference by The Freedom Forum in Arlington, Va. (October 29–30, 1996). Retrieved 20 June 2002, from http://www.ksg.harvard.edu/iip/doeconf/carey.html.

Playing video games with others connected on a broadband network is just one example of changes broadband Internet access can bring.

high-bandwidth users are hard to interpret, because those who have access to broadband capabilities in 2002 are, in general, what are called "early adopters." They tend to have more income, are more educated, and are likely to be two-parent households. They are different by nature than the late adopters, and it may be in part these differences that account for the differences in how they connect to the Internet.

The World of Online Media

In a sense, talking about online mass communication means talking about all of mass communication. Today, countless offline mass communication products, whether print or electronic, also exist in some form online, whether for free or fee. The *American Journalism Review* counts 4925 online newspaper sites, and all of the top-50 magazines by circulation have Web sites, as do thousands of specialized periodicals. Some use their Web sites mainly to showcase their printed material, but others publish original material online as well.

As bandwidth increases, most television stations will place more of their content online, just as an increasing number of radio stations do already. Similarly, more of the cinema and recording arts will become available online as connectivity and bandwidth continue to increase.

Many mass communication sites originally created solely online are also available, from one-person operations to major endeavors by large companies such as Microsoft in their creation of the online magazine *Slate*. Even companies not traditionally involved with mass communication have found that maintaining their own Web sites is an excellent way to communicate directly to a large audience.

The following discussion describes both the current state of and emerging trends in online mass communication and digital media beyond what was touched upon in earlier chapters with the various types of traditional media.

Media Future: Wireless Broadband Advances on the Horizon

Wireless broadband services are on the horizon in what is sometimes referred to as the third generation of wireless technology (3G). The first generation was analog cellular, and the second generation was digital. At its most basic, 3G wireless involves using digital technology to send voice, video, and other data signals over very high radio frequencies. The benefit? Information is sent at fiber-optic speeds while maintaining security and communications clarity. It works by installing small antennae throughout communities and on towers in the countryside.

There are many social implications that go with a wireless broadband world, including issues of privacy, who controls what information is released publicly about individuals, identity theft, and changing social behaviors because of the ability to communicate instantly with different groups of people who are also mobile. Already changes in social dynamics are being seen in countries like Finland and Japan, where a practice called "swarming" has begun. This is when loose-knit groups of people communicating wirelessly in real time through text messaging or via mobile phones make changing plans to meet at a restaurant, coffee shop, or bar. Swarming behavior can also occur through wireless networks when someone sends a message about the sighting of a famous person at a nearby restaurant; others in the neighborhood then quickly converge on the spot to see the celebrity.

Business owners see great potential in targeting advertisements using wireless broadband networks. Limited-time offers based not only on a person's demographics, but also on his or her geographics (i.e., proximity to a certain shop) could flash on screens and be the electronic equivalent of impulse-buy items. Just how much personal data a person is sending out through her or his wireless devices is one of the important issues that will arise as wireless broadband services become more widespread. Some people may feel their privacy is being invaded when their PDA flashes a screen advertising their favorite coffee at the nearest coffee shop (information having been gathered from the store's database, based on recent purchases), while others may welcome a chance of a 20 percent discount at the store they see a block away.

Online Books

Digital books offer a variety of advantages over printed books, including permitting the reader not only to read the text but to make electronic annotations and bookmarks, access the content of the book via an interactive table of contents, and keyword search the entire text. Digital books and their sale online also point to a fundamental issue in the future of how mass communication industries will derive much if not most of their revenue: from online transactions, or what is called e-commerce.

Digital books allow readers to electronically annotate text, make bookmarks, and do keyword searches, among other useful functions. Screen clarity can still be an issue for the public, however, as reading text by computer screen for long periods can tire the eyes.

Although few people still may want to read a book on a standard computer screen, the Internet has brought a growing number of books online and made them available universally. Much of the content of these online books may be most valuable as a research tool, but many may also find them a potentially viable way to read for pleasure. Segments of a book can be printed out, for example, saving weight and space when traveling, and as computer screen technology gets better and creates sharper images, reading on-screen will not be as tiring as it can be today.

In the late 1990s, major publishers prepared for a growing surge in consumer demand for electronic books, and many experimented with the online sale and distribution of digital books. However, after the economic slowdown in 2000, which hit technology and Internet companies particularly hard, and a subsequent slowdown in sales of digital books, publishers started to adopt a slower, more cautious approach.

However, many believe that just as young people powered the paperback revolution, the young are showing a voracious appetite for digital books. Dennis Dillon, a librarian at the University of Texas, was initially surprised at the popularity of electronic books.

"No one was sure whether anyone was going to read any digital books," said Dillon, the university's head of collections and information resources. "We were somewhat skeptical." After minimal promotion of the University of Texas's newly purchased electronic books, with titles from *Euthanasia: A Reference Handbook* to *From Barbie to Mortal Kombat: Gender and Computer Games*, they are suddenly the most popular titles in the library. "Usually a book has a one-third chance of being checked out. So to have some titles checked out 25 times in two months— that's shocking."[11]

Some of the leading online book publishers and distributors conduct their business exclusively online. Among the leaders are netLibrary, peanutpress, 1stBooks and Xlibris. NetLibrary and peanutpress sell and distribute exclusively digital books online. They carry large numbers of titles, ranging from books published by university presses to trade books. Xlibris and 1stBooks are print-on-demand (POD) publishers who specialize in helping authors publish their own books, but they also offer digital books for online distribution.

Weblink

netLibrary
[www.netlibrary.com]

peanutpress
[www.peanutpress.com]

1stBooks
[www.1stbooks.com]

Xlibris
[www.xlibris.com]

Online Newspapers

Newspapers are among the leading providers of online news. Almost half of the top-20 news sites were newspaper Web sites in August 2002, including NYTimes.com, Washingtonpost.com, Gannet Newspapers and Newspaper Division, and Hearst Newspaper Digital.[12] One notable difference between the online and offline worlds, however, is that these "newspaper" sites are in direct competition with the leading national "broadcast" and "cable" television news sites, including the top news site since the terrorist attacks on September 11, 2001, CNN.com, second-place MSNBC.com, and fifth-place ABC.com.

Online newspaper sites also face direct competition on a number of other fronts in the online arena, including to some degree the general public, who can put online eyewitness accounts of events. Matt Drudge's site was ranked twentieth in August 2002 of top news sites. News services such as AP or Reuters offer their breaking news content online on news aggregator/portal sites such as Yahoo! News, which was in third place. Newspaper Web sites have the potential to take back some of the ground in breaking news coverage that they lost to television, but this can create an odd situation of a newspaper Web site "scooping" its more established print version, which comes out on a set schedule.

The competition online newspapers face with cable and broadcast television news channels shows in part the complexity of the online mass communication world. For example, there is nothing stopping a newspaper from training some of their journalists to shoot and edit video footage, which could then be webcast on the newspaper's site. The same could apply to audio recording. This is exactly what some newspapers have been doing, such as the Tribune Company, whose flagship newspaper the *Chicago Tribune* and flagship television station WGN are part of a converged news operation providing considerable quality online video news.

Advertising is another big area in which newspaper companies are threatened by the Internet, especially classified ads. Classified ads make up a large portion of advertising revenues for most newspapers, but online classified ads aggregators can allow people to search far more ads than are usually covered in a newspaper's circulation area. If a consumer wants to look for an item in a region that is covered by four or five different newspapers, there is no reason for that person to go to each newspaper's Web site to look at classifieds when he or she can see them all on one Web site. Likewise, a consumer can visit an online auction site like eBay and reach a nationwide group of potential sellers or buyers.

Online Magazines

Despite the low bandwidth requirements for online text, online magazines have not been very successful to date. There are very few purely online magazines,

Media Timeline: Selected Milestones in the Development of Online Media Content

1982
Eleven U.S. newspapers began daily electronic versions via Compuserve, which then had 10,000 subscribers.

1985
Stewart Brand and Larry Brilliant founded the Whole Earth 'Lectronic Link (WELL), the first significant online community.

1990
The Albuquerque Tribune launched the first PC-based electronic newspaper system, *The Electronic Trib.*

January 19, 1994
The Palo Alto Weekly in California became the first newspaper to publish regularly on the Web.

1996
The New York Times launched its Web site, as did many other major newspapers (e.g, *The Wall Street Journal, Chicago Tribune, The Washington Post*).

1997
Streaming audio and video were delivered via the Internet on a regular basis.

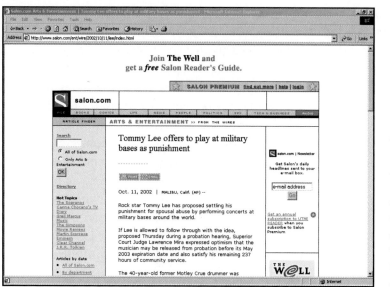

Online magazines have had difficulty attracting readers, but better screen resolutions and more portable devices may overcome the reluctance some people have to reading online.

Slate.com and *Salon.com* being two of the most prominent ones, but even these two online magazines have not been profitable despite publishing articles from world-class writers. Print-based magazines have done little original online content, preferring to use online versions of their magazines mainly for promoting print stories or archiving past issues.

There are several likely reasons that online magazines have fared poorly, despite the apparent benefits the online world would seem to bring to magazines and long-form nonfiction writing in particular because of the lack of space limitations. One of the main reasons is technological; reading long blocks of text on computer monitors becomes tiresome because the resolution of computer monitors has not reached the same quality as text on a printed page. Even once computer monitors do achieve higher resolutions, there is still the issue of portability. In other words, unless monitors can compete with a printed magazine in terms of clarity and portability (and to some extent disposability), there is likely to be a barrier among people in reading anything of any length in a digital format. This of course is not unique to magazines, as digital books and newspapers face the same issues. E-ink or some other digital form of paper may solve this problem, but this will not reach consumers for a few years yet.

1998
Online gossip columnist Matt Drudge broke the Clinton–Lewinsky scandal via his Web site, *The Drudge Report.*

1999
ABC Television began the first regularly scheduled network-sponsored live Internet news program featuring one of its top correspondents.

September 26, 1999
NFL.com became the first major sports league to use the Internet to transmit video of its in-progress regular season games.

2001
With 55 million unique visitors to the entire site each month, Yahoo! became the number-one destination on the entire World Wide Web.

2001
WSJ.com had over 500,000 paid subscribers, making it the second largest paid news and information site on the Web (*Consumer Reports Online* had 600,000.)

Changing behavior among the public in how they consume media is another factor weighing against long-form, text-based narratives like those found in *The New Yorker* or *The Atlantic Monthly*. With greater competition for their attention during the day, the public seems less willing to spend the time necessary to read long articles. In an online environment, readers are also more likely to click on hyperlinks to get more information rather than wait for the author to fully explain a point. Likewise, an article may be a starting point for a much more robust discussion among Web users in the form of online discussion groups.

However, there could be an important niche for magazines to provide a measure of distance and perspective on issues and to thereby be a voice of authority in their specialized area. If a magazine is perceived as having suitable authority and is respected highly enough by its readers, it seems that the public is willing to pay for online subscriptions. *Consumer Reports Online* is one of the few success stories in the online magazine world, with over 580,000 subscribers who can access archived articles and reviews on various products.

Online Music

The MP3 file format represents an interesting example to illustrate how the new networked digital marketplace works. It's indicative how the recording industry is likely to sell much of its music in the future. The $5 billion recording industry is faced with a dramatic shift as users embrace digital audio and all the flexibility and power it affords them.

The MP3 file format is used to compress near-CD-quality audio of music, which then lets the files, which generally range between 2 and 4 MB in size, be distributed easily over the Internet. There is nothing inherently illegal in the MP3 file format itself; it is simply the technology used to compress audio files. The problems with the recording industry arise because consumers can copy, download, and distribute music largely for free through file-swapping services such as KaZaA. The recording industry has long held that it is acceptable for an individual who purchases an album, cassette, or CD to make a copy for personal use, and it is of course not uncommon for friends to exchange copies of music among themselves. File-sharing of online music takes these exchanges to completely new levels, however. At any given time during the day, it is not unusual for 1.8 million users to be on a service such as KaZaA, exchanging close to 300 million files. These are not simply audio, of course, and can include video, text, and images as well, but it would be safe to say most of the files being shared are music files.

KaZaA, Morpheus, Grokster, the now-defunct Napster, and many other online peer-to-peer file sharing systems have been at the core of this phenomenon. The issues surrounding peer-to-peer networking, especially regarding the lawsuits against Napster and its subsequent demise, as well as the public sharing music online, are discussed in Chapter 9.

For now, suffice it to say that the major labels and everyone else in the recording industry value chain are enormously threatened by this development. They lose significant control and, they say, their profits and investments are being reduced along with the piracy of their intellectual property. In 2001, the major record labels finally began getting into the online music business themselves even as they maintained their lawsuits against file-swapping services.

Media Spotlight: Project Gutenberg: Reading the Classics Online

One of the most impressive collections of online books has been created by Project Gutenberg, with more than 3000 books from the public domain available digitally free via the Internet. In fact, many classic texts required for college English literature and other classes are in the public domain and available for free at this site, so students interested in cutting costs on required books might look online for considerable savings.

Project Gutenberg was started in 1971 by Michael Hart. There are three main categories of books in etext form; "light" literature such as *Alice in Wonderland* or *Peter Pan,* "heavy" literature such as *Moby Dick* or *Paradise Lost,* and reference works such as encyclopedias and almanacs. Etexts are downloadable as plain text files or zipped files, which makes them viewable on the widest number of computer platforms and also makes the text easily searchable with a word processing program. Because of copyright restrictions, they usually do not have books published after 1923. Books are submitted by volunteers, who scan or type in the public domain works and submit them to Project Gutenberg.

W

Weblink
Project Gutenberg
[promo.net/pg/]

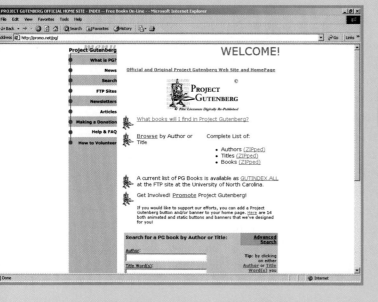

Warner Brothers, BMG, EMI, Arista, Virgin, Jive/Zomba, and others teamed up to launch MusicNet.com, a for-profit online music distribution service. Consumers pay $9.95 a month to RealOne, which uses Real Networks to enable music downloads.

Even as the labels become more involved in digital distribution of their music—belatedly, many would say—other industries within the current music distribution industry will also be faced with drastic changes, such as those in the plastics industry, distributors, and retailers.

Finding new songs and artists that you may like may become more difficult than ever in the digital age. As production and distribution costs decrease, more people can create their own professional-sounding (although not necessarily good) recordings and distribute them digitally. One solution that is emerging is the use of intelligent agent-based collaborative filtering, a sort of music club for the digital age. Amazon.com and other e-commerce organizations already are making use of collaborative filtering to alert their customers to new books and music that they would be likely to find appealing, based on previous purchases and the purchasing patterns of people with similar buying tastes.

The music industry is trying to find ways to negate the threat digital media have on their business model and profits.

Online Radio

Music is one of the most popular forms of online entertainment. Thousands of radio stations offer live webcasts of their regular over-the-air transmissions, although there are unsettled issues regarding royalty payments for webcasts of recorded music. In 2002, the U.S. Copyright Office decided that webcasters must pay 70 cents per song heard by 1000 listeners, half of what a government panel recommended they pay in a decision in February 2000 but still less than what the recording industry was asking. Webcasters also have to pay royalties retroactively from 1998, and many of them said the rates and retroactive payments would cost them hundreds of thousands of dollars and force them to shut down. Traditional radio stations are exempt from this new royalty payment method, successfully arguing in 1998 that they are helping promote the music.

The term *radio* is itself somewhat meaningless in an online digital world in which music is not broadcast over the air but retrieved by users on demand over the Internet. In that way, online "radio" is technically audio programming, and in some ways will seem much closer to the current state of on-demand online music downloads, even though the term *radio* may stay with us or change its meaning.

Regardless of the technical approach, online-only radio stations such as spinner.com are free of many FCC regulations and don't require a license to operate. Moreover, they reach a global audience, and there's no potential for signal interference. As a result, there are hundreds, possibly thousands of online radio stations. Many of these stations operate independently of any broadcast parent, although legislation is being drafted that will bring them under some of the same rules broadcasters face.

Online radio stations must abide by the **Digital Millennium Copyright Act,** however, which prohibits the advance posting of playlists, which would permit users to plan in advance when to copy songs. Even before the 2002 rulings on royalty payments for webcasts, some online radio stations paid royalties to one of the two music licensers in the United States, the American Society of Composers, Authors and Publishers (ASCAP), or Broadcast Music Inc. (BMI).

Live transmissions of sports events have emerged as an important part of online radio. In the case of major league baseball, Internet users must pay a fee ($14.95 in 2002) to listen to live audio webcasts of professional baseball games. Some other professional sports, such as the National Football League (NFL), make the audiocasts of their games available for free online.

One of the challenges of listening to online radio is finding stations that are available. One list with more than 10,000 Internet radio stations from all around the world was created by WMBR-FM at the Massachusetts Institute of Technology. It allows for searches by country or region, call letters, format, or frequency.

Online Film

The Internet has proven a valuable means of distribution for film, especially independent and short films, which have traditionally found distribution to be the most vexing bottleneck in becoming successful. Because independent and short films vary widely in quality and style and are produced outside the mainstream of Hollywood, few theaters, or theater chains, have been interested in showing them. Because of the low cost of online distribution and the potential to

Weblink

Spinner.com
[www.spinner.com]

Weblink

Radio-Locator
[www.radio-locator.com
/cgi-bin/nation]

Digital Millennium Copyright Act (DMCA)—an act of Congress in 1998 that reformed copyright law comprehensively in trying to update copyright laws for the digital age. Key provisions included the circumvention of copyright protection systems, fair use in a digital environment, and Internet service provider (ISP) liability for content sent through their lines.

build audiences over time and space, a growing number of Web sites provide extensive independent and short films online, typically for free viewing.

Two of the leading independent film sites are Indie Films and ifilm. These advertising and e-commerce-supported sites feature hundreds of independent films and film trailers for free viewing. BMW Films is another interesting example of an online film site, in this case funding the production of independent short films—as long as all funded and shown films feature BMW cars. As commercially oriented as this may sound, the films produced have been of very high quality and not too crass in their commercialism. The quality of the online films available on the site, some done by famous directors, have been praised widely by leading independent critics.

Weblink
Indie Films
[indie.hollywood.com/]
ifilm
[www.ifilm.com]
BMW Films
[www.bmwfilms.com/

Online TV and Video

There is a wide variety of sources of video content online. Most television stations and all major networks maintain Web sites. A small but growing number of them provide at least some of their programming via the Web. An even smaller but growing number of these and other programmers provide near-broadcast-quality video programming via the Web, some of it on demand.

One television station that is delivering video programming in real-time or on-demand via the Internet is San Francisco's KRON-TV, the local NBC affiliate. Viewers can go to the station's Web site and select from a variety of news and information options, including stories reported in text, audio, or video format. These various formats help add depth to the stories that video-only formats simply are not able to do because of the need for interesting visuals, sometimes at the expense of exploring related issues to a story.

Weblink
KRON-TV Web site
[www.kron.com]

Costs of Digital TV and Online Video

For established broadcast or cable stations, changing to a digital format that allows them to take full advantage of the capabilities of online video can be expensive. Jim Topping, former general manager of KGO-TV (KRON's ABC-owned competition in San Francisco) and then senior vice president (now retired) at ABC-owned TV stations, notes that the installation of a powerful video server cost KGO-TV $9 million. Other technology to help the station become digital cost another $12 to 14 million. This investment gives KGO-TV the capability of delivering any of its programming at high quality and on-demand via the Internet or other broadband media. However, the investment KGO-TV made is prohibitive for the majority of stations, especially those in smaller markets.

Of course, a $9 million investment is not necessary to start transmitting digital video on the Internet. One small-market station has found a way around the high price tag. In Kingsport, Tennessee, DMA 93, WKPT got a digital signal on air for just $125,000. George DeVault, president of Holston Valley Broadcasting Corp., owner of the ABC-affiliated station, decided to forego HDTV initially and bought and installed a digital system to put a standard definition television signal on air. This low-cost approach is what has opened the door to many independent producers who are now transmitting television-like programming on the Internet.

Public television stations are also converting to digital television. Jerry Butler, senior director for the DTV strategic services group at PBS, reports that as of May 2001, 29 of its member stations were broadcasting digital signals, covering

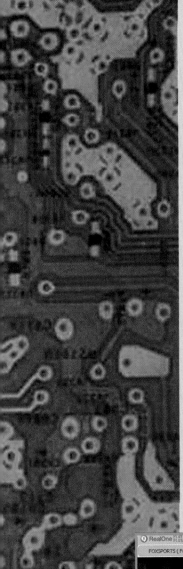

Media **Technology**

Streaming Media

The term *streaming media* refers to a method of delivering audio and video in real time over the Internet either live or on-demand. The quality of streaming media received by the audience depends on several factors, especially how the media content was encoded in the first place (at what level of quality the producer digitized the material, such as the video resolution and frame rate) and the available bandwidth.

For streaming media, a software program known as a codec (compression/decompression) buffers a few seconds of the video, and then the program begins playing on the client's (audience member's) computer, with a few more seconds of material continually being sent via the Internet. In today's network, if there's a great deal of demand on the server or the network, streaming may not always provide an uninterrupted flow of content, thus causing video frames to freeze or become jerky. Most of the video streamed via the Internet today is fairly poor quality. It is often fuzzy, only a few frames per second, and only a few inches in image size, and often breaks up or is interrupted by network congestion. As the network improves, and as consumers get access to more bandwidth, streaming media will continue to improve in quality and reliability.

The main alternative to streaming media is downloading media content (i.e., transferring the entire video file to a hard drive). Downloading files can be very slow, even if the user has a broadband connection, because despite compression that greatly reduces the size of video files, they can be very large, even gigabytes in the case of high-quality feature-length motion pictures.

38 percent of U.S. households. Eight of the digital stations were in the top ten markets, and eleven are in the top twenty markets.

Online Programming

A June 1999 Arbitron NewMedia Internet study showed that at that time almost three-quarters of Internet users in the United States spent up to 30 minutes a week watching streaming video. Nearly half planned to watch more streaming video in the future.

The development of television programming on the Internet has given rise to at least two main types of online video programming: that which has been transferred from off-line television and original Internet video programming. Because so much of online video or television is still in its infancy and still largely constrained by technological issues such as bandwidth, computer storage capacity, and screen resolution, it is likely that these two types will morph or change in ways that we cannot foresee and create some kind of as yet uninvented form of online programming.

An early example of the type of hybrid that may develop is Alternative Entertainment Network TV (AENTV), which combines original Internet video programming and aggregates digital video originally aired on television. AENTV was named one of the "10 Great Video Sites on the Internet" by *Broadcasting & Cable* magazine and has collected hundreds of hours of programming from a variety of TV shows, all available on-demand and for free.

Weblink
AENTV
[www.aentv.com/]

Transferred from Television Programming

This type of programming, which simply serves up programming originally produced for television, is still perhaps most common, although there is no definitive study yet available to prove this. Although there are examples from virtually every type of programming category, most "television" programming of this type is simply promotional. Trailers, soap opera clips, and sit-com excerpts are put online to generate viewer interest in an upcoming show that will appear on television. One exception is Comedy Central, which provides much of its television programming online on-demand.

The most common type of nonpromotional programming thus far from over-the-air television stations is news and public affairs. CNN.com, MSNBC.com, CBS News, ABC News, Fox News, and NBC News are among the leaders in providing online video news. The CBS Boston affiliate WBZ provides exceptional regional online video news, as do Seattle CBS affiliate KIRO and NBC San Francisco affiliate KRON. A leading provider of international video news online is the BBC World, which provides live video news feeds online.

Viacom's 2000 acquisition of CBS has begun opening up greater opportunities for television, or video, on the Internet. With its new Internet division, MTVi, including both MTV and VH1, as well as its recently acquired SonicNet, Viacom CBS is positioned well to provide not only online music but also online music video. Combined with CBS video news strength, the Viacom CBS empire is poised to take a leadership position on many online television fronts.

DTV can be interactive, which opens the door to more participation and interest in shows among viewers. ABC's Enhanced TV synchronizes customized interactive content over the Web during many of its programs, such as *Who*

Wants to be a Millionaire and *Monday Night Football,* which offers an interactive play-along synchronized game as well as live statistics and facts about the players and teams.

ABC has initially focused on the "two-screen" platform whereby viewers have an Internet-connected computer in the same room as their television, so it's not truly interactive television. There are more than 40 million homes that today are capable of such TV-Internet convergence, which is closer to a critical mass than the current set-top box installation numbers. Currently several companies are trying to make the convergence complete, either as a PC-turned-TV or a TV-turned-PC.

Original Internet Video Programming

Television programming typically has been provided to the public by a limited set of program providers. They have made their programming available on a scheduled basis, packaged for mass audiences and broadcast according to a controlled schedule. Just as online music distribution opens the music recording industry to potentially thousands of new artists (i.e., program providers), the Internet opens the TV business to thousands, perhaps millions, of new TV program providers.

Internet-original programming began with web cams, tiny cameras that attach to a computer that have enjoyed enormous popularity around the world. Web cams have provided typically live feeds of everything from a coffee pot at Oxford University to a seemingly endless series of individuals inviting the public to pay to watch their uncensored private lives.

This early experimentation among amateurs has given rise to much more serious original online video programming, however. Some of the most interesting are web cams set up by researchers to allow viewers from around the world to observe important, unusual, or simply interesting experiments or other research in action. Universities and not-for-profit organizations have also used online video to show lectures from famous guest speakers, panel discussions, or to highlight on-the-scene video footage shot elsewhere in the world that does not make it to mainstream media.

Navigating the Million-Channel Universe

Online programming guides, also known as electronic program guides (EPGs) in digital television or video, are becoming a necessity as Liberty Media chairman John Malone's outdated notion of a "500-channel universe" is replaced by a "million-channel universe." Leading the way in the online program guides today is tvguide.com, the online version of *TV Guide,* with 50 million subscribers. Tvguide.com offers viewers a fully interactive and keyword-searchable guide to the coming week's television programming from terrestrial broadcast to cable, satellite, and the Internet. The site also features daily news about television and other media, a database on more than 40,000 movies, and digital video.

Will DTV Learn Online Music's Lessons?

The same developments that have challenged the recording industry will start to emerge in the television industry as digital television enters the marketplace and broadband use increases, allowing for fast downloads of large files. Digital video files are much larger than what most people can accommodate in downloads, which has hampered the popularity of video file-swapping online. Fixed media,

Media Spotlight: **CBS, FOX, and ESPN**

CBS and Fox networks, although behind ABC and NBC in rolling out DTV terrestrial broadcasting, stand out in their use of digital production technology. CBS News and Special Events has been in the forefront in their use of digital technology for producing innovative news and information programming. Dan Dubno, producer and technologist, CBS News and Special Events, has spearheaded the use of a variety of digital tools for news gathering and storytelling. Among the most impressive uses to date have been Dubno's application of remote sensing imagery to generate three-dimensional "extrusions" of a variety of geographic locations, buildings, cities, and regions for various news reports, including "fly-throughs" of the Middle East; Washington, DC; and other venues for major news stories.

Fox and ESPN have implemented digital technology in sports programming. Among their applications have been the use of digital objects in motion video, including the layering of a "first down marker" on the football field during National Football League games, as well as digital commercial messages layered into the field, the stands, and other locations. Fox also used a three-dimensional digital audio technology to broadcast immersive audio during Superbowl XXXV. Of course, only a few households could experience this immersive audio experience, but it was a sign of things to come.

such as videotapes or DVDs, are still primarily used for on-demand, repeated viewing, although new technologies could easily change this as well and make fixed media obsolete.

The television industry has been closely watching what the recording industry is doing with the hope that they will not repeat the same mistakes. However, concerns about intellectual property theft and unwanted competition have limited some programmers' forays online. Large television companies, broadcasters, and cable companies generally see the Internet and digital video as threatening their loss of control and their existing franchises, and whether they learn from the experiences of the recording industry or follow them in litigation and political lobbying to stop potential threats to their control remains to be seen.

So far, attempts at creating secure digital media have not been successful. They have either been extremely clumsy and overly restricted consumers' ability to play media such as a CD on a variety of devices, have been foiled by low-tech

Universities and other organizations are beginning to use the Web to show video lectures of professors or guest speakers.

mechanisms such as using a black marker pen to mask digital encoding, or have been extremely unpopular with consumers and thus failed, such as what happened with the DIVX format that forced consumers to pay per use of a digital video they "bought."

Digital Media Economics

Traditionally, media enterprises, like other industrial-age businesses, required heavy capital investment. Capital was required to build the transmission towers for television and radio stations. It was required to buy printing presses and to build cable systems. Not only was the infrastructure expensive, but it created enormous barriers to entry for prospective competition.

In the digital age, these rules are changing. Some of the most significant barriers to entry are shrinking. Capital costs are reduced, as anyone can go online and create a Web site and potentially compete with established media companies. It's part of why relative newcomers such as AOL, Yahoo!, and eBay have been so successful. Of course, the cost of producing quality original content is still relatively high, especially for video but less so for text or audio. Moreover, few media enterprises have found a formula for making profits in the online world, as most people seem unwilling to pay for content and advertising does not seem to be very effective.

Most large online media outlets have the backing of traditional media companies behind them, such as MSNBC.com, a joint venture between NBC and Microsoft, or CNBC.com. With advertising and other revenues being generated from the parent companies, these online endeavors can afford to take losses for a while as online revenue models can be tried and tested. Many smaller, independent media dot-com companies were not so fortunate, especially after the economy and stock market spiralled downward from spring 2000. Some severely scaled back their business plans, and others, such as award-winning online crime news Web site APBNews.com, went out of business. Other online media enterprises such as *Salon.com,* which are still creating quality original content, are now charging for what used to be free.

Revenue Models for Digital Media

One of the most significant challenges all online media properties face is building a revenue stream not only to cover costs but to return a profit. As of this writing, few content sites had found a way to produce a substantial revenue stream, and, with the tightening economy of 2001–2002 and a substantial drop in venture capital and advertising revenues, the situation is even more difficult. There are several ways online media companies can generate revenues—at least in theory. These include traditional methods such as advertising, subscriptions, and syndication, as well as methods that are either unique or feasible in an online environment, such as e-commerce and micropayments. However, none so far have proven to be inherently better than other methods, and dot-com companies as well as online media companies are still experimenting with methods to earn profits. It is likely that more advanced technology will open the door to creative revenue generating models that are unavailable today.

Media Spotlight: **BNNTV**

One of the most innovative developers of quality programming in the online arena is also one of the best independent program producers in the offline television world. BNNTV (Broadcast News Network Television) is a 15-year-old company that embraces a philosophy that is much more tightly in tune with the redefined rulebook of new media.

Founder and BNNTV executive producer Steven Rosenbaum explains BNNTV's objective is to empower viewers to make television and act as an agent to package and polish the content to enhance value. He says *MTV Unfiltered*—which BNNTV helped launch in 1996—was slightly ahead of its time, and they had viewers call in, request cameras, and shoot their own stories, with extraordinary results. Rosenbaum believes that user content will demand stations to rethink the broadcast model by creating new communities around digital video and storytelling that let the audience tell the broadcasters if that's what they want.

Rosenbaum believes this new mode of "participatory programming" will expand far beyond news and information.

Since its founding, BNNTV has grown with network clients including *CBS News, 48 Hours,* A&E's *Investigative Reports,* Court TV, The Sci-Fi Channel, the History Channel, MTV, Fox Family, MetroChannels, and VH1.

Weblink
CameraPlanet
[www.cameraplanet.com]
BNNTV
[www.cameraplanet.com/divisions/bnn/]

For the time being, the revenue streams that appear most viable for content sites involve a combination of advertising, subscription, and micropayments. AOL produces substantial revenues, but mostly from its monthly subscription fees, which are actually charges for online service rather than content per se. AOL does produce some revenue from online transactions in the form of online shopping. This may grow significantly in the future as more consumers become used to buying online.

Advertising

Advertising has proved disappointing in generating revenues for all but the largest portal or content sites, such as Yahoo! or MSNBC.com, which attract millions of visitors. Media companies both offline and online charge advertisers for the cost per thousand (CPM) of audience members. This means a magazine with a circulation of 100,000 can receive more for carrying ads than a magazine with a circulation of 10,000.

In the online media environment, technology allows Web site owners not only to see exactly how many people have visited a given page on the site but to track whether people clicked on the advertisement on that page or not. Because the average numbers of click-throughs on ads are generally extremely low (ranging between 0.75 percent for standard banner ads to 1.5 percent for large oversize ads in the center of the screen), advertisers have become more cautious about placing their ads online based simply on the numbers of visitors to a site. It may well be that ads are similarly ineffective in the analog world, but there is of course no way to measure that in the concrete terms that the online world can provide.

Online companies have tried a number of things to improve click-through rates on ads and thereby increase revenues. Larger ads, animated ads, pop-up and pop-under ads have all been tried, but with minimal success. In fact, most computer users seem much less patient with advertising than they are on television and radio. This could be because the online media world is still relatively new and established rules of behavior have still not been agreed upon, or because media consumers are much more active in getting their media content so that intrusions in the form of advertising are more frustrating than in a passive medium like television, where there is little choice but to change the channel.

Subscriptions

The most successful revenue-producing media sites have been those that have carved out an important content niche; produced original, quality content; and designed an effective, efficient online presence—and charged a subscription for their site. The two best examples are *The Wall Street Journal Interactive* and *Consumer Reports Online*. *Consumer Reports Online* provides all the content from its well-known magazine, plus additional customizable information and reports on product testing and ratings. With a fee of less than $50 a year, *Consumer Reports Online* has captured 580,000 paid subscribers. This is only a fraction of the 3 million paid subscribers to its printed magazine, but it is nevertheless a significant number and revenue stream (nearly $30 million a year).

Most other sites that have tried subscription models, however, have not been as successful. Financial news Web site TheStreet.com, for example, started with a subscription model when it launched but then switched to a free model in June 2000. After a while it moved to a partial subscription model, offering most content for free but charging subscriptions of from $200 to $2200 for specialty newsletters or other "premium content." This partial subscription model is being tried by a number of online media companies as they look for what types of content the public is willing to pay for in a medium that started out and still has most of its information available for free.

Syndication

Syndication is a long-held part of the business model in publishing and broadcasting, where content providers have licensed everything from opinion columns and comic strips to situation comedies to other content distributors. As the syndication model has migrated to the Internet, content providers such as Reuters, CBS, and Dun & Bradstreet have begun to license their content to Web sites, which subscribe to or pay to republish the content.

Moreover, traditional technologies for distributing syndicated content have proven unreliable and unscalable, which means they break down when large volumes of content need to be moved in short periods of time. For example, in August 2000 the satellite the Associated Press normally uses to distribute its content to its member newspapers and other news providers twice failed in a one-week period, interrupting the flow of news at critical times.

Internet-based content delivery, because of its noncentralized design, is very reliable by comparison. As a result, media content syndication of text, images, sound, and video via the Internet is forecast to become a more than $6 billion industry by 2005 and will be a fundamental component of the media business model in the digital age.

Weblink
The Wall Street Journal Interactive
[www.wsj.com]

Consumer Reports Online
[www.consumerreports.org/]

E-commerce

E-commerce refers to the electronic commercial environment that emerged in the 1990s, primarily on the Internet. Although the potential of e-commerce was probably overhyped in the late 1990s, it could be argued that it has likewise been looked at overly skeptically in the post-dot-com boom era.

Yet, e-commerce presents an interesting opportunity in the long run for media businesses operating in the digital age. The online arena is an environment in which consumers can not only get information about products on demand, but, conversely, media and other organizations can deliver promotional messages specifically targeted to individuals based on their online profiles. In many cases consumers can also purchase those products or services and even have them delivered digitally via the Internet, as is the case for music, computer software, digital books, videogames, and some other products. For those that can't be delivered electronically, most are shipped via commercial delivery services anywhere in the world.

A major issue for online media organizations is how to provide a secure environment for payments for online transactions. Many consumers are concerned about the safety of providing a credit card number via the Internet and thus are afraid of venturing online to make a purchase of any type.

Another issue that online media organizations must consider when venturing into e-commerce is maintaining viewer trust in their content and disclosing potential conflicts of interest or even the appearance of conflicts of interest. For example, an online magazine may have a book review on its site, along with a link to online bookseller Amazon.com. It would seem to be a convenient way for a reader who likes the review to buy the book, and it is. However, if the Web site is an affiliate member of Amazon, a common program in which a member receives a commission on each book sold if consumers come to Amazon through a link on the member's site, then the Web site's or reviewer's journalistic objectivity could be called into question. It is in their best financial interest to get people to buy that book, making it appear less likely that a reviewer would give a negative review or write reviews on books that might not sell very well. This kind of behavior, for which several large media organizations have been called to task in the past several years, further erodes public trust in content produced by media companies.

Micropayments

Micropayments are small fees paid for each online transaction, perhaps as little as a penny or even less. The idea is that micropayments would be much like water or gas bills, in which the charged units are so small that users do not object to the costs and are based only on what is actually used. In an online environment, this would mean charging users for downloading media content, such as songs, text articles, or video. Currently, charges for individual songs, for example, are considered high and thus are not popular, and the technology to allow for payments less than a cent is not fully developed. It may seem economically infeasible to charge as little as ten cents or even a penny for a song, for example, but consider the revenue stream if that song is downloaded by millions of users and there are no added distribution or production costs to the producer of the content.

Micropayments could encourage the use of digital cash, a relatively secure form of online payment. With such purchases, a consumer would spend digital cash rather than give a credit card number. There are different digital cash models, but one of the most common is to pay in advance with an online bank account and

micropayments—small fees, even under a penny, paid for each online transaction, such as downloading a song or text article.

then have charges deducted from that account. Another option is to place charges on one's monthly ISP bill.

The Business Challenge to Media Organizations

Broadband digital media present both an opportunity and a threat for those in the media and communication industries. On the one hand, long-standing corporations, institutions, and entire industries are being turned upside down by the digital revolution. Businesses built on analog technologies of production and distribution are trying to figure out how to adapt in the digital age. New efficiencies of creating and delivering content in a digital, networked environment are emerging throughout the world. Long-held, highly profitable business models based on the analog world are less viable in a digital marketplace.

Yet, uncertainty prevails in the largely digital world. Dot-com stocks have plummeted. Converting to digital production and distribution costs a lot of money, and the returns are not guaranteed. No wonder so many executives in the media business are nervous about digitization choice and change.

Nevertheless, the new digital world means new business opportunities. It means opening new markets that formerly were restricted by political, economic, and geographic boundaries. It means new storytelling formats that bring true interactivity to television and radio. It means creating immersive audio and video on demand for consumers who want their media, in all its forms, customized according not only to their preferences but also to their current geographic location and many other factors.

Overall, the digitization of television and radio means an expansion of the business pie. In other words, the size of the marketplace is growing, which means extraordinary business opportunities for those brave enough, talented enough, and persistent enough to enter the fray in a creative manner. Established businesses face the additional hurdle of having to deal with their own corporate culture that insists on placing a priority on protecting their existing business interests. This short-sighted thinking opens new opportunities for entrepreneurial startups nimble enough to adapt to an uncertain and rapidly changing marketplace.

The Convergence of Technology and Mass Communication in Leading Companies

There is perhaps no better example of how convergence of telecommunications companies and media companies is affecting mass communication than AOL Time Warner. There is certainly no larger example, as after Internet service provider (ISP) America Online acquired media giant Time Warner in January 2000 it became the largest media company in the world. The Time Warner portion of the company has already been discussed in previous chapters, with its interests in print, music recordings, film, video, and television. Here we will emphasize the AOL portion to see how it can be seen as a mass communication company in its own right as well, although its roots and strengths lie in the technology and Internet side of the business. Other Internet-only companies or technology companies such as Microsoft, CNET, and RealNetworks are also looked at for similar reasons. The list is not meant to be comprehensive but simply to demonstrate how convergence blurs the lines between technology and media companies.

AOL

America Online is the world's largest online communications service provider, with 34 million subscribers as of July 2002 and localized versions of AOL in eight languages in 17 countries. There are 120 million registered users of its popular instant messaging service, ICQ, which is available to non-AOL Internet users as well. AOL operates a unique, proprietary online communications service based on its own computer software authoring environment, as well as providing access to the Internet. This makes it the world's largest ISP as well.

Founded in 1985, the Dulles, Virginia-based firm in 1998 acquired the number-two ISP, Compuserve, which was among the earliest online services along with its then 2 million customers (now 3 million). In 1999, AOL acquired Netscape, a popular Web browser with 48 million users, positioning AOL for global leadership in the Internet and online communications markets. It also put the company in direct competition with Microsoft, which has the leading Web browser, Internet Explorer, and operates its own ISP, Microsoft Network (MSN).

AOL provides its members (what AOL calls its subscribers) with a wide variety of online services, including e-mail, Web browsing, online shopping, and instant messaging. In addition, AOL provides extensive content channels, including news, sports, and entertainment. Most content is provided to AOL by a variety of media content producers, including CNN, CBS News, and the Associated Press (AP). Entertainment content providers include *TV Guide,* EW.com *(Entertainment Weekly),* E Online, and *People,* while music and music-related news and entertainment is provided by sources such as *Rolling Stone* and Sonicnet.

AOL does produce some original content, mostly through its AOL TV, which is distributed both online and via DBS provider DirecTV. Mostly, though, AOL offers its users a convenient, user-friendly bundle of content and services packaged uniquely for AOL's members. An example would be AOL's nicely produced special interactive section on the 2001 Emmy Awards. It featured extensive coverage on the nominees, including text, audio, and video.

All this comes at a price, with subscribers paying an annual fee of about $270, or a monthly rate of about $25. Importantly, AOL is easy to install and use, making it a popular service among less technologically sophisticated users and leading to the charge by critics of AOL that it is "the Internet on training wheels." However, predictions by Internet pundits that once users became accustomed to being online they would then leave AOL and its pop-up ads in droves have not come true, although AOL's rate of growth in getting new subscribers has fallen off markedly in the past couple of years.

AOL's 2000 fiscal year (ended June) revenues were $7.7 billion. AOL employed 15,000 (this is only a portion of the total employed by AOL Time Warner). AOL founder Stephen M. Case is now chairman of AOL Time Warner, the only executive from AOL still left in AOL Time Warner's top-level executive ranks. After the merger with Time Warner, and in the post-dot-com boom, AOL Time Warner's stock fell sharply, leading many investors and analysts to blame AOL for dragging Time Warner down rather than being the engine of growth it was touted to be before the merger. After an executive shakeup in July 2002 that saw former AOL COO Robert Pittman forced to resign, Don Logan, previously chairman of the Time Inc. magazine division, was named chairman of a newly formed media group that includes AOL and Time Warner Cable as well as the books and magazine divisions. Jeff Bewkes, previously chairman of HBO, was named chairman of a newly formed entertainment division that includes television networks, film and television studios, and music.

Microsoft

Ranked seventy-second in the Fortune 500, and with founder and Chairman Bill Gates ranked as the world's richest man, Microsoft is mentioned here primarily because of its powerful market influence in software that can in turn determine what types of media are available online. Most computer users look at and use Microsoft products. Although Microsoft is still primarily a technology or Internet company, its forays into content creation and development make it a potentially powerful force in the world of digital media. A merger with a media giant that has lots of content, such as Sony or Viacom, would create a media monolith along the lines of AOL Time Warner.

Microsoft is involved in every aspect of the technology behind content creation and distribution on the Internet. Its Windows Media Player to watch or listen to streaming media was created to compete with RealNetworks RealPlayer and Apple's QuickTime. Microsoft started integrating its Windows Media Player into its Windows operating system, making it easy for consumers to use.

Because Windows Media Player is incompatible with either of the other two proprietary streaming media formats, however, streaming content creators have to duplicate their streaming content for all formats if they want to reach the largest possible audience, which increases production costs. Hardware makers and media content companies in television and Hollywood are wary of relying on a single proprietary standard, however, and are likely to put pressure on streaming media makers to use an open, common standard such as MPEG-4, although these issues are still unresolved.

Microsoft is also an ISP, with its MSN network, and is increasing its broadband capabilities. Its .Net Passport services attempt to give Internet users an easy way to access various types of content and to conduct e-commerce in a secure environment. In a partnership with NBC, Microsoft is part of cable channel and popular news Web site MSNBC.

They have started competing with video game makers with their Xbox video game console and have been involved in development of interactive television, first with WebTV and then with UltimateTV, but cut back on research in the area as of early 2002 as their interactive television ventures had not met with great success.

In 2001, Microsoft had sales of $25 billion and revenues of $7.3 billion. They have almost 48,000 employees.

CNET

CNET Networks is one of the top Internet companies, ranking as the Internet's thirteenth largest U.S. property in 2001 and one that most resembles a traditional media company in terms of what it creates. CNET Networks covers news in the technology industry through its CNET, ZDNet, TechRepublic, News.com, CNET Radio, and CNET Channel, as well as owning download.com and *Computer Shopper* magazine. In 2001, CNET had revenues of $286 million, down from $428 million in 2000.

RealNetworks

RealNetworks makes the popular RealPlayer software that lets consumers locate and listen to streaming audio and video over the Internet. More than 250 million people have downloaded RealPlayer to stream audio, video, and other multimedia content. It used to be the dominant streaming media software, but Microsoft has made great inroads into its area by bundling its proprietary Windows Media Player for free into its operating system, much as they did with Internet Explorer when they started competing with Netscape's Web browser.

RealNetworks, although it still gets almost 60 percent of its sales from licensing its software to consumers and content providers, has also been striking deals with content providers such as MLB.com for the rights to stream games over the Internet. It is also embracing the open MPEG-4 video compression standard rather than its proprietary RealPlayer standard in order to better partner with mobile hardware production companies. In 2001 it had $188 million in sales, growing almost 22 percent from the previous year, although it still lost $75 million in 2001.

Direction in Online and Digital Media

Digitization of media has lowered production costs and lessened training needed to create professional-quality media content (at least in terms of technical proficiency, if not always in terms of content quality). The Internet has created a networked environment that lets anyone reach a potential audience of millions of people for very little cost. The changes have threatened and will continue to threaten the interests of many established media companies unless they learn to adapt to the changing media environment.

Although rapid improvements in technology make it impossible to accurately predict what specific changes will affect media in the future, there are several basic trends that will influence online and digital media in the coming years. Some of these trends simply accelerate changes that have already been taking place with analog media, while others are unique to the digital, Internet-connected media world.

From Scarcity to Plenty

It is already very easy to become overwhelmed by the amount of media available, and this trend is only likely to increase. The media world has gone from one of scarcity, where it was difficult to find certain items like rare editions of books, film, or music, to a world in which more than you could ever want can be found largely online or, if not there, then the Internet can show you where to find it.

Issues of space or time that publishers or broadcasters dealt with are no longer a factor online. There is no physical reason to cut a story to 300 words so it fits on a page, although there very well may be reasons of clarity or design to cut a story online. Likewise, it does not matter if an online video segment is longer than three minutes, as there are no advertisers who will get angry that their ad was not broadcast at a certain commercial break. Of course, these analog media limitations can be, and in some cases have been, placed on digital media, but there is no inevitable law that says it must be so.

What this means for media professionals is that they are no longer the gatekeepers of information, deciding what is deemed important enough, given limited resources, to be sent through the media system to be distributed to the public. Rather, they will be filters or matchmakers of information, processing the raw material that almost anyone can access, and shortening, clarifying, and putting it in a larger context for the audience.

This means media consumers will need to become more discriminating about what media they consume so they do not waste time or drown in information overload. Technologies such as collaborative filtering are likely to play a role in helping bring only the type of media content that a person wants.

Greater Audience Fragmentation

Just as magazine audiences fragmented with the advent of television, and broadcast television audiences fragmented with the advent of cable, audiences are fragmenting even further in an online environment.

This audience fragmentation will have profound effects on advertising revenues, because under the current advertising-supported models media companies get more revenue when they can attract a larger audience.

Greater fragmentation also means that it is less likely that large groups of people will share media experiences and will therefore have less in common than they otherwise would have. The flip side of that argument is that those who do interact with a group that shares their interest can perhaps feel closer to others than if they were in a more homogenized, less fragmented media world.

Lower Media Production Costs

Costs have always been relatively low for writers—a typewriter, paper, and some perseverance, and a person could see his or her name in print fairly easily, even if the published work did not receive a wide distribution. Computers and word processing software of course helped this process. Video and television production, however, have been a different story until recently.

At present, for less than $10,000 someone can buy all the necessary equipment (computer, camera, and software) to digitally edit video at professional levels of quality, suitable for broadcast by mainstream media. It may still seem like a lot of money, but considering that even 15 years ago the costs for a similar set-up were more along the lines of $100,000, costs have dropped considerably.

This is not to say that anyone can—or should—plan to be a television producer simply because it's possible. It takes practice and skill to learn to use technologically sophisticated equipment such as digital video cameras and computers proficiently, as well as learning the media grammar of video in terms of cuts, staging shots, and lighting. However, the fact that someone with the necessary training, practice, and skills can create something without years of apprenticeship in a traditional media company is a dramatic shift and will lead to more participation among the general public in creating and interacting with mass media.

The relatively low costs to create and produce media such as music or video will open the field to many more people creating media content. As with the text-heavy Internet now, much of that content will not be very good, causing some to long for the days of gatekeepers such as strict editors and record label executives who screened the abysmal from the mediocre, but there will be many more voices available to be heard and seen that would have otherwise been silenced in the traditional media world, and some of these will be worth listening to or watching, even if they do not have mass-market appeal.

Widespread Broadband Connectivity

As broadband connections reach more and more households, the way the public uses the Internet will change. Online video and graphics will become a viable choice for receiving content, thereby changing the Web from its current text emphasis to a more visual, video-oriented medium. Text will still play a role, however, but could well be pushed to a largely secondary or supporting role when someone wants more in-depth content on a topic. Text will also continue on the Web simply because it is likely to be some time before broadband penetrates enough homes for content producers to ignore those with dial-up modems.

Television/PC Convergence

It is still unclear at this stage whether the television will absorb the PC or the PC will absorb the television; but, as should be clear from points made earlier in this chapter, there will increasingly be little difference between the two. When one can watch a rerun of *Seinfeld* on demand and can do instant messaging with friends or check e-mail on the same screen while watching it, it will matter little to consumers whether that device is defined as a PC or a TV, because it will function as both.

Interactivity at some level will be an expected part of the "television" viewing experience, although there will also be times when the public are more than willing to be passive media consumers again and simply sit back and watch what they want. But for media and technology companies, the direction in which the PC/TV goes can be a matter of success or failure. Where will computer maker Dell be, for example, if the public starts buying Sony equipment that meets their computing *and* entertainment-viewing needs?

Video-on-demand will largely make the concept of programming at specific times obsolete, except for live shows, special events, or breaking news. Audiences will not need to tune into a specific channel at a certain time to see a rerun of *The Simpsons*. It will, in a sense, always be "on"—just as all other episodes will be—all available from an on-screen menu that's keyword searchable and that lets you choose what show or shows you wish to see.

SUMMARY

All media of communication or information, including telephony, broadcasting, motion pictures, recorded music, books, newspapers, and magazines, are converting from their traditional analog or noncomputerized form to digital, computerized form. Digital media, in other words, are not simply a "new type" of media but encompass all types of media and mediated telecommunication currently used.

Many of these changes take place in areas of media production that are not seen by most of the general public, who still get much of their media in analog form as final end products. However, the analog product is usually only a small portion of the whole production and distribution process and will become increasingly less important as digital display devices become better and ubiquitous. The Internet, in connecting computer users to each other in decentralized networks, has played a key role in making digital media readily accessible to a worldwide audience.

Different media types have different levels of digitization and have been affected differently by it and the Internet. Many established media companies are severely threatened by the changes online digital media are bringing, with the recording industry and MP3 file-sharing services being the most commonly cited example. However, the same forces that have undermined the recording industry's position also have the potential to undermine publishing and television. For different reasons (technological as well as social), they have so far not had the same effect on publishing and television or video.

Media companies are experimenting with various revenue-generating models online, as advertising, the most profitable model in the analog media world, has so far not been very successful. Some models include, besides advertising, syndicating content, subscriptions, e-commerce, and micropayments. None has established itself as a guaranteed success, and it is likely that some kind of hybrid system, or a system not thought of yet, will prove its worth.

What exactly constitutes a media company is also changing, as technology companies become involved in content creation and distribution or merge with traditional media companies. A company like AOL Time Warner can have a profound effect on what its over 50 million users worldwide see in terms of media content.

Digital media has accelerated some media trends, such as audience fragmentation, and created new trends, such as audience interactivity, lower costs and skill levels needed to produce and distribute media content, and the eventual obsolescence of television and radio programming as we currently know them. It will be less important to define media devices as PCs, radios, or televisions than it will be to answer how well a media device meets consumers needs in terms of delivering the kind of media content—interactive, personalized, and multimedia—that they want.

Discussion Questions

1. If electrical power was to go out, thus shutting down all computers, which mass media type would be most likely to be able to keep operating, if any? Why?

2. If online news Web sites merged into combined newspaper/radio/television news stations or channels, which group do you think would be better prepared to learn new skills—print journalists learning broadcast skills or broadcast journalists learning print skills? Why do you think so?

3. What are the primary reasons the recording industry is so threatened by file-sharing services? Are their reasons justified?

4. Why haven't the publishing industry and television, video, or film industries been as vocal in their opposition to online file-sharing as the recording industry?

5. Which revenue models have the most potential to be successful for digital media? Why?

6. Try to create the perfect media/technology company by taking units from various existing companies. What would the strengths and weaknesses of your company be? How could you enhance the strengths and reduce the weaknesses?

7. Describe your vision of how the media world will be for most consumers five years from now. Discuss audience behavior, expectations, media industries, and the ways people will access media content.

Storing, Representing, and Retrieving Digital Content

7

Imagine a world without paper. No books, magazines, or newspapers as we know them. There would still be libraries to store knowledge, of course, but they would have to be vastly bigger to store the material in whatever form was most common—probably parchment, or specially treated animal skins. Checking out books—if it was allowed at all for fear of them getting lost or damaged—would mean a cumbersome trek. No easy way to read today's news unless you went to the news bulletin board, probably a large chalkboard or whiteboard that would allow for relatively quick updates and rewrites of various events. No slipping a note to a friend in class, no fast and convenient way to transfer knowledge that is written down.

Now imagine a world much like ours today except in which MP3 audio files used a device

the size of a brick to store a single song. Would you be downloading a dozen songs and taking the music with you when going out? Would the recording industry have to worry about lost revenue because people weren't buying CDs?

These two extreme examples demonstrate that how we store and retrieve information can have dramatic effects on how we use and interact with media, which in turn affect everything from social relations to culture to the economy. And, like knowing about user interface and digital distribution, understanding digital storage of content will help you have a better understanding of how digital media have fundamentally altered the mass communications landscape.

OBJECTIVES

In this chapter we will:

- List the five fundamental principles that make something a storage technology and explain how they relate to mass communication issues.
- Compare and contrast various historical and current storage technologies in terms of how well they meet the five fundamental principles.
- Contrast the development and elements of nonelectronic media vs. electronic media.
- Describe the historical development of traditional analog storage media.
- Evaluate the impact digital and optical storage media have had on mass communication and the role they continue to play.
- Describe the consequences of storage technologies for mass communication and society.
- Outline the state-of-the-art of storage media and coming technological trends.

Prologue

This chapter focuses on the evolution of storage technologies from analog to digital formats and their implications for mass communication. Being able to store information so that it can be retrieved later is a crucial element not only in mass communication, but in such fields as education, business, and law. Imagine trying to educate young people, conduct business, or uphold laws solely by relying on peoples' memories rather than having the information stored and accessible.

The term **storage technology** simply refers to any type of device or medium in which information can be kept for later retrieval. An ideal storage technology will be strong in five components common to all storage technologies: longevity, capacity, portability, accessibility, and reproducibility. However, throughout history various technologies have been strong in one or some aspects but not others, and attempts to find a perfect balance continue today. In addition, digital technology and the information concerns of the modern age bring their own unique issues to storing and retrieving content in a mass communication context.

Among the most important mass communication issues we'll examine are how text, still images, sound, and video are stored, indexed, and represented for fast, efficient, and easy retrieval.

Characteristics of Storage, Representation, and Retrieval

How information is stored is critical to mediated communication, whether analog or digital. Because only a portion of media content is distributed live, or without storage, an overwhelming amount of the media content we see or hear has first been stored for subsequent editing, distribution, and access, which of course applies to printed matter as well. Moreover, in order to be stored, information must somehow be represented. Whether through letters on a page, a magnetic tracing on a computer disk, or etchings on an optical drive, information must be represented in a fashion that allows for people to access it. The following discussion identifies the five concepts of longevity, capacity, portability, accessibility, and reproducibility that help to define the nature and quality of storage media.

Longevity

In one sense, longevity, or how long information can be retained in a medium, is most critical. The oldest known media, petroglyphs or cave paintings, have lasted for many millennia, as have hieroglyphics, also painted on rock. Their longevity has given us a window into the past and a glimpse into the world of early humans.

Information storage technologies have generally sacrificed longevity for increases in the four other characteristics, such as capacity or portability. In other words, storage technologies such as paper, film, or magnetic storage do not last nearly as long as some of the earliest storage technologies of petroglyphs, for

storage technology—any type of device or medium in which information can be maintained for later retrieval.

1. (True/False) Kilobytes are named after Anastasios H. Kilobyte, the nineteenth-century Greek mathematician who discovered them.
2. Put the following in order of smallest to largest: gigabyte, kilobyte, petabyte, megabyte, terabyte, exabyte.
3. (True/False) Until humans invented writing, there was no way to store information or knowledge.
4. (True/False) Out of all the fundamental characteristics of storage media, longevity has improved the least and in many respects has decreased compared to older storage media.
5. (True/False) MP3 stands for MPEG-3, a type of audio compression format.
6. Which was the last network to switch from film to videotape for its news coverage? In what year did they switch, and why?
7. How many pages of text can a single CD-ROM hold?
8. (True/false) Even the best search engines only cover about 30 percent of the Web.

See answers on page 245.

---

example. Compare the lifespan of 4000-year-old hieroglyphics in Egyptian tombs with that of cinema film stock from the early 1900s, which is already disintegrating less than 100 years after it was created.

Capacity

Newer storage technologies have greatly increased capacity to store information but at the expense of shorter lifespans. Papyrus and parchment can record far more information than cave paintings in a small amount of space but decay far

Petroglyphs, the oldest form of stored communication, also have excellent longevity—but at the expense of other storage technology characteristics.

Papyrus and parchment were revolutionary developments in making written communication more portable.

more rapidly. Books and other print media, such as newspapers and magazines, can retain even greater amounts of information but begin to decay almost immediately and are unlikely to survive more than a few hundred years.

Consider the size of a floppy diskette and how much more information it can store in a smaller space than a book that contains the same amount of printed text. Expand that to CD-ROMs (700 MB versus 1.2 MB for diskette) and then to DVDs, which store up to 4.7 GB (9.4 GB double-sided) in the same amount of physical space as a CD; and that doesn't include using compression algorithms that can cram even more material into the same amount of disk space.

Portability

Tied closely with increasing capacity has been increasing portability. Although cave paintings endure, they are essentially immovable. Stone or clay tablets improved portability of information—although not by much. Papyrus and parchment, first developed in Egypt and widely used in the Greek and Roman worlds of the late fourth century BCE until the middle of the seventh century AD, created a dramatic improvement in portability of information.

The development of paper and printing also helped increase the portability of information and therefore made distribution easier as well. A CD-ROM, because of its relatively high capacity to store information, can hold the text of a number of books and is thus very portable compared to carrying around the actual books, but isn't as accessible as a printed book unless a CD-player or computer is available.

Accessibility

Better accessibility of stored information can be looked at from two perspectives. On one hand, the need to use technology such as a television, radio, or computer in order to access information can be seen as limiting when compared to reading a book or looking at hieroglyphics or a photograph, which can be read or looked at directly by a person. Without a television set you simply cannot access the airwaves to retrieve the information being broadcast.

Computer storage allows for much greater access to information in a small space than previous storage technologies allowed.

International standards and devices to retrieve the information on digital storage media continue to change so rapidly that in just a few years it can become virtually impossible to access the content stored on a particular device. For example, try to find an eight-track tape player, or even a 5.25-inch computer floppy disk drive—storage media that were common in the 1970s and 1980s. Will DVD players manufactured in the early twenty-first century have a longer lifespan? Will a member of a human civilization living 3000 years from now—or even 300—be able to find a machine to play a DVD?

On the other hand, modern electronic storage technology, especially in digital form, provides much greater access to information to a larger number of people than ever before if they have the right equipment. A person does not have to be present at the cave to see the cave drawings, or have an actual photograph to see it, or wait months for a book or magazine to arrive by post. Today, people anywhere in the world can use the Internet to instantly access information of any type stored on computer hard drives, no matter where they reside, as long as they are connected to the network.

Reproducibility

In many ways digital media can be seen as improving on trends that have continued for thousands of years in storage technology, but in terms of reproducibility digital media are a radical departure from anything that has come before them, for a number of reasons. The ease and accuracy of reproduction in digital media far surpass analog media. Prior to the printing press, the only way to copy written text was by hand-copying it—a laborious, time-consuming, and error-prone process. Visual media could be hand-copied or copied through woodblocks or engravings until the nineteenth century, when photography helped further "automate" the copying process to some extent.

Digital media can be easily reproduced because the data exist only as bits and bytes and not as anything physical. In other words, the very fact that digital media are not physical objects of any sort ironically makes it easier to copy as well as allowing for an infinite number of copies without reducing the number of copies available. This same characteristic also makes it possible to reproduce not only perfect copies of the original, but *better* versions than the original, such as when imperfections of sound recordings are removed digitally. In analog media, copies of the original are inevitably changed and lose some quality compared to the original version—again, think of audio recordings, in which a third- or fourth-generation audiocassette copy of a recording from a CD is noticeably poorer in sound quality. In digital media it is much easier to retain the same quality as the original, although for storage space reasons reduced-quality versions are often saved.

Implications for Mass Communication

Contemporary U.S. society places a premium on immediate technological solutions, often regardless of the ultimate cost or consequences. Canadian media scholar Harold Innis and his famous protégé Marshall McLuhan formulated well-known hypotheses about the longevity and portability of media and their resulting cultural meanings. It is worth reading McLuhan's book *Understanding Media: The Extensions of Man* (with Lewis H. Lapham) or Innis's *The Bias of Communication* for a detailed understanding of how the lifespan and portability of a medium might affect the nature and role of communications media in a society.

Innis argued that from papyrus to printing, the social and political development of the Western world has been profoundly shaped by the qualities of media storage technology. Papyrus lent itself to political organization, by enabling laws and other information to be recorded and distributed, thus facilitating the development of early civilizations such as that of ancient Egypt. In the European Renaissance, the adaptability of the alphabet to printing became the foundation for literacy, advertising, and trade. In the late 1800s and early 1900s, books and newspapers reinforced the position of language as a basis of nationalism (e.g., consider the role of these print media in fostering the belief that anyone living in the United States should speak English).

Nonelectronic Media vs. Electronic Media

In terms of storage technology, there is a fundamental difference between nonelectronic media such as print, painting, or photography (including film) and electronic media such as radio and television. The storage capacity of the former types of mediated communication is inherent in the medium itself. In other words, in painting a picture or writing words on paper (or stone, or parchment) the information is being stored. Because these types of communication have been around much longer than electronic media, they have had more time to be changed or improved upon in order to overcome their inherent weaknesses.

For example, books have medium- to long-term longevity (in modern terms), are very portable, and are fairly easy to reproduce. They are accessible, assuming one can read, but their accessibility drops markedly if one is searching for a specific piece of information. Think of searching for a favorite quote or passage in a novel read long ago. In storage technology terms they can be described as **"sequential access memory"** devices; i.e., a reader must go through each page to find some specific piece of information in the book. Developments of the book such as using page numbers, creating a table of contents, and indexing (neither of which are of any use without page numbers) all help make the book more of a **"random access memory"** device and thus help increase its accessibility of random content. Today we take these book characteristics for granted, but it is important to note that they only developed gradually as printed matter became more widespread. Dictionaries, encyclopedias, and telephone books, where information is listed either alphabetically or by some other logical categories, are examples of books created *as* random access memory devices.

Electronic media, on the other hand, can be broadcast live and unrecorded. In fact, one way of looking at electronic media such as radio and television is that in their purest forms they are not storage technologies at all—once they are broadcast they have absolutely zero longevity and cannot be "stored" in any real

sequential access memory—a type of media in which a reader, viewer, or user must go through the media in the order they received it in order to find specific information they are looking for.

random access memory—usually used for a type of computer memory and abbreviated to RAM, in storage technology terms it is a type of media that allows for readers or viewers to randomly obtain specific pieces of content they are looking for by doing searches, using an index, or taking some other action.

sense except through the memories of listeners or viewers. Imagine living in a world in which every television show, every news broadcast, and every radio song was done live over the air.

Finding a way to store, or record, audio and later video was crucial if they were to be fully utilized as mass media. Overcoming this challenge occupied a great many scientific and engineering minds over the past 130 years, but it still did not address the issue that, like a book with no page numbers, table of contents, or index, there was no way to quickly and randomly access specific segments of audio or video.

Digital media, and its capacity for easy random access memory, has changed that. Random access memory enables nonlinear playback, search and retrieval of text, audio, video, or any other content type. For example, when you run a keyword search on a computerized text document, the computer searches the entire document and goes instantly to the first occurrence of that key word. So far search and retrieval of video and audio has lagged behind text developments, just as it did in the analog world, but technology developments are changing that as well.

However, the road to the present in making audio and video true storage technologies was a fascinating one that can provide insights into some of the developments currently taking place in the digital realm.

Development of Audio and Video as Storage Media

The roots of trying to record sounds lie as far back as 1875, when inventor Thomas Alva Edison successfully recorded and played back the song "Mary's Little Lamb" from a strip of tinfoil wrapped around a spinning cylinder, which he demonstrated at the offices of *Scientific American,* giving birth to the phonograph. A decade later, the American inventor Oberlin Smith introduced the concept of recording sound on magnetic tape in an article he published in 1888. Magnetic recording involves placing tiny iron-based magnetic particles in substrate, such as a plastic film. The particles can be modified, or "written," by magnetizing them in either a north or south pole direction, thereby encoding or storing information.

The Telegraphone

magnetic recording—a type of recording that involves placing tiny iron-based magnetic particles in substrate, such as a plastic film. The particles can be modified, or "written," by magnetizing them in either a north or south pole direction, thereby encoding or storing information.

The first operating **magnetic recording** device (analog and linear) was produced in 1898 when the Danish engineer Valdemar Poulson developed his prototype system, the Telegraphone, to record audio. Poulson's device recorded audio by running a thin wire past an electromagnet. Each portion of the wire would store a corresponding electromagnetic charge, thus recording the sound. Poulson's device could also play back sound, but only softly. There was no way to amplify the signal, and the Telegraphone had little initial success.

But two years later, in 1900, Austrian Emperor Franz Josef recorded his voice with the Telegraphone at the Paris Exposition. It caused a sensation, as the press and the public began to realize the implications of recording a human voice, especially a great public figure. Among other things, one could now hear someone's voice without having to be present when that person spoke; it became possible to hear someone "speak" even after he or she had died.

The Blattnerphone

The first three decades of the twentieth century saw important developments in the evolution of magnetic recording. In 1928, Austrian chemist Fritz Pfleumer invented a recorder using lightweight tape coated with magnetic particles. During the 1930s Englishman Louis Blattner's Blattnerphone magnetic recorder was used by the British Broadcasting Corporation, or BBC, for its radio programs. The Blattnerphone was a remarkable and imposing machine that featured as its magnetic recording medium massive steel ribbons that required two people to install. The extreme tension of the steel ribbons created an environment not only dominated by their sheer size but one that was extremely dangerous. If the bands snapped, they could have killed anyone in the room.

Stereo Audio Recording

Although as early as the 1870s Clement Ader had used carbon microphones and armature headphones to inadvertently create a stereo effect, in which sound is recorded and played back in the same three-dimensional space as it was originally produced, it was not until 1930 that stereo recording was invented. Under the employment of Electrical and Musical Industries (EMI) in London, Alan Blumlein wrote a paper outlining the concept of stereo recording and obtained a patent for his idea. Arthur Keller and others at Bell Labs in the United States tested the idea and built a working device.

The Magnetophon

In 1936, the Magnetophon, another magnetic recording device, was used to record a performance of the London Philharmonic Orchestra in concert in Ludwigshafen, Germany. The device is among the oldest known surviving magnetic recordings of its type. The Magnetophon employed plastic tape coated with iron oxide. This was an extremely important development because it eliminated the dangerous characteristics of the Blattnerphone and made magnetic recording cheap and easy to use.

First Media Applications of Magnetic Storage: Bing Crosby

In 1947, the first major radio broadcast using magnetic recording occurred in the United States when crooner Bing Crosby switched his radio show from the National Broadcasting Corporation (NBC) to the American Broadcasting Corporation (ABC) radio network in order to use the Magnetophon.

Austrian Emperor Franz Josef recorded his voice on the telegraphone at the 1900 Paris Exposition.

Popular singer Bing Crosby was one of the pioneers in using magnetic recording technology.

ABC agreed to let him record his new show as long as the ratings did not fall too low, and they did not. The technical staff of the *Bing Crosby Show* on ABC arranged to rerecord original disk recordings of the show onto tape and then edit them for airing. Bing Crosby Enterprises negotiated financing for Ampex, the leading producer of magnetic recording technology, for exclusive distribution rights. As the exclusive distributor for Ampex products, Bing Crosby Enterprises sold hundreds of recorders to radio stations and master recording studios. In 1951, Bing Crosby Electronic Division was spun off to handle the development of audio instrumentation and video recording.[1]

Advent of Videotape

In 1956, Ampex Corp. manufactured the first practical magnetic videotape recorder, the VR-1000, for use by television stations. But the cost was very steep: $50,000. More than simply a means of recording video, the Ampex VR-1000 represented a whole new model for television programming, including television news. Essentially it meant not all programming or news needed to be either live or recorded on the slow-to-process and expensive medium of film. The features of the recorder made at least two new capabilities possible.

First was the instant replay feature of the recorder, which made it particularly attractive in comparison with the slow development time of film. Instant replay has of course transformed sports coverage. Second, the use of the recorder has also made it possible for journalists to edit video news even when they are close to deadline. This was a matter of importance to mass communication in the 1970s, as will be discussed shortly.

A drawback of the large, complex Ampex video recording machine was its use of two-inch-wide tape, which was cumbersome and difficult to work with.

The Ampex VR-1000 was the first practical magnetic videotape recorder, created in 1956. However, it had a steep $50,000 price tag.

Advances in Video Recording Technology

In 1961 the Society of Motion Picture and Television Engineers (SMPTE) established the standard for time code format on recorded audio and video (first on tape, but now on any storage medium). This is important because time coding (which indicates the seconds and minutes of the recording) is the basis for modern post-production or editing. Both audio and video are edited based on time code.

In 1963 Philips introduced the compact audiocassette recorder, followed by the eight-track recorder and microcassette.[2] In 1968 the first portable video recording equipment was invented in Europe. Portability meant journalists and other media professionals could work with video outside the studio. Prior to the development of portable video recording technology, only film could be shot in the field, whether for news, a commercial shoot, or a motion picture. Since its development, portable video recording has become a mainstay in the field production toolkit for contemporary media professionals.

Digital Tape Recording

It's also important to note that videotape does not necessarily mean a recording is analog. There are in fact many digital videotape recorders. Introduced in Japan in 1986, digital audiotape (DAT) emerged in the 1990s as a popular format for recording audio of all types and is widely used by mass communication professionals. Many video cameras also use digital videotape, and many mainframe and other computers use digital magnetic tape to store data.

The Social and Political Impact of Recording Audio and Video

Why do these developments matter to mass communication and society? Not only has the video recorder directly affected mass communication and how media professionals do their jobs, but it has affected news events, public affairs, and cultural phenomena themselves.

From the Kitchen Debate to Watergate

A dramatic example is the so-called "kitchen debate" in 1960, the height of the Cold War. U.S. Vice President Richard M. Nixon, who himself would later become President, was visiting the Soviet Union. While there, Nixon met with Soviet Premier Nikita Khrushchev. An impromptu debate occurred between Khrushchev and Nixon while the two were touring an exhibit of American home appliances in Moscow. Thanks to the "miracle" of recently invented portable magnetic video tape recorders, the "kitchen debate" was caught on videotape and subsequently replayed to 72 million TV viewers in the United States.

The impromptu "kitchen debate" between then U.S. Vice President Richard Nixon and Soviet Premier Nikita Krushchev could be watched by millions of people because of videotape.

Weblink
watergate.info
[watergate.info/]

In 1974 President Richard M. Nixon resigned after audiotapes (despite missing portions of the tapes) documented his role in the 1972 cover-up of the break-in of the office of the Democratic National Committee in the Watergate office complex.

From Rodney King to the Oval Office

More recently, in 1991 an amateur videotape of Rodney King being beaten at the hands of the police lead to riots in Los Angeles. This tape provided a record of the controversial use of force by police in arresting an African American suspect. It also offered a window for the entire U.S. population into the simmering racial tensions of the second-largest city in the country, in addition to showing how portable video recording technology made recording events much more ubiquitous.

In 1998, Linda Tripp's secret telephone audio tapings of her conversations with White House intern Monica Lewinsky lead to a sex scandal involving President Bill Clinton. After a major investigation by the office of the independent counsel, on December 19, 1998, President Clinton was impeached by the U.S. House of Representatives but acquitted of impeachment charges by the Senate on February 12, 1999.

The Media Impact of Recording Audio and Video

In the media, videotape has exerted a significant influence on news and programming production and distribution. Among the first media organizations to feel the effect of video recording technology were the television networks. They were among the earliest adopters of video recorders because they produced a great deal of motion picture content; but because it aired on television, it did not need to be of as high a quality as film. Film may have been needed for theatrical display, but

An assassination attempt on President Gerald Ford in San Francisco in September 1975 forced NBC News to realize they needed to switch to videotape, as the other two networks already had, in order to broadcast breaking news in a timely manner.

on the home television sets of the day the lower resolution of video was more than adequate. Moreover, the faster and easier editing made possible by video recording offered even further advantages to the networks, which produced many hours of motion picture programming each day.

By the mid-1970s both the ABC and CBS network news operations had converted from film to tape in their news-gathering processes, while NBC, with its parent RCA, had not—largely because, as news veteran Reese Schonfeld points out, RCA hadn't started producing tape. The 1975 assassination attempt on President Gerald Ford was the catalyst NBC needed to change from film to videotape.

In San Francisco, Calif., on Sept. 22, 1975, a would-be assassin fired a gun at President Gerald R. Ford. ABC and CBS recorded the attempted assassination on videotape, while NBC had it only on film. ABC and CBS were able to broadcast tape of the San Francisco shooting during their 7 PM news broadcasts, while NBC couldn't, because of the longer processing time required for film. After borrowing a copy of the video, NBC finally reported the event using the tape at 8:15 PM. The next day, Schonfeld recalls, NBC News put in the order to replace all its film equipment with videotape technology.

Managing Information: Development of Digital Storage Devices

We have become used to rapid changes in technology and particularly to changes in storage capacity so that we take developments largely for granted. But the gains in storage technology, especially storage capacity, are happening with a speed previously unseen in the development of media.

A first step toward automated computation and digital storage of various types of data was the introduction of punched cards, which were first successfully used in connection with computing in 1890 by Herman Hollerith working for the U.S. Census Bureau. Hollerith developed a device that could automatically read census information that had been punched onto a card. Hollerith, who also developed the

Media Technology
Information Bytes

Following are the most commonly used storage terms for digital media, with some of the higher-end terms to become more common as storage needs and capacity increase. A **byte** is eight bits of data, such as 0110011, and is the common unit used to denote memory storage:

kilobyte (KB)—1024 bytes

megabyte (MB)—1024 kilobytes; a floppy diskette is 1.2 MB, while a CD-ROM is usually about 700 MB

gigabyte (GB)—1024 megabytes; today's computer hard drives are commonly between 20 and 40 GB, while a DVD has 4.7 GB or 9.4 GB on a double-sided DVD

terabyte (TB)—1024 gigabytes; it is likely to be a few years before desktop computers have terabyte-capable hard drives, but this level of storage is needed for large, detailed and information-intensive images such as working with satellite imagery

petabyte (PB)—1024 terabytes

exabyte (EB)—1024 petabytes

For the sake of convenience, it is standard to round down to 1000 when calculating the amount of storage a given unit has. Note that the increases in storage capacity are exponential. That is, a gigabyte doesn't store 2000 times more than a kilobyte but a *million* times more (i.e., a thousand thousands).

Researchers in 2001 calculated that approximately 1.5 exabytes of new information is produced each year, or enough to fill 50 million iMacs. And that's not including information that is simply copied.[3]

A comparison of a 1996 IBM disk drive to the first IBM disk drive, introduced in 1956.

first electromechanical tabulator, got his idea from watching a train conductor punch tickets. As a result of Hollerith's invention, reading errors in the Census were consequently greatly reduced, workflow was increased, and, more important, stacks of punched cards could be used as an accessible memory store of almost unlimited capacity. Furthermore, different problems could be stored on different batches of cards and worked on as needed. Hollerith later went on to establish his own firm to market his electromechanical tabulator, a company that later became International Business Machines (IBM).

In 1964, Rex Schaeffer of the *Rochester Times-Union and Democrat & Chronicle* suggested the idea of using a punched-card subject index for a clip file collection in a newspaper morgue. In 1968 *The Toronto Globe and Mail* began to store photo negatives on aperture cards and index them with a computer for easy retrieval. Although punch cards continued to serve as an important part of computing and computing memory well into the 1980s, the 1950s witnessed the development of magnetic recording technologies central to computer memory and recording.

Digital Storage Technology

Core memory, hard disk, and magnetic tape storage devices were developed in the early 1950s, although their capacity was quite limited by today's standards. In 1952, for example, the core memory of the Whirlwind I computer could store just 256 bits of data. Compare that to the standard multigigabits of magnetic storage a basic personal computer came equipped with by 2002. IBM shipped its first hard-disk computer storage device in 1957. Its capacity: 50 disks that could store a combined 56 megabytes. Today's PC and laptop hard drives are usually 20 gigabytes or more.

In 1971, the floppy disk was introduced, first in 8-inch format, then 5.25-inch and later 3.5-inch. The key developments were, and continue to be, miniaturization of storage, higher storage capacity, and random access. Memory sticks, introduced by Sony in 1999, as well as other miniature memory cards by other makers that go by a variety of names, are used in digital cameras, handheld PDAs, and other devices. They are about half the size of credit cards or even smaller and can hold many megabytes (MB) of information. In 2001, Sony introduced memory sticks holding up to 128 MB—the equivalent of about one hundred 3.5-inch floppy diskettes—in a device approximately the size of a stick of chewing gum. Flash cards, the size of a large postage stamp, can hold several MB of information, enough for dozens of Web-quality digital photos, for example.

Optical Storage

In 1982, Sony and Philips N.V. of the Netherlands introduced the compact disc–read only memory **optical storage** device (CD-ROM). CD-ROMs were the first optical, digital storage medium and, as such, the first storage medium with truly massive recording capabilities. CD-ROMs, like other optical storage media, do not record information using the magnetic properties employed on computer floppy disks, memory sticks, or audio/videotape. Instead, optical storage media use light, in the form of lasers, to store and read data of all types, whether text,

byte—the most common base unit used to measure computer storage and information, it consists of eight bits, or some combination of os and 1s, to form letters, numbers, and all modes of computer information that are displayed.

optical storage—uses light in the form of lasers to store and read data of all types, whether text, audio, or video. Using light is highly efficient and permits storage devices to record vastly greater amounts of data in small spaces and enable faster retrieval of the stored data than do magnetic storage devices.

Media Future: Nanotechnology: It's Going to Be Big

Nanotechnology refers to ultra-small technology, involving devices built or operating at nanometer sizes, or one billionth of a meter. Nanotechnology promises to transform a variety of fields, including electronics, manufacturing, and information storage and retrieval. The science of nanoscale research is relatively new, having developed since the invention of atomic force microscopes in the mid-1980s.

With the theoretical physical limits nearing of conventional silicon-based storage media, nanotechnology may one day produce the only viable information storage media capable of storing massive quantities of media data on incredibly miniature devices. Nanoscale storage media will be capable of manipulating data at an atomic or subatomic scale. This means that the contents of the entire Library of Congress of the United States, the largest library in the world, could be stored on a single device no larger than the tip of a finger. The content of today's Library of Congress in analog format (e.g., words and pictures on paper, audio, and video on tape) comprises more than a million cubic feet on approximately 530 miles of bookshelves in three buildings. The Library of Congress's collections include 120 million items, including 18 million books, 2.5 million recordings (including audio and video, such as television shows and movies), 12 million photographs, 4.5 million maps, and 54 million manuscripts.[4]

Because of its enormous potential, researchers expect nanotechnology to be an increasingly important and significant part of information storage and other fields in the twenty-first century. In 2001, the National Science Foundation awarded funding for the establishment of national nanoscale research centers at six major research universities.

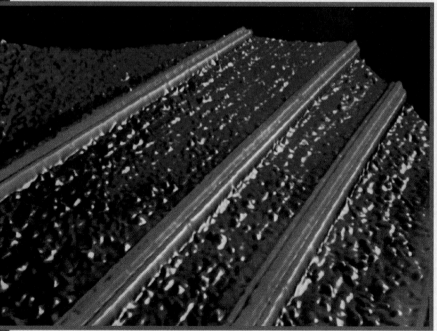

audio, or video. Using light is highly efficient and permits storage devices to record vastly greater amounts of data in small spaces and enable faster retrieval of the stored data.

CD-ROMs

A single CD-ROM can store up to 300,000 pages of text, more than an hour of audio (explaining the popularity of the CD for music distribution) or about a half-hour of video. CD-ROM technology, like many other optical and other digital recording media, has a limited expected lifespan. Experts project that a typical CD-ROM has a life expectancy of about 50 to 75 years. At this time, the content will begin to disintegrate or the devices to play or access the content contained on the CD-ROM will have become obsolete. Compared to other digital devices, this is about the typical life expectancy. But compared to some analog devices, this life expectancy is somewhat inferior. Although newsprint and videotape disintegrates in a similar fashion, books can last much longer than half a century and accessibility does not depend on technology. However, a book of course cannot record sound or motion pictures.

DVDs

The CD-ROM was the precursor to the DVD (digital video disk or digital versatile disk), introduced in 1997. DVDs are the first optical medium that can store an entire two-hour feature-length movie in digital format. For this reason, DVD has emerged as an important medium for delivering movies to the home. From Disney to Warner Brothers, all the major Hollywood movie studios now release for sale or rental new, older, and classic titles on DVD. Many titles include never-before-seen footage, interviews with the actors and filmmakers, and "making of" footage shot while the movie was being made.

DVDs also provide better visual and sound quality than videotape, as well as additional content. VHS resolution is 210 horizontal lines, while laser disc has 425 lines and DVD 540 lines of resolution. The viewer also has more control over the viewing experience, choosing among various screen formats, such as wide-screen (cinematic) or conventional TV viewing. Viewers typically also can choose the language in which they listen to a movie on a DVD, usually English, French, or Spanish. DVDs offer high sound quality, with a higher sampling rate than audio CDs, as well as Dolby Surround Sound, with six audio channels. DVD discs look just like audio CDs, being $4^{3}/_{4}$ inches in diameter.

By 2002, more than 5000 movie titles were available on DVD, and more than 20 million DVD discs were sold the previous year. *Titanic* sold more than a million units on DVD. Consumers have purchased more than 20 million DVD players, and the price of DVD players has fallen below the $100 level.

Recordable DVDs, or systems that allow users to record their own DVDs, entered the commercial market in 2000. As digital storage prices continue to fall and recordable DVDs become more widespread, it is believed that they will supersede and eventually completely replace CD-ROMs in computers.

Digital Personal Video Recorders

An important development in the digital television (DTV) consumer marketplace is the introduction of digital video recording and playback devices, including such products as ReplayTV, TiVo, and UltimateTV. The Web sites for these products

Personal Video Recorders promise to further redefine the relationship with television audiences and programmers.

describe their systems as "personalized television." Some call them **personal video recorders** (PVRs).

PVRs use advanced digital television technology to record analog or digital television signals delivered over the air, by satellite, cable, or DSL to the recording and playback device, for either live or delayed viewing, usually a large hard-drive storage device of 10 gigabytes or more.

They offer a variety of features that many viewers find compelling, such as easy recording of TV shows without commercials; the ability to pause, rewind, and fast-forward live TV; instant replay; compatibility with all cable set-top boxes; and convenient search functions that allow programmed recording of all shows by criteria such as one's favorite actor or director.

Mass Media Implications for Digital Storage Technology

It is easy to see the benefits of CD-ROMs or DVDs in terms of how they improve most of the fundamental aspects of storage technology, except perhaps for longevity. It is much easier to carry around a CD-ROM containing the text of more than 500 books than it is to carry the books themselves around. Likewise, DVDs increase the portability of movies over videotapes or reels of film. And although the portability gain may seem minimal in the case of videotapes, DVDs can play on more devices, such as computers and DVD players, and are thus more accessible, not to mention their higher storage capacity that allows them to provide the audience with more types of content.

PVR systems promise to further alter the relationship between audience and program provider. They are not simply competition for the video rental store and VCR industry. They fundamentally change the relationship between the program provider and the viewer by placing much greater control in the hands of the viewer and providing a low-cost, consumer video-on-demand service. One simple example already visible today is how they change the way viewers will—or will not—get their TV advertising.

The consequences to date have been at least twofold. First, because the traditional video providers recognize the importance of these digital recorders for how people watch television and advertising, they are themselves investing in the development of digital recorders. Among the investors in TiVo are America Online (AOL), Advance/Newhouse, CBS, Comcast Corporation, Cox Communications, Discovery Communications, Encore Media Group, Liberty Media, NBC, Showtime Networks, Sony, TV Guide Interactive, and The Walt Disney Company.[5]

Second, traditional video providers are increasingly developing programming where commercial messages are embedded directly into the programming. Such **product placement,** as it is called, is not new to television. Network television programming from the 1950s often featured actors, hosts, or even news anchors holding a product from a sponsor or sitting on a set featuring the name of a sponsor. But in the digital age, product placement is often of a virtual nature, where the product that appears on screen is inserted electronically and is not physically present on the set or in the studio. Further, as interactive television develops, the virtual products are themselves interactive and permit the viewer to click a mouse

personal video recorders (PVRs)—another term for digital video recording and playback devices, including such products as ReplayTV, TiVo, and UltimateTV. Devices like these, which allow many hours of recording and several other features, will fundamentally alter the relationship between the TV viewer and broadcaster.

product placement—the practice of having actual products shown prominently and used in television shows and movies, which advertisers pay for.

How Digital Media Are Changing Our World   www.ablongman.com/pavlik1e

or remote control device, or use voice command to select the product, drop it into their virtual shopping basket, and purchase it for home delivery.

As a result, James F. McCaffrey, senior vice president, Strategic Planning, Turner Entertainment Group, says ReplayTV and TiVo are at the point where established broadcasters can't simply ignore them. "We are exploring the implications of this new technology on our business and industry and will closely examine all our options," he said.[6]

Managing Information: Compression of Digital Audio and Video

The technological development of digital storage and distribution has not developed at an even pace. Although we have vastly more storage available to us than even a few years ago in increasingly smaller devices, audio takes much more capacity than text and video even more than audio. In other words, as our ability to store information digitally increases, our desire to store more memory-hungry content seems to increase as well.

What has not kept pace with increases in storage capacity is the storage capacity of the lines, or "pipes" used to transmit that data between users in a network. Twisted-pair copper wires for telephone lines, which are fine for voice communication and which most people use to access the Internet through dial-up modems, do not have enough capacity to transmit large amounts of data. This is one reason why it is necessary to compress digital data. A useful analogy might be the need to roll up and stuff a sleeping bag into its original cover bag in order to easily carry it from one campsite to another. Once it is finally in a compact form, it can be carried relatively easily. And like the contortions and struggles that go into cramming a down sleeping bag into a space the size of two loaves of bread, engineers have had similar troubles trying to compress audio and video so they too can be easily transported.

How MPEG Works

MPEG, or the Motion Pictures Experts Group, was established in 1988 under the leadership of **Leonardo Chiariglione,** who is now heading the secure digital music standard for the international music recording industry. MPEG is also the name for the encoding process used to compactly represent digital video and audio for general distribution.

The MPEG encoding process transforms a stream of discrete samples captured from the original audio and video into a stream of data that takes less space than the original but is just as clear to the eye or ear. This transformation, or digital representation of sight and sound, exploits characteristics of human perception that allow people to fill in missing data as well as some actual statistical redundancies in the sampled data.

MPEG compresses, or squeezes, the video or audio by removing any redundant information from one frame of video to the next. In other words, it removes

MPEG—Motion Pictures Experts Group, established in 1988 and responsible for creating the standards for digital and audio compression. Also used for the types of compression, such as MPEG-1, MPEG-4, and so on.

Chiariglione, Leonardo—former leader of MPEG and now in charge of the Secure Digital Music Initiative, a group created by the recording industry to examine ways to protect copyrights and stop unauthorized copying of music in the digital age.

An MP3 Player.

Weblink
MPEG Web site
[www.cselt.it/mpeg/].

the part that doesn't change and only transmits the part that changes from frame to frame. Occasionally, however, a small amount of important information is lost in the process. As a result, compression sometimes does not work well with video in which there is a lot of movement, such as a sporting event.

MP3 and Common MPEG Formats

The audio component of MPEG (Motion Pictures Experts Group-1, Audio Layer III) emerged in the mid-1990s as an ad hoc standard for pirated digital audio and is today known simply by its nickname, MP3. There is a wide range of software players available for listening to MP3 audio files on a computer. A variety of portable MP3 players, or hand-held devices for listening to MP3 files, also emerged in the late 1990s.

MPEG-2 was approved in 1992 and was the compression standard in 2002 for broadcast-quality digital video. It's what's being distributed via current terrestrial DTV broadcasts, direct broadcast satellite (DBS) systems, high-density CD-ROMs, and digital video/versatile disks (DVD).

MPEG-4 represents an important next generation of digital video. MPEG-4 is the standard for a type called object-oriented digital video, in which the individual components of a digital video stream can be encoded separately. For example, imagine a video of the pit at an automobile racetrack. The car is an object, the members of the pit crew are objects, the equipment can be objects.

What does this mean for media producers and the audience? In a scene with separate objects, each object can be encoded with additional information, such as its identity, or textual labels or annotations, or even pointers to related Web pages.

MPEG-21 represents the convergence of all the existing MPEG standards, integrated into an international digital video standard for the twenty-first century. At this writing, the final specifications of MPEG-21 are still being crafted but are likely to contain the specifications of the earlier MPEG levels, plus important specifications for digital watermarks to protect copyright of digital content and security for electronic commerce.

The Media Implications of MP3 and MPEG Formats

The implications of MPEG compression and its various standards are significant for mass communication. Importantly for both media organizations and consumers, MPEG compression greatly reduces the amount of bandwidth needed to store and send video in digital format. This makes it easier and more economical for media organizations and consumers to store digital content, as well as deliver or access it via a network, even with a dial-up modem connection. With MPEG formats currently in development, such as MPEG-4 and MPEG-21, they will enhance the interactive capabilities of digital video even more.

MP3 has at least three important implications for mass communication. First, MP3 has become a de facto standard for high-quality digital audio distributed via the Internet. MP3 file sizes are typically 1 MB per minute of music. This small size makes them easy to transport and copy onto other media, as well as turns an average desktop computer into a digital jukebox. Consequently, all traditional music distributors, including the major and minor record labels, have been forced to seriously consider how they can adapt their traditional distribution systems—which have relied on the use of CDs—to accommodate this immensely popular and powerful form of online music compression and its subsequent distribution.

Second, online distribution of MP3 music files has significantly challenged conventional wisdom on copyright and intellectual property rights. Courts, companies, consumers, and artists are today embroiled in legal battles and battles in the court of public opinion to resolve questions of who owns the rights to digital music and how to accommodate and protect those rights in the age of online communications.

Third, the pricing structure for music distributed online in MP3 form is being revisited. There was a certain logic that underlay the pricing structure for music distributed on fixed media such as CDs, records, or tapes. This logic was based on the combination of a variety of factors, including costs for music production, marketing and manufacturing and distributing the physical items that contained the music. Music distributed online in MP3 format no longer follows this same formula, because manufacturing and distribution costs have been radically revised, if not eliminated.

Managing Information: Finding and Retrieving Digital Content

With vast amounts of information available to us at the touch of a few keystrokes, finding and retrieving the information that is specifically wanted becomes a crucial issue. It serves little purpose if a library of information is stored in the space of a desktop computer if there is no easy way to randomly access information. Indexing has long been a useful tool for text-based information and continues to be used for Web search engines. However, indexing has been more difficult for digital audio and video, although new technologies are changing that. Further, researchers are investigating radical new ways that information can be accessed and retrieved, including the use of intelligent agents and other such methods that used to be imagined only in science-fiction.

Search Engines

Search engines are tools for locating content on the Web. With millions of Web pages, users employ keyword search engines in which the user types in the unique word or set of words that identify the subject of interest to find the pages of content they are looking for. Search engines include various types of tools or capabilities, including keyword searches, multimedia search tools, and even language translation.

Yahoo! and many of the several other major search engines have developed into what are called "portals," or gateways into Web content. As such, they have evolved new forms of content access and presentation that go far beyond simple content searches. For example, Yahoo! offers My Yahoo!, which includes customizable news, chat, travel services, and much more. Many traditional mass communication organizations are seeking to develop their own "portal" sites, often partnering with major search engines. These portals also include directories of Web content, typically organized into more than a dozen main content areas such as news, health, and entertainment.

Problems with Web Search Engines

One of the problems with search engines in general is that none of them include all Web pages. In fact, a study by the NEC Research Institute shows that total search engine coverage, including all search engines, is actually dropping over time as more sites are published. There are more than 30 million Web sites, and many billions of Web pages).[7] In 1997, total search engine coverage was 60 percent; by 2001 that percentage had fallen to less than 50 percent.

No single engine indexes more than about one-fifth of the web. As a result, many mass communication professionals may find combined-search engine searches useful. Such tools are called metasearch engines. One popular metasearch engine is metacrawler. Although it doesn't offer effective advanced or refined features on concept searches, it does allow the user to enter a search term once and simultaneously search multiple search engines, including Excite, AltaVista, and Google. Such metasearches allow for easy expanded coverage of the Web.

Content-Based Systems: Searching for Audio and Video

Empowered by improved digital storage technologies, an important development in the late 1990s and early twenty-first century has been the development of what are known as **content-based systems** for storage, indexing, and retrieval. These content-based systems permit communication professionals and others to access and retrieve visual and audio content based on the attributes of that content, not just the text-only access that has dominated for so long. That is, images and audio have been accessible primarily through two methods. First, users could watch or listen to the images or audio tape to find what they're looking for. Second, based on how someone had manually indexed those images or audio clips using text descriptors, users could conduct a keyword search of the content. In either case, the process was slow, expensive, and not terribly efficient, which has meant that many local or small media organizations have made limited use of multimedia archives.

New content-based techniques allow searches based on the visual or sound features of the content itself, greatly improving efficiency and speed of retrieval and thereby making it possible to do new things with that content. For example, imagine you are editing video and have four hours of video to search through for a specific, 30-second clip of interest, such as a sports sequence in which a baseball player hits a home run. In the past, unless you manually indexed every sequence within the video, or had already watched the video (perhaps while it was being recorded), the only way to find what you are looking for would be to watch the entire video, looking for the frames of video where the batter hits the ball out of the park.

content-based systems— search and retrieval systems that allow searches based on the attributes of content, such as visual or audio features of a piece of content regardless of the details of what is shown or heard.

Using content-based video search and retrieval, you would use a visual search engine to sketch out your ideas and query the video database. That is, using a visual tool box much like the simple painting or drawing programs that come with most computers, you would draw on a digital sketch pad a circle to represent the ball and then drag it across the pad to represent the motion of the ball being hit out of the park for a home run. Utilizing random access memory, the visual search engine would then automatically search the four hours of video for an action or sequence similar to what you had sketched on the digital pad. After a few moments, a series of frames would appear on your screen indicating the matches identified from the video. You would then quickly scan each one to identify the precise sequence of interest. The entire process might take you less than three or four minutes, a significant time savings over watching the entire four hours of video, even if scanned on fast forward.

Intelligent video and audio search tools are now capable of automatically scanning video for objects or actions of significance, such as automatically detecting scene changes or significant events in sports contests such as a soccer player scoring a goal.[8] For mass communication professionals this can be of special value, especially when operating on a tight deadline.

Intelligent Agents

Search engines often use "spiders," or intelligent agents (sometimes called "knowledge robots," or "knowbots," or even just "bots"), to search the Web for content and accept site registrations and thus compile databases. Intelligent agents are software robots that act autonomously (i.e., they act independently, traveling the Web, making decisions, evaluating the content they find, and categorizing it into a database) on behalf of another entity (typically a human, but it may be another software robot, for example). They are becoming increasingly common on the Web as tools for:

- sorting and sifting through the millions of pages of Web content;
- conducting specific assigned tasks (such as booking a reservation for a flight);
- making an online purchase or searching through newsgroups.

Many of these agents are now being used in online journalism products, from the automatic handling of subscriptions to online news products and services to sorting through thousands of Usenet newsgroups and thousands of news stories from hundreds of online news sources every day and compiling easily digested summaries.

Transforming Information Indexing and Retrieval

An emerging set of technologies is transforming how information is sorted and retrieved in a digital media storage system. These systems take advantage of the combination of improvements in digital storage capabilities and advances in computer processing power. They promise to make much of the time-consuming, expensive manual labor involved in searching, indexing, and retrieving specific content—especially audio or video content—much easier. This will improve the quality of information journalists can send in their stories, as they will have more time to evaluate and compare data as opposed to logging time codes or transcribing.

Columbia Newsblaster

The Columbia Newsblaster is a natural language processing system designed as a tool for summarizing news from the Internet . Leading the Newsblaster research has been Kathy McKeown, professor and chairman of the computer science department at Columbia University. Newsblaster provides links to live news sources and articles, then classifies, summarizes, and presents the summaries. Newsblaster uses advanced artificial intelligence algorithms to extract salient bits of information—for example, the death toll in a terrorist attack—from different news sources and then presents results to the user as updates become available. One demonstration of the system has successfully tracked the 2001 World Trade Center terrorist attack. Tests of the Newsblaster technology have also analyzed and summarized multimedia news, presenting maps of the area and images of the scene of the World Trade Center attack.

Weblink
Columbia Newsblaster
[www.cs.columbia.edu/nlp
/newsblaster]

Automatic Transcription

A variety of institutions are conducting research on storage, retrieval, and summarization technologies. Consider a system called Rough'n'Ready developed by GTE Internetworking / BBN Technologies in Cambridge, Massachusetts. Rough'n'Ready is an audio indexing system that produces rough transcriptions of audio files that can be prepared for browsing in minutes on a standard personal computer. In other words, Rough'n'Ready automatically records and roughly transcribes the proceedings of meetings, presentations, or conferences.

Rough'n'Ready also can be used to automatically transcribe radio or television broadcasts, cablecasts, or webcasts. Moreover, using a proprietary large vocabulary speech-recognition system called Byblos, Rough'n'Ready has a summarization tool that can automatically provide a summary of the entire transcript. The software can also identify and label each speaker and classify by topics, which permits the automatic indexing of a transcript based on stories or subjects, people, places, and organizations.[9]

Weblink
Rough'n'Ready
[www.bbn.com/speech
/roughnready.html]

SUMMARY

This chapter has examined what is meant by the term *storage technology*, the key issues underlying it, and the importance that it has to mass communication in the digital age. Among the fundamental elements for any storage technology are longevity, capacity, portability, accessibility, and

reproducibility of storage media. The evolution of media can to some extent be seen as improvements in each of these fundamental elements, although advances in some areas have traded off regression in other areas. The relatively short lifespan of chemical, magnetic, or optical media is a step backward from the longevity of stone tablets, for example, although in almost every other category they are a vast improvement.

The historical development of storage media for audio and later video started in the nineteenth century and continues today. Mass communication, and especially entertainment, has been a driving force behind technological developments in recording. Entertainment continues to be crucial in giving incentive to media companies to innovate and develop better storage technologies in the digital age.

Media professionals and organizations have used a variety of recording media to create, edit, and distribute text, audio, and video programming. Not only have these storage media influenced media production and distribution processes, but they have influenced the audiences and societies accessing those media.

The state-of-the-art of storage media is increasingly becoming digital, super-fast, massive, and optical in nature. Emerging storage technologies are poised to expand storage capacities even further, although not without creating new problems that must be overcome, such as how to easily find material in a randomized yet specific manner. Media organizations and professionals look to use these technologies to improve storage and retrieval efficiency, cost effectiveness, and control over intellectual property. Meanwhile, consumers look to use these devices to give them more personalized and portable access to digital multimedia content.

Discussion Questions

1. Which characteristic of storage technology do you think is most important for a society to run day-to-day business? What about to preserve its cultural heritage? Do you think the relative importance of storage technology characteristics has changed with the advent of digital media? Why or why not?

2. Imagine a world in which audio or video could not be recorded. Discuss how media would be different in terms of content creation, performance or distribution, media organizations, and economics.

3. Some contend that secretly recording conversations or activities in audio or video format, even when the acts recorded occurred in a public space, is a violation of privacy. State and defend your position on the matter.

4. How might increased portability or accessibility of a media storage device change the way people interact with media content? What implications could this have for people, media companies, and society in general?

5. Personal video recorders (PVRs) such as TiVo or ReplayTV provide vast amounts of storage capacity. Discuss their weaknesses in terms of other fundamentals of storage technology and suggest ways that they could overcome these weaknesses. How might these changes affect how they are used by consumers?

6. Discuss ways in which you would like to see search engines improved.

7. Compare the benefits and drawbacks for media professionals of having large amounts of information readily at hand. How might the balance of information versus ease of retrieval affect how journalists do their jobs?

8. If almost all information was available to anyone at any time on a compact, easy-to-use device, how do you think this would affect the level of people's general knowledge or education? Would people become more knowledgeable and more active in society? Would they become more apathetic, or would they be more or less the same? How might this device affect different people within society, such as rich vs. poor, or various ethnic or language groups?

MEDIA ? Quiz

1. False; it is 1000 (kilo) bytes.
2. kilobyte, megabyte, gigabyte, terabyte, petabyte, exabyte.
3. False, cave paintings and petroglyphs are forms of information storage that predate writing systems.
4. True, such current media as videotape and DVDs are expected to last only about 50 to 75 years.
5. False, it stands for MPEG-1, Audio Layer-III.
6. NBC, after the assassination attempt on President Ford in 1975
7. Approximately 300,000 pages of text.
8. True.

BUILDING STATUS

- Not Affected
- Needs Cleaning
- Damaged But Stable Ready for Occupancy With Repairs/Cleaning
- Major Structural Damage Occupancy Not Permitted
- Destroyed
- In Danger of Collapse

User Interface: Interacting with Digital Content

8

In the aftermath of the terrorist attack on the World Trade Center in New York City on September 11, 2001, many people turned to online sources of information for details on what happened, how, and why.

Among the most powerful tools available to explain the attack, its impact, and context were various forms of advanced interactive visualizations made possible only in a digital environment. At CNN.com, for example, viewers had access to a series of more than three dozen 3-D maps, animated diagrams, and other interactive features explaining the damage done to the World Trade Center, the rescue and recovery, the potential for biological attacks, and much more.

Online slideshows, interactive timelines, video clips, and active chat rooms and discussion groups were also part of the unique news environment available to the public to help them understand and come to terms with the tragedy.

Weblink
[http://www6.cnn.com
/SPECIALS/2001/trade.center
/interactives.html].

Prologue

The term **user interface** is a technological way of referring to the junction between a medium of communication and the people who use it. We are usually familiar with our everyday media and so don't give user interface a second thought. Nobody has to remind you how to turn a page in a book, for example, or how to find the sports section in the newspaper or tune a radio dial.

However, it is easy to forget that the knowledge of using everyday media did not come naturally, but was learned. Watch a baby with a children's book to see how she explores the book. She chews the corners of the book, holds it upside down, shakes it, and randomly goes through the pages. It does not take long for her to figure out that she should turn the pages in sequence, even long before she can actually read.

Comparing a baby exploring the world with rational, thinking adults might not seem completely fair. But consider a case in which many adults are left as helpless as a baby—programming a VCR. Or think about the last time you were able to immediately turn on someone else's television and stereo system with an unfamiliar remote control. Chances are you needed to ask the owner for help in doing so, even though it was probably just a matter of pushing a couple of buttons. But knowing which buttons to push in what order made all the difference.

Computers, because of their newness for most people and relative complexity, make us even more aware of user interface issues. Even something as simple for computer users as using a mouse is a completely new and nonintuitive experience for a computer novice, let alone the functions that right clicking a mouse or double-clicking can accomplish. Even after the mechanics of mouse clicking and manipulation have been mastered, there is still an entirely new world of user control with the interface that must be learned, including the concepts of adjusting window sizes and moving or hiding windows within the screen.

The previous example exemplifies how computers have brought a new aspect of user interface to mass communication—the ability of the audience to interact with and control what they see and how they see it. This does not apply only to

user interface—the junction between a medium of communication and the people who use it.

Computer users have the ability to interact far more with media content than do viewers of traditional media.

changing the desktop background or screen resolution, but also to how they get their news and entertainment, whether in words, images, video, or sound.

In the past, the audience has been limited largely to the role of passive recipient of mediated news and entertainment. Newspapers, magazines, or books could be limited by locale and could only contain a certain amount of news or information. Likewise, radio and television stations covered only specific geographic areas. The advent of cable and satellite television largely eliminated the issue of limited televised content, but the audience was still by and large passive. Media content was sent by a publisher or broadcaster to a large audience who could do little about changing how they experienced what was sent.

In today's media environment, the audience can choose not only what type of content they see and from what media source, but in many cases how they want to experience it. They could choose audio to listen to news while they work on other things, or watch a video clip of an interview, or get the full text transcript of that interview to read later. They could also choose to get the content in a format that they could easily download to a digital appliance such as a Palm Pilot.

These are dramatic changes in how the public receives—and perceives—its media. The increased control in the hands of the audience as to how they see their media content and a better awareness of user interface issues can help generate more active media consumers who are more likely to have a higher level of media literacy.

The Importance of User Interface

Audiences have always used traditional media in terms of receiving content. But they are not "users" of the media in the same sense that they are users of a computer to run applications such as word processing, a Web browser, or e-mail. With the rise of digital media, the audience have become more active users, and the interface has become a key element in shaping that use.

The interface transformation is in many ways about empowering the user, or audience. The user is critical to the future of mass communication. The user interface, or how the user interacts with a medium or its content, is a cornerstone for media success. If a user can't find her or his way to a Web site, the 500-channel universe, or an electronic program guide, then even great media content will essentially be hidden from view. To be practical, the user interface should be intuitive and natural, yet appropriate to the medium and its content and customizable to each user's preferences. For a field such as journalism, utilizing a good user interface means potentially re-engaging an increasingly alienated news audience. This is why the user interface is critical to mass communication in the digital age.

Current Problems with User Interface

There are advantages to a simple, unchanging user interface. The user always knows what to expect, always knows where to find things, and doesn't need a user's guide each time he or she tunes in a new channel, reads a different newspaper, or opens a new book. As long as the user interface is well designed, a static design offers efficiency to the user. Traditional media have had decades—or even centuries—to create the most efficient user interface. They have evolved slowly, carefully, and thoughtfully into highly effective systems.

This is unfortunately not the case with digital media and the Internet. User interface has become a critical issue for a number of reasons. First, digital media are very new and have not had time to evolve. Second, rapid advances in technology radically alter any user interface assumptions that can be made. Think of how different content may appear in a world in which tiny screens on cell phones with keypads are the primary method of accessing media, as opposed to one in which tiny lenses embedded in a pair of glasses give the appearance of wall-sized screen with crystal clarity and are activated by voice commands. Third, varying computer standards mean not all technology is accepted, so what may appear in one browser may not appear correctly—or at all—in a different, or older, browser. Finally, the audience too often remains media illiterate from a technological standpoint, making them unable to access media simply because they do not understand how to do the online equivalent of turning a page in a book. To be fair, it is not always the public's fault; too often poor or confusing design choices by Web site designers create confusion.

However, most of these problems will eventually sort themselves out over time and become less of an issue compared to traditional media. It is likely to take some time, however, and will happen only after many stops and starts. These kinds of problems are to be expected with digital media, which are fundamentally challenging the centuries-old model of a relatively noninteractive media system and a static user interface.

Development of the User Interface

From an historical perspective, the evolution of the electronic user interface, or how people access mass communication content, began with the development of

How Digital Media Are Changing Our World   www.ablongman.com/pavlik1e

Most computer monitors today employ exactly the same CRT technology used by the vast majority of televisions.

radio and television, two important electronic media whose "user" interfaces were critical to their success.

Yet before the development of the computer, we did not generally employ the term "user interface" in discussions of the media. This is because the traditional, analog media were not designed to be interactive, and what we call the user interface was generally unchanging. It was easy to understand how to turn a dial or push a button to receive content, which appeared in the same way everywhere it was broadcast.

There are two main elements in the development of the electronic user interface. One is the technological innovations that have given us the computer and other items in the modern era. The other element is the social aspect, or getting people used to using new technologies in a mass communication context.

Before examining the technological innovations, we will first examine an unlikely source that unknowingly helped prepare the public mentally for interacting with computers in the digital age—television.

The Television Screen

Except for laptops or flat-panel displays, computer monitors use the identical **cathode-ray tube (CRT)** technology that TVs utilize. Technological improvements in computer monitors, once they became the standard interface with computers, have largely been driven by giving them more television-like qualities that we have come to expect from a screen such as color, a certain size, sound, and crisp images. Of course some of these elements have nothing to do with the monitor itself, such as sound, but the point is that we have come to see our televisions as single units that produce sounds and moving pictures.

The fact that computer monitors largely adopt the screen **aspect ratio** of television screens has affected a great many subsequent design and user interface choices. The fact that a "page" of text cannot be seen and read in its entirety on a screen sometimes bothers new computer users, for example, who would like to see an overview of where items are spaced on a page at a glance *and* read text at the same time. For word processing, it would seem more natural to have a vertically oriented screen, as if the standard monitor were turned on its side.

cathode ray tube (CRT)—a device that is still used in most television screens and computer monitors in which electrons are transmitted to a screen for viewing.

aspect ratio—the ratio of a screen's height to its width. The incompatible aspect ratios of films and television mean that films either have to be cropped to fit within a television screen or, in order to keep the original aspect ratio, black borders must appear on the top and bottom of the screen.

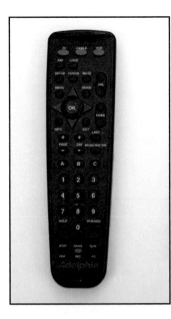

Remote controls have become far more complex than the earliest models, just as more media appliances can be controlled remotely.

multitasking—in a computer environment, doing several activities at once with a variety of programs, such as simultaneously doing word-processing, spreadsheet, and database work, while conducting real-time chat through an instant messenger service.

When people start to watch more movies on their computer monitors, the aspect ratio will also have an effect on how they are seen, because the aspect ratios between films and television are different (thus either forcing movies on television to cut off part of a scene or keep the original aspect ratio but have black spaces above and below the scenes).

It is interesting to note that although computer makers originally borrowed from television in creating monitors, television has returned the favor in borrowing from the online world of screen windows, scrolling text or tickers, and multiple items on various topics on a single screen. This can especially be seen in newscasts, although the results are often confusing when done on television.

Television and the Remote Control

The TV remote control is not only one of the most important transformational technologies in television but has also often been the source of friction between the sexes and family members. The first TV remote control was introduced in 1950.[1] Zenith introduced the Lazy Bones, a remote control connected by a wire to a TV set. In 1955, Zenith introduced the Flashmatic, the first wireless TV remote, which used a flashlight to change channels. Then, in 1956, Zenith's Space Command (remember, it was the dawn of the space age) used ultrasound to change channels, also producing interesting effects on household pets. Most modern TV remote controls use infrared technology.

The remote control, besides being one of the earliest examples of consumers using wireless technology in the home (aside from the radio), had important effects on TV viewers. Perhaps most importantly and obviously, it enabled easy channel changing. Before the remote control, viewers had to get up and walk to the set to change the channel, which significantly inhibited channel changing. The remote control altered viewing habits, as viewers could now easily move back and forth between channels, or channel surf, and avoid commercials or uninteresting segments in programs or simply watch multiple sports events. In other words, they were almost effortlessly interacting with their televisions, albeit in a very limited way as of course they could not actually change the content they were receiving.

In addition, frequently changing channels could be considered a simple form of **multitasking,** a common phenomenon in the computer environment in which people do several simultaneous activities. The decreased patience in watching content can also be seen in the way computer users use digital media as they access a number of different media outlets in pursuing their objectives without spending a long time on any specific item.

However much remote controls are taken for granted today, they did play an important role in subtly altering and expanding the parameters of media usage. The computer of course has played a much more prominent role in bringing user interface issues to the forefront of mass communication.

The Computer Interface

Because computers and humans use different languages, some kind of interface, or "translator," is needed to allow communication between the two. In the earliest days of computing, the user interface was anything but simple. Usually, only the inventor or a highly trained specialist could operate a computer, interact with it, or access information contained within it.

Data was entered on punch cards, often requiring hundreds of cards to represent even a simple piece of information, such as a series of numbers or names. The output of a computer analysis was typically printed on paper, which might take many minutes or even hours to print with a slow, dot-matrix printer. If computers were to be more useful for people, they would not only need to become more powerful but would also have to have a better interface both for inputting information and for output.

From the 1970s, personal computers started having electronic monitors, which were generally monochrome, either a black screen with white text or black screen with luminous green text. The display let users input information or see output without having to wait for a printout.

The development of speakers to use with a computer to play back sound was critical to creating a full, multisensory experience for the user. This laid the foundation for a multimedia computer. Today, it is standard for every computer to have an electronic display with audio capability, and most come with a microphone or microphone port so users can input audio information. All this makes a computer a potentially complete digital media production facility.

The Creation of Intuitive Interfaces

In the 1960s, an important series of advances were made in the computer user interface. Most of these developments helped make the computer simpler and more natural, or intuitive, to use, more efficient to work with (i.e., to enter information and access information contained in the computer) and more capable of dealing with multimedia content such as audio, video, photos, and graphics. The process is evolving even today as improvements and refinements are made in the interface methods discussed below.

The Keyboard

Typewriters were developed in the 1870s as a way to make writing faster. At first, the typewriter keyboard was arranged alphabetically, but it turned out this was a poor design because some keys were used more often than others, and, if typed too quickly, the keys would jam together. Instead, Christopher Latham Sholes developed what is known as the QWERTY keyboard (the letters in the first row of keys in the upper-left-hand corner of the keyboard), which has the most frequently typed keys spread far apart (such as "a" and "t"). The QWERTY keyboard slows down the user and prevents the keys from jamming in a typewriter.

Jamming keys became a nonissue with the invention of electric typewriters, but the QWERTY keyboard was by then standard and is what most people are trained on today. A keyboard certainly makes it easier to enter information into a computer than the old punch card system, but the QWERTY keyboard is actually poorly designed for computer use. Because there are no keys to jam on a computer keyboard, it would make far more sense to have a keyboard that is designed for maximum typing efficiency, such as the Dvorak keyboard. Unfortunately, the QWERTY keyboard is a standard part of the computer user interface, and such legacies are very hard to change, even when changing them would greatly improve things.

Media **Inventors and Innovators**

August Dvorak

Designed by August Dvorak in the 1930s, the Dvorak keyboard is designed for maximum typing efficiency. His keyboard allows the user to type more than 3000 words without the user needing to reach with her or his fingers. With a Dvorak keyboard, the typical typist's fingers would travel about one mile a day—with a QWERTY keyboard her or his fingers would travel an astounding twelve miles a day. A demonstration project showed that users could type nearly twice as fast with the Dvorak keyboard and with more than 50 percent improvement in accuracy—and this was a demonstration using a typewriter, not a computer

keyboard. On a computer, the gains might be even greater.

The standard QWERTY keyboard can be reprogrammed to the Dvorak layout quite easily. The software to automatically reprogram a QWERTY keyboard is available for free downloading. Once the keyboard has been reprogrammed, the user sim

ply installs new key caps with the letters corresponding to the new layout as needed.

Weblink
Switch Your Computer to Dvorak
[www.mwbrooks.com/dvorak
/support.html]

Dvorak keyboard.

Besides inherited inefficiencies in the QWERTY keyboard, the keyboard also suffers from other drawbacks in making it an intuitive interface. First is the need for literacy to understand its use and second is the need for typing training in order to make the use of a keyboard more efficient. An intuitive interface should not need hours of training to learn how to adequately use it. It is also slower as an input device than simply speaking to a computer, for example.

As computers and other media devices have become smaller, the keyboard has also proved to be a limited input device, as keys can become no smaller than what can be comfortably typed, or smaller than the fingertips. Small keyboards often leave users with cramped hands or hitting the wrong keys. Users also get used to the "feel" of keyboards they are familiar with, and adjusting to new types of keyboards can often take time.

One benefit the keyboard does have over some other types of interfaces is the ability to input information privately. Typing, unlike a voice interface, can be done without disturbing others in the vicinity.

The Computer Mouse

A major development in the evolution of the intuitive computer user interface occurred in 1968 when Douglas C. Engelbart invented the computer mouse. His invention was made of wood and was used with a companion keyboard. He demonstrated his invention in San Francisco at the Fall Joint Computer Conference in December of that year, but the germ of the idea had occurred in 1945, during WWII.

Douglas Engelbart created the computer mouse in 1968, a huge step forward in creating a more intuitive computer user interface.

Engelbart worked as a radar technician in the South Pacific, and he realized the potential for people to interact with a monitor. His inspiration came while reading a now-classic article in the July 1945 edition of *The Atlantic Monthly* by Vannevar Bush, then science adviser to President Harry S. Truman, titled "As We May Think." The article discussed how the computer could be a desktop tool to help people in their work.

Engelbart initially proposed his idea for a better computer user interface in 1963 when he wrote an article titled, "A Conceptual Framework for the Augmentation of Man's Intellect." In the article he said that, through a better-designed computer interface, "people could cope better with complex, urgent things." His vision involved creating better intuitive tools for people to interact with and control the information they input, access, and process in a computer. The computer mouse was one of the most important tools he developed for implementing his vision. The mouse allowed the computer user to easily manipulate data in the computer, pointing and clicking as desired.

The mouse is important for mass communication because it makes it easier not only for content producers to work more effectively and quickly, but also for the audience to access and obtain information. Suddenly the screen has coordinates, which the mouse cursor uses to "see" where it is, and it can be navigated, much like a map, with different areas of the screen having different functions that can be controlled.

Despite the huge leap in creating a more intuitive interface that the computer mouse represents, it still has its limitations. First, the functions of buttons or wheels on a mouse are not immediately clear and have to be learned.

Second, there is still a disjunct between moving a mouse across the desktop and where the cursor actually goes. This is why computer novices often have

Weblink
"As We May Think"
[www.theatlantic.com/unbound/flashbks/computer/bushf.htm]

trouble at first using a mouse—a small hand movement on the horizontal plane toward the computer actually corresponds to a relatively large upward movement on the computer screen, which isn't initially intuitive. It takes practice to become accustomed to how hand movements translate to cursor movements. There have been stories of computer novices putting the mouse on their screens and clicking when asked to click on objects, for example.

The Touch-Sensitive Screen

Another important development in the evolution of a more intuitive computer user interface occurred in 1974. In that year, the Control Data Corporation (CDC) introduced PLATO (Programmed Logic for Automated Teaching Operations), the first computer system to have a touch-sensitive video display terminal.[2]

One of CDC's leaders, William C. Norris, was keenly interested in applications of computers to education, and the introduction of a touch-sensitive screen was a significant opportunity to extend the computer to young learners as well as the general public, who were not accustomed to computers and keyboards.

The importance of a touch-sensitive screen is that it greatly simplifies the human–computer interaction. With PLATO, children and adults alike, without any prior training, could spend many minutes or hours playing word games and other applications on the system, all by simply touching the screen with their fingers.

Despite being perhaps one of the most intuitive interfaces, there are several drawbacks to touch-sensitive screens as a standard interface. First is the need to be within reach of the screen to touch it, which means screen sizes ideally should only be as large as is comfortable to sit in front of and still reach. Second, the interface is primarily limited to pushing virtual buttons—moving or resizing windows by dragging, such as is possible with a mouse, is not possible with touch-sensitive screens. Third, extremely small screen sizes limit interaction, just as with keyboards, because items that can be manipulated can be only as small as a fingertip can comfortably push. A stylus or other thin device can help overcome this latter drawback, however, as well as playing a key role in the next type of interface.

Handwriting Recognition

Another advance in user-friendly technology occurred in 1979 with the introduction of the Micropad, the first computer to accept handwritten data, unveiled by Quest Automation. Micropad allowed the user to write with an electronic pen, or stylus, and thereby capture the characters written. At the time, the characters were not translated into computer-readable text, however. This did not occur until the Newton MessagePad, almost two decades later.

The late 1990s saw some other important developments in handwriting interface design. In 1997, the second generation of handwriting recognition software with products such as the Newton MessagePad 2000, offering about 95 percent reliability, appeared. Other even newer devices such as the Palm feature a handwriting recognition program called "Graffiti" that is very close to standard handwriting and has very high reliability but requires the user to learn to slightly modify his or her handwriting in order for the device to recognize it.

CrossPad allows handwriting using pen or pencil on paper laid on top of a digital pad, with all writing stored digitally while only selected text is indexed in

HAL, the speaking, hearing, thinking, and lip-reading computer in the 1968 science-fiction classic *2001: A Space Odyssey*, is an example of how computers with voice recognition capabilities have long been seen in popular entertainment.

machine-readable format. Importantly, it allows journalists to write and have access to all notes in digital format in real time.

Handwriting recognition still has a way to go before it can easily translate a person's natural scrawl into machine-readable text, however. It will also always have limitations for portable computing devices, as the writing surface must be big enough to write comfortably, so must be at least the size of a small notepad.

Voice Recognition and Speech Synthesis

One of the most natural, or intuitive, user interfaces has also been one of the most elusive. Computer voice recognition and speech synthesis have been a hallmark of science fiction for generations and are slowly becoming a central part of the real-world computing environment. Isaac Asimov's 1950s science-fiction novel *I, Robot* featured not just his immortal three laws of robotics but also robots that fully understood human speech and could talk fluently. In the 1968 film *2001: A Space Odyssey*, by Arthur C. Clarke and Stanley Kubrick, HAL is a computer that can see, speak, hear, and think like its human colleagues aboard a spaceship.

The reality of computer speech and voice recognition has lagged far behind the realm of science fiction. Early efforts of the 1970s and 1980s were fairly primitive, clunky, and slow. Even those speech recognition systems that had a fairly effective range of understanding took many hours of training, and required the speaker to pronounce his or her commands in a staccato style, with a momentary pause between each word spoken, what is called discrete speech. Most had highly restricted vocabularies and were limited to specialized applications, such as medical patient logs.

In 1976 Kurzweil Computer Products introduced the Kurzweil Reading Machine, which read aloud any printed text presented to it and could recognize text in any font. It was intended to be a sensory aid for the blind. Most of the early current voice recognition systems are really nothing more than voice typewriters, translating spoken words into printed ones. Some can respond to simple, preset commands, such as "open file," but have no understanding of semantics. They are speaker dependent, which means they do not recognize speaking from others who have not used the system, or their rate of recognition is greatly reduced, making them of limited use to journalists hoping to avoid tedious transcribing of interviews.

Speech recognition could greatly simplify many interactions with computers, although it is not without its weaknesses as well. One issue, especially for people in urban areas or in public spaces, is noise. Imagine the noise level in a classroom if all students had to speak to their computers to input information, or the noise on a city bus as all the riders spoke not into cell phones but to their portable computers.

Graphical User Interface

The foundation for modern **graphical user interfaces (GUIs)** was created, like so many other computer innovations, at Xerox Palo Alto Research Center (PARC). In 1974 Xerox created the Alto, a 64K computer that used a mouse and bit-mapped monitor and was connected by Ethernet to other Altos. With a graphical user interface, users could simply point and click various objects on the screen to access applications or files.

The Alto, apparently ahead of its time, never caught on. It took a visit to Xerox PARC by Apple cofounder Steve Jobs to see Xerox's graphical user interface and to decide to use that with Apple computers. Several years later Microsoft's Windows followed Apple's lead in using a graphical user interface (GUI) for its operating system.

Prior to the GUI (pronounced GOO-ey), computer users had to memorize or have at hand a series of arcane commands to open, save, and move files as well as to use applications. When the GUI was introduced, there was a widespread feeling among established computer users that it "dumbed down" computer use and was not a good development, despite (or perhaps because of) its ease of use and the way it opened up computer use to the nontechnical public.

The Desktop Metaphor

Most computer users, whether using Macs or Windows, are familiar with the graphical user interface of the computer desktop. Software applications are represented as icons and placed within the screen space in resizable "windows," which can be layered on top of one another or moved around. Computer files are "placed" in folders that sit on the screen or that exist within other folders.

Some of the earliest graphical user interfaces for the PC even tried to carry the desktop metaphor further, by having images of an actual desk as if the user was sitting at it and with images of items like a Rolodex (for contacts and addresses), file cabinet, and other office equipment to represent various computing functions. These kinds of attempts at realistic user interfaces failed primarily for a couple reasons. One reason was the computing power needed to show detailed 3D images, which was beyond the capacity of most PCs until fairly recently; and another reason was that the realistic interface imposed real-world constraints on obtaining and manipulating information that computers would otherwise not have.

Some computer interface designers have said that the desktop user interface has outlived its usefulness. It was fine in the early stages of GUIs, when computers

graphical user interface (GUI)—a computer interface that shows graphical representations of file structures, applications, and files in the form of folders, icons, and windows.

How Digital Media Are Changing Our World   www.ablongman.com/pavlik1e

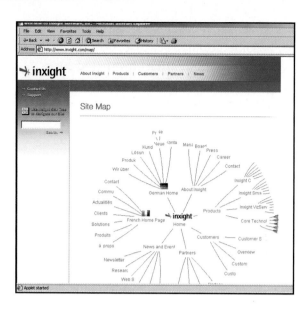

Some computer experts are claiming that the desktop metaphor is too cumbersome in today's computing environment and are experimenting with radically new types of user interface designs.

were less powerful and computer users mostly had text files rather than a range of multimedia types and far less storage for files. But nowadays, the desktop can actually hinder the most efficient way of getting or manipulating information for the user. The office iconography of the standard desktop can also be confusing at first to people who are not familiar with such Western office standards as file folders, printers, or floppy diskettes.

Consider the time spent searching for lost files, either in directories filled with hundreds of various files, or in sub- sub- sub-folders of different categories. The windowed environment does not help matters in that regard, either. In exchange for better interactivity and manipulability of content windows, computer users have lost stability in the interface, as windows can appear not only in different sizes but in different places on the screen. For example, when turning on the television, never will a part of the screen appear in the upper right corner while another channel suddenly appears in the lower left corner. But with computers, windows sometimes resize by a mistaken click of the mouse or because of some default setting when opening a program or file. And that's not even considering issues that arise when others use the same computer and adjust the settings to their preferences.

There are some interesting attempts to create a better PC user interface that can more fully accommodate the complex media needs of today's computer user. One attempt by Microsoft, called TaskGallery, makes the screen look as if it is opening into a 3D room, with Web sites or files "hanging" from the walls. Users put related files in virtual rooms and enter those rooms through the room they are in. This is meant to assist users in remembering where they put certain files. Another, called Scopeware, uses a diary metaphor and relies on the assumption that computer users access certain files more frequently than others, so the more frequently accessed files always show up toward the top of a series of cascaded files on the screen, making finding files easier. Yet another interface in development, StarTree, tries to show relationships between files rather than in the hierarchical structure that people are familiar with in the desktop file folder system.

Whether any of these new types of user interfaces will catch on and replace today's desktop interface is impossible to predict. It could well be that they are relegated to the position of the Dvorak keyboard; a widely recognized improvement on a current system that will not become popular because most users are already familiar with the system currently in use, no matter how inefficient it may be. On the other hand, user interface design is still in an early enough stage that a radically new system that makes using a computer much easier could catch on rapidly, just as the GUI garnered widespread use over the command-line interface in a very short time.

Key Elements of Modern User Interface

The GUI for personal computers and later for the World Wide Web probably had the single greatest impact in changing the public's behavior and attitude toward computers. If computer scientists and programmers can be compared to literate monks and scribes in the Middle Ages, then the GUI is the equivalent of the printing press that brought greater literacy in the Renaissance. Specialized knowledge to use a computer—even, to some extent, the need for literacy—became unnecessary when using a computer with a GUI. Once basic knowledge such as what mouse buttons to click or where to search for files was learned, much could be done on a computer even without being able to read. The graphical browser took the Web out of the realm of only the computer scientist or engineer and into the realm of the ordinary citizen.

A similar opening up to a mass audience occurred with the Internet and specifically the World Wide Web when the first widespread use of a graphical browser, Mosaic, was released in 1992. Mosaic later became Netscape, and it was not long before Microsoft offered its own graphical Web browser, Internet Explorer, to compete against Netscape's dominance.

Whether the GUI is for the PC or for the Web, the modern computer user interface consists of some primary characteristics that are unlikely to substantially change. These characteristics, as will be explained later in this chapter, have crucial effects on mass communication and how the public interacts with media.

Point-and-Click Functionality

It is likely to be quite a few years before voice-recognition interfaces become commonplace, and even when they are there will still be many instances in which a computer user will want to interact with the computer silently or without letting others around them know what they are inputting or searching for. Therefore, some type of input device such as a mouse or stylus is likely to always be with us.

The ability to move a screen cursor by a mouse and select material on the screen is called **point-and-click functionality**. It is the foundation of a user interacting with on-screen content in a GUI. Pointing and clicking allows a user to navigate within or between Web sites by clicking on various links; lets them play multimedia such as audio or video, as well as giving them the ability to pause or rewind it; and lets them resize windows or manipulate content, such as moving paragraphs on a page. Pointing and clicking is much more efficient than typing

point-and-click functionality— the ability to use a mouse to move a cursor on the screen and to click a mouse button to interact with what is being pointed to, such as opening a folder with files or starting a program by clicking on its icon.

icons—small images or graphics that represent an object, function, or command.

How Digital Media Are Changing Our World   www.ablongman.com/pavlik1e

commands for many situations. A main difference between pointing and clicking of a remote control and pointing and clicking of a mouse is that the latter lets the user change content or appearances *within* the screen as well as changing the entire screen content (e.g., changing the channel).

Iconic and Visual Language

The use of **icons,** or small images or graphics that represent functions, objects, or commands, enables computer users to see relatively large amounts of information in a small space. One example on television where icons are frequently used is weather reports. It is much easier to see a series of images of sun or clouds than to have to read text descriptions of the weather forecast.

In a computer environment, icons can represent not only information, but files, applications, and even actions. Many icons are based on precomputer objects in the real world, such as paper clips to represent an attachment, a clipboard, or scissors to represent the "cut" function in a word processing document, while other icons are based on objects associated with computers (a printer to represent the "print" function and a floppy diskette for "save," for example).

It has been mentioned that one drawback to icons is that they presuppose the user is familiar with the real-world objects they represent. Someone unfamiliar with a printer, for example, would have no way to intuitively know what the icon is meant to represent. Some icons can become obsolete as well, which can also cause confusion. It is easy to imagine the floppy diskette icon for "save" in Microsoft Word will need to be replaced at some point as the floppy diskette slowly gets phased out in favor of other types of storage media such as DVDs.

Iconic language can be even more abstract, however. The use of a blue border around images or graphics to denote that they can be clicked on, rather than using an accompanying text description saying "please click here to see a larger version of this image," is an example of abstract iconic usage. There are no logical reasons, other than convention, that a blue line should represent a clickable object, for example. So far, however, there is very little agreement on what types of standards there should be to denote even something as basic as clickable images on the Web.

Graphics combined with short text, such as online "buttons," can also help computer users navigate and find various types of information easily. Text-image combinations can help clarify what particular icons may mean and in many cases can impart even more information in a small amount of space than icons alone.

With the increased use of icons, combined with more multimedia usage, it is likely that text will play a less dominant role than it does today in the user interface of the future. This will have an effect on how media stories, entertainment, and information are presented, as well as affecting the way the audience processes information.

Windowed Environment

The use of windows, which are essentially screens that appear on top of or within screens, lets users have layers of information on a topic or topics. Even an action as simple as resizing two screens side-by-side so two different articles can be compared line-by-line greatly empowers the media user in terms of controlling the information she or he sees and how that information is interpreted. On a computer, a similar activity could be performed by watching two streaming videos from competing TV news networks, for example, to easily compare how each one covers the news.

Being able to access "layered information" easily, such as through hyperlinks on the Web, drop-down menus, or pop-up windows, is another unique development in the computer user interface that is changing how people interact with media. Links can open to new windows of archived stories on the topic, original source sites such as from the government or relevant groups, or other types of media by which to experience the story, such as photo slideshows or video footage.

Implications of User Interface on Mass Communication

The modern user interface changes not only how the audience can access and utilize information, transforming them from passive media consumers to active media users, it also changes how media organizations must create, produce, and present stories. In terms of journalism, news stories must attract the attention of computer users immediately and hold their attention—no easy task in a colorful, online multimedia environment full of entertainment. The need to get attention quickly will affect not only how a given story is designed and presented on the screen, but how it may be written or even what types of stories may be more likely to appear.

However, the GUI also holds the potential to bring news, information, and entertainment to audiences in ways that engage, educate, and entertain that were unimaginable with analog media. Sometimes information in news stories could be presented as interactive content that encourages the user to learn and explore. Online quizzes, surveys, or games are currently being used on many news Web sites, but these often do not take full advantage of the user interface and often do not go beyond asking trivia questions. This type of limited interactivity with generally unchallenging material might have novelty appeal but is unlikely to be the type of content that truly engages people over the long term.

Likewise, simply presenting lists of hyperlinked news stories and Web sites on a topic does not help the audience understand the issue in context. Through a combination of graphics, animations, and other multimedia, along with utilizing layered information and clear navigation, audience members can become much more engaged in content than they had been before. Some news Web sites are starting to utilize the Web's multimedia capabilities better. During the 2002 Winter Olympics, NYTimes.com, the Web site for the *New York Times,* had interactive, user-controlled animations of various events such as the luge or the skiing competitions embedded into articles about the events. This enabled users unfamiliar with the sport to rapidly learn the basics of it and to see what the course looked like and where areas were that had caused difficulty for competitors. One of the strong points of these animations, besides their clear, uncluttered artwork, was the fact that users could progress through them at their own pace, clicking on the next segment only when they were ready. They did not have to sit through a video or animation lasting a few minutes with no way to stop the flow of information.

Maps and timelines are two other areas in which good user interface can make stories or education more robust. The images or graphics are not only nicer to look at but they also present material in contextual terms that aids its comprehension and retention. This is especially important for international news stories, for example, an area of news generally underreported in the U.S. media and that a small segment of U.S. news consumers shows interest in. According to a survey by the Pew Research Center for the People and the Press released in June 2002, 60 percent of the respondents who do not follow international news closely said their primary reason was a lack of background on the subject. Interactive maps of regions that highlight the history, culture, languages, and politics could be a useful tool in allowing people to easily learn background information that they otherwise don't bother learning about.

What does this mean for media professionals? It means that they must maintain current standards of media professionalism while at least being aware of unique possibilities in presenting information that modern computer user interface design allows. There is little point in working hard on an intricately plotted text narrative of 5000 words if the story could be better presented in short chunks of text on separate screens or combined with animations or graphics. It also means that media professionals will have to be even more aware of likely related sources, issues, and Web sites that could be included in stories in order to give the audience the most complete, interesting media package possible.

Graphical browsers also helped lead to the commercialization of the Web and the Internet (and some would say its destruction) as businesses sought to reach the growing number of consumers online. Examples of a windowed environment that most computer users are unfortunately all too familiar with are the growing number of pop-up ads or animated ads that must have their windows closed before being able to access content.

For those who are not convinced that user interface has become an important issue, consider the lawsuit filed by the U.S. Department of Justice and 18 states in May 1998 against Microsoft, accusing the company of violating antitrust laws. One of the key issues was whether Microsoft used its near monopoly of the operating system market (90 percent of PCs run Windows) to unfairly promote its Internet Explorer browser by making it part of the Windows operating system. The rapid adoption rate of Internet Explorer at the expense of Netscape, which did not come automatically bundled with new operating systems, was pointed out in the case as evidence of Microsoft's unfair tactics.

Although Microsoft eventually emerged largely unscathed from the original suit (nine states are continuing separate action against Microsoft as of this writing), for a while during the trial there seemed to be the very real possibility of Microsoft being broken up into three separate companies. What was one of the main factors in an event that could have seen the breakup of one of the world's richest and most powerful computer corporations? The software that created a graphical user interface for the Web. So user interface can also become the subject of news stories as well as the means to view those news stories.

Media Future: Flat Panel Displays

Flat panel displays, especially those with digital high resolution, provide extremely crisp images and take up very little cubic space, unlike a CRT, which has much more depth; but they can be expensive: a Philips Electronics 42-inch, flat-panel plasma display cost $15,000 in 1999, although 15-inch consumer flat panel displays in 2001 cost about $600. As prices fall, flat panel displays are likely to become much more common. They are already familiar to anyone who has a laptop computer or a hand-held device, such as a Palm Pilot. These devices use flat panel displays, as do various hand-held video game players. The future of media may include ubiquitous flat screens embedded not only in expected places, such as a living room wall where one watches television, but in some unexpected locations, such as in a table top, a refrigerator door, or even a gas station pump.

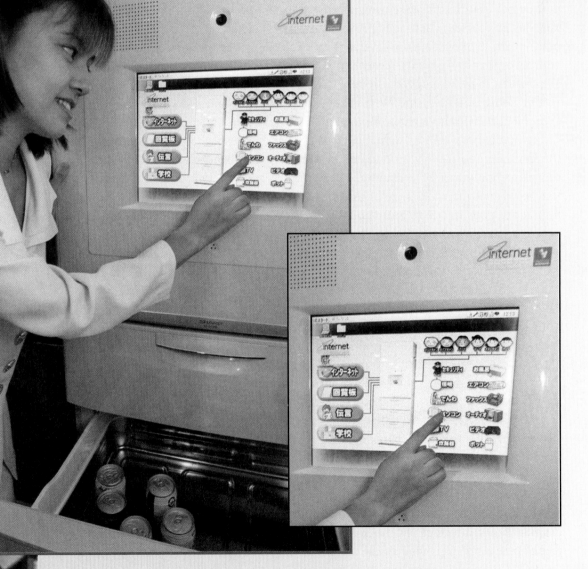

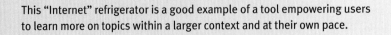

This "Internet" refrigerator is a good example of a tool empowering users to learn more on topics within a larger context and at their own pace.

TV/PC Convergence: Implications for User Interface

Television video games transform the television into an interactive entertainment center.

It is still too early to predict whether the television will absorb the functions of the PC or the PC will adopt more TV-like functions, but either way what we know today as two separate items (essentially two separate monitors) will merge into one, and in the end it largely won't matter. That's not to say that most households will have only one monitor; it can almost be guaranteed that American households will maintain their multimonitor way of life, just as they have TVs in various rooms today. If anything, it is likely that households will have more screens than they do today, as flat panel monitors become prevalent and are placed on or embedded in walls, refrigerator doors, or other areas in the house that currently do not have screens.

Business decisions will play a large role in determining which way the convergence goes—toward the PC or toward the TV—but user interface issues will also play an important role. First, consider screen size and viewing distance from the screen. Computer users sit much closer to their monitors than TV viewers do, making the experience of interaction much more personal, even for monitors of comparable size. Viewing distance from the screen will affect how "socially interactive" the PC/TV becomes. The fact that most computer users sit relatively close to the screen (between one and two feet), makes it difficult for other people to sit around and share in the experience without seeming as though they are looking over the computer user's shoulder. TV, on the other hand, can be easily shared with others as everyone sits further away (five feet or more) and at indirect angles to the TV screen.

Second, screen resolution is important so that text and other detailed graphics that may be interactive can be displayed clearly on a large TV screen. Computer monitors must display text clearly and therefore must have a higher resolution than television monitors. To test the resolution of the PC monitor compared to the television monitor, try putting your face as close to the PC screen as you can before what you see becomes illegible. Then try with a television. Chances are, unless you have a digital television, you can get much closer to the PC screen before things become blurry than the television screen. Reading text from a distance, even with fairly high screen resolution, can quickly become tiring.

Third, the type of content and the way the audience interacts with that content will affect how the PC and TV converge. Currently, the PC is far more interactive and requires far more action than the television. With computers, users are actively involved in getting information or communicating, whereas with traditional television viewers are largely passive and in fact do not have any way to communicate directly either with other audience members or with media producers. Early attempts at interactive TV partially address some of these issues, however.

The main exception to passively watching television is television video games. Video games, which will be discussed in a mass communication context

Gameshows such as *Who Wants to Be a Millionaire?* have encouraged viewers to go online and participate in quizzes. In the future, this type of functionality will become seamless as part of the television environment.

in more detail in Chapter 11, are one of the few activities that have transformed the passive television box into an interactive (some say addictive) entertainment center. Computers also allow for games, but television videogames such as Nintendo Gamecube and Sony Playstation are far more popular. Because the public is now comfortable with using the television as a dual-purpose device (active gaming and passive television viewing), an Internet-connected television may well be easier for the public to accept than an antenna-ready PC. The perception could be enhancing a TV versus "dumbing down" a PC in terms of what each currently does.

Fourth, devices to interact with on-screen content are likely to have to be revised. The relatively simple multibutton devices for gaming or remote controls do not offer the same level of control and manipulation over content that a mouse can offer, with its ability to select parts of a screen by dragging (holding down the button while moving the mouse), for example. Keyboards will likely remain the primary input device for text for some time, which means they would be necessary for activities like online chat or e-mails while watching a show. In fact, keyboards or some other silent input devices are perfect examples of why they will remain necessary as part of a user interface—the audience will not want to miss what is being spoken by announcers or actors by either talking themselves or hearing someone else speak. By typing in messages, they can simultaneously listen while they communicate. How exactly someone will balance a keyboard in his or her lap while holding a drink and eating chips while watching a sports game is a matter for engineers to ponder.

Finally, the type of content that is made available for interactivity will affect how the user interface develops for the converged PC/TV of the future. If media companies only create or encourage interactive content for such programs as gameshows or popular programs, then it is likely that interactivity with the "television" will be less than what is done with the "computer." This could mean screens have different looks to them, with the ability for the user to simply switch to "TV mode" and have less of the screen area taken up by interactive options than if they are in "computer mode" and actively seeking information on the Internet. This type of flexibility in deciding what type of content exists on a screen and how it looks is exactly the kind of thing computer users today deal with as they collapse menus or floating toolbars when using different types of programs.

At any rate, the Internet will become more TV-like in how it is presented as broadband becomes more common and video and other multimedia can be shown over the Internet more easily. This means text will likely become less predominant as people choose to watch or listen to something rather than read about it. But text will also influence how TV is presented, as people will also want the choice to read about an event in more depth or to simply have the text visible so they can reread a part that they may have missed or didn't understand.

The eventual convergence of the PC and TV is not some futuristic fantasy; it is happening today in ways that we often do not realize because it is taking place in small, gradual steps and with many dead-ends, stops, and starts. Let's look at some ways it is happening, thanks largely to the move toward digital television and the role it is playing in user interface issues.

Digital Television: Preparing the Way for Convergence

Although electronic television has always utilized a video display terminal, the user interface has evolved through several important stages. In the first stage (the 1950s), the video display was relatively small and black and white, with monophonic, low-fidelity sound (i.e., no directionality and not high quality). In the second stage (the 1960s and 1970s), color television and stereophonic sound were developed, greatly increasing the realism of the viewing experience. All the while, the level of resolution of the display was relatively unchanged.

The third stage of the television user interface arrived in 1981, when NHK (Japan Broadcasting Corporation) engineers demonstrated analog **high definition television (HDTV),** calling it Hi-Vision. HDTV was a significant advance in the television interface because it presents a much higher-resolution image, sharper color, a wider aspect ratio, and superior audio. NHK had begun its research on HDTV in 1973, long before the digital revolution was on the global radar screen.

In 1990, General Instrument Corporation proposed an all-digital television system, something initially deemed technically impossible, especially for over-the-air broadcasting. But this proved not to be the case. **Digital television (DTV)** became the accepted global standard for next next-generation TV. It is important to note that DTV and HDTV are not the same thing. HDTV as invented by the Japanese was analog in format. DTV was invented in the United States as a response to the Japanese invention of HDTV. HDTV can be digital, and digital can be HDTV, but the two are not one and the same.

Why DTV Matters in Mass Communication

In comparison to analog TV, digital TV provides higher-resolution video images, better color, and digital sound. HDTV offers even higher resolution and a wider aspect ratio (more cinematic wide screen). These advantages make it possible to use DTV or HDTV effectively in the presentation of text. Prior television displays were too low in resolution to effectively permit text for reading.

In some ways DTV is more important than HDTV from the point of view of media programming. Digital TV enables the convergence of computing, television, and telecommunications and the possibility of interactivity. This means that with DTV new storytelling techniques are possible, as well as the ability to link to **multicast** (also known as multiplex) or to simultaneously transmit multiple channels of compressed content, or in some cases the same content but at different times. DTV brings the possibilities of functionality that has been experimented with or used on computers or the Web in recent years. Whether journalists and TV programmers take full advantage of these capabilities remains to be seen.

The Capabilities of DTV

DTV has many capabilities simply not possible with analog television. It makes possible a wide variety of creative options for novel program formats. It also

high-definition television (HDTV)—a new form of television with much higher resolution than standard television, as well as a different screen size ratio.

digital television (DTV)—television programming that is created, distributed, and shown using digital means, which offers much sharper pictures and more functionality than traditional analog TV.

multicast—simultaneously transmitting multiple channels of compressed digital content over the television airwaves.

enables more user control and navigation throughout the video, including VCR functionality for video delivered on demand or in real time. Among the opportunities are:

- Enhanced TV, linking video to the Internet and Web. WebTV represents perhaps the most widely available current form of interactive television by converging television with the Internet, though it is perhaps better thought of as enhanced TV (or TV with something extra).
- 360-degree video, or panoramic views, allowing the viewer to use a remote control or voice command to pan, tilt, or zoom through 360-degree still or fullmotion video to look around a scene.
- Object-oriented multimedia, or layering in interactive objects into a motion video the way objects are incorporated into today's static Web sites. This is an important capability that will permit digital TV programs to include embedded information graphics in the news, commercial product placements in entertainment programming, and pointers to related Web sites.
- Meta-data manipulation, which allows producers to process any of the digital objects in the video. This enables a variety of new procedures, such as a fascinating "motion tracking" application developed at Lucent Technologies that can then overlay information such as player movements on a tennis court during a match and show percentages of winning shots or break points. Such technologies can be used to help analysis in sports as well in other applications such as traffic reporting.
- 3D, or three-dimensional video and graphics and animations that allow the viewer to explore an entire scene or virtual location using a remote control, mouse, or even voice command. These tools are used in digital TV production for news and entertainment but are now becoming available for the viewer to interact with.

Electronic Program Guides

One aspect of the user's interface unique to the realm of DTV, and which marketers sometimes claim as interactive TV, is the provision of **electronic program guides (EPG),** which help inform users of what is on which channel and when as well as allowing some simple interactivity such as ordering pay-per-view programming. Their functionality is perhaps better considered as a form of enhanced TV rather than interactive TV, if for no other reason than to differentiate the limited functionality currently available from the kind of interactivity that will be possible in the future.

At present, these EPGs are still relatively primitive, such as the electronic program guide provided with DirecTV, which offers users an on-screen, on-demand list of programs, with program descriptions, language options, and the like. Cable television EPGs are more sophisticated, offering not only on-screen program descriptions but also multiple windows where the video can be displayed in one portion of the screen and program descriptions displayed in another portion of the screen. Future systems will be much more powerful, allowing viewers to search for their favorite program by keyword, instructing an intelligent agent to automatically record your favorite shows, and other features.

electronic program guides (EPG)—guides available on television that provide program listings and some simple interactivity such as ordering pay-per-view programs through the television or buying CDs or DVDs of music or shows that are listed.

Future Developments Affecting User Interface

Computing technology changes rapidly, sometimes radically altering the industry and the way people use computers. The convergence of computing, telecommunications, and media means that technological changes can have a strong ripple effect on media and mass communication. One example is how the increase in computer processing power created better opportunities for a graphical user interface and how the GUI then made computers much more accessible to the average person, which in turn helped drive even more innovation. It is likely that advances in technology will further alter the way we interact with computers in ways that we cannot foresee. A cheap way to connect the public to broadband Internet connections, for example, would have profound effects on how audiences access media content on the Web.

General patterns can be looked at to get a sense of what transformations might take place regarding user interface. These can be divided roughly by categories: evolution and standardization of user interface, media devices, and ways to access media.

The Evolution and Standardization of User Interface

Within the Internet's limitations of bandwidth and various types of browsers and versions of software, user interface design will evolve almost imperceptibly as audience Web usage patterns emerge over the coming years. Stringent attempts at standardizing the Web are likely to be counterproductive because of the differences in how the audience may see content depending on what type of computers, browsers, software, and devices they have. Media companies will continue to redesign their sites to improve navigation and ease of use, and from these attempts some general consensus will gradually arise as to what elements in user interface design work best.

More multimedia will be available as the number of broadband users increases, although there will still be influential calls to keep the Web simple and primarily text-based to accommodate the still large numbers of users who do not have fast connections.

Although the desire to standardize some elements of user interface will be strong, technological developments could quickly make what previously worked well obsolete or limiting, so the evolution of user interface design is likely to have many setbacks as technology changes the way people access media content.

From ways to let the audience mark and store content they may want to access later to giving them the ability to create their own designs and presentation of media, user interface issues will make it difficult to devise one single standard that can be applied to all people. Rather, general principles will probably be developed that can be applied in certain situations or with certain types of audiences; but it is unlikely, given the highly interactive and personal nature of online media, that a one-size-fits-all approach to user interface will work.

Media Devices

Wireless and handheld devices, or personal digital appliances (PDAs) such as the Palm Pilot or video-enabled cell phones, will become more commonplace and raise important user interface questions for content on small screens and input using tiny keypads. Handheld devices are likely to stop shrinking and become gradually larger in order to accommodate the multiple demands the public will place on them as they seek one portable device that can act as phone, e-mail, and Internet connection with multimedia capabilities. However, possibilities in wearable computing, in which a tiny screen embedded in a pair of glasses looks to the user as though it is projected on a screen two feet away, may help merge the large-screen user interface and portable, small-screen user interface. Some sort of input mechanism will still be needed, such as an electronic pad or arm-mounted or foldable keyboard.

Another possibility that could alter user interface issues having to do with small screens is the use of electronic paper. This could make writing electronically as easy as writing on a sheet of paper, and if electronic paper proves to be as portable and flexible as real paper, or nearly so, then larger design elements can be placed on the larger pages while still making the material portable.

Geography and location will become more important as more devices are equipped with GPS receivers. From a user interface perspective, this means that mapping and maps will become increasingly important as on-screen graphics that also contain different types of information. Map-based GUIs can provide everything from information on the nearest restaurant to local points of cultural or historical interest.

Ways to Access Media

Accessing media content will be increasingly easy, but accessing the content one *wants* may be harder than ever unless sound principles in user interface design are applied to search and find functions. New computing power, faster connections, or a number of other developments in computing could have drastic effects on providing new ways to access media. Content-based visual search tools are one example, such as a visual search tool now available on Google. More advanced visual search tools are currently in development by various researchers that can allow searches not only by keyword, but by color, shape, texture, or face or pattern recognition. As the Web becomes more visually and multimedia based, visual search tools will become more important than they are today.

Voice Recognition

Advances in handwriting recognition and voice recognition will also provide new ways to access media content and present new challenges in user interface designs. Voice recognition especially will have to combine elements of audio with something visual (speech-generated text or menu options that can be glanced at rather than the user having to memorize various options presented by computer aurally).

The potential advantages of an easy voice-recognition system for journalists are great. Voice recognition could save time currently spent transcribing interviews and could also provide an immediate written record of what was said, giving journalists a better chance to recognize a line of questioning that they may not have seen had they simply listened and taken notes.

Immersive Media

Emerging in the online broadband arena is a variety of forms of immersive media. These include three-dimensional (3D) visualizations, 360-degree photography and video, virtual reality, and immersive audio.

3D Visualizations

In 3D online content, the user may be immersed in a virtual space where he or she can turn in any direction and move about in any direction, potentially interacting with other people, places, and objects in that 3D space. Or, the user may encounter 3D objects placed in a two-dimensional environment. For example, the user might visit a standard Web page, but on that page she or he may find a 3D representation of an object from the real world, such as a statue, a building, or a car. Using a mouse, the user might turn that object in a 360 space, turn it over, or move closer to inspect it in detail or move farther away to see it from a wider perspective. This type of activity presents interesting issues in user interface design; namely, how best to show a readily understandable real-world, 3D functionality such as picking up an object and holding it closer, in the two-dimensional environment of the screen.

360-Degree Photography

Traditional cameras have a relatively narrow field of view, about 105 degrees, which roughly corresponds to the field of view of humans. New, digital technologies have made possible cameras with unusually large fields of view, even an entire circle, or hemispheric view, a full 360-degree view. This means this new class of digital cameras (that can shoot still or full-motion video) have the ability to take in an entire scene, allowing the viewer to look in any direction without panning (i.e., turning the camera left or right) the camera.

A wide variety of uses of wide-view and 360-degree imaging have been tested, ranging from online campus tours to real estate listings. Portions of the image can consist of items that are hyperlinked to other photos, Web sites, or explanatory material. Figuring out ways to best show this type of functionality, as well as showing the ability to move around—literally—on the screen and zoom in are important user interface issues.

Weblink

360-Degree Tour of Tikal Mayan Ruins in Guatemala [www.studio360.com/tikal.htm]

Quicktime VR Tours www.apple.com /quicktime/products/gallery/]

CAVE Virtual Reality [www.evl.uic.edu/pape/CAVE /oldCAVE/CAVE.overview.html]

Virtual Reality

Virtual reality environments are extensions of 3D spaces, sometimes adding additional sensory data to enrich the user's experience. For example, force-feedback devices such as a data glove or body suit enable the user to "feel" objects or people encountered in a virtual space. Using a data glove a user might pick up an object such as a ball and feel its shape, texture, or weight. Such tactile feedback can add dramatically to the apparent reality of a virtual experience. Some researchers even say it is more important than the visualization aspect of virtual reality.

Important research on next-generation user interfaces is happening in a number of places, including the Integrated Media Systems Center (IMSC) at USC, Carnegie Mellon University, and elsewhere. Among these projects is breakthrough work developing immersive virtual reality. Immersive virtual reality

Virtual reality environments not only promise to be very engaging to audiences but are likely to create new possibilities for user interface design.

means enabling the user to enter via a desktop or head-worn display into high-resolution, realistic three-dimensional imagery, including full-motion video. The video is accompanied by three-dimensional audio and possibly with tactile or force-feedback via a data glove or body suit.

However, the massive computing power needed to create complete, realistic virtual reality environments is still probably many years off for the average consumer. In some ways, creating a user interface for a virtual reality environment will be easier than doing so for today's computer users. Not only will user interface principles have evolved by that time; but, because it looks like reality, graphics of actual real-life objects would and should be used. But that's not to say that objects couldn't be used to represent abstract things or certain kinds of data. The U.S. Department of Defense is firmly convinced that VR is real and has invested $40 million in a new VR training facility at the University of Southern California.

Immersive Audio   One of the more novel immersive media presentation environments under development is called Personal AudioCast. Personal AudioCast refers to a 3D, immersive audio technology now under joint development by the University of Southern California (USC) Integrated Media Systems Center; the Annenberg School for Communications, including its School of Journalism and Online Journalism Program; and Columbia University's Center for New Media. Three-dimensional audio incorporates depth of sound sources, in addition to the directional quality provided by stereophonic audio. These programs are designing a multiyear project to develop and test the Personal AudioCast system as a means of delivering real-time, customized, on-demand audio news and information (accessed on voice command using advanced speech recognition technology) transmitted from a dynamic, online multimedia news and information database.

Similar user interface issues to voice recognition technology arise with immersive audio. At times accessing content through voice commands will be the most efficient, but other times a user may want to read a transcript of a previous speech while listening to a speech being delivered live. In this case, being able to switch back and forth between a visually based user interface and a spoken one is important.

SUMMARY

The modern user interface allows people to access media content and to interact with others through that medium in a digital, networked environment.

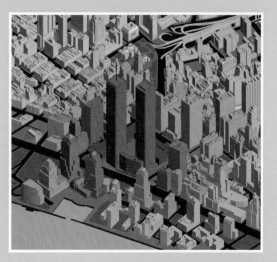

Although there has always been some sort of interface between media and their audiences, it was not until the advent of the computer that the notion of a user interface emerged widely in discussions of media. The user interface for traditional media was largely static and changed relatively slowly over time. In addition, the audience was largely passive in receiving content. Even with these limitations, television especially had components that helped make people better able to accept computers when they became available for the general public.

In a computer environment the audience is active and involved with media content and has far more ability to change how the content they receive looks. The user interface in the digital environment is far more variable than traditional media. Although it gives users more control over the media they see and interact with, it can also cause confusion that can hinder media consumption.

All interface devices such as the keyboard, mouse, touch-sensitive screen, and voice recognition have strong and weak points. The graphical user interface (GUI) played a key role in making computers and the Web more accessible to average people, which helped popularize computer and Internet use.

The PC and TV will eventually converge into one unit, although it is still too early to tell which will be perceived as merging into the other. Digital television (DTV) is playing and will continue to play an important role in helping this process of convergence, as many computerlike features previously unavailable with TVs will be possible. These include on-screen searchable electronic program guides, interactive objects embedded within video programs, and choices over changing the screens or viewpoints on the video display.

Future developments are likely to move the user interface into even more intuitive designs, more multimedia capabilities, and immersive media such as navigable 360-degree video, 3D surround sound, and virtual reality. Each of these developments will present its own unique challenges in the evolution of the user interface but also will enable media producers to find ever more interesting and engaging ways to tell stories.

Discussion Questions

1. Spend a day following your normal media consumption habits but without using a remote control device of any kind and instead changing stations or channels manually. Take notes on whether your media consumption changes and if so, in what ways. Are the changes a good or bad thing? Why?

2. Compare the user interface of a newspaper with that of the newspaper's Web site. What elements are similar and what elements differ? Explain why they may be so.

3. Visit three different Web sites within a specific industry (such as car rental agencies, airlines, newspapers, etc.) and note user interface differences between them. What elements did you like and dislike about each site? Why? How could they be improved?

4. Which do you think is more likely to happen, the PC becomes part of the television and a home entertainment center, or the TV becomes part of the desktop PC? Explain your reasons.

5. How might the eventual convergence of the PC and TV alter how they are used compared to today? Are these potential changes good, bad, or neutral?

6. Is the development of new types of technologies such as virtual reality and immersive media environments a good thing? Why or why not?

Bringing the Masses to Mass Communication: Distribution of Digital Content

9

Mahir Cagri was just another Turkish journalist until November 1999. Then his cell phone and home phone began ringing constantly, with people from all over the world who wanted to talk to him about his home page.

Even in the earliest days of the Web in the early 1990s, his home page would be considered technically crude. Visitors were greeted by:

> This is my page . . .
> WELCOME TO MY HOME PAGE !!!!!!!!!
> I KISS YOU !!!!!

This was followed by a picture of a smiling Cagri in a brown suit, then:

> I like music , I have many many musicenstrumans my
>   home I can play
> I like sport , swiming , basketball, tenis , volayball ,
>   walk ....
> I like sex
> I like travel I go 3–4 country every year

Several pictures of Cagri followed—playing table tennis, lying on a beach in a red Speedo—interspersed

by similar English statements, and at the bottom he invited anyone to visit him in Turkey and gave his phone numbers. If Cagri's grasp of written English was as tenuous as his grasp of HTML coding and Web site design, it didn't stop him from becoming a Web sensation. Within days a million people had visited his page.

Cagri said that apparently someone in Turkey copied his home page and republished it to another site, sending it to some friends as a joke. From there it quickly made the rounds of the Web. The interest in his site peaked at the end of 1999, but numerous parody sites sprang up and some advertising firms tried to copy the style to pitch products. Cagri recorded a pop single, "I Kiss You," and an ad for a British Internet company. He has also written a book. His Web site also gave him the chance to meet many women, some who specifically came to Izmir to see him, and he has become a local celebrity.

Internet commentator and author David Weinberger said it would be a mistake to dismiss Cagri and his home page. "The absurdity is the point," says Weinberger. "Hollywood has been cynically handing us stars, and we reveled in showing that now we are the ones who will decide who to notice. I think the general Web reaction was: 'We made this relentlessly ordinary guy a star! Cool!' "[1]

Weblink
I Kiss You home page
[www.ikissyou.org/mahir/mahirilk.hm]

OBJECTIVES

In this chapter we will:

- Outline the characteristics that distinguish digital distribution from traditional forms of distribution of media content.
- Examine the implications new forms of digital distribution have on mass communication and media organizations.
- Describe the historical development of telecommunications and networks that have created the current status of digital distribution.
- Examine different types of online communities and file-sharing services.
- Highlight the future development and potential problems of digital distribution.

Prologue

Digital distribution is in many ways the most crucial and visible aspect of how digitization and the Internet are transforming mass communication. Computerized production and editing technologies, storage media, and interface design have important implications for mass communication, how it is practiced, the content of news and entertainment media, and the way media organizations conduct business. But none of these would be such important issues if media distribution remained largely unchanged.

Digital distribution has altered the dynamics of distribution. It has gone from a unidirectional model in the analog world, in which large media companies primarily control distribution channels of media content, to one in which the public can distribute content as widely as an established media company.

The continuing battle the recording industry is having over file sharing services such as KaZaA and Morpheus, although framed in terms of intellectual property and copyright infringement, is an issue primarily because of changes brought about in distribution. The public is behaving no differently than they did prior to the Internet, when a music fan would make an audiocassette copy of an album for a friend or compile songs from a favorite band onto a cassette to be listened to in the car. A primary difference is that rather than making a tape or two and giving them to friends, millions of people can now get free copies of music and send those copies to others throughout the Internet.

A. J. Liebling once said, "Freedom of the press is guaranteed only to those who own one." With digital media and the Internet, now practically anyone has a "printing press" that can distribute not only printed text but audio or video as well.

Characteristics of Digital Distribution

Digitization of media, as we have seen in earlier chapters, has radically altered many aspects of mass communication. Distribution is no different—and for some of the same fundamental reasons that have caused changes with other aspects of media. Some of these characteristics have been mentioned before, but they will be touched on again here in order to give a complete characterization of what makes digital distribution so different from analog distribution.

Distributing Bits

A fundamental characteristic of digital media, that it consists of electrons rather than anything physical, is the cornerstone of the characteristics that follow. Although data still must be stored in some physical location, compared to analog media, which consist of physical items such as printed matter on paper, digital media can exist in such small physical spaces as to be virtually nonexistent. Enough books can be stored on a computer the size of a small suitcase to fill a small library if they were in physical form. As we have seen, digital data can of course be put into a physical form, such as a printed book, DVD, or CD, but it does not *need* to be put into such a form to be seen as long as someone has access to a computer network and the information is stored in that network.

With digital media there is no need for warehousing or for large amounts of physical storage space; this reduces the costs of media products.

Low Distribution Costs

With nothing to physically send, distribution costs are greatly reduced. There is no need for trucks, trains, or planes to move products from manufacturing or printing plant to warehouses and then to retail stores—and no need to send back unsold copies. Media content can travel at the speed of light over hair-thin wires directly to computers. This does not mean that distribution over the Internet is free, however. Internet users must still pay for access to the Internet, and distributors of content often have to pay the Web hosting companies for the amount of bandwidth they use as the public requests streaming audio or video. Sometimes these costs can be quite substantial—several thousand dollars a month—for popular Web sites that contain video clips. Although the costs are technically not distribution costs, they act much the same way because an individual or company unable to pay the extra costs for Internet traffic essentially has its Web site closed to further visitors after its monthly limit has been reached.

Perfect Infinite Copies

A factor in reducing distribution costs is that creating copies of digital content is largely free. Unlike with analog media, in which there are fixed costs associated with creating physical copies of media such as books or albums, digital media has no such restrictions. This is because, unlike analog media, a digital piece of content never runs out. A member of the public downloading a book from a publisher's Web site does not mean that there is one less book for somebody else to download or that the publisher will have to order more copies of the book in order to meet demand. The consumer simply has downloaded a perfect copy to his or her computer, taken from a digital version of the book on the publisher's Web site that is still there and available to anyone else.

The ability of anyone to create an infinite number of copies of digital media and make them available to anyone else on the Internet is the crux of what concerns media companies about their current business models. It is also the primary motivation behind the various initiatives to create secure digital content that cannot be copied without the copyright holder's permission.

Instantaneous Distribution

Although not truly instantaneous, by analog media standards the ability to distribute media content over the Internet is instantaneous. A click of a mouse can send content to tens of thousands or hundreds of thousands of people, nearly at the speed of light. Although network congestion and dial-up connections can slow down how quickly something is actually received, material can reach a wide audience in an extremely short period of time and much faster than what it takes to create and send a physical product.

Consider the case in May 2002 when rapper Eminem's long-awaited CD "The Eminem Show" was released. Its release date had already been moved up twice by the record label because of piracy concerns, but even before the record hit the stores it was already the second-most-played CD in computer drives around the world, according to Gracenote, a company that tracks online listening habits. Gracenote did not even consider the CD in MP3 format; it looked only at *physical* CDs playing in peoples' computers, which means CDs that were either copied from friends or bought from bootleggers off the street.[2]

In May 2002, rapper Eminem's CD "The Eminem Show" was the second-most-played CD on the Internet—even before it was officially released.

New Distribution Dynamics

The fact that once a piece of digital content is available on the Internet there is currently essentially no way to completely control how it is distributed is another cause for serious concern among media companies. Let's look at an example such as a photograph from a local online newspaper. It is a simple matter for a user to copy the picture to his or her local drive separate from the article it was associated with (it is also easy for the user to manipulate the photo, but for our purposes here that is not important). He or she could then send the digital photo as an attachment by e-mail to 20 of the people in his or her e-mail address book. Assume that only half of those 20 people like the photo enough to send it to 20 other people in each of their address books and half of those people do the same. Within three "generations" of sending the photo from the original sender, it could be seen by over 2200 people, all within a matter of minutes and at virtually no cost to the senders. Add one more generation of senders and the number jumps to over 20,000—again for no cost. This example does not even take into account somebody putting the photograph on his or her own Web site, which could have tens of thousands more visitors, or posting it to a discussion board.

This example shows that distribution is no longer dependent on a central location sending out content to a passive audience. Distribution has essentially become decentralized and takes place "at the edges" of the computer network. In other words, rather than central servers containing media content that the public accesses, the audience can now store media content on their own computers and make it available to others on the Internet. It replaces a few, centralized distribution points with many, localized distribution points. This is the basis for **peer-to-peer (P2P)** applications, of which file sharing services such as KaZaA and Morpheus are examples. P2P will be discussed in more detail later in this chapter.

The Audience as Distributor

Decentralization of distribution means a loss of distribution control for media companies, since a single company cannot dictate what every single PC among the public may or may not distribute. This translates into potential lost revenues as copies are made and shared among millions of Internet users without paying the copyright holders. This is precisely what is happening with the case of music online, although some studies have countered the music industry's claims that they are losing revenues in lost CD sales by showing that increased exposure to different music and artists actually helps increase sales. Through file sharing services, each member of the public who uses these applications becomes a potential distributor of content merely by the fact that he or she has certain files other people would like to download. This "distributor" doesn't have to send anything.

A benefit is that widely distributed content among the public makes it far less likely that the content would become unavailable should a central company server go down. In a P2P system, as long as someone with that content is online, then it can be downloaded.

The Implications for Mass Communication

New distribution patterns through the Internet can greatly diminish the importance of established distribution channels that media organizations currently use. Just how large media organizations will adjust to these changes in distribution or how they will find viable business models within these new dynamics is still unclear. What is clear is that media organizations have much less control over how their content is distributed than they used to, unless they choose to put technological constraints on digital media to give it certain analog characteristics, such as making it hard or impossible to copy from one format to another. However, attempts at these kinds of limitations have met with resistance from consumers and the creation of programs that allow the public to sidestep security measures.

The Internet has added a new element to the traditional one-to-many distribution method, in which media content was sent by one organization to the public through clearly defined distribution channels according to fixed procedures and rules. A person who wrote and self-published a book, for example, would be unable to have it carried by major bookstores because the writer would not have access to the distribution channels needed to send copies of the book to the different outlets. Nor would he or she have the same access to book reviewers in major media outlets, making it difficult for the public to learn about the book and review it even if they could easily purchase a copy at a bookstore. The same obstacles could be applied to other content creators outside of mainstream media, from musicians to aspiring filmmakers.

peer-to-peer network (P2P)—a network in which all computers on the network are considered equal (peers) and can send and receive information equally well. This is the basis of file sharing services such as KaZaA and Morpheus.

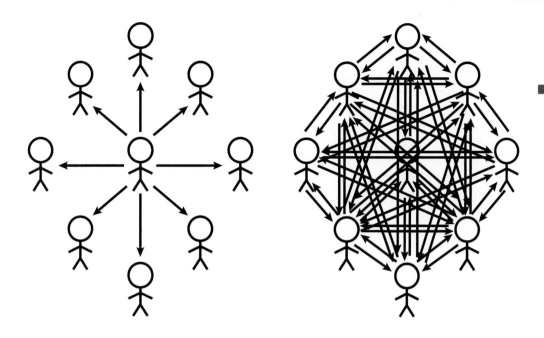

Figure 9-1 One-to-many and many-to-many distribution models. In the traditional one-to-many distribution model (left), one person or organization creates media content and distributes it from a central location to the audience. In a many-to-many model (right), such as that with P2P networks, everyone in a network can create and distribute content to everyone else without having to go through a centralized location.

The many-to-many distribution model made possible by the Internet completely sidesteps traditional distribution networks that favored established media companies. Now any content creator can reach millions worldwide simply by putting content on the Internet and especially the World Wide Web. And, as already mentioned, there are no unit production costs associated with making more copies of media content. Members of the public who download media content from a Web site are creating a new copy. If they are connected to a P2P-type network, then this copy is also available to others on the network.

The Internet also lets the public completely bypass established media outlets and communicate directly with each other through e-mail, online discussion boards, instant messaging services, and online chat rooms. Much of what people talk about may well be derived from what they see in the media, but it doesn't have to be.

This is not to say that there is no place for established media companies and their distribution networks in an online distribution environment. As even a short visit to the Web will show, publishers, record labels, film production companies, and other media companies act as quality control gatekeepers of sorts, filtering out substandard content and supporting higher-quality content. This of course may not always seem to be the case when looking at new books, television shows, films, or music being released, but the fact is that the financial support of the media companies not only increases production quality of media content but also helps greatly in marketing content they do produce. If anything, in the new world of digital distribution this act of filtering types and quality of content will become more important than ever, as most people will not want to spend lots of time trying to find quality content that they like from the flood of material that is available.

Media content is likely to coexist in some kind of dual-distribution system, in which "mainstream" content is accessible through traditional distribution outlets but also available in downloads or on-demand formats from the Internet. Content creators outside of mainstream media will largely rely on Internet distribution and **viral marketing,** or information on the content spread by word of mouth through

viral marketing—spreading news and information about media content through word of mouth, usually via online discussion groups, chats, and e-mails, without utilizing traditional advertising and marketing methods.

online chats, e-mails, and discussion groups, to get noticed by a large audience. Some content creators that seem to have mass market appeal will get offers from mainstream media and then have traditional marketing and distribution channels at their disposal as well.

Media companies will have to be aware of the trends and shifting desires of the online audience if they want to capitalize on networked distribution. To distribute media content, what previously took months of careful marketing and advertising planning, as well as producing multiple copies and sending the items to stores, can now take place in a matter of weeks or even days if the online audience decides they like something. And as in the case of the Eminem CD already mentioned, the public can even beat the media companies at making physical products widely available through bootleg downloads and copying technology.

To better understand how radically telecommunications and networks are affecting media distribution, let's look briefly at the historical development of distributional technologies.

The Historical Development of Telecommunications

Let's begin with a review of the historical development of the modern system of network and publishing technologies. These have played crucial roles in shortening the time for communication to take place and in turn allowing for wider, more rapid distribution of communication or media content.

Fundamentally, the invention of the mechanical printing press in 1455 made possible easier production and therefore distribution of content over distance and time. It represents a shift in the nature of human communication. It also made possible the creation of modern mass communication.

It is tempting to think that the age of rapid telecommunications is a late-twentieth century invention, but in fact the origins of high-speed data transmission over long distances can actually be traced to the eighteenth century.[3]

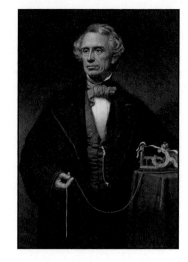

Samuel F. B. Morse, inventor of the telegraph.

Telegraphy

In 1794, French clergyman Claude Chappe and Swedish nobleman Abraham Niclas Edelcrantz built the first high-speed data network, the optical telegraph, so that news could be brought from Finland to Sweden and Stockholm and from Denmark to the Scandinavian coast and from there to the capital. The optical telegraph worked by building a series of signaling stations, each within sight of the next, usually less than a kilometer or so apart. A person standing in a look-out platform on the station would watch the next tower for a visual signal, which would represent a letter, word, or number. A series of signals could represent a message, which would then be relayed to the next tower, and so on. Experienced signalers could transmit even a fairly complex message quickly.

In 1837, American Samuel Morse invented the electromagnetic telegraph, which marked the beginning of today's information age. Morse's invention was the first technology that could transform information into electric form and transmit it reliably over great distances. Many in the newspaper business saw the important role the telegraph could play in the rapid delivery of news and in getting news to their readers more quickly than competing newspapers. The telegraph had effects on journalism beyond more rapid transmission of news. Because telegraph lines could go down during transmission, it was important to put the most important facts of a news story first and include facts of lesser importance later. This led to the style of news writing still practiced today, the inverted pyramid style.

Information Railroad

The notion of a national electronic communication infrastructure stretches back nearly a century and a half to the telegraph, when two entrepreneurial visionaries issued a public call to build an information railroad. In 1853, Hiram O. Alden and James Eddy lobbied the U.S. Congress for "a right of way through the public lands of the United States, for the construction of a subterranean line of telegraph." On behalf of the House of Representatives Committee on Territories, Ephraim Farley subsequently issued a report on their proposal. Farley's report, which outlines many of the benefits of the proposed enterprise, foreshadowed the arguments of the early 1990s in support of an information superhighway. Prior to 1861, when coast-to-coast telegraph service became available, the most rapid form of long-distance communication between the East Coast and the West Coast of the United States, as well as many other parts of the country, depended on the speed of the fastest horse.

Universal Service

The notion of universal service is present in the 1853 suggestion by Ephraim Farley that every home "would be in immediate communication with each other." Farley outlined the plan for a subterranean line of two wires that would reach from the Atlantic to Pacific coasts and stated that such an "information railroad" would help encourage business growth, especially in the West. Although seriously

In the mid-19th century there was a proposal put before Congress to fund creation of a coast-to-coast telegraphy network.

considered by Congress, the estimated $2,760,000 price tag for creating the underground lines was finally deemed too expensive and best left to private industry to create if they wanted it. Had the government decided to provide the right of way for the proposal, perhaps the 1990s debate about building a national information infrastructure would have had a decidedly different tone.

Telephony

packet switching—a type of switching that occurs within a network in which information is divided up into pieces, or packets, and transported as separate packets using the least congested routes. At the end of the route the packets are reassembled in their proper order and delivered over the telephone line or Internet.

circuit switching—the original system used for telephony in which circuits connected two people communicating. Once the circuit was connected, or "on," the people on either end of the circuit used the whole circuit exclusively, even if they didn't speak. When they hung up, the circuit was disconnected by an operator and available for others to use.

Bell's 1876 invention of the telephone launched the national system of telephony, which used the same basic infrastructure as the telegraph. The American Telephone and Telegraph Company (AT&T) and the American Bell Telephone Company existed as regulated legal monopolies for most of their history based on the principles outlined by former AT&T president Theodore Vail in 1907. He said that the telephone, by the nature of the underlying technology, could operate most efficiently as a monopoly providing universal service. Competing telephone systems, in which users of one telephone system could not communicate with users of other telephone systems, would hurt the growth of telecommunication. This principle guided U.S. telecommunications policy for most of the twentieth century. Although it may well have helped ease the early adoption of telephones, the monopoly control AT&T had over telecommunications systems also slowed innovation.

As some of the early researchers into what would eventually become the Internet learned, AT&T blocked attempts to test a digital, **packet-switched** network via telephone lines when first approached with the idea in the early 1960s. Paul Baran, who conceived of the Internet's architecture in the early 1960s, said that even when the Air Force offered to give AT&T money to develop a digital, packet-switched network they said, "It's not going to work. And furthermore, we're not going into competition with ourselves." Analog telephone systems that relied on **circuit switching** were centralized in five-level hierarchies. Messages transmitted through switching centers would degrade in quality, just as third or fourth generation videotape dubs degrade the quality of the original recorded video. If a central switching center was destroyed, the entire telephone system could be incapacitated.[4]

Today, the basic architecture of the telephone system is digital and packet switched, just like the Internet.

Satellites

Communication satellites were first proposed in 1945 by science fiction writer Arthur C. Clarke. Clarke was trained in communications and helped invent radar during World War II. On October 4, 1957, the Soviet Union launched Sputnik I ("traveling companion"), the first communications satellite. Sputnik I was a 23-inch, 184-pound ball of metal that contained a radio receiver and transmitter, using what is today the Citizens Band, or CB radio frequency, and signaled not only the beginning of instantaneous global communications but an important milestone in the Cold War. It was the Soviet's launch of Sputnik that led four years later U.S. President John F. Kennedy to declare that the United States would be the first country to put a human on the moon.

Sputnik I, the first artificial satellite, launched on October 4, 1957.

Although some scholars have questioned the importance of the invention of the communications satellite as a transformative technology, Arthur C. Clarke disagrees, saying that claiming it is simply an extension of existing communication technologies is like claiming the atomic bomb was simply an extension of conventional warfare.

Communication satellites have substantially upgraded mediated communication in at least two ways. First, they have substantial bandwidth, or communications capacity. This means more information, communications, or media content can be distributed. Second, because they are positioned high above the earth (typically 22,000 miles), satellites permit ground-based media to communicate with parties in remote corners of the Earth for which terrestrial communication might be impossible or prohibitively expensive. That is, a signal can be sent from one location on Earth, bounced off the satellite, and relayed to a distant location that also has a line of sight with the satellite. The two terrestrial locations might be thousands of miles apart and, because of the curvature of the earth, would be unable to reach each other with wireless terrestrial communications.

Fiber Optics

In many respects, the story of fiber optics goes all the way back to the optical telegraph created by Claude Chappe and Abraham Niclas Edelcrantz, because it used light to transmit information. Subsequent developments in telegraphy by Morse and later in telephony used electromagnetic waves at different wavelengths than light to transmit information. The concept of transmitting information with light was not forgotten, however. Alexander Graham Bell patented an optical telephone system, the Photophone, in 1880, but his earlier telephone was more practical, and his Photophone was donated to the Smithsonian Institution.

Transmitting light through the air, as with the Photophone, had numerous problems. The light not only became diffused but also was dependent on weather conditions for the clarity of the signal. Numerous inventors and scientists worked on the problem of somehow concentrating and focusing the light, usually through glass tubing of some type. In the 1950s and 1960s, two developments helped make the transmission of information by light a reality: covering the glass or plastic fibers that helped reduce light leakage from the fibers and the invention of the laser in 1960.

Sending light long distances without degrading the signal still proved to be problematic, making fiber optics not practical as a communication medium until further technological improvements in 1970.

Today's fiber optics can send information through hair-thin glass or plastic fiber by laser almost 100 miles without using a repeater, or device that boosts the signal. Fiber not only has much more capacity to carry information than traditional copper wires, it moves information much faster—the speed of light, in fact. Almost all of the major communication lines within the United States now use fiber optics to send information. However, laying fiber optic lines directly to homes is still not cost effective for telecommunications companies, so most information travels by fiber optics to switching stations near the destinations, where it is sent by copper wires or coaxial cable, both of which are much slower.

Fiber optics can send information through hair-thin glass or plastic fibers at many times the speed of data passing through traditional copper wires.

Networks

Some characteristics of networks have already been discussed in earlier chapters, and here we will examine two basic types of networks that have been mentioned but not thoroughly explained, as well as discussing issues related to connectivity and quality of network service.

The Client/Server Model

The **client/server** model is what the Internet, for a number of technical reasons such as limited bandwidth, Internet Protocol (IP) addresses, and the rapid rise in popularity of the Internet via the Web, largely developed into. This model of a network simply means there is a centralized computer, or server, that stores content that the audience (clients) can access on the network. It is a hierarchical system in which most computer users do not contribute content to the Internet; they simply receive content.

A client/server network model has strong points and weak points. Among its strong points is that information is stored in a centralized location, making it easy to find (it always has the same virtual address, in the case of the Web shown by a Web site's URL). Among its weak points is that a single server can easily become overloaded if many clients request content from it at the same time. The single location also makes it vulnerable to attack or destruction. If the server or servers with the hard drives that contain the information are destroyed, such as in a fire, the information is lost unless backup copies were made and stored somewhere else.

Servers are an important part of how mass communication content is moved about in a digital, networked environment. Audience members access a growing portion of the content produced by media organizations via Web servers.

The Peer-to-Peer Model

client/server network—a model of network computing in which some computers store and send information to other computers on the network (clients). For a number of technical reasons, this has been the primary model used for the Internet.

The peer-to-peer (P2P) network model represents what the Internet was initially supposed to be: an interconnected group of computers, all of which were essentially "equal" in their ability to send, store, and receive information; i.e., a network of peers. P2P networking is by its nature decentralized and nonhierarchical.

Usenet, discussed later, is an early example of a P2P network and one that highlights some of P2P's flaws in the current Internet environment. Before the

How Digital Media Are Changing Our World   www.ablongman.com/pavlik1

commercialization of the Internet, **spamming,** or sending mass e-mails advertising products or business services, was an action that would quickly create outrage among Internet users. Now it is commonplace, and a service like Usenet has no inherent mechanism to stop spammers. Spammers not only take away bandwidth from legitimate Internet users, slowing the system down, they also clog inboxes with advertising messages not related to the topics being discussed that are designed to trick users into reading them. The result? People avoid visiting discussions on Usenet, diminishing its usefulness.

Another hurdle for P2P applications reaching their full potential on today's Internet is the amount of bandwidth available to upload content. Because in a P2P network anyone can be a content distributor, users need as much bandwidth to upload content as they do when they download content. Unfortunately, broadband providers such as cable modems and satellite services, in order to conserve the amount of total bandwidth on the network, limit the upload speeds for users.

Many of the best applications being developed on the Internet combine aspects of client/server networks and P2P. Napster, for example, was not a true P2P application because they used a central server to store information on which files were available for downloading. This classic client/server network characteristic, although helping searches, also helped make them an easy target when they were sued by the RIAA, which will be discussed later.

Connectivity

Connectivity can be defined in terms of the ability of people and their computers, digital television sets, or other digital devices to link to the Internet and other media of online communications. Connectivity is critical for at least two reasons.

First, without a connection, the citizen, or media consumer, has no access to the online communications network. This means he or she cannot communicate electronically with others or access content published online.

Second, the value of the communications network rises as the comprehensiveness of connectivity in the society to that network rises. This is summarized in what is known as **Metcalfe's Law,** which states that the value of a network is equal to the square of the number of people on that network. Imagine if the telephone had just been invented, and only one person had a phone. It wouldn't be of any value. Adding a second person to the phone system greatly increases the system's overall value. The same principle applies for people going online. The more people who are online, the more valuable the network system is as a means of mass communication. This is a foundational principle in network economics.

Although some in the industry would argue that universal service, or connectivity, is too expensive, the reality is that in network economics complete connectivity increases the value of the system to the entire society and is of ultimate economic benefit to the whole. Without complete connectivity in the society, not only will the economics of online communications fail, but the function of mass communication in democratic society also fails. It is necessary for all citizens to have access to basic information, even if that access is unequal. Access will always be and always has been unequal, even in the days of analog media. But, it is critically important that all citizens at least be connected to the system of communication, online or off.

spam—unwanted e-mail sent out by advertisers as a mass mailing.

Metcalfe's Law—the value of a network rises in proportion to the square of the number of people on that network. In other words, the more people who are connected to a network such as the Internet, the more valuable that network becomes.

Napster creator Shawn Fanning saw his company eventually close because of lawsuits brought against it by the record labels and bands such as Metallica.

Quality of Service

Quality of service, or the reliability, efficiency, and effectiveness of one's online connection, is an important element in the world of online communications and networks. If one cannot rely on one's online connection, then it is impossible to make it a cornerstone of civil society, much less commerce and culture. Today's Internet cannot guarantee a high quality of service. Its strength is that anyone can access it, any time, from anywhere to send or receive content.

Some critics of the Internet contend the Internet, by its very nature, will never be able to provide a high level of quality of service. Instead, because it is an open architecture (i.e., anyone can use it at virtually no marginal cost), it means that at any specific moment a user may not get the bandwidth needed for high-quality video or audio or may not be able to access the server needed or wanted for a critical journalistic or e-commerce transaction.

This argument may be true. As a result, some point to alternative proprietary high-bandwidth telecommunications transmission systems where quality of service is guaranteed—but at a cost. Broadcasters pay for the use of satellites or private fiber optics networks to reliably transmit their video to affiliate stations. Another solution is to use a combination of the Internet and private networks. However, using private networks could create a new kind of digital divide in which the majority of Internet users have a cheap or free network with severe limitations on transmitting or uploading multimedia content, while large media corporations or wealthy individuals could have high-quality, high-speed private networks that transmit content to a paying audience.

File Sharing Services

File sharing services using P2P networks started making the news in late 1999 primarily because of the rapid rise in popularity of Napster, a program created by 18-year-old Northeastern University student Shawn Fanning. Napster let Internet users easily share MP3 files, a compression format for digital music. College campus networks slowed as millions of students downloaded and shared music files, and the music industry got a rude awakening to the power of digital distribution of media content.

Although music files and their widespread free distribution among users led the Recording Industry Association of America (RIAA) and the major record labels to take legal action against Napster and other file sharing services, P2P networks can and are being used for a variety of other purposes as well. These range from looking for signs of extraterrestrial intelligence to solving complex model simulation problems to creating an information network that is impossible to shut down or censor.

File sharing services can work in different ways, and some have been created with various goals in mind. Let's examine some of the most common ones.

Napster

It is ironic that the program and company largely responsible for starting the rapid popularity of P2P file sharing services does not even follow a true P2P model. Napster used central servers to store information on what music files were available on what users' computers. Napster users would search the Napster database, see the music they wished to download, and then connect directly with that user to download the song. Napster simply facilitated searches and was not involved in actually transferring files between users.

But this ability to easily search and share files for free is exactly what the record labels saw as a threat, and in December 1999 they filed suit against Napster saying that they facilitated massive piracy among their tens of millions of users. Napster claimed that its service exposed emerging and unknown musicians to the general public and said that any copying of music files should be considered **fair use.** Napster also argued that they should be protected under the 1992 Audio Home Recording Act, which allows consumers to make digital recordings for their personal use. Because they were simply facilitating this process, albeit on a much larger scale, they should be protected under the act, they said.

The court did not agree. Initially, Napster was told to shut down completely but received a stay of that injunction for six months. Under a court-brokered agreement, Napster blocked access to any copyrighted songs they did not have license agreements for even as they started negotiations with one of the record labels in the original lawsuit, Bertelsmann AG's BMG label, to develop a fee-based service that would give them access to all songs in the BMG music archive. The other major labels maintained their lawsuit while they developed two music subscription services of their own, Musicnet and Pressplay.

Bertelsmann invested about $85 million in Napster as they tried to establish a subscription service and kept the struggling company on life support. Napster was finally shut down in July 2001. In May 2002 Bertelsmann bought Napster's assets for $8 million, and in June 2002 Napster declared Chapter 11 bankruptcy. The bankruptcy filing put a hold on the still-unsettled copyright infringement claims by the major record labels, although they can bring their claims before bankruptcy court. It is unclear what a new Napster may be after executive changes at Bertelsmann later in the summer of 2002, or even if it can be a viable music sharing site, let alone have the same popularity it once did.

fair use—an exception to copyright law that allows someone to use an excerpt of a work without paying for its use. Quotations from works in reviews or their use in commentary or criticism are examples of fair use.

As ABCNews legal analyst Jeffrey Toobin said, "The technology is changing so fast Napster is not the worst problem the music companies face because at least Napster is a centrally controlled switching point for this music."[5]

Other Music File Sharing Services

Napster's centralized servers made it an easy target to shut down through legal action. During Napster's struggles, several other music file sharing services sprang up. Some were small and threatened with legal action by the record labels and subsequently shut down before they could catch on. Austin-based Audiogalaxy, which included in-house music reviews and tried to promote obscure bands, was sued quickly after the record labels' success against Napster and paid the labels a "substantial sum" that neither party disclosed before shutting down. But others may prove to be much more difficult to bring to court.

KaZaA

KaZaA is the name of the software distributed by Sharman Networks, a company with headquarters in Sydney, Australia, but registered in Vanuatu, an island in the South Pacific. KaZaA allows sharing of music, image, video, and text files among users, and it too has been sued by the record labels. In May 2002, KaZaA withdrew their defense in a lawsuit filed against them and Morpheus in Los Angeles, claiming they could not afford legal costs, but the fact is it will be nearly impossible for the labels to successfully sue a company registered in Vanuatu and with no central servers as Napster had.

Sharman Networks distributed a new version of its software, available for free download over the Internet, which includes a subscription service. KaZaA also includes advertising along the bottom of its window, although the company was getting what some would call poetic justice as users have manipulated the KaZaA software to allow for a stripped-down, ads-free version. The very same distribution dynamics that are allowing for easy music file sharing are making it easy for users to download the ads-free version of the software, thereby depriving KaZaA of a potential revenue source.

Morpheus

Like KaZaA and Audiogalaxy, the company that created and distributes Morpheus file sharing software, StreamCast, was sued by the record labels in May 2002. And like KaZaA, they withdrew their defense, citing lack of funds.

StreamCast looks more vulnerable to lawsuits than the internationally based Sharman Networks, and several delays in a new version of Morpheus following an unexpected shutdown of the service in spring 2002 have hurt its standing with the file sharing audience. StreamCast plans to add a for-pay section to its software as well, which would include features such as long-distance telephone service, an instant messaging service, and video conferencing to AOL Instant Messaging (AIM) users, of which AOL claims there are 140 million. Whether the additional services the new software offers will be enough to create a viable business model and stave off lawsuits from the record labels remains to be seen. "We are still running toward peer to peer with our arms open," said StreamCast Chief Executive Steve Griffin. "We think it's the technology of the future, and we want to be an active part in it."[6]

Other P2P Applications and Services

Sharing music files is not the only thing that P2P networks can be used for. Other applications have been developed that take advantage of P2P's inherent strengths—specifically the amount of unused computing power on individual PCs that are at the edges of the network and the inability to track the numerous computers at the edges.

Gnutella

Gnutella's existence owes much to the mass communication power among Internet users. Gnutella gets its name from GNU (GNU's Not Unix) and Nutella, a hazelnut and chocolate spread. Gnutella was created over two weeks in March 2000 by two developers, Justin Frankel and Tom Pepper, who had a few years earlier created the program Winamp, which allowed digital music files to be played. AOL, who had bought their company in 1999, deemed Gnutella an unauthorized research project and quashed it.

However, **open source** developers were able to post Gnutella's code to other developers as well as give them access to a type of chat room from which they could communicate with each other in real time as they worked on developing Gnutella. Through this loose-knit collaborative network of volunteer developers, Gnutella was improved and distributed on the Internet as an open source program that nobody could claim ownership of.

Although Gnutella started out as an application, it has transformed into a P2P protocol. Gnutella lets users exchange not only music files but other kinds of files as well. Late Gnutella developer Gene Kan said Gnutella's strength is in how it mimics natural communication. He compared a request made over the Gnutella network for a file to someone arriving at a crowded cocktail party and asking where the sushi is. The query goes from one person to another through the crowd until it reaches people with sushi and they say "It's here!" The news is passed back to the person wanting sushi, who goes through the crowd to get it. The truly decentralized nature of Gnutella makes it extremely difficult, if not impossible, for any one company or person to control. Drawbacks to Gnutella are that it sometimes takes longer for queries to "ripple through" the network to find what one is looking for than if there were a central server that had a database of everything that was available. Two popular Gnutella-based software programs are Bearshare and Limewire.[7]

Weblink
Gnutella.com
[www.gnutella.com]

Bearshare
[www.bearshare.com/]

Limewire
[www.limewire.com/]

Freenet

Freenet was created as a system utilizing a P2P network structure that would allow people to freely publish or view all types of information from all over the world. Like Gnutella, it is an open source system in which volunteers work on developing and improving the application. Ian Clarke first outlined the Freenet system while he was at the University of Edinburgh in a 1999 paper entitled, "A distributed decentralized information storage and retrieval system," and he began work on it with some volunteers shortly after that.

According to Freenet's founders, its main goals include:

- Uncensorable dissemination of controversial information;
- Efficient distribution of high-bandwidth content; and
- Universal personal publishing.[8]

open source—any program in which the programmer allows the source code of the program to be seen by others. This lets others improve upon and modify a program's source code. Most proprietary software programs do not allow the public to see their source code.

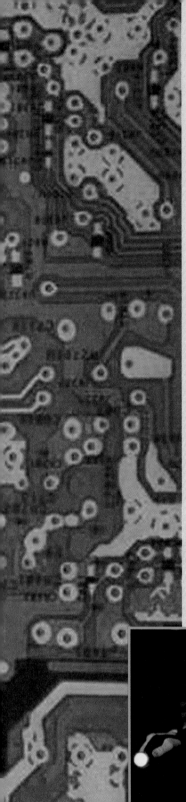

Media **Technology**

Is There Anybody Out There?

Mass communication does not stop at the communication satellites circling the earth. Ever since the first radio stations started transmitting their signals, the earth has inadvertently been broadcasting into space. It occurred to some astronomers that if there is extraterrestrial intelligent life in the universe, they would also be sending out electromagnetic waves as byproducts of their technological development in communication. The search for extraterrestrial intelligence (SETI) began.

SETI is a massive project that involves radio telescopes pointing at small slivers of the sky and recording radio waves, which emanate from many types of celestial bodies, and then trying to determine if there are patterns among the waves that would demonstrate signs of intelligent life. Processing the massive amounts of data being returned is beyond even the most powerful supercomputer.

SETI@home was developed to utilize the unused computing power among millions of home PCs to analyze the radio data that have been transmitted. Volunteers in the project download the software and data at certain intervals, and their computers work through the information even as the computer owners use their computers normally. When each segment is complete, it is transmitted back to a central computer, and a new packet of data is sent. There are safeguards in the system to make sure users cannot tamper with the data.

Although not purely peer-to-peer computing, because a central server and database keeps track and stores the information, SETI@home is a good example of how digital distribution can be used. Any number of volunteers can assist a project without inconveniencing themselves, because the program works in the background; and the free computing power amassed by the various users is many times more than what any research project could afford. The Web site also informs people of progress being made, thereby engaging the public in a field they otherwise might not get involved in.

Weblink
SETI@home
[setiathome.ssl.berkeley.edu/]

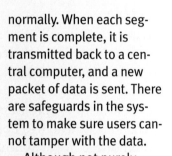

The movie "Contact," based on the novel by Carl Sagan, was based on the premise that the SETI program did establish contact with aliens.

Although the second goal has attracted the most media attention as well as the wrath of media companies because of the potential to distribute audio and video files, the first and third goals could have much more of an effect on online mass communication. Freenet protects freedom of speech by enabling anonymous and uncensorable publication of material ranging from grassroots alternative journalism to banned exposés. This could have important implications for distributing news that otherwise would not be seen in the mainstream press. By letting anyone have a Web site, even if they don't own a computer, Freenet essentially gives every member of the public a printing press.

Weblink
Freenet Project
[freenetproject.org/cgi-bin
/twiki/view/Main/WebHome]

Jabber

Jabber, as its name suggests, concentrates on real-time messaging, much like other instant messaging (IM) systems such as AOL's Instant Messenger (AIM), ICQ, or Yahoo! Messenger. One problem with proprietary IM systems currently is that users of one system cannot communicate with users of another system. It is the equivalent of a person on an AT&T telephone system not being able to communicate with someone on a Verizon system. This obviously reduces the effectiveness of IM systems. Jabber uses a set of XML-based communication protocols that do allow users from a variety of platforms to communicate with each other, although some companies have blocked or frequently changed their protocols so Jabber no longer works with them.

Jabber was created in 1998 by Jeremie Miller, and it now has many volunteers working on developing and improving Jabber. Miller says future plans for Jabber include applications such as whiteboarding and the extension of Jabber to wireless devices.

Weblink
Jabber Software Foundation
[www.jabber.org]

Online Communities

With the new distribution capabilities of the Internet, any member of the public can communicate directly with thousands and even millions of others. No longer is a traditional mass communication media channel, such as newspapers' letters-to-the-editor section or radio call-in shows, needed to reach other members of the public. Online communities have sprung up in which people are not bound by geography but by common interests, religious beliefs, ethnic origins, and other characteristics. The communities exist only online and are in this sense "virtual" communities that are not dependent on specific locales or times to "meet" and communicate with each other.

People become involved in online communities to meet others, discuss ideas or opinions, flirt (or more), learn, be entertained, and argue. Because of their high degree of interactivity and the fact that members in an online community are talking among each other as peers rather than passively receiving information from an authoritative media source, online communities can become quite engaging and even addictive. That is not to say that online communities ignore the world of media, however. Often discussions center around news or entertainment read or seen in the media.

There are various types of online communities, depending on the purpose of the members for gathering and the type of communication they use over the

The WELL: A Brilliant and Brand Brainchild

One of the earliest popular online communities was The WELL, which stands for Whole Earth 'Lectronic Link. Stewart Brand and Larry Brilliant founded the Whole Earth 'Lectronic Link in 1985 in Sausalito as a way for the writers and readers of the *Whole Earth Review* to have a dialogue with each other. The WELL initially had a limited audience but eventually expanded beyond users in northern California and the Bay Area and covers many other social, political, and artistic topics as well.

It has maintained a relatively high level of discussion and literacy among its members, who pay $10 a month for the ad-free discussion boards, called WELL Conferences. It is not uncommon to see names such as John Perry Barlow, a former lyricist for the Grateful Dead and a cofounder of the Electronic Frontier Foundation; musician David Crosby; science-fiction writer Bruce

Sterling; or other artists, writers, and leading thinkers posting messages as members of the WELL community.

Weblink
The WELL
[www.well.com]

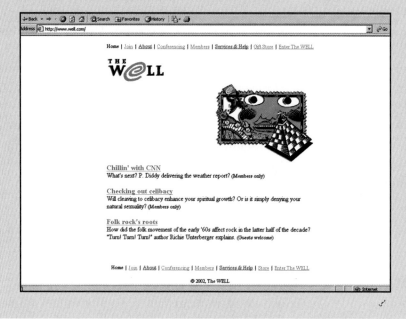

Internet. Some, such as chat rooms, are short-lived and at times chaotic. Others, such as discussion groups, can be highly literate with topics being discussed for months. Internet users usually belong to several different communities.

Online communities continue to change with technology. Right now most communication on the Internet is text-based, which lets people easily try new identities or personas as they communicate with others. How online communities will change when broadband becomes more common, along with computer video feeds to the Internet, remains to be seen.

Some online communities, such as Palace.com, encourage users to select or create **avatars,** or graphical representations of themselves. Another development that is likely to make participating in online communities much better is some kind of member rating or trust system, similar to that used in an auction site such as eBay or a product review site such as Epinions, in which a member can establish "levels of trust" with other users and thereby automatically block or delete messages from certain members they do not want to hear from. This kind

avatar—a graphical representation of an Internet user, which can be used in online communities or to otherwise represent oneself on the Web.

Dave Winer writes the influential and opinionated blog *Scripting News.*

of informal rating system will help encourage the distribution of worthwhile content and discourage poor content by inhibiting (although not eliminating) distribution of it.

Blogs

Weblogs, or **blogs**, are Web pages of short, frequently updated postings by an individual that are arranged chronologically, much like a series of diary entries or journal pages. Blogs can contain thoughts, links to sites of interest, rants, or whatever the blogger wants to write about. Some blogs by noted programmers or computer experts such as Dave Winer's *Scripting News* can be heavily visited and are quite influential, having an **agenda setting function** much like mainstream media. This is when a topic is covered by the media and therefore becomes a subject of discussion among the public.

Blogs are probably closest to a traditional publishing model than any other online community, because they often do not have interactive features for readers to easily reply publicly to specific postings. In this respect, a blog without a discussion board, or one that does not post e-mail replies to entries, is much like reading an article in a newspaper or magazine, and the only sense of "community" that is developed is among fellow readers.

One strong point about blogs is that they can be easily updated, without the poster needing to know any HTML code or manually uploading pages to the Web. Blogs can be effective in letting project members keep each other updated on developments or plans as well as letting family members keep each other up-to-date on family or friend news.

Discussion Boards

A discussion board is a type of online "bulletin board" where Internet users can post messages that can be seen by others coming to the discussion board and in which they can post responses to previous messages, or posts, or create their own

Weblink

palace.com
[www.palace.com]

eBay.com
[www.ebay.com]

Epinions
[www.epinions.com]

Weblink

Scripting News
[www.scripting.com/]

Blogger
[www.blogger.com]

weblog or blog—a type of Web site on which a person posts regular journal or diary entries; the posts are arranged chronologically.

agenda setting function—a role the media plays during the course of deciding which topics to cover that, by virtue of being covered in the media, become topics of discussion and perceived importance to the public.

message on a new topic. Series of messages that reply to a certain post are organized by threads according to their subject headers, making it easier for users coming to a discussion topic to follow the thread of the discussion back to earlier replies and the original posting that started the discussions in the first place.

Usenet provides thousands of discussion boards, each separated by categories called **newsgroups.** Separating newsgroups by general categories, as well as letting anyone create their own newsgroup on any topic, helps make finding discussions of interest to users easier and facilitates users starting their own communities.

Some online news Web sites such as CNET.com or WSJ.com encourage readers to post messages to discussion boards from within specific articles. Depending on the subject of the article, the subsequent discussion board postings can often take on a life of their own as readers discuss and argue with each other over points made by the writer or correct factual errors.

The ability for audiences to respond almost immediately to aspects of an article is an important shift in the balance of power between media producer and media consumer. Responses on discussion boards within articles can be read by all and compared to the article, unlike official corrections made by newspapers a few days after an article has appeared, making them appear out of context. However, because the public is not held to the same stringent standards of fact-checking that journalists are, it is easy for a reader to point out an "error" in the original article that is in fact correct but is simply something that reader disagrees with. It could be a never-ending spiral for a journalist to have to reconfirm every single fact in an article to prove he or she was right in the first place.

Partly because of the ease of sending messages to discussion boards, they often suffer from a few individuals who either send messages not related to the discussion board topic or send numerous messages on variations of the same topic, effectively monopolizing the "board space." Some discussion boards are moderated, which means a moderator either approves all messages before they are posted or has the ability to kick anyone off the discussion board or block their posts. Kicking someone off a discussion board often becomes a subject of much-heated debate when it happens and can lead to new discussion boards being formed as people stop going to the original one. Another weakness of discussion boards is the difficulty in fully exploring an issue, especially when many people are commenting on various aspects of a complex topic, and the speed in which members can go off topic.

Discussion boards are a vital form of mass communication on the Internet. Their format and asynchronous nature (i.e., not requiring users to be online at the same time) allow for relatively lengthy expositions on topics written whenever is convenient for the person sending the message. They also provide value even to board members who do not post messages but simply read what others are writing, a practice called **lurking.** Some discussion board creators encourage newcomers to lurk for a while so they can become familiar with the tone and type of topics being discussed on the board.

newsgroup—a category for discussion groups within Usenet.

lurker—a person on an online discussion board who does not contribute to discussions by posting messages but who simply reads what others write.

Chat Rooms

A chat room is a "virtual room" in which a community of users can visit and talk with each other through text messages in real time. Like discussion groups, chat

How Digital Media Are Changing Our World   www.ablongman.com/pavlik1

Media Spotlight: France's Minitel

Perhaps ahead of its time, France in 1980 launched its videotex service, or text delivery over the air or by cable for presentation on television screens or other electronic displays, known then as Teletel and today as Minitel. Minitel survives to this day, and in the 1980s was pointed to as an example of an early successful interactive online information service. Minitel worked because the government subsidized it and provided access devices to every home. Its biggest problem ultimately turned out to be the emergence of the World Wide Web, which has made the stand-alone Minitel model, with its slow modem speeds and clunky graphics, obsolete. One part of Minitel that really did point the way toward how popular the Web would become was the so-called "blue rooms," or adult-oriented chat rooms, which were the only part of the service that generated a significant revenue stream.

rooms are usually divided by the types of topics that are meant to be discussed, ranging from highly technical computer issues to pop stars to sex. Chat rooms differ from instant messaging, which also takes place in real time, in that instant messaging usually involves an online conversation between two or at most a few people. In addition, with instant messaging special software is needed, and users of one instant messaging system such as AOL's Instant Messenger cannot communicate with users of other instant messaging systems. For the most part, chat rooms have no such limitations.

Because chat rooms are synchronous, or take place in real time, they can be effectively used by media organizations to promote special guests online and let the audience "speak" to them, much as a radio station would have a musician visit the station and talk to callers. Drawbacks to doing something like this could include slowing down servers as many people try to send their messages at the same time and choosing which postings to respond to.

Even without a star attraction, chat rooms can often be chaotic, much like trying to talk to someone across the room at a crowded, noisy party. The immediate nature of chat rooms and the very short responses often encourage verbal abuse of others that may or may not be intentional. It can also be difficult to tell who is being addressed, although some chat rooms have general rules and guidelines posted for proper behavior.

Although messages may be sent in real time, the fact that they must be typed inevitably slows down the give-and-take that occurs during natural conversations, which can lead to confusion as one chat room member may be responding to something asked two questions ago. Some chatters can monopolize the conversation as well or repeatedly post the same message, a practice called scrolling, which quickly draws the ire of other chatters in the room.

Chat rooms are perhaps best used when the topic of conversation is focused and relatively narrow. Viewers of a television show, for example, could be in a chat room during the show and discuss aspects of the stars, plot, or series with each other. This type of interactivity, although not directly part of the show, greatly empowers the media audience as they establish connections of like-minded individuals in online communities and inform, educate, and entertain each other and perhaps even the show's producers.

E-mail

E-mail, or electronic mail, was one of the first uses of the Internet and is still the most popular use, accounting for most of the traffic on the Internet. Although e-mail is an exchange of messages by telecommunication between two people, it is quite easy for an individual to create a mailing list that sends out a single message to multiple people, in a sense "broadcasting" the message. This characteristic has caused more than a few red faces, as anyone who has been on a mailing list in which a member of the list replied with embarrassing remarks about another person on the list, not realizing the message was being sent to everyone and not only the original sender.

Mailing lists differ from discussion boards in that messages posted get sent directly to subscribers' e-mail inboxes rather than remaining in a location that a member must visit in order to read the messages. **Listservers** are automated mailing list administrators that allow for easy subscription, subscription cancellation, and sending of e-mails to subscribers on the list.

Mailing lists offer some of the same benefits of discussion boards in that longer, more complex explorations on various topics can be conducted asynchronously. They also have the added benefit of arriving directly in a member's e-mail inbox, making it more likely members will read or at least scan posted messages. Drawbacks of mailing lists, besides posts sometimes mistakenly sent to the members, include information overload as the inbox gets full of messages and potential monopolization of the list by one or a few members sending multiple posts each day. Large e-mails with photos or file attachments can also slow download speeds, especially for those online via dial-up modem.

News organizations have taken advantage of mailing lists to help attract Internet users to their sites or to specific stories that subscribers have said they may be interested in. These mailings are often in the form of e-mail newsletters and usually consist of plain ASCII text to keep the size of the e-mail to a minimum, with hyperlinks to stories on the sender's Web site. They have been more effective than other methods in bringing the audience to a media organization's Web site.

The principles that allow for easy creation of mailing lists is also responsible for what many consider the scourge of e-mail: spam, or unsolicited e-mail advertising. Spam, once rare and considered extremely bad form in the early days of the Internet, is now unfortunately all too common. Companies buy lists of e-mail addresses much as print publishers buy mailing addresses from other magazines or organizations. They create a bulk mailing list and send mass mailings advertising their products or services.

Spammers have become increasingly clever in what they include in their subject lines, making it appear as if the e-mail was coming from a long-lost friend or contained information on "the item you asked about." Sometimes the spam has a link in the message that says "Remove Me from This List." This is usually a trick and simply confirms to the spammer that the e-mail address they sent to is valid and still being used, which enables them to include that e-mail address in future mailings and put it on lists that they can sell to other spammers.

Despite the fact that response rates are extremely low with spam and spam seems to generate more ill will toward a company than whatever sales are generated with spam, it is likely to continue because the costs for sending spam are so

listservers—also known as listservs, these are automated mailing list administrators that allow for easy subscription, subscription cancellation, and sending of e-mails to subscribers on the e-mail list.

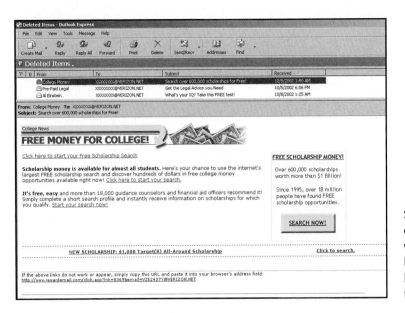

Spam, or junk e-mail, often clogs inboxes with messages that look like they could be from friends or family.

low. Just as lowered costs of distribution on the Internet have helped create online communities and have given the public a chance to distribute media content on a par with established media companies, these lowered costs have also made it easier for individuals and companies to abuse that distribution system, making it less valuable for all. Legislators are fighting back in several states, however, with increasingly stringent antispam laws that penalize spammers.

New Distribution Technologies, New Legal and Social Issues

Along with the amazing empowerment that digital distribution brings to the general audience, there is also the potential for abuse of this system—from media companies as well as from the general public—that could hamper the development of a democratized, participatory, and informational mass communication system. Some of these have been mentioned, such as the effect spam has on participation in discussion groups, or how services like Freenet are trying to make information as freely available as possible without having whistleblowers suffer when publicizing their stories.

Record labels and other large media companies are relatively unsympathetic targets of the changes wrought by the Internet and digital media. Considering rising prices for entertainment, the homogenous nature of much of the media that is produced, and the often disappointing content, it is hard to feel sorry for large media corporations that claim they are losing revenues as old distribution models are disrupted by new technologies. The differences look especially stark when contrasted with the volunteer open source movement of software programmers and developers, in which information is freely shared and all efforts go toward a "virtual commons" from which all can benefit and the proprietary and copyrighted material from companies trying to maximize their profits in which consumers have very little say.

Along with new technologies must come new thinking on not only social but legal issues and responsibilities.

Legal Issues

Media organizations and writers, artists, musicians—anyone creating media content for a living that has a copyright—want to be fairly compensated for their work. Otherwise, the reasoning goes, there would be no incentive for an artist to create something only to have it rapidly copied and distributed without the creator reaping the financial rewards of the popularity of his or her work. With digital media, the very notion of copyright has been called into question, and several lawsuits are working their way through the court system that in some ways could increase control for copyright holders, which, in most cases, are media organizations and not individuals.

Digital **watermarks,** which allow content to be visibly or invisibly marked so it either cannot be altered, can be traced as it is distributed, or shows a history of how it has been altered, will be needed to make digital distribution more secure. However, many experts say this is a losing battle, as media companies spend millions trying to make digital content conform to real-world constraints. Whenever a new secure system is proposed, it is guaranteed that a crack, or way to break the system, is not far behind. Rather than deal with this fundamental issue, media organizations have tried to have laws changed that favor the nondigital systems over the digital and have taken people to court who even publicize the fact that there are security weaknesses in encrypted or watermark systems.

Other legal issues involve the status of messages sent by private citizens. Is a posting to a discussion board considered "publishing," and could a poster be sued for libel? What if that poster wrote something libelous in a private e-mail to a friend and that friend included the e-mail in a discussion board topic? Who could be sued for libel? These and many other similar legal issues have yet to be resolved.

In other words, the public will have to start considering issues of privacy, libel, defamation, and possibly lawsuits—all issues traditional media companies' must consider every day—as they gain access to a worldwide distribution network.

Social Issues

It is useful to revisit some of media guru Marshall McLuhan's observations, even though he died in 1980 and his comments on electronic media were made before the Internet revolution. McLuhan argued that print media disconnected people from their basic tribal emotions and behavior, which were generally visual, oral, and interactive. McLuhan suggested that satellite-based electronic media were retribalizing society. By reconstituting a worldwide oral tradition and bringing all senses into full play, the electronic media were leading to the creation of a "global village." McLuhan argued the electronic media help put people back in touch with basic tribal emotions and reconnect with each other around the world.

Consider how McLuhan's notion of a global village might today be applied to the Internet and other online media. With its global reach and interactivity, the Internet takes us even further toward a notion of simultaneous worldwide communications. E-mail may have the potential to reconnect people to their tribal emo-

watermark—a symbol or mark embedded in a photograph that identifies who owns the copyright for that photograph. With digital media, any piece of content can be watermarked and the watermark, itself digital, can be completely invisible.

Almost (and Unwillingly) Famous

We have mostly concentrated on media organizations and how digital distribution affects them. However, now that anybody can essentially be a publisher with his or her own Web site, sometimes private individuals can unwillingly be thrust into the public eye.

Let's return to Mahir Cagri's experience mentioned at the beginning of this chapter, in which his unintentionally humorous home page was sent by others as a joke and seen by millions of people within days. What if the subject isn't able to make light of the situation, but instead suffers public humiliation or loss of employment because of something he or she put on the Web? Is it that person's fault for putting it on the Web in the first place, or do the people who distribute it share some of the responsibility?

Some Web sites advertise nude photographs of ex-girlfriends or ex-wives, presumably taken by boyfriends or husbands in happier, more care-free, and trusting times. Sent to Web sites out of spite or greed, these photos can now be seen by millions worldwide.

Or consider a case involving Bill Owens, whose online persona was Buck Hunter. He claimed he was pressured to leave his job at Home Depot and suffered sexual harassment from female coworkers after they learned of a pay-per-view pornographic Web site he and his wife ran from home that contained streaming video and pictures of them in various sexual acts. Cases like this are becoming more common as employers realize how widely a Web site can be seen and worry how it may reflect on a company's image. Several similar cases are currently working their way through the courts. The defendants argue that what they do in their private life away from the company is none of the company's business.

What implications are there for citizens who act as publishers on the Web? Should they be afforded traditional First Amendment rights? If so, what rights do others whom they may defame or embarrass have to seek damages?

tions, even though it is still primarily text-based. Imagine the transformations that can take place when e-mail or other communication technologies are video based.

There are still many unresolved issues regarding how people socialize with each other online. Almost everyone who has been on discussion groups or in chat rooms has seen or been the victim of someone making verbal attacks, often far more abusive than those the attacker ever would make if he or she were speaking in person. Others may find the comments offensive, but there is little they can currently do except chastise the attacker either by e-mail or on the discussion board—and perhaps get attacked as well.

With greater ability to mass distribute messages also comes greater responsibility in thinking how that distribution will affect others. This even applies to the level of forwarding a humorous photograph received by e-mail. Will the busy colleague really appreciate receiving this? Will the relative using a dial-up modem who is charged by the minute while online? Could this be considered offensive to others who may receive this?

Some of the socialization issues regarding the Internet will gradually work themselves out as general rules of behavior form and become accepted. Technology will also help in making it easy to filter out people who consistently break those rules. Peer-review systems like those on eBay, Amazon, or Epinions will also encourage responsible social behavior and better-quality information.

New issues are likely to arise because of improvements in technology as well. With video-based chats or e-mails it will be harder to hide one's true identity, and using digitally-created avatars may not be adequate substitutes for people who want "face-to-face" telecommunication. Social mores could change so that someone who chooses not to use video communication is assumed to have something to hide and is therefore taken less seriously, just as people who post to discussion groups who do not identify themselves are today. Old prejudices regarding race, gender, and looks could also resurface in a video-based system.

Discussion Questions

1. Make a list of types of jobs involved in the media industry that may become obsolete by new distributional technologies. What could be done to find new types of employment for those displaced?

2. Discuss parallels between today and the proposals in the mid-nineteenth century for the U.S. government to create a nationwide underground telegraph service. How do you think the telecommunication landscape might be different today if the government had supported such a project?

3. Discuss the comparative strengths and weaknesses between client/server network models and peer-to-peer network models. How might some of the weaknesses of each be minimized?

4. Choose one of the common methods of online communication (discussion groups, e-mail, chat rooms, blogs) and think of how it could be improved in terms of facilitating communication between people, ensuring quality communication, and enabling a greatest number of users to distribute information.

5. Discuss possible social, political, and economic ramifications of a completely anonymous free information service such as Freenet. Does such a service need to have guidelines; and, if so, what kinds of guidelines? Are guidelines even possible with such a service?

6. Should someone who runs a pornographic Web site of him or herself have the same rights to privacy and job security as someone who posts a Web site that disagrees with an employer's political views? Why or why not?

7. With increased broadband availability, do you think people will be more inclined to share files of copyrighted material? Why?

SUMMARY

Online distribution of digital media content has been the lightning rod for many of the changes digital media and the Internet are bringing to mass communication. Although music file sharing programs such as KaZaA, Morpheus, and the now-defunct Napster are in the media spotlight, they only demonstrate one aspect of the changes coming with digital distribution.

Digital distribution has several unique characteristics. Like other aspects of digitization, it replaces physical objects with electrons, which makes the material essentially "formless." Because of its lack of physical properties, production, storage, and distribution costs are dramatically reduced. Perfect copies can also be made an unlimited number of times, which further reduces costs of media, and can be distributed over the Internet almost instantly. This has given rise to new distributional dynamics; primarily a decentralization of distributed content. On the Internet, a private citizen can distribute content as easily as a large media organization.

None of this would be possible without the convergence of telecommunications and computers. From the telegraph, telephone, satellite and now fiber optics and the Internet, rapid communication among a widely accessible network is crucial for this kind of distribution model to work.

For several technical reasons, the Internet has been dominated by a server/client model, in which content resides on a central server and is sent to computers. However, peer-to-peer networking, in which all computers on the network can both serve and receive content, is changing many aspects of online communication among the public, not the least of which is music file sharing. Other applications using peer-to-peer networks are being developed, however, including ones that can allow the publishing of anonymous information and others that utilize individual PCs as part of a larger research project in searching for extraterrestrial intelligence.

Vibrant and active online communities have arisen around the ability to communicate widely with others, even before peer-to-peer networks. These include discussion boards, chat rooms, weblogs, instant messaging, and of course e-mail. These communities tend to gather based on topics of interest rather than based on geography, and the tools can enhance the communicative ability between members of a traditional community.

With new power to distribute information also come new responsibilities among private citizens regarding legal issues such as libel suits and copyright infringement. Social issues will also be important as people learn how to best communicate online in a civil manner.

Journalism

A grisly 2002 Memorial Day slaying at a Maryland beachfront condominium caused a minor confrontation among three news organizations covering the crime. The victims were a couple from Fairfax, Virginia; the suspects lived in Pennsylvania; and, because the crime took place in an area covered by the *Washington Post,* that newspaper took an interest in the story. The conflict touches on several types of ethical issues and questions modern journalists must face in the digital world.

A reporter for the *Washington Post* covering the murders posted a note on the online bulletin board of a competing daily also covering the murders, the *Free Lance-Star* in Fredericksburg, Virginia, asking for readers who knew the suspects or victims to contact him with information or tips. *Free Lance-Star* reporters and editors objected to their Web site being used by a rival to find sources. "I think it's crossing a line," said Web Editor Chris Muldrow. *Post* reporter Nelson Hernandez did not feel he did anything wrong. "Anything on

the Internet is open," he told *Editor & Publisher.* "It did not occur to me to be a breach of ethics." He added that a reporter from the *Altoona* (Pennsylvania) *Mirror,* in the suspects' hometown, also posted a similar message on the *Free Lance-Star* bulletin board. Bill Kibler, the *Mirror* staff writer who posted the note, said their papers did not compete with each other so he did not cross any ethical boundaries.

The *Altoona Mirror,* meanwhile, had been criticized for not posting stories about the murder case online, despite receiving dozens of requests from people who wanted information about it. Managing Editor Ray Eckenrode said the *Mirror* has never posted news stories on its Web site. "We do not give away content," he said. *Mirror* Publisher Edward Kruger described the practice of providing free Web content as "flawed thinking."

OBJECTIVES

In this chapter we will:

■ Explain what journalism is and its role in mass communication and society.

■ Outline important historical developments in journalism that affect how it is practiced today.

■ Discuss journalism today, types of journalism, and what the future may hold for journalism in a convergent digital media environment.

■ Outline legal and ethical issues in the practice of journalism, with special emphasis on ethical issues in the analog and digital world.

■ Highlight some aspects of the business of journalism and how they affect the practice of journalism.

■ Examine how convergence is affecting business models in journalism.

Prologue

Journalism's purpose, according to some journalists, is to "comfort the afflicted and afflict the comfortable." The societal roles and responsibilities of journalism have often been discussed—as government watchdog, as advocate of the common citizen, as panderer to baser tastes among the public, as big business, as influencer of public opinions and discussions. Heated discussions on how well journalism is fulfilling its roles continue to this day in letters to the editor pages, on call-in talk shows, and on the Internet. These discussions should not be seen as some inherent failure of journalism as a type of mass communication; rather, they should be understood as signs of how important journalism continues to be in the modern world.

Journalism plays an important part in three of the four main functions of mass communication: **surveillance, correlation,** and **cultural transmission.** They can also play a major role in **mobilizing** the public. These functions are carried out by the coverage of news. The public learns of events and happenings in their areas and around the world and put the events in a context that helps them form a picture of what the world is like. Through articles and shows on cultural and artistic figures, culture is transmitted and the public learns the mores of society. To a lesser extent, journalism also serves the **entertainment** function of mass communication through coverage of entertainment events or news on popular stars.

In order to get a good understanding of journalism, however, it is important to first understand what news is.

What Is News?

The journalist's old adage that news is "when man bites dog" rings true in the sense that news is something out of the ordinary that occurs. News usually is about recent events in the case of breaking news, such as a fire or accident, or recent discoveries of events that took place that affect the public, such as financial wrongdoing by corporate executives or politicians.

Several issues arise when looking at this basic assumption of the definition of news. First is the often-heard complaint made by the public that news concentrates too much on negative events—crime, accidents, wrongdoing, and the like. Critics say that this overwhelmingly negative coverage gives the public a misleading impression that things may be worse than they actually are, such as making it seem that local crime is rising by intense coverage on a spate of robberies when in fact the crime rate has dropped. News organizations do include positive news, such as heartwarming stories on rescues or human-interest stories, but then they can be accused of acting as a public relations mouthpiece for organizations or individuals and not adequately informing the public.

Conventional wisdom suggests that news means reporting the unexpected. But the truth is that a large portion, perhaps sometimes the majority, of news is

surveillance—primarily the journalism function of mass communication, which provides information about the processes, issues, events, and other developments in society.

correlation—primarily the interpretation of aspects of society as a function of mass communication, and the individual to society, including how journalism, advertising, and public relations shape public opinion through comments or criticism or through propaganda.

cultural transmission—primarily refers to the transference of the dominant culture as a function of mass communication, as well as its subcultures, from one generation to the next, or to immigrants. This function includes socialization, which the media perform in helping persons learn society's rules, or how to fit into society.

mobilization—a function of mass communication in which the media can influence the public, especially regarding political issues or movements.

entertainment—a function of mass communication that is performed in part by all three of the other four main functions (surveillance, correlation, cultural transmission) but also involves the generation of content designed specifically and exclusively to entertain.

On soft news days, editors include stories or photographs that would not appear in the newspaper if important events had taken place.

soft news day—a day in which not much of importance happens so editors are more likely to add features that may not be of real news value, such as human-interest stories.

agenda-setting function—a role the media play during the course of deciding which topics to cover that, by virtue of being covered in the media, become topics of discussion and perceived importance to the public.

largely predictable either a day, a week, a month, or sometimes years in advance. It is vital that media consumers realize this, because news just doesn't happen. It is in many ways manufactured and influenced by a wide variety of people, organizations, and forces, many of which are outside the media, and much of the information comes in the form of advertising and public relations. Historian and Pulitzer Prize–winning author Daniel Boorstin describes what he calls pseudo events, such as press conferences or other staged events like marches and rallies, as an example of how groups can influence what is covered in the news. These events are often known about days or weeks in advance.

What kind of news shows up on television or in a newspaper depends on what other events are happening that day. A **soft news day** happens when editors feel not much has happened that is newsworthy and therefore will air programming or include articles such as human-interest stories. A flood in India that kills 500 people may get put on the front page of a local newspaper on a soft news day, whereas it may only be included as a "World News Brief" on an inside page—or not be included at all—on a day that has important local news. How do editors decide that a story on a popular local high school athlete killed in a traffic accident is more important than a story about 500 killed in India? They try to determine what is of most interest to their readership. In this way, journalists have an important **agenda-setting function,** which means they can influence by their coverage what is seen as important by their audience and what is therefore more likely to be discussed by the public.

Although journalism has a strong public service mission, it is nevertheless subject to the realities of the commercial media system. Without significant audiences and typically substantial advertising revenues, most newspapers, news magazines, and news programs on television and radio would cease to exist. Most newspapers and magazines are actually made up of more advertising than news, in terms of the amount of space devoted to each type of content.

Let's look at the historical development of journalism as a profession and business to see how each has influenced the practice of modern journalism.

The *New York Times* was first published on September 18, 1851, competing in the New York City area with 15 other newspapers. Although the *Times* cost a penny during its first year and again from October 10, 1898, to January 26, 1918, it was not one of the so-called penny press. The *Times* differentiated itself by taking a more serious approach to reporting the news than many of its competitors. Within a week and a half of its launch, it grew to 10,000 copies sold a day. But the paper began to fail, losing as much as $1000 a day, and it was the 1896 purchase of the paper by newspaper publisher Adolph S. Ochs that saved the *Times*.[1]

Ochs emphasized clinical, nonpartisan news reporting, and the paper began to grow again. On August 16, 1896, he published on the front page his vision for the paper: "It will be my earnest aim that the *New York Times* give the news, all the news, in concise and attractive form, in language that is parliamentary in good society . . . to give the news impartially, without fear or favor, regardless of any party, sect or interest involved; to make the columns of the *New York Times* a forum for the consideration of all questions of public importance, and to that end to invite intelligent discussion from all shades of opinion."[2]

The *Times* is today known especially for its extensive coverage of international events and is generally regarded as the nation's best daily newspaper.

The Historical Development of Journalism

The advent of the **penny press** and mass distribution of newspapers in the early 19th century, discussed in Chapter 3, brought about a sea change in the concept and definition of journalism. Prior to that, editors of newspapers mostly relied on "news" brought to their offices by citizens or from information they or a small staff could gather, as well as liberally copying from other newspapers, often without crediting the sources. Editor's or publisher's (they were often the same person) opinions were often freely mixed with other editorial content, and no thought was given to presenting all sides of an issue fairly.

With the need to appeal to as wide a readership as possible, however, newspaper publishers often toned down opinions in articles and concentrated more on covering sensational crimes or events. In order to fill their pages, they also had to hire reporters who looked for news to cover rather than passively waiting for news to come to them.

Further fueling the transformation of newspapers were competitors such as **James Gordon Bennett,** who founded the *New York Herald* in 1835. He added a number of features that are now staples in modern journalism, including a financial page, editorial commentary, and public affairs reporting.

In order to maintain their objective stance throughout the rest of the paper, or at least the public appearance of impartiality, newspaper editors began publishing their points of view exclusively on a special page dubbed the "editorial" page, which is a tradition maintained today by the Western press. Editorials provide a valuable service to the public, helping to guide public opinion on matters of public importance, such as endorsements for candidates for public office or referenda.

The penny press in the early 19th century changed the journalism industry in many ways.

penny press—newspapers that sold for a penny, making them accessible to everyone. They differed from older newspaper forms in that they tried to attract as large an audience as possible and were supported by advertising rather than subscriptions.

Bennett, James Gordon—founder of the *New York Herald* in 1835. He started many features found in modern newspapers, including a financial page, editorial commentary, and public affairs reporting.

Two Newspaper Women: Mary Shadd Cary and Ida B. Wells

Born a free black in 1823 to Abraham and Harriet Shadd of Wilmington, Delaware, Mary and her family fled to Windsor, Canada, after the Fugitive Slave Act was passed in the United States in 1850, threatening to return free northern blacks and escaped slaves to slavery. In response to a vigorous campaign to deter runaway slaves from escaping to Canada, Mary wrote a 44-page pamphlet, "Notes on Canada," outlining the opportunities for blacks in Canada. Building on the success of this widely read publication, Mary established her weekly newspaper, the *Provincial Freeman,* targeting blacks and especially fugitive slaves. Her newspaper reported on a variety of important topics, among them the lies being spread in the United States that African Americans in Canada were starving.

Another important African American woman journalist in the 19th century was **Ida B. Wells.** Born a slave in 1862, six months before the signing of the Emancipation Proclamation, Wells spent her adult life fighting against racism and especially the lynching of African Americans. Wells wrote for the religious weekly, *The Living Way,* and for various African American newspapers, including the *Free Speech* and *Headlight.* She was elected secretary of the Afro-American Press Association in 1889. Wells married attorney Ferdinand L. Barnett, editor and founder of the Chicago *Conservator.*

Weblink

The Associated Press
[www.ap.org]

Wells, Ida B.—a female African American journalist in the latter 19th century who wrote and fought against racism and the lynching of blacks.

objectivity—a journalistic principle that says journalists should be impartial and free of bias in their reporting. This principle has come under attack in recent years because of the impossibility of people being completely objective and has largely been replaced by the concepts of fairness and balance.

Associated Press (AP)— founded as a not-for-profit members' cooperative in 1848 by a group of six New York newspaper publishers in order to share the costs of gathering news by telegraph. Today 1700 newspapers and 5000 television and radio stations are members of this news-gathering organization.

Objectivity and the Associated Press

The notion of what is news continued to evolve and was shaped by its relationship to the democratization of politics, the expansion of the market economy, and the growing impact of an entrepreneurial middle class. One reason news became less partisan or more impartial and free of bias—what is known in journalism as **objectivity**—was due to the emergence of the news wire service in the 1840s. In 1848 publishers of six New York newspapers organized the **Associated Press (AP),** in large part to take advantage of the capabilities made possible by the telegraph as a high-speed communications medium. Telegraphy was too expensive for any single newspaper to afford, so a consortium, or association of leading press organizations, made economic sense.

Because the AP gathered news for half a dozen newspapers with varying political viewpoints, it needed to publish news reports that were politically neutral, and thus acceptable to all its member papers. By the dawn of the 20th century, AP dispatches had become virtually free from editorial comment.

The Associated Press is still based in New York and is the world's largest news-gathering organization, providing textual, audio, and video news; photos; and graphics to its members. The AP is a not-for-profit members' cooperative including 1700 newspapers and 5000 radio and television news operations. That means that the members provide much of the content distributed by the AP, and in turn any member can use the content distributed by the AP. The AP also has its own staff of journalists, employing 3700 in 242 news bureaus in 70 countries.

Minority Newspapers

Also important during the 1800s was the rise of various minority or ethnic newspapers. These newspapers served the needs of niche audiences, including Native

American, African American, Jewish, and other ethnic groups. Among the earliest minority newspapers was *El Misisipí,* the first U.S. Spanish-language newspaper, which began publication in 1808 in New Orleans.[3] The first Native American newspaper, the *Cherokee Phoenix,* began publication in 1828. The first African-American daily, the *New Orleans Daily Creole,* began publication in 1856.

American abolitionist and former slave Frederick Douglass was not only a great statesman but also a journalist, publishing an antislavery paper called the *North Star.* Among the most notable minority newspapers of the day was the *Provincial Freeman,* a newspaper founded and edited by **Mary Shadd Cary,** the first African American woman in North America to edit a weekly newspaper.

Frederick Douglass.

Pulitzer and Hearst: The Circulation Wars, Sensationalism, and Standards

Although the practice of objective reporting became the norm for the AP, it was well into the 20th century before most newspapers had adopted this model of reporting for their own staff. Throughout the latter half of the 19th and early in the 20th century another form of reporting became prevalent at many U.S. newspapers. **Sensational journalism,** or news that exaggerated or featured lurid details and depictions, came to dominate much newspaper content of this period. Two of the greatest newspaper publishing titans of this era were **William Randolph Hearst,** publisher of the *San Francisco Examiner* and of the *New York Journal,* and **Joseph Pulitzer,** publisher of the *New York World,* the *St. Louis Post-Dispatch,* and other papers.

Joseph Pulitzer

Pulitzer built the circulation of the *New York World* to 300,000 by the early 1890s by mixing good, solid reporting with sensational photographs, comic strips, and "crusades" against corrupt politicians, support for increased taxes, and civil service reform. Pulitzer wanted his papers to focus on city news and encouraged his reporters to seek out original, dramatic, and compelling news, especially humorous, odd, romantic, or thrilling stories, written accurately and with attention to detail.

One of Pulitzer's most successful undertakings was the introduction of color printing of comics in his Sunday papers. The most notable example was *The Yellow Kid,* a comic strip drawn as busy, single-panel illustrations. Although *The Yellow Kid* was not the first newspaper cartoon, its innovative style contributed much of the comic strip format many today take for granted.[4]

The Yellow Kid was a creation of cartoonist Richard Felton Outcault during the Pulitzer–Hearst newspaper circulation war in the 1890s and was characterized by rude, vulgar, and brash behavior on the back streets of Hogan's Alley. In some ways, *The Yellow Kid* was a late-19th century precursor to the crude kids of South Park created during the cable and broadcast television ratings battles of the late 20th century.

The Yellow Kid quickly became a central figure in the circulation battles between newspaper giants Pulitzer and Hearst when Hearst hired Outcault away from the *World.* The brashness of *The Yellow Kid* reflected well the *Journal*'s overall dramatic style. Because of the Kid's well-known yellow shirt, critics coined the term **yellow journalism** as a reference to the sensational style of journalism characteristic of the newspapers of Pulitzer and his competitor, Hearst.

Cary, Mary Shadd—the first African American woman to edit a weekly newspaper. She founded and edited the *Provincial Freeman* in Canada after leaving the United States to avoid being captured and put into slavery under the Fugitive Slave Act.

sensational journalism—news that exaggerates or features lurid details and depictions of events in order to get a larger audience.

Hearst, William Randolph—newspaper publisher and media magnate who owned several major newspapers. His circulation wars and rivalry with Joseph Pulitzer's newspapers helped sparked the term "yellow journalism" because of the sensational, and sometimes false, coverage before and during the Spanish-American War in 1898.

Pulitzer, Joseph—newspaper publisher and owner of the *St. Louis Post-Dispatch,* the *New York Post,* and the *New York World.* After the sensational coverage of the Spanish-American War in 1898, Pulitzer advocated professionalism in journalism and bequeathed money to found the Graduate School of Journalism at Columbia University.

yellow journalism—a style of journalism practiced especially by publishers Joseph Pulitzer and William Randolph Hearst during the late 1890s in which stories were sensationalized and often partly or wholly made up in order to be more dramatic.

Setting the Standard for Newspapers: Joseph Pulitzer

Joseph Pulitzer was born on April 10, 1847, in Budapest, Hungary. He emigrated to the United States in 1864, serving in the Union Army during the Civil War. In 1868 he moved to St. Louis and went to work as a reporter for a German-language paper. Pulitzer purchased the bankrupt *St. Louis Dispatch* in 1878, later merging it with the *Evening Post* and thus creating the *St. Louis Post-Dispatch*. In 1883 he bought the *New York Post* and later the *New York World*.

He was elected to the 49th Congress of the United States but resigned after three months because of failing health. His health continued to deteriorate, however, and by 1890 he was almost completely blind and became extremely sensitive to sounds. Despite officially resigning as editor of the *World,* he continued his involvement by communicating through secretaries and assistants while he sought various treatments.

He became embroiled with Hearst in the newspaper circulation wars during the 1890s, using frequent illustrations, a racy style, and colorful headlines to build the circulation of the *World*. After the four-month Spanish-American War in 1898, Pulitzer withdrew from the sensational tools and techniques that had helped build his news-papers' circulations and replaced them with a vision of journalistic excellence, which he outlined in a 1904 article for the *North American Review*.[5]

During this time, Pulitzer was instrumental in the passage of antitrust legislation and regulation of the insurance industry because of investigative stories his papers ran. This emphasis on public service journalism and accurate reporting is still a cornerstone of the annual Pulitzer Prizes, which he bequeathed along with an endowment for the Columbia University Graduate School of Journalism, at his death in 1911.

Joseph Pulitzer.

William Randolph Hearst

Later immortalized in Orson Welles's cinematic triumph, *Citizen Kane,* William Randolph Hearst sensationalized the news by printing colorful banner headlines and splashy photography, and some say even inventing the news. Hearst's stories did not always capture the truth, and his readers probably knew it; but they enjoyed reading the accounts, and his newspapers' circulation increased tremendously.

One historian has summarized Hearst's actions as inflammatory. Ernest L. Meyer wrote:

> Mr. Hearst in his long and not laudable career has inflamed Americans against Spaniards, Americans against Japanese, Americans against Filipinos, Americans against Russians, and in the pursuit of his incendiary campaign he has printed downright lies, forged documents, faked atrocity stories, inflammatory editorials, sensational cartoons and photographs and other devices by which he abetted his jingoistic ends.[6]

The Muckrakers

Just as the efforts of renowned newspaper publishers Hearst and Pulitzer laid a foundation for many of the practices of contemporary journalism, so did a number of very important magazine journalists, or reporters, from the late 19th and early 20th centuries. Among the most important were the **muckrakers.** Journalists such as Ida Minerva Tarbell, Joseph Lincoln Steffens, and Upton Sinclair (author of *The Jungle*) were dubbed muckrakers by a disapproving President Theodore Roosevelt, because these reporters pioneered investigative reporting of corrupt practices and problems in government or business, a process analogous to raking muck, the polite term for the manure, mud, and straw mixture found in stables. Many of the most important muckrakers reported for magazines of the day, in large part because their investigations required considerable time and were more amenable to the publishing cycles and longer deadlines of magazines than in newspapers.

Edward R. Murrow.

The Decline of Print Journalism and Rise of Electronic Journalism

The golden age of newspapers started its decline when radio became a medium of mass communication in the 1920s. The public did not have to wait a day or more for news of events as they did with newspapers, and furthermore radio was "free," as it was entirely advertising supported. But it was television news that started a steep decline in the prominence of newspapers as the public's main source of news.

The late 1940s and early 1950s marked the beginning of television news. News was and still is an important part of how broadcast television fulfills its federal mandate to serve in the public interest, a topic discussed in more detail in Chapter 14.

Many of the early news programs were produced by the television network news divisions in New York. In 1947, NBC debuted *Meet the Press,* a made-for-TV news conference, with journalists asking questions of various news makers, often government officials. The program continues today and is the oldest series on network TV. In the 1950s, NBC introduced the *Today* show, the first and still-running early-morning network news show. *Today* had a decidedly entertainment quality back then, with host Dave Garroway joined by chimpanzee sidekick J. Fred Muggs.

Murrow and News in TV's Golden Age

Setting the standard for television news during television's Golden Age in the late 1940s and 1950s was the distinguished journalist **Edward R. Murrow,** who first achieved fame by broadcasting dramatic news reports via radio from London during World War II. Murrow produced the popular television programs *See It Now* and *Person to Person* at CBS News.

Murrow's comments on television at the Radio-Television News Directors Association (RTNDA) on October 15, 1958, ring equally true today of television as they do the Internet: "This instrument can teach, it can illuminate, and yes, it can inspire. But it can do so only to the extent that humans are determined to use it to those ends. Otherwise it is nothing but wires and lights in a box." The same year he also wrote in *TV Guide* that viewers must realize "television in the main is being used to distract, delude, amuse and insulate us."

Changes in Television News Coverage

The introduction of video cameras into the television newsroom brought important changes to television news. **Electronic news gathering (ENG)** equipment allowed journalists in the field to capture and send videotaped news by satellite to the

Murrow, Edward R.—a radio and later television journalist and announcer who set the standard for journalistic excellence on television during television's Golden Age.

electronic news gathering (ENG)—tools such as video cameras and satellite dishes that allow journalists to gather and broadcast news much more quickly than in the past.

Citizen Kane: William Randolph Hearst

William Randolph Hearst was born in San Francisco on April 29, 1863, the son of a self-made multimillionaire miner and rancher in northern California. Hearst studied at Harvard and became "proprietor" of his first newspaper, the *San Francisco Examiner,* in 1887 at the age of 23. His father had acquired the paper as payment for a gambling debt. The younger Hearst then acquired in 1895 the *New York Morning Journal* and debuted the *Evening Journal* a year later, hiring away many of Joseph Pulitzer's best reporters and editors by offering them higher pay. He increased his

newspaper and periodical chain nationwide to include the *Boston American* and *Chicago Examiner,* as well as magazines *Cosmopolitan* and *Harper's Bazaar.*

Hearst was elected to the U.S. House of Representatives (1903–1907) but failed in his efforts to become mayor of New York City and governor of the state. Hearst's ornate, 130-room mansion, San Simeon, built in the 1920s and nicknamed the Hearst Castle, today stands as a California landmark.

Often criticized for his sensational tactics, Hearst nevertheless

articulated news standards that resonate even today. W.R. Hearst's editorial guidelines from 1933 stated: "Make the news thorough. Print all the news. Condense it if necessary. Frequently it is better when intelligently condensed. But get it in." In 1945 Hearst established The Hearst Foundation (now the William Randolph Hearst Foundation), which today provides important support for journalism education and other concerns, including health and culture. Hearst died at age 88 on August 14, 1951, in Beverly Hills, California.

network where it could be edited and broadcast much more quickly than film. This has influenced the nature of video storytelling. The late CBS news veteran Bud Benjamin likened it to "NTV," or the video journalism equivalent of "MTV," or music television, with rapid-paced cuts and entertainment values becoming increasingly paramount to journalism.

The growth of cable television has also led to an increasing number of local 24-hour cable news operations. A 1999 survey by the Radio-Television News Directors Foundation (RTNDF) reveals that 24-hour all-news television channels are operating in 34 cities or regions throughout the United States. One of the authors of the RTNDF report, Mark Thalhimer, says 24-hour local news offers a "preview of a 24-Hour DTV [digital television] future." Thalhimer suggests that there will be even more widespread proliferation of 24-hour local news as U.S. television shifts to digital frequencies in the coming years. TV stations will often split their new digital channel into four or more simultaneous program feeds, what is called multicasting, and will offer 24-hour news as one inexpensive programming option. "In the future, the development of digital television and the Internet will force all news managers to consider a 24-hour news cycle," Thalhimer said.

Foundational Aspects of Journalism

Digital technology and the Internet have brought and will continue to bring transformative changes to journalism, but journalism today is still largely practiced as it has been in terms of reporters covering and writing about news, editors selecting what news is published or aired, and business economics affecting what gets covered and what doesn't. Digital technology will not change the fact that reporters need to visit places and interview people, for example. Nor will digital technology replace an experienced editor's judgment on where to place a certain story or how long to make that story.

In order to understand what aspects of journalism have changed and can continue to change in a converged media environment, we will first look at basic issues of journalistic responsibility and how journalism is practiced.

The Hutchins Commission and *A Free and Responsible Press*

In 1947 the **Hutchins Commission** published a landmark report titled *A Free and Responsible Press,* offering a critique of the state of the press in the United States. The 133-page report of the Commission on Freedom of the Press was written by Robert Maynard Hutchins and a dozen other leading intellectuals. The report argued that the public has a right to information that affects it and that the press has a responsibility to present that information. Because the press enjoys constitutionally guaranteed freedom, it carries an additional moral responsibility to fulfill this responsibility. The commission recommended that the government, the public, and the press could all take steps to improve the functioning of a healthy press. Among these steps, the commission recommended that the government should recognize that all media should be given the same constitutional guarantees traditionally enjoyed only by print media.

For the press, the commission recommended that the agencies of mass communication assume the responsibility of financing new, experimental activities in their fields. Moreover, the members of the press should engage in vigorous mutual criticism, which is available today in the form of various journalism reviews. The commission called upon the public to create academic–professional centers of advanced study, research, and publication in the field of communications. Among the first such centers was the Media Studies Center, founded in 1984 by the Freedom Forum. The commission also recommended that existing schools of journalism exploit the total resources of their universities so their students may obtain the broadest and most liberal training. Finally, the commission recommended the establishment of a new and independent agency to appraise and report annually upon the performance of the press. This notion has been tried at a national level, in the form of a National Press Council, but has failed, although a similar idea has had marginal success in some states.

The Separation of Editorial and Business Operations

Commonly called the "separation of church and state," this is a basic principle in ensuring that news coverage is not influenced by business decisions or advertisers who threaten to stop advertising because they do not like coverage of an issue. This separation is supposed to carry over to the pages of a newspaper or magazine as well by showing clear differences between advertising and editorial content.

However, many media critics complain that this separation has been breaking down in recent years as publishers or large media corporations that own

Hutchins Commission—a commission that issued an influential report on the press in 1947 called *A Free and Responsible Press* that outlines the responsibilities the press has toward public service and states that if news organizations fail in that responsibility then some other agency should carry them out.

news organizations increasingly let business decisions influence editorial content. This can happen blatantly, such as the case in which the owner of the *Los Angeles Times* used staff reporters and editors to create a special "news" section on the Staples Center that was entirely sponsored (and had content approved by) Staples without explicitly saying so; or it could be more insidious, as when corporate management lays off editorial staff with the effect of hampering original reporting and forcing the paper to rely on cheaper, but perhaps less relevant, wire service news.

Fairness and Balance in News Coverage

Fairness and **balance** in news coverage have replaced the goal of objectivity in journalism. Objectivity, or the principle that news is reported on and presented in a completely unbiased manner, has come under attack in recent years. Critics say that people cannot be completely unbiased, and to claim objectivity in a given situation is simply masking the bias of the reporter. In addition, everything from the subsequent editing of a story, or placement of a story in a newspaper, to the time slot for a news segment can reflect biased coverage, even if the reporter has no strong bias when he or she wrote the story. Unintended biases can also show up in the people a journalist decides to interview and the choice of story assignments an editor makes.

Journalists now strive for fairness and balance in news coverage. These terms mean that journalists try to present all sides of a topic equally and in a way that does not present one side in a more favorable light than the other. Fairness and balance do not mean that all players in an issue get equal space for their views, however. A small radical political group of 50 people supporting a local political candidate would not get the same amount of coverage as a popular candidate from a major political party simply because they are fielding a candidate in an election. Factors such as the relative importance within the context of the story and validity or authority of the news source must be considered when a journalist decides how much coverage to give a person or group.

Framing the News

Traditional news media often decide how they will "frame" a story before the reporting is completed and sometimes before it has even begun. This is called "the angle," and it is one of the biggest problems in journalism today. It is a problem because frequently the facts of a story are forced to fit into the frame, or angle, regardless of reality. Balance, or fairness, is often not achieved.

The imbalance caused by framing can easily be seen in reporting about the Internet. Traditional media can employ the "Internet is good" frame. This frame is most often seen in reports about the valuable role of the Internet in education, science, or health care. They can also employ the "Internet is bad" frame, which is seen in articles about child pornography on the Internet or sexual predators online.

One of the problems with the use of these two frames is that rarely are they used in the same story to show that the Internet might have both good and bad effects. Instead, each story portrays life on the Internet as either paradise found or paradise lost.

fairness—in news coverage, the concept of covering all relevant sides of an issue and allowing spokespeople representing those various sides a chance to be covered in the same way.

balance—in news coverage, the concept of presenting sides equally or of reporting on a broad range of news events.

In one survey, nearly 90 percent of "expert" sources on network newscasts were men, and more than 90 percent were white.

Perhaps even more problematic, however, is the fact that frequently the reporting of events in the real world is forced into an existing frame, when reality is in fact more complex and defies framing.

Expert Sources

A related issue to framing and another problem in the media, especially on television, is in the use of "expert" sources, who are used to not only give the news more credibility but also to place it in the context of an authority. At the three main television networks, ABC, CBS, and NBC, speakers selected to give their views during the news or other public affairs programs are almost always white and male. The 10th Annual Women, Men and Media Study, conducted by ADT Research in conjunction with the Freedom Forum, shows that during the first six months of 1998, "Nearly nine of ten 'expert' sound bites (87 percent) on the network newscasts were provided by men, and *more* than nine in 10 (92 percent) were provided by whites." Women were featured in just 13 percent of expert sound bites and people of color in just 6 percent. In contrast, nonexperts on network news programs are much more likely to be of diverse backgrounds.

"Individuals of either sex, any age and all races can be heard from on the network news, as long as they are not wielding power or offering expertise. The networks' 'golden rolodexes' of expert consultants are badly in need of updating," said Andrew Tyndall, director of the study, titled *Who Speaks For America? Sex, Age and Race on the Network News.* Research about other mainstream media, including important print media such as news magazines *Time, Newsweek,* and *U.S. News & World Report,* shows similar results.

The News Agendas of Newspapers

An important change in newspaper content has to do with the basic news agenda of newspapers. Research by the Pew Research Center for the People & the Press, an independent opinion research center sponsored by the Pew Charitable Trusts, indicates that in 1980 the front page of the average daily newspaper was quite different in its news agenda than it is today.

Two of the most important differences are: In 1980 one of every three front page news stories dealt with government or public affairs. Today, just one in every five stories deals with government or public affairs. Government and public affairs matters are traditionally considered the cornerstone of journalism in a democracy. Second, in 1980 only one in every 50 front page daily newspaper stories dealt with celebrities, popular entertainment, and other related subjects. Today, one in every 14 front page daily newspaper stories deals with celebrities and the like.

Together, these trends mean that the front pages of U.S. daily newspapers, which reflect the core agenda of daily newspapers, have shifted dramatically away from public affairs and toward popular entertainment. There are a number of reasons for this. An increasingly competitive media environment, in which newspapers must compete against electronic entertainment media, is one reason. Also important is the changing ownership structure and economics of newspapers. Further, technological change is contributing to this transformation, as newspapers struggle to reinvent themselves in an online, digital age.

The News Agendas of Television News

Television news counts on interesting visuals to help tell its stories, and this can often dictate the ordering of stories in a newscast as well as even whether a story is aired or not. Stories with dramatic video footage, such as fires or accidents, are more likely to air than stories in which stock footage is needed or that have poor-quality video.

Time constraints of less than 30 minutes or an hour to cover local, national, and international news; business news; sports; and weather also place limitations on how long particular stories can be within a newscast. In-depth looks at newsworthy issues must be sacrificed in order to cover a wider range of news stories. The need for scheduled commercial breaks often means that guest experts invited to speak are asked to explain complex subjects in less than a minute so the station can go to commercial break.

Perhaps because of the visual nature of television, television news has always had an eye on the entertainment aspect of media, as demonstrated as far back as the early days of the *Today* show mentioned earlier. The rise of 24-hour news channels also means that there is much more of a **news hole** to fill, which encourages stations to be less discriminating on what they consider newsworthy. Sometimes this is a good thing, as events that would otherwise not reach a televised audience are covered, but other times the material serves mainly a public relations or entertainment purpose.

From Event to Public Eye:
How News Is Created

news hole—typically used with newspapers, it is the amount of total space available after advertisement space has been blocked out.

In journalism there must always be news to fill the regularly scheduled evening news on television, the morning's paper, or the weekly news magazine. Like an accordion, news can expand or contract as required by the day's events, but only to a limited degree. The fact is, whether anything important happens today or not, the networks will still have at least a 30-minute newscast (actually, 22 minutes, after subtracting the time for commercials). Sometimes, they will extend the news

Journalists gather news by interviewing various witnesses to an event.

to an hour or even have continuous coverage during a major breaking news event, such as the September 11, 2001, World Trade Center and Pentagon attacks.

Newsgathering, reporting, and presenting the news to the public involve techniques that have been refined over the years and that have changed surprisingly little. There are variations between techniques that print journalists and television journalists must use, of course, but the basic principles are largely the same. We will look at some of the basic steps in the newsgathering process.

Gathering the News

The Associated Press news service publishes for its members a daily listing of upcoming news events such as important court cases, demonstrations, and press conferences. It's called the AP day book, and most journalists or assignment editors refer to it the night before to get ideas for stories to cover the next day. The day book is a pretty good predictor of the next day's news.

Some media critics claim that much news is actually manufactured by media organizations with the help of public relations professionals sending press releases and creating pseudo events such as press conferences, marches, or organized demonstrations with the sole purpose of getting the attention of the press or public. It is a well-known phenomenon that people can act out of the ordinary when cameras are rolling specifically so they do attract media attention, thereby possibly causing a tense situation to erupt into violence and perhaps making it newsworthy because of the subsequent violence.

Although news covering pseudo events or based on press releases may well be "manufactured," the fact is journalists must largely rely on these sources to be informed of what is happening. But journalists also use sources they have developed through experience covering a **beat,** or subject area that they may specialize in. Initially beats covered geographic areas, much like a beat a police officer may cover in his or her daily rounds, and sometimes there still are geographically based beats. Increasingly, though, beats cover specific subject areas, such as education, city hall, the state capital, or science. Through their reporting, journalists become aware of interesting developments that may be newsworthy and can cultivate

beat—a geographic or subject area of coverage by a reporter that he or she specializes in. Common beats in large- or medium-sized newspapers can include education, crime, or state politics.

sources that can inform them of newsworthy events in that area. Small newspapers cannot afford to have highly specialized reporters and often simply have general assignment reporters who cover a range of topics.

Moreover, the media tend to spotlight selected issues and stories. These stories often resonate through the entire media system, whether it is the release of a highly anticipated movie such as 2001's blockbuster *Harry Potter and the Sorcerer's Stone,* an earthquake in Turkey, or a U.S. presidential campaign. An unusual advertising campaign for a movie, for example, may trigger news stories on the campaign and its effect on the success of the movie, which in turn generates more publicity for that movie that adds to its popularity. Some news filters up through the media network, starting as a story in a local paper that is then covered by a regional television station that is seen by a reporter for a national newsweekly who does the story and reaches a national audience.

Producing the News

Once a story has been assigned or decided on and the raw material such as interviews, background facts, or video footage has been gathered, the reporter then has to make sense out of it all and shape it into a compelling story that accurately reflects the facts yet will attract an audience. Depending on whether the story involves breaking news or not, the journalist sometimes has very little time to write or produce the story before deadline. Few journalists have the luxury of putting a story aside for a week to ponder word choices or polish stories.

In newspapers, editors decide which stories are most important and where they will be placed in the newspaper in meetings several hours before story deadlines, and these spaces are blocked out (advertising space has already been blocked out). Sometimes breaking news or an unexpected event may push planned stories from their slots or from the newspaper entirely.

Editors look for logical weaknesses or errors in stories, often asking reporters to get more information or make more calls to make the story more complete. Fact-checkers research all facts stated in the story for accuracy and, depending on the media organization and laziness of the reporter, sometimes have to replace many TK's (used in journalism to mean "to come") in a "finished" story with hard facts based on their research. Copyeditors correct writing errors and make sure everything is written according to the proper style. In larger newspapers, headline and caption writers read the stories and come up with headlines and photo captions that fit within the space allotted to the story. In smaller newspapers, journalists may have more than one role or may be responsible for fact-checking or suggesting headlines as well.

Design and page layout artists put the copyedited articles and graphics in a digital version of the paper using a page layout program such as QuarkXpress. Proofreaders check to make sure editorial errors have not been missed or inserted; and, after the issue is approved by an editor, it is sent to the printer for printing. This used to be done by taking negative photographs of hard copies of the pages, but now it is mostly done entirely electronically with the printer receiving the pages digitally through a high-speed Internet connection.

In television news, camera crews and reporters usually return to the station to edit footage shot on location and to add voice-overs and graphics to the video.

Because time is so critical in television news, news segments are edited and rehearsed down to the second to fit into their selected time slots. With breaking or international news, reporters will report live from location, often broadcasting via satellite.

Television news, because of the amount of equipment needed to shoot video, requires many more people to gather and produce a story. A camera crew of two people, including the reporter, is usually needed. Digital video technology has helped reduce the number needed to shoot broadcast-quality video, but there are still many more technical steps involved in assembling a television news package.

At the station, the producer and reporter decide on what to edit and how the story will be put together, usually working with video editors or other technicians to carry out their instructions. At some stations, news anchors also have a role in editorial decisions, although in other stations they simply present the news.

Distributing the News

The goal of both print and electronic media in distributing the news is the same: to attract as large an audience as possible. The reasoning is simple; a larger audience means a higher advertising rate and more income for the media organization.

Newspapers and magazines will use colorful or dramatic photos on their front pages or covers, often with what the editors have decided is the most enticing story or stories. Some magazines may send press releases about what they feel are particularly noteworthy stories that will be coming out in the next issue with the hope that other media outlets report on these and generate more sales. Individual stories can be syndicated and appear in other print media outlets.

Print media are distributed through subscriptions and newsstand sales. Subscribers are more valuable to media organizations because they represent a stable revenue base and provide mailing lists that can be sold or rented to other organizations. Material costs for print media, ranging from paper to ink to delivery trucks, can be quite high.

Television stations will have short teasers during commercial breaks throughout the evening, usually asking a provocative question such as, "Could the food you are eating be dangerous? Find out at 11." Often the stories that have acted as the bait to get viewers to watch the news are not the lead story but appear later in the program in order to keep people watching. This is the reason weather forecasts usually come toward the middle or end of a news broadcast. National news shows are transmitted by the network to affiliate stations, sometimes with time slots available for additional local news content to be added. Networks also send video feeds of international and national news coverage to local affiliates so they can use the footage in their news reports.

Types of Journalism

The basic outline of how news is produced belies the rich variety of journalism types or specialties that have arisen in attempting to adequately cover the world in all its richness and complexity. Some types follow traditional journalistic principles

Entertainment journalism can range from simply providing a forum for stars to promote their latest movie to covering business news regarding the entertainment industry.

yet have special characteristics because of the topics they cover, such as science journalism or health journalism. Other types, often quite controversial, have arisen from dissatisfaction with the characteristics of mainstream journalism.

Specialized Journalism Types

With an increasingly complex world, not only do reporters often specialize in a subject area in order to better cover that topic, but whole branches of journalism have specialized in various areas, complete with their own support organizations. The following list is by no means complete, as it does not cover beats like education or local or national politics, but it should give a general idea of the range of specialized types of journalism.

Business and Financial Journalism

Business news is often read by a highly educated, knowledgeable audience seeking specific information. It can be difficult for journalists to penetrate an organization's public relations office to get access to executives, and when they do it can be hard to get candid information from them. Understanding business practices such as accounting procedures and being able to read and understand various complex forms are important, as is being able to write about complicated issues such as changes in tax laws that much of the general public may find boring. On the other hand, investors are usually very interested in learning the truth about companies, and financial journalists must be able to separate the hype from the reality.

Arts and Entertainment Journalism

As mentioned earlier, entertainment-related stories have become more prominent in the news in recent years. Much of entertainment journalism, especially on television on programs like *Entertainment Tonight,* is little more than orchestrated interviews and video shoots with artists or stars that essentially help them promote their latest film. "Behind-the-scenes" segments serve this purpose as well and help the public feel as though they are seeing the "real" person behind the star, even though there is little of true informational value in such features.

On the other hand, cultural and art criticism play an important role in helping define public tastes and form cultural trends in everything from fashion to film. Book reviews in prestigious magazines like the *New York Times Book Review* can be the deciding factor for a book's success. Coverage of the entertainment industry as a business can yield important information on corporate changes occurring with media companies.

Sports Journalism

Sports journalism shares many of the same characteristics of both arts and entertainment journalism and business journalism. Like popular singers or movie stars, popular athletes can be almost impossible to approach for in-depth interviews, and journalists may mostly get the usual mumbled platitudes in the locker room after the game.

Owning a sports franchise is a business, and the owners treat it as such, jealously guarding company secrets just like businesses everywhere, yet sometimes asking for public funds to build facilities like stadiums. In addition, media access is strictly controlled by the various leagues, making it easy for journalists who pry too closely into touchy issues to be barred from further access to the team or players. This can have a dampening effect on thorough coverage of important issues, such as drug use or illegal activities by players or business practices by team owners.

Health or Medical Journalism

Health or medical news is almost always of high interest to the public, and journalists in this area have an especially important responsibility to report information accurately and fairly. Claiming that a drug company will have a cure for cancer within three years, despite what the company may say, only gives cancer sufferers and their families' false hope. Journalists specializing in health and medicine must not only have a good grasp of medical terms and drugs, but they must also be able to read and understand the medical literature and critically analyze statistics and complex studies. They must also know the business side of the health care and pharmaceutical industries and report this complex information in a way that engages the audience. Access to company scientists and executives can be difficult, just as in business journalism.

Science and Technology Journalism

Science journalists have a double challenge in covering their areas, as the U.S. public generally does not understand basic scientific principles or care about science-related topics compared to other types of news such as sports or entertainment. The science journalist must interpret and explain complex concepts or findings in an easy-to-understand way and show why the public should care about the topic. Hot-button issues such as cloning or genetically modified foods have many facets that defy quick explanations and are often misreported. Scientists are notoriously hesitant to announce findings with the kind of certainty or sound-bites that journalists seek in order to make a good story.

Technology coverage has many of the same issues, in addition to difficulties in accessing executives of technology companies and getting beyond corporate PR hype. Much of the technology press failed miserably in predicting the dot-com collapse or pointing out weak companies. Sometimes technology companies were out of business by the time a glowing profile of them appeared in a magazine, such as *Business 2.0*'s positive feature in their June 2000 issue on APBNews.com, which had gone bankrupt earlier that month.

Environmental Journalism

Like science journalism, environmental journalists often have to explain complex concepts in interesting and clear ways that the general public can understand. Because many environmental processes take place slowly and there is often disagreement over what a finding may mean, it is often hard to find a solid angle within the traditional media framework for environmental stories. Environmental catastrophes such as oil spills often become major news events but suffer from the media spotlight effect, in which there is intense coverage for a short time and then the media flock moves on to another news item. Environmental journalism started out as a form of advocacy journalism but has shifted in recent years to be more impartial in environmental coverage.

Breaking from Journalism Tradition

Much serious questioning of journalism took place during the 1960s, when social upheavals led many to question norms in established society. Leading reporters such as James "Scottie" Reston of the *New York Times* and Paul Anderson of the *St. Louis Post-Dispatch* perceived the limits of "objective" news reportage that simply stated the facts in a story and developed the beginnings of **interpretive reporting,** which tried to explain the story by placing the facts into broader context.

Critics of interpretive reporting argue that it does no better at adequately representing the complexity of reality than does objective reporting. Still, interpretive reporting opened the door to a variety of journalistic writing styles during the 1960s, including New Journalism, literary journalism, alternative journalism, and advocacy journalism. Civic journalism, although not growing out of this movement per se, also has the goal of putting stories in context in addition to making stories more relevant to the audience and getting them more involved in civic affairs.

New Journalism

New Journalism developed in the 1960s and 1970s during a time of great social, political, and economic upheaval in the United States. Many journalists sought to present a true account of the complexity of the times reflected in that upheaval. What emerged was a form of reporting that often used literary techniques such as point of view, exploration of emotions of characters, or first-person narrative. Topics often covered popular social issues of the day and the drug culture. Truman Capote, Tom Wolfe, and Norman Mailer were three prominent writers using New Journalism techniques in their books. Critics charged that the literary style often blurred the line between fact and fiction, even though New Journalists said they reported facts.

interpretive reporting—a type of reporting that tries to put the facts of a story into a broader context by relying on knowledge and experience the reporter has about the subject.

The *Boston Phoenix* is one of the most influential alternative weeklies in the United States.

Literary Journalism

Literary journalism is similar to New Journalism and could be considered its less flamboyant, more traditional cousin. Literary journalism generally does not employ the same fiction techniques used by New Journalists. Literary journalism stays closer to true, observable narrative in its storytelling, although its pace may be slow with frequent lengthy side trips on other topics. One of the finest literary journalists is John McPhee, who has written books on everything from a single tennis match between Jimmy Connors and Arthur Ashe to geologic formations in the western United States. He combines immersive reporting, solid research, and excellent writing to create engaging stories that are not necessarily framed (and thus not newsworthy in the traditional journalistic sense) but that are interesting and memorable nonetheless. Other practitioners of literary journalism include Joan Didion, James Fallows, and Robert Kaplan, all of whom write on a range of issues, including foreign affairs and politics.

Alternative Journalism

Alternative journalism departed considerably from the traditions of objective reporting. It offered a personal, individual point of view. Its manner was aggressive and its approach antiestablishment. It reflected closely the energy of the civil rights movement. Leading alternative journalists included Eugene Cervi, editor of the *Rocky Mountain Journal,* known for expressing through his work the conviction that "good journalism begets good environment"; and Bruce Brugman, who in 1966 founded the alternative weekly newspaper *The Guardian* in San Francisco. Alternative journalism is still alive today in the form of many alternative news weeklies, especially in urban areas, such as the *Boston Phoenix, Miami New Times,* or *Houston Press.*

Advocacy Journalism

Advocacy journalism maintains a strong commitment to political and social reform. Leading examples of advocacy journalism were Gloria Steinem (founder of *Ms. Magazine* and a leader of the women's movement), Pete Hamill (one-time editor of *The Daily News* in New York), and Nicholas Von Hoffman. Much of early environmental journalism was a type of advocacy journalism.

Civic Journalism

Civic journalism developed in the early 1990s out of dissatisfaction among some editors and journalists over how poorly traditional journalism seemed to be covering important social and political issues. They saw the growing cynicism and apathy among the general public in civic affairs and increased distrust of the media and wondered if perhaps traditional journalism coverage had an influence on those attitudes.

Civic journalism expands on the watchdog role of journalism but tries to engage the citizenry more closely with creating and discussing the news. Civic journalism also tries to avoid the framing of news in terms of conflict and extremes and examines the news in a more nuanced fashion, sometimes using New Journalism writing techniques.

Newspapers experimenting with civic journalism around the country have reported a higher level of trust toward the press by their readership and some signs of increased civic participation and awareness of social and political issues. Critics of civic journalism charge that it is little more than boosterism or advocacy journalism and weakens the role of the press as a sometimes unpopular and critical voice of a community's conscience because it tends to pander to its audience.

Journalism in the Digital World

The digital tools available to journalists to help them do their jobs more effectively have been slow to be adopted, although from 2000 more and more journalists are seeing the value in using one tool—the Internet—in making their jobs easier. Electronic databases, spreadsheet programs, and interactive multimedia graphics have all gained slow acceptance as commonly used journalism tools among journalists. Busy work schedules and unwillingness on the part of media corporations to subsidize professional training and development for their journalists play a part in the slowness to fully utilize digital media.

The increased power of the audience to communicate with journalists and with each other in a public forum also can be threatening to some journalists who are accustomed to being the gatekeepers of information. Now readers and viewers online can point out, quite publicly, when a journalist errs, and they often have the same or similar resources from which to draw information and have a more or less equal ability to that of the journalism organization to distribute that information online.

Print and electronic journalists face increased competition for audience attention not only from other traditional media outlets but from the online world as well, where the audience is much more active and has even more choices for content than anything the traditional media world can offer. In addition, there are

Media Spotlight: Trends in Online Journalism

The "Media in Cyberspace" study is an annual survey conducted by Dan Middleberg, Chairman and CEO, Middleberg + Associates; and Steve Ross, Columbia journalism associate professor of professional practice. Trend information from the seventh annual study in 2000 is based on more than 4000 responses and reveals that journalists are making increasing and significant use of the Internet and other online resources in their work. The most important findings of the landmark study include:

- 98% of respondents go online at least once daily to check for e-mail. Journalists spent about 15 hours per week online reading and sending e-mail.

- 27% said they have had training in computer-assisted reporting, and half that number trained on their own initiative.

- 45% of print media sites "never or almost never" allow the Web site to scoop the print product.

This is down significantly from 1999, when it was 58%.

- E-mail matched the telephone for the first time as the preferred method for interviewing new sources.

- 32% said their organizations are preparing for delivery of high-bandwidth or wireless content, even though they felt consumers would want that.

- 70% said they or their colleagues participate in dialogues with readers via e-mail or discussion groups, up from 54% in 1999.

- 56% said they had never used instant messaging, down from 76% in 1999.

- 61% of newspaper respondents and 46% of magazine respondents said they prefer to receive digital photography rather than slides and photos.

often rivalries inside media companies between the traditional journalism product and its online counterpart.

In June 2002 half the top-20 U.S. news Web sites were affiliated with newspapers, up from seven the previous month. Although the top spots were primarily news Web sites derived from television media, just as television news draws larger audiences than most newspapers, newspapers did seem to be making inroads into attracting Internet users. CNN.com, MSNBC.com, Yahoo!News (which mainly utilizes news feeds from wire services and other news organizations), NYTimes.com, and ABCNews.com were the top five in June 2002.

Google's automated news system compiles news stories from sources worldwide without using human editors.

Although advances in technology can bring about changes in how people use the Internet, thereby changing the role online news may play in the public's overall picture of media use, some trends can be pointed out that may show the way to the niche online journalism fills in providing news and information to the public.

The 24/7 News Cycle

Online news is not tied to a printer's schedule or specific broadcast slot, which means that online news can be presented 24 hours, 7 days a week. This has the potential to cause the increasingly common situation in which a media organization's Web site scoops its print newspaper or television news show. Many media companies avoid this by putting an embargo, or temporary hold, on publishing the news on the Web until the traditional media product has published or aired the story, although this practice is becoming less frequent. A non-deadline-driven news cycle wreaks havoc on how news is usually processed and could add to production costs as more reporting and editing staff are needed to process news around the clock.

Nontraditional News Sources

Accessing nontraditional news sources has two aspects: getting news from traditional news outlets that are not usually viewed or read by the public and getting news from individuals or groups who do not claim to be professional journalists but who nevertheless provide information and news on topics of interest to the user. A good example of the former category is viewing an online newspaper from the Middle East to see how a story is covered there. Even looking at media coverage of international issues from the U.K. can often be a valuable and educational experience for U.S. media consumers, who receive a fairly narrow range of international news and commentary. With nonjournalistic, nontraditional sources, users should have a high degree of media literacy so they can weigh sources of news and any biases the Web site creator may have.

News sources are increasingly viewing themselves as content providers who can publish their own content, without relying on a traditional journalistic publisher or gateway. NBA.com, for example, publishes extensive news about its basketball games and even includes video clips. Why would a viewer go to CNN or ESPN when he or she can get their sports news straight from the source?

The danger for the news consumer using nontraditional news sources like these is that the sources may not have the same commitment to fairness and balance of coverage that a professional news organization would have. It is unlikely a user would find an expose on NBA.com about financial wrongdoing by the league, for example. On the other hand, many members of the public may not care about such news and simply want to get basketball scores and news on the latest trades. In that case, going to a site like NBA.com may be fine.

But consider this same situation in political coverage. If an Internet user can go directly to a free Web site created by a political candidate, which ostensibly has political news, will they be as inclined to go to a professionally produced news Web site, especially if they have to pay a subscription?

Weblink
Online Newspapers.com
[www.onlinenewspapers.com/]

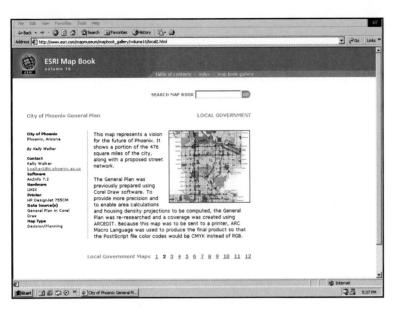

Interactive online maps can help users personalize their news and create unique news stories.

Online Users' Media Habits

Online users' media habits differ from traditional media use in a number of ways. First, online users are generally more active in their media use and can easily visit different Web sites to find the information they are seeking. This shorter attention span for viewing media content means that news stories have to compete harder for the audience's attention. Because of current display technologies and established media-use patterns, most members of the public do not like to read large amounts of material online. This encourages producing shorter printed stories or stories with interactive graphics or multimedia.

Users want to quickly understand not only the essential facts in a story but its context as well and will readily use hyperlinks to click to related stories or other Web sites to seek the information they are looking for. However, from a business standpoint, media organizations do not want visitors to leave their Web site, so there is a natural tension regarding what types of hyperlinks to provide and how to provide them that allows users to explore further yet encourages them to remain on the Web site.

Personalization

The Internet allows users to personalize the type of content they receive, ranging from localized weather forecasts to choosing news on favorite sports teams or companies in a stock portfolio. Personalization is one of the unique features of online media that traditional media simply cannot compete with, and its development will play a key role in making online news an increasingly important source for news. Personalization could lead to changes in how journalists write or produce stories. For example, a standard version of a story could be written that could include various hyperlinked informational modules, or types of sidebars, that may be of interest to users in specific demographics and can be called up on demand.

Journalists will obviously not be able to write individual stories for each user, but it is likely that elements of stories could be broken up by computer and reconstituted in a personalized format.

Contextualization of News

Using personalization and other digital tools journalists will have a greater ability to contextualize the news without trying to frame it in a predetermined manner that may distort coverage.

However, users will still want some kind of context regarding raw data. For example, a user may click on an interactive crime map when reading an online news story about a certain crime in a different part of town and then select his or her own ZIP code to call up an interactive map of his or her neighborhood. The user can see on the map what types of crimes have been committed within the neighborhood within the past year. Currently, for news sites with features like this, that's all he or she can do. Ideally, the user will also be able to click on a crime type or location and get more information on what the crime is, when it occurred, what the crime rate is for that crime, and whether it's increasing or decreasing, with possible explanations from expert sources on why. Hyperlinks to archived news stories of the crime, if there are any, would also help put the interactive map in context.

An excellent example of how online journalism can improve the contextualization of the news is provided at the National Journal.com, a leading journal covering U.S. politics. It features, among other things, a section called "Ad Spotlight." Ad Spotlight provides reporting, analysis, and commentary on political advertising from local, state, and national political campaigns throughout the United States. Unlike traditional analog media reports on political advertising, the National Journal.com incorporates digital versions of the actual advertisements being evaluated. Visitors to the site can watch and listen to the ads via RealPlayer to put the reporting into better context and decide for themselves whether the reporting is accurate. Moreover, inaccuracies can be instantly noted through e-mail to reporters and editors and in chat rooms and other online forums. Visitors can also attach electronic "post-it notes" digitally to a Web site for others to read. All these characteristics force reporters for online content providers to pay particular attention to detail and to the precision of their analysis. Perhaps it is this heightened attention to accuracy that has led the National Journal.com to emerge as one of the first commercial success stories in online content.

Multimedia

Online video, audio, and interactive graphics are increasingly being used with text stories to enhance and supplement stories. Likewise, text can be added to primarily video stories that can not only offer different ways to access the information but that can provide more depth and context to a story than video or audio alone can do. Journalists will have to become versed in the various tools of online journalism, including video, audio, and writing.

A truly interactive multimedia experience that allows the user to stop or replay segments at will, skip information already known, or to learn background information on topics he or she does not know about, will help differentiate online journalism from its analog counterparts.

New Journalism Tools

Technology can change not only the production and presentation of the news but how it is gathered. Advancements in handheld digital video cameras, laptop

Weblink
National Journal
[nationaljournal.com/]

computers, and satellite phones, combined with increased access for journalists by the military, allowed reporters covering the 2003 war with Iraq to provide news audiences with an intimate view of the war. Reporters on the battlefields, "embedded" with military personnel, were allowed with few restrictions to capture any images they wished. They could provide the footage as live feeds directly to news outlets or prepare complete video packages that they digitally edited and produced on the spot. Although much of the video footage never appeared on air or online, the fact that many more journalists were shooting video footage provided a huge potential archive of video material that the news outlets can use at some later point or even sell to other media outlets.

Omnidirectional Imaging

Other technologies can be utilized in an online environment that takes advantage of both digital media and active news consumers. Omnidirectional imaging or video, for example, in which a journalist takes a 360-degree digital picture and adds in hyperlinks to other images, video clips, or text stories, can be a unique way to present news stories and put them in a natural context. An inflammatory speaker at a protest rally may not seem so threatening when the user can pan around the scene online and see they are speaking to disinterested passersby. A crime scene can be shot with omnidirectional photos or video, letting the viewer "stand" in the place and get a sense of all the surroundings rather than simply a limited view chosen by a photographer. One simple example of this involves the 1999 accidental shooting death of West African immigrant Amadou Diallo by New York City police officers. Viewers can pan around the vestibule of his apartment where he was shot and zoom in to see the bullet holes in the wall, along with messages left by sympathizers after the shooting. Clicking on parts of the photo takes the viewer to where roughly the police officers stood when they shot him 19 times, as well as a view of the street and apartments across the street.

Remote-Sensing and Satellite Imagery

Unmanned air vehicles (UAVs) are currently used by law enforcement and the military for surveillance. Their use in journalism could improve news coverage of scenes where the physical presence of journalists could be dangerous or hamper rescue efforts. They could also be used where the presence of journalists with cameras may help ignite a tense situation as protestors vie for media attention.

Satellite imagery can play an important role in covering environmental, political, or military conflict stories. Mass graves can be seen on satellite images, for example, proving or disproving claims by different parties of wartime atrocities.

Satellite imagery can be used to tell important geographically or environmentally based stories.

Media Future: The Mobile Journalist's Workstation

A collaborative project between the Center for New Media at the Columbia University Graduate School of Journalism and the Columbia University Graphics and User Interfaces Lab illustrates the potential of digital tools for the journalist of the near future. The collaborative project, known as a Mobile Journalist's Workstation (MJW), is a wearable computer and communications system that puts the full functionality of a central newsroom into the hands of a field reporter. For the news consumer, it provides the immersive storytelling capability of augmented reality into mass communication. Designed by Professor Steven Feiner and his students, the MJW system is a hybrid of technologies involving:

- a head-worn see-through display with a head orientation measure;
- augmented reality (a cousin of virtual reality in which visual, aural, or other information is layered onto the user's direct observation of reality);
- high-speed wireless Internet access; and
- a Global Positioning System (GPS) receiver.

Wearable computers such as this remove the remaining tethers of computer users to their desktop PCs, just as laptop computers and wireless networks started to do. It's important to emphasize that the prototype research system shown here is not the one we would expect anyone to actually wear in the field. One would expect a commercial version of the MJW to be much smaller, perhaps the size of a Sony Walkman. In fact, such miniaturized wearable computers are already being manufactured. IBM has announced plans for a wearable computer about the size of a hand-held PC.

Satellite images showing soil erosion or other environmental damage, when compared to older images that were taken, can provide a stark picture of an otherwise complex subject.

Journalism Ethics

Because of journalism's unique role in society, its protection by the First Amendment and its public service mission, many ethical dilemmas arise in the course of practicing journalism. Ethical questions play a role in the entire news gathering and production process, and many questions do not have easy answers. Editors must consider whether headlines and captions accurately reflect the important points of a story or simply titillate. Privacy issues play a role when private citizens are thrust by circumstance into the media spotlight. Reporters must consider fairness and balance in their choice of interview subjects. Photo editors and designers must avoid the temptation to alter elements of photos to make them more dramatic. Societal mores and cultural values of the audience must be considered when determining what qualifies as news and how it is reported, although newspapers must also sometimes take highly unpopular stands on issues when acting as the public's conscience.

Privacy Rights Versus the Public's Right to Know

Although there is no actual law stating the public has a "right to know," it is often cited as a commonly understood principle when journalists are trying to obtain information that can help the public make better-informed decisions regarding everything from political candidates to corporate wrongdoing to potentially dangerous foods, drugs, or buildings.

Gathering proof of wrongdoing is one of the biggest challenges journalists face. Admissions of guilt are unlikely to come out during an interview—even if the subject agrees to an interview, which is often not the case. Journalists are often barred from the very locations they need to visit in order to gather information. Employees are forbidden by management to speak to journalists or threatened with losing their jobs if they do; police or public officials refuse to see or talk to journalists or are slow in providing requested documentation, even if the documents are public documents.

New technology such as miniature microphones and cameras or going under-cover may seem to be an easy answer to the journalists' dilemma. But the ethics and legality of these tools and actions must be considered. Sometimes these techniques are the only ones that will give access to people engaged in illegal or unethical behavior, such as selling drugs or arms.

Federal law prohibits the media or anyone else from intentionally intercepting, or attempting to intercept anyone's communication either by wire, oral, or electronic means. Citizens have a reasonable expectation of privacy for oral, or spoken, communications, including via a telephone or over the Internet. However, this issue is complicated in that states have varying laws on whether only one person or both people in a conversation must give consent to have a communication recorded.

Regardless of the legality of intercepting communications, is it ethical? There is no easy answer, as it depends on the circumstances. It also depends on whether print or broadcast media are involved. The FCC generally prohibits the use of wireless microphones to overhear private conversations unless all parties to the communication have given prior consent. Conversations that take place in a public place, such as a bar, however, would not be subject to the same prohibition, because people in public places cannot expect the same right to privacy. Broadcast television or radio stations may not record telephone conversations without the consent of all parties, and they must notify the parties prior to broadcasting any of the recorded content. Long-distance calls can only be recorded under limited circumstances, including an announcement made at the beginning of the call indicating it will be recorded or possibly broadcast. Violation of these rules can result in the forfeiture of the station's license, fines, or other penalties.

Weblink
Hidden Cameras, Hidden
Microphones
[www.rtnda.org/resources
/hiddencamera/]

Going Undercover

The legality and ethics of journalists going undercover are also not settled. In many ways they depend on how ethical or responsible the media professional was in using these techniques. Questions that may be asked in a court of law include: Were the media being fair? Does going under cover or using hidden cameras somehow manipulate or distort the situation? Do the undercover techniques help build meaningful information or simply sensationalize the story? If a media professional (or anyone else for that matter) is convicted of violating the law in going under cover, there are a variety of potential penalties, including substantial prison terms and fines.

The Internet raises new questions about journalists not announcing their identity. If they engage in a discussion in a child pornography online discussion group, for example, is it ethical to use posts by others in a story without their permission? Is it ethical to pose as someone other than a journalist in order to get people to talk as they naturally would in an online forum?

Victimizing the Victims

Crime victims can feel doubly victimized when their names are made public by the media, especially with crimes such as rape that still carry a social stigma. Most newspapers and television stations do not make rape victims' names public, although critics of this practice argue that it further stigmatizes rape rather than educating the public about the crime of violence that it is.

Publicizing details of crimes can also contribute to copycat crimes, and journalists must always consider what kinds of information in a story are important and what are simply lurid or titillating details. Needlessly mentioning race, gender, or sexual orientation can often be unethical in portraying a subject in a certain light that may reinforce social stereotypes.

Photographs and video sometimes have a power to tell a story in a way that words alone cannot. Yet, in many cases, publicly presented dramatic photos or footage are not always justified for their news value alone. In fact, in cases of human tragedy, sadness, or crime, personal grief has been violated by the repeated presentation of pictures or video in newspapers, in magazines, or on television.

Do the Ends Justify the Means?

On November 5, 1992, ABC's *PrimeTime Live,* a weekly newsmagazine show, broadcast a report claiming labor and food-handling problems at Food Lion, a nonunion supermarket chain and at the time the fastest growing supermarket chain in the United States, with more than 1000 stores. The program's producers had been contacted by the United Food and Commercial Worker's union (UFCW) in early 1992 about doing a story about alleged unsanitary conditions at the supermarket chain.

The show's producers designed a scheme to obtain hidden camera footage from inside Food Lion stores. The scheme required *PrimeTime Live* producers to obtain jobs at Food Lion under false identities and fraudulent employment applications. Once they started working at Food Lion, the producers brought in hidden cameras and recorded what they saw inside the stores, including harried employees, unsanitary conditions, and wasted food. The problem was that much of the conditions observed were due to the ABC employees neglecting their own cleaning duties as Food Lion employees.

Food Lion objected to the airing of this report and sued ABC, which during the course of litigation was purchased by the Walt Disney Company in 1995. The case went to trial in late 1996 and concluded in January 1997. The jury found for Food Lion on all counts and against Disney/ABC. The jury concluded that *PrimeTime Live* based its report on unlawfully obtained videotape and that the program's producers had committed fraud and illegal trespass.

Do you think the decision against ABC was justified? What other ways could the journalists have obtained the kind of information they did on unsanitary practices at the supermarket chain?

On Sunday, June 11, 2000, the annual Puerto Rican Day Parade in New York City was marred by a group of 15 to 25 men who assaulted women attending the parade. Amateur video documented many of the assaults, and the footage was used by the police to apprehend suspects. Television also aired much of the video, and newspapers published print photos extracted from the video, sometimes revealing the identities of the women who were being assaulted.

This is an example of a decision a news director or editor must typically make when deciding what to print or air as news. There is no doubt that footage and pictures of seminude women would attract a larger audience (along with vociferous complaints from various groups), but the ethics of showing such material must be considered in the effects it would have on the victims and their families.

The Society of Professional Journalists' Code of Ethics

The Society of Professional Journalists (SPJ) is a large organization of working journalists and student chapters that tries to ensure journalism is being practiced professionally and ethically and that it is fulfilling its role in society. The society's code of ethics says journalists should "seek truth and report it" and that "journalists should be honest, fair and courageous in gathering, reporting and interpreting information." Other principles in their code of ethics include:

- Test the accuracy of information from all sources and exercise care to avoid inadvertent error. Deliberate distortion is never permissible.
- Diligently seek out subjects of news stories to give them the opportunity to respond to allegations of wrongdoing.
- Identify sources whenever feasible. The public is entitled to as much information as possible on sources' reliability.
- Make certain that headlines, news teases, promotional material, photos, video, audio, graphics, sound bites, and quotations do not misrepresent. They should not oversimplify or highlight incidents out of context.
- Never distort the content of news photos or video. Image enhancement for technical clarity is always permissible. Label montages and photo illustrations.
- Avoid misleading re-enactments or staged news events. If re-enactment is necessary to tell a story, label it.
- Support the open exchange of views, even views the journalist (or the majority of the public) may find repugnant.
- Avoid undercover or other surreptitious methods of gathering information except when traditional open methods will not yield information vital to the public. Use of such methods should be explained as part of the story.

Weblink
SPJ Code of Ethics
[www.spj.org/ethics_code.asp]

The Business of Journalism

The early years of the 21st century have been especially challenging for the media business, especially for news organizations. Advertising revenues took a sharp downturn after the dot-com bust in 2000 and have only slowly been growing again. Many media companies laid off significant numbers of staff in 2000 and 2001. By one estimate, U.S. media enterprises laid off as many as 100,000 employees during this period.[7]

Some media companies that predicted new business opportunities in media convergence, such as AOL-Time Warner or Bertelsmann, spent large amounts to provide services or media that never made a profit. Other media companies that adopted a more cautious approach with digital media see even fewer reasons to invest in new technologies. However, even the executives who have been burned say the changes will come and that they simply moved too quickly.

Deeply affecting the media at the start of the 21st century is the war on terrorism. "The quality of our journalism is at the heart of our company's success, and we will do everything we can to continue providing our readers and viewers and listeners and users with world-class news reports," Times Co. Chairman Arthur Sulzberger Jr. told employees shortly after the September 11, 2001, attack on the World Trade Center and the Pentagon.

He also warned that the declining economy and the high costs of reporting the attack and military activity that followed would cause the company to miss its annual earnings goal. His sentiments are echoed by many other media executives, who are concerned that the high cost of the war may adversely affect the quality and extent of news coverage. Estimates show that U.S. news companies spent at least $100 million more than their existing budgets in covering the first few weeks of conflict. Moreover, U.S. television networks lost more than $500 million in advertising revenue in the days following the attacks as they converted to 24-hour news reporting.[8]

In order to cut costs, news organizations may use several methods short of firing editorial staff that nevertheless affect the quality of the final news product. It has already been mentioned that using a greater percentage of wire service copy rather than original local reporting saves money, at the cost of making the news less relevant to a local audience. Investigative journalism is usually scaled back substantially when a news organization is trying to cut costs. Publishers may increase the advertising percentage in a newspaper or raise advertising rates in order to increase revenues, although there is debate as to whether these practices hurt a newspaper in the long run.

There will always be a tension between the business side and the editorial side in a news organization. In line with the adage that journalism should "comfort the afflicted and afflict the comfortable," the editorial side of the business is looking for stories that do just that, and often publishers or their corporate parent are "the comfortable." Journalists can sometimes face severe pressures or even get fired if they do not go along with a publisher's wishes in either killing a story on a subject that a powerful advertiser does not want to see or downplaying news that is embarrassing to the publisher's associates or friends. Rare are the media owners who are willing to turn the investigative spotlight on themselves as readily and thoroughly as they are on others.

Careers in Journalism

The employment outlook for journalists in the digital age is uncertain, as it largely reflects how well the overall economy is doing. After a decade of strong growth in employment and business, the 21st century has gotten off to a troubled start, and media and technology companies have been especially hard hit with the downturn in the economy.

However, this is an exciting time to be a journalist. Online journalism is still in its infancy and plays a fairly small but increasingly important role in the overall journalism picture, and there are still many possibilities for journalists in traditional print, radio, and television. Combined with the various types of journalism available, such as financial journalism or science journalism, there are an almost endless number of journalism niches that can be pursued as a career.

Salaries

Salaries for journalism and mass communication professionals vary according to several factors, including the type of medium one works in (television is the highest paid, print media the lowest), the location or market (i.e., the larger the market, the higher the pay), the type of position one occupies (positions farther up in management, ownership, or celebrity status correlate positively with pay), experience, and a variety of other less definite factors, including gender, with men generally still being paid more than women, as unfair as that may be. Salaries and overall compensation vary so widely—from $15,000 a year to many millions of dollars—that crude averages are relatively meaningless.

In general, network television offers the highest salaries for midlevel jobs as producers. National magazines and newspapers offer fairly good pay, while papers in mid- and small-sized markets offer relatively poor salaries. Internet media offer fairly good salaries, and until the dot-com bust their stock option plans made a lucky few journalists instant millionaires when the companies went public. Many more people missed that train than rode it, however, as Internet media companies started going bankrupt.

Vernon Stone, of the University of Missouri, has conducted surveys on the salaries of television and radio newspeople. His data show that in 1991 the median salary for all radio newspeople was $19,000. The mean was $24,500 and the range was $8,000 to $120,000. Stone reports the median radio salary in 2000 was $24,700; the mean, $31,800; and the range $10,400 to $156,000.

For TV newspeople the salaries in 1990–1991 were: $30,000 median and $39,700 mean, with an $8000 to $1,800,000 range. In 2000, the median salary was $39,000, the mean $51,600, and the range $10,400 to $2,340,000.

Salaries for newspaper reporters have been examined since the late 1980s by Lee Becker of the University of Georgia. Becker's national survey of 3134 respondents shows that entry-level daily newspaper salaries were at a record high of more than $25,000 a year in 1999, $1000 more than the previous year.

Women and Minorities in the Newsroom

Circumstances in American media have been slow to change. In 1950, African American journalist Marvel Cooke (1903–2000) was hired as a reporter and feature writer for the *New York Daily Compass*. She was the only woman and the only black on the staff of the white-owned paper and was among the first blacks to have worked for any white-owned daily newspaper.

In 1998 the American Society of Newspaper Editors (ASNE) sponsored an industry-wide survey on employment of women and minorities by U.S. daily newspapers. The ASNE survey found that just 18 percent of employees are minorities, with slightly more men than women, 10 percent and 8 percent. African Americans make up the largest portion of minority newspaper employees at 10 percent, with Hispanics at 5 percent, Asian Americans at 2 percent, and Native Americans at 1 percent. Minorities make up just 11 percent of newspaper executives and managers.

Vernon Stone conducted a survey, sponsored by the RTNDA, to look at women and minorities in television newsrooms. Stone reported, "The typical TV journalist surveyed in 1990–91 was a 30-year-old married white man." In a 1994 survey, Stone found that television newsrooms are predominantly white (82 percent), with a small percentage of African Americans (10 percent), Hispanics (5 percent), Asians (2 percent), and Native Americans (1 percent). These numbers are nearly identical for radio, Stone reports, and quite similar across all media types.

With regard to gender, the television and radio newsroom has changed greatly since the 1950s. Women made up about 10 percent of the television and newsroom workforce in the 1950s. In 1994 women were 36 percent of the TV newsroom staff and 31 percent of the radio newsroom.

Condace Pressley, assistant program director for WSB radio in Atlanta and 2001–2003 president of the National Association of Black Journalists, is one of the few women minorities in a newsroom management position.

SUMMARY

Journalism plays a crucial role in informing the public of important events taking place domestically and internationally and providing a context that helps people understand the world better. News is the bedrock of journalism, although news is often manufactured by public relations professionals, individuals, or organizations, and the amount of news coverage on any specific topic can change from day to day depending on the perceived importance of other news events.

Modern journalism grew out of the penny press in the 19th century, when business economics and technology helped make the concept of objectivity one of the principles of journalism, even if it wasn't always practiced. There continues to be a tension between the temptation to sensationalize the news to create a larger audience and to report the news in a fair and balanced manner but that may not seem as exciting. This tension also exists in television news, which is the primary source of news for the public.

The press has special privileges in its role as government and societal watchdog but also special responsibilities. Journalism should provide fair and balanced coverage, but some practices such as framing the news and using a select group of expert sources can hamper this goal. Newspapers and television serve an important agenda-setting function by what they publish or air as those items usually are perceived as important because they appeared in the news.

Even with changes brought by digitization of media, journalism follows certain general steps in gathering, producing, and distributing the news. There are several types of journalism that have unique characteristics in terms of reaching sources or reporting. These include business or financial journalism, sports journalism, and health and medical journalism, among others.

Some journalists, especially during the social upheaval of the 1960s and early 1970s, were dissatisfied with inadequacies in journalistic coverage of important social issues and sought to expand the boundaries of journalism. New journalism types were developed, most of which continue to this day. These include New Journalism, literary journalism, alternative journalism, and advocacy journalism. Civic journalism was created in the 1990s to re-engage the public in society and the political process and to expand the role of journalism in a dialogue with the public.

Despite the fact that some basic aspects of journalism practices will not change, digitization and online media are bringing many substantial changes to the world of journalism. These include a 24/7 news cycle, nontraditional news sources, personalization of news by users, better contextualization of news, and new reporting tools such as 360-degree photos and video and satellite imagery.

Ethical questions in journalism arise constantly and at every stage of making the news. Everything from the privacy of citizens to going undercover to how people are portrayed in the media potentially involves ethical issues.

The media business relies heavily on advertising, and when there is an economic downturn companies advertise less, bringing in less revenue for media companies and requiring cutbacks in investments and sometimes even layoffs, as happened from 2000 after the dot-com bust. Online advertising sales never reached predicted numbers and media companies have yet to figure out ways to make profits from online subscription models.

Most newsrooms still do not reflect the cultural diversity found in America, although strides have been made in the past 50 years. Still, an extremely small number of minorities and women can be found in management or executive positions in news media. Salaries for journalists range according to what type of market the journalist works in, his or her experience level, and the type of media. Television tends to pay best at higher levels but pays less than newspapers at entry-level positions.

Discussion Questions

1. Look at the front page of your local paper and analyze the placement of stories and photographs. What reasons could there have been for placing the stories where they were? Think about placing the stories in other places on the front page or moving a story from the inside to the front page. How would this change your impression of the news?

2. Choose an article from your local paper and see if you can find a likely source for the article from a public relations department. Compare the original press release, if available, with the final article.

3. Discuss a current event being covered in the news and how it is being framed. Examine how this framing may affect how the topic is being covered and suggest ways that may allow for more balanced, complete coverage.

4. Choose one of the alternative journalism types and explain potential pitfalls of that type and how these pitfalls may be overcome, if they can be.

5. Keep track of your news reading habits online for a day or two, including every Web site you visit to get news and any hyperlinks you click on and why. Discuss what you learned.

6. Should there be penalties for breaches of ethics by journalists? What kinds of penalties should there be, if any? Who should enforce the penalties? What effects could these have on the practice of journalism?

Entertainment

While movie stars and popular singers enter our homes every night through television, stereos, and home entertainment systems, in 2002 MTV turned the standard model on its head by inviting viewers into the home of rock star Ozzy Osbourne and his family. The voyeuristic and frequently bleeped show *The Osbournes* became a huge success, and MTV's highest-rated episode reached 11 million viewers—better than average for many network shows and even more spectacular because MTV reaches only about 80 percent of the audience that network television does.

The 10-week series had barely ended when stars of yesterday and today—but mostly yesterday—started pitching their own reality series with themselves as the stars. Actress Cybil Shepherd, rapper and clothing entrepreneur Sean Combs, pop singer Brandy, rock singer Courtney Love, lead singer of Kiss Gene Simmons, and former lead singer of Van Halen David Lee Roth were all promoting themselves.

The sudden self-marketing of stars to be on reality television is an interesting twist on the

traditional star image, in which fame is hard-won and privacy is jealously guarded. Some media watchers say that the popularity of reality-based shows featuring regular people has left stars wondering if anyone cares what they have to say. Others say that reality television would allow stars to control their image more thoroughly, while providing the illusion that they are just like everyone else.

In a rock and roll life full of crazy stunts and excess that most would see as having little to do with reality, Ozzy Osbourne remains remarkably level-headed about the show's success. "I'm flavor of the month, hottest ticket in town, but eventually we'll be yesterday's news," he told BBC's *Radio Times*. "And then I'll have serenity again."

OBJECTIVES

In this chapter we will:

- Examine the functions of entertainment.
- Outline the historical development of entertainment content in books, magazines, comics, television, movies, music, and video games.
- Explore the role of entertainment content in our perceptions of and interactions with media.
- Compare the changing dynamics between methods of media distribution and media types, such as movies, television, videocassettes, and DVDs.
- Review ethical issues involved in entertainment media.
- Explore how digital media are affecting the entertainment industry.

Prologue

Regardless of whether reality shows such as *The Osbournes* are a passing fad or a trend toward new styles of entertainment, they are yet another example of how media, and especially entertainment media, have thoroughly infiltrated our lives and blurred boundaries between reality and fiction. Fiction is still of course popular, but now the public considers watching someone else's daily home life to be entertainment.

In addition, *The Osbournes,* like other reality shows, is heavily produced and edited, despite its look of voyeuristic realism. Although the degree of access the Osbourne family gave to MTV is perhaps unusual for stars, the fact that a media professional or professionals had to sort through thousands of hours of videotape to select the segments to fit within a 30-minute show (less, with commercials), plus the sound, lighting, and camera crews who videotaped the Osbournes, in many respects makes it no less contrived than a fictional TV series.

The prevalence of media in our lives today and fragmentation of media channels have placed greater demands on different media formats to get our attention. Because of the popularity of entertainment, media professionals in fields such as journalism, advertising, and public relations can sometimes be under strong pressures to provide more entertainment-oriented material, or media products that are entertaining. This is a criticism especially of some modern journalism practices, which at times have been accused of concentrating too much on entertaining the public at the expense of the public service mission to inform citizens of important issues and news.

Entertainment media covers a wide range of activities, including sports events, performing arts, televised or filmed dramatic series in a variety of fiction genres, music, books, magazines, and video games, just to name a few. The entertainment industry has always been greatly affected by new media technologies and in many cases is the driving force behind developing new technologies. The historical development of technologies for recording and playing music can be seen as being driven by entertainment needs as consumers seek high-quality recordings of music that are also portable and that can be played on a number of devices.

The development of new technology and its adoption by consumers can outpace the business models of the entertainment industry, however, as media companies are learning in regards to the Internet and digital media. File sharing services using **peer-to-peer (P2P)** networks would not be a threat to large media companies if the public restricted themselves to sharing classic works of philosophy and literature in the public domain over the Internet, but they are not doing so. They are sharing the latest popular music, TV shows, and movies without paying the companies that produced the content or the copyright owners of that content.

It is estimated that in industrial countries people are able to spend 30 percent of their time for leisure activities, although in the United States that number is 35 percent, with 28 percent of the time being spent for work and the rest for maintenance of daily living.[1] Despite what seem like incredibly busy schedules, people today have more leisure time than ever, and that trend promises to continue.

peer-to-peer network (P2P)—a network in which all computers on the network are considered equal (peers) and can send and receive information equally well. This is the basis of file-sharing services such as KaZaA and Morpheus.

MEDIA Quiz   Are You an Entertainment Junkie?

1. Did you have a TV in your bedroom while growing up? A VCR?

2. Did you have a personal computer in your bedroom while growing up?

3. Did your family have videogames?

4. Do you schedule certain aspects of your social life and study time in order not to miss your favorite program or programs?

5. Have you ever changed your hairstyle, clothes, or mannerisms to reflect an admired singer or movie star?

6. Do you use catchphrases from TV shows or movies in your conversational speech?

7. Do you regularly attend concerts or sporting events?

8. What is the first media appliance you turn on in the morning—the radio, the TV, or the computer? How long after you wake up do you turn it on?

9. What is the first section you usually turn to in a newspaper?

10. Have you ever participated in online discussions or chats with people about entertainment or entertainment figures?

If you answered yes to most of these, it doesn't necessarily mean you are an entertainment junkie; it simply shows how pervasive entertainment is in your life and the effect it can have on you, your sense of self, and your perceptions of society.

Functions of Entertainment

One function of entertainment, as its name would indicate, is of course to **entertain.** However, in fulfilling this function entertainment also has other important mass communication functions, including **cultural transmission** and **mobilization.**

Through the types of media entertainment that are seen in publications, over the airwaves, or on the Internet, a society's dominant cultural values are transmitted to the public. In fact, this was a frequent criticism of media entertainment, especially on television, in which shows had primarily white characters and plots that appealed mostly to white, middle-class viewers.

When minorities did appear, they were usually in stereotypical or one-dimensional roles. Although a greater number of media outlets such as cable channels have given greater visibility to programming that features diverse groups or characters outside of mainstream society, some cultural critics charge that entertainment still mostly transmits the values of society's dominant group. However, there is no doubt that there is more cross-cultural transmission than there used to be, as suburban youth adopt fashions and mannerisms derived from entertainment such as hip-hop or gangsta rap, which originated in black urban youth culture.

Entertainment can also mobilize the public to action, although it is often not for the better. City riots, such as those that took place in Los Angeles in June 2000 after the Los Angeles Lakers won the NBA championship, left the realm of entertainment and entered the realm of the evening news. Entertainment-oriented television programs or movies about real events, although usually produced well after the event, can nevertheless influence public perceptions of that event and the people involved, even though the show may have been heavily dramatized and bears little resemblance to actual events. Perhaps the best example of entertainment mobilizing the public is Orson Welles's radio dramatization of *War of the Worlds* in 1938, when many listeners thought an invasion from Mars had occurred and took various steps to protect themselves.

The Historical Development of Entertainment

Entertainment developed only after humans were able to hone hunting and agricultural skills enough so they had extra time in which they did not need to gather food. Neolithic animal hide drums have been found, showing that even primitive humans created some form of music, although it is not known whether this music was primarily used for religious purposes or simply to entertain.

Although little is known about mass entertainment in ancient times, it is known from records that the ruling classes in such civilizations as Egypt and China enjoyed lavish banquets that included acrobats, musicians, and dancers. It is assumed the lower classes had similar entertainment available to them, although presumably on a much less extravagant scale. Greece had plays and sporting contests, while later Rome had chariot races, gladiatorial combat, and

entertainment—a function of mass communication that is performed in part by all three of the other four main functions (surveillance, correlation, cultural transmission) but also involves the generation of content designed specifically and exclusively to entertain.

cultural transmission—primarily refers to the transference of the dominant culture as a function of mass communication, as well as its subcultures, from one generation to the next, or to immigrants. This function includes socialization, which the media perform in helping persons learn society's rules, or how to fit into society.

mobilization—a function of mass communication in which the media can influence the public, especially regarding political issues or movements.

other forms of mass entertainment in order to help pacify the public. The Circus Maximus in Rome, where chariot races were held, could hold 250,000 spectators—about five times the size of the average modern football stadium. By the fourth century, Rome had 200 holidays a year; every other day was dedicated to state-sponsored entertainments.[2]

In the Western world, the rise of Christianity saw restrictions placed on entertainment, although occasional attempts to ban entertainment outright usually failed after a short while. Fairs throughout medieval Europe presented morality plays to townspeople on traveling stages, which became the precursors to permanent theaters such as those created in London in the late 1500s. Cockfighting and animal baiting were popular spectator events in Europe and America among commoners and nobility well into the 19th century, even after laws were enacted that made such blood sports illegal.

During the Renaissance and later, printed books and magazines reached mass audiences and gave the public a range of fictional styles and stories. With industrialization, more leisure time meant more demand for entertainment, a need that recorded music, then films, then radio, then television helped fulfill. The Internet and digital media, although not created with entertainment in mind, now play a huge entertainment role as they contain all other types of entertainment and provide new forms, such as interactive multiplayer video games.

The Entertainment Media

Entertainment covers a huge swath of activities that can include travel and tourism, gambling, and recreational pastimes, as well as live performing arts or visual arts such as painting and sculpture. Although these and other forms of entertainment play important roles in society and culture and are important elements to varying degrees in the economy, we will look only at entertainment in a mass communication or digital media context.

The typical child in the United States spends an average of five and a half hours a day—or 38 hours a week—consuming various types of media, according to a 1999 study by the Kaiser Family Foundation. That amount is even higher among kids eight or older, who spend an average of six and three-quarter hours a day. "Watching TV, playing video games, listening to music and surfing the Internet have become a full-time job for the typical American child," said Dr. Drew Altman, president of the Kaiser Family Foundation.

In previous chapters we examined media development, characteristics, and issues primarily from a technological perspective. Here we will look more closely at how various entertainment genres evolved within their specific media. We will also examine how digital media and the Internet are affecting entertainment within each of these media types.

Television

Out of the five and a half hours a day children between 2 and 18 years old spend using media, almost half that time (2 hours, 46 minutes) is spent watching television. If this trend continues, by the time today's teens are 75 years old, they will have spent over 12 full years of their lives watching television.

Television as a mass medium is just over 50 years old, yet it has become the most common mode in which we receive our news, entertainment, and advertising, despite numerous critics of the medium. The late drama critic John Mason Brown said that "some television programs are so much chewing gum for the eyes." The passivity that TV seems to induce in viewers, and the realism by which it can portray events (so that viewers can mistake those events for reality rather than fiction), are two common complaints about television.

Although television viewers from 1953 would be likely to be impressed with wide-screen, high-definition television; surround sound; and the multitude of channels to choose from, they would readily recognize many of the types of programming—and they might even be able to see some of the programs or movies they watched 50 years ago.

The Golden Age: Television's First Decade of Programming

The late 1940s and 1950s saw the emergence of innovative programming that not only adapted programs from other media, but introduced quality programs of a variety of types. Many of the programs of this period were performed and broadcast live, largely because the only effective recording medium at the time was film, and film processing was slow and expensive. It was not until improved magnetic tape recording was developed in the late 1950s and subsequently diffused in the 1960s that recorded television programs became the norm.

Much early TV programming came directly from radio, where talented actors and comedians such as Jack Benny had begun their careers. These performers adapted their routines in radio for television. The Broadway stage also lent much to early television. Hollywood studios initially resisted putting movies on television, because they felt that threatened their control over the movie distribution system. They also promised to blacklist actors who acted for television studios. After several years of legal battles, studios finally realized that television could be another revenue source in the movie distribution chain after movies had played themselves out in second- and third-run movie theaters.

The first decade of television programming is often referred to as "The Golden Age" of television because of the many successful programs that were produced then. Many of the programs created during this period were critically acclaimed commercial successes. They have established themselves as classics, shown time and again to new generations of viewers who still enjoy and watch the programs.

Among the most memorable entertainment shows to emerge in television's Golden Age was *The Ed Sullivan Show,* originally called *Toast of the Town,* which debuted in June 1948. The show established the format for a variety series and continued on CBS until 1971, frequently with 50 percent of all U.S. television households tuned to the show. In 1964, the show introduced the British pop group the Beatles to America, a show that attracted 73 million viewers nationwide. Milton Berle made his TV debut in September 1948 as the master of ceremonies on *The Texaco Star Theater.* Berle's show earned the highest ratings for the new medium: 86.7 percent of all TV households.

The 1950s witnessed the rise of television as a medium of mass communication in the United States. The post-war generation was the first to grow up with

The Ed Sullivan Show debuted in 1948 and stayed on the air until 1971. The variety show frequently had 50 percent of the television audience tuning in.

the medium, and many of the programs of that period have become classics. Among the most enduring programs are Jackie Gleason's *The Honeymooners*; Rod Serling's *The Twilight Zone*; *I Love Lucy,* the first half-hour filmed TV sitcom; the children's show *Howdy Doody*; *The Tonight Show*, NBC's late-night talk show, now hosted by Jay Leno; and *Gunsmoke,* a classic Western.

The 1960s: The Birth of PBS

The Public Broadcasting Service (PBS) began in 1969 after being authorized by the Public Broadcasting Act of 1967, and in November 1969 launched *Sesame Street,* one of the most influential programs for children on TV then and today.

The British Broadcasting Corporation (BBC), another important public broadcasting service, was started in the United Kingdom in 1936. The BBC was based on a very different funding model than in the United States. The BBC receives an annual fee collected by the government in the form of a broadcasting tax levied on all TV and radio receivers. PBS, on the other hand, depends on a combination of annual federal appropriations, corporate sponsorships, and private viewer contributions. The BBC model of supporting public broadcasting has never been adopted in the United States, although the system in the United Kingdom has produced high-quality public television programming.

The Public Broadcasting Service operates as a private, not-for-profit corporation owned by its member stations. In 2001, there were some 350 PBS member television stations in all 50 states, Puerto Rico, Guam, and the U.S. Virgin Islands. In 1997–1998, PBS programs won more Peabody Awards than any of the commercial broadcast or cable networks and one-third of the duPont–Columbia Awards for television and radio journalism; and its children's programming, such as *Sesame Street* and *Mr. Rogers,* won more Daytime Emmys than any other shows on broadcast and cable networks.

The 1970s: Pushing the Programming Envelope

The 1970s saw a number of significant program developments. Among them were programs of various formats that introduced more complex, realistic characters into formerly one-dimensional program genres. The highest-rated program of the decade was *All in the Family,* a controversial situation comedy that used a bigoted character, Archie Bunker, to address many of the social, gender, and civil rights issues that were being discussed in society. In today's politically correct environment, it is unlikely a show such as *All in the Family,* with its racial stereotypes and slurs, would appear on network television, even if it was intended to be satirical.

Other notable developments in the 1970s included the 1977 ABC airing of its 26-hour miniseries *Roots,* based on the novel by Alex Haley. The January 30 episode became the third most-watched TV program in history.

The 1980s: The MTV Generation

The growing availability of cable and satellite television threatened the programming dominance the three networks had enjoyed since television first became a mass medium. Suddenly viewers found themselves with programming choices far beyond three network channels and public television. The networks were generally slow to respond to this growing threat to their audience by introducing innovative programming of their own, choosing to instead offer variations of tried-and-true formulas.

One exception was a new genre of gritty police drama introduced in September 1980 on NBC by producer Steven Bochco called *Hill Street Blues.* The show had several prominent characters, all with various storylines and a realistic, often chaotic quality that added dramatic elements of soap operas to the story. Bochco continued to evolve the genre in the 1990s with ABC's *NYPD Blue.*

Music Television, or MTV, debuted in 1981 as a cable channel, showing the music video "Video Killed the Radio Star." MTV has not only dramatically changed how music is promoted, but it has continued to introduce innovative, although not always culture-enhancing, programs in the 1990s such as *Real World, Jackass,* and in 2002, *The Osbournes.* Since the debut of MTV, many critics have charged that oftentimes the emphasis in music is now on the video and not on the quality of music. But the music video format has proven popular, and since the launch of MTV a variety of other music channels have emerged, devoted to specific music genres.

What MTV represented and was part of was a sea change in television programming, from a limited, one-size-fits-all approach as on network television, to a fragmented and specialized programming approach on cable or satellite television. Channels devoted to travel, sports, movie classics, television classics, cartoons,

MTV's 24-hour format of music videos changed not only aspects of television, but how music was promoted as well.

science, science fiction, animals, law, history, even specific sports such as golf, are now common on cable or satellite TV.

Reflecting the growing Latin American population in the United States, in the 1980s the Reliance Capital Group launched the Spanish-language television network Telemundo Group. Cable and satellite television have also encouraged the growth of more channels that target certain ethnic groups, as well as giving groups access to some programming from their ancestral home countries.

Today: Cable Starts to Get Respect

With the increased fragmentation of the television viewing audience, it is perhaps bitterly ironic to the networks to see some cable channels such as HBO—which is only in about 30 million homes, or a third of the number that get network television and the big cable channels—attract more viewers for some original programming than many network shows. On September 15, 2002, the fourth-season premiere of HBO's hit Mob series *The Sopranos* attracted 13.4 million viewers, making it the most-watched show in the history of the cable channel. Not only that, but *The Sopranos* attracted the most viewers of any show that Sunday night, while placing fifth overall in viewership for the week. One senior network executive told the *New York Times* that the *Sopranos* results "should make everybody else nervous about their Sunday night shows this season." HBO had already been making original feature films for several years, but their original series such as *The Sopranos, Six Feet Under*, and *Sex and the City,* the latter two each drawing between 7 and 8 million viewers, and all winning several Emmy awards, are making the networks finally take notice of cable television programming.

It is not just an "only on HBO" phenomenon, either. The FX Channel is trying to generate its own buzz with cutting-edge programming and attracted 5 million viewers for the premiere episode of its police drama *The Shield*. The Learning Channel (TLC), hardly on the networks' radar a few years ago, is now attracting 6 million viewers a week for its Saturday night reality decorating series *Trading Spaces*—about six times what some shows on the networks average for Saturday night viewers.

Critics of network television programming say the networks have only themselves to blame for large-scale defections of viewers to cable channels. They cite a risk-averse corporate culture among television networks that encourages copying popular programming types rather than trying to be innovative. They also charge that networks became complacent because they knew that most viewers had nothing else to watch. However, cable TV programming can be more innovative and edgy because cable companies do not have the same content restrictions from the FCC that broadcast networks face, as users of public and limited electromagnetic spectrum. Another factor that works against networks is their need to attract as large an audience as possible in order to charge higher rates for commercials, something that subscriber-based channels such as HBO do not have to consider.

Types of Programming

In the early days of television, several enduring television programming types were either refined from their radio formats or were developed originally for TV. These included hosted children's shows, variety shows, situation comedies, dramatic anthologies, Western series, sports, and news talk shows. These various program types laid the foundation for the development of three broad programming categories, which eventually emerged as formal divisions within the commercial television networks. These three divisions are entertainment, sports, and news.

We will examine entertainment and sports here and show how these types of programming differ from each other, such as their varying production requirements. Although there are some "location" shoots in entertainment shows, they generally require studio space and involve extensive script preparation and postproduction, such as editing. Sports often involves live coverage of unscripted competitive sporting events.

Changes in Media, Changes in Programming   Some programming has survived for decades across media, but because of the rise of the multichannel universe of cable, satellite, and other new media, many are now facing extinction or undergoing revolutions. An example is the **soap opera,** one of the staples of radio programming that has endured on television. Soaps, as they are called, were so named not because of the content of the programs, but because first on radio and then on television, the principal advertising sponsors were soap and other household products aimed at the daytime serial programs' primary audience, homemakers. *The Guiding Light* is the oldest soap, having begun on radio in 1937 and shown on television since 1952. As a production of Procter & Gamble Productions, *The Guiding Light* and other long-running soaps, such as P & G's *As the World Turns* (on the air since 1956), have for decades appealed primarily to the women who stayed at home both to raise their children and to maintain their homes. Procter & Gamble is, of course, one of the world's largest makers of household products, especially cleaning materials.

But the 1990s brought profound changes to the soaps and their audiences and sponsors. One by one, the soaps have died as their audiences have shrunk, as more women entered the workforce. After 8891 episodes and 35 years on the air, NBC's *Another World* ended its run in 1999. Ratings show that the soaps have lost a quarter of their audience since the 1980s. P & G Productions once produced 13 soap operas and now is down to two. Two of the five weekly publications that covered the soaps have ceased publication, and no new English-language soaps have been introduced during the 1990s.

Soaps have also lost audience to the Internet, where many teens who might have once watched soaps now log onto their favorite Web sites. Some teens who enjoy episodic domestic drama also watch MTV's real-world soap opera, *The Real World*, which offers up the romantic intrigue of real-life 20-somethings.

Many fans wax nostalgic over the loss of soaps such as *Another World*, pointing out that the show set important new standards for daytime television by introducing discussion of topics such as abortion and illegitimate pregnancy. The show also introduced some of today's biggest movie and television stars, such as Morgan Freeman, Kelsey Grammer, Anne Heche, Ray Liotta, and Brad Pitt.

Filling the Days   One of the greatest sensations in commercial television's first full decade was the game or quiz show, a format that had been successful in radio as well. Nearly everyone with a television set in his or her home tuned in each week to a favorite quiz show. These shows drew enormous audiences partly

soap opera—a type of programming that began on radio and successfully moved to television but that is now threatened with the rise of media types and changes in lifestyles. Soap operas are dramatic story series involving numerous characters and aimed at a daytime audience of homemakers.

because it was easy to identify with the contestants, many of whom came from ordinary walks of life, and the stakes were large. By the end of the 1958 TV season, there were 22 network quiz shows, or one of every five shows. It turned out that many of the quiz shows were rigged, and after a public scandal involving the popular quiz show *Twenty-One* and a Congressional investigation, new rules for regulating game shows emerged.

Like soaps, game shows during daytime programming have been in decline as other types of programming that is cheaper to produce, such as talk shows, replace them. Today the only daytime game show is the long-running *The Price Is Right,* with host Bob Barker. Talk shows such as Oprah, Jenny Jones, Rikki Lake, and Jerry Springer have taken much of the role that soaps used to play in bringing controversial or sensitive issues to the public arena as guests talk about a wide range of personal issues.

Filling the Nights The popularity of the prime time game show was revived when ABC's *Who Wants to Be a Millionaire* became a ratings leader after its debut in 1999. Although its success was relatively short-lived, getting cancelled after only three years, it helped spawn a number of other prime time shows that followed a game show or quiz show format. Notably, some of the most popular game shows were copies of shows that originated in Europe, as did *Who Wants to Be a Millionaire.* Other foreign imports included *Survivor* and the short-lived *The Weakest Link* with its acerbic British hostess Anne Robinson. This reversed a long trend of European television programming copying successful game shows from the United States. Despite the rapid fall and disappearance of some of the prime time game shows, others that have appeared before prime time have proved more long-lasting, such as *Jeopardy!* and *Wheel of Fortune.*

It is hard to say exactly what caused the resurgence of interest in the prime time quiz and game shows, but one factor is that the new shows have raised the

Long-running evening quiz show *Jeopardy* has outlasted many others that offered higher prizes or that used gimmicks to attain their popularity.

Truth or Consequences was a popular NBC radio quiz show during the 1940s and 1950s that later became one of the earliest television quiz shows. The show's producer, Ralph Edwards, wanted to celebrate the show's tenth anniversary in 1950 in a special way and thought it would be interesting if the citizens of a town in the United States respected the show so much that they would be willing to name their town after the show.

Hot Springs, New Mexico, a small desert spa town on Interstate 25 between El Paso and Albuquerque, decided that changing their name could be the boost the sleepy resort town could use, and after a vote a majority of the citizens agreed. In 1950 Edwards brought the *Truth or Consequences* radio show to Truth or Consequences, New Mexico, for a live broadcast.

Two subsequent referendums in the 1960s on whether to keep the Truth or Consequences name both passed, and every year Edwards visits the town with Hollywood friends to celebrate the anniversary of their name change (and to generate publicity for the town), even though the radio show has long been off the air.

stakes considerably, with contestants potentially winning millions of dollars. Another factor is the potential for viewers to interact, albeit still in a limited way, with the shows through the Web. Although the shows of course thoroughly screen contestants, they are not professional actors, which gives the shows a sense of credibility that allows viewers to imagine themselves as participants.

Prime time network programming is dominated by dramatic series and situation comedies, with occasional made-for-TV movies or broadcasts of popular movies that had appeared in theaters. This latter venue has become less important than it once was, however, as many viewers choose to see uncut movies without commercial interruptions on videotape or cable.

Sports   Today, sports and television are almost synonymous. Some of the biggest television events involve sports, such as the Super Bowl, which annually draws one of television's largest audiences in the United States. Every four years the World Cup, the quadrennial soccer tournament, draws one of the largest worldwide television audiences. Television commentator Les Brown explains that sports is considered by many the perfect program form for television. "At once topical and entertaining, performed live and suspensefully without a script, peopled with heroes and villains, full of action and human interest and laced with pageantry and ritual. The medium and the events have become so intertwined that playing rules often are altered for the exigencies of TV."[3]

One of the most enduring sports programs launched in the 1960s was the ABC sports anthology *Wide World of Sports*. Broadcast on Saturday afternoons, the program debuted in 1961, carrying a wide range of sports, from fringe sports such as ping pong to mainstream events such as auto racing. Today sports-only cable channels such as ESPN provide even more venues to show a variety of sports that otherwise would not have a large audience.

Sports has also been an ongoing venue for technical experimentation. The introduction of instant replay in the early 1960s added a new dimension to televised sports during its debut in a telecast of an Army–Navy football game. In

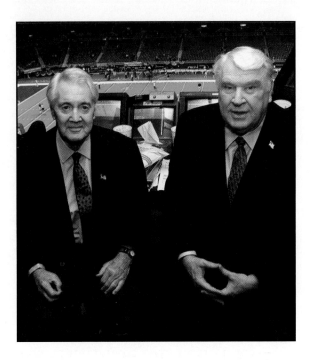

Pat Summerall (left) and John Madden (right) were two of the more popular sports commentators for NFL football.

1964 it became a standard technique and continues to play an important though controversial role in the NFL. Advances in video and audio technologies have led to miniature cameras, allowing viewers to see what referees see on the field, for example, or to hear selected sounds of a baseball game when a player or manager has a microphone attached to them. Some digital cable channels allow viewers to select various static camera angles during a game, in effect giving them simple directorial control over what they watch.

Professional wrestling offers a blend of sports entertainment that has proved popular over the years, although its popularity seems to rise and wane in cycles. In the late 1990s and early 2000s it reached a peak of popularity and commercial success with the World Wrestling Federation (WWF), a company headed by Vincent McMahon. McMahon's genius was to more or less admit that the bouts were staged (although it was obvious that the wrestlers did take actual physical punishment) and to add ample doses of sexuality, show business flash, and character-driven storylines from week to week with himself and a few cronies cast as the crooked bad guys who cheated popular wrestlers of their rightful titles.

Revenues for the WWF company in the fiscal year ending April 2002 were $422 million, up more than fivefold from $81.9 million in 1997. Most of this increase came from television revenues, especially from advertising on cable television and pay-per-view buys at between $10 and $20 per ticket, which increased from 2.25 million in 1997 to more than 6 million in 2002. Professional wrestling had a marked drop in popularity after the events of September 11, and McMahon's failed attempt to establish a new professional football league called the XFL, which ended after only one season, hurt company earnings. Professional wrestling is a controversial form of entertainment, however, as critics say it glamorizes violence while some of its mostly young male fans injure themselves as they attempt similar wrestling techniques at home with friends.

Questionable Programming

Although it is popular to complain about the poor quality of television programs, some programs draw more criticism than others. Outlandish television talk show host Jerry Springer brought television to new depths of vulgarity as he encouraged and sometimes choreographed on-air fights between guests. Radio shock-jock Howard Stern had two different controversial television shows, both eventually cancelled, that featured adolescent sexual humor and strange guests.

Bill Maher's celebrity argue fest on various social and political topics, *Politically Incorrect,* was cancelled at the end of the season by ABC in 2001 after Maher made a comment when the United States started bombing Afghanistan that military leaders were cowards. Although he apologized for the comment and said it had been misunderstood, ABC did not reinstate the show.

MTV has had its share of controversial programming as well. *Jackass,* in which members of the public perform stupid and sometimes dangerous stunts, has been criticized for encouraging reckless behavior. One female victim of one of the show's pranks sued the show in October 2002, even as *Jackass: The Movie* topped box office charts the first week of its release that same month.

Movies

Despite competition from a variety of other media sources, movies continue to play a large role in entertainment. From a high of 510 films released in U.S. theaters in 1997, the number has dropped to 482 films released in 2001—almost the same number that were released in 1950. Predictions that movie theaters would close as people stayed home with cable television, large-screen, high-definition television sets, and surround sound, have proven unfounded, although it took until 1996 for the number of films released each year to reach the level of 1950.

Going to movies is as much a social activity as it is a mass media entertainment activity, as it gives theater-goers an entertainment environment that even the best home entertainment center cannot match. One sign of this is that single adults attend more movies than married adults do, according to MPAA Worldwide Market Research.

In 2001, gross box office receipts in the United States rose almost 10 percent from the previous year, reaching an all-time high of $8.41 billion, according to research done by the Motion Picture Association of America (MPAA). Keep in mind that this is only what was made at U.S. movie theaters and does not include additional income from foreign box office sales (which make up 40 percent of the total revenues for Hollywood movies), videotape sales and rentals, and other income sources such as soundtrack CDs or books that were derived from movies.

People 40 and older continue to be the largest group of movie-goers, making up 40 percent of the total audience in 2001. However, the percentage of people 12 to 24 years old rose to 30 percent in 2001, equal to the percentage of 25-to-39-year-olds. Teens are an important part of the movie-going audience because they attend movies more frequently than older people. Fifty-one percent of teens 12 to 17 years old reported they go to movies at least once a month, while only 24 percent of people 18 and over said they did.

With whole cable television channels devoted to almost nothing but films—such as the Independent Film Channel, Turner Movie Classics, American Movie

Although other forms of entertainment have eclipsed revenues from box office receipts, movies continue to play an important part in the entertainment landscape.

Classics, Home Box Office, Cinemax, and Showtime—in addition to commercial and cable channels frequently (and repeatedly) showing movies, a movie may remain as part of the entertainment landscape long after it has left the theaters.

Movies are not the leading entertainment force they were before television and the Internet, however. Today, movies are often created from popular television programs, plays, books, and even video games. The movie version of a novel, game, or show can often drive increased interest in the original version and spur it to have a renewed life of its own for a time.

Film Genres

There are a variety of types, or **genres,** of film content in modern cinema. These genres help to define the character of the cinema industry and reflect both public tastes as well as approaches to filmmaking around the world and among different types of filmmakers. Two basic distinctions are between nonfiction films, or documentaries, and fiction films. Fiction films are by far the dominant type, and it is rare in the United States for documentaries to be shown in multiplex cinemas. If they are released theatrically at all, they are shown mostly in urban art-house theaters to limited audiences.

Among the most familiar and popular genres of fiction film are action/adventure, comedies, romance, science fiction, suspense, historical, horror, Western, fantasy, musical, biography, and drama. In many cases there are subgenres, such as crime drama, and some films cut across two or more genres, such as romantic comedy.

A variety of forces influence filmmaking. Economics, technology, audience tastes, and many other factors all influence the subjects, styles, and substance of film. Three important influences are examined here: the film director as auteur, technological influences on movie genres and popularity, and other media entertainment as sources for movies.

The Director as Auteur

French film critic Andre Bazin in the years after World War II introduced the notion of the filmmaker as author, or **auteur,** of his or her films. Although some

genre—a type of story that has recognizable and defined elements, usually with the same types of characters, plot development, and story structure.

auteur—French for *author,* this term is usually used in the context of filmmakers who stamp their vision on the films they make, as opposed to a form of filmmaking in which the director has but one role among many other professionals in the making of a film.

of the early filmmakers such as D.W. Griffith and Sergei Eisenstein could be seen as auteurs of their films, in the intervening years filmmaking became much more of a collaborative, corporate enterprise, a trend promoted by Hollywood's studio system, in which directors, actors, screenwriters, and others involved in filmmaking had assigned tasks within the overall process.

The French New Wave directors in the 1950s helped in popularizing the concept of director as auteur, and a number of important French directors emerged during this period. These included Jean Luc Godard, who made *Breathless* (1959); Louis Malle, who made *Zazie dans le metro* (1960); and Francois Truffaut, who made *The 400 Blows* (1959). These directors used camera techniques innovative for their day, such as hand-held cameras and freeze frames, which have now become common in many films.

Swedish filmmaker Ingmar Bergman is another of the great international film auteurs whose work has left a lasting impression. *The Seventh Seal* (1957), *The Virgin Spring* (1960), and *Wild Strawberries* (1957) are among his greatest and darkest masterpieces.

One of the most influential international film auteurs was Japanese director Akira Kurosawa. One of his greatest films, *Rashomon* (1951), tells the story of a woman's rape and murder from the perspective of four characters. Some of Kurosawa's other early films, such as *Seven Samurai* (1954), were remade by others as Westerns. *Seven Samurai* became *The Magnificent Seven* (1960) starring Yul Brynner and Steve McQueen, and *Yojimbo* (1961) was remade in 1964 by Sergio Leone as *A Fistful of Dollars*, starring Clint Eastwood, becoming a worldwide hit. Two characters in the classic *The Hidden Fortress* (1958) are said to be the models from which director George Lucas, a great admirer of Kurosawa and Japanese cinema, based his C3PO and R2D2 robot characters and relationship in *Star Wars* (1977). Kurosawa also borrowed from the West in making his films. Two of his films, *Throne of Blood* (1957) and *Ran* (1985), are based on Shakespeare's plays (*Macbeth* and *King Lear*, respectively).

A number of important American filmmakers have also contributed to the auteur movement in cinema. Among them are Blake Edwards, who directed *Days of Wine and Roses* (1962), and Stanley Kubrick, who directed *2001: A Space Odyssey* (1968), *Dr. Strangelove* (1964), and *Eyes Wide Shut* (1999), his final film. Other notable contemporary American film auteurs include Martin Scorsese, whose films include *Taxi Driver* (1976), *The King of Comedy* (1983), and *The Age of Innocence* (1993); David Lynch, who made *Eraserhead* (1977), *Blue Velvet* (1986), and *Wild at Heart* (1990); and Spike Lee, whose movie *Do the Right Thing* (1988) examines the sensitive topic of race relations in the context of a Brooklyn pizzeria suffering from the strain of a very hot summer in New York City, and who also directed *Summer of Sam* (1999).

Also worth noting is the reemergence of important documentary work in the late 1980s and 1990s. Michael Moore's *Roger and Me* (1989) provides a window into the commercial motivations and interests of Ford in Moore's hometown of Flint, Michigan. *Bowling for Columbine* (2002) is a documentary that examined with a critical eye the widespread availability of guns in the United States.

Documentary filmmaker Michael Moore, director of films such as *Roger and Me* and the Academy Award–winning *Bowling for Columbine*.

Technological Influences on Movie Genres

Technology has always influenced filmmaking, from the times that short film reels only allowed films of five minutes or less, which hampered creation of complex stories, to the development of synchronized sound in film that made the cameras stationary and changed movies from action-oriented to speaking-oriented styles.

Today, digital technologies allow filmmakers to make entire worlds realistically and to even populate those worlds with lifelike characters. George Lucas, with his *Star Wars* movies, is at the forefront of using computers to create spectacular special effects, although critics charge this is often at the expense of good old-fashioned storytelling and character development. Likewise, digital technology has allowed for more realistic animations, and studios such as Disney and Pixar are utilizing the fact that animated movies now are much less labor-intensive (although it is still questionable how much money is saved after the costs for high-end computer systems is factored in to the budget) than they used to be and have made several successful animated feature films for young audiences.

New technologies also can have an effect on what movies are popular. High-tech gadgetry in our daily lives and today's fast-paced media environment have parallels to many of the science-fiction and technology-oriented movies that have been coming out. Slower-paced, character-driven movies based on historical events have less appeal to younger audiences. Plots can also be interpreted differently because of changes in technology. A suspense movie made in the 1980s in which tension is created by the main character's difficulties in finding a public telephone would likely make young viewers today wonder why the character doesn't simply use his or her cell phone or borrow someone else's to make the call.

Other Entertainment Sources For Movies

Movies have always relied heavily on other media as their sources for stories. Some of the earliest films were nothing more than filmed stage plays, including Shakespearean dramas. Other movies took their inspiration from popular novels or stories, as many movies do today.

It used to be that successful original movies would sometimes lead to the creation of TV series based on the movie, such as *M*A*S*H* (1970) and the subsequent television series of the same name that ran from 1972 to 1983—eight years longer than the Korean War, the time frame in which the story took place. Although it still occasionally occurs, such as with TV's *Highlander* series that originated from the *Highlander* movie series, today movies are equally as likely to derive their inspiration from popular TV series, video games, cartoons, and even the Web.

Although *Spider-Man* (2002) was a huge success, many other movies that have been created from TV, comics, or video games have not been nearly as successful. In the past several years a spate of movies based on popular television sitcoms and cartoons were released, such as two *The Addams Family* (1991, 1998) films, *The Beverly Hillbillies* (1993), two *The Brady Bunch* movies (1995, 1996), and *Scooby-Doo* (2002), with another *Scooby-Doo* movie planned for release in 2004.

The movie *Undercover Brother* (2002), a parody on blaxploitation films of the 1970s, was one of the first movies derived from an animated series that originated on the Web, on a site called Urban Entertainment. A bidding war started among studios for the rights to make a movie of *Undercover Brother,* showing how studios are mining the creative resources that appear on the Web for story ideas. The Web also allows studios to see how popular animations or stories may be as news of an entertaining animated series or story spreads over the Internet without traditional marketing efforts.

Tapping other media sources for movie material is not without its pitfalls, however, as any disappointed reader can say after watching a movie version of a favorite novel. The medium invariably not only changes how scenes may appear, but also can change the order of scenes and even alter characters or remove some completely. This happens for a variety of reasons. Sometimes the producers see a different vision for the film than what the book emphasized, usually much material must be cut out to keep the movie within a standard 90-minute or 2-hour time frame, and often studio politics plays a role as studios alter storylines and characters to make the movie appeal to the widest possible audience.

Studios have tried to cash in on the popularity of some video games, such as *Super Mario Bros.* or *Tomb Raider,* by either making movies based on the games or making the game characters the main characters in the story. *Super Mario Bros.* (1993) did poorly at the box office, and although critics panned *Lara Croft: Tomb Raider* (2001), it did well enough to spawn a sequel for 2003. Exciting special effects, fast-paced action, and the fact that Angelina Jolie as Lara Croft is more interesting to watch than Bob Hoskins as Mario Mario probably had something to do with *Tomb Raider's* greater success. Experts in the video game industry doubt that video games can be successfully transplanted to movies, however. Steven Poole, author of *Trigger Happy: Videogames and the Entertainment Revolution,* says that the very things that make video games so

Weblink
Urban Entertainment
[www.urbanentertainment.com]

Angelina Jolie played Lara Croft in the movie *Tomb Raider,* from the video game of the same name. Hollywood is using popular video games as sources for movies.

addictive and popular—their interactive nature and fact that the user to some extent controls the flow of the story, such as it is—are taken away from movie-goers, who must sit passively and watch what their favorite characters do.

Videotapes and DVDs

It is estimated by Nielsen Media Research that in 2001 96.2 million U.S. households out of 105.5 million households with TVs, or 91.2 percent, had VCRs. On average, children watch videos 39 minutes a day, fourth after watching TV, listening to music, and reading for fun.

The movie industry strongly resisted the introduction of consumer video cassette recorder models when they first became available in the 1970s, even taking VCR manufacturer Sony to court for encouraging copyright infringement, claiming that videocassettes would ruin the movie industry as people illegally copied movies. This of course did not happen, and in fact video sales and rentals now bring in more revenue for studios than box office receipts. In 2001, consumers spent a record $16 billion buying and renting videos, up 21 percent over 2000 and double the revenue from box office receipts.

The lower production costs for videotape created new opportunities for filmmakers who would not otherwise have a chance to make movies that would be distributed as feature films. Some movies are made with the intention of going straight to video, while others that have not fared well at the box office go to video sooner than popular movies. One area of entertainment that has changed dramatically because of videotape has been that of adult entertainment.

Adult Entertainment

Adult, or sexually oriented, entertainment has been a significant subject of photography and film since the early days of the industry. In the digital age, adult entertainment is proving to be among the most important money makers.

The rising popularity of VCRs in the home meant that people did not have to visit an adult movie theater to watch pornographic movies; they could rent them and watch them in their own homes. Some commentators have noted that this may have played a factor in making VCRs more popular. Video also changed the nature of adult movie-making, as most adult movies were shot on video rather than film, which made them much cheaper to produce, edit, and distribute.

By the mid-1990s, the adult movie business had become quite large, with 8000 titles released in 1996 and adult movie rentals producing $3.1 billion in revenue.[4] The advent of digital technology, which made movie production substantially less expensive, brought further financial success to the adult movie business. Moreover, with online distribution of adult movies making it even easier for viewers to see adult entertainment, the U.S. pornographic movie business grew to $10 billion in annual revenues in 2001, with adults spending $4 billion annually on graphic sex videos rented from video outlets and another $800 million a year on milder sex videos. Pay-per-view adult movies on satellite and cable television generated a combined $545 million revenues in 2001, with digital, direct broadcast satellite making up the majority ($324 million, or 60 percent).[5]

DVDs

DVDs, or digital versatile disks (also called digital video disks), are likely to completely replace videocassettes as the primary portable storage medium for watching entertainment. Not only are they more compact, they are also not as subject to wearing down or breaking as videotape cassettes are after repeated viewing. DVD players are now in 25 percent of U.S. homes, reaching a level of market penetration faster than any other consumer electronics product. In 2001, consumers spent $6 billion on DVD purchases and rentals combined, and DVD sales outpaced videotape sales for the first time—an extraordinary accomplishment given that only 25 million households have DVD players as opposed to the 96 million households with VCRs.

Like video, the primary purpose of DVDs is to watch movies, and the added features DVDs provide in terms of behind-the-scenes looks at the making of a movie, interviews with directors and actors, multilingual capabilities for viewing, and other features make DVDs an attractive format for watching movies at home. DVDs are still so new that it is unclear what impact they may have in shaping how movies are made or what movies are made, but for the time being it is likely that studios will continue to simply add extra material or outtakes to DVDs so the audience feels as though they have the opportunity to watch more than just the movie.

Video Games

Children spend an average of 20 minutes a day playing video games, according to the Kaiser Family Foundation report "Kids & Media @ the New Millennium," although another study by a video game industry group says they play video games for up to 90 minutes a day. Video game and hardware sales were $9.3 billion in 2001, outranking for the first time the amount spent on movies at the box office. The *Mario Bros.* video game is set to surpass the $10 billion revenue mark by the end of 2002, 19 years after its first release in the game *Donkey Kong*, making Mario's earnings higher than megastars such as Harrison Ford.[6]

Massively multiplayer online games (MMOGs) have proven very popular, and video game makers are looking to move toward online games rather than console-based games.

Video Games: When Fantasy and Reality Collide

Many people who play video games say they are addictive, but they usually mean it only in the figurative sense. But for some people, they truly are addictive in all senses of the word.

A Wisconsin woman blamed the game *EverQuest* for the March 2002 suicide of her 21-year-old son, who had a history of mental health problems and who was an obsessive *EverQuest* player. In 2001, the game was linked to the death of an infant in Tampa, Florida, whose father reportedly played the game so much he fatally neglected his son. There have been cases of people losing their jobs and spouses because of playing the game. Some have dubbed it "Evercrack" because of its addictive nature.

"It's a huge and growing problem with older teenage males and young adult males," said Dr. Timothy Miller, a Stockton, California, clinical psychologist. "I've seen a number of cases with 17- or 18-year-old males where they have a broadband (Internet) connection and they basically haven't left the house for years. I had one young man who was trying to get on Social Security disability for agoraphobia," he said. "He didn't have a mental disorder; he just didn't want to leave *EverQuest* or instant messaging."[7]

According to mental health experts, signs of addiction include:

- Inability to stop the activity or playing much longer than anticipated.
- Neglect of family and friends.
- Lying to employers and family about activities.
- Problems with school or job.
- Carpal tunnel syndrome.
- Dry eyes.
- Failure to attend to personal hygiene.
- Sleep disturbances or changes in sleep patterns.

Psychologists say that part of the reason online games like *EverQuest* are so addictive is that they give people who feel as though they do not fit into regular society a chance to interact easily with others and to redefine themselves.

What responsibility do video game makers have when their fans become addicted to their games, if any? What steps may be taken to minimize risks of video game addiction in this relatively new entertainment format?

---

massively multiplayer online games (MMOGs)—a type of video game played online with tens of thousands of other players who are also online. The format allows for real-time communication and trading items, as well as fighting each other or working together toward common goals.

Video games are dominated by Sony's Playstation, Nintendo, and Microsoft's Xbox, with a much smaller percentage going to computer games. The most popular games are usually fast-paced action or sports games in which multiple players can play against each other. However, that format is being challenged by **massively multiplayer online games (MMOGs)** such as Sony's *EverQuest* or Funcom's *Anarchy Online*. In these types of games, players adopt roles and go online to engage in quests or missions, working with others online in real-time using chats and text messaging to join in teams, fight with or against each other, and gain treasure or experience. After purchasing the game on a CD, players must pay between $13 to $20 a month to keep playing. Console video game makers see this area as one with lots of potential and are moving to establish their own MMOGs. *EverQuest*, the most popular MMOG to date, has 430,000 players.

Many game-related Web sites have very active discussion groups in which fans of a particular game help each other with questions, trade tips or taunts, and complain about aspects of the game they do not like. This is the kind of dedication to an entertainment product that many other media companies would love to have, but it is not without its dangers (see the Real World Ethics Dilemma).

Despite the potential pitfalls of creating movies from popular video games, as mentioned earlier, Hollywood continues to hope to capitalize on the popularity of some games. In August 2002 it was announced that Columbia Pictures had bought the rights to make a movie based on Activision's popular video game *Return to Castle Wolfenstein*. Many role-playing or first-person video games actually use quite a few cinematic techniques as they develop their storylines, and most video games have cinematic introduction scenes complete with sweeping panoramic views, pans, and complex tracking shots—all computer-generated, of course. Video games that employ some sort of narrative or character development, as opposed to simple shooter or arcade-style games, usually use techniques of plot and character development borrowed from Hollywood genres. The main difference between movies and video games in these cases is that games are interactive and the player has some degree of control as to the fate of his or her character and how the story develops.

Some experts initially thought that the video game market would be inherently limited primarily to young males in their teens or younger. However, as the first generation of young people who grew up with home console video games reach their 20s and 30s, research has shown that they not only keep playing video games, but that females are playing more games than in the past as well. Still, video games remain a primarily youth-oriented, male pastime, although it will be interesting to track how video game playing changes as video game fans age.

Music

Second only to watching television, children spend almost 90 minutes a day on average listening to music, according to the Kaiser Family Foundation. However, some groups such as the Parents Music Resource Center say children spend much more time than that, listening to some 10,500 hours of music between the seventh and twelfth grades—almost one-third of their waking hours. Regardless of the amount of time actually spent, there is no doubt that music plays a large role in the entertainment environment of many people, especially young people. Musical tastes help people define themselves with other social groups and help ease some of the awkwardness young people often feel as they create their self-identities. By imitating clothing and hair styles of certain musicians, people can easily create a public image that gives others a message about who they feel they are or at least who they would like to be.

Music is often playing in the background as people go about their daily activities or are engaged with other types of media such as playing video games or reading. Couples often have "their" song that holds special meaning for them or seems to speak to their particular relationship (despite the fact that the song was written for mass appeal), and many a teen has played air guitar in front of the mirror while listening to (usually) his favorite singer, dreaming of rock stardom.

Music also plays an important role in movies and television, acting as audio cues to viewers on what to expect or feel in particular scenes. The low, threatening music in the movie *Jaws* (1975) whenever the shark was going to appear heightened tension as viewers wondered whom it would strike next. The theme became so well-known that it entered other movies as parody and even daily conversation as people used the theme to humorously denote imminent trouble.

A Brief History of Popular Music: From Tin Pan Alley to Rock and Roll

In the early days of the recorded music industry, much of the popular music in America was generated in New York's historic Tin Pan Alley, an area in Manhattan on West 28th Street between Broadway and Sixth Avenue where music publishers had located to be near the theaters and vaudeville houses. Before record players became widespread, people usually bought sheet music for voice and piano of songs they had heard in vaudeville shows or the theaters so they could play them at home. As the years passed, Tin Pan Alley became a generic reference to the music publishing business that hired composers and lyricists on a permanent basis to write popular songs. Tin Pan Alley continued for about 70 years, until roughly 1950, when radio and television became more important in the promotion of music.

Although there were many great composers during the early days of Tin Pan Alley, from George and Ira Gershwin to Cole Porter, perhaps the one name most synonymous with the time is Irving Berlin. Berlin achieved stardom in 1911 when his song *Alexander's Ragtime Band* became an international hit. He went on to pen such classics as *Blue Skies, God Bless America, White Christmas,* and *There's No Business Like Show Business.* Today he is remembered as one of the greatest songwriters of the 20th century's recorded music industry.

As Hollywood developed and motion pictures with sound emerged in the late 1920s and early 1930s, a recorded music industry also emerged in Los Angeles, where it continues today. Perhaps the greatest songwriter of this era is little known today, although his music is familiar to many. Harry Warren began writing popular hit songs for movies during the Great Depression of the 1930s and wrote such hits as *That's Amore* (recorded by Dean Martin), *Jeepers Creepers, Chattanooga Choo-Choo,* and many other swing classics. Between 1935 and 1950, Warren had 42 hits on *Your Hit Parade* (a popular weekly radio and later television program), nine more than even Irving Berlin.

The emergence of the recording industry and radio in the first half of the century enabled musicians and music fans to hear many musical forms. Both black and white artists created songs with audience crossover appeal and laid the foundation for much of popular music today, including rap and other formats.

Roots of Rock and Roll   The roots of rock and roll lie in a blend of musical forms, including blues-oriented vocalizations, black gospel musical structures, urban rhythm and blues (R&B) instrumentals, and white Western and "hillbilly" strains, or rockabilly. In the late 1940s and early 1950s the combination of country artists such as the Delmore Brothers, Hank Williams, and Tennessee Ernie Ford and R&B artists such as T-Bone Walker, Fats Domino, B. B. King, Ruth Brown, and Muddy Waters helped shape the early character of rock and roll.

Weblink

Charles A. Templeton Sheet Music Collection [library.msstate.edu/ragtime /main.html]

Ray Charles has been an enduring icon on the R&B and rock music scene.

From about 1954 to 1959 rock and roll took form and emerged as a popular sensation, with artists such as Bill Haley & His Comets (Western swing crossover), Ray Charles (gospel/R&B), Elvis Presley (rockabilly), Chuck Berry (R&B), and Buddy Holly (rockabilly) leading the way. Popular rock vocal groups included the Platters, the Penguins, and Dion & The Belmonts, and teen idols such as Frankie Avalon and Brenda Lee.

Rock continued to evolve and in the 1960s rock took a variety of new turns, including soul, "girl groups," Motown, surf rock, and folk rock. Many of these popular groups and musicians had not only a musical impact but also a social influence. They influenced social trends and tastes, from clothing to hair styles, and many of the groups, especially folk rock artists, shaped public thoughts and social movements against the war in Vietnam, to protect the environment, and to expand civil rights. Reflecting his broad social influence and the artistry of his work, in 1997 Bob Dylan was nominated for a Nobel Prize in Literature.

Redefining Rock   Redefining rock in the mid- to late 1960s was "the British invasion," with groups such as the Beatles, the Rolling Stones, and the Who bringing a new level of energy and popularity to rock and roll. It was at this time that experimentation with drugs grew in popularity, both among the young in general and rock musicians in particular, who helped shape popular opinion in this regard. Some new strains of rock emerged, including psychedelic rock, jazz rock, and the beginnings of heavy metal. Forty years later, some of the bands and artists popular in the late 1960s who helped promote youth culture are still touring and performing, even though many of the performers are in their early 60s.

In the 1970s music moved from socially conscious and experimental types to highly produced glam rock or bands like KISS, with their flamboyant make-up and stage shows. Disco also appeared for a brief time in the mid-1970s. Punk rock, which also started in the mid-1970s, was partly a response to the perceived over-commercialization of popular music. The 1980s saw heavy metal music become popular, while pop music from bands like Culture Club and Wham! sang of love and infatuation. Rap music left the urban streets and started to enter mainstream music from the late 1980s but became more widespread in the early 1990s. In the late 1980s and early 1990s Seattle bands such as Nirvana, Soundgarden,

Berry Gordy, Jr.'s, Motown Record Company

When rock and roll started in the 1950s, although much of the music owed its inspiration to black artists, few black musicians reaped any of the rewards. From Elvis Presley to Bill Haley and His Comets, most of the successful rock stars of the day were white. All that changed, thanks to Detroit's Berry Gordy, Jr., and the record company he started, Motown Record Company. Gordy was a musician himself, but as the songwriter of a successful song recorded by Jackie Wilson, he had received few profits.

Gordy decided to try creating his own music recording company in the Motor City, Detroit, his hometown and a city with a historically large black population. With $700 borrowed from his sister and a makeshift studio in the basement, Gordy signed a kid off the street named Smokey Robinson and his backup singers, The Miracles, and started producing their music. The group quickly pro-duced a string of hits, and other successes followed, with Gordy signing and producing the music of Diana Ross and the Supremes, Marvin Gaye, Stevie Wonder, the Jackson Five (with Michael Jackson), and many more talented black artists. By 1983, Motown was the largest black-owned company in the United States, with annual revenues of $104 million. In 1988, Gordy sold Motown to MCA Records.

and Alice in Chains developed a dark sound that has been dubbed alternative or progressive rock.

Musical genres continue to evolve and splinter as they wax and wane in popularity. Sometimes even older musical genres, such as swing, enjoy a short resurgence in popularity. Mainstream country music has come to sound much more like country rock, for example, and some hit songs enjoy popularity on pop and country charts. One element that has changed the music industry in the past 20 years is the development of MTV, or music television.

Music and MTV

The launching of MTV in 1981 provided a new venue for promoting music. The 24-hour format required many music videos to fill the air time, and it changed the nature of how music was promoted and, to a large extent, what artists or bands were promoted. Suddenly, it became just as important how a band looked on television as how they sounded.

Music videos have often been criticized by various groups as promoting sexual or violent imagery, sexism, antisocial behavior, and even Satanism. Studies have shown that viewers like watching music videos more than just listening to music, and when controversial lyrics are combined with controversial video, it is feared that music videos could be teaching young people socially unacceptable messages.

Researchers have reported that between 40 percent and 75 percent of music videos contained sexual imagery, although it was generally mild and nongraphic. Sexism remains strong, however, with over half the women dressed provocatively but only 10 percent of the men dressed so, with women much more likely to be treated as sex objects or dominated by men than the other way around.[8]

New music channels began on cable in the 1990s, including channels devoted to specific genres of music or targeting specific audiences, such as country music

The Dave Matthews Band.

fans or blacks. Because any music video must have interesting visual elements throughout the entire song, it is interesting to ponder what effect music videos may have on slower-paced songs that do not lend themselves to the quick cuts seen in many music videos.

Books and Magazines

Despite the perception among many adults that young people do not read anymore, "reading for fun" was a surprising third on the list in the Kaiser Family Foundation report in terms of amount of time spent each day with media, coming in behind watching TV and listening to music, at 44 minutes a day on average. As with other measures, the study did not differentiate between using one or more media at the same time, so it is likely that some reading took place while listening to music or watching TV or videos.

The portability and inexpensiveness of magazines and, to some extent, books when compared to other entertainment media will likely make them a part of the entertainment landscape for quite some time. Revenues from books in 2001 were $16.5 billion, more than double movie box office receipts and about the same as video tape revenues.

Novels can engage media consumers in their stories as few other media can, because characters, scenes, and situations are pictured in readers' minds. Every genre is available, appealing to a variety of literary (and not so literary) tastes. Magazines help guide people in their social behavior and better understand what the culture deems as standard or normal.

Digital Entertainment

All other types of entertainment mentioned in this chapter can of course be produced, provided, and experienced digitally, and in some cases like video games can be used only in a digital format. Interactivity is really the major unique element that digital entertainment can provide, and it is an important one. Interactivity is best exemplified in the form of video games or online games, but some functions of interactivity could be applied to other media entertainment types as well, even with current technologies.

Distribution and mixing of music using digital technology has become remarkably cheap and easy, much to the chagrin of the major record labels, and similar activities with digital film and video are available as well, although they require more technical skill and bandwidth to work with and distribute. These differences will gradually disappear, however.

Increased interactivity could be a great boon for some types of entertainment while leaving others little changed. Readers may not want an interactive novel, for example, in which they have to frequently choose between plot points to determine the course of the story they are reading; they may well simply want an author they trust and like to give them a tale well told. This is likewise true when watching a movie or television program. In the latter case, interactivity may be best when viewers limit it to mark certain parts of a movie to either learn about something or to click on a part of the screen to order an item, such as a piece of clothing an actor or actress is wearing.

Interactivity may well prove popular in sports programs, as viewers could gather specific statistics and even choose their own camera angles or watch instant replays as they dictate. With frequent pauses and breaks even in fast-paced sports like football, viewers would have many opportunities to conduct such activities as clicking on a player or choosing from a player roster and learning more about the player and his or her statistics.

Take this level of interactivity one step further and apply it to a gaming environment, in which sports fans could communicate with others online while watching a game, even trading players or creating fantasy sports league teams while they watch.

Limited bandwidth continues to hamper full development of the Web as an entertainment medium, although even now full-length videos and films are available online, as well as many original animated short series and of course text-based and audio stories. Humorous Web sites or entertainment have been very popular on the Web, often spreading quickly among Web users by e-mail or word of mouth.

Pornography is also widespread on the Web, and in many ways adult Web sites have led the way in pushing online technology to get better as an entertainment medium. For a monthly subscription fee, members of online pornographic Web sites expect online, on-demand video, and often can chat live with someone with or without a video feed, as well as receiving regularly updated images, video, and stories. Some sites even include interactive pornographic games. Pop-up advertising that is so prevalent on the Web today was started by adult Web sites as they tried to attract users to sponsoring or supporting Web sites. Online pornographic Web sites are some of the very few online businesses that have been earning revenue.

Entertainment Ethics

With the important role that entertainment plays in our lives, an especially sensitive issue that media entertainment companies must constantly deal with is how to mitigate and eliminate messages of negative social values or harmful stereotypes their content may contain. Even apparently minor decisions, such as how some characters dress compared to others, may promote gender or ethnic stereotyping, for example. Repeated viewings of certain ethnic groups or minorities in a bad light or in stereotypical "bad guy" roles may cause an unconscious shift in attitudes among some viewers that all such people are bad.

Portrayals of sex and violence have often been issues for which groups criticize media companies. Although the old adage "sex sells" is usually true, entertainment companies have an ethical responsibility not to pander to baser instincts among the public simply to increase their revenues.

Despite some progress in more balanced, fully developed portrayals of women and ethnic groups, there are still many instances in which media companies fall short. For at least three reasons, the U.S. media industries have often sought to regulate themselves. First, self-regulation can be a responsible form of self-discipline, which can improve the actions of the media. Second, and as a related consequence, in the court of public opinion self-regulation can improve the reputation of the media by signalling a willingness to act responsibly. Third, self-regulation can avoid or reduce the possibility of unwanted government regulation by solving or reducing problems before they produce the need for government action.

The Censorship of Comics

A fascinating historical and continuing case of censorship is the comic book. Popular among both children and adults, comics have long been under the scrutiny of critics in both government and the public. Criticism and censorship reached a peak in the McCarthy-era 1950s when psychologist Frederic Wertham, M.D., published his book, *Seduction of the Innocent,* which contended that the reading of violent and sexually graphic comic books caused juvenile delinquency and worse. Wertham's book captured public and media attention and quickly led to intense pressure from the government and other groups to curtail the graphic sexual and gruesome violent content of comic books, especially the horror comics such as *Tales from the Crypt, Haunt of Fear,* and *Vault of Horror.*

Comics have long been in the forefront of calls for censorship.

Wertham based his argument on his own observations of juvenile delinquents. He found that many delinquents read a lot of comic books, especially horror comics. He also found that many of these kids were poor readers. Wertham therefore concluded that reading comics, especially horror comics, caused both juvenile delinquency and illiteracy. Although his reasoning and methodology were flawed, in response to Wertham's claims the U.S. Senate conducted a full-scale investigation in 1954 into the nature and effects of comics on children.

The Senate did not take any formal legal action against the comics industry. Instead, a consortium of comics publishers called the Association of Comic Magazine Publishers formed the Comics Code Authority (CCA), a sort of industry censorship review board. The CCA began reading every comic book published and effectively put a ban on all sexual and violent content, at least the most graphic material popular in many horror comics of the day, including torture, sadism, and detailed discussion of criminal acts. A CCA seal of approval then was emblazoned on the cover of acceptable comics. As a result of the CCA action, many of the most graphic horror comics were put out of business.

The Motion Picture Production Code of 1930 (the Hays Code)

In 1922, the Motion Picture Producers and Distributors of America (MPPDA) selected President Harding's Administration Postmaster General, Will H. Hays, to supervise the industry's content. The Hays Office, or the "the Hays organization," as it was more commonly known at the time, focused on three areas of film content: violence, sex, and crime. The codes provided the production standards that all films were to adhere to. If they did not, they were not allowed to be shown in theaters that were part of the MPPDA, which included virtually all theaters nationwide.

The Hays code outlined three general moral principles. First among these principles was the intention to prevent any motion picture from being produced that would "lower the moral standards of those who see it. Hence the sympathy

The Hays Code created guidelines for filmmakers that involved depictions of violence, sex, and crime.

of the audience should never be thrown to the side of crime, wrongdoing, evil or sin." Second, every picture was to present "correct standards of life, subject only to the requirements of drama and entertainment." Third, no picture was to ridicule "natural or human" law.

The Code went on to prescribe the proper depiction of content in 12 specific areas, including criminal activity, sex, and religion. By today's standards, although some seem well-intentioned, many of these prescriptions seem quaint, and in some cases are offensive, racist, or at least politically incorrect.

The Hays production code ended in 1968 and was replaced by a voluntary Motion Picture Association rating system including G, M, R, and X, today modified as G, PG, PG-13, R, and NC-17. The movie ratings code has served as a model for industry self-censorship "ratings" for music, television, and computer software.

The entertainment industry is constantly searching for new trends to capitalize on.

The Business of Entertainment

Media entertainment companies have usually been the driving force behind most of the large mergers of media companies that have led to the concentration of media ownership in the past several years. Either they have tried to swallow competitors or other entertainment properties in order to provide more types of entertainment to the public, or they have been swallowed up by larger companies that see their media content as powerful assets in order to enter the media entertainment field.

The entertainment industry touches many more people than simply the various writers, actors, directors, producers, and other creators of entertainment. For television, ratings are extremely important to determine how much can be charged for advertising, and a network that consistently has weak shows and that places third hurts the chances for affiliate stations to earn money through higher advertising prices. In movies, movie theaters and their employees, not to mention all the behind-the-cameras staff ranging from lighting technicians to construction workers, rely on the industry for their jobs. At its peak in 1999, the movie industry alone employed almost 600,000 people. CD and DVD manufacturers, plus jewel case manufacturers, printers, and shippers are counting on the growing popularity of these formats for their livelihoods.

Costs for most mainstream entertainment remain too high to allow for an individual outside of the industry to enter on his or her own with entertainment content. The average cost of movies is now $48 million, and without distribution deals with U.S. theaters, there is little hope of a movie being seen by a mass audience in theaters, even if someone was willing to spend that much to make a movie. Book production costs are far lower, but distribution channels remain extremely limited without a major publisher, and a lack of marketing for any media content would likewise hamper its chances of success.

Although it seems that entertainment would be one of the first items on people's budgets to be cut when economic times are hard, that is not the case. Although some entertainment sectors have downturns in slow economic times, other areas remain immune. For example, during the Great Depression in the 1930s Hollywood still produced many films, offering often escapist fare and musicals to the public.

SUMMARY

We live in an entertainment society. Everywhere we are bombarded with messages trying to get our attention, usually by trying to entertain us. We often talk about entertainment we have seen with friends and family, and entertainment likes and dislikes help us define ourselves as a part of a group or groups within society.

Entertainment plays an important role in transmitting cultural values, although some critics argue that entertainment generally transmits only the values of the dominant societal group at the expense of other groups.

Children and teens 8 to 18 years old spend an average of six hours and 43 minutes using media each day. By far the most common media usage is watching television, at two hours and 43 minutes. This is followed by listening to music, reading for fun, and watching videos. Some media usage takes place simultaneously, so it is difficult to break down separate usage very accurately.

Television has changed from three major networks to a multichannel universe of cable and satellite TV that has fragmented the television audience and eroded the power of the three networks. In recent years, some popular cable shows have eclipsed network shows in terms of numbers of viewers, even though far fewer homes have cable television than have network television.

Although movie box office receipts are smaller than revenues generated from CD sales and even video games, movies have a strong cultural influence as they help generate other media entertainment and filter through the media network from movie theaters to video or DVD, cable channels, and finally to commercial television. Videotapes are starting to be replaced by DVDs, which are more compact, show content with a higher quality, and give the viewer more options to choose from when watching a movie or show.

Music touches our lives in many ways. Musical genres continue to shift and evolve with popular music styles; as new types go out of fashion, older genres are sometimes revived.

Video game revenues in 2001 outpaced box office receipts for the first time, and sales are expected to continue to grow. Video game makers are moving into the realm of multiplayer online games rather than console games, as the popularity of games such as *EverQuest* seems to bode well for the success of an online interactive gaming environment.

Digital entertainment promises to provide interactivity never before seen in entertainment, although it is likely audiences will utilize interactivity only in select situations. Sports programming is one area that is likely to be conducive to interactivity among viewers, while frequent interactivity when watching movies is unlikely.

Because of the prominence entertainment plays in our lives, it is important for professionals who create entertainment not to propagate racial or gender stereotypes. The entertainment industry has made some improvement in that regard but still has a way to go. In order to avoid government regulations, the entertainment industry has tended to censor itself or create self-regulating guidelines such as the movie rating system.

The business of entertainment should continue to grow, despite changes in digital technologies that will harm some areas of entertainment while helping others or creating new opportunities.

Discussion Questions

1. Count the maximum number of TVs, VCRs, stereos, CD players, and other media devices your family had at a certain time. How do your numbers compare with the national average? If you had a higher-than-average number of media devices, discuss what factors led to getting these and the effect they had on you and family life after getting them. If you had fewer-than-average numbers of media devices, discuss what effect that had on family life.

2. Keep a daily log for one week of how many conversations you have with friends, classmates, and family that have to do with media entertainment. This can range from talking about an episode of a TV show the previous night, an upcoming movie, or any entertainment-related area. Write down when the conversations took place and how long they lasted and compare your log with classmates.

3. Keep a daily log of how much time you actually spend with media entertainment, either watching TV, listening to the radio, playing video or computer games, or going to concerts, sporting events, or movies. Compare this amount of time with the time spent discussing the entertainment event and share the information with classmates.

4. What factors in a movie would make it seem better if seen in a movie theater than on video? Could the opposite happen, in which a movie made for video is better on video than if it was shown on a movie screen? Why or why not?

5. Make a short list of some of your favorite TV series or movies and see if you can research where the ideas for these shows or movies came from. Are they remakes of much older shows? If they are original, what influences did the producer or filmmaker have when he or she made these?

6. Most people do not like to watch a movie or read a book more than once or twice. However, people can often play the same video game for hours on end, repeating levels and characters. Why do you think this is so?

7. How might negative ethnic or gender stereotypes have a greater impact on players of video games than those same stereotypes when shown on a TV show?

8. Discuss whether you think the movie rating system, and the music and video game rating systems that are based on it, are a good thing and useful.

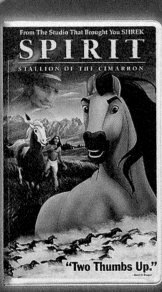

Advertising and Public Relations

Some critics argued it was pushing the limits of good taste, but for NBC and Baskin-Robbins, the integrated marketing deal they struck in July 2002 was sweet.

Baskin-Robbins agreed to add even more flavors to its rotating stock of over 1000 different flavors with such concoctions as Fear Factor Sundae, Will & Grace's Rocky Road of Romance, Good Morning Miami Mint, Stuckey Bowled-Over Brownie, and Pralines 'n American Dreams.

If the names ring a bell, it's because they are not only popular ice cream flavors but also some of the popular programs on the top-rated network's line-up for viewers 18 to 49, a prime advertising audience. Baskin-Robbins became associated with NBC and got advertising on the network, while NBC got to adorn Baskin-Robbins 4500 stores with signs of NBC shows. A series of sweepstakes associated with the shows was also promoted.

It was not the first time Baskin-Robbins had worked with a media company in that way. In 2001 Baskin-Robbins teamed up with Dreamworks Pictures in creating Shrek's Swirl ice cream and Shrek's Swamp Fizz, a drink that fizzed after it was stirred, to tie into the theatrical release of the animated movie.

Whether or not other entertainment companies will strike similar deals with food or beverage companies remains to be seen, but in the summer and fall of 2002 NBC and Baskin-Robbins were milking the campaign for all it was worth, with NBC estimating they probably received about $2 million worth of media and public exposure.

OBJECTIVES

In this chapter we will:

- Provide an overview of advertising and public relations and the theoretical foundations that underlie these media support industries.
- Examine the purpose and form of advertising and public relations.
- Outline the history and structure of the advertising and public relations industries.
- Identify the impact of digital technologies on advertising and public relations.
- Review the ethical challenges of persuasive communications.
- Discuss the role of evaluation research in advertising and public relations.

Prologue

Many diverse forces shape the media of mass communication. Among the most important are advertising and public relations. This chapter examines the nature and history of these two essential media support industries and how they are adapting to the shifting nature of mass communication in the age of digitization and convergence. Advertising has traditionally been the method by which companies or stores reach a mass audience, utilizing the distribution system that newspapers and other media outlets have created. Public relations involves managing the public "persona" of a company, again through using media outlets and their mass distribution networks.

In a digital, networked world, however, the power to distribute information cheaply by almost anyone has been greatly enhanced, which would seem to eclipse the need for advertisers or public relations professionals. However, this is not the case. Just as not everyone can be—or wants to be—a journalist, musician, or filmmaker simply because he or she has the tools and distribution network to do so online, companies still need the expertise that advertising and public relations professionals can provide in how to best reach their target audiences and deliver their messages. The modes of communication and distribution structure may change, but the ability to reach audiences with powerful messages will not.

Although getting news and entertainment are the reasons most people use media, in reality advertising is the most prevalent form of media content. This can easily be seen in print media, where the typical **news hole,** or portion of the product devoted to editorial or news content, is just about one-third of the total space. In other words, two-thirds of most newspapers and magazines are filled with advertisements (not including advertising inserts). And even though most television programming time is devoted to content rather than commercials, consider the number of times the audience sees the same commercial repeatedly during the course of a program.

Advertisements, whether in print, in the form of commercials on broadcast radio and television, or online, provide the basic financial revenue, or support, for the rest of the media's content. Moreover, sometimes consumers intentionally use the media specifically to access the advertising content, including both display and classified advertising. Classified advertising has found an ideal home in online media for both the seller and the buyer, making it a system of almost perfect information distribution.

Public relations also plays a vital supporting role for the media of journalism and mass communication. Although public relations is really about managing relations among organizations, people, and their relevant publics, much of the public relations function involves media relations in the form of publicity and other influences on media. Many organizations have historically sought to influence media content and thereby public opinion. They have done everything from generating publicity to staging events to get the attention of the press. Further, most news organizations are dependent on the public relations function of organizations—whether corporations, government agencies, or not-for-profit groups—for information. This includes everything from scheduled announcements and report releases, such as government reports on the economy, to corporate financial statements and information during crises.

news hole—typically used with newspapers, this term refers to the amount of total space available after advertisement space has been blocked out.

The news media are largely dependent on public relations for information, and press conferences are an easy way to provide information to the press and thereby the public.

Strategic Communications

Advertising and public relations represent what can be called strategic communications. Strategic communications refers to media-based communication campaigns that are designed to influence the audience in some way. Advertising does this by purchasing media space or time where commercial messages can be presented to the public, often in the hopes of influencing people to buy a product or service. Public relations is a broader enterprise that includes the use of communication campaigns in which media time or space are obtained free of charge to convey messages

Advertising tries to persuade individuals to adopt a new position, attitude, or behavior—in this case, encouraging consumers to want to buy the product.

designed to influence the public's opinion about a person, issue, or group. For example, a government official might call a press conference in the hopes that media will report favorably on her new policy on public school vouchers.

Advertising and public relations are based on various principles of **persuasive communication.** Persuasive communication refers to the process of using mediated messages to influence others to adopt a new position, opinion, attitude, or behavior. Persuasive communication has its roots at least as far back as Aristotle, who used the term *rhetoric* to describe persuasive communication in an interpersonal communication context. There were a number of techniques that classical rhetoricians could use to strengthen their arguments, although unlike logic or philosophy, rhetoric was not concerned with the truth of a matter but only whether one could persuade others.

There are at least two dozen theories of persuasive communication and audience decision-making. These theories help explain or provide models of how persuasive communications work, as well as guide the strategic communication campaigns that advertising and public relations professionals create and carry out via the media.

The Role of Media in Persuasion

At the core of most of these theories is the following three-part notion linking the public, the media, and strategic communicators:

1. People's behavior or actions are somehow linked to their cognitions (knowledge or beliefs) and affect (attitudes and emotions).

2. Mediated communications can somehow influence these cognitions and affect, which in turn can result in behavioral change.

3. Media-based communication campaigns can be strategically designed to produce the cognitive, affective, or behavioral changes organizations or individuals might desire.

One of the most long-standing models of how advertising is derived from this notion is called in somewhat operatic fashion, **AIDA,** although it is not in reference to a musical love story. AIDA stands for attention (sometimes, awareness), interest, desire, and action. This traditional model of how advertising works suggests that the first step in getting people to buy or do something is to get their attention or make them aware of an issue or product. Once you've got their attention, you've got to get their interest. Once they are interested, you need to get them to desire to do the intended behavior. Finally, desire leads to action.

Four Factors That Affect Mediated Persuasion

There are many factors that affect the process of mediated persuasion. Among the most important are:

- **Media differences.**
- **Message characteristics.**
- **Audience fragmentation.**
- **Individual characteristics and conditions.**

persuasive communication— the process of using messages to influence others to adopt a new position, opinion, attitude, or behavior.

AIDA—a foundational principle of effective advertising, this refers to attention (sometimes, awareness), interest, desire, and action.

media differences—along with message characteristics, audience fragmentation, and individual characteristics and conditions, one of four basic factors that affect mediated persuasive communication. Media differences are the qualities that distinguish the various media of mass communication, such as print vs. electronic and interactive vs. passive.

message characteristics— along with media differences, audience fragmentation, and individual characteristics and conditions, one of four basic factors that affect mediated persuasive communication. Message characteristics are the qualities of the communications themselves, such as the level of complexity, credibility, or emotional or informational quality of a message.

audience fragmentation— along with media differences, message characteristics, and individual characteristics and conditions, this is one of the four basic factors that affect mediated persuasive communication. The growth in media channels over the course of the 20th century essentially splintered the audience for mass communication.

individual characteristics— along with media differences, message characteristics, and audience fragmentation, one of four basic factors that affect mediated persuasive communication. Individual characteristics are the various identifiable qualities, such as demographic factors, geographic location, and media habits that account for or shape public tastes, preferences, opinions, knowledge, and behaviors.

For advertisers, teens are a highly sought-after demographic.

Media differences are the qualities that distinguish the various media of mass communication, such as print vs. electronic and interactive vs. passive.

Message characteristics are the qualities of the communications themselves, such as the level of complexity, credibility, or emotional or informational quality of a message.

Audience fragmentation refers to the fact that national media channels grew dramatically in number and variety over the course of the 20th century, with a resulting splintering of the audience. In the early 1970s, the U. S. public had fewer media choices than we do today, and it was relatively simple (though expensive) for advertising and public relations campaigns to reach a large, or mass, audience. By the dawn of the 21st century, however, most people in the United States had access to many more media choices. It has therefore become substantially more difficult and complicated for strategic communicators to reach large audiences.

Individual characteristics and conditions are the various identifiable qualities, such as demographic factors (e.g., age, gender, and race or ethnic background), geographic location (e.g., where they live), psychographic factors (e.g., what people may think or intend), and media habits that account for or shape public tastes, preferences, opinions, knowledge, and behaviors.

Consequently, most advertising and public relations emphasize targeted campaigns or communication strategies that are designed to use carefully selected media vehicles such as print, broadcast, or online, to reach specialized or segmented audiences. In electronic media this is called **narrowcasting,** where specialized media channels are used to deliver messages to highly targeted audiences, audiences defined by their demographic, geographic, or other characteristics.

narrowcasting—specialized media channels used to deliver messages to highly targeted audiences that can be defined by interests, demographics, or some other specific focus.

advertising—an ancient form of human communication generally designed to inform or persuade members of the public with regard to some product or service.

Advertising

Advertising is an ancient form of human communication generally designed to inform or persuade members of the public with regard to some product or service. In the modern age, advertising has taken its basic shape as sponsored, or paid-for, communications designed to inform and persuade the receiver of a message to buy a good or service, to accept a point of view, or act in some fashion desired by the sender of the commercial message.

Print and electronic media have developed around this advertising model and in effect are in the business of selling mass audiences to advertisers who wish to reach these audiences. From a business perspective, the media exist primarily as the means to gather an audience; but many communications professionals, although recognizing an element of truth in this view, would counter that audiences will not gather if media content is not interesting, useful, or entertaining to them in some way. Media organizations determine how much they can charge advertisers for space in their publication or air time on their station based on the audience reached or delivered to the advertiser. In broadcasting, this number is called the **rating.** In print and online media, it is called the **CPM,** or **cost per thousand** audience members. The online model is still evolving, however, and CPM may include the cost per 1000 hits or page views, as well as unique visitors to a site or Web page. **Performance-based advertising** has also been used online, in which advertisers only pay for results of an advertisement, such as actual click-throughs to the advertiser's site, rather than the total page views a site has.

Advertising rates within media or specific media vehicles vary as well according to the size and quality of the target audience. In radio, for example, the most expensive time to purchase advertising is AM and PM drive time. These are the morning and afternoon prime radio time slots for advertising and programming, when audiences are at their peak. An advertiser for a youth-oriented product may choose to show its commercial on prime-time MTV rather than a late-night slot on a network because, although the viewing audience may be smaller than on a broadcast network, it is a more targeted audience that is more likely to want the product.

The Historical Development of Advertising

In its earliest form, advertising was conducted as face-to-face, word-of-mouth communication with buyers and sellers negotiating for the best bartered arrangement for a good or service. In ancient Egypt, advertisements for products and service were written on papyrus and posted in common, public areas for passersby to see. The advent of the printing press in the15th century gave rise to advertising in mass communication settings, usually in the form of posters, flyers, or broadsheets. Broadsheet advertisements to emigrate to the New World were a popular technique for attracting people to the colonies. Colonists in the 18th and 19th centuries could obtain information from advertising about everything from where to buy groceries and patent medicines to seeing ship schedules.

The Rise in Prominence of Advertising

By the mid-1800s, advertising had become a mainstay of how U.S. firms marketed their products and services. With the advent of the penny press, newspaper publishers relied more heavily on advertising revenue to make up for the lost revenues in subscription income. Advertisements became more prominent and were designed to stand out better from surrounding editorial content. Individuals also used advertising to promote their unique services. In 1856, photographer Mathew Brady advertised his services of "photographs, ambrotypes and daguerreotypes" in the *New York Herald* paper. Also that same year, publisher

rating—used in broadcast media to explain the numbers of households that watched a particular show.

cost per thousand (CPM)—the standard unit for measuring advertising rates for publications, based on circulation.

performance-based advertising—any form of online ad buying in which an advertiser pays for results rather than paying for the size of the publisher's audience, or CPM.

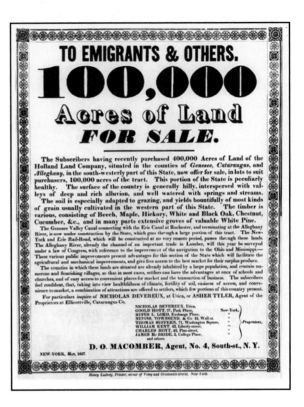

Advertising was widely used to attract European immigrants to the New World.

Robert Bonner ran the first full-page advertisement in a newspaper to promote his own literary paper, the *New York Ledger*.[1] At this time there were no standards in advertising, and medicinal advertisers often made extravagant and untrue claims as to the curative powers of the products they were selling.

The early 20th century brought the rise of mass-produced, packaged goods and the automobile industry. Today, the automobile industry is the largest advertiser, followed by retail, business, and consumer services. Advertising for cigarettes and other tobacco products grew during the 20th century, but not without criticism. In 1919, the magazine *Printer's Ink* warned against "an insidious campaign to create women smokers" in reaction to the portrayal of women shown smoking in cigarette ads.

The rise of electronic media in the 20th century drew heavily upon the resources of the advertising industry, which effectively used radio and television to promote a wide variety of products and services to audiences throughout the

In the early 20th century, cigarette makers targeted women in their advertisements in order to reach a largely untapped market.

United States and internationally. Television quickly surpassed print media as the main vehicle for reaching a national advertising market.

The Growth of Commercial Television

There was never any widespread debate on whether or not television should be publicly funded or run on a commercial basis, as there had been in the early days of radio. It was assumed that television would be advertising supported, just as the radio networks—which were three out of the four early TV networks—had become. The questions raised were not whether to support television through advertising, but what would be the best way to do it.

Commercials quickly became a mainstay on television. The year 1948 established an early high watermark for advertising, with 933 sponsors buying TV time, an increase of 515 percent over 1947. *Variety* reported in 1957 that during a typical week, viewers saw 420 commercials totaling 5 hours, 8 minutes. In the early days of television, advertisers often sponsored whole shows and had their names included as part of show titles, such as *Texaco Star Theater.*

The Television Bureau of Advertising was also launched in the mid-1950s, responding to the emergence of television as the leading medium for advertising. The bureau is a not-for-profit trade association of America's broadcast television industry and provides a variety of tools and resources to support the use of television as an advertising medium.

Weblink
Television Bureau of Advertising
[www.tvb.org/]

Commercial developments have continued to reshape the TV landscape. In the 1960s, ABC extended the station break between programs from 30 to 40 seconds in order to increase its profits, with other networks soon following suit. The longer station break allowed more commercial time to be sold and thereby made more money for the network. Within a few years the breaks had become even longer, and standard commercial lengths had reached one minute. By 1971, the networks cut the standard commercial length from 60 seconds to 30 seconds in order to increase profits even further. This cut the length of the standard commercial in half although rates for a 30-second spot were not reduced by a corresponding 50 percent. Networks began the practice of advertising "piggybacking," or running messages for two related products from one company in the same one-minute commercial.

In 1969, New York's WOR-TV became the first station to air a program made up of exclusively commercial messages. This is called **paid programming,** or an "infomercial."

Also in 1969, the U.S. Supreme Court applied the **Fairness Doctrine** to cigarette advertising, giving antismoking groups access to "equal time" on the air to reply to tobacco commercials. The FCC also issued a Notice of Proposed Rulemaking to ban cigarette ads on TV and radio, as Congress debated the issue. Tobacco companies finally agreed to stop advertising cigarettes on the air. In 1970, a Congressional ban on radio and TV cigarette advertising took effect, costing the broadcast business roughly $220 million in advertising. The hard liquor industry has had a voluntary ban on TV advertising for the past 50 years, although they have been testing the regulatory waters in recent years by airing ads on local cable TV stations. NBC announced in 2001 that it would air liquor ads in late-night time slots, although this drew a number of protests from civic groups, and the network reconsidered the plan.

paid programming—also called "infomercials," these are 30- or 60-minute television shows that seek to sell a product and that usually involve a celebrity spokesperson and testimony from customers about how good the product is.

Fairness Doctrine—adopted by the FCC in 1949, it required broadcasters to seek out and present all sides of a controversial issue they were covering. It was discarded by the FCC in 1987.

The Commercialization of the Web

The first advertisements on the Web appeared on Hotwired, the online version of *Wired* magazine, in October 1994. Hotwired offered space on the Web site to 14 advertisers in the form of the now-familiar **banner ad.** However, because online connection speeds were slow in 1994, the ads could not be large graphics, so remained fairly small and primarily HTML text. After the programming language Java was created, it allowed for interactive and animated graphics of relatively small file sizes, creating an opportunity for better-designed ads.

Today, increased bandwidth has allowed multimedia ads to appear, and advertisers have looked into new types of advertising to further attract consumers' attention as tracking consumers online has shown that banner ads have a very low click-through rate, meaning a very low percentage of users actually click on banner ads—fewer than 1 percent.

Types of Advertising

There are two basic types of advertising:

1. **Product/service.**
2. **Institutional/issue.**

Product/Service

Product and service advertising is by far the most common in the media of mass communication. Any time an ad selling a product or service is seen or heard, the audience is being exposed to this type of advertising. Although these ads ultimately are designed to get consumers to act (i.e., buy something), frequently the ads' initial purposes are to raise awareness of a product or service, what is called "top of mind awareness." The goal is to make the message stand out among the cacophony of commercial messages audiences are bombarded with daily.

Institutional/Issue

Institutional and issue ads are less common than product/service ads but are still widely seen and heard. These are ads designed to sell not a particular good or service but rather an idea or point of view. Institutional advertising does not usually tell the reader or viewer what to do. It is sometimes called "image" advertising, and its goal is often to improve the image of the company in the mind of the audience.

Companies, nonprofit organizations, and individuals will often pay for ads, even organize entire advertising campaigns, to influence public opinion. In recent years, there have been institutional ads designed to influence opinion on gun control, land development, and many other issues. The National Rifle Association (NRA) has organized a variety of institutional or issue advertising campaigns over the past decades to reinforce the public's commitment to the Second Amendment to the U.S. Constitution, which stipulates the public's right to bear arms. The NRA generally opposes legislation designed to restrict public ownership of firearms and believes that mobilizing more public support for its position will decrease the political will to pass such legislation. The NRA sees media advertising as an important communication strategy in reaching and shaping public opinion in this regard.

banner ad—an advertisement across the top of a Web page; the original form of advertising on the Web.

product/service—one of the two basic types of advertising and the most common. It tells the audience what to do in getting them to buy a product or use a service.

institutional/issue—one of the two basic types of advertising. It usually tries to improve the image of an organization or persuade people to have a more favorable viewpoint on an issue.

The National Rifle Association has made effective use of advertising to promote its stance on the public's right to own guns.

Among the NRA's most memorable institutional advertisements have been the scores of television, radio, and print commercials featuring its long-time president, actor Charlton Heston, speaking on behalf of the public's right to own guns.

Political advertising falls into the institutional/issue category, although some might effectively argue that it is really simply selling a good—a political candidate who wants your vote.

Other Advertising Types

In addition to the two basic types of advertising, there are two other types of advertising that can often combine aspects of both basic types: public service announcements and branding.

Public Service Announcements   Closely related to advertising is the not-for-profit version of persuasive messages in the mass media. These are commonly known as **public service announcements (PSAs),** which are advertising-like messages for which the media donate time or space to organizations with a worthy purpose that ostensibly benefits the public, such as advertisements for the Red Cross. Although it is not sponsored or paid for, the purpose of a PSA can combine aspects of both basic types of advertising. Like commercial advertising, PSAs can try to persuade someone to do something, such as make a donation. And like institutional/issue advertising, they can raise awareness of general societal issues or the existence of an organization.

PSAs are usually part of a **public information campaign,** which is a media program funded by the government and designed to achieve some social goal, or what might be called social engineering. Some public information campaigns have been designed to get people, especially young people, to stop smoking, or never start smoking. Others have been designed to get people to practice safer sex. Many of these campaigns have involved federal grants from programs such as the National Institutes of Health.

Branding   **Branding** refers to the process of creating in the consumer's mind a clear identity for a particular company's product or trademark. Branding via advertising developed in the 1890s and early 1900s as products sought to differentiate their brand from others in an increasingly cluttered and competitive marketplace and to have high brand-name recognition among consumers.

Sometimes, the actual qualities that might differentiate one brand from another were quite few. As a result, advertising is used to create an image of one brand's uniqueness. This is typically done by creating a catchy slogan and distinctive visual identity that are memorable and then advertising the brand across

public service announcement (PSA)—advertising-like message for which the media donate time or space to organizations with a worthy purpose that ostensibly benefits the public.

public information campaign—media program often funded by the government and designed to achieve some social goal, or what might be called social engineering.

branding—the process of creating in the consumer's mind a clear identity for a particular company's product, logo, or trademark.

British Petroleum changed its shield logo to a more environmental-looking logo and does not use its name in its television commercials, saying "BP" stands for "beyond petroleum."

multiple media, so the desired audience segment or target group gets frequent exposure to the product. Among the first to successfully do this was Campbell's soup, which used the artwork of Grace Weidersein in 1904 depicting "The Campbell's Kids." Campbell's includes Weidersein's artwork in its advertising to this day. Another highly successful advertising campaign was launched in 1970 to promote Coca-Cola. In that year, "Coke" introduced its "I'd Like to Teach the World to Sing" commercial, with the song becoming an instant hit. Coca-Cola sold a million records featuring a noncommercial version of the popular advertising jingle.

Some advertising campaigns have been so successful (some would say too successful) that their brands have become synonymous with the product itself. For example, advertising for Kleenex® (introduced in 1924) has branded the product so well that many consumers consider a "Kleenex" to simply be the generic name for a facial tissue. This can be both good and bad for the advertiser. On the one hand, this level of branding means that consumers will have extremely high brand-name awareness, but on the other hand, they may go shopping for what they are calling "Kleenex" but actually buy another brand.

Advertising Formats

Advertising formats vary by type of medium of mass communication and can include some formats, such as billboards, direct mail, or telemarketing, that are usually not thought of in mass communication terms. Each format has specific characteristics that affect what kind of message is delivered and how it is delivered, as well as what kind of audience it is expected to reach.

Advertising in Print Media

In newspapers and magazines, commercial messages come in either of two forms, **classified advertising** or **display advertising.** Classifieds are short messages appearing together in a special classified section and posted by individuals and organizations

classified advertising—a type of advertising usually found in print media, especially newspapers but also in some magazines and now increasingly online; messages are posted by individuals and organizations to sell specific goods or services.

display advertising—a type of advertising in print media that usually consists of illustrations or images and text and that can be anywhere from a small section of a page to a full-page or multipage advertisement. Because of their high costs, they are usually bought by large companies or organizations.

Media Spotlight: **Super Bowl Advertisements**

Advertisements for the Super Bowl have practically become a media event in and of themselves, with advertisers jockeying to have the most clever or creative ad so people will be talking about them the day after the game.

Advertisers pay for the privilege, however. A commercial spot cost just $42,000 for Super Bowl I played in 1967. By 2001, the price had increased 50-fold, to $2.3 million for a 30-second television spot in Super Bowl XXXV, compared to costs between $90,000 and $200,000 for a 30-second spot on a regular Sunday afternoon football game, depending on the network. During the dot-com boom, some Internet start-ups used substantial portions of their start-up funding for marketing on Super Bowl ads in order to get as much recognition as possible. This did not help many of them when the boom was over and they had to shut down. One of the ads for Super Bowl XXXVI in 2002 parodied the many dot-com companies that had gone out of business, showing a ghost town of bankrupt dot-com companies and the popular Pets.com sock puppet.

Advertisements during the Super Bowl have become known for being more clever or creative—as well as extremely expensive.

in order to sell specific goods or services. Display ads are much larger, typically a quarter to a full page or two devoted to a company's goods or services. Costs of running these ads vary by both size and location of the ad both on the page and within the publication (back cover placement is usually the most expensive), as well as whether color is used. A type of display ad that is created to look like an actual article in the publication is called an **advertorial** and usually has tiny print either on the top or bottom of the page that says "paid advertisement."

Publishing companies create a **rate card,** which lists the various advertising rates based on size and placement of an ad and any discounts available for multiple ads. Usually rate cards are simply used as rough guides, as big advertisers have much leeway to negotiate advertising rates down in the highly competitive print media world.

Advertising in Electronic Media

Advertisements on radio or television are called commercials, or "spots," and typically run for 30 seconds. Although the length of time for commercials has gone down and audiences continue to fragment, advertising costs on electronic media are generally high compared to advertising in print media. A primary reason is the larger audience electronic media can command compared to most print outlets. Even large-circulation magazines of over a million readers reach an audience considered relatively small by television standards.

Paid programming, or an infomercial, is typically a 30- or 60-minute program in which a product is demonstrated or promoted for purchase, oftentimes with a celebrity endorsement or endorsements from highly satisfied consumers, who are typically paid or otherwise compensated.

advertorial—a type of display advertisement that is created to look like an article within the publication, although most publications have the words "advertisement" or "paid advertisement" in tiny print somewhere near the advertorial.

rate card—a listing of advertising rates by size, placement, and other characteristics such as whether ads are black-and-white or full-color. Frequency discounts are also usually offered, and the listed rates are usually negotiable, especially for large advertisers.

Ted Turner: From Outdoor Advertiser to Media Mogul

Ted Turner, founder of Turner Broadcasting and the Cable News Network, now part of AOL Time Warner, and the largest single shareholder of AOL Time Warner, built his fortune off the outdoor advertising business. Turner was the son of a Savannah, Georgia, businessman who owned a small but successful outdoor advertising business. When Ted was 24 his alcoholic and abusive father committed suicide, leaving his son the business. The younger Turner was able to transform his inheritance into a global media empire.

In 1970 Turner bought Atlanta's WJRJ-TV Channel 17, a UHF station, for $2.5 million, and turned it around from an operation losing a $1 million a year to a profitable enterprise within 12 months. He renamed the station WTCG, standing for Turner Communications Group. In 1973 he struck a deal for the television station to air the games of the Atlanta Braves, a team he eventually bought.

A man with a keen sense of the potential of new technology, Turner struck deals with cable operators nationwide, especially TCI's CEO John Malone, who thought Turner would never get FCC approval for his ideas but loved them anyway. Inspired by the success of HBO, in the mid-1970s the flamboyant Turner realized the potential to go national with his local station by using satellite distribution to local cable operators. On Dec. 17, 1976, the FCC gave Turner permission to beam WTCG via Satcom I (a communications satellite), and Turner was on his way to building the first "superstation," which he shortly renamed WTBS, for Turner Broadcasting System.

Turner's biggest challenge was getting advertisers to buy into the idea of advertising on his national cable channel. The idea was so novel, and advertisers were so conservative, that few could be convinced that they could advertise nationally on anything other than

one of the three big television networks. But without advertising, WTBS couldn't succeed. Eventually, Turner established a rate card based on his station's national audience as measured by A. C. Nielsen, and that convinced advertisers to give it a try. Soon the advertisers were lining up, and the money was piling up. Today, Turner has amassed a personal fortune of more than $6 billion and has pledged more than $100 million to support the United Nations.

Ted Turner

Another way advertisers get their products noticed is through **product placement,** or having products shown or being used by the characters in a show. This practice also happens in the movies and is increasingly being used by advertisers.

Advertising Online

Online advertising includes both aspects of print advertising, the classified ad and display ad—originally called a banner ad on a Web site—and all aspects of electronic media, because there can be video or audio commercials online as well. Some media technology companies, such as Real.com, force users to listen to or watch a brief advertisement before being allowed to watch a video clip.

There are also new types of online ads being developed, including larger display ads on a Web page; animated ads that move across a page; pop-up ads, called interstitial ads; and pop-under ads that appear beneath the browser window that is open. Some companies even make their Web site become a user's

product placement—the practice of having actual products shown prominently and used in television shows and movies; advertisers pay for this exposure.

homepage without their immediate knowledge or send a software program called spyware that sends back information on the user's computer and browsing habits without the user knowing. Almost all Web sites leave "cookies" on users' computers, which are small programs that identify a specific user and make it easy for companies to see what computers are visiting their sites and where they are going. Any time a Web site "remembers" a visitor, such as after registering for a site but returning days later, that is because of a cookie.

Because it is much easier to track advertisement response rates on line, advertisers have come to expect more from online ads than in other media types, which are largely impossible to track regarding effectiveness. This has hurt the development of online advertising and led to the development of new ad types, most of which still receive very low response rates (usually no more than 1 or 2 percent). The lack of success with online advertising has been largely responsible for the demise of many dot-com companies, especially media-related companies, that relied on an advertising-supported business model.

Advertising in Public Spaces

From billboards to store signs to ads on taxis, buses, and bus stops, the public is bombarded with more advertising messages than most people realize simply because advertising is so ubiquitous in public spaces, often called outdoor advertising. Even wearing brand-name clothing effectively makes the wearer a walking advertisement for the company—and what is good from a company standpoint is that the consumer is paying *them* to advertise their product!

Store signs are some of the oldest forms of public advertising, although their reach is limited to people passing by the particular store. Increasingly, municipalities are allowing corporate sponsorship of public vehicles and spaces to help shore up government budgets. Technologies such as low-power video monitors are allowing advertisements to appear in new public spaces such as above cash registers or in elevators, where news content is delivered alongside advertisements.

Advertising to People Directly

Direct mail marketing, commonly called "junk mail" by its recipients, includes ads for everything from lower insurance rates to credit card offers to pleas to donate to various charities or subscribe to magazines. Some companies use tactics to make it appear that the recipient has won a drawing or lottery and needs to send in the material to claim their prize.

Telemarketing involves calling people at home to offer them such things as telephone services or new credit cards. Many people find the calls intrusive and annoying and actively screen calls with their answering machine or with functions like caller ID before answering the phone. Telemarketers use a thoroughly prepared script when giving their sales pitches, complete with prepared responses to a range of expected answers.

The Telephone Consumer Protection Act of 1991 is a federal law that lays out strict guidelines on what times telemarketers can call and that allow people to be removed from their mailing list. Some states have implemented "Do Not Call" registries that serve the same purpose. Because of the proliferation of cell phones, some using numbers that were previously land lines, some consumers have been getting telemarketing calls on their cell phones, a practice that they find particularly irksome because they are paying for the call or use their cell phones primarily for emergencies. Some states are beginning to look in to legislation to ban telemarketing calls to cell phones.

The Advertising Business

Hoovers.com estimates that total spending on advertising in the United States is about $279 billion a year. This figure counts not only the media of mass communication, including television (the largest medium by advertising sales), radio, newspapers, magazines, outdoor billboards, and Web-based media, but also other media, including telephone directories and direct mail. Total advertising revenues were growing about 7 percent per year until the global economic slowdown that commenced in 2001. Advertising revenues leveled off after that but started rising again by mid-2002.

The dominant player in the world's advertising industry is the United States, representing nearly two-thirds (62 percent) of total worldwide expenditures ($450 billion), with companies outside the United States spending roughly $171 billion a year. Japan is the second-largest advertiser, with some 15 percent of the world market. Germany, Brazil, and the United Kingdom are also important. Just as in other areas of the media business, advertising firms have been hot on the acquisition trail, with larger advertising firms buying smaller ones, thereby becoming even larger. Advertising is also become increasing global, with the largest advertising firms increasingly transnational in nature.

Critical to the success of advertising firms is their creative work, and size doesn't necessarily translate into being the best or most creative. In 2001, for example, a top advertising industry award, the Clio Gold Award, went to a little-known local advertising firm based in Berlin, Germany. The Scholz & Friends advertising agency won a Clio Gold Award for innovative media use for an outdoor advertising campaign designed to promote Fiona Bennett's hats.

General Motors is the largest single advertiser, followed by Procter & Gamble. Internet companies such as Primestar and AOL Time Warner are spending greatly on advertising, although less than in the late 1990s since the decline of the dot coms and the fall-off of the U.S. and global economies.

Advertising Agencies

Advertising agencies are the foundation of much of the advertising business. They perform many important functions in helping create and sell advertising across all media and provide a vital link between media and marketing firms (i.e., the company seeking to sell a product or service). There are more than 500 U.S. advertising agencies that employ more than 70,000 people.

Advertising agencies have four main areas of operation, including:

1. *Creative:* the area of the business where the content of advertising is produced, with copywriters and others working under the direction of creative and art directors.

2. *Client management:* working with the client, usually handled by account executives.

3. *Media buying*: media planners and buyers determining and making the purchase of media time or space; the area that traditionally has produced agency revenues.

4. *Research*: researchers collecting and analyzing data on consumer characteristics and media and purchase behaviors.

The Development of the Advertising Agency

Early advertisers bought newspaper space and primarily targeted local audiences. It was not until the 1860s that advertising went national via nationally distributed monthly magazines.

Among the most successful early sellers of newspaper advertising space was Volney B. Palmer, who gave birth to both the first advertising agency in 1841 and the long-standing business model for the ad agency industry. Palmer provided his advertising clients with circulation data, gave them copies of the ads, and deducted an **ad agency commission** from the advertising fee to the publication as compensation for his effort.

The advertising business grew quickly as the penny press grew into mass-circulation media. By the 1860s, there were more than 20 advertising agencies in New York City. N. W. Ayer & Partners, an advertising agency founded in 1869 by Francis Wayland Ayer, bought Palmer's firm, and the trend toward consolidation of the advertising business had begun. Ayer built on Palmer's basic media billing model, which charged clients a fee for placing ads in newspapers and magazines, and established a standardized ad agency commission: 15 per cent of the total media billings.

N. W. Ayer also set the standard for creative services, with some of the most-well-known ad slogans of the 20th century, including the DeBeers tag line, "A diamond is forever," AT&T's "Reach out and touch someone," and Camel cigarettes' "I'd walk a mile for a Camel." N. W. Ayer & Partners is now part of Bcom3 Group, Inc., one of the world's largest advertising firms.

Today, instead of relying exclusively on the 15 percent commission from media billings, most leading advertising firms now charge a fee to their clients based on a more complex set of factors, including the types of services provided, hours worked, performance-based measures (i.e., of the impact of the advertising on sales of the product or service), as well as media billings.

Today's Largest Advertising Agencies

Early on, many advertising firms were independent agencies. Leo Burnett, a leading advertising agency founded in 1935 that kept some of its clients for as long as 60 years, was eventually acquired by larger companies that could facilitate economies of scale.

Today, most of the world's leading advertising agencies are owned by much larger advertising and media services companies, and 90 of the top 100 firms have international operations. Most of these firms also operate both advertising and public relations enterprises, making them what are called full-service companies. These types of firms handle all aspects of the communications business, from campaign planning to creative execution, media buying, and public relations. On the opposite end of the spectrum are boutique agencies, or small, specialty advertising agencies.

ad agency commission—a percentage amount of the cost of an advertisement taken by the advertising agency that helped create and sell the ad.

Tony Schwartz

One of the most talented advertising professionals of the audiovisual realm is Tony Schwartz. Born in 1923, Schwartz had a career in advertising spanning most of the 20th century. He has produced more than 20,000 radio and television spots for a wide range of products, including more than 200 political candidates and not-for-profit public interest groups. Schwartz' television spots are widely regarded for their impact and their effective use of images and audio. He is the master of using implied messages to their greatest effect.

He achieved perhaps his greatest fame in the realm of political advertising for a spot known harmlessly as "The Daisy Spot." Aired initially in 1964 during the height of the Cold War, the commercial begins with a pastoral view of a young girl in a field picking the petals of a daisy. Then a male voice-over begins a countdown, evoking the sense of a missile countdown. The spot ends with a nuclear mushroom cloud. Never in the spot does it say, "Don't vote for Barry Goldwater." Neither does it say "Vote for President Lyndon Johnson," who had taken office after the assassination of President John F. Kennedy. But the message was clear to voters in 1964: Senator Barry Goldwater, who was known as a hawk, would be likely to get us involved in a nuclear war.

The spot ran only once as a paid political advertisement, but it ran countless times on newscasts, not to mention in most political science and mass communication classrooms ever since. Political communication scholar Kathleen Hall Jamieson considers The Daisy Spot to be among the most powerful political ads ever aired. "Television can pair previously disconnected images with a speed and seamlessness that defies the scrutiny of the suspicious."[2]

Tony Schwartz.

Table 12-1 presents data on the world's five largest advertising and media services firms, ranked by their annual worldwide billing in 2001, and their advertising and public relations operations.

Advertising in a Digital World

Traditionally, most commercial media organizations have based their business model on advertising revenues, with 70 percent or more of their revenues coming from advertising. Media organizations also are now seeing their advertising business, the economic foundation of the media, transformed by digital technology. Advertisers have more ability to track consumers and to see what kinds of advertisements work best. They are also finding that traditional advertising techniques do not work as well on the Web, where the audience tends to be more media-savvy than average and is often looking for specific information. Interactivity, such as online quizzes or giveaways, is also being used to attract consumers to an advertisers' Web site.

Because the Web is such an excellent distribution medium, some of the most successful advertising online has been without the use of advertising agencies or

Table 12-1 World's Five Largest Advertising and Media Services Companies

Rank	Firm	Worldwide billing in 2001 (in millions)	Advertising	Public Relations	Headquarters
1	WPP Group	$75,711	Ogilvy & Mather, J. Walter Thompson, MindShare, Young & Rubicam	Communications Consulting Worldwide	London
2	Interpublic	$58,080	McCann-Erickson WorldGroup, Foote, Cone & Belding Worldwide, The Lowe Group, Bozell, Temerlin McClain	DraftWorldwide, Initiative Media, and Octagon	New York
3	Omnicom	$58,080	BBDO Worldwide, DDB Worldwide, TBWA Worldwide	Hill and Knowlton, Burson-Marsteller	New York
4	Publicis Groupe/ Bcom3	$52,892	Publicis Worldwide, Saatchi & Saatchi, Fallon Worldwide, Leo Burnett	None	Paris
5	Dentsu	$20,848			Tokyo

Sources: Advertising Age, Hoovers.com.

expensive marketing campaigns. Rather, it is in the form of **viral marketing,** or brand promotion via person-to-person online communications such as in chat rooms, online discussion groups, or e-mails. For companies that generate sufficient interest in their product among online users, the consumers end up not only endorsing the product but publicizing it to others—basically marketing for the company. Companies have also taken advantage of this aspect of online communications by offering incentives to users to send multiple e-mails to other friends online who then register on the company's site.

Online Advertising Revenues

Until the late 1990s, the relative share of each analog medium of total advertising revenue stayed fairly constant. Television received the lion's share of the advertising revenue, roughly 39 percent of all advertising dollars, with most of this coming in the form of national advertising. Newspapers have been second in total advertising revenues, with most of this coming in the form of local retail and classified advertising, because most newspapers are distributed within cities or local regions. Magazines are third in overall revenues, with about 12.9 percent.

viral marketing—spreading news and information about media content through word-of-mouth, usually via online discussion groups, chats, and e-mails, without utilizing traditional advertising and marketing methods.

Radio is a distant fourth to television but still has a respectable 10 percent of total advertising revenues. Internet advertising has been growing faster than traditional media advertising, but it still makes up less than one percent of total advertising expenditures. Although still small, it is likely to be the beginning of a trend in which advertisers spend increasing amounts online, thus taking away ad dollars from traditional analog media, especially newspapers.

Jupiter and Forrester forecast that by 2004, online advertising will reach $33 billion worldwide, more than the total revenues for media giant Time Warner (now AOL Time Warner) in 1998.[3] Roughly one-third of this will be outside the United States. Forrester expects the Internet to draw $22 to 27 billion—or some 10 percent—of all United States ad spending, including a sizeable chunk away from traditional media, by 2004. Advertising spending dropped sharply after the bursting of the dot-com bubble, although it started rising again in the latter half of 2002.

Online Advertising Formats

There are a number of online advertising formats, many of which are unique to the online world, although they often borrow aspects from the print and electronic media world.

Banner Ads   Banner ads have continued to evolve since they were introduced as the first type of display advertising on the Web, and they still make up nearly 50 percent of all online advertising formats. They are now considered to be largely ineffectual in getting users to click on them to the advertisers' Web sites. However, some online advertising agencies say that banner ads do help build brand recognition even if they are not clicked on. Some advertisers have used techniques such as making the ad look like a standard Windows warning although it takes the user to the advertisers' Web site. These types of ads have drawn strong criticism because they take advantage of the fact that many computer users are still not very computer literate and may mistake the ad as a legitimate warning about their computer.

New types of banner ads have been used on many commercial Web sites since 2001. These include larger banners in the traditional location across the top of the page, so-called "tower ads" or extramercials, which are rectangular vertical banner ads down the right-hand side of a Web page, and large display ads in the middle of a page of editorial content.

Pop-up Ads   There are two main types of pop-up ads. One is the traditional pop-up, which appears in a new window when a Web site is opened, and can be either an **interstitial ad** or a **superstitial ad.** Interstitial ads load as the page is loading, which can slow down page download times. Although they get noticed by users, they have proven unpopular among users because they must close the ad browser window in order to see the Web site they originally wanted to see, and users are not as likely to click on the product as they do with superstitial ads. There are also multiple interstitial ads in which more than one browser window opens, forcing the user to close multiple windows.

Superstitial ads are pre-stored on pages and only show up when some action is performed, such as clicking the mouse. Not only are they perceived as less

interstitial ad—a type of pop-up ad on the Web that opens a new browser window when a Web site is clicked on, forcing users to close the window to see the Web site they originally wanted to see.

superstitial ad—a type of pop-up ad on the Web that opens underneath the Web site that was clicked on and is not apparent until closing browser windows.

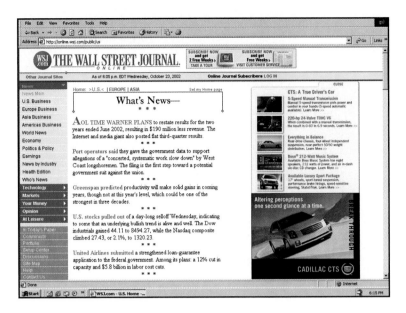

Superstitial ads, although more expensive to produce than other types of online advertising, have garnered more attention and are not seen as obtrusive as other types of pop-up ads.

obtrusive, but they allow for a range of multimedia effects that are making the superstitial ads better integrated with content than other types of online ads.

Another type of pop-up ad is technically a pop-under ad, which also opens a new window but underneath the Web site. Users may not even know a new window has been opened until they close their original browser window.

Webmercials Webmercials look and feel much like regular TV commercials and usually come on while the user is waiting for content to download. These types of ads can be seen on sites like RealNetworks as a user waits for an audio or video file to stream. Video-oriented sites are more likely to use Webmercials than print-oriented sites, although their use is becoming more common.

Advertorials/Infomercials The formats of advertorials in the print world or infomercials in the television world are making their way to the Web. Two major factors have made advertorials an especially attractive form of advertising on the Web. First, many Web sites have a great need for updated content, making them less selective about what type of content they put on their sites to look like editorial content. Also, users have a greater difficulty in differentiating editorial from marketing content on the Web.

Some advertisers, such as Sony, have taken advantage of these two factors. In 2002, Sony hired freelance writers to write about some of their products and then tried to syndicate the features simply labeled with a small subhead that said "Feature by Sony" rather than explicitly saying it was an advertorial. The New York Times on the Web refused to run the advertorials unless they were clearly marked as such, something Sony refused to do, countering that they were informative, independent articles. This is one example of how advertisers can blur the lines between journalism and marketing on the Web, making it harder for users to know if they can trust the source of what they're seeing or reading about.

Classified Ads Classified ads are very popular on the Web and are in fact threatening the income newspapers have traditionally received from their classified

Some Web-based companies have utilized traditional media outlets to attract users to their site.

ads. Online search and personalization tools make finding specific ads faster than in traditional media. The nongeographic nature of the Web also lets users search a wider area—even worldwide—for something they are looking for or want to sell. Similar to classifieds, online auction sites such as eBay have proved to be extremely popular.

E-mail Marketing Commonly called **spam** and greatly derided by most Internet users, mass e-mail mailings are cheap. Spammers are facing increasingly tough hurdles as some states are enacting antispam legislation, and software is available that can block spam. In addition, people or organizations caught spamming can have their addresses blocked from sending any messages over the Internet, and ISPs can close them down. Spam usually has a short, enticing note in the subject line of the e-mail and has a link the recipient can click on. Messages are usually all text to keep file sizes down, although some may have images in the e-mail.

Many companies have been using opt-in e-mail marketing, also called permission e-mail marketing, in which users give their permission to receive periodic e-mails highlighting special deals or sales the company may have.

Convergent Media Buying

Advertisers are also looking increasingly to exploit the potential of **convergent media buying.** Convergent media buying means purchasing online banner ads while also purchasing complementary space or time on the parent media company's other media properties, including newspapers, magazines, television, or radio. These convergent buys can benefit the advertiser in a number of ways, providing for more frequency of exposure to the advertising message, reinforcing the message in multiple media and modalities, and reaching the audience across various situations (e.g., at home, at work, while mobile). Convergent media buys also benefit the media, by increasing overall advertising revenues. Traditional media outlets such as television commercials and billboards have become useful to drive users to Web sites.

Interactive Advertising Agencies

Although traditional advertising firms still dominate the advertising landscape and have created interactive divisions within their corporations, a number of Internet-original firms emerged in the late 1990s. Among the most important are online design firms and those that specialize in online network services, although most have lost substantial revenues in the dot-com bust. There was a 28.6 per-

spam—unwanted email sent out by advertisers as a mass mailing.

convergent media buying—purchasing online ads as well as complementary space or time on the parent media company's other media properties, including newspaper, magazine, television, or radio.

cent drop ($2.3 billion in revenues in 2001) compared to 2000 ($3.2 billion) for the top 200 ad agencies for providing interactive advertising services.

Previously top-ranked interactive ad agency Scient, which merged with competitor iXL in August 2001, dropped to the number-two position among interactive ad agencies as its 2001 revenues declined 76 percent over 2000 revenues. Other Internet-only firms such as Razorfish, Agency.com, and Organic either dropped substantially or were bought by other companies in 2001. Some of the interactive ad agencies with traditional advertising agency parents fared better in the dot-com bust.

Ethical Issues in Advertising

Mass media are a powerful vehicle to influence the public's opinions, even when they are simply trying to inform or educate and not trying to persuade, as advertising does. Otherwise companies wouldn't spend billions of dollars on advertising each year trying to persuade people to buy their products. From snake oil salesmen of the 19th century to complaints about billboards in the 20th century, from claims of invasion of privacy against telemarketers and false and deceptive advertising in the mass media to actors paid to give "customer testimonials," numerous ethical issues have been raised that may cause the discerning consumer to have a jaundiced eye toward advertising.

Advertising is an important part of how goods and services are marketed in a capitalist economy, and some advertising contains useful product information. Advertising is also the economic engine that drives much of the system of mass communication. If consumers had to pay the entire cost of a daily newspaper, for example, they would be likely to see the cost of that paper rise to more than $5 a copy, instead of about 50 cents.

The advertising industry has been less successful at regulating itself than the entertainment industry, and usually the government eventually steps in to create new laws or regulations regarding advertising after receiving consumer complaints or sometimes after long campaigns regarding certain advertising practices. The Federal Trade Commission (FTC) and the Food and Drug Administration (FDA) are responsible for regulating the advertising industry. Industry self-regulation comes from a variety of trade organizations, including the National Advertising Division of the Council of Better Business Bureaus. One of the main issues regarding advertising ethics from a mass communication perspective deals with false or deceptive advertising.

The public learns to take a jaundiced eye about advertising claims early when products don't match what they have seen.

Puffery, a statement of opinion that cannot be proven as true or false, is allowed by the FTC.

False or Deceptive Advertising

In some cases, advertisers give clearly false or misleading information, but this practice is illegal only if it is deceptive. Falsity in advertising is not illegal, because in some cases, falsity is not trying to deceive the public. For instance, ice cubes photographed in a beverage ad may not be authentic ice cubes. Actual ice might melt under the photographer's hot lights, but because the fake cubes don't mislead anyone, it's fine to use them.

In other cases, however, false or misleading claims are made with the intention to deceive the consumer. A division of the Federal Trade Commission is assigned responsibility to ferret out such deception and can force such advertising from mass media or even levy fines.

The FTC once found a commercial for a toy car deceptive even though it was not false. The toy was filmed in extreme close-up next to the track, so that the car seemed to move very rapidly and appeared as a blur on the screen. The FTC ruled that children would be deceived into believing the car actually moves so fast that it is a blur, and the ad had to be canceled or modified.

Puffery

Nevertheless, there is great temptation among those selling goods and services, as well as those sponsoring ads, to exaggerate their claims. This is called **puffery,** and it is an ethical and legal gray area (i.e., sometimes allowed, sometimes not). Puffery usually involves an opinion statement about the product. Examples include these familiar advertising slogans:

- "The best in the business" (AT&T).
- "The best part of waking up is Folger's in your cup."
- "Trojan: America's #1 condom."

In each case, there is no way to prove the truth or falsehood of the claim, and the advertiser cannot document the claim. The FTC's position is that audiences do not believe the opinion claims of these commercials because they do not perceive them to be factual. Consequently, the FTC permits most puffery, because it feels people are not deceived. Yet, the nation's leading scholarly authority on puffery disagrees. Ivan Preston, a long-time professor of advertising at the University of Wisconsin, has conducted extensive research on puffery. He is firmly convinced that people do in fact believe the claims implied by puffery. "Puffery is used because it works," Preston concludes.[4]

Weblink
FTC
[www.ftc.gov]

puffery—exaggerated advertising claims deemed allowable by the FTC because they are unverifiable statements of opinion that cannot be tested.

Banned Advertising

Because of their power to persuade, radio and television are not permitted by the federal regulators to broadcast advertising of certain legal products, including cigarettes.

Some industries have also treated advertising on the electronic media with special care. Since the late 1940s, the distilled beverages industry had exercised a voluntary ban on advertising hard liquor on television. But in June 1996, Joseph E. Seagrams & Sons Co. broke the ban and ran advertising for its liquor products on television. Less than a year later, the Distilled Spirits Council of the United States revised its Code of Good Practice to permit its members to advertise their hard liquor products on radio and television.

Public Relations

Just as advertising agencies straddle the world between advertisers and media, public relations firms straddle the world between companies wishing to promote themselves to the public and media organizations who can widely distribute that message.

Public relations has been described and defined in many ways. To many journalists, public relations represents at best a necessary evil. To others, it is far worse. It is the enemy. And to still others, public relations is viewed as a vital part of the three-way relationship among organizations, their publics, and the media. The term *public* refers to the many groups, organizations, or collectives with whom an organization or individual may have some sort of relationship.

Although the phrase "the public" is often used to refer to the general population, there are in fact many "publics" with whom an organization might be concerned. For example, a company has many relevant publics, including its employees, consumers, shareholders, activists (who might oppose certain corporate policies), regulators, and of course the media, which is the primary vehicle by which the general public hears about the company. When a company is

Media **Inventors and Innovators**

P. T. Barnum

Phineas Taylor "P. T." Barnum (1810–1891) used various techniques to communicate with the public and had his greatest success with staged events, or publicity stunts, to attract attention. In the 1830s, Barnum entered the world of promotion, press manipulation, and show business.

One of his first successes was the establishment of Barnum's American Museum in the center of New York, where in 1842 he debuted Charles Sherwood Stratton, a dwarf 25 inches tall and weighing 15 pounds, as "General Tom Thumb" to help promote his new museum.

But it was not until 1870 at the age of 60 that he founded P. T. Barnum's Grand Traveling Menagerie, Caravan and Circus. It grossed $400,000 its first year; and, in 1887, Barnum asked James Bailey to join him in the new Barnum and Bailey Circus, which he dubbed the "Greatest Show on Earth."

P. T. Barnum was a master showman and had a knack for creating events that attracted widespread public interest.

in trouble or there is potentially damaging information about the company, public relations professionals work to mitigate the negative stories about the company. When there is good news, they seek to promote the news heavily to media outlets.

Edward L. Bernays, the late father of modern public relations, used to say that propaganda was better than impropaganda. The same might be said of public relations. It all depends on how it's done.

The Historical Stages of PR Development

There are some who say public relations is the world's second-oldest profession, but the modern field of public relations has evolved through at least three phases of development beginning in the latter half of the 19th century. Prior to that, a number of publishing activities that today we would separate as journalism or public relations were conducted with little sense of differentiation between them. Thomas Paine's pro-revolution pamphlets in the 1770s or the sympathetic writings in newspapers on the Boston Massacre, for examples, would be considered public relations by today's standards rather than journalism.

Phase I: Press Agentry

> **press agentry**—the practice of getting publicity for clients by getting them mentioned in media outlets, such as news stories or feature articles, as well as on television or radio.

During the 19th century and early 20th century, the first stage of public relations emerged. This area might best be called the age of **press agentry.** Press agentry refers to the practice of getting publicity in the press (or other media) for a client. It is based on the premise that just about any publicity is good publicity, as long as the client's name is spelled right. It operates on a **one-way symmetric public relations** model, in which information is almost exclusively from companies to the public, usually via the media.

Press agentry flourished under the practice of Phineas Taylor "P. T." Barnum, the great showman and founder of the famous American circus that still bears his name.

Press agentry features a wide spectrum of PR activities such as special events or stunts. These stunts have ranged from the spectacular to the sublime. In one case, debutantes were invited to march in the 1928 Easter Parade in New York City holding their "torches of freedom"—otherwise known as lit cigarettes—to help get media attention and thereby build public support for women smoking in public at a time when society frowned upon it. The occasion was sponsored by the American Tobacco Co., manufacturers of Lucky Strike cigarettes.

The Pseudo Event   One of the most enduring legacies from the early days of modern public relations is the creation of what Daniel Boorstin calls "the pseudo event." Pseudo events are events manufactured by individuals or organizations, typically to capture the attention of the media and thereby the public. Press conferences, protests, and parades are all examples of pseudo events and are a form of media manipulation. But the media have become dependent on them. In fact, studies show that as much as 75 percent of the news content in even the best of the nation's newspapers such as the *Washington Post* was in someway influenced by a pseudo event. Only occasionally is a story generated through pure "enterprise" or original reporting, with no public relations influence.[5]

Ivy Lee   Although the term had not yet been coined, it was former journalist Ivy Ledbetter Lee who was perhaps the first true public relations practitioner. Lee was a master of managing the press and the press agentry model, which essentially viewed the public as a mass audience waiting to be manipulated. He once observed, "Crowds are led by symbols and phrases." He employed a variety of innovative techniques that are staples of modern public relations practice, including press conferences, staged events, and newsreels, which today are known as video press releases.

One of Lee's most visible clients was John D. Rockefeller, Sr., the founder of the Standard Oil Trust and the world's first billionaire, who managed his companies and employees ruthlessly, even by standards of the day. After he had the Colorado state militia put down a miner's strike by killing dozens of miners, including some women and children, his son realized that public opinion must also be won and brought in Ivy Lee. Lee produced reports stating that women and children victims in a house fire started by the militia died because of an overturned stove, not as a result of the militia's actions. In response, muckraking journalist Upton Sinclair, author of *The Jungle,* described Lee as "Poison Ivy."

During the years to follow, Lee continued to produce massive amounts of favorable press materials on John D. Rockefeller, Sr. Among Lee's successes was the production of newsreels showing "John D." giving out dimes to poor children. Lee became legendary internationally for his ability to manipulate the media and the masses, and in the 1930s the Third Reich of Nazi Germany hired Lee to present a more favorable face for the "New Germany" in the United States.[6]

one-way symmetric public relations—a model of public relations used in the press agentry format, in which information about a company is almost exclusively sent by the company via the media to the public.

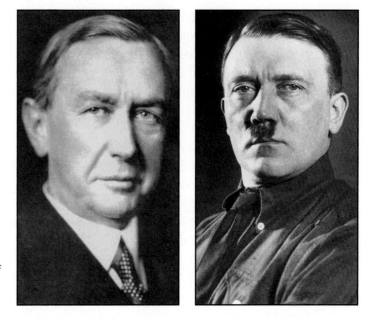

Ivy Lee was such a successful public relations professional that he was hired by Nazi Germany in the 1930s to help improve the image of the "New Germany" to Americans.

Phase II: Edward L. Bernays and Two-Way Asymmetric Public Relations

The term *public relations* was coined by Edward L. Bernays, who managed some of the first public relations campaigns of the 20th century. Bernays also ushered in the second phase in the evolution of public relations, what public relations scholars James Grunig and Todd Hunt describe as **two-way asymmetric public relations.** This term refers to the fact that public relations conducted in this framework involves a two-way flow of information between organizations and their publics, but that the flow is dominated by the organizations. Moreover, the organization is dominant in the relationship, intending to influence the knowledge, attitudes, or behaviors of the public. Feedback is used as a means by which to gauge public opinion and to effectively design messages to influence it.

Trained during World War I as a member of the Foreign Press Bureau of the U.S. Committee on Public Information (CPI), essentially the propaganda arm of the U.S. government, Bernays was a nephew of psychologist Sigmund Freud and often dined with his famous uncle. Bernays mastered Freud's theories and in fact produced the first English-language translation of Freud's books. After the war, Bernays applied both the principles of Freudian psychology and social science, a then-budding field, to the strategic influence and shaping of public opinion. He went on to write a classic book, *The Engineering of Consent*.

Phase III: Two-Way Symmetric Public Relations

The third phase of public relations began to take shape in the 1980s and is still developing today. This phase is by no means a complete transformation, but it is best characterized as the emergence of a **two-way symmetric model of public relations.** This model emphasizes public relations as a system of managing relationships between organizations and individuals and their many publics, including both internal and external. Communication via the media of mass communication is one tool in this system of relationship management. Emphasis is on building mutual understanding as much as on influencing public opinion.

two-way asymmetric public relations—public relations conducted within a framework of two-way information flow between an organization and the public, but with the flow dominated by the organization.

two-way symmetric public relations—a model of public relations that emphasizes a system of managing relationships between organizations and their many publics, of which communication through the mass media is one tool to manage the relationship.

Research by Grunig and others shows that organizational excellence (as defined in terms of achieving both short- and long-term organizational objectives) is achieved most effectively when this model of two-way symmetric public relations is practiced. The two-way symmetric model also incorporates the public relations function into the senior management and decision-making of the organization, and both formal and informal techniques are used to assess the attitudes, knowledge, behaviors and intentions of various publics. The symmetric model places a premium on the ethical practice of public relations.

Of course, many practitioners of both public relations and journalism still equate public relations with publicity and media relations, but in the emerging symmetric model this represents merely one activity within the repertoire of tools used in the ethical management of organizational relationships.

One of the best examples of two-way symmetric public relations comes from the story of how Johnson & Johnson handled the well-known Tylenol tampering case in 1982, when seven people died of cyanide poisoning after taking tainted Extra-Strength Tylenol capsules. After the first reported poisoning in the Chicago, Illinois, area, Johnson & Johnson took immediate steps to prevent further tragedy and established clear and open communications lines with both the media and the public.

Among its efforts, both Johnson & Johnson and its parent, McNeil Consumer Products Co., established a hot line for people to call and offered a $100,000 reward for the arrest and conviction of the person or persons responsible for the deaths. Johnson & Johnson instituted a nationwide recall of all Extra-Strength Tylenol capsules at a cost of some $100 million to remove and destroy all 31 million bottles. The company received thousands of calls requesting information and opened regional poison control centers to dispense information and assistance.

The capsules were successfully reintroduced into the market in January 1983 with triple-sealed, tamper-resistant packaging. Johnson & Johnson and McNeil Consumer Products Co. were cleared of any legal liability for the deaths and poisonings, and Tylenol sales have recovered. In 1991, Johnson & Johnson and McNeil Consumer Products Co. provided the families of the seven victims with an undisclosed settlement, estimated to be as much as $50 million.

Despite the overwhelmingly negative nature of the event, coverage of the Tylenol tragedy generally portrayed Johnson & Johnson and its parent in a favorable light. Companies during a crisis are often criticized by journalists for hiding

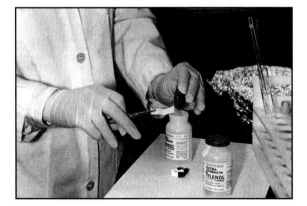

Johnson & Johnson, the makers of Tylenol, were widely praised for their rapid response and openness during the Tylenol tampering incident in which seven people died.

information from the press and the public, but many journalists have praised Johnson & Johnson for its openness and the immediacy of its response to the poisonings. John O'Brien of the *Chicago Tribune* said, "The public relations people were knowledgeable and available when the media needed to talk to them. They didn't try to sugar-coat anything."

PR and Media Relations

Although public relations professionals engage in a wide variety of activities, most typically devote a large portion, if not a majority, of their efforts to working with the media, including journalists, producers, and others who are responsible for the content of those media. By developing and maintaining good working relationships with the media, public relations professionals anticipate that they will be more successful in obtaining fair or positive coverage of their organizations in those media. When a negative story does occur, having maintained a good relationship with the media increases an organization's opportunity to at least communicate clearly and responsibly with the media. If the media err in reporting a story, a public relations professional who has maintained a good relationship with the media will be more effective in obtaining a correction.

Distributing News to the Media in the Digital Age

An important development in media relations is the distribution of corporate or other organization news, information, and data (whether statistical or multimedia, including audio and video). This was and in many cases still is done largely with analog media, such as publication-quality photos, artwork, or video footage distributed to journalists in press kits that news organizations can use.

However, increasingly PR firms are relying on online distribution of content and media, either via the Web or some other means. The Middleberg/Ross study *Media in Cyberspace* has confirmed the value of online content distribution to media organizations, especially journalists, who are increasingly relying on these feeds, and in fact oftentimes preferring them to content delivered in other formats.

The Middleberg and Ross data show that, as stated in the study, "Journalists cite financial information as being the most useful element to a Web site, followed by photos and press releases."

Three-quarters (73 percent) of journalists go online to find press releases, and more than half (53 percent) like to receive story pitches online. Digital photography is increasingly preferred over slides and photos in the magazine industry. Nearly half (46 percent) of magazine editors favor digital images, compared to just a quarter (26 percent) who prefer slides or camera-ready art. An even higher percentage of photo editors at newspapers prefer to receive images in digital format. More than half (61 percent) prefer digital photos to film. A third of broadcasters want to receive audio files from Web sites, and one-fifth want video files.

Journalists prefer digital content as being easier to look at and evaluate for newsworthiness because the journalist simply downloads the material to his or her desktop computer. Digital media are also easier and faster to edit, store, and retrieve than analog content. In an age of information clutter, digital content is also easier to ignore or discard.

Journalists increasingly prefer to receive public relations information digitally rather than through a traditional press kit.

Leading Online PR News Services

Founded in 1954, New York–based PR Newswire has been a pioneer in delivering extensive corporate and other public relations news via online media. PR Newswire serves 40,000 customers who pay an annual fee to distribute more than 1000 news releases and photos sent each day over the service to 22,000 media organizations and 40,000 journalists. PR Newswire also distributes content to 2600 Web sites and databases and provides multimedia broadcasts through cable and satellite systems.

Top competitors to PR Newswire include the Business Wire, MediaLink, and Bloomberg. Business Wire is based in San Francisco and offers 40,000 clients an international business news wire service, delivered largely online. MediaLink is another New York-based business service, specializing in video and audio production and distribution, including video news releases sent to television stations and material sent to more than 6000 online news sites. With some 1600 clients, the company had 1998 revenues of $56 million and 320 employees.

Finding Sources Online

Facilitating the media–public relations relationship has been the growth of various **expert source clearinghouses** in the online arena. Although such clearinghouses have functioned in the off-line world for many years in a variety of forms (such as media guides published by universities, or *The Yearbook of Experts, Authorities & Spokespersons*), they have thrived in the online arena for many of the same reasons that classified advertising works well online: Online media allow highly efficient targeting of communications and searching. *The Yearbook of Experts, Authorities & Spokespersons* is now available online, greatly facilitating the process of finding experts and authorities, especially when on deadline.

Perhaps the biggest of these clearinghouses is ProfNet, an online service that connects more than 6000 news and information officers at colleges and universities, businesses, research centers, medical centers, nonprofit organizations, and public relations agencies with journalists all around the world.

Weblink

PR Newswire
[www.prnewswire.com]

Businesswire
[www.businesswire.com]

MediaLink
[www.medialink.com]

Weblink

The Yearbook of Experts, Authorities & Spokespersons
[www.expertclick.com/]

ProfNet
[www3.profnet.com/]

expert source clearinghouse— a company that maintains lists of expert sources in various fields from which journalists can draw when they need an authoritative source to comment on some news story.

Finding experts in various fields is greatly facilitated by online databases and services such as ProfNet.

The way this clearinghouse works is simple. A reporter submits a query to ProfNet (online or via an 800 number), and the query is then dispatched to appropriate organizations included in the more than 2000 institutions that participate in ProfNet. The query contains a description of the story the reporter is working on, the name of her or his news organization and deadline, as well as the preferred means of communication. The journalist also selects which types of organizations she or he would like the query submitted to, such as colleges and universities, corporations, or government agencies. Typically, in less than 24 hours various experts are identified at these institutions by their public relations officers, and the journalist making the query is notified of the appropriate experts and is able to contact them directly.

Before an online clearinghouse such as ProfNet, journalists would have to either scour related articles in the publication's archives, called a **morgue,** to get an idea of who has been interviewed in the past or telephone contacts they knew who might know experts with whom to get in touch. With that information, they would then get the number of the expert or the public information office of the expert's institution and explain whom they want to talk to and why over the phone, or try to call the expert directly.

The speed and convenience of an online service such as ProfNet means that many different experts can be contacted on a topic rather than relying on a limited network of professional relationships for sources. Drawbacks to ProfNet include that it sometimes becomes too easy to rely on it rather than doing one's own research to find the best possible expert to comment on a topic.

ProfNet maintains an "experts database" containing the names and descriptions of more than 2000 experts already known to the system. ProfNet was started in 1992 by Daniel Forbush, then a public relations officer at the State University of New York at Stony Brook. ProfNet is now owned by the PR Newswire.

PR Firms and the PR Industry

The U.S. public relations industry enjoyed substantial growth in the economic boom of the late 1990s but suffered accordingly as the economy turned down and many of the technology-related companies they had as clients (which made up 40 percent of revenues in 2000) either went out of business or severely cut back their marketing budgets. Overall revenue for the $4.2 billion industry fell 10 to 15 percent in 2001, according to the Council of Public Relations Firms.

morgue—an archive of news articles or photographs from a publication and other publications on various topics that can be used as a background reference source for a journalist doing a story.

In public relations, revenues are based on a combination of sources of income. These include primarily fees for public relations consulting and services; income from specialized communications services such as research, interactive communications, and employee communications, and mark-ups for production services and other media materials.

The 1990s saw considerable consolidation among public relations firms. But acquisition has slowed considerably in the first years of the 21st century, with most consolidation still occurring internationally. Major buyers are European holding companies such as Incepta Group, Havas, Publicis, and Cordiant. Omnicom is the one major U.S. communications firm that acquired several technology firms for Fleishman-Hillard.

Although most large organizations maintain their own internal public relations unit or office, many hire public relations firms to help in their efforts, particularly with more specialized services such as media relations. Media relations can be extremely complex and can require extensive experience with not just local but national media. Oftentimes, public relations firms maintain their own specialists who have the necessary experience to help clients manage their media relations, particularly during campaigns or crises.

PR firms are organized into three main areas:

1. *Core practice areas,* or the type of relationships the client needs managed, including marketing communications or consumer relations, investor relations, public, nonprofit, and governmental affairs; corporate and employee communications; political communications; and community relations.

2. *Services,* or the type of activity the firm provides to its clients, including media relations, research, interactive or online communications, writing, lobbying, fund-raising, and crisis management.

3. *Industries,* or the business sectors the clients operate within, including utilities, technology, retail, manufacturing, health care, financial services, and consumer products.

Many firms specialize in one or more core practice areas, services, or industries. This enables them to focus resources in one or more areas, yet achieve a high enough level of expertise needed to serve clients operating on a national or global scale. A good example is Padilla-Speer-Beardsley, a Minneapolis-based firm with a national and international reach. Although the firm employs just 100 people, it is able to compete with much larger firms employing thousands and to do so with large clients with national or international interests.

Some PR firms also offer integrated communication programs, sometimes called integrated marketing communications. This means the firm provides a comprehensive set of communication management and services to clients as well as public relations and advertising activities. Most of the larger PR firms provide integrated communication programs.

Table 12-2 provides data on the top-10 U.S. public relations firms according to total worldwide revenues for 2001. The largest public relations firm in the world is Weber Shandwick Worldwide, which displaced Fleishman-Hillard from the top spot despite an almost 16 percent drop in growth in 2001. Most of the PR firms had revenue losses or lackluster performances in 2001, largely because

Weblink
Council of Public Relations Firms
[www.prfirms.org]

Weblink
Padilla-Speer-Beardsley
[www.psbpr.com]

Table 12-2 Top Public Relations Firms, 2001: Worldwide Revenues

Rank	Agency Name	Employees	2001 Revenues	Growth from 2000
1	Weber Shandwick Worldwide	2838	$426,572,018	–15.94%
2	Fleishman-Hillard Inc.	2288	$345,098,241	1.97%
3	Hill and Knowlton, Inc.	1117	$325,119,000	7.38%
4	INCEPTA (CITIGATE)	2236	$266,018,371	9.05%
5	Burson-Marsteller	1613	$259,112,000	–14.73%
6	Edelman Public Relations Worldwide	1973	$223,708,535	–4.16%
7	Ketchum, Inc.	1066	$185,221,000	10.09%
8	Porter Novelli International	1553	$179,294,000	–13.87%
9	GCI Group/APCO Worldwide	1282	$151,081,645	0.28%
10	Ogilvy Public Relations Worldwide	1110	$145,949,285	–13.87%

Source: http://www.prfirms.org/resources/rankings/2001_rankings.asp.

of the downturn in the economy and the events of September 11. Many firms laid off employees, with Burson-Marsteller laying off 15 percent of its staff in 2001 and Edelman laying off 10 percent of its staff, just to name two examples. The performances in 2001 are in stark contrast to growth in 2000, with some companies such as Fleishman-Hillard posting 60 percent growth over the previous year.

Ethical Issues in Public Relations

Public relations people face a unique set of ethical issues compared to journalists, media entertainment professionals, and advertising people. Like advertising professionals, their loyalties lie with the message their client wants to give to their publics, but like journalists their credibility and that of their clients can be severely damaged if they present false or misleading information. In addition, although some public relations practitioners like to claim they are the "conscience of the client," the fact is they do not always have access to the corporate channels of power to head off possibly disastrous management decisions before they happen. Often they are called in after damage has been done and are asked to minimize or negate the damage from a public relations standpoint.

Because public relations deals with trying to present an image to the public or change public opinions on a topic or organization in order to create a more favorable light, a clear-cut line between ethical and unethical behavior is often hard to discern. Guidelines for ethical public relations practices are articulated by professional associations such as the Public Relations Society of America (PRSA) and the International Association of Business Communicators.

According to the PRSA, unethical behavior for PR practitioners includes lying by omission, such as failing to release financial information from a corpo-

Hill and Knowlton: Selling a War

Hill and Knowlton is considered one of the most power-ful PR firms in the world, with 57 offices in 32 countries as well as an extensive associates network.

The company was widely criticized for its clandestine efforts to influence the U.S. government and the American public during the Gulf War. The firm was hired at a cost of more than half a million dollars by the government of Kuwait to foster support among the American public and the U.S. Congress.

Hill and Knowlton produced and distributed dozens of video news releases (VNRs) to television news operations around the country. Many of the stations aired the VNRs without identifying their source as either Hill and Knowlton or the government of Kuwait. Many of the stations aired the propaganda without editing it, presenting it as impartial journalism.

Hill and Knowlton also helped organize the so-called "Congressional Human Rights Caucus," which held hearings on Capitol Hill. Chaired by California Democrat Tom Lantos and Illinois Republican John Porter, the cau-cus was housed in Hill and Knowlton's Washington, D.C., office. In a caucus hearing on Capitol Hill on October 10, 1990, a 15-year-old Kuwaiti girl, known only as Nayirah, spoke in tears, saying, "I volunteered at the al-Addan hospital. While I was there, I saw the Iraqi soldiers come into the hospital with guns, and go into the room where . . . babies were in incuba-tors. They took the babies out of the incubators, took the incubators, and left the babies on the cold floor to die."

For months after her testimony, the Iraqi soldiers' killing of babies was repeated in the media and even by President George H. Bush as rationale for the U.S. presence in the region. Later it was revealed that Nayirah was a member of the Kuwaiti royal family, that her testimony was a fabrication, and that a Hill and Knowlton vice president had coached Nayirah on what to say during her testimony. After the end of the war, the Canadian Broadcasting Corporation produced an Emmy Award–winning documentary on the Hill and Knowlton campaign entitled, *To Sell a War.*

Who should bear the brunt of the responsibility for this misleading cam-paign, PR firm Hill and Knowlton—or the journalists who did not bother to check the sources of media they were getting?

PR firm Hill and Knowlton was widely criticized for manipulating the media and public with mislead-ing information and false testimony on atrocities commited by Iraqi soldiers during their invasion of Kuwait.

ration or giving a misleading impression of a corporation's performance; deceiving the public by employing people to pose as volunteers to speak at public hearings or in "grass roots" campaigns; and giving expensive goods or gifts to journalists or politicians in order to influence their opinion on a product or issue. On the other hand, their guidelines also state that members must protect the privacy rights of clients and safeguard their confidential information, as well as advise appropriate authorities if they discover that an employee is divulging confidential information. It is easy to see how an ethical conflict could arise for a PR professional who learns information about the poor financial situation of a company and is asked by the company to encourage positive news reports on its financial health, rather than negative ones.

Digital media present new and unique temptations to public relations professionals. Shortly after Infoseek's Executive Vice President Patrick Naughton was arrested in September 1999 for allegedly planning a sexual encounter with a minor he'd met over the Internet (who turned out to be an undercover policewoman), Naughton was not only fired from Infoseek and had his management bio removed from the site, but the public relations department tried to delete all mention of his name in their archived press releases online to make it seem as if he never worked there. There were protests about this clumsy attempt to rewrite history *1984* style, and within 24 hours his name was back in most of the press releases and Infoseek claimed it was "an accident."[7] The ease by which not only current information, but archival information, can be changed could be a temptation for other companies or individuals who would like to rewrite history.

Weblink
Public Relations Society of America
[www.prsa.org/]
International Association of Business Communicators
[www.iabc.com/]

SUMMARY

This chapter has provided an overview of the media support industries, advertising and public relations. Although news and entertainment are the content most people go to the media for, in reality the most common form of content is advertising, while much of the editorial content or programming has been inspired or influenced by public relations.

Underlying these media support institutions are theoretical principles of persuasive communication. Four concepts are especially important:

1. Media differences.
2. Message characteristics.
3. Audience fragmentation.
4. Individual characteristics and conditions.

Both fields face changes in their roles and how they carry them out with digital media.

Advertising has so far failed to be a great success on the Web. Technology allows for greater accountability of response rates to advertisements, and the low response-rate numbers have not made advertisers feel their money is well-spent online. As a result, advertising agencies have been trying new types of advertisements online, with mixed results and with some Internet user backlash at larger, more obtrusive ads.

The Web has given all groups the ability to publicize their messages, although public relations firms will continue to be vital in making sure organizations get noticed in the mainstream media and managing the public face a corporation or group presents to the public.

Practitioners of advertising and public relations face important ethical challenges as they engage in communications designed strategically to influence members of the public.

Discussion Questions

1. Keep track of every advertising message you receive from the time you wake up to the time you reach your school or workplace. Don't forget to include not only the number of radio and television commercials or ads you see in the morning paper, but advertising on Web sites and ads on objects like cereal boxes, buses, taxis, telephone booths, and outside and inside stores.
2. How effective is persuasive communication? What could make it more effective in today's crowded media environment?
3. Some brands have such successful marketing that the brand name becomes synonymous with the product itself, such as the trademarked name Kleenex being used generically for facial tissues. Can you name other trademarked brands that have become commonly used for the generic products?
4. Discuss which advertising format you feel is the most effective and why. Are there some products that are better advertised in a certain format as opposed to other formats? Why do you think this is?
5. Discuss strengths and weaknesses of the large advertising agency model common today. Do you think the trend to ever larger agencies is good or bad? Why?
6. Which profession faces greater challenges in a digital media world, advertising or public relations? Explain your reasons.

Media Research and Effects: From Film to the Internet

13

Research on media has long focused on the question of the possible harmful effects of television viewing on young viewers. Some early studies examined the possible harmful psychological effects of watching television, especially viewing violence.

A string of violent acts, such as school shootings by preteens and teens in the late 1990s, the most notorious of which happened at Columbine High School in 1999, prompted more calls to examine the role of TV, movies, music videos, and violent video games in influencing children's behavior.

But questioning the potentially harmful effects of media on young people also has a long history. Ancient Greek philosophers worried about the corrupting influence of written poetry, and many books have been banned in

the United States and elsewhere, all with the justification that exposure to them would be harmful to young people. Even comics, perhaps because of their graphical nature, have fallen under severe scrutiny for the harm they may cause to young people.

However, the rise of electronic media seemed to spur many more studies on the effects of media. Recently, researchers have started asking questions about interactive media, such as video games, as they study how the interactivity and participatory nature of such games may differ from passive viewing of violence, such as on television or in movies, and how this may change behavior and attitudes.

Prologue

Since early television studies, research has not only confirmed the negative physiological effects of television viewing but has diagnosed a host of other problems as well, such as increased aggressiveness among TV viewers of frequent violence. Research suggests nonviolent programming can have positive effects on children as well, including improvements in reading ability, mathematics, and social skills. How the balance tips in the years ahead will depend on many factors, including how the next generation of mass communication professionals incorporate the findings of media research into creating better future media programming for everyone.

We will look at media effects research over roughly the past 75 years, since the systematic inquiry of mass communication began in earnest. Our focus is on the effects of media on individuals, groups, and society.

About Media Research

Media research is the systematic and scientific investigation of mass communication processes and effects. Media research methodology, or how research is carried out, takes many forms. It can range from social scientific research using quantitative tools, such as surveys and experiments employing statistical analysis of the data, to critical studies employing qualitative methods, such as ethnographic studies.

We can best understand the nature of media research in the context of three factors:

1. The methodology used to conduct mass communication research.
2. The theories that guide mass communication research.
3. How mass communicators, the public, and policy makers use mass communication research.

Research Methodologies

Researchers use many methods such as experiments, surveys, and case studies to conduct studies of mass communication effects. We can group these methods into two broad areas of research methodologies, **quantitative studies** and **critical–cultural studies,** which are sometimes called qualitative studies.

Quantitative Studies

Quantitative studies include the familiar methods of experiments, surveys, or content analyses. The exact type of method used depends on several factors, but especially on the goals or purposes of the research. If a study is intended to establish causality, such as whether watching violent programming on television causes increased levels of violence among children, then experimental or quasi-experimental methods are especially appropriate.

If a study is meant to document how much violence is on television, then a content analysis should be conducted. If an investigation is designed to determine

quantitative studies—studies that focus on numbers and measures and experimentation to describe phenomena. Researchers usually have a hypothesis they are trying to prove or disprove through controlled experimentation.

critical–cultural studies—studies that describe phenomena in words instead of numbers or measures. Ethnographic studies, such as interviews with people to learn about beliefs or trends, are an example of critical–cultural studies. Also called qualitative studies.

Quantitative studies are carefully designed according to specific research goals and are carried out to test a hypothesis.

validity—in experimental terms, the measure of how well the results or conclusions can be inferred from the data.

reliability—in media research terms, the extent of how accurate or repeatable a certain result is in an experiment.

ethnographic studies—taken from methods used in anthropology, a researcher enters a culture or milieu and studies how the population behaves in its natural setting, trying to create as little impact as possible while conducting his or her studies.

how much televised violence children see, then a survey or direct observation is in order.

In any case, research methods are never perfect indicators, and each study offers a certain level of validity and reliability. **Validity** means that the results or conclusions can be correctly inferred or deduced from the data. For example, a study of television violence viewing would have little validity if it relied exclusively on how much violence children told their parents they saw on television. Many children would likely under-report how much violence they watched either for fear their parents might restrict their television watching or because they may not even define some violent programming as such. Direct observation through an electronic meter or some other method would be needed to get a more valid measure.

Reliability refers to the accuracy, or repeatability, of a measure. A yardstick that is 37 inches long would provide a reliable measure of distance, but it would be invalid, because it should be 36 inches in length. In terms of the media, a survey that asks viewers how much television they watched last night might provide a reliable and valid measure (i.e., the same person asked the same question twice might answer it the same both times).

Critical–Cultural Studies

Critical–cultural, or qualitative, investigations are often used to provide more depth or texture to quantitative studies. A popular critical–cultural method in media research involves the use of ethnographies, or ethnographic investigations. **Ethnographic studies** involve the application of a technique developed in anthropology, where the researcher enters into a culture, immersing her- or himself, to directly observe the culture, while minimizing her or his impact on the functioning of that culture.

In the context of the media, an ethnographer might enter into a household, a newsroom, or an advertising agency and spend hours, days, weeks, or even months directly observing the media behaviors of the people or organization involved. The ethnographer might video and audio record the observed activities as a way of documenting her or his research. Then, she or he would subsequently conduct a detailed analysis of what was observed. The results might be used in isolation or in combination with other methods to draw conclusions with regard to the media effects or processes under investigation.

Ideally, media researchers employ a combination of at least three methods to triangulate on the desired effect or process they are studying. Triangulating with three or more methods is more expensive and laborious than a single or dual method, but it provides the most reliable and valid results. Sometimes, researchers use the results of their own single-method study in combination with other studies that may have used other methods to increase the generalizability of their research results. Such an investigation is called a meta investigation.

The Levels or Types of Media Effects: Individual, Group, Societal

Media theory takes many forms. There is no single overarching theory of media effects. But one way to organize the many disparate theories is to consider the impact of media on three hierarchical levels, or levels of abstraction:

1. Individual.
2. Group.
3. Societal.

Individual effects are those that are manifested on individuals, with mass influences totaled across populations. For example, viewing media violence may influence an individual's attitudes and behaviors, whether she or he is part of any larger group or not. Individual-level effects are the most commonly understood and discussed in society.

Group effects are those in which media effects are seen on some sort of social organization, from an interpersonal pair to the public. An example here might involve the impact of media exposure on family communication patterns.

Societal media effects are those that manifest themselves on an entire culture or societal grouping, or even on global society. These effects are typically longer term than the other effects and often harder to measure or see, but they may be the most important of all. An example might involve the impact of the international dominance of Western media, with their core signs, symbols, and values, on global culture. Such effects might manifest themselves in the form of the growing use of the English language online.

Media scholar Marshall McLuhan.

Media scholars Marshall and Eric McLuhan offer another view of media effects in their book *Laws of Media*. They suggest that every human innovation, media included, produces at least four basic effects. These effects may not always be visible but are always present, whether latent or manifest:

1. *Amplification:* The invention of the automobile greatly increased human mobility.

2. *Displacement:* The horse-drawn carriage was all but eliminated.

3. *Retrieval:* Already-existing roads were used even more and greatly expanded and improved.

4. *Conversion:* Suburban sprawl became a defining characteristic of the late 20th-century Western landscape, due largely to the mobility resulting from the invention of the automobile.

These effects can be at the individual, group, or societal level. For example, consider the Internet in the context of these four laws and from the point of view of the three levels of effects:

1. *Amplification:* The Internet amplifies, or causes to increase, human to human communication (e.g., consider the rapidly growing numbers of e-mails sent by Internet users).

2. *Displacement:* The Internet displaces other forms of communication (e.g., not as many letters are being sent by conventional post).

3. *Retrieval:* The Internet is leading to the retrieval of written communication (e.g., rather than using the telephone, people are sending e-mails or using online instant messages).

4. *Conversion:* The ubiquity of the Internet has changed many people's behavior as they access the Internet throughout the day but also are deluged with information.

The Role of Research for Mass Communicators, the Public, and Policy Makers

Research on the effects of mass communication plays a vital role in shaping the work of professional mass communicators. Research also influences public understanding of media effects and the decisions of policy makers regarding the role of media in contemporary society. Professional mass communicators use research to better gauge their audiences and their appetite for and response to media content. For example, ratings research in television and radio shapes the programming mass communicators create and offer to their audiences. It also affects media economics by influencing what advertisers will spend for commercial airtime corresponding to a particular show or program.

The public often takes great interest in media effects, such as how popular music might affect the behavior of youth or how children learn from different types of media. Correspondingly, policy makers take great interest in and may fund research on media effects to better gauge the policies that affect those media.

Early Concerns on Media Effects

For more than a century, public concern has arisen about the possible effects of each new medium of mass communication as it has emerged. Questions have been asked about each medium's impact on public culture, political processes, the values and behaviors children learn, and the like. In the 1920s, much of the public became concerned about the depiction of sex, violence, and lawlessness depicted in film. This is true not only for the electronic media that were developed mostly in the 20th century, but goes back much farther.

In the 1800s, critics warned that newspapers caused juvenile crime. Moralists believed that the flow of sensational news stories about crime and vice would lead people to imitate that immoral behavior. In 1888, *Punch* magazine attributed crimes committed in Whitechapel to "highly coloured pictorial advertisements."

Concern about the effects of media on children has even deeper roots. We know that even in ancient Greece, philosophers Socrates and Plato worried greatly about the influence of literacy on children. Plato was concerned especially about the morally corrupting influence of poetry, particularly allegorical tales such as Homer's *Battles of the Gods*, and sought its ban.[1] In 360 BC, Plato offered this reasoning:

> Children cannot distinguish between what is allegory and what isn't, and opinions formed at that age are usually difficult to eradicate or change; it is therefore of the utmost importance that the first stories they hear shall aim at producing the right moral effect.

> Plato, *The Republic*

These and other concerns have laid the foundation for much of the research conducted on the nature and impact of mass communication in society, research that was based on the development of social science research using scientific principles.

Four Research Epochs

There are many views and models of media effects throughout the 19th and 20th centuries. This book proposes that most media effects research has tended to focus on the new media of the day. This proposition was introduced and tested by media scholars Ellen Wartella and Byron Reeves in a 1985 article in the *Journal of Communication*. Wartella and Reeve's investigation showed that for each new medium there was a positive correlation between the diffusion of that medium and the number of studies about that medium and its impact. There is a positive correlation between annual film audience data during the early part of the 20th century, for example, and studies of film viewing effects on children. There is a similar correlation between the diffusion of radio receivers and radio research during the 1930s. The number of television receivers in use by year is even more highly correlated with the number of studies on television published each year, Wartella and Reeves report, during the early decades of television's diffusion. Notably, as each new medium arose, research on the previous medium showed a marked decline, despite a continued high level of audience usage of the older media.

Although Wartella and Reeves' research was conducted in the pre-Internet days and included only the audiovisual mass media that existed at that time (e.g., film, radio, television), the basic hypothesis appears to be as true as ever today. In fact, it even explains 19th century interest in the effects of popular newspapers and magazines, although there was little formal research at the time to test this concern.

There have been four epochs of media effects research dating back to the beginning of the 20th century. These epochs (which sometimes overlap) are:

1. Film effects, 1904–1945.
2. Radio effects, 1930–1940.
3. Television effects, 1948–1990.
4. Internet effects, 1993–the present.

Plato was one of the ancient philosophers who worried about the negative effect literature could have on children.

Epoch One: Film Effects, 1904–1945

Although we now can identify four research epochs, Wartella and Reeves in 1985 identified just three research epochs. An epoch is defined in terms of the preponderance of published research dealing with a particular medium, and the research usually starts appearing a few years after the introduction and dissemination of a new medium of mass communication. It does not imply that no other research on an older medium has been conducted since the end of the epoch. Rather, the end of an epoch merely marks the period of dominance of research focusing on the new medium of mass communication.

The film epoch began in 1904, as film began to emerge as an important medium of mass communication, and ended in the mid-1940s with the end of World War II. The film epoch peaked in the early 1930s, Wartella and Reeves suggest, when film had become a form of mass entertainment and with the publication of the so-called **Payne Fund studies** of film and children. The Payne Fund studies, named after the source of funding for the research, were published in 1933 and included a 12-volume report on the impact of film viewing on

Payne Fund studies—a 12-volume series of media effects research on film conducted between 1928 and 1933 by some of the most prominent psychologists, educators, and sociologists of the day. It helped further the move for the movie industry's self-regulation and laid the foundation for the movie rating system.

Sex and violence in early movies led to calls for regulating the film industry as well as subsequent studies on the effects films may have on audiences.

children.[2] Research during the film epoch laid the foundation for the movie ratings system that would emerge later in the middle of the 20th century.

The Payne Fund

The Payne Fund studies were conducted between 1928 and 1933 by some of the most prominent psychologists, sociologists, and educators of the day. The trigger for the Payne Fund studies was the industry's self-regulation in the form of the so-called **Hays Code,** introduced in 1930 as a mechanism to control the amount and depiction of sex, violence, and crime in movies of the day, or at least to appease public criticism of such content. The studies provided a detailed examination of the effects of film on wide-ranging subjects, including sleep patterns, attitudes about violence and delinquent behavior, and knowledge about foreign cultures.

The Payne Fund studies concluded that the same film would influence children differently depending on those children's varying backgrounds and characteristics, including age, sex, life experience, predispositions, social environment, and parental influence. One study of movies, delinquency and crime, for instance, concluded that the impact of film on criminal behavior may vary depending on both the range of themes presented in the film as well as the social context, attitudes, and interests of the viewer.

Although much of the Payne Fund research started from the assumption that movies would have a variety of negative effects, the research also revealed a variety of positive effects of film. For example, some research found that children could learn positive lessons from film, and that information retention was a function of grade in school.[3] Children remembered action especially when it involved sports, and when the information had an emotional component.

The Hypodermic Needle Model

Another important thread of research during the film epoch was spun during World War I. During this time, both the United States and Germany employed film and other media (including posters) as instruments of propaganda to shape

Hays Code—a code established in 1930 by the movie industry to censor itself regarding showing of nudity or glorifying antisocial acts in movies. Officials for the Hays office had to approve each film that was distributed to a mass audience.

Media Spotlight: **Field of Dreams**

One strange media effect occurs when a motion picture redefines real life or when some people confuse movies with reality. Consider the bizarre case of the 1989 film *Field of Dreams,* a movie starring Kevin Costner as a farmer who hears a voice saying, "If you build it, they will come." The farmer eventually realizes he is meant to build a baseball field in his corn field and does so. The movie was shot in part on a real plot of farmland in eastern Iowa. And today, tourists come from hundreds, sometimes thousands of miles away to see the actual corn field. What makes the case especially unusual is that the field lies on the property of two different farmers, and they have both staked commercial claim to the "real" field of dreams. They have created mazes, souvenir shops, and a baseball field next to a corn field, charging visitors to tour their property. The two owners are now suing each other over the right to claim they have the "real" field of dreams.[4]

public opinion and generate support for their positions in the war. Political scientist Harold Lasswell coined the term "hypodermic needle" during his analysis of World War I propaganda efforts to describe the notion that media can act like a drug being injected into an almost indefensible audience. The **hypodermic needle model** is based on the assumption that messages have a profound, direct, and uniform impact on individuals. This model has also been called the "magic bullet" model of communication, and derives largely from learning theory and simple stimulus–response models in behavioral psychology.

Major studies of a series of films conducted during World War II illustrate this model. In 1942, General George C. Marshall, the Chief of Staff of the U.S. Army, commissioned celebrated Hollywood filmmaker Frank Capra to direct a series of films titled *Why We Fight.* Capra (whose film credits include *It Happened One Night, It's a Wonderful Life,* and *Mr. Smith Goes to Washington*) directed seven 50-minute documentaries explaining to U.S. soldiers why the United States got

hypodermic needle model—a model of media effects, also called the "magic bullet" model, largely derived from learning theory and simple stimulus–response models in behavioral psychology, that states media has a profound, direct, and uniform impact on the public.

involved in the war. The films were meant to convince the soldiers to fight against the Nazis and the Japanese. *Prelude to War, Divide and Conquer,* and *The Battle of Britain* were among the most important of the films studied by the research team. The research team set up controlled experiments to test the impact of the *Why We Fight* films. In the case of *The Battle of Britain,* for example, 2100 soldiers were studied in a carefully designed before-and-after experiment with a control group, while another 2100 were studied in an after-only with control group design. The results showed that the films succeeded. They had a strong impact on knowledge, with soldiers who saw the film in either experimental group exhibiting a significant increase in knowledge about the battle, which involved Nazi bombing of Britain, including the fire-bombing raids that destroyed much of Coventry. The film also negatively influenced the opinions of the soldiers of the Nazis and helped convince them that the Nazis' intent was to "invade and conquer England." The film had less impact on the overall attitudes of the soldiers toward the British.

Epoch Two: Radio Effects, 1930–1940

The radio epoch began in 1930 and ended just before World War II. By 1930, radio had emerged as a leading form of live, mass communication, and by the end of the epoch it had become a ubiquitous medium of mass communication. Meanwhile, newspapers had fallen in popularity. The electronic media had begun their dominance in American mass communication, and research attention followed suit.

Studies of Radio's Impact on Children

Also included in this epoch was a series of Payne Fund studies of radio. The Payne Fund sought in 1927–1928 to create a "school of the air," which would use radio to educate children on a variety of subjects.[5] This led to the formation of the National Committee on Education by Radio (NCER), as well as the allocation of some $300,000 in the early 1930s to support a reform of U.S. broadcasting, which at that time meant radio. Some of this funding supported early radio research. The research suggested that radio could be effective as an educational tool, with evidence that children listened attentively and acquired much of the information being disseminated.

A 1936 study offered the first major look at the impact of radio on children.[6] Based on a survey of more than 3000 New York children and their parents, the study examined the link between radio listening and children's preferences for radio programs and children's learning about the world, their imitation of radio characters' language and behavior, and requests for advertised products.

In 1941 further research on children's radio listening provided evidence that children not only acquired information but also learned standards of conduct from radio.[7] The research also demonstrated that age differences explained much in the way of children's tastes and preferences for radio programming. Other studies of radio in the 1940s documented the ability of radio drama to produce emotional reactions in children, and even to influence performance in school as well as to solicit requests for products advertised on the air. These studies also demonstrated that children were differentially able to distinguish between reality and fantasy.

Media Spotlight: Orson Welles's War of the Worlds

At 8 PM on October 30, 1938, the Columbia Broadcasting System's Mercury Theater of the Air began its radio broadcast from a New York City studio. Regular listeners and others who heard the introduction understood perfectly well what was about to follow. It was simply a radio adaptation of the science-fiction writer H.G. Wells's famous 1897 novel, *War of the Worlds*, produced that night as a Halloween joke by Howard Koch and starring a 21-year-old baritone named Orson Welles.

But many who did not hear the introduction found themselves lulled into a state of calm as the program brought them a supposedly live orchestral performance. When the program was interrupted for a news flash, the calm was shattered by the announcement that Martians had landed at a farm near Grovers Mills, New Jersey. The increasingly frequent and intense news flashes reported in the broadcast sounded very much like a Walter Winchell report, whose hurried tenor was familiar to millions and was the radio standard of the day.

As the Martian invasion ensued and it became apparent that the Martians had vastly superior weaponry, many who lived along the eastern seaboard, especially the New York and New Jersey area, panicked. Many listeners gathered their personal belongings and fled their homes or hid in basements. The broadcast made news headlines for weeks because of the widespread panic that ensued. A study by a psychologist showed that one in six listeners—one million people—thought the show was a real broadcast and that Martians were invading (although not all one million panicked and fled).

Studies of children and media at the Columbia Bureau of Applied Social Research during the 1940s found a direct link between children's newspaper readership and radio news listenership and their knowledge of current affairs, even when accounting for other factors, such as age, sex, and intelligence.

Radio's Wider Impact

Radio had other effects in society that reached far beyond the realm of children. Consider the events that unfolded on the night of October 30, 1938, when Orson Welles broadcast a radio program created to sound like a news event, called *War of the Worlds*.

Television content has been the subject of much media research for almost 60 years.

Together, studies of the War of the Worlds broadcast and other radio programming demonstrated that media effects could be quite dramatic, but that media did not produce uniform effects across the population. The research indicated that a variety of factors, including individual differences such as personality, demographic, and psychological variables such as good critical thinking ability could mediate audience members' response to media exposure. Studies of the *War of the Worlds* broadcast led to intense public scrutiny of the role of radio in society and triggered an intense public debate over whether or how to regulate this new medium.

This event focused attention of Americans on the power of mass communication in the form of radio and triggered one of the first major research investigations of a media program on the subject of social panic and mass hysteria, as well as a debate about the government's control over the radio industry.

Epoch Three: Television Effects, 1948–1990s

The advent of World War II slowed the funding for research on mass communication as well as the development of television, and it was not until well after the end of the war in 1945 that a commercial consumer market for television began and, with it, studies on the effects of television. The diffusion of television was the most rapid of any new medium up to that time. From availability to the general public in 1948, it took less than six years for 50 percent of U.S. households to own a television. By 1954, 55 percent of American households had a television set, and the epoch of television research was well underway. Households with children were more than twice as likely to have a television set than those without children, and researchers undertook increasing numbers of studies of television's impact on the young. Although television had reached market saturation by the late 1960s, a high level of research activity endured into the 1990s, partly in response to the continued evolution of the medium, as channel capacity increased, audiences fragmented, and the beginnings of digitization emerged.

As television achieved its ubiquitous presence in modern U.S. society, researchers undertook thousands of studies of its effects. These studies have addressed many issues and topics, but three broad questions have received an abundance of attention:

1. How does television viewing influence children?

2. How can television be used strategically, or intentionally and by design, as a medium for shaping society in general in a positive, or prosocial, way?

3. How do viewers use television? This third question essentially turns the effects question around and looks at the notion of how an active audience might use a medium for its own purposes.

We'll begin our discussion with an examination of what research tells us about the influence of television viewing on children.

Television's Influence on Children

Since the 1950s, there have been thousands of studies on the impact of television viewing on children. Many times the results of these studies have been inconsistent if not contradictory. Although it is difficult to draw many clear-cut conclusions from this massive body of research, some general effects have been observed. All children are not influenced equally by the same television programs. Rather, television's effects vary depending on a variety of factors, including the child's background, gender, and overall media habits. Moreover, the effects are often subject to various mitigating or intervening circumstances, especially environmental factors, such as parenting style. Finally, repeated exposure to television programming over time increases its impact.

Although much television programming is educational and entertaining, much of it is laced with violence, sex, and profanity. Consequently, many adult viewers and policy makers have pondered what effect all this extended television viewing may be having on the minds, bodies, and souls of society's next generation. Is viewing television violence eroding children's morals? Are children learning to be overly aggressive, in imitation of what they see on the television screen? Are they learning more about the Three Stooges than the three branches of government?

Researchers have studied many questions about television's effects on children, but two broad topics have received a preponderance of attention:[8]

1. How children learn from television.
2. Consequences of violence viewing.

How Children Learn from Television   Basic to how children learn from television is a process known as **developmental learning.** Developmental learning is a theoretical approach that posits learning as a progressive process in which a child's intellectual capacity grows through several stages of increasing ability.

Swiss psychologist Jean Piaget's research laid the foundation for much of the developmental learning approach. Piaget (1896–1980) sought to understand how children learn. He considered himself a "natural scientist" and conducted much of his research by observing his own children, Jacqueline, Lucienne, and Laurent, and watching their intellectual development from infancy on. He concluded that the development of knowledge in a child proceeds through four stages of increasing cognitive capability.[9] These stages are:

1. *Sensorimotor:* During the first one to two years of life, infants are aware of sensorimotor experiences and do not connect their experiences to things outside of themselves. They understand little about how things will react, so they frequently experiment, pulling on things, putting things in their mouths, shaking them, all in an effort to learn by trial and error.

2. *Preoperational:* From about 18–24 months to roughly age 7, children are in the preoperational stage, where they begin to think about things in symbolic terms, especially language. They develop their imaginations, can verbalize their thoughts, understand concepts of the future and the past, and can begin to distinguish between fantasy and reality.

3. *Concrete operations:* Ages 7 to 12 bring the ability to analyze problems systematically and see things from others' perspectives.

4. *Formal operations:* After age 12, children begin to think in abstract forms; are able to formulate hypotheses and contemplate abstractions such as justice, economics, and democracy; and consider all the logical consequences of actions.

Jean Piaget.

Weblink
Jean Piaget Society
www.piaget.org/

developmental learning—a theoretical approach, based on psychologist Jean Piaget's research, that posits learning as a progressive process in which a child's intellectual capacity grows through several stages of increasing ability.

Many communication researchers have employed Piaget's theories to understand how children learn from television and other media. Research shows that children of all ages can learn from television. What they learn is influenced significantly by their stage of development. Children in stage one are largely preliterate (i.e., they cannot read or write), yet they can learn a great deal from watching television, especially in the context of learning about what is right and wrong, what is rewarded and punished. In stage two, children begin to learn to read and write and can learn the symbolic messages of television, such as the roles of men and women, stereotypes, and commercialism. Parents and teachers can help children in this stage learn that commercials are different than programs and that they are designed to get people to spend their money to buy things.

Children in stage three, or ages 7 to 12, can learn a great deal from television and are especially likely to bring a critical eye to what they see. Research suggests that during this stage it is imperative that parents, teachers, and others take an active role in encouraging media literacy and critical thinking about television, including notions of the role of media in civic affairs and the political process. By stage four, children can engage television on a higher level intellectually. They can learn lessons about not only sex and violence, but history, science, and freedom of speech. Yet, children in this stage live in the highly social phase of life known as adolescence, and the social meaning of television takes on paramount value. Children's appetites for television, research similarly shows, tend to mature through these stages from cartoons to comedy, from Barney to Britney and beyond.

Learning to Buy   Some research has examined how children learn to buy from watching television commercials. Developmental studies suggest that younger viewers in stages one and two are especially vulnerable to commercial messages but that children in stage three or beyond can be taught by teachers, parents, or others to be critical television viewers.[10] They have the capacity to understand the selling intent of a commercial and to question the veracity of a commercial's claim. Children in these stages can learn to effectively challenge inflated advertising claims and to understand that the fun someone apparently has in a commercial playing with a toy or even using a cleaner to mop the floor is only the result of paid acting.

Learning Social Lessons and Stereotypes   As children develop, they also learn a great deal from television about social roles and human behavior. Television programming contains many lessons about how people are expected to behave in society. Research indicates that television programs that present various types of groups not in the mainstream in diverse, positive roles can positively influence the views of children. Programs that do this, such as HBO Family's *Fairy Tales for Every Child*, are, regrettably, not in the majority.

Although the situation is slowly improving, television and movies shown on television in general tend to provide few depictions of women in heroic roles, such as the ones played by Sarah Michelle Gellar on *Buffy the Vampire Slayer*, Jessica Alba in *Dark Angel*, and Sigourney Weaver in *Aliens*.

Television also teaches children a great deal about what to expect of members of minority and other ethnic groups. Even today, blacks star in disproportionately

Dark Angel is one of the few television shows that portrayed a strong and independent female protagonist.

fewer dramas than comedies. When they are shown in dramas, minorities are often cast in the role of criminals. Even news programs more often show blacks and other minorities as involved in crime than as expert sources interviewed for their knowledge or authority.

These programs provide few positive role models for young minority group members to emulate. Prime-time television is improving, but only slowly, and what it teaches the next generation of viewers is still fraught with problems.

The Impact of Viewing Television Violence   When looking at data on children's television violence viewing, it is obvious that most U.S. children are heavy viewers of television, and much of what they see is violent in nature. Evidence accumulated over the past half century indicates that this heavy violence viewing increases aggressiveness, especially among young boys, although the effects are present among girls as well.

Hundreds of studies have been conducted and millions of dollars have been spent to investigate the effects of TV violence on children who viewed it. Among the first investigations into the effects of television on young viewers was a study that introduced the notion that television had become the new "Pied Piper." In this view, television was seen as providing a model for children to imitate, oftentimes not a very good model.

Yet few early studies could provide conclusive evidence that exposure to TV violence would necessarily produce identifiable negative consequences in the real world. Laboratory research in the 1950s by psychologist Albert Bandura and others had shown that children exposed to TV violence were more likely to repeat the behavior they had witnessed (e.g., beating a "Bobo doll") as well as become more aggressive—while they were still in the lab. Although these studies

Media Spotlight: Statistics on Children's Viewing of TV Violence

- By age 12, the average American child sees 8000 murders and 100,000 acts of violence on television.[11]
- By age 18, that child has seen on TV 200,000 acts of violence, including 40,000 acts of murder.[12]
- Longitudinal studies show that 8-year-old boys who viewed the most violent programs were more likely to act aggressively and engage in delinquent behavior by age 18 and commit criminal behavior by age 30.[13]
- Fifty-four percent of children have a television set in their own bedroom and often watch with a friend, unsupervised.[14]
- Nearly half (47 percent) of the violent actions show no depiction of pain.[15]
- A national survey of 2000 boys and girls showed that nearly one in ten (9.1 percent) of boys and one in fifty (2.2 percent) of girls said they were victims of genital assault (being kicked or hit with an object in the genitals) as a result of children imitating movies and television programs such as *The Jungle Book*, *Dumb and Dumber*, and *Three Ninjas*.[16]

By age 12, the average American child will have seen 8000 murders and 100,000 acts of violence on television.

showed that children learned by observing, or watching others, the effects could be documented initially only within a laboratory setting. The researchers could not confirm that the children continued to be more aggressive once they had left the laboratory and returned to their everyday lives.

Subsequent studies, however, have extended these laboratory findings to the real world. One study from the 1970s found that youths who observed criminal acts on television were likely to imitate those behaviors in the real world.[17] Imitation was especially likely to occur when the perpetrators of the crime were portrayed as suffering few or delayed consequences for their acts.

Limited Effects View　A landmark research investigation of the impact of television on children in North America was conducted by Wilbur Schramm, Jack Lyle, and Edwin Parker in 1960. In their study, *Television in the Lives of Our Children*, Schramm, Lyle, and Parker concluded that some children under some conditions were likely to exhibit some negative consequences of exposure to television violence. But there was no magic bullet of media effects. Based on 11 studies conducted in 10 American and Canadian communities between 1958 and 1960, the investigation reviewed the physical, emotional, cognitive, and behavioral effects of television on children. The investigation showed that the content of television was "extremely violent," featuring considerable fighting, shooting, and murder.[18]

Studies of TV violence conducted in the field (that is, when children in their normal, daily lives were observed) did not yield clear-cut results regarding how children learned aggressive behaviors. Schramm, Lyle, and Parker argued that television could contribute to violent and delinquent behavior in some cases. A child who confuses the rules of the fantasy world, as shown on television, might imitate that behavior. The researchers cautioned that television was only a contributing factor in causing violent and delinquent behaviors and not a sufficient condition by itself.

The research of this period led to a model referred to as the **limited effects** view. In this view, media are seen as a component in a much larger, and more fundamental, system of influences to which all are subject. Institutions such as the family, school, and religion were seen as much more fundamental in their influence on the individual. These other institutions were viewed as providing the basic set of forces shaping the individual's tastes, attitudes, and behaviors. Media were seen as contributing to and often reinforcing the individual's world view, but media exposure was clearly secondary to these other influences.

Catharsis   Some research also suggested that watching televised violence (or other content) might have a beneficial effect by purging one's negative feelings. **Catharsis** is an idea derived from ancient Greek theater and first scientifically tested by Sigmund Freud. When Freud had placed a patient in a hypnotic state, her symptoms would become terribly powerful and dramatic. But afterward, her feelings would be purged and she would be freed from her psychological stress. This powerful and sometimes traumatic emotional transfer of a memory was dubbed catharsis. Most research has failed to confirm the catharsis effect in a media or any other context. Venting anger through physical aggression, such as hitting a pillow, does not decrease one's anger. In fact, it may actually cause a person's hostility level to increase.[19]

1960s: Violence and the Media Report   The 1960s saw a dramatic rise in social unrest and much domestic violence, much of it politically motivated. In response, President Lyndon B. Johnson in 1968 convened the National Commission on the Causes and Prevention of Violence. He was concerned about a broad range of violence and its social causes, but one major part was the media. Emerging from the Commission's media task force in 1969 was a massive three-part report called *Violence and the Media*. It focused on not only the quantity of violence on entertainment television, but also its quality. How did the media portray violence? Who used which weapons to kill whom, and what were their motivations and the consequences of their acts? Did the aggressors find reward or punishment? Professor George Gerbner of the Annenberg School for Communication at the University of Pennsylvania was selected as the head of the team to conduct the content analysis. His study defined violence as "the overt expression of force intended to hurt or kill."

Overall, Gerbner and his colleagues found the consequences of television violence were unrealistic. There was rarely pain or much blood. Good guys were often as violent as bad buys, but did not suffer the negative consequences of their action. Bad guys usually got their punishment not from the courts but from the cops. Whites were often the victims, and young black males and other people of color, as well as immigrants, were typically the perpetrators of crime. A follow-up report by Gerbner reached many of the same conclusions.

limited effects—a view that sees media as a minor component in a much larger, and more fundamental, system of societal and institutional influences to which all are subject.

catharsis—in media effects research, the belief that watching violent television content may purge violent feelings from the viewer and thereby have a beneficial effect, rather than a negative one as is commonly thought. Research has failed to confirm the cathartic effect, however.

Ronnie Zamora, then 15, murdered his 80-year-old neighbor in 1977 and claimed that he was not responsible for his actions because he had been influenced by television violence. He was found guilty of murder and sentenced to life imprisonment.

Producers of television programming differed in their views, insisting that TV violence was like real life. But other research supported Gerbner. Monroe Lefkowitz and his associates conducted one study involving a 10-year study that showed how the television habits of 8-year-old boys shaped their aggressive behavior later in life. The more violence they watched as children, the more aggressive they were as teenagers. Although these studies had methodological flaws, together they influenced public policy and public perceptions by leading policy makers to call for stricter controls on television programming aimed at children.

1970s and 1980s: Cultivation Analysis   During the 1970s concerns about the effects of TV violence continued to escalate. In 1977 a teenage boy named Ronnie Zamora was charged with murdering his 80-year-old neighbor. In a sensational case that was captured on film and later shown on television, the 15-year-old Zamora's defense was "television intoxication." He claimed to have been so influenced by television violence that he was not responsible for his actions and that he was legally insane. His defense team even planned to subpoena Telly Savalas, star of the TV show *Kojak*, to testify in his defense. The judge ruled Savalas's testimony out of order, and in the end, the jury found Zamora guilty. But the stage was set for even more research on the effects of TV violence. Gerbner and others have also argued that TV violence not only causes aggressiveness, it can also alter our perceptions of the world.

Gerbner's research examined the long-term impact of television watching and led to a theory known as **cultivation analysis.** In this view, television cultivates audiences to view reality in a manner similar to the world portrayed in television programs. Rather than emphasizing the impact of individual programs on individual viewers, cultivation analysis posits that the cumulative effect of viewing thousands of murders on television is to create viewers who see the world as a more dangerous place than it actually is. This is known as the "mean world syndrome." Because television programs are designed as mainstream entertainment and are easy to understand, they provide a means by which people, especially children, are socialized.

Research by Gerbner and others has provided evidence that those who watch more television are not only more likely to believe the real world is a more dangerous place, but are also more likely to be stronger supporters of a more powerful system of law enforcement. Senior citizens who watch more television are more inclined to stay at home because they are more fearful of perceived dangers in the real world. Cultivation effects are not uniform, however. People who talk about what they watch, especially children and teenagers who talk with their parents, are less likely to conform their view of reality to what they see on television.

The 1980s and the 1990s witnessed continued research on TV violence. In 1992, the American Psychological Association issued its TV violence report, *Big World, Small Screen: The Role of Television in American Society*. It argued that, "The accumulated research clearly demonstrates a correlation between viewing violence and aggressive behavior. Children and adults who watch a large number of aggressive programs also tend to hold attitudes and values that favor the use of violence." It is important to note that correlation does not equal causation, so although there may be a relationship between television violence viewing and aggressive behavior, the one does not necessarily cause the other.

cultivation analysis—a theory of media effects that states television cultivates audiences to view reality in a manner similar to the world portrayed in television programs. For example, it posits that viewing thousands of murders on television is unlikely to increase the chances that an individual will commit murder but does lead to a belief that the world is a more dangerous place than it actually is.

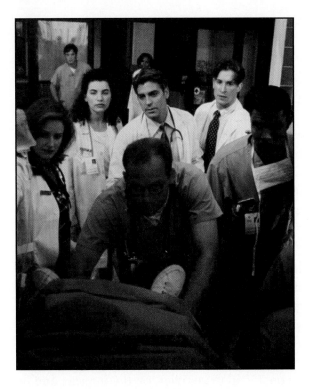

ER and other realistic hospital or crime dramas portray the consequences and complexity of violence more than do most programs.

1990s: UCLA Television Violence Report   One of the most important studies of TV violence in the 1990s was conducted by a team of researchers at UCLA led by Jeffrey Cole. Cole's research shows that U.S. network television series programming has gotten somewhat less violent in recent years, but that the emergence of "shockumentary" reality-based specials have increased dramatically. Funded by the networks themselves at a cost of $450,000, the third annual *UCLA Television Violence Report* showed that overall violence decreased on ABC, CBS, Fox, and NBC during the 1996–1997 season. But the reality-based programs are especially violence-filled and are most commonly encountered on Fox. These programs feature real and recreated footage of police shootouts, car chases and crashes, and animals attacking people, in some cases killing them on air. Typical programs are *World's Most Dangerous Animals, The World's Scariest Police Shootouts,* and *Video Justice: Crime Caught on Tape.*

Weblink
UCLA Television Violence Report
[ccp.ucla.edu/Webreport95
/otherfin.htm]

Out of 107 network series in the 1996–1997 season, just two portrayed violence especially graphically or glorified it as heroic. Some programs, such as *Law & Order* and *ER,* were especially noteworthy in their presentation of the consequences and complexity of violence.

Criticisms of Television Violence Studies   Television violence effects studies have been subject to a number of criticisms. First, many studies rely on correlational data, or data based on measurements of the relationship between two or more variables. One of the severest limitations of correlational studies is that they do not permit the researcher to infer causation (i.e., that TV violence viewing causes violent or aggressive behavior in the viewer).

Experimental studies are often conducted as an attempt to test causality. Although the properly designed experiment does permit causal interpretation, many television violence experiments have been conducted under conditions far different from real-life viewing experiences, thereby limiting the usefulness of the results in their ability to be generalized across society.

Case studies in television violence viewing represent a third class of research and one that addresses the real-life constraint of many experimental investigations. Although case studies often feature prominently in the media and many public debates about the effects of TV violence viewing, case studies are nonetheless highly questionable as to their intrinsic validity as a research methodology. Although they may provide vivid illustration of a possible media effect (for example, convicted serial rapist and killer Ted Bundy's defense rested in part on his having had extensive exposure to pornography), case studies are limited on a number of bases, including the lack of a control or comparison group or the fact that the viewer at issue is unlike the typical viewer.

AAP Recommendations for Limiting Children's Television Viewing

Based on the collective findings of a half century of research, as well as Piaget's conceptual framework, the American Academy of Pediatrics (AAP) has issued a set of recommendations for limiting children's television viewing. In particular, the AAP recommends that children under age 2 should not watch television at all. The AAP states, "Increase awareness of the impact of media violence. Children need to know that violence on TV, in the movies, on the Internet and in video games is not real. In real life, children have alternatives when dealing with conflict and anger."

It's also based on Piaget's theories of how children learn that the AAP also argues that TV (and other media) can be used constructively to help children learn, especially when properly used and when parents and teachers work interactively with children to help them interpret and understand TV programming (and other media content). The AAP states, "In addition, pediatricians, parents and teachers should help children develop critical thinking and viewing skills about what and how things are portrayed in the media. Children who are 'media educated' are less likely to be influenced by media messages and more likely to withstand potentially harmful effects."

Weblink
American Academy of Pediatrics
[www.aap.org]

Using Television for Positive Social Change

The second broad question addressed by much research on television has examined how the medium could be used strategically for shaping society in a positive way. This research had its roots in early studies of persuasion as well as investigations of public communication campaigns designed to achieve social objectives, such as getting people to quit smoking, wear seat belts, or to adopt healthier lifestyles in general. We'll begin our discussion with a look at what research tells us about persuasion and television.

Communication and Persuasion   Much important work during the television research epoch examined the ability of mediated messages to persuade the audience. This research has its roots in early investigations of how the media in general, including print and electronic media, could persuade audiences. Many of these studies posited that media effects would likely be dependent on a number of conditions being met. These conditions were conceptualized as having to do with at least four sets of factors:

1. Characteristics of the source, or communicator.
2. The nature of the message.
3. Channel, or media, characteristics.
4. Audience factors.

Among the most important research of this early period were the investigations of Carl Hovland, Irving Janis, and Harold H. Kelley. Hovland, Janis, and Kelley conducted their research at Yale University between 1946 and 1961, and their research is sometimes referred to as the Yale Program of Research on Communication and Attitude Change. They conducted their research in controlled laboratory settings rather than in the field using the actual media system. They designed their research in this fashion in order to control for other factors in the environment and to more reliably and validly test their theoretical ideas, which were based on a stimulus–response model (i.e., the message, source, or other factor is the stimulus, and the response is the attitude change in the audience).[20]

Their research demonstrated that credibility of the source or communicator is an important variable in shaping the persuasiveness of a mediated message. Credibility was defined largely as either the expertness of the source (i.e., the authoritativeness) and the trustworthiness (i.e., does the source have an ulterior motive; is he or she honest?). More expert or trustworthy sources were found to be more persuasive than those less authoritative or who had perhaps something to gain. Hovland and his colleagues, for example, showed that a story attributed to *Fortune* magazine was more convincing than the same article attributed to a gossip columnist.

Hovland and his colleagues also found that certain message factors could influence the persuasiveness of a communication. For example, fear appeals sometimes were found to provide a motivation to act; although, if too strong, a fear appeal could have the reverse effect. The structure of a message can also be important. For example, presenting both sides of an argument can be persuasive, if it properly "inoculated" the recipient (i.e., it could persuade by refuting the counter argument). Audience factors were also found to be important in Hovland and his colleagues' research. They found that personality factors, group membership, and the extent to which the audience member is involved in the message could all play a role in a message's persuasiveness.

Other researchers have studied the importance of media-related factors in persuasiveness. Some research has shown that in agenda-setting processes, newspapers can be especially important in establishing the basic agenda of issues, whereas television plays a central role in establishing priorities (i.e., which of the agenda items are most important).

Teaching Children Prosocial Lessons   Developmental models have been tested not only in possible negative effects on television for children, but in the context of how children learn prosocial lessons from television. In fact, entire educational programs have been created based on the fundamental notions of developmental learning. One of the most familiar is *Sesame Street* on public television. *Sesame Street* designs its educational programs for children at different developmental stages and has been successful in using this approach to teach children basic literacy skills, mathematics abilities, and more.

Sesame Street is a good example of programming that is educational and teaches children prosocial messages.

The growth of cable and satellite television has led to a huge growth in the amount and diversity of programming available for younger audiences, especially children in developmental stages three and four. HBO Family, the Discovery Channel, and National Geographic are three channels available on cable and satellite television that deliver a great deal of educational and entertaining programming for youth audiences in these stages. Research indicates that programs on these channels, such as *Bill Nye, The Science Guy,* which uses a variety of innovative educational strategies to entertain and teach children about science, are highly effective at both engaging young audiences and in nurturing their knowledge in a variety of fields, from natural history to political affairs. If similar programs are produced in greater numbers, the prosocial value of television for younger audiences may increase.

Public Communication Campaigns   Research on television and persuasion has been especially important to the development of modern advertising, public relations, and public information campaigns, the areas of strategic mass communication. This is particularly the case because all the media can be important in shaping knowledge, opinions, attitudes, or emotions, and research suggests that the most influential media for the public in general are frequently those that involve both sight and sound. During the film research epoch, for example, considerable research examined the nature and impact of film as a vehicle for propaganda designed to generate attitudes of support for a government's military activity. Early research also suggested radio could be used effectively to shape attitudes and knowledge.

More recently, television has been used and studied widely as a vehicle for conducting strategic public communication, advertising, and public relations campaigns. In the 1960s, television-based campaigns were utilized to shape public views about cigarette smoking. When depicted in film, cigarette smoking has often been associated with attractive characters. As a result, young viewers especially have been shaped in their views of smoking as a behavior associated with being sexy, powerful, or otherwise attractive. Government-sponsored antismoking campaigns have utilized television as a means to fight these notions, and research has demonstrated their effectiveness.

Government-sponsored antismoking advertising campaigns seem to have had some success in reducing the rate of teen smoking, but there has been less success with antidrug messages.

Television-based campaigns have been engineered to influence social norms, attitudes, and behaviors in a variety of areas, including health (e.g., heart disease prevention, AIDS awareness, cancer treatment), public safety (e.g., seat belt wearing), and gift giving (e.g., making charitable donations to nonprofit groups and causes).

As newer communication media have emerged, including the Internet, World Wide Web, and e-mail, researchers have found that not only are the findings of earlier investigations confirmed, but these newer media facilitate communication campaigns by enabling interactivity as well. Interactivity engages audiences in ways possible before mainly through face-to-face or interpersonal communication.

Weblink
The Ad Council
[www.adcouncil.org/]

The Active Television Audience

The third broad question that research on the effects of television has addressed asks how viewers use television. This question turns the effects question around and looks at the notion of the audience somehow acting on the media, rather than vice versa.

Uses and Gratifications Research   First formulated in the 1940s for research on listenership of radio soap operas, so-called **uses and gratifications** research looks at *why* people use particular media. It examines what people do with the media rather than what the media do to people. Uses and gratifications research saw a revival of research interest in the 1970s and 1980s and offered a **functionalist paradigm** for media research, especially studies of TV usage. This paradigm posits that people have certain needs, especially psychological and social, which they seek to satisfy through media usage. Blumler and Katz presented research that showed how people used the media to gratify (or satisfy) a variety of social or psychological needs of the individual. Their research suggests that people use the media for at least four purposes:

1. *Obtaining information:* To learn.

2. *Personal identification:* Finding models of behavior or reinforcing one's personal values.

3. *Social interaction or integration:* Substituting for real-life companionship.

4. *Entertainment:* Escape, relaxation, sexual arousal.[21]

uses and gratifications research—a branch of research on media effects that looks at why people use certain types and looks at what people do with media rather than what media do to them.

functionalist paradigm—a research paradigm that posits that people have certain needs, especially psychological and social, which they seek to satisfy through media usage.

Users of the Internet report that it is replacing the television as their favorite medium of escape.

The uses and gratifications approach has also been applied to the study of other media, including the Internet, especially in comparison to television. One study by BBDO New York, an advertising unit of BBDO Worldwide, found in 1999 that respondents to a survey said they used the Internet for escape and mental stimulation as well as to get specific information on business, health, and travel. In fact, users said the Internet had replaced television as their favorite medium of escape. "Respondents said using the Internet gave them feelings of innovation, intelligence, creativity, power and accomplishment," said the BBDO report. The study was limited to 104 adults, ages 22 to 34, interviewed in eight markets across the United States in September 1999, and is largely exploratory.[22]

Because uses and gratifications research is based on a model of a more active rather than passive audience (i.e., audience members seek to satisfy certain needs based on their media use), this research model may see a return to center stage during the age of the Internet and DTV, both of which are similarly based on an active audience model. Of course, uses and gratifications research has been criticized for being somewhat circular in its reasoning and hard to test empirically. In other words, it's hard to know which came first—the social/psychological need or the media use. Uses and gratifications research has been criticized on a number of levels, including the difficulty that media audiences may have in articulating why they used the media and what gratification they derived from it.

Selective Perception, Retention, and Exposure   Another important aspect of the active audience involves what is known as **selective processing,** including selective perception, retention, and exposure. This says that the way we understand mediated messages depends on how we can use those messages in the context of what we already know or believe to be true. For example, imagine that a person believes that Osama bin Laden was responsible for the attacks on the U.S. embassy in Africa in 1998. Then, that same person hears allegations that bin Laden was similarly responsible for the terrorist attack on the World Trade

selective processing—a belief in media effects research that media processing by individuals is selective and that they accept information that tends to confirm what they feel they already know to be true.

Advertising and Its Potential Negative Effects on Women

Advertising is designed to achieve a variety of goals, most typically to persuade people in some manner, in order to sell goods and services or to get people to act in some fashion, such as to vote for a particular candidate. Extensive research is conducted by the industry to measure the effectiveness of particular advertising campaigns. But frequently there are side-effects, perhaps unintended. Among the most significant possible side-effects are the attitudes and behaviors of young viewers who may be influenced by the characters in television commercials they see depicted in a variety of stereotypical, demeaning, or self-destructive behaviors or situations.

One group has been particularly outspoken in its criticism of such advertising, the Advertising Women of New York. On September 28, 1999, the group released a study of 556 young women ages 12 to 19. The group had commissioned Smart Girl Internette Inc. in New York to conduct the investigation. The study showed that 55 percent of respondents answered "Yes, I see them all the time" to the question "Have you ever seen an ad that made you feel like you needed to go on a diet?" With a high level of teenage girls suffering from eating disorders, the findings are particularly disturbing.

"That's frightening," said Ellen Flahive, president of Advertising Women of New York.

Respondents also said many commercials "offend" them by portraying women as if they "only care about their looks" from depicting models as "too skinny" to skewing camera angles to "focus on sexy body parts." One of the most offending commercials in 1999 was produced by the Frito-Lay unit of Pepsico Inc. and BBDO New York of the Omnicom Group. The commercial is for barbecue-flavored Doritos snack chips and shows a library filled with male students studying human anatomy in the form of the model Ali Landry as she saunters by in a clinging dress.[23]

Television and other media make a sizeable portion of their revenues from such advertising. If you were the president of one of the major commercial television networks, would you consider banning such advertising, knowing it would significantly reduce revenues and might result in the loss of jobs at the network?

The group Advertising Women of New York has been outspoken about the portrayals of women in advertising.

Center on September 11, 2001. That person would be especially likely to believe the new allegations are true, because they are consistent with what he or she already knows to be the case.

Epoch Four: The Internet, 1993–the Present

Research on television has begun to wane with the rise of the Internet as a medium of mass communication in the 1990s. In turn, the Internet epoch of mass communication research has emerged. Early research on the Internet has focused on three developments:

1. Increasing Internet usage.
2. Evolving differences between online and off-line content.
3. Changing relationships between media and their publics.

Internet Usage

The United States has the greatest number of Internet users, with 164 million people online. But the global dominance of the United States on the Internet is rapidly changing as more people from various countries get online. In 1995, some 90 percent of all Internet users worldwide were in the United States. By February 2002, North America made up 33 percent of all Internet users worldwide and Asia-Pacific was making rapid gains in Internet usage as it approached 30 percent of worldwide Internet users, primarily in Japan, China, and Korea. Latin America, the Middle East, and Africa lagged far behind in Internet users (see Table 13-1).

It is projected that in most of the advanced industrial nations, Internet penetration will reach 50 percent by the year 2005. The United States already has 58.5 percent of its population on the Internet, and some of the northern European countries either match or exceed that rate of Internet penetration, especially in Scandinavia, where some countries have over 60 percent of the population on the Internet, according to NUA Internet Surveys.

Table 13-1 Global Internet Users, February 2002	
Region	**Numbers of Internet Users**
North America	181.23 million
Europe	171.35 million
Asia-Pacific	157.49 million
Latin America	25.33 million
Middle East	4.65 million
Africa	4.15 million
World Total	544.2 million

Source: NUA Internet Surveys [www.nua.ie], February 2002.

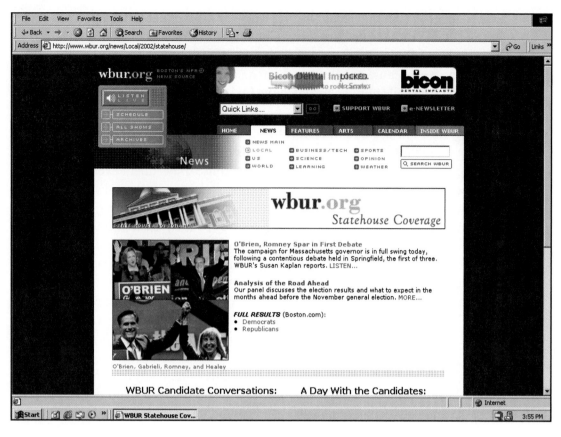

Links to candidates' homepages, platform positions, and earlier articles on the candidate and their opponents can help citizens get more information easier than they can from traditional media sources.

Differences between Users and Viewers

In contrasting online media with the traditional analog media, perhaps the most basic distinction is that the online audience is highly active. Although there is evidence that audiences use television and other media to fulfill certain needs or wants and are in that sense active, the audience for online communication goes beyond this basic view of activity. The audience online is in many ways a full participant in the process of online communication.

In fact, the term "audience" must be used guardedly when discussing online media such as the Internet. A better term is "user," because what happens online is that people actively "do" something. People who go to Web sites are called "visitors." People "send" e-mail. E-commerce permits people to shop and buy things.

Consider the terms used to describe consumers of traditional analog media. People who "use" radio or recorded music are "listeners." People who consume newspapers, books, or magazines "read" them. People who watch TV or movies are "viewers." All of these, of course, are activities, but they are essentially passive activities. Media content washes over the audience member who passively absorbs its message.

Online, although there are certainly passive media experiences, they only happen after the user has first engaged them. Most often, however, users actively seek media content, or they publish their own. Although there is relatively little research to date to explore the active audience online, this will become one of the most important areas of Internet research in the 21st century. The change from viewer to user affects media organizations, the way news and entertainment is presented, and even what types of news or entertainment will likely be consumed. Of course, it would be misleading to suggest that the traditional media experience was completely passive, because people would often talk back to their televisions or do other activities while nominally watching TV.

Framing News in the Old Millennium   An important area of mass communication research involves what is called **media framing.** A frame refers to the notion of using a central organizing idea for making sense of pertinent events and processes. News and information presented in isolation can have little intrinsic meaning. Thus, when the media report the news, they tend to place the facts into some sort of context to provide coherence. This context is the connecting tissue that ties isolated facts into a whole. Importantly, it is the frame that can shape how the public views an issue, group, or event, casting it in either a positive or negative light.

A variety of mass communication scholars have conducted research on framing. This work delineates between strategy versus policy analysis in a framing context. Research shows that the public's mistrust of institutions is a byproduct, at least in part, of how media frame issues. News that uses strategic frames promotes greater audience mistrust or cynicism than value-neutral, policy-oriented frames. A political campaign story that emphasizes the issues and where the candidates stand on those issues, rather than candidate character traits, is much less likely to elicit audience feelings of institutional mistrust or cynicism.

Research that looks at the framing effects of news coverage on public opinion and political choice suggests two forms of media frames, episodic and thematic framing.

Television news routinely reports events in the context of specific events, or **episodic framing.** This is in contrast to print news coverage, which is more likely to use **thematic framing** in which stories are placed in more general context. Episodic framing depicts concrete events that illustrate issues, while thematic framing presents collective or general evidence. Research shows that broadcast media are particularly apt to use an episodic frame for public affairs reporting in which community issues are portrayed in terms of concrete instances.

Contextualizing News in the New Millennium   The advent of online communications, and evolving forms of journalism in the age of digital media, present important implications for the framing of news stories. Unlike their analog media counterparts, digital media are not constrained by space or time limitations. Moreover, through hyperlinks, news reports on the World Wide Web can place stories in much greater context without the need to put the story within a sometimes narrow media frame. This is called **contextualization.** These stories can provide links to related sites, in-depth background, and source material. Moreover, an increasing amount of research suggests that readers, especially young readers who are turning in the greatest numbers to online news, welcome the diversity of online news sources and perspectives.

Although some might say that providing too much context may result in information overload, the Pew Center for Research suggests this is not happening to online news consumers:

media framing—the practice of organizing news and information within a central idea or theme to provide some sort of context so the information makes sense as part of a greater whole.

episodic framing—a type of media framing mostly used by television news that portrays a story in terms of concrete events that highlight real issues, such as covering a local crime by focusing on the perpetrator. This is in contrast to thematic framing.

thematic framing—a type of media framing that depicts news events in a general context or as part of larger issues. This contrasts with episodic framing.

contextualization—the act of putting online news into a larger context by adding hyperlinks to other news sites on related issues, organizational Web sites, expert or primary sources, and online communities.

Major news Web sites saw huge jumps in traffic in the aftermath of the attacks on the World Trade Center and Pentagon.

Not unsurprisingly, the Internet audience is comfortable with today's news environment, which like the Internet itself, offers a seemingly endless stream of information and choices . . . Americans who go online also place a slightly higher priority than non-computer users on getting news that is timely and up-to-date, and Internet users care less about having news delivered in an entertaining or caring manner. For example, 29 percent of non-computer users rank "enjoyable and entertaining" as extremely important news qualities, compared to just 15 percent of those who go online.[24]

Weblink
The Pew Research Center for the People and the Press
[people-press.org/]

Changing Relationships

Emerging research suggests that perhaps the most important impact of the Internet may be on the evolving relationships between and among media organizations, communication professionals, and their many publics. The Internet revolution is something of a myth. In reality, the real revolution is how the Internet changes and redefines relationships, between individuals as well as between organizations and individuals.[25]

In journalism, for example, the most important relationships are being transformed by new media. Not only does the presentation of news differ, as noted in the earlier discussion on media framing versus contextualization of news, but news sources are no longer dependent on the news media to present their messages. This can be seen from organizations such as sports franchises or leagues to political or business organizations that post press releases and updates on their Web sites. If a member of the public can go directly to NBA.com to watch clips of his or her favorite team that played earlier that night, why watch a sports broadcast on the evening news or go to a sports Web site? Will the public be as willing to accept information directly from politicians' Web sites as trusted news as they are from media organizations?

Answers to these questions are only beginning to emerge in research on the Internet. Early signs are that most voters will be drawn to quality content, and the challenge to online news providers is to increase the value they add to the political and other information they report. A recent study by the Pew Research Center in

Making the Internet accessible to as many people as possible will help bridge the digital divide that exists between Internet users and nonusers.

Washington, D.C., showed that a large (and apparently increasing) percentage of Americans are turning to the Internet for breaking news. In the aftermath of the World Trade Center attacks on September 11, 2001, at least 12.5 million unique users logged onto MSNBC's Web site in the 24 hours following the first plane crash.[26]

Redefining Audiences and News Relationships

Perhaps most important, however, is the changing relationship between media organizations and their audiences. Audiences are rapidly shifting from almost exclusively local geographic communities to communities of interest that transcend geographic, political, ethnic, and cultural boundaries. Accessing the *New York Times* on the Web is as easy from New York as it is from Nepal.

The relationship between the audience and news is in the midst of a paradigm shift, and what shape it will ultimately take is difficult to say. One thing is certain: Tomorrow's audience will have access to much more news and information than any previous generation. Whether it will be high-quality news and information will depend not only on developments in new media but also on how news organizations adapt and apply these new tools.

The Digital Divide

One of the most important audience issues related to online usage has to do with access among society's haves and have-nots. This gap is commonly called the digital divide, and research has shown that from the early days of public use of the Internet, especially from the first graphical Web browsers, Internet access tended to be much higher among society's economically advantaged, those with higher education and a legacy of higher overall print media use. Economically disadvantaged groups and those with lower income, especially minority groups and the rural poor, tended to have less Internet access and lower Internet and overall online usage. Yet, the gap has closed dramatically if not disappeared in some cases by 2000. Women, for example, now make up the majority of U.S. Internet users, with 50.2 percent of all adult Internet users being female as of 2000.

Problems of equity of access to online media will not disappear soon, however, and online journalists and other media professionals concerned about their

Table 13-2 Media as Important Information Source

Medium	Percent of U.S. adults who say medium is important source of information
Book	73.1%
Newspapers	69.3%
Internet	67.3%
Television	53.1%
Radio	46.8%

Source: UCLA Center for Communication Policy.

role in a democracy must be aware of the uneven distribution of computers and online services throughout the United States and around the world.

The Effects of the Internet and Other Online Content

Because of the newness of the Internet, there is a growing amount of research on the impact of time spent online, whether on children or adults. A major study was launched in 1999 to examine the social, cultural, and commercial impacts of the Internet. Funded by a consortium of major companies interested in online communication, the study is headed by Jeffrey Cole, director of the UCLA Center for Communication Policy, who had earlier headed the UCLA Television Violence Study. Among the companies sponsoring the 20-year longitudinal investigation are Microsoft, America Online, Disney, and Sony. Researchers are studying a variety of questions, including how family time, political leanings, and social life are influenced by Internet usage. The study is also designed to examine online banking, shopping, and buying habits, comfort with using credit cards online, and other issues related to e-commerce. The initial panel includes 2000 persons selected from a national sample, with later years adding international representatives to the study.[27]

The first results were released in 2000 and the initial results are quite significant. They show that among the most popular of online activities is e-mail. And for those who do use e-mail, 72 percent check their e-mail daily. As shown in Table 13-2, results also show that the credibility of online news and information rivals that of newspapers and other traditional media. "The fact that the vast majority of Americans who use the Internet consider it an important information source—even though it has been commonly available for only a few years—vividly demonstrates how this technology is transforming the political process and the knowledge of voters," said Cole.

Media Future: Digital Broadband Media: 2002 and Beyond

Research on the process, nature, and effects of digital broadband media is now beginning to emerge. The questions researchers are asking are wide ranging and include a continuing public concern over the effects of television violence on children, uncertainty about how people use broadband online media, and whether learning is enhanced through the interactive broadband experience. Digital broadband media, offering both new audio and video formats and programming, as well as a confluence with the Internet and other digital media (such as digital television and computer/video games), may mark the beginning of what is a new epoch in media research: the digital broadband media epoch.

Early findings show that people's media habits change dramatically with the advent of digital broadband media. For one thing, people use digital broadband media much more heavily than they do digital narrowband media. A study released in September 2000 showed that the average American spends 33 percent of his or her average media day with television, 28 percent with radio, and 11 percent with the Internet. But in homes with broadband connections, Internet usage soars to 21 percent of total media time, roughly the same as television (24 percent) and equal to radio (21 percent). Further, the study shows that broadband users spend more than two hours daily online (134 minutes), 61 percent more than people in homes with dial-up connections.[28] A June 2002 study conducted by the Pew Research Center found that users with broadband spent an average of four hours more online per week than dial-up users and were twice as likely to contribute content to the Web rather than simply to consume it. Contributing content included creating Web sites, engaging in online discussions, or sharing files with other Internet users.

It is still not known how much violent video games affect children, but researchers suspect that their interactivity and high degree of engagement with the player may have more serious effects than simply viewing television violence.

Data on Internet usage, including traffic to specific journalism and mass communication Web sites, are coming from a variety of sources and sometimes vary in their reliability. The premier provider of television ratings, A. C. Nielsen, launched an Internet ratings service known as "eratings.com" in 2000. It promises to help to provide a more stable audience measurement basis in the future for the mass communication industry.

Research on the effects of video games, including how they may reinforce negative gender or racial stereotypes, is being conducted. How violent video games influence children is not as well known or researched as is the impact of violent television programming. Yet, evidence consistently shows that children have a great ability to imitate actions they observe. It is especially true that young children under 5 years of age do not always have the ability to determine whether such violent actions are appropriate or properly motivated or justified. Moreover, the highly repetitive and interactive nature of videogames in which the player is often attempting to kill or brutalize a facsimile of a real human being would lead one to expect these negative effects to be even greater than with television viewing.

SUMMARY

This chapter has presented what research tells us about the effects of media in society. We have defined research as a form of systematic inquiry using a wide range of methodologies, including both quantitative and critical–cultural techniques.

Our examination has identified four primary epochs in the development of media research, including early research on film, studies of radio, investigations of television, and most recently research on the Internet and other forms of online mass communication. Research of course continues in older forms of media, but because research tends to be an expensive undertaking, new media have tended to receive the greatest amount of funding support because policy makers and others who have funding to give, as well as the scholars undertaking the research, have a natural interest in understanding the new, unexplored media.

In each epoch there have been a wide range of studies, but many have focused on the effects of viewing mediated violence, sex, and advertising. Attention has been paid especially to the possible physical and emotional harm of mediated violence, including changes in children's and teenager's knowledge, attitudes, and behaviors. Guiding this large and growing body of media effects research is a set of theoretical notions that help to explain, describe, and predict the patterns seen.

The Internet epoch is still relatively new, so not as much research has been done about the Internet as with other media; but even so it is already apparent that the Internet is dramatically changing relationships between the media and the public. There are other important issues that also must be addressed by policy makers, including making sure that all segments of society have equal opportunity and access to the Internet.

Discussion Questions

1. Find some recent media or social science studies reported on in the news and determine if they are quantitative or qualitative types of research. What are the strengths and weaknesses of the approaches used in these?

2. Could the analytic framework presented by Marshall and Eric McLuhan of amplification, displacement, retrieval, and conversion help to better understand the impact of digital media? Pick a traditional media type and try to apply this framework to it in terms of digital media.

3. Which type of media do you think may have the strongest influence on people, radio, film, television, or the Internet? Why?

4. Describe some of your own experiences in seeing how television may have affected the behavior of you or your friends in terms of your actions, fashion sense, or career goals. Were these changes short- or long-term?

5. Write a list of your television or film heroes from your teens to the present, along with a brief sentence on why you like them. Compare your list with a classmate of either a different ethnic group or the other gender and discuss your choices.

6. What implications for media on the Internet could there be as more people from different countries start using the Internet? Do you think these implications are good or bad for an American, English-speaking audience? Why?

Communication Law and Regulation in the Digital Age

14

The anonymity the Internet seems to provide Netizens can often make people forget that with freedom of speech also comes responsibility. An increasing number of companies have been obtaining the identities of chat room posters who the companies claim have defamed them. Usually, the Internet Service Provider (ISP), not willing to spend funds fighting someone else's legal battles, hands over the names.

However, in 2000 some discussion board members, who had been heavily criticizing the president and chairman of the board of Hvide Marine (now Seabulk International) and even hinting at illegal conduct on his part, were tipped off that the ISP was being subpoenaed. They filed their own suit to quash the request for their names, fighting to keep their right to post anonymously.

The fight for the right to publish anonymously now taking place in chat rooms and online discussion groups is at least as old as the United States itself. In the debate over the U.S. Constitution in 1787 and 1788, Alexander Hamilton, James Madison, and John Jay wrote a series of essays, which later became the Federalist Papers, under the pseudo-nym "Publius."

Critics of anonymous writings on the Internet say that one person can cause a company millions of dollars of damage by posting false information. Civil rights groups and consumer action groups disagree, saying that anonymous postings allow the broadest possible exchange of ideas and opinions.

Courts have decided both ways, although there seems to be a trend toward requiring companies to prove actual damage from each incident of defamation they are claiming. Still, some courts have granted aggrieved companies the right to get specific names of anonymous posters, and others have supported the rights of the posters. Like much else in communication law in the digital age, the law has a long way to go before it catches up with how people are communicating on the Internet.

OBJECTIVES

In this chapter we will:

- Outline a legal framework for understanding the nature of freedom of speech and press and how media are regulated in the United States.
- Review the historical development of media law in the United States.
- Describe the key concepts in law protecting and restricting freedom of speech and press, including threats to national security, libel, and censorship.
- Review the regulation of content in the United States, especially regarding commercial speech, political speech, and children's programming.
- Discuss the principal legislation that defines communication regulation in the United States and the principal federal communications regulatory agency, the Federal Communications Commission.
- Review the Freedom of Information Act (FOIA).
- Discuss intellectual property issues, especially copyright and how it is affected in the digital age.

Prologue

> Congress shall make no law respecting an establishment of religion, or prohibiting the free exercise thereof; or abridging the freedom of speech, or of the press; or the right of the people peaceably to assemble, and to petition the government for a redress of grievances.
> —First Amendment to the Constitution of the United States

Thomas Jefferson was a strong believer in a free and open press.

Although the **First Amendment** guarantees that Congress shall make no law restricting freedom of speech or of the press, it has been interpreted by the courts, elected officials, and legal scholars, not to mention many others including some in the public and private sectors, to permit some level of regulatory and legal restriction, rules, and requirements on the media of journalism and mass communication. Some of these laws deal with matters of libel, obscenity, and other aspects of media content. Others deal with technical issues related to broadcast station operation, such as to prevent one station from interfering with another's operations, and others pertain to matters of media ownership, intellectual property rights, and fulfilling the requirements of broadcasting licenses.

The Legal Framework

When printing began in Renaissance Europe, political and religious authorities were quick to realize the power of publishing in spreading not only religious teachings but political edicts as well. However, political and religious dissidents found printing presses equally as useful in disseminating their views against authority. The tension between government control of the press and using the press as a means to be free of political or religious control continues to this day.

The reasons underlying the value of freedom from governmental control were perhaps best articulated by U.S. President Thomas Jefferson, one of the principal crafters of the Bill of Rights to the Constitution, who said that "information is the currency of democracy." When the first U.S. Congress passed the Bill of Rights in 1789, there were fewer than three dozen printing presses in the country. Despite this small number, the importance of the press was recognized by the nation's founders. Jefferson said, "Were it left for me to decide whether we should have a government without newspapers, or newspapers without a government, I should not hesitate a moment to prefer the latter."

The press is a critical watchdog of government, as well as other powerful institutions in society, including business. But it is the press as an unofficial "fourth branch" of government, or **fourth estate,** that justifies the necessity for a press free from government censorship or control.

In societies where government control over the press, or media, is substantial, as in China or other authoritarian countries where journalists must be licensed to operate or where paper and printing are controlled by the government, the press suffers from an inability to criticize the government, its policies, or representatives. More often than not, the press becomes a puppet to the government and is

First Amendment—amendment to the U.S. Constitution that guarantees that Congress shall make no law restricting freedom of speech, press, or religion.

fourth estate—another term for the press, or journalism, in which it acts as a fourth branch of government and one that watches the other branches (executive, legislative, and judicial).

Test your legal knowledge as it relates to the First Amendment, media regulations, and copyright. Mark whether the statements are true or false:

1. Libel and slander are simply two different legal terms for the same thing.

2. It is impossible for politicians, but not public figures such as movie stars, to sue for libel.

3. The government can restrict free speech if they feel it will harm national security.

4. Journalists can protect themselves from libel as long as they properly attribute the questionable material by showing who said it.

5. Broadcasting media face more regulations than print because it is felt they have a greater impact on the audience.

6. Only accredited journalists or freelance writers under contract can use the Freedom of Information Act to request public records from the federal government.

7. The FCC enforces its broadcasting regulations by examining station and network programming and flagging material that is objectionable.

8. Copyright law is being threatened by new technology.

See answers on page 485.

used to promote government positions rather than independently evaluate them. In the United States and other democratic societies, the press acts as an independent balance of power, complementary in the U.S. case to the three constitutionally mandated branches of government, the executive (the president), the legislative (Congress), and the judicial (courts). However, concentration of ownership, commercialism, and other issues can adversely affect the ability of the press and other media to act responsibly or effectively in their role as watchdog of powerful societal institutions.

Despite the early Constitutional admonitions to protect freedom of speech and press, there have been many attempts by the government at all levels to infringe upon the independence of the press and to commit acts of censorship. The following discussion details some of the most significant cases and their legal resolution. In addition, a second problem has plagued the media with regard to acts of general governmental control. This problem is one of the failure of the government, in each of its three branches, to extend full First Amendment protection to the media in all its forms. Instead, only the print media have received full protection. In *Miami Herald Publishing Co. v. Tornillo* (1974), for instance, the U.S. Supreme Court struck down a Florida statute that required newspapers to give space at no cost to political candidates whose personal or professional character the paper had criticized. However, television or radio stations must provide air time should the station itself editorially endorse or oppose a candidate.

Radio, television, cinema, and today the Internet have received much less protection than print media, and only through extended legal battles have they won a certain degree of freedom. In fact, during the first half of the 20th century, cinema was not provided any First Amendment protection. Not until the Supreme Court's 1952 *Miracle* decision *(Joseph Burstyn, Inc. v. Wilson)*, in which the court ruled that the showing of a film could not be prohibited because a censor deemed it sacrilegious, did any constitutional protection extend to the world of motion pictures.

There are at least three major areas in which limits on government control over the media have been established in the courts. These are national security, libel, and censorship (including graphic violence and obscenity).

National Security

Justice Hugo Black is a renowned defender of the First Amendment.

In an opinion in *Beauharnais* v. *Illinois* (1952) Supreme Court Justice Hugo Black, a renowned defender of the First Amendment, wrote that the First Amendment mandates "no law abridging the freedom of speech or of the press . . . without any ifs, buts, or whereases." But despite Justice Black's clarity of thought on the matter, there are nevertheless numerous federal, state, and local laws and regulations that restrict speech and press activities.

As Donald Gillmor, a distinguished First Amendment scholar and coauthor of *Justice Hugo Black and the First Amendment: "No Law" Means No Law* has noted, it is difficult to defend the idea of a "First Amendment absolutist." An "absolutist" believes that because the First Amendment declares "no law" shall abridge the freedom of speech or of the press, then speech and press are absolutely protected from interference by the government, with no exceptions.[1] Although some media theorists subscribe to this view, the fact is that sometimes one right conflicts with another, and in those cases there must be compromise. In the case of the First Amendment, although some would argue it should take precedence over all rights because it comes first in the Bill of Rights, the U.S. Supreme Court has consistently ruled that there are conditions under which there must be legal restrictions on freedom of expression.

In his book *Mass Media Law,* Don Pember describes a **preferred position balancing theory** that has particular utility in this regard. In this theory, there is a balance that must be struck between speech and other rights, but speech is given a preferred position (especially print media), and limitations on freedom of speech in print are usually illegal. The burden of proof falls on the government to show that some speech or expression information is harmful to national security; it is not journalists or media organizations that must prove that it is not harmful.

preferred position balancing theory—a theory stated by Don Pember that states there must be a balance between speech and other rights, with speech given a preferred position (especially print media) and limitations on freedom of speech usually being illegal.

Clear and Present Danger

The most basic restriction occurs when the speech in question meets both of the following conditions:

1. It is intended to incite or produce dangerous activity (such as falsely shouting fire in a crowded theater).
2. It is likely to succeed in achieving the purported result.

This two-part framework is known as the **clear and present danger** test and is subject to the appropriate criminal law enforcement authorities and to the judicial system rather than regulatory authorities.

The clear and present danger test emerged from *Schenck* v. *United States* (1919). In that case, the U.S. Supreme Court unanimously upheld the conviction

clear and present danger—a restriction on speech when it meets both of the following conditions: 1) It is intended to incite or produce dangerous activity (such as falsely shouting fire in a crowded theater); and 2) it is likely to succeed in achieving the purported result.

The Supreme Court ruled shortly after World War I that in wartime ordinary Constitutional rules do not apply.

of Charles T. Schenck for violating the Espionage Act of 1917. Schenck had been distributing handbills urging resistance to U.S. involvement in World War I. He was a Communist but did not commit any violent acts. The Court based its decision on not only the notion that the First Amendment is not absolute, but that in wartime ordinary Constitutional rules do not apply.

Prior Restraint

An important ruling came in the 1931 Supreme Court ruling in *Near* v. *Minnesota*. Minnesota courts had stopped the publication of an anti-Semitic weekly on the basis that it was a "malicious, scandalous and defamatory" periodical in violation of the state's nuisance law. The Supreme Court reversed the decision, saying that **prior restraint,** or the government preventing or blocking the publication, broadcasting, showing, or otherwise distributing of media content, whether in print, over the air, or in movie theaters, must only be used in cases of serious or grave threats to national security.

In 1971, the Supreme Court made another important ruling in this regard in the case of *New York Times* v. *U.S.* In this case, the Supreme Court overturned a lower court ruling that had stopped the *Times* from publishing "The Pentagon Papers," a top-secret Pentagon study of U.S. involvement in the Vietnam War. The government failed to prove that national security interest outweighed a heavy presumption against prior restraint.

In 1979, a district court stopped *The Progressive* magazine (*U.S.* v. *Progressive*) from publishing "The H-Bomb Secret." The magazine had obtained its information from publicly available documents, and six months later the court injunction was lifted after others published similar material.

In sum, the courts have ruled that freedom of speech is not an absolute, especially during time of war. There is, however, a strong presumption against permitting the government any form of prior restraint on publication or distribution of speech, and it is incumbent on the government to clearly show that publication poses a clear and present threat to national security. This framework seems especially relevant in the aftermath of the September 11, 2001, terrorist attacks on the World Trade Center and Pentagon.

prior restraint—situation in which the government prevents or blocks the publication, broadcasting, showing, or distribution of media content, whether in print, over the air, in movie theaters, or online.

Libel

Libel is a type of defamation, such as a false attack on a person's character, that-damages a person's reputation. Libel is different historically from **slander** in that slander involves the spoken word while libel involves the written word, as in a publication such as a newspaper or magazine.

With the rise of electronic media in the 20th century, libel has been extended to broadcasting on television or radio, as well as online communications, even though broadcast media are technically spoken rather than printed.

In the case of *Phipps v. Clark Oil & Ref. Corp.* (1987), the Minnesota court ruled that libel occurs when a publication "tends to injure the plaintiff's reputation and expose the plaintiff to public hatred, contempt, ridicule, or degradation."

Colonial Roots: From Zenger to Sedition

Much of the foundation for freedom of expression in the U.S. was shaped in the colonial era of America. Foremost is the case of **John Peter Zenger,** a New York printer and journalist who faced a libel suit from the publication of the *New York Weekly Journal,* a political journal opposed to the colonial governor, William Cosby. As publisher of the *Journal,* Zenger was responsible for the articles that frequently featured scathing attacks on the governor. In November 1734 Zenger was arrested for libel and spent nearly 10 months in prison awaiting trial. Zenger's attorney, Andrew Hamilton, requested the jury rule on the veracity of Zenger's printed statements, and in August 1735 Zenger was acquitted of libel. This important precedent established the principle of freedom of press from an early stage in America and one that differs from how libel is viewed in England even today, in which someone can successfully be sued for libel even if the statements printed by them are true but damage their reputation.

In 1798 a series of four acts limiting freedom of speech were passed by the recently formed U.S. Congress. The **Alien and Sedition Acts** were passed by the Federalist-controlled U.S. Congress as a response to a threat of war with France and were meant to crush the position of the Jeffersonian Republicans, who were sympathetic to France. Among other things, the Acts prohibited sedition, or spoken or written criticism of the U.S. government, and imposed penalties of a fine or imprisonment upon conviction.

With the end of the threat of war, the Sedition Act expired in 1801, but other sedition acts have resurfaced throughout U.S. history, especially during times of war.[2]

The New York Times v. *Sullivan* (1964)

Media historians and legal scholars tend to agree that the most important legal decision to establish a free press in the United States was the 1964 Supreme Court ruling in *New York Times* v. *Sullivan.*

In 1960, the *New York Times* printed a fund-raising advertisement for the civil rights movement, which contained several minor factual errors. L. B. Sullivan, a Montgomery, Alabama, city commissioner in charge of the police, said that some

libel—a type of defamation that is written and published, such as a false attack on a person's character, that damages a person's reputation.

slander—a type of defamation that is spoken, as opposed to written (libel), that damages a person's reputation or otherwise harms them.

Zenger, John Peter—a New York printer and journalist who published *New York Weekly Journal,* a political journal opposed to the colonial governor, William Cosby. He was acquitted by a jury of libel in August 1735, establishing an important precedent in the American colonies for the principle of press freedom.

Alien and Sedition Acts—a series of four acts passed by the U.S. Congress in 1798 that, among other things, prohibited sedition, or spoken or written criticism of the U.S. government, and imposed penalties of a fine or imprisonment upon conviction. Although they expired in 1801, other sedition acts have been passed periodically, especially during times of war.

Media **Inventors and Innovators**

Vanessa Leggett

On January 4, 2002, Vanessa Leggett walked out of the Federal Detention Center in Houston and into the history books after spending 168 days in prison and being the longest-jailed journalist in U.S. history. Her crime? Refusing to surrender her notes, including conversations with confidential sources, to a grand jury criminal investigation.

Leggett, 33, was a virtually unpublished writer who planned to write a true-crime book on a high-profile murder case. At first she cooperated with FBI agents investigating the case, who assured her they did not want her to reveal her confidential sources. But when they started asking her for these sources, she refused to give them names, claiming reporter's privilege under the U.S. Constitution,

and was jailed when the judge ruled that reporters have no such privileges when required to divulge information—confidential or non-confidential—in a criminal case.

Leggett was released when the grand jury to which she was supposed to testify ended its investigation. However, a new grand jury could be called, and she could again face the same choices between her principles and her freedom. Her case on whether or not journalists must relinquish their notes or divulge confidential sources for grand jury or criminal investigations will likely work its way to the Supreme Court. In April 2002 Leggett received the $25,000 PEN/Newman's Own First Amendment Award for her fight in maintaining First Amendment rights.[3]

Vanessa Leggett spent 168 days in prison for refusing to hand over her notes to a grand jury investigating a criminal case.

of the false statements in the advertisement regarding Montgomery police actions defamed him, even though he was not mentioned by name. A jury agreed and awarded him a half million dollars. The *New York Times* appealed the case, and it eventually went to the Supreme Court, which overturned the lower court ruling.

The Supreme Court ruled that public figures (defined as publicly prominent) and public officials (defined as public policy makers) may not file suit for libel unless they can prove "actual malice." For nonpublic figures (private citizens), the standard for libel is less stringent, requiring merely that the plaintiff show objectively that a "reasonable person" knew or should have known the defamatory statement was false.

The court defined actual malice in terms of either 1) the intent of the defendant was malicious or 2) that he or she knew the statement was false, or acted with reckless disregard for the truth, and published it regardless. This is known as the "actual malice" test. The Court ruled that the common law of defamation violated the guarantee of free speech under the First Amendment and ruled the citizen's right to criticize government officials is too important to be intolerant of speech that may contain even harmful falsehoods. The result of the ruling has been to maintain a more robust environment for media to publish criticisms of public figures, knowing that they can be found libelous only if they meet the stringent actual malice test.

Protecting Journalists against Libel

Most media organizations have libel insurance to protect journalists. Freelance journalists, however, often do not have libel insurance, so the threat of libel can be particularly chilling. This is especially true for online journalists or others who operate on a shoestring budget or who are not widely recognized by media organizations as "real" journalists but who nonetheless report on events and publish them on the Web.

Moreover, although there is no prior restraint for libel cases, journalists can be imprisoned for contempt, whether in libel or other cases. Most typically this happens when a journalist is protecting his or her sources (i.e., refuses to release their identities), but it can also occur for other reasons, such as failing to release one's notes.

There are at least five steps journalists or other mass communication professionals can take to minimize their chances of committing an act of libel. These are:

1. One must engage in thorough research, including investigating the facts and maintaining good records, establishing written criteria in making decisions about when and what to publish and adhering to those, and using reliable sources.

2. One must confirm the identity of the target of a report.

3. The journalist must use quotations whenever possible and attribute statements to sources.

4. The journalist must report facts only and avoid language that draws conclusions (i.e., avoiding taking sides, not saying someone is dishonest without substantial facts to substantiate this claim).

5. The journalist must avoid bias in reports and strive for balance (i.e., give the different sides in a debate fair play).

Shield Laws

Shield laws are laws intended to protect journalists from legal challenges to their freedom to report the news. Journalists have received neither blanket protection from the Supreme Court nor a national protective law from the Congress, however. Yet 30 states have enacted laws to protect journalists from being required to answer every subpoena.[4] In these states, journalists are not required to testify or produce materials obtained from sources in confidence. Most of the other states and territories (15 of the 21 without shield laws) provide some court protection for journalists. Without these shield laws, unrestrained legal action might exert a chilling effect on journalists, some suggest, including Reed Hundt, former chairman of the FCC.[5] "Newsgatherers might be less aggressive and cease to pursue confidential sources or information. Whistle-blowers and other sources could be left without any legal protection from discovery," Reed said.

How effective are shield laws? Evidence suggests they have limited effectiveness. As reported by The Reporters Committee for Freedom of the Press, in the states with shield laws, as well as the District of Columbia, news organizations in

Weblink
The Reporters Committee for Freedom of the Press
[www.rcfp.org/]

shield laws—laws intended to protect journalists from legal challenges to their freedom to report the news.

The Supreme Court has ruled that school-sponsored publications such as student newspapers do not enjoy full First Amendment protection.

1997 reported being served with 1655 subpoenas, 61 percent of all subpoenas served that year in those states (and DC). This is actually a worse percentage than in the states without shield laws. In those states in 1997, news organizations were served with 1070 subpoenas, 39 percent of all subpoenas reported.[6]

Censorship

Censorship, the third major dimension of government control over media, refers to the act of prohibiting certain expression or content. In a sense, it is a form of prior restraint; only, rather than prohibiting an entire publication, it targets specific content within that publication, broadcast, film, or Web site. Censorship is not generally permitted in the United States, although it is routine in some countries, especially authoritarian regimes where criticism of the government or the countries' rulers is often prohibited. In the United States, censorship is most common in two areas: 1) during wartime, when content, especially that being reported from the battlefield, is subject to censorship under the principle of national security; and 2) pornographic or obscene content, which can sometimes include graphic violence or detailed accounts of criminal behavior.

An important censorship case is *Hazelwood School District* v. *Kuhlmeier* (1988). This case established that not all citizens have the same First Amendment rights. In particular, people still in school, typically but not necessarily those under 18, are not afforded full First Amendment protection. In this case, a school principal was permitted to censor school newspaper articles dealing with pregnancy and divorce. The court found that school-sponsored publications are not a public forum and thus may be subject to censorship to protect the young from harm.

Indecent Content

Although not prohibited, **indecent speech** is also subject to federal regulation. Broadcasters may not air indecent speech when children are likely to be in the audience, or between 6 AM and 10 PM. This has been called a safe harbor period, and other topics such as portrayals of violence or sex are sometimes requested to be excluded during the time period as well by concerned groups.

censorship—the act of prohibiting certain expression or content. Censors usually do not target the whole publication, program, or Web site, but seek to prohibit some part of the content.

indecent speech—language or material that, in context, depicts or describes, in terms patently offensive as measured by contemporary community standards for the broadcast medium, sexual or excretory organs or activities.

Federal law defines indecent speech as "language or material that, in context, depicts or describes, in terms patently offensive as measured by contemporary community standards for the broadcast medium, sexual or excretory organs or activities." Exempted from this definition is profanity that is neither indecent nor obscene. "Damn" is an example of a permitted word. Indecent speech was put to the test in a landmark First Amendment case involving comedian George Carlin.

Carlin recorded before a live California audience a 12-minute monologue titled "Filthy Words." He opened his routine by contemplating "the words you couldn't say on the public airwaves, the ones you definitely wouldn't say, ever." He then listed those words and repeated them in a variety of contexts. The Supreme Court decision in *Federal Communications Commission* v. *Pacifica Foundation* (1978) was the basis for subsequent regulations on indecent speech for broadcasters.

Other entertainers have tested and pushed the limits of freedom of speech in the electronic media as well, including radio "shock jock" Howard Stern, whose frequently crude and vulgar on-air commentary has drawn criticism not only from citizen groups but from government regulators. In 1995, Infinity Broadcasting Corp. (owned by CBS), the producer and broadcaster of Stern's radio show, agreed to pay $1.7 million without admitting guilt to settle a variety of indecency charges that had been leveled by the FCC against Stern since 1989, whose comments are frequently sexually graphic.

As part of the **Telecommunications Act of 1996,** the first sweeping federal legislation to rewrite the foundation of communications regulation in the United States since 1934, legislators had sought to curb "indecent" speech online, but the Communications Decency Act (CDA) passed as part (Title V) of the Act was ultimately struck down by the U.S. Supreme Court in *ACLU* v. *Janet Reno* (1998). The Act made it illegal to "depict or describe" anything considered indecent on the Internet and made no distinctions between scientific or literary works and pornography. The ACLU filed a lawsuit against the government on the same day the Telecommunications Act was passed, and a lower court ruled the CDA unconstitutional, which the Supreme Court affirmed.

Obscenity

Pornography, or **obscenity,** is one of the major forms of speech deemed unprotected by the First Amendment and is subject to censorship by the government. A landmark case in this regard was *Miller* v. *California* (1973), in which Miller had been convicted in California of mailing unsolicited pornographic brochures. He appealed his conviction on the grounds that it inhibited his right to free speech, but the court disagreed and outlined guidelines for determining whether content is obscene. In the case, the U.S. Supreme Court set out a three-part test, or identified three criteria, that must be met in order to be considered obscene:

1. An average individual applying her or his contemporary community standards must believe the content, taken as a whole, appeals to prurient interest.

2. The content must show or describe in an offensive manner sexual conduct.

3. The content on the whole must lack serious literary, artistic, political, or scientific value.

Comedian George Carlin's monologue "Filthy Words" was the origin of a Supreme Court case that ruled on indecent words.

Weblink
"Filthy Words" by George Carlin transcript
[www.law.umkc.edu/faculty /projects/ftrials/conlaw /filthywords.html]

Telecommunications Act of 1996—the first major overhaul of regulations regarding the telecommunications industry since 1934, this legislation was designed to open the telecommunications field to greater competition by deregulating many aspects of the industry.

obscenity—one of the forms of speech not protected by the First Amendment and thus subject to censorship. Although the exact definition of the term has been difficult to achieve in various court cases, generally a three-part standard is applied for media: the material must appeal to prurient interests as defined by community standards; the content must show in an offensive manner sexual conduct; and the content on the whole must lack serious artistic, literary, political, or scientific value.

Defining obscenity, however, is difficult, and some would say simply that "I know it when I see it (or hear it)."

The digital age has created unique issues for obscenity cases. One issue is the ease with which pornography can be distributed across local or national boundaries. Another issue is computer-generated pornography in which increasingly realistic images can be created. In April 2002, the Supreme Court reaffirmed that free speech principles applied online when it struck down provisions in the Child Pornography Prevention Act of 1996 that made it a crime to create, distribute, or possess "virtual" child pornography, or computer-generated images of children in sexual acts as opposed to images of actual children. Justice Anthony M. Kennedy wrote for the majority, saying the Act "prohibits speech that records no crime and creates no victims by its production." Although some justices voted in favor of keeping penalties for computer-generated images, and the government argued that real children could be harmed and exploited when a market for virtual child pornography could be sustained, Justice Kennedy said that, "The mere tendency of speech to encourage unlawful acts is not a sufficient reason for banning it."[7]

Criticism, Ridicule, or Humor

As objectionable as they may be, stereotypes and other offensive material are protected by the U.S. Constitution. Criticism, ridicule, or jokes about individuals (including government officials), groups, or institutions based on race, religion, gender, national background, or other factors is protected speech, whether in print or electronic media, and may not be regulated by the FCC. In the case of licensed broadcasters, it is incumbent upon station owners and operators to act responsibly in offering programming that meets the needs of the communities they serve.

The Federal Communications Commission (FCC)

The **FCC** is the principal communications regulatory body at the federal level in the United States. Some would say the FCC is also a lightning rod for criticism because of its prominent position on the communications regulatory landscape. Oftentimes, regardless how the commission rules, someone or group is left unhappy and frequently is quite vocal in expressing their displeasure.

The principal mandate of the FCC is "regulating interstate and foreign commerce in communication by wire and radio so as to make available, so far as possible, to all the people of the United States a rapid, efficient, nation-wide, and world-wide wire and radio communications service . . ." In this sense, the term *radio* is interpreted to include television. The Commission is authorized to "make such regulations not inconsistent with law as it may deem necessary to prevent interference between stations and to carry out the provisions of [the] Act." The FCC mandate was reaffirmed under the Telecommunications Act of 1996, which supplanted the 1934 Act. The new act added an emphasis on fostering competition in the newly converged digital landscape, in the hopes of both supporting

Federal Communications Commission (FCC)—the principal communications regulatory body at the federal level in the United States, established in 1934.

and expanding the communications industry and in bringing a greater range of communications services at an affordable price to the American public.

FCC Commissioners

The FCC consists of five presidentially appointed commissioners, each of whom must be confirmed by the Senate. The commission must include at least two representatives of each of the major parties, helping insure the nonpartisan nature of the FCC. As of this writing, the chairman of the FCC is Michael K. Powell, appointed in 2001 by President George W. Bush. Powell, who is the second African American to head the commission following William E. Kennard, appointed in 1997 by President Bill Clinton, is the son of U.S. Secretary of State Colin L. Powell.

Weblink
FCC Web site
[www.fcc.gov]

Regulating Radio and Television

Among its principal duties for journalism and mass communication, the FCC allocates new broadcast radio and television stations and renews the licenses of existing stations, ensuring that each licensee is complying with the laws mandated by Congress. The FCC does not license TV or radio networks, such as CBS, NBC, ABC, Fox, UPN, WB, or PBS, except when they are owners of stations.

The commission considers two basic sets of factors regarding the allocation of new stations. First, it evaluates the relative needs of communities for additional broadcast outlets. This depends on a variety of considerations, including a community's population and its heterogeneity. Second, the commission considers various engineering standards that eliminate interference between stations.

In fulfilling its duties, the FCC invites public comment on its proposed rules, publishes those rules, and implements them through a set of seven bureaus and eleven offices. The bureaus include the Mass Media Bureau, which regulates radio and television stations and which absorbed the Cable Services Bureau, which had regulated cable television; and the Common Carrier Bureau, which regulates wireline and wireless telephony.

Cable and satellite television are not under the same FCC rules as broadcast, or those transmitted via terrestrial frequencies. Cable TV and satellite channels are available only to subscribers and have many fewer rules to abide by than network broadcasters. Among the most important rules administered by the Cable Services Bureau are:

- Basic service, which is the lowest level of cable service a subscriber can buy. It includes, at a minimum, all over-the-air television broadcast signals carried pursuant to the must-carry requirements of the Communications Act and any public, educational, or government access channels required by the system's franchise agreement.

- Must-carry, in which every broadcast TV station, whether commercial or noncommercial, is entitled to have its programming carried on any local cable TV system. The station receives no compensation, but its programming is carried via the cable system. A broadcaster may opt instead to grant permission to the cable system to carry the station and receive compensation for the programming. This is called retransmission consent and is available only to commercial TV stations.

The FCC and Station Activities

Each station must air identification (i.e., station IDs) announcements as it signs on and off each day and must air announcements hourly, at what the Commission calls "a natural programming break." The requirements for station identification foster a certain level of uniformity in programming style in the broadcast media, but they do not mandate that programmers insert station IDs at the top of the hour and at other well-defined intervals. The fact that most programmers or stations do so is largely a result of competitive pressures and inertia—the fact that stations have done so for a long time. TBS, one of the "superstations," in fact breaks five minutes past the hour partly as a means to differentiate itself from other programmers.

License Renewal

The FCC licenses stations to operate either as commercial or noncommercial-educational (public) broadcasters for up to eight years, after which the station must renew its license. This is the case for either radio or television broadcasters licensed to transmit their signals via terrestrial frequencies.

At the time of license renewal, a station must meet five basic requirements, including primarily that it has served in the public interest and met all legal requirements. A station must also accept and respond to viewer or listener complaints.

Audience members, journalists, or anyone else may also review what is called the station's Public Inspection File. Technically, an appointment is not required to view the file, but it might help. In any event, the file may be stored in analog or digital format. If it is analog, the requester will probably need to go to the station to see its contents. If it's digital, one may still need to go to the station, which must provide access via a computer, but the file may also be available on the Internet on the station's Web site.

The Public Inspection File contains a wide variety of materials about the station and its programming. Among the contents are the station's license, including all technical specifications and any special conditions imposed by the FCC. Noncommercial stations must also provide lists of donors who have supported specific programs during the past two years. In 1999, a number of Public Broadcasting Service stations got into trouble when it was revealed that 28 stations had shared their donor lists with political organizations, a practice dating to at least 1981. Although not technically illegal, this practice undermines the credibility of the public broadcasters by bringing their impartiality into doubt.

FCC Limits on Stations

There are a variety of station activities that are either regulated or prohibited by federal law. Among these regulated activities are station-conducted contests, television games or quiz shows, and broadcasting telephone calls. When a station hosts a contest, it must fully disclose all terms and rules of the contest, including this in any advertising promoting the contest. Stations are required to inform any parties to a phone call before recording it for broadcast, or broadcasting it live,

The FCC licenses stations to broadcast publicly for up to eight years.

although there are certain exceptions, such as call-in shows, when the caller can reasonably be expected to understand that his or her call may be broadcast.

Generally, only the stations themselves are responsible for selecting the material they air, including coverage of local issues, news, public affairs, religion, sports events, and other subjects. The **Communication Act of 1934** prohibits the FCC from censoring broadcast programming, and stations are not required to air material submitted or recommended to them. Nor are they required to air public service announcements. If a licensee violates the rules, the FCC is authorized to levy a fine or even to revoke a station's license. Among the programming concerns for which the FCC may levy fines or revoke licenses are primarily the airing of obscene or indecent language when children are likely to be viewing and nudity. The FCC does not advise stations regarding artistic standards, format, or grammar. Stations must rely on their own judgment.

Among the prohibited activities for stations are knowingly broadcasting a hoax, including false information regarding a crime or catastrophe (defined as a disaster), especially when a broadcast might cause public harm. This rule came about largely as a result of the 1938 *War of the Worlds* radio broadcast. Stations are also prohibited from airing any advertising for a lottery, or information concerning a lottery, with the exception of lotteries conducted by a state, gaming conducted by an Indian tribe, lotteries conducted by nonprofit organizations, and lotteries conducted by commercial activities but which are done on an occasional basis and are done as promotional activities.

Regulating Content

In addition to the federal controls over libel, obscenity, and speech that threaten national security, there are at least eight other types of content restrictions in the United States. These are largely unique to the broadcast media, though not exclusively so. These restrictions are primarily aimed at protecting children, controlling political communication, and limiting commercial speech.

In the cases of libel, copyright, clear and present danger, or obscenity and pornography, the judicial system has authority over the broadcast or publication of such material. In the case of false or deceptive advertising, the Federal Trade Commission has primary responsibility, although the Food and Drug Administration (FDA) has authority when food or drugs are involved. These issues are discussed in more detail later in this chapter. Most of the remaining content restrictions are subject to the jurisdiction of the FCC.

Commercial Speech

Commercial speech, including advertising, has generally been afforded less First Amendment protection than other forms of speech, especially political speech or the news. In a landmark decision, the U.S. Supreme Court ruled in 1942 in *Valentine* v. *Chrestensen* that "purely commercial advertising" was unprotected by the First Amendment. Chrestensen was a businessman who was displaying a World War I–era submarine at a pier in New York City and dispersed leaflets

Communications Act of 1934—an Act that established the FCC and gave it power to regulate broadcasting such as in licensing stations, assigning call letters and radio frequencies, and levying fines on stations that did not meet its regulations. The Act was superseded by the Telecommunication Act of 1996.

advertising tours of the submarine. The leaflets were becoming litter, and the police commissioner in New York forbade him from distributing the leaflets. Even though Chrestensen attempted to subvert the ruling by adding political messages on the opposite side of his advertising leaflets, the city still barred him from distributing them, and the Supreme Court agreed, giving commercial speech no protection under the First Amendment.

In the 1970s the broad powers granted to government regarding commercial speech were restricted somewhat by cases that allowed some First Amendment protection to commercial speech, although not on par with other forms of speech. In 1976, the Court ruled in *Virginia Board of Pharmacy* v. *Virginia Citizens Consumer Council, Inc.,* that speech that does "no more than propose a commercial transaction" is entitled to at least some First Amendment protection. This was in response to a case brought by some citizens' groups in Virginia that wanted to see pharmacies advertise prices of drugs, which the state legislature had prohibited.

In some cases, however, commercial speech has been afforded more protection than one might expect. An interesting example comes from a case involving former New York City Mayor Rudolph Giuliani. Giuliani was lampooned in an advertising campaign by *New York* magazine in 1997 on the city buses of New York, which said that the magazine was "possibly the only good thing in New York that Rudy hasn't taken credit for." Giuliani, who had often taken credit for everything from drops in the crime rate to a booming economy, found the ads to be offensive and ordered them removed from the buses. In this case, commercial speech won. Consider the conclusion of U.S. District Judge Shira Scheindelin, who said, "Who would have dreamed that the mayor would object to more publicity?" She ruled that Giuliani's administration violated the First Amendment when it ordered city buses to remove paid ads.

Tobacco Advertising

Most legal products are legally advertised on electronic media under the jurisdiction of the FCC. However, one type of legal product may not be legally advertised by broadcasters: most products containing tobacco. Advertising cigarettes, small cigars, smokeless tobacco, and chewing tobacco are all prohibited on radio and television or any other electronic medium regulated by the FCC, such as telephony. It is permissible to advertise smoking accessories, cigars, pipes, pipe tobacco, or cigarette-making machines. There are no federal laws or FCC regulations prohibiting the advertising of alcoholic beverages, such as beer, wine, or liquor, on electronic media, including television and radio. However, most hard liquor makers follow a voluntary ban on advertising on television.

False Advertising

One other area of commercial speech that is subject to federal regulation is false or deceptive advertising. However, this form of commercial speech is regulated by the Federal Trade Commission (FTC), not the FCC. In the case of food or drug products, the Food and Drug Administration is also involved. Other areas of commercial speech that are not regulated or prohibited by any federal law or agency, including either the FCC or the FTC, include loud commercials (which the FCC has shown through research are only perceived as louder than programs but actually aren't), offensive advertising, or subliminal programming. In the latter case, the FCC states that use of subliminal messages, which are meant to be perceived only on a subconscious level, are "inconsistent with a station's obligation to serve the public interest." However, it does not officially prohibit subliminal programming. Research does not provide conclusive evidence that subliminal messages are even understood or have an influence on behavior.

Political Speech

Historically, the heart of freedom of expression revolves around political speech, or speech that deals with the political process, government, elected officials, or elections. Some go so far as to contend that the only speech the founders intended when they wrote the First Amendment was political speech. Political speech is also one area where federal regulations have been most extensive.

The Equal-Time Provision

Until October 2000, stations had been required to adhere to an **equal-time provision** outlined in the 1934 Communications Act, which required broadcasters to give "equal air time" to candidates running in elections. Under this provision, if a station permitted a qualified candidate for public office to use its facilities, including commentaries or paid commercials, the station was required to "afford equal opportunities to all other such candidates for that office." Two circumstances were exempted from the equal-time provision: 1) when the candidate appears in a newscast, during an interview, or in a documentary; and 2) if the candidate appears during on-the-scene coverage of a news event.

Section 312(a)(7) of the 1934 Act laid out the basic right of access to the media for political candidates. The U.S. Supreme Court ruled in 1981 in support of this section, saying that Section 312

> . . . as defined by the FCC and applied here, does not violate the First Amendment rights of broadcasters by unduly circumscribing their editorial discretion, but instead properly balances the First Amendment rights of federal candidates, the public, and broadcasters. Although the broadcasting industry is entitled under the First Amendment to exercise "the widest journalistic freedom consistent with its public [duties]," *Columbia Broadcasting System, Inc.* v. *Democratic National Committee,* supra, at 110, "[i]t is the right of the viewers and listeners, not the right of the broadcasters, which is paramount."

In early October 2000, the FCC suspended its rules requiring "radio and television stations to provide free reply time for opponents of political candidates endorsed by the stations and for candidates and others whose integrity had been attacked."[8] Then, on October 11, 2000, a federal court overturned the provision entirely, ruling that the FCC had not demonstrated the value to the public of the equal-time provision given the limitation it places on broadcasters' First Amendment rights. Given this ruling, it is not clear what the future of the equal-time provision may be. Ultimately, the case may find its way to the U.S. Supreme Court, which may affirm or overturn its earlier decision.

The equal-time provision was the last vestige of the **Fairness Doctrine,** which the FCC had adopted in 1949, requiring broadcasters to seek out and present all

equal-time provision—the requirement that broadcasters give equal air time to opposing candidates running for election for commentaries and commercials. It did not apply to candidates appearing in newscasts, as part of documentaries, or in news event coverage. The provision was thrown out by the FCC in October 2000, and its future is unclear as it works its way to a hearing by the Supreme Court.

Fairness Doctrine—adopted by the FCC in 1949, it required broadcasters to seek out and present all sides of a controversial issue they were covering. It was discarded by the FCC in 1987.

sides of an issue when covering a controversy. In 1969, in *Red Lion Broadcasting Co. v. FCC*, in which Red Lion Broadcasting was forced to provide equal air time for a politician's response to an attack on them, the Court held that because of the scarcity of broadcasting frequencies the government might require a broadcast licensee "to share his frequency with others and to conduct himself as a proxy or fiduciary with obligations to present those views and voices which are representative of his community and which would otherwise, by necessity, be barred from the airwaves." The Court thus gave the public a right of access "to social, political, esthetic, moral, and other ideas and experiences." The Fairness Doctrine is no longer required, having been discarded by the FCC in 1987. Despite a number of attempts to resuscitate the Fairness Doctrine, the FCC has resisted on the basis that the Doctrine never really produced more diversity in programming and with channel proliferation there's more diversity than could have been hoped for when television was dominated by three major commercial networks.

Political Editorials

The FCC defines a political editorial as "when a station endorses or opposes a legally qualified candidate(s) during a broadcast of *its own* opinion." It distinguishes the opinions of third parties broadcast by the station as "comments" or "commentaries," which are thus exempt from these rules. The Commission does not require a station to identify political editorials but generally expects them to do so. A station has 24 hours to provide other qualified candidates for the same office or the candidates that were opposed in the editorial with these three things: 1) notice of the date and time of the editorial, 2) a tape or script of the editorial, and 3) free and comparable airtime in which to respond.

The FCC may not attempt to influence the opinions expressed on any station or influence its selection of subjects on which to report or editorialize. Nor may it review the qualifications to "gather, edit, announce, or comment on the news; these decisions are the station's responsibility."

Personal Attacks

The FCC defines a personal attack as the situation when "during the presentation of views on a controversial issue of public importance, someone attacks the honesty, character, integrity, or like personal qualities of an identified person or group." When this occurs, the station has one week to provide the attacked party with the same three things that candidates receive regarding political editorials. Stations are not required to maintain copies of the material they broadcast, with two exceptions: personal attacks and political editorials.

Children's Programming Protections

Parents, elected officials, and others have long sought not only to protect children from unwanted or offensive speech but to create a media system that actively nurtures and nourishes children. As such, there has been considerable

There are many regulations broadcasters must follow regarding children's television programming.

regulation designed to both protect and promote children's welfare in the context of the media, especially the electronic media. Among the most important pieces of regulation in this regard is the **Children's Television Act.**

The Children's Television Act

The Children's Television Act (CTA) took effect in 1990. It placed limits on the amount of commercial content permitted in children's TV programming (including broadcast, satellite, and cable). The Act also mandates that each television station provide programming specifically designed to meet the educational and information needs of children age 16 and younger. The FCC determination of whether programming meets this criterion is based on four standards:

1. The programming is primarily designed to meet children's educational and information needs (i.e., it can't be primarily entertainment, such as a cartoon, and have as a byproduct some educational value).

2. It is broadcast between 6 AM and 10 PM, hours when children are likely to be viewing.

3. It is scheduled to run regularly each week.

4. It is at least a one-half hour program.

In addition, commercial stations are required to identify their educational programs for children at the beginning of those programs; they must identify these programs to publishers of program guides as well. Moreover, all programs aimed at children 12 and younger may not contain more than 10.5 minutes of advertising per hour on weekends and 12 minutes on weekdays. The FCC also established that stations that air at least three hours of core children's programming a week would be in fulfillment of their obligations under the CTA, *core* being defined primarily in terms of item one, above.

Violent and Sexual Programming: The V-Chip

Violent and sexual programming receives special attention from the FCC because of concern about the implications of such material for young viewers. With the

Children's Television Act— created in 1990, it places limits on the amount of commercial content that programming can carry and forces stations to carry certain amounts of educational programming for children 16 and under, among other provisions to help protect children.

In 1997 President Clinton pushed heavily for the V-chip to be included in all televisions, although critics say it raises important questions as to whether or not technology can replace or adequately assist close parental supervision.

passage of the Telecommunication Act of 1996, the federal government began regulating televised violent content in addition to sexual content, which it already regulated. The Act seeks to give parents greater control over their children's viewing of violent and sexual programming. The Act begins by summarizing research findings that demonstrate the negative impact of television violence viewing on children. It notes that, "Parents express grave concern over violent and sexual video programming and strongly support technology that would give them greater control to block video programming in the home that they consider harmful to their children."

In order to give parents knowledge and control over what kind of programming their children are able to watch, the government mandated that now all television sets 13 inches or larger come equipped with what is called a **V-chip,** or "violence chip." The V-chip is a computer device that enables parents or any other viewers to program their TV sets to block access to programs containing violent and sexual content based on the program rating. The FCC phased in the V-chip, requiring by July 1, 1999, that half of all new televisions with screens 13 inches and larger have the V-chip, and by January 1, 2000, that all such sets sold have the V-chip.

The rating system developed for the V-chip is also called the "TV Parental Guidelines." At the request of the government, the television industry was asked to create its own voluntary ratings system and to agree voluntarily to broadcast signals that contain ratings of their programming, which could be detected by the V-chip. The ratings are shown on the TV screen for the first 15 seconds of rated programming and permit viewers to use the V-chip to block those programs from being displayed on their sets. On the basis of the First Amendment, all news programming is exempted from the V-chip.

Arising from this development is a set of important questions. First, will most parents use, or be able to use, the V-chip technology? Imagine the technical challenge a technophobic parent might face when trying to configure a smart

V-chip—a computer device that enables parents or any other viewers to program their TV sets to block access to programs containing violent and sexual content based on the program rating.

Media Spotlight: **The TV Parental Guidelines**

The new television rating system identifies six categories of programming. The first two refer to programming designed solely for children, and the final one is programming aimed solely for adults. The middle three ratings refer to programming that has not been designed for children but that may be suitable for some children, and it is up to parents to decide. The rating system is similar to the system developed for motion pictures. Following are the categories and their official definitions.

Programs designed specifically for children are:

- *TV-Y* (All children; this program is designed to be appropriate for all children): Whether animated or live action, the themes and elements in this program are specifically designed for a very young audience, including children from ages 2 through 6. This program is not expected to frighten younger children.
- *TV-Y7* (Directed to older children; this program is designed for children age 7 and above): It may be more appropriate for children who have acquired the developmental skills needed to distinguish between make-believe and reality. Themes and elements in this program may include mild fantasy or comedic violence or may frighten children under the age of 7. Programs where fantasy violence may be more intense or more combative than other programs in this category will be designated TV-Y7-FV.

Programs not designed for children, but possibly suitable for audiences including at least older children, are:

- *TV-G* (General audience; most parents would find this program suitable for all ages): Although this rating does not signify a program designed specifically for children, most parents may let younger children watch this program unattended. It contains little or no violence, no strong language, and little or no sexual dialogue or situations.
- *TV-PG* (Parental guidance suggested; this program contains material that parents may find unsuitable for younger children): Many parents may want to watch it with their younger children. The theme itself may call for parental guidance, and/or the program contains one or more of the following: moderate violence (V), some sexual situations (S), infrequent coarse language (L), or some suggestive dialogue (D).
- *TV-14* (Parents strongly cautioned; this program contains some material that many parents would find unsuitable for children under 14 years of age): Parents are strongly urged to exercise greater care in monitoring this program and are cautioned against letting children under the age of 14 watch unattended. This program contains one or more of the following: intense violence (V); intense sexual situations (S); strong, coarse language (L); or intensely suggestive dialogue (D).

Programs designed only for adult audiences are:

- *TV-MA* (Mature audience only; this program is specifically designed to be viewed by adults and therefore may be unsuitable for children under 17): This program contains one or more of the following: graphic violence (V); explicit sexual activity (S); or crude, indecent language (L).

The TV ratings system is meant to help parents decide what is appropriate programming for their children.

agent to keep his or her technologically sophisticated and hormonally driven teenager from surfing prohibited channels.

More importantly, how will programming change as a result of the V-chip? It will not change dramatically, at least not at first. Television set manufacturers have started producing and selling the next generation of V-chip–enhanced sets, but it will take close to a decade (according to most data on rates at which American consumers replace their television sets) to replace more than 50 percent of household TV sets. As a result, most American's won't even have access to the V-chip technology until well into the decade. One subtle change will likely occur, however. Those producing programming designed for a general audience will increasingly use innuendo to communicate sex or violence themes and acts, rather than depicting them graphically, so they can get a more children-friendly rating and larger audience.

In the digital age, the V-chip is no longer the only tool at parents' disposal to restrict television viewing among their children. All digital media systems, including digital cable and satellite television, contain software controls that can block individual programs, entire channels, or classes of programs based on their ratings. That is not to say many parents make use of these filtering features. One study by the Kaiser Family Foundation in 2001 showed that just 7 percent of parents were using the chip, despite the fact that 40 percent of U.S. households have sets equipped with the V-chip.[9]

The Press Freedom Model

The following seven-part **press freedom model** is an adaptation of psychologist Harold Lasswell's famous media effects question. It provides a guide for understanding the legal framework for restricting media freedom in the United States. The model asks:

1. What is said (is it obscene; is it political or commercial speech?).

2. By whom it is said (are they protesting repressive governments or promoting hate speech?).

3. To which audience it is said (children are generally afforded less freedom of speech protection).

4. Through which medium it is distributed (print media have historically enjoyed much greater freedom than electronic or audiovisual media).

5. By whom it is censored (this is typically discussed in the context of the government, but industry or companies—including media companies—can also censor or self-regulate).

6. Which tools are used (by humans in the analog world, by humans or automation and filtering in the digital world).

7. What harmful effect is intended to be prevented (typically to prevent harming children, a person's reputation or income, or national defense).

press freedom model—an adaptation of a famous question on media effects first posed by psychologist Harold Lasswell, it provides a guide for understanding the legal framework for restricting media freedom in the United States by asking seven questions.

Radio was primarily used in its earliest days as a way to increase safety on ships, which could send distress calls.

The Evolution of Regulation of Electronic Media

The origins of U.S. electronic communications regulation rest in the development of broadcasting in the early part of the 20th century, starting with radio and later including television after that was developed. The approach taken has evolved considerably over the years, in large part as a result of the technical and economic factors surrounding and underpinning those media. The following discussion examines the evolution and nature of electronic media regulation in the United States.

Stage One (1911–1926): Early Days and the Radio Act of 1912

The regulation of broadcasting in the United States has evolved through a series of four stages. Prior to 1911, there was no regulatory authority for broadcasting, which at the time meant specifically radio transmissions. The technology of radio was in its infancy, and so little was known about the new medium or its potential that there was little to regulate. Because radio emerged initially as a vital medium for ships at sea, especially for making distress calls, in 1911 the Commerce Department's Bureau of Navigation hired three inspectors to make sure that large ocean vessels would carry radio equipment as required by a June 24, 1910, act of Congress. That act was later amended to become the **Radio Act of 1912,** which at that time meant "ship to shore" radio transmission. Responsibility for radio regulation rested with the Commerce Department until 1927.

During this period, radio broadcasting was done largely by amateur technology enthusiasts. The process of obtaining a frequency on which to broadcast was very informal. As broadcast historian Mark Goodman points out, "By mailing a postcard to Secretary of Commerce Herbert Hoover, anyone with a radio

Radio Act of 1912—Act that assigned three- and four-letter codes to radio stations and assigned frequencies to the stations, as well as limiting broadcasting to the 360-meter wavelength.

transmitter, ranging from college students experimenting in science classes, to amateur inventors who ordered kits, to newspaper-operated stations, could broadcast on the frequency chosen by Hoover."[10] Despite new regulations by the Commerce Department that limited the number of people who could operate a radio transmitter, by 1926 there were 15,111 amateur radio stations, 1902 ship stations, 553 land stations for maritime use, and 536 broadcasting stations in the United States. The government allocated just 89 wavelengths for these 536 broadcasting stations. Despite geographic separation of radio transmitters and various power restrictions on those transmitters, there was a great amount of interference among the different stations' signals. Radio became what historian Erik Barnouw calls "a Tower of Babel" and the need for regulation grew. In the 1920s much public attention became focused on the new medium of radio and how the government was attempting to regulate it.[11]

Stage Two (1927–1933): Increasing Regulation and the Federal Radio Commission

"The airwaves by 1927 were an open forum for anyone with the expertise and equipment to reach a forum with 25 million listeners," explains Mark Goodman.[12] But the rapid and largely uncontrolled growth of the new medium required a new regulatory structure. The **Radio Act of 1927** was signed into law in February and borrowed from railroad regulations. It said that anyone who owned a radio frequency and radio should operate for the "public convenience, interest, or necessity"—even though the Act didn't define those terms.[13]

The Federal Radio Commission (FRC) was also established by the Act. The FRC was comprised of five politically appointed commissioners and limited staff whose mandate was to sort out the mess in radio. They revoked over 18,000 radio licenses and instituted a new system that favored fewer, high-powered stations over many low-powered stations.[14]

Stage Three (1934–1995): The Communications Act and Spectrum Scarcity

In 1934, Congress enacted the Communications Act, which became the foundation of communications law for the next 62 years. The Act was based on the premise established in the Radio Act of 1927 that the airwaves were a public good, a limited natural resource that belonged to the people. Broadcasters were granted licenses to use those airwaves at no cost, but they were public trustees who bore a responsibility to use the airwaves in "the public interest, convenience or necessity." Because of the limited nature of the airwaves, the Act established regulations based on the notion of "spectrum scarcity," or limited channel capacity. It was under this model that news, whether profitable or not, came to meet the public service requirements for radio and television broadcasters.

The Communications Act of 1934 established the FCC, with five political appointees, including one chair, and a series of bureaus, each assigned responsibility for an area of the growing radio industry. The FCC would eventually assume regulatory responsibility for the emerging medium of television as well.

Radio Act of 1927— Act that replaced the Radio Act of 1912 and created the Federal Radio Commission, the precursor to the FCC, and gave the government greater regulatory and enforcement powers over radio, as well as establishing the premise that the airwaves were a public good and limited.

Stage Four (1996–present): The Telecommunications Act and Its Effects

Congress enacted the Telecommunications Act of 1996 as a response to the technological transformation of the communications system in the United States and around the world. The convergence of telecommunications, computing, and traditional media in a digital, networked environment created the need for a basic reconstruction of the regulatory framework for the media of mass communication.

The Act introduced that new framework. Although it preserved the requirement to serve in the "public interest, convenience and necessity," the Act's new mandate was to foster competition in the communications marketplace. The preamble of the Act states it is intended "To promote competition and reduce regulation in order to secure lower prices and higher quality services for American telecommunications consumers and encourage the rapid deployment of new telecommunications technologies." The motivation for this new mandate was the digital revolution that made the premise of channel scarcity virtually obsolete. The public no longer only had three or four network channels to watch—they now had broadcasting choices ranging from cable to satellite television and, increasingly, to Internet-based programming.

More than 100 pages in length, the complex Telecommunications Act of 1996 raises a variety of issues that affect not just the structure of the communications industry and how it is regulated but the nature of programming and production as well. The Act permits and promotes direct competition among all telecommunications providers, including terrestrial broadcasters, direct broadcast satellite providers, mobile communication services, cable providers, and the regional Bell telephone companies. Further, the Act specifically targets two forms of programming: violent or sexual programming and interactive services.

Since passage of the Act, there have been dramatic changes in media ownership involving radio stations; similar concentration of ownership has been happening in television and technology companies and will likely accelerate in the coming years. Whether this trend will have the stated desired effect of fostering competition or creating powerful media cartels has been a subject of some debate. Another trend has been an increase in alternate media service providers in which cable companies are allowed to provide telephone service, for example, and telephone companies could provide, in theory, programming content.

Expansion of Ownership Limits

The Act puts no limit on the number of television stations a single person or organization may own in the United States, as long as the combined reach is no more than 35 percent of U.S. households. This also will spur greater concentration of ownership, which has already occurred in the radio industry, where concentration of ownership has increased dramatically since passage of the Act. In fact, because of the lifting of ownership restrictions, one company founded in 1997 has already become the third-largest radio station owner-operator in the United States. Cumulus has acquired or has under contract 232 FM and AM radio stations in 44 U.S. cities, plus the Caribbean, making it the nation's third-largest owner-operator in terms of number of stations and the twelfth largest in revenues, with nearly 82,000 local, regional, and national advertisers. It employs some 2500 professionals and serves more than 5 million listeners. As a result of these regulatory, economic, and technological trends, Eli Noam and Robert Schapiro point out that the media offer unprecedented programming diversity at the national level and ever-dwindling diversity at the local level.[15]

Alternative Service Providers

Because the Act eliminates the legal barriers preventing telephone and television companies from competing in the areas of telephone and video services, consumers will see an increased array of alternative service providers, at least initially. Similarly, consumers will see an increase in the range of both phone and video services, including video, news, advertising on demand, and transaction-based services.

Most importantly, however, the next decade will see a rapid rise in the production and direct-to-home delivery of video programming created not by traditional programming providers but by corporate organizations, advertisers, direct marketers, public relations firms, even political strategists, all interested in reaching the U.S. and international markets directly, without going through the traditional news programming gateway. Increased channel capacity, increased bandwidth availability, and growth of video delivery through multiple media: all are driving this shift, which is directly fueled by provisions of the Telecommunications Act.

Television and Persons with Disabilities

Building upon the television industry tradition of providing closed-captioning for hearing impaired, the Act mandates that the FCC undertake a study to evaluate the use of video descriptions on video programming in order to provide accessibility of video programming to persons with visual impairments. Video description refers to the insertion of audio narrated descriptions of a television program's key visual elements into natural pauses within the program's dialogue. Such video description has been used extensively in live theatrical productions and tested in video trials. The art of audio description is explained by Joel Snyder of the National Endowment for the Arts. He observes that in audio description one makes the visual oral and aural. For example, don't say, "He is angry" or "She is sad." Rather, "He's clenching his fist," or "She is crying." With an estimated 13 million Americans legally blind, audio description will serve as an empowering tool in the next generation of television programming.

Universal Access

Another important item for the FCC's future agenda will be the definition of universal service, a long-cherished notion central to the 1934 Act. The Act does not go so far as to provide a definition of universal service, however. It states that "Universal service is an evolving level of telecommunications services that the Commission shall establish periodically under this section." It identifies six principles central to this evolving notion of universal service. They are to provide:

1. Quality services at reasonable and affordable rates.

2. Access to advanced telecommunications and information services throughout the United States.

3. Access in rural and high-cost areas.

4. Equitable and nondiscriminatory contributions to the preservation and advancement of universal service.

5. Specific, predictable, and sufficient federal and state mechanisms to preserve and advance universal service.

6. Access to advanced telecommunications services in elementary and secondary schools and classrooms, health care providers, and libraries.

The outcome of this evolving notion is a new model of universal service. In one scenario, this model would make fully interoperable high-bandwidth, two-way communication service—the 21st century equivalent of "plain old telephone service" (POTS) mandated in the 1934 Act. This would create a powerful network engine to drive a new information infrastructure linking wired and wireless technologies and empower the development of fully interactive, multimedia communications. An alternative paradigm, however, would simply mandate that all homes have access to at least two communication service providers capable of delivering both traditional and new media services (including the Internet), with low-income households receiving the equivalent of information stamps, as once proposed by media mogul Ted Turner.

Access to Information: FOIA and Public Records

In the United States, there are laws that give journalists and everyone else legal access to certain types of information. Most notably, the **Freedom of Information Act (FOIA),** passed in 1966, provides legal access to public records maintained by the federal government. There are also state freedom of information laws pertaining to state and local jurisdictions.

Public records are owned by the public, and the public has legal access to them. Public records often take the form of transactional records, such as the records maintained by the Internal Revenue Service on tax payments, political donations, criminal records, and driving records, but virtually every government agency maintains records, many of which are classified as public. In many cases, it is necessary to file a formal request for these records via the Freedom of Information Act (or law, if it is at a state level). The Reporters Committee for Freedom of the Press provides details on submitting FOIA requests and has online forms. In virtually all cases, at least at the federal level and increasingly at the state and local levels, records are kept in digital form. In the past they were often kept on paper only. With the growth of the Internet and the World Wide Web, many public records have been placed on the Internet. However, after the terrorist attacks on September 11, 2001, many government agencies have removed previously accessible public information and have been encouraged by U.S. Attorney General John Ashcroft to be cautious in granting FOIA requests that, prior to the attacks, would have been likely to be granted.

On September 6, 1996, the "Electronic Freedom of Information Act Amendments of 1996" (E-FOIA) passed into law. Among other things, it required that

Freedom of Information Act (FOIA)—an act that provides legal access to public records maintained by the federal government. States and local jurisdictions also have freedom of information laws that allow public access to state or local records.

electronic public records be provided at a cost in line with the actual cost of producing the data electronically. Before the E-FOIA, some government agencies had tried to charge excessive fees for data, arguing that if they had charged, for instance, one dollar a record in print, and an electronic database of 1 million records was now desired, then the appropriate fee would be $1 million—when in reality the cost of producing the database electronically would be only a small fraction of that cost.

Intellectual Property Rights: Copyright Protection

Weblink

U.S. Copyright Office
[lcweb.loc.gov/copyright/]

intellectual property (IP)— ideas that have commercial value, such as literary or artistic works, patents, business methods, and industrial processes.

copyright—the exclusive right to use, publish, and distribute a work such as a piece of writing, music, film, or video.

patent law—protects the right to produce and sell an invention, rather than a literary or artistic work, which is covered by copyright law.

Digital Millennium Copyright Act (DMCA)—a 1998 act of Congress that reformed copyright law comprehensively in trying to update copyright laws for the digital age. Key provisions included the circumvention of copyright protection systems, fair use in a digital environment, and Internet service providers' (ISP) liability for content sent through their lines.

fair use—an exception to copyright law that allows someone to use an excerpt of a work without paying for its use. Reviews of works or their use in commentary or criticism are examples of fair use.

Of significant and growing concern to those in mass communication is protecting their **intellectual property (IP)**. The term *IP* refers to ideas that have commercial value, such as literary or artistic works, patents, software programs, business methods, and industrial processes, particularly in the form of **copyright** protection. Copyright law ("copy-right" refers to the legal right to make a copy of a work) is one form of intellectual property rights protection that deals with protecting specific expressions of ideas.

A second form of IP protection is patent law. One of the first laws enacted by the U.S. government, in 1790, was regarding **patent law.** Patents are intended to protect a specific form of intellectual property known as inventions. To stop someone from copying it, an inventor or his or her organization applies for a patent from the U.S. government, and the government issues a patent if the invention is deemed new and useful. Once granted, a patent prohibits anyone from copying the invention, pattern, or design. Anyone can apply for a patent, as long as the idea is new. The life of a patent depends on what kind of patent it is and can last from 14 to 17 years.

A patent cannot be issued for written material, although certain areas of software code are something of a gray area and may be patented if they perform some function. A book or an article is protected by a copyright, not a patent.

Copyright law protects a wide range of expression, primarily the creations of authors. Included are literary works (including newspapers, books, magazines), musical works, dramatic works, pantomimes, choreographic works, pictorial and graphic works, sculpture, motion pictures and other audiovisual works, sound recordings, and architectural works. **The Digital Millennium Copyright Act** extends to digital works as well, including those on the Internet or other online media.

Fair Use

Holding a copyright to a work provides the owner an exclusive right to reproduce, distribute (over any media), perform, display, or license that work. There are limited exceptions to the rights under copyright law, including primarily for **fair use** of an expression, such as in a movie or book review where the reviewer might take an excerpt of a work and include it in the review or in criticism or commentary. In general, there are four factors considered in deciding whether the use of another's copyrighted work is legal under the "fair use" provision of the Act:

Media Spotlight: **APBNews**

In 1999, APBNews submitted a FOIA request to obtain the financial records of all U.S. federal judges. These records are vitally important in establishing accountability in the judicial system, where investigations in the past have sometimes revealed instances in which a judge has ruled in a case where he or she had held a financial stake in one of the parties to the case and should have been disqualified because of a conflict of interest. The judges agreed to APB's request until they realized the news organization planned to post the public records online. The judges then objected, saying that although the records are public, putting them online would make them "too public."

In 2000, APB won its case, and it set an important precedent for freedom of speech and online access to public records in the digital age.

This does not mean that journalists or anyone else is free to be irresponsible online or off. In fact, it is just the opposite; those who would access or use public records have a mandate to be responsible or face the legal consequences, including libel or other litigation. Digitization of public records in a way facilitates responsible use of those records by making it far easier to delete any information that is irrelevant that might be an invasion of privacy. For example, in the case of income tax information, it is relatively straightforward to provide journalists tax returns with any personal identification information removed.

1. The purpose and nature of the use (i.e., whether it is purely commercial, educational, or for the news, the latter two of which are generally more likely to qualify).

2. The character of the copyrighted work (some works are inherently more protected; this is a subjective matter determined by the courts).

3. The amount and extent of the excerpt used in proportion to the copyrighted work in its entirety (this is more qualitatively than quantitatively determined, however, and there are no exact rules on the permissible number or words one may borrow from a text or the amount of video or audio or image size one may excerpt, because even a short clip may represent the most significant creative aspect of the work).

4. The effect of the use on copyrighted work's market potential (i.e., in dollar terms), especially when the copyrighted work is used as the basis for a derivative work (i.e., a movie based on a book).

Creating Copyright

A copyright exists from the moment a work is created in its fixed form, although establishing a copyright can prove difficult if it is not published and widely circulated. Inserting a © symbol (although in the case of a musical recording the symbol is a P in a circle, but that symbol may be hard to find on your keyboard) along with a date and the name of the copyright owner also helps. In the case of a work for hire, the employer generally owns the copyright. A copyright is in effect for the lifetime of the author, plus 70 years, although it may be up to 125 years in the case of a work for hire. The rationale of a copyright is to protect not only the intellectual product but also the author/owner's financial interests. In

Weblink
The Copyright Web site
[http://www.benedict.com/]

1989, the United States joined the Berne Convention for the Protection of Literary and Artistic Works, extending copyright protection globally.

Intellectual Property Rights and Royalties

One of the most contested notions in the recorded music industry is control of intellectual property, or ideas and their expression, and **royalties,** or payments artists or copyright holders receive for the sales or other revenues from their work.

In June 2002 a bill regarding royalty rates for songs streamed over the Internet was passed, threatening to put thousands of small webcasters out of business. The royalty rate per song per listener was established by the Library of Congress at .07 cents, less than what the recording industry was asking for but more than what the nascent Internet radio industry said it could pay. A further blow to Internet radio was the ruling that the companies would have to pay going back to 1998.

Radio is not saddled with these royalty payments because they have successfully argued that they promote the music and are providing a service. The Internet radio industry tried to make the same claim, but it was rejected. Small webcasters were granted a delay in negotiating payments, although large ones are expected to start paying. It is still unclear what effect this will have on Internet radio.

Freelancers and IP Online

On June 25, 2001, the U.S. Supreme Court agreed with an appeals court ruling on Sept. 24, 1999, that will have important ramifications for freelancers and publishers, as well as possibly influencing disputes in book and music publishing.

The case involved the *New York Times'* resell of freelance writers' material to Lexis-Nexis, the leading online legal and newspaper database. A three-judge panel of the U.S. Court of Appeals, Second Circuit, ruled in *New York Times Co., Inc.,* v. *Tasini* that the *New York Times,* Lexis-Nexis, and other publishers and online databases must have the expressed approval of freelance authors of newspaper and magazine articles before they can resell them for distribution on electronic databases. The appeals court decision overturned an earlier opinion issued by former Federal District Court Judge Sonia Sotomayor, who interpreted the Copyright Act to permit publishers to reuse freelance materials in creating a "revision" of a print article into electronic form.

The publishers argued that putting articles in electronic databases was merely a "revision" of the article that they already had paid for. The Supreme Court, supporting the appeals court ruling, rejected the publishers' argument. Justice Ruth Bader Ginsburg, writing for the majority, said, "The Database no more constitutes a 'revision' of each constituent edition than a 400-page novel quoting a sonnet in passing would represent a 'revision' of that poem."[16]

As a result of the ruling, the *New York Times* and other publishers such as Time Inc. started removing freelance articles from their databases to avoid lawsuits from writers. Historians and researchers have complained about these actions, saying it will hurt research efforts. Critics of the publishers' actions claim that most publishers revised their freelance contracts in the mid-1990s anyway to force freelancers to give up electronic reprint rights, so only a small fraction of material would be affected by the ruling.

royalties—the payments artists or copyright holders receive for the works they produce, paid as a percentage of the income from the number of works sold.

Digital Watermarks

Digital watermarks are a very important part of the standards for digital content. Watermarks are computer code (usually invisible, but sometimes visible) inserted into any digital content, whether images, graphics, audio, video, or even text documents, that authenticates the source of that content. Copyright owners value watermarks because they can protect media assets, or intellectual property, from theft.

For example, if a media company sends digital video over the Internet and someone else tries to copy the video and distribute it without obtaining permission, the original copyright holder, an end user, or even an intelligent software agent, can examine the content for an embedded digital watermark. If the watermark is present and is that of the original copyright holder, then it can be easily demonstrated that the redistributor is in violation of copyright law. In essence, the digital watermark is analogous to a cattle rancher placing a brand on her or his cattle to deter or catch cattle rustlers.

There are at least three types of digital watermarks: fragile, semifragile, and robust. Robust watermarks can survive any kind of manipulation of the content, whether editing or any other kind of change. Fragile watermarks disintegrate when any change is made to the watermarked content. Semifragile watermarks permit certain types of changes, such as compression, but disintegrate when more malicious types of changes are made, such as a hacker editing the content.

Visible watermarks can often be seen on images online, but invisible watermarks can also be created digitally.

Uses for Media Organizations

Media professionals and organizations are increasingly using digital watermarks to protect their content. Although there is still considerable research going on in the development of digital watermarks, a number of companies are already providing commercially available digital watermarking technology to protect media assets. One of the leading commercial providers of digital watermarks is Digimarc. Digimarc's patented digital watermarking technology is invisible but can perform a variety of functions for media professionals and organizations. Digimarc's watermarking technology can:

- Deflect potential theft of digital assets.
- Monitor video broadcasts.
- Protect video assets.
- Communicate copyright information.
- Prevent digital counterfeiting.
- Manage media assets and e-commerce.

A related software tool called a spider (an intelligent agent software program) can track watermarked digital images across the Web and enable digital material to link to Web content. Advanced digital watermarking allows users to embed image- or transaction-specific watermarks in each image or video. Thus, media organizations can grant permission to others to publish, broadcast, or webcast their content a specific number of times and use a digital watermark to control and charge for the number of uses.

Uses for Media Professionals

Increasingly, image-editing software enables consumers and media professionals alike to use watermarking technology, including that of Digimarc, to embed

digital watermark—computer code (usually invisible, but sometimes visible) inserted into any digital content, whether images, graphics, audio, video, or even text documents, that authenticates the source of that content.

watermarks in their photos and graphics. Adobe Photoshop, one of the leading image-editing software packages used by media professionals, allows the user to embed a digital watermark in any image, photo, or graphic.

Some cameras also permit the embedding of watermarks at the point of image acquisition. Kodak, for instance, sells digital cameras that allow photographers to watermark images automatically. In many cases, these watermarks are not terribly sophisticated, consisting simply of either the date and/or time, or a text message.

Some are more sophisticated, however. In one case, a global positioning system (GPS) receiver is attached to the camera, automatically embedding a GPS stamp (including the exact longitude, latitude, altitude, date, and time—per Greenwich mean time—into each photo). Such a GPS stamp can be an invaluable tool in establishing the authenticity (i.e., the exact location and date) of a photo. This can be invaluable for pictures documenting a wartime atrocity (e.g., a mass grave) or human rights violation, for example.

S U M M A R Y

The legal framework for freedom of expression is guaranteed in the First Amendment to the U.S. Constitution. But this has not permitted the media to enjoy unrestricted freedom, and broadcasting media have traditionally been more restricted than print media. In particular, print and broadcast media have been restricted in three major areas: threats to national security, libel, and obscenity. Commercial speech and broadcasting content for children have also been regulated, but broadcasters have attempted to regulate themselves as much as possible in order to show they are using public airwaves responsibly and to avoid further government regulation in their industry.

The early years of radio broadcasting were largely unregulated, but as the airwaves became more cluttered, the government gradually increased its regulatory activities, culminating in the Communications Act of 1934. In part, the Act created the Federal Communications Commission (FCC), which plays a key role in regulating radio and television broadcasting, especially regarding commercial speech, political speech, and children's programming, as well as licensing stations. The 1934 Act operated on the principle of spectrum scarcity and managing the airwaves for the public good, and governed broadcasting until 1996, when the Telecommunications Act took effect.

The Telecommunications Act, which operates under the principle of spectrum abundance because of the proliferation of cable, satellite, and Internet access to media, adds a new emphasis to fostering competition between telecommunication providers in order to give the audience as many media options as possible. Whether this has achieved the desired effect or simply increased the power of increasingly larger media organizations is under debate.

The Freedom of Information Act (FOIA) allows journalists and the public to request public documents from the federal government, just as FOIA laws allow access to state and local governments, where those laws exist. Government agencies have removed much previously accessible public information from their Web sites after the terrorist attacks of September 11, 2001, however, and have been encouraged by U.S. Attorney General John Ashcroft to be more stringent in granting FOIA requests.

Intellectual property (IP) issues, especially pertaining to copyright, are undergoing dramatic changes because of digital media. Questions remain on how best to compensate content creators or copyright holders in a medium that allows for perfect copies and easy, widespread distribution. Being able to digitally watermark a piece of content will likely be a key way to protect copyright and to ensure that content has not been altered.

Discussion Questions

1. In light of the terrorist attacks on the World Trade Center and Pentagon on September 11, 2001, do you think the government should have more or less control to exercise prior restraint and block publication or broadcast material that they feel might hurt national security interests? What would some of the effects be, both positive and negative, if they adopted your opinion?

2. Tobacco and tobacco products cannot be advertised on electronic media such as TV and radio, yet alcohol can. What could the reasons for this be? Do you think both should be banned, alcohol but not tobacco banned, or neither banned from the airwaves? Why?

3. Can traditional standards of what makes a "community" be applied on the Internet when dealing with such things as Internet obscenity or pornography? If so, what would those criteria be? If not, what standards could be applied?

4. What are the implications for journalists and their confidential sources if journalists must divulge the names of their sources and their interview notes to a grand jury or to law enforcement authorities? Should journalists do this if they know the confidential source is responsible for a crime? Why or why not?

5. Do you think television and movie rating systems are effective in protecting children? Why or why not? Could there be a better system than ratings to protect children from seeing objectionable content?

MEDIA Quiz

1. F	5. T
2. F	6. F
3. T	7. F
4. F	8. T

6. What dangers are there in a media industry that regulates itself or self-censors? Why could self-censorship be a good thing?

7. Put yourself in the role of a freelance writer or struggling musician who is trying to make a living writing or making music. Would you oppose or support greater government or corporate control on copyright if the technology promised that unauthorized copies of your work could not be circulated?

Mass Communication and Politics in the Digital Age

15

Like many people in the United States during the summer of 1998, Joan Blades and Wes Boyd, two Silicon Valley entrepreneurs, were tired of the lack of congressional leadership and slow-moving process toward impeachment of President Bill Clinton. In September 1998 they decided to do something about it and started the "Censure and Move On" campaign on their newly created Moveon.org Web site. Initially an online petition drive to get Congress to simply censure Clinton and "move on" to more pressing matters, it quickly grew to more. Within a month they had 250,000 signatures for their online petition, at the time the largest ever, and by the end of October had constituents hand-deliver hard copies of the petition to 44 district offices. By the end of the failed impeachment proceedings, Moveon.org had helped organize over 250,000 phone calls and had over 1 million e-mails sent to Congress.

Moveon continues to help organize grassroots efforts for various causes, and their stated goal is "to bring ordinary citizens back into politics." Because money often drives politics, Blades and Boyd have shown they can play that game as well and have collected over $2 million from 10,000 citizens, which they have donated to select election campaigns. Although that is still a far cry from the $6 million former presidential candidate John McCain raised online, it does show the organizational, communicative, and fund-raising ability of the Web for average citizens.

Now several organizations sell software and advice not only to politicians running for office but to activist groups who want to get the electorate more involved in politics than they have been. "Democracy is a growth business," says John Aristotle Phillips, CEO of voter list company Aristotle Publishing.

Weblink
Moveon.org
[www.moveon.org]

Prologue

The United States is a media society, and the media are the tools of the political communication process. As society heads deeper into the new millennium, the role of mass communication in this political process is characterized by three basic dimensions.

First, mass media communicators consider their core mission to be the foundation for the democratic process. Journalism is the mechanism through which the public obtains unbiased, impartial information about candidates for office, sitting elected officials, and the agencies they represent and operate. Although this is the goal, media critics contend the media are anything but unbiased. Consider the words of Joseph Pulitzer, the former publisher of the *New York World,* and the founder of the Pulitzer Prizes, the highest award for journalistic excellence. In support of his proposal for the founding of a school of journalism, Pulitzer summarized his credo:

> Our Republic and its press will rise or fall together. An able, disinterested, public-spirited press, with trained intelligence to know the right and courage to do it, can preserve that public virtue without which popular government is a sham and a mockery. A cynical, mercenary, demagogic press will produce in time a people as base as itself. The power to mould the future of the Republic will be in the hands of the journalists of future generations.[1]

Second, it is more than journalism, however, that drives the media–political engine. In fact, especially in times of presidential election campaigns, it is advertising that drives this machine. In the 2000 presidential election, candidates Bush and Gore alone spent more than $100 million on political advertising. Political advertising, especially on television, is how most candidates, particularly presidential candidates, reach most voters most often. Negative political advertising is one of the mainstays of the U.S. political world, and it has been extensively researched. Political advertising also provides substantial income for media organizations.

The third dimension of mass communication in the political process is the Internet and other forms of online communication. Research on this emerging dimension of the political communication arena is only beginning to take shape, but it is clear that a number of issues will change the current mass communication and political landscape. These issues include the ability of people to communicate with each other on a mass scale without using a centralized media outlet; continuing legal battles involving copyright, privacy, and security online; and more sources of information available to the public on politicians, political campaigns, and financing.

The following discussion examines what research tells us about the process and effects of journalism and mass communication in the sphere of political communications.

Political campaigns are becoming increasingly expensive, partly due to the extensive marketing and advertising candidates must do.

Theories of Mediated Political Communication

The roots of today's understanding of mediated political communication lie in the research on political campaigns in the 1940s and 1950s. Among the most significant research of this period was that conducted at the Columbia University Bureau of Applied Social Research. Paul F. Lazarsfeld (1901–1976), an Austrian-American sociologist born in Vienna, was one of the most important researchers of this era. After emigrating to the United States in 1933, he cofounded with Robert K. Merton the Columbia University Bureau of Applied Social Research. In 1940, Lazarsfeld teamed with Bernard Berelson and Hazel Gaudet in one of the most important mass communication studies of this or any other epoch. Published in 1948, *The People's Choice* still stands as a classic investigation into the effects of mass communication in the political process.

The Two-Step Flow Hypothesis

Lazarsfeld, Berelson, and Gaudet conducted a multiyear longitudinal study to determine the role of media exposure and personal influence in political decision-making. They interviewed people more than once over time throughout the presidential election of 1940. Based on data collected from voters in Erie County, Ohio, the team found that "ideas often flow from radio and print to the opinion leaders and from them to the less active sections of the population." They dubbed this the **two-step flow hypothesis.** Opinion leaders could include anyone from entertainment or sports figures to respected local community leaders who would further reinforce what was initially printed or broadcast during the course of their discussions with members of the public.

For many years to follow this hypothesis became the dominant model for understanding mass communication in a variety of contexts, especially advertising and marketing of goods and services, such as product choices, fashion, and movie attendance.

two-step flow hypothesis—a theory about how mass communication affects the public; states that information flows from print or electronic media to opinion leaders and then to less active members of the population.

The media serve an important agenda-setting function in defining what issues the public sees as important, which can in turn affect what issues political candidates stress in their campaigns.

The Agenda-Setting Function of the Media

In the early days of the 2000 presidential election campaign (actually begun in 1999), then Vice President Al Gore spent considerable time and energy discussing what he considered one of the biggest issues facing the country: suburban sprawl. He also talked a great deal about the Internet and its role in education and commerce. His objectives were, at least in part, to get the attention of the media and have his views reported to the general citizenry.

One of the reasons Gore and any other candidate seeks out media coverage is because of a concept first explained by Paul F. Lazarsfeld and Robert K. Merton in 1948. Lazarsfeld and Merton explained that one of the primary functions of the media is to confer status on those who appear in them. The process of singling someone out from the large, heterogeneous masses tends to bestow prestige and authority on those so identified. "The audiences of mass media apparently subscribe to the circular belief that if you matter, you will be at the focus of mass attention and, if you are at the focus of mass attention, then surely you must really matter," wrote Lazarsfeld and Merton.[2]

By extension, media scholars have argued that the media are **agenda setters.** As such they can shape our perception of what issues are important and how important they are, depending on their prominence in the mass media. Of course, opinion leaders such as former vice president Al Gore play an important role in shaping the agenda of the media, a role confirmed by both research and common sense.

This agenda-setting notion was perhaps first suggested by psychologist and social scientist Harold Lasswell in observations he made about the 1948 post–World War II presidential election in which Truman beat Dewey. Political scientist Bernard Cohen more clearly articulated the agenda-setting model when he wrote, "The press may not be successful much of the time in telling people what to think, but it is stunningly successful in telling its readers what to think about."[3]

Research by communication scholars Max McCombs and Donald Shaw tested and further articulated this phenomenon in the 1970s and demonstrated that in fact the media are especially effective at influencing public views on the importance of various issues. Moreover, McCombs and Shaw's research showed that different media tend to play a different role in the agenda-setting process. In particular, newspapers have historically tended to set the general agenda of public issues. For example, newspapers might tend to determine which issues the public is likely to see as important, such as taxes, education, crime, or health care.

agenda setting function—a role the media play during the course of deciding what topics to cover, which then, by virtue of being covered in the media, become topics of discussion and perceived importance to the public.

Meanwhile, the electronic media of television and radio are especially effective at shaping the public's views of which of those issues are most important. In other words, these media shape the ranking of the issues on the list. And of course the electronic media excel at covering breaking news such as the attacks on September 11, 2001, or the nine coal miners in Pennsylvania who were rescued in July 2002 after three days of being trapped underground when their mine flooded. Heavy media coverage of the sniper attacks that took place during September and October 2002 in the Washington, D.C., area also played a role in alerting the public as to the make of car the suspects were in, prompting a call from one citizen who saw the car at a rest stop, leading to the suspects' capture.

A major question emerged in the 1990s regarding the role of the Internet and other online media in the agenda-setting process. Although many researchers have followed in the footsteps of pioneers McCombs and Shaw to test and refine the agenda-setting model, little research to date has examined how communication via the Internet and other online media affects public opinion, especially with regard to the perception of importance of different issues.

The Spiral of Silence Hypothesis

The **spiral of silence hypothesis** was developed by German communication scholar Elisabeth Noelle-Neumann to explain why people may be unwilling to publicly express their opinions when they believe they are in the minority. Her analysis is based on her own observations of Germans during the Nazi regime in the 1930s and 1940s. Because of her association with the Nazis, however, Noelle-Neumann has herself become a controversial figure in communication research, and her work has been seen as an excuse for public apathy during the Holocaust.

The spiral of silence hypothesis has been widely tested and shown to be valid under a variety of circumstances. It is based on three premises:

1. People have a natural fear of isolation.

2. Out of fear of isolation, people are reluctant to express publicly views that they feel are in the minority.

3. People have a "quasi-statistical organ," a sort of sixth sense, that allows them to gauge the prevailing climate of opinion and determine what the majority views are on matters of public importance.

How people gauge the climate of opinion is based on a variety of factors, including their interactions with others and past experiences, but it is especially shaped by the media. A person who feels her or his point of view is in alignment with the prevailing climate of opinion will feel more comfortable publicly expressing that viewpoint. On the other hand, a person who feels out of step with public opinion will be increasingly less likely to express that opinion, thus leading to a possible spiral of silence. In some instances, it is possible that even a majority opinion, if perceived to be the minority (possibly through biased media reporting), may not be expressed publicly.

The Third-Person Effect of Communication

Among the most interesting of media effects was first observed outside the United States, although its implications are not limited to the international

spiral of silence hypothesis— states that people are naturally afraid of isolation, realize that if they are in the minority on a issue they are likely to be isolated, and have a kind of sixth sense that helps them gauge when their opinions are contrary to the majority, which makes them refrain from expressing their opinions.

The third-person effect of communication can take place when early poll results on the east coast may influence voters on the west coast where the polls have not yet closed.

arena. It is known as the **third-person effect of communication,** and it occurs when a media message does not affect the behavior or beliefs of the intended audience but does affect a different group who also receives the message and who may act in the belief that the message will affect the intended audience.

The third-person effect of communication was first recognized from examining records from World War II in which the Japanese dropped propaganda leaflets to black servicemen stationed in the South Pacific, saying the Japanese were fighting against the white imperialists and had no ill will toward blacks. It encouraged them to surrender and promised them good treatment until after the war was over, by which time they could return home. Although records show this campaign had no effect on the black servicemen it targeted, it did cause the white officers of these black troops to transfer soldiers away from areas where they could be targets of the propaganda in order to avoid any potential loss of morale.

Many researchers have since studied the third-person effect of communication and demonstrated its widespread effect in society and in many different circumstances. Car manufacturers learned to use this to their advantage after some expensive mistakes. When conducting market research in the early 1960s, Ford asked people what kind of car they would like to have. The answers—functional, safe, durable, and the like—made sense, and Ford built a car that met those specifications. The car was a flop. They went back and asked people what kind of car they thought their *neighbor* would like to have and, based on those answers, created a new car. The result? The popular and now classic Ford Mustang.

In the political communication arena the third-person effect of communication may play a role in election outcomes if the media publicizes results too early. If the election outcome seems to be decided early on by exit polls, many people may decide not to bother voting because it won't seem to make a difference anyway. After the confusing and contradictory results announced by the media during the 2000 presidential elections, news organizations promised to show restraint in reporting on early results in the midterm 2002 elections, in which the Republicans took control of Congress. By all accounts the media did show restraint, although how much of that was due to being chastened two years earlier or simply because they had no exit polls available, because the company providing them was revamping their computer system, is not known.

third-person effect of communication—a media characteristic in which a media message does not affect its intended audience but does affect the behavior of a third party who takes action with the belief that the media message will affect the intended audience.

Another interesting aspect of this effect comes from the experiences of one of the authors when he would give his undergraduate students in a mass media and society class a one-question quiz asking them whether their voting would be affected by exit polls. The catch to the quiz is that there were two versions randomly distributed; half the students got that question while the other half received one that asked if they thought other people would be affected in their voting by exit polls. Inevitably, the students who were asked about themselves said exit polls would have no effect on their voting, while students who were asked about others said exit polls would have a moderate or great effect.

Bear in mind the third-person effect of communication the next time someone in the media says there may be a shortage of a particular item next summer, say gasoline, canning jar lids, or Pokemon cards. There may very well be a shortage, but not necessarily because of the popularity of those products or a shortage in their supply. It may simply be the third-person effect of communication at work. People may think that others will in fact buy up these goods to avoid being caught short-handed; and, as a result, they will buy or even hoard them, thereby causing the shortage where none might otherwise have occurred. It may even have been a clever marketing ploy in the first place.

The Role of Media in Political Elections

Since the earliest days of the republic, the media have been intimately involved in our political process. The earliest colonial newspapers were a "partisan" press, typically aligned with a particular political party or persuasion. Media also played a role in helping the revolutionary cause. Journalism in the 19th century evolved into an impartial press, but it still considers its core mission to provide the information citizens need to make informed decisions and thereby serve as the engine of democracy.

Since the first use of radio in political campaigning in 1924, the electronic media have played an increasingly important part in political elections. In both 1936 and 1940, while the majority of U.S. newspapers openly endorsed Republican candidates for office, radio had become the more heavily used medium by Democrats. President Roosevelt was masterful in his use of radio to reach the masses, providing his regular "Fireside Chats" during the 1930s and 1940s. Radio had emerged as the politically potent medium of mass communication in this epoch, with even greater impact than the printed media of newspapers and magazines, and radio itself was soon to be replaced by television as the dominant medium in the 1950s. It had begun an era in which the personal qualities of candidates would take center stage in the campaign process.

Sound Bites and Horse Races

With the rise of electronic media, especially television in the past half century, the process of political communication and debate in the media has been transformed from one of at least some substance into one increasingly characterized by superficial examination of the issues. More often than not, the horse-race

Media Spotlight: **Sound Bite Shakespeare**

University of San Diego Professor Daniel C. Hallin puts the shrinking sound bite into context.[4] In 1968, if a commercial network television reporter had included a sound bite from William Shakespeare's *Julius Caesar* (Act III, Scene II, at the Forum), he would have had time to include the following statement from Antony:

> Friends, Romans, countrymen, lend me your ears;
> I come to bury Caesar, not to praise him.
> The evil that men do lives after them;
> The good is oft interred with their bones;
> So let it be with Caesar. The noble Brutus
> Hath told you Caesar was ambitious:
> If it were so, it was a grievous fault,
> And grievously hath Caesar answer'd it.
> Here, under leave of Brutus and the rest—
> For Brutus is an honourable man;
> So are they all, all honourable men—
> Come I to speak in Caesar's funeral.
> He was my friend, faithful and just to me:
> But Brutus says he was ambitious;
> And Brutus is an honourable man.

Here's what we'd hear from Antony today (or by 1988) on the commercial network television evening news:

> Friends, Romans, countrymen, lend me your ears;
> I come to bury Caesar, not to praise him.

A couple of caveats are in order. To begin, Hallin's research was specific to the evening network newscasts of three major U.S. commercial television networks of the day, ABC, CBS, and NBC. Other television news options and National Public Radio provide sound bites that are actually often substantially longer. Annenberg Dean Kathleen Hall Jamieson notes in her book *Dirty Politics* (1992) that on PBS's the *MacNeil–Lehrer NewsHour* (now the *NewsHour with Jim Lehrer*), almost half (45 percent) of political sound bites are 60 seconds or longer. On ABC's *Nightline* (with Ted Koppel) sound bites are not as long as on PBS, but are substantially longer than on commercial network evening newscasts, with 15 percent of sound bites being 60 seconds or longer.

It is also important to note that the "10-second sound bite" should not necessarily be synonymous with the trivialization of news. As Hallin notes, "In many ways modern TV news is much better journalism than it was twenty years ago." Television journalists are less likely to simply put candidates on camera and let them talk. The candidates' words are "raw material to be taken apart, combined with other sounds and images, and reintegrated into a new narrative."[5]

Nevertheless, the sound-bite culture has affected not only the media but politics as well. As Jamieson points out, a scan of C-SPAN (the cable television channel that focuses largely on the proceedings of Congress) reveals that politicians often structure their speeches for sound bites and anecdotes rather than to provide detailed analyses of issues and their positions on them.

Research has shown that politicians often structure their speeches for sound bites and anecdotes rather than providing detailed analysis of issues.

aspect of the campaign, or chronicling who's ahead, who's behind, and what their latest campaign tactic might be to move ahead in the polls, becomes the whole story at the expense of coverage of issues. Consider that in 1968 Kiku Adatto of Harvard University did a study on political **sound bites** in the media, or how long a source in a news story is allowed to speak without being edited by the reporter in television news. In 1968 the average sound bite was 42.3 seconds. Nearly a quarter of all political sound bites were at least a minute in length, providing considerable room for context. Twenty years later, in 1988, the average TV sound bite of a political candidate had shrunk by some 80 percent to just 9.8 seconds, and virtually none were a minute or longer—in fact, entire stories were often not a minute in length. By 2000, sound bites had continued to shrink, although there is a limit to how short they can go—at least in analog television where time is a significant constraint on the evening news.

The Changing Tone of Television Political Coverage

The tone of television political coverage has also changed. Consider the research findings of Syracuse University political scientist Thomas Patterson, author of *Out of Order*. He found that in the 1960 presidential election, three-quarters (75 percent) of the news reports about leading candidates John F. Kennedy and Richard M. Nixon were positive in tone; only a quarter (25 percent) were negative. Thirty years later, in the 1992 presidential election, news reports had become predominantly negative in tone; more than half (60 percent) of the reports about then candidate Bill Clinton and then President George H. Bush were negative and less than half (40 percent) were positive. Patterson's research also shows that the length of candidate statements in election stories on the front page of the *New York Times* had similarly shrunk. In 1960 the average quote was 14 lines. In 1992, the average quote was fewer than seven lines.

Has this situation changed with the rise of online news? Not by much. Although there is scant research evidence yet to point to, the fact is that much of the online political coverage (or other coverage) is no different than the political coverage in other media, because much of that coverage is lifted and repurposed from other media, including television, radio, newspapers, or magazines. The sound bites are the same, and the quotes are the same.

Many of the better online news operations, such as CBS News online, typically add further reporting to stories that are adapted from on-air coverage, turning the text of a 60-second video report (what might be fewer than 200 words) into a 500-word or longer report with more depth and possibly additional quotes. Such quotes are sometimes the same length but are occasionally longer than in the broadcast text. Much of the additional reporting is drawn from wire service copy (e.g., Reuters, the Associated Press) pulled off the Internet or sometimes from original reporting conducted via telephone or e-mail interviews. Increasingly illustrations such as maps are being used as well.

Opinion Polls

Campaign coverage has also become heavily driven by **opinion polls.** Patterson's research shows that the news becomes more favorable when a candidate's support in the polls increases markedly or if he or she leads by a wide margin in the

sound bite—the length of time a news subject is allowed to speak without being edited by a reporter. It also has come to refer to short utterances that are catchy and designed to capture the media's attention.

opinion poll—a poll that is usually conducted by professional polling organizations asking members of the public their opinions on issues or political candidates.

Many traditional pollsters say that Internet polls are not scientific and do not capture a true cross section of the American public.

polls. Conversely, media coverage becomes more negative if there is a drop in the candidate's standing in the polls or if he or she trails significantly in the polls.

Media organizations usually use one of several professional polling organizations, such as Gallup, to conduct polls. These polling organizations try to take random samples of the public in order to assess what the population as a whole is likely feeling about a candidate or issue. However, lower telephone response rates in recent years as people screen calls to avoid telemarketers have made conducting telephone polls more expensive.

Opinion polls or surveys have been increasingly showing up on news Web sites, although these are not considered scientifically valid because the answers represent only users who have visited the Web site and chosen to answer the poll. Online polls are being used by some polling organizations such as Harris Interactive, although these are largely derided by other organizations and the American Association for Public Opinion Research (AAPOR) as being nonscientific. Internet users do not fairly represent a broad sampling of the general populace because they tend to be more affluent than average, white, and male. They also have voluntarily signed up to participate in online polls, usually with the promise or chance of winning prizes, and are therefore a self-selected group that is also not considered to be representative of even the online population. Despite the poor image of online polling among some polling professionals, their use increased during the 2000 election campaigns.

Sometimes telephone "polls," called **push polls**, are actually political advertising. Push polls try to sway voters by giving them false or misleading information about opposing candidates under the guise of taking a poll.

Political Advertising

Partly as a result of the shrinking sound bite, the poll-driven horse-race media coverage of campaigns, and the political candidates' and parties' interest in controlling their own messages to the voter, candidates have turned increasingly to paid advertising to reach the voter. Of course, candidates have historically used a wide variety of techniques to reach as many people as possible directly, from

Weblink
Gallup
[www.gallup.com]

Harris Interactive
[www.harrisinteractive.com]

American Association for Public Opinion Research
[www.aapor.org]

push poll—a type of negative political advertising that appears to be a telephone poll but is actually a telemarketing campaign to sway voters by giving them false or misleading information about opposing candidates.

Table 15-1 Political Campaign Expenditures and Amount Spent on Political Advertising

Year	Total amount spent on political campaigns	Portion spent on purchasing advertising (mostly radio and television airtime)
1952	$140 million	5%
1988	$2 billion	20%
2000	$5 billion	30%

whistle-stop speeches to political rallies. However, campaigning has become increasingly expensive in the United States as campaigns and technology become more complex and candidates attempt to reach people through the media.[6]

Total political campaign spending in the United States grew 15-fold between 1952 and 1988, from $140 million to nearly $2 billion. As shown in Table 15-1, much of the increase is a result of increased spending for political advertising and other media-related expenses. In 1952, just 5 percent of campaign expenditures were spent on radio and television time. Dwight Eisenhower's presidential campaign in 1956 was the first to rely extensively on television commercials. In the 1972 Nixon–McGovern presidential contest, the portion of campaign dollars spent on political advertising had climbed to 15 percent. By 1988, some 20 percent of nearly $2 billion spent on political campaigns was spent to purchase airtime. Factoring in the salaries of media consultants and advertising production costs, more than 40 percent of campaign dollars was spent on media-related expenditures in 1988.[7] By 2000, the portion of campaign dollars spent on advertising had swelled to more than 30 percent, and the total for all media-related expenses topped 50 percent. Political advertising for presidential campaigns begins with the primaries, and here it has grown as well.

Impact of Negative Advertising

Some people say that political advertising is no different than other product advertising, except that in a political campaign there is a one-day sale. It is this mentality that drives the industry. As a result, many candidates gravitate toward negative advertising. Based on an examination of more than 1100 political commercials, political communications scholar Larry Sabato concluded that:

> Even when television is used to communicate political truth (at least from one candidate's perspective), the truth can be negatively packaged—attacking the opponent's character and record rather than supporting one's own. If there is a single trend obvious to most American consultants, it is the increasing proportion of negative political advertising. . . . At least a third of all spot commercials in recent campaigns have been negative, and in a minority of campaigns half or more of the spots are negative in tone or substance.[8]

Although some of the paid political spots on television are intended to simply provide information about the candidate and his or her position on the issues, the ads that have captured the most criticism and research have been the negative ads that are intended to attack the candidate's opposition, rather than shed light on the issues. The rise of political advertising has also led news media to increasingly focus their coverage of the candidates on their advertising.

Much of the negative political advertising has been problematic for a number of reasons. One of the biggest problems, as Kathleen Hall Jamieson points out, is that many of the ads contain falsehoods or lead the audience to make false inferences.[9] Among the most notorious examples is the so-called "Willie Horton" negative television advertising from the 1988 presidential campaign. The advertising accused the Democratic candidate Michael Dukakis with being soft on crime. As Jamieson explains, the advertising contained three false statements and a false inference that as governor of Massachusetts Dukakis furloughed 268 first-degree murderers who had then gone on to rape and kidnap, when in fact there had been only one such case, that of William Horton.

Theoretical Explanations on Negative Advertising

A variety of scholars have conducted research to explain the use of negative advertising. Research suggests at least three possible theoretical explanations as to the popularity of negative ads in campaigns.

Expectancy Theory   The first is based on **expectancy theory.** Expectancy theory is a motivational framework that proposes an individual will act in a certain way based on the anticipation that the act will be followed by a given outcome and on the attractiveness of that outcome to the individual. As negative advertising has gotten a foothold in the political campaign world, candidates and their campaign managers have employed negative advertising in an attempt to lower the attractiveness of opposing candidates and thus lower the motivation of voters to put their support behind those candidates.

Cognitive Response Model   Second is the **cognitive response model.** This model proposes that the persuasion that occurs during or following a communication is in fact *self*-persuasion. That is, the receiver of the communication convinces him- or herself while reading, listening to, or watching the message to accept the position advocated in the communication. Persuasion has less to do with the facts presented in the message than it does with certain message attributes. Fear appeals, source credibility, or the feelings evoked in the message, especially if they coincide with the receiver's own feelings or beliefs, all increase the likelihood that this self-persuasion will occur. Confirming this notion, a number of studies have shown that subjects' opinions oftentimes continue to be positive toward a candidate (or issue) even though the subjects can't actually remember any supportive arguments. The cognitive response model suggests that negative advertising might exert a cumulative effect on those exposed to the message, leading the candidate sponsoring the ad to develop greater support than his or her opponent.

Hierarchy of Effects Model   Third, the **hierarchy of effects model** suggests that negative ads might help voters differentiate among candidates. The hierarchy of effects model is based on a classification of media effects into three categories:

1. *The cognitive:* the knowledge or intellectual realm (e.g., learning about a candidate).

expectancy theory—a motivational framework that proposes an individual will act in a certain way based on the anticipation that the act will be followed by a given outcome and on the attractiveness of that outcome to the individual.

cognitive response model—a theoretical model explaining how negative political advertising works that proposes the persuasion that occurs during or following a communication is in fact *self*-persuasion.

hierarchy of effects model—a theoretical model that proposes how negative political advertising works based on a classification of media effects into three categories: the cognitive (knowledge or intellectual realm), the affective (emotional or motivational realm), and the conative (behavioral realm).

2. *The affective*: the emotional and motivational realm (e.g., supporting or opposing a candidate).

3. *The conative*: the behavioral component (e.g., voting for a candidate).

This three-part model suggests advertising might influence voters' knowledge level, attitudes, or intentions to vote for a particular candidate. Based on this model, advertising scholar Gina Garramone and her colleagues argue that negative ads can be very effective when differentiating or discriminating candidates' images.

On a theoretical level, a negative political ad that contains concrete, substantive information would allow voters to distinguish candidate qualities, positions, and performance more readily than would other types of political information that provide less explicit information. Also, the greater perceived differences between candidates may lead voters to greater attitude polarization regarding the candidates. As a result, by discerning clear differences between or among candidates, voters may be more likely to strongly like one candidate while strongly disliking another and subsequently voting for the preferred candidate. Yet, most negative ads are devoid of concrete information. Rather, most negative ads tend to attack opposing candidates. Consequently, negative political advertising tends to be relatively ineffective. The following discussion reviews the findings of research on negative advertising effectiveness.

Negative Advertising Effectiveness

Researchers Richard Lau and Lee Sigelman tested three hypotheses regarding negative political advertisements: 1) that they work (i.e., they get voters to endorse the candidate doing the attacking); 2) that voters dislike negative ads; and 3) that negative ads tend to have an unintended side effect of disenfranchising the electorate.

Regarding the first hypothesis, Lau and Sigelman found in a study of voters in 1997 that negative ads do not work; they actually decreased the favorability of voters' attitudes toward the candidate whose campaign ran the negative ad. Conversely, the favorability of voters' attitudes toward the "target" of the ads increased. A study of the 1992 campaign similarly revealed that candidates who initiated negative ads lost 18 out of 25 elections. They also found there was no strong preponderance of evidence indicating that negative political ads were more memorable than positive ads.

Regarding the second hypothesis, that voters dislike negative ads, the results are clear again. "Six of the nine studies found negative political ads being rated less ethical, less fair, and otherwise less liked than positive political ads, while two studies came to the opposite conclusions and one uncovered no significant differences," Lau and Sigelman report.

Third, whether negative ads contribute to voter apathy or disenfranchisement, the results are somewhat mixed. Although there is some evidence to support this hypothesis, it is not clear. "Of the 20 relevant findings, ten report no significant differences and two associate positive outcomes with negative political ads (e.g., higher turnout), but eight report significant negative consequences," Lau and Sigelman explain. "This pattern of results is not strong enough, in our judgment, to serve as an empirical basis for urging policy makers to begin regu-

Good media literacy is especially important when it comes to understanding how political advertising can influence voters regardless of issues or qualifications of candidates. Following are ten questions to consider when watching a political advertisement:

1. Who is the advertisement targeting?

2. What or whom is the ad trying to sell?

3. How does the ad convey its message in terms of production techniques, camera angles, music, quick edits?

4. What kind of appeal is it employing, emotional or logical?

5. Does the ad present a positive or negative view of a candidate?

6. What facts, if any, are presented in the ad? Can they be readily checked?

7. Are the facts it presents useful to voters?

8. Who is paying for the ad?

9. How effective was the ad in influencing your views and why?

10. Did the ad enable better understanding of the candidate's position on an issue or issues?

lating the content of political ads, but it *is* strong enough to heighten the interest of scholars and others concerned about the American political scene."

Some research indicates that one of the most important effects of negative political advertising is to alienate young viewers from the political process. Negative political advertising increases the level of cynicism among young viewers and decreases their interest in becoming politically active and involved.

Political Debates

One of the most important areas of political communication is the debate. From the great debates between Abraham Lincoln and Stephen A. Douglas during the U.S. Senate race of 1856, debates have been a proving ground for candidates to test their mettle against an opponent and for the voting public to better understand both the character and the content of each candidate. Notably, these early debates were in many ways quite different than the televised debates the public has come to know since the first televised debate in 1960. For example, a debate between Lincoln and Douglas might last more than five hours, with each candidate offering detailed commentary of an hour or more on a single issue, such as abolition, which was the topic of the first joint debate, held on August 21, 1858. Further, because television or radio did not yet exist, these debates were not heard by any one other than those persons present for the live event, although the public could read about them in newspapers.

Arguably the most important debate between U.S. presidential candidates in the 20th century occurred in 1960, when for the first time presidential candidates debated live on broadcast television and radio. The debate pitted John F. Kennedy and Richard M. Nixon against each other. Research conducted at the time showed that among those who watched the debate on television, Kennedy, who was handsome and well-groomed, was clearly perceived to be superior. Nixon, whose dark stubble of beard and "shifty" eyes gave him a more sinister look (the debate was scheduled for the evening and Nixon had not shaved since

In the famous televised debate between 1960 presidental candidates John F. Kennedy and Richard M. Nixon, television viewers felt that Kennedy won the debate while radio listeners felt that Nixon had won.

the morning) was deemed to have lost. Meanwhile, on radio, with listeners able only to hear the candidates' voices, the clear winner was deemed to be Nixon because it seemed he had the more convincing arguments. Kennedy ultimately won the presidential contest in an extremely close election, and it is not clear whether the debate was the deciding factor in the election. But it has been the touchstone for televised campaigning ever since. Today it is a given that one's television persona is an essential quality in winning an election. More recent evidence on televised debates from the 1988 campaign indicates that the candidate with the strongest personal image, the greatest credibility, and the strongest emotional appeals often emerges the victor.

Vox Politics: Talk Shows and Candidates

Although many journalists may think they are the public's most important source of political news during an election, research suggests otherwise. Not only is political advertising an important source for many voters, television and radio (and increasingly online) talk shows have emerged as vital sources of candidate information to voters. The Freedom Forum Media Studies Center found this to be a growing part of the presidential campaign process as early as 1992.

"Politicians on talk shows are usually a bust for ratings," noted Larry McGill, then manager of news audience research for NBC (and now with the Freedom Forum), "But this year (1992) they seem to be bucking that trend." In fact, the *Today* show averaged a 3.8 rating in 1992, but drew a rating of 4.1 for Clinton's June 9 appearance and a 6.0 rating when Ross Perot came on the show. In recognition of the importance of talk shows in reaching voters, the candidates in 1992 made extensive appearances on the talk shows. Between January and July 1992, Clinton appeared on TV talk shows 23 times, including eight times on *CBS This Morning*. Perot appeared on talk shows 14 times, five times on *Today*. George Bush appeared just twice.[10] Could this have explained the results of the 1992 election? Although this may dismay some journalists, Freedom Forum research also shows that many viewers don't discriminate between talk shows and other network programs—including news—in terms of where they get their information about the candidates.

Candidates are showing up more on talk shows in order to speak directly to the public, especially younger viewers.

The Internet and Political Campaigns

One phenomenon that has emerged in the 1990s as a strong force in political elections is the direct-access medium of the Internet. Never before have candidates and the public had such great ability to directly communicate with each other. Voters can simply go online and visit a candidate's Web site to obtain information about where a candidate may stand on an issue, to make a campaign contribution, or to volunteer to help the candidate's party. Conversely, the voter can also create a Web site voicing his or her approval or disapproval of a candidate or support for or opposition to an issue. Some have even bought Web site domain names to create Web sites that make fun of a candidate. Research by the Freedom Forum and others show that direct-access media are increasingly important in the political process. Voters use these resources to supplement their knowledge of the candidates and to compare what the candidates have to say with what the news media report.

However, although citizens may tend to think of candidates' use of new media such as the Internet as the beginning of direct communication between candidates and voters, the phenomenon is not new. In fact, a century ago, in 1901, the *Saturday Evening Post,* with a circulation of 250,000, continued to increase its readership by adding an "A-list" of political leaders to its writing corps. "In 1912, the *Post* featured a wealth of political monographs by several former and future presidents, William Howard Taft and Theodore Roosevelt among them, seeking to reach the public, directly and unfiltered. That same year, the *Post* ran an article by Woodrow Wilson on civil service reform and a piece by Warren G. Harding titled 'The Conscience of the Republic,'" according to a Freedom Forum report.

What is different today is the online media permit access to the candidates on demand, and they permit active voter participation and interactivity between the candidates (or at least their staff) and the voter. Moreover, there is an almost inexhaustible set of well-developed online resources of all types for those interested in the world of politics, campaigns, and public issues. Online news sites are creating well-rounded sections covering politics on their Web sites that include links to various articles and other Web sites that let users learn about topics that specifically interest them. Online discussion forums are also important outlets for people to communicate with each other regarding candidates. In the 2000 presidential

In the early 20th century, the *Saturday Evening Post* had leading political figures write articles on various topics, letting them speak directly to the public.

election the Green Party used an online petition that gathered over 75,000 signatures in support of having the Green Party candidate, Ralph Nader, participate in the presidential debates, although the petition drive was unsuccessful in having him join the debates.

It's also the case that many online political resources offer the public information in a package unlike that of traditional journalism, yet it performs the journalistic function of putting news and information in a larger context. One of the most interesting political news and information sites is Politics.com, a site founded by Howard Baer.

Baer and his colleagues have created a political site that features a wide range of useful news and information, including details on the candidates and their positions on the issues, the results of various opinion polls, an exhaustive directory of online political information and resources, an opinion and analysis section, and a diverse set of interactive forums where voters (or nonvoters) can voice their own opinions and knowledge and read what others have to say.

One especially useful feature of Politics.com, which is only possible online, is the site's money trail. Not only does the site provide an up-to-date report on the dollars raised by the candidates as well as a "soft money leader board" (soft money refers to contributions by corporations and individuals to parties for "party-building" activities, reports the site), but it allows visitors to customize information on demand about any U.S. community or any person who may have contributed to a candidate, using data from the Federal Election Commission. The user simply enters a ZIP code and immediately obtains a list of everyone in that geographic area who has contributed to 2000 federal campaign committees.

Media Spotlight: Net Election 2000 by the Numbers

The presidential candidates in 2000 used their official Web sites to communicate directly with voters, to state their positions on issues, to help organize volunteers or direct online petition drives, and to sell items ranging from bumper stickers to shirts and cufflinks to increase their campaign funds. In late September 2000, the *Industry Standard* collated various numbers about some of the candidates' Web sites and the political leanings of Internet users:

■ Percentage of Americans online who are registered Republicans: 36.8 percent.

■ Percentage of Americans online who are not registered with a party or affiliated with other parties: 35.3 percent.

■ Percentage of Americans online who are registered Democrats: 27.9 percent.

■ Percentage of total candidates (House, Senate, gubernatorial, and presidential) nationwide with Web sites: 56.6 percent.

■ Percentage of Republican candidates nationwide with Web sites: 71.9 percent.

■ Percentage of Democratic candidates nationwide with Web sites: 63.4 percent.

■ Percentage of third-party candidates nationwide with Web sites: 35.8 percent.

■ Most expensive item for sale at George W. Bush's online store: W. 2000 silver cufflinks for $95 per pair.

■ Most expensive item for sale at Al Gore's online store: XX large–XXX large Gore 2000 denim shirt for $48.

Alternatively, the user can enter the first three or more letters of a person's last name and obtain a detailed inventory of her or his contributions during any election cycle dating to 1990.

The database is maintained by Opensecrets.org, which also offers a wide range of other useful online political information, such as details on the activities of Political Action Committees (PACs), the spending of lobbyists (which can be extremely revealing in how organizations or industries are trying to shape the nation's political agenda), and which political races have raised and spent the most. Not everyone thinks making public records such as these widely available on the Internet is a good idea, however.

Weblink

Politics.com
[www.politics.com/]

Vote Smart
[www.vote-smart.org]

Open Secrets.org
[www.opensecrets.org/]

The Center for Voting and Democracy
[www.fairvote.org/]

Politics.com.

Online Media and Political Communications

Political elections are not the only arena in which online media are affecting political communications. Political activists have found the Web to be an effective place to organize people as well as to distribute their messages. Web site e.thePeople encourages citizens to e-mail their politicians, create and sign online petitions, and discuss various political topics with others online. There are a couple potential problems with online petitions, however, besides the fact that it is easier to fake names on an online list, and therefore such lists may not carry as much weight as an actual petition. The first is that with online petitions it often is not clear who will be sending the final petition to the recipient, nor do they let signers know when it has been sent. The other potential problem is that these online petitions can be used by unscrupulous marketers as a source of mailing list rentals, because signers are often asked to put their names and addresses.

E-mail initially seemed to promise a faster, more efficient way for constituents to communicate directly with their members of Congress, but a report released in 2001 by George Washington University and the Congress Management Foundation as part of the Congress Online Project said that the reality of e-mail communications did not bear out that promise. There was growing frustration on the part of constituents who felt that their politicians were not responding to their communications and likewise a frustration on the part of politicians who felt that the public did not adequately understand how Congress worked and had unrealistic expectations of how quickly they could receive responses. Some House offices were receiving 8000 e-mails a month, and some Senate offices were getting 55,000 e-mails a month, far more than their staff could read—let alone answer—in addition to doing their various regular duties. The report also said that there was a general perception among politicians that e-mails were a more casual form of communication than a telephone call or written letter and were thus given lower priority than those other forms of contact.

As we have seen, the government has become more active in recent years in writing bills that attempt to counter some of the trends online communication has brought, such as the general breakdown in the ability of media companies to protect copyrighted material. One proposed bill in 2002 would even have allowed media companies to legally hack people's computers who use file-sharing systems that transmit copyrighted material that has not been authorized to be distributed, although it is doubtful the bill will pass in its original form. Another 2002 bill proposed that manufacturers of electronic equipment be required to install security devices that would block unauthorized digital copies of content. Consumer groups have complained about this, saying that the proposed legislation would mean consumers could not even copy a movie from a DVD to a computer elsewhere in their own house, and the manufacturers are wary of installing expensive equipment that is likely to be hacked relatively soon anyway. Hollywood counters that they will not embrace video over digital distribution systems until they can be assured their content won't be copied and distributed illegally.

Weblink
e.thePeople
[www.e-thepeople.com/]

Weblink
Congress Online Project
[www.congressonlineproject
.org/index.html]

Wireless networks and text messaging can allow large groups of people to mobilize and organize relatively quickly, as happened with organized protests against Philippine President Joseph Estrada in 2001.

These and issues regarding online privacy, encryption, and online pornography are likely to continue to be hot topics that involve politicians and the court system for some time.

Some political activists are also using online media to not only organize online but to physically gather as well. Dubbed **smart mobs** by author Howard Rheingold, these groups use cellular phones and wireless networks to communicate rapidly with each other and organize. Smart mobs contributed to the overthrow of President Suharto in Indonesia in 1998 and to the overthrow in 2001 of Philippine President Joseph Estrada, as organizers orchestrated demonstrations against him via forwarded cell phone text messages. Protestors at the World Trade Organization meeting in Seattle in 1999 were able to check the electronic network to see which way the tear gas was blowing. Through the use of wireless technology, mass demonstrations in various parts of a city can be roughly coordinated in real time, giving protestors almost as good a communication network as police or military might have in such a situation.

smart mob—a term coined by author Howard Rheingold to define a group of people communicating with each other via text messaging or wireless networks that allow them to coordinate their activities even though they are in different places.

SUMMARY

Among the most important functions of mass communication in society is its role in the democratic process. Mass communication provides much of the information voters rely upon to make informed decisions about the candidates and the issues.

Among the most important effects of media is its agenda-setting influence, which is not limited to political issues but is perhaps most often visible in this context. Through the media, old or new, politicians, candidates, and journalists alike all influence, or attempt to influence, the public's views on what is or is not important. There is little to suggest that the agenda-setting function will become any less important in the digital age.

Research tells us that political communications has undergone a sea change in the past half century in the United States. Media reporting of campaigns in particular is characterized by sound bites and the horse-race dimension of elections. Although journalists ostensibly are exercising great care in fashioning impartial intelligence in daily news reports on the candidates for office, the voices of the candidates are increasingly limited to short sound bites, often ten seconds or less. The depth or substance of such "bites" is necessarily limited.

Opinion polls frequently drive media coverage of campaigns as well, with attention more often focused on who's ahead or behind than on their position on the issues. Debates and media coverage of the debate also exert important influence on voters and other citizens.

Paid messages from the candidates are often dominated by negative advertising, which typically takes the form of personal attacks, sometimes filled with falsehoods or misleading innuendo. Political advertising campaigns are increasingly expensive, with presidential campaigns often costing $100 million or more, senatorial campaigns costing $30 million or more, and even campaigns for the House costing several million dollars. The only clear winners in this costly contest are the media, who gladly take the millions in paid political sponsorships.

Many of the stories reported in traditional media are repackaged for online, digital media with little revision or added substance. Some online original sites, however, depart from the traditional model, and offer much greater depth of analysis and commentary, as well as links directly to candidates' sites or other sites about politics or the issues in a campaign. Moreover, these online sites offer interactive forums and personalized campaign finance information that only online media can provide. Although little research is available, early indications are that the U.S. public, at least the 52 percent online as of 2000, is finding this type of online engagement increasingly attractive and compelling.

Candidates see the online media as especially desirable, since they can not only direct their message to highly targeted audiences, but they can solicit campaign donations and other contributions such as volunteering directly via the Internet.

Although elections tend to be the focal point of the junction between media and politics, changes in digital media and networked communications are also allowing citizens easier access to their representatives—at least in theory. In reality, the overwhelming numbers of e-mails politicians receive, and their own bias toward weighing letters or phone calls as more important, mean that most people sending e-mails do not receive personal responses, or any response at all.

Activists have used wireless networks domestically and internationally to organize smart mobs, or groups of people who communicate with text messaging or cell phones to act in concert during demonstrations or protests.

Discussion Questions

1. Do you agree with Joseph Pulitzer's statement on the importance of the press in preserving American democracy? Why or why not? What trends and events both historical and current support your views?

2. In today's digital, networked world, does the two-step flow hypothesis still seem to apply? If so, who are opinion leaders on the Internet, and how do they become opinion leaders?

3. Discuss some of the important trends in media coverage of elections such as sound bites and horse-race coverage and what can be done to change these trends, if you feel they are detrimental to good journalism and the political process.

4. Considering that most media organizations rely heavily on advertising for revenue, is it fair to deny them the revenues that come from political advertising? Are there any potential conflicts of interest that could come from a media organization's coverage of fundraising or election issues because of the current arrangement? How might this situation be changed so that media companies can still earn money, politicians can effectively reach the public, and the audience can be thoroughly informed on issues?

5. Look at the numbers in the Media Spotlight box on the percentage of registered voters online by party and those who are not registered or belong to other parties and compare that with the number of candidates who had Web sites in the 2000 elections. Do some parties seem to be using the Web more effectively than others? What could some segments do to better reach potential voters?

6. If you go to a nonnews Web site to get information on candidates, what do you look for in a Web site that makes you trust the information it provides? Do you visit more than one site to read about a particular candidate, or do you stay with one site?

Media and Convergence: International Perspectives

16

In many parts of Europe, 50 percent of 8- to 16-year-olds have their own mobile phones. In the United States, many parents and educators have looked disapprovingly on children or teenagers having their own mobile phones, for a variety of reasons. Parents and educators typically have viewed mobile phones as at best a distraction for kids and an expensive one at that.

Although mobile phones and other wireless communication technologies such as portable text messaging systems have fallen in price dramatically over the past few years, the United States is still behind several other countries in their widespread adoption.

Text messaging has been the focus of mobile phone burnings in India, where the practice has been blamed for causing divorces and for introducing young people to Western social behavior.

It has also been widely adopted in Japan, where crowded public spaces make it difficult to carry on a private conversation with a cell phone. Text messaging has become such a phenomenon that a new term to describe these people was created—*oya yubi sedai* ("thumb tribe," or "thumb generation"), which refers to how young people use their thumbs to rapidly type messages.

What ways will people in other nations find to use new and developing communication technologies? What power will governments have in controlling access to information in an increasingly wired world? How will local cultures and beliefs be affected if citizens in developing nations have equal access to the many entertainment options promised in a digital, networked world?

OBJECTIVES

In this chapter we will:

- Provide an overview of media around the world and a comparative framework for their analysis.
- Outline four theories of the media in an international context.
- Review three major issues in international mass communication, including the role of media in economic development, globalization, and press freedom.
- Examine the general state of media in six regions of the world.
- Describe the state of media in several countries representative of each of those regions.

Prologue

U.S. media have a dominant, and some would say dominating, presence on the global communications scene. The three largest media companies in the world are U.S.–based. Hollywood produces blockbuster films popular the world over. U.S. record labels produce much of the most popular music. CNN and other U.S. news media are seen across the planet.

Yet, as prevalent as U.S. mass communications are around the globe, many international voices share this worldwide stage. In fact, much of the most important and intriguing media technology and integration into daily use originates outside the United States in countries such as Finland, Sweden, and Japan, among others. New communication technologies are being utilized by developing countries as well in novel ways that are changing their societal practices and power structures. These developments are usually not reported on in the general U.S. media and often only are haphazardly covered in specialized publications.

Understanding how mass communication models and media work in other countries and how convergence and new technologies are affecting them provides an excellent mirror to see the strengths and weaknesses in the U.S. system and may give ideas on how some aspects in the United States could be improved upon.

Four Theories of International Mass Communication

Four theories of types of international mass communication were presented in 1956 by social scientists Frederick S. Siebert, Wilbur Schramm, and Theodore Peterson.[1] They offered four theories of how the press operates in different political, historical, and cultural environments around the world. Although they referred specifically to "the press," we can extend their theories to embrace all the media of mass communication, including television, radio, and online.

Siebert, Schramm, and Peterson's four theories of the press are:

1. The authoritarian theory.
2. The libertarian theory.
3. The social responsibility theory.
4. The soviet theory.

The Authoritarian Theory

The **authoritarian theory** describes the oldest system of mass communication, with its roots in 16th and 17th century England. This system exists under authoritarian states in which government exerts direct control of the mass media. Countries where government consists of a limited and small ruling-class are especially likely to have an authoritarian media system.

Media in an authoritarian system are not permitted to print, broadcast, or webcast anything the government feels might undermine its authority. Content

authoritarian theory of the press—a theory of how the mass media works in which authoritarian governments exert direct control over the media.

John Milton.

that threatens or challenges the existing political system and its values is strictly prohibited. Anyone who violates the rules is subject to harsh punishment, including imprisonment, expulsion, or even death.

Government uses the media to not only inform the public of important events but also to shape public opinion in support of its policies. Although ownership of media can be private or public, media professionals are not permitted to have editorial independence within their organizations. Foreign media are subordinate to governmental authority. Countries where the authoritarian theory best describes current systems of mass communication include China, Cuba, and Myanmar.

The Libertarian Theory

The **libertarian theory** is often also called the free-press theory. Libertarian theory rests on the notion that the individual should be free to publish whatever he or she likes. Its roots lie in the work of 17th century philosopher and writer John Milton, whose *Areopagitica* (1644) argued, "All the winds of doctrine were let loose to play upon the earth, so Truth be in the field, we do injuriously by licensing and prohibiting to misdoubt her strength. Let her and Falsehood grapple; who ever knew Truth put the worse, in a free and open encounter."

In the libertarian theory, criticism of the government and its policies is accepted and even encouraged. There are no restrictions on the import or export of media messages across the national borders. Media professionals have full autonomy within their media organization.

In some ways, however, the libertarian theory is an ideal type, and not one that realistically applies in full anywhere. There are few if any countries where the libertarian theory perfectly describes the system of mass communication. Yet there are many countries where elements of the theory clearly play a role in the media system. The United Kingdom, Australia, and Mexico embrace many of the qualities of the libertarian theory.

The Social Responsibility Theory

The **social responsibility theory** best describes the systems of mass communication in most democratic societies. The theory rests on the notion that the media play a vital role in informing citizens in a democratic society and as such should be free from most governmental constraints in order to provide the best, most reliable, and most impartial information to the public.

To operate effectively in this environment, the media must exercise self-restraint and act responsibly. The Commission on Freedom of the Press (known as the Hutchins Commission) in 1947 articulated media's obligations to society. These included being informative, truthful, accurate, objective, balanced, and diverse. The Commission argued that a responsible media system must do more than simply report the facts. It must place them in context. This means the media must provide analysis, explanation, and interpretation.

Although the social responsibility theory may best describe the system of mass communication in democracies such as the United States, Canada, and France, the growth of global corporate media organizations challenges media to place the public good over profits and to do so internationally as well as domestically. Siebert, Peterson, and Schramm cautioned, "The power and near monopoly position of the media impose on them an obligation to be socially responsible, to see that all sides are fairly presented and that the public has enough information to decide; and that if the media do not take on themselves such responsibility it may be necessary for some other agency of the public to enforce it."

Siebert, Peterson, and Schramm add that, "Freedom of expression under the social responsibility theory is not an absolute right, as under pure libertarian theory. . . . One's right to free expression must be balanced against the private rights of others and against vital social interests." For example, a socially responsible news organization would exercise extreme care in reporting about terrorist activities, especially those that might detail how bioterrorism is conducted or that may provide information on a city's disaster plans.

The Soviet Theory

The **soviet theory** of the press is based on a specific ideology: the communist system of government practiced in the former Soviet Union. Siebert traced the roots of this theory to the 1917 Russian Revolution and the views of Karl Marx and Friedrich Engels. According to the soviet theory, media should serve the interests of the working class and should be publicly owned, not privately owned.

Although there are some similarities between the soviet and authoritarian systems, such as the media being subordinate to government, there are also important differences. In particular, the soviet theory posits that the media should recognize their responsibility to the people, and the media should self-regulate their own content. Government censorship is not to be the norm. With the demise of the Soviet Union in the 1980s, however, this theory is most useful as an historical reference point.

Issues in International Mass Communication

The theories of international mass communication may give a good general framework from which to understand how media may be organized, but there are issues that are outside of these theories that are also affecting media worldwide. These issues transcend individual countries or regions, while affecting them all to various degrees. The main cross-border issues in mass communication are adoption of mass communication technologies in developing countries, globalization, and threats to press freedom.

Adoption of Technologies in Developing Countries

The media and accompanying communication technologies are instruments for economic development throughout the world and can have exceptional potential to improve the economy in developing nations. Western companies looking to establish factories overseas to take advantage of cheap labor costs look for developed aspects of infrastructure, such as passable roads and access to telephone

soviet theory—a theory of international mass communication that states the media should be publicly owned and used to further the needs of the working class.

lines, although wireless technologies and satellites have lessened the need for telephone land lines to some degree.

Radio and television are often used to reach persons in remote agricultural regions to provide information on agricultural techniques. Broadcast stations are often among the first places taken in a coup, as those in power—or those wishing to gain power—realize the importance of controlling the means of distributing information. Print media are often used to foster the business development of a region, although their effectiveness is limited in countries with low literacy rates or where many different languages are spoken.

Countries such as India have become sources for relatively cheap software developers and computer programming workers, as well as database centers or information processing centers. A generally well-educated work force that speaks English has positioned India nicely to take advantage of "low-end" information economy needs, such as scanning documents, transcribing documents, and providing technical support for computer makers.

Some countries in Africa have been making moves toward similarly fulfilling information processing needs of industrial countries. A data-processing company in Ghana, for example, inputs tickets in a database from minor violations ranging from parking tickets to jaywalking that occur in New York City. For Ghanian workers the pay is better than other jobs, and the working conditions are better than in many other industries, although hours are long and breaks are short by Western standards.

Although some critics charge that moving information processing work overseas is no different than sending factories overseas to obtain cheaper labor and avoid dealing with issues such as pollution, others have supported this trend. They claim that the information technology (IT) industry is not like industrial-era factories; these businesses are generally not polluting, they can be created using existing buildings, and the type of work raises the level of education of the workers and better positions them for other jobs within information societies. In short, it is hoped that developing countries can skip the worst results of the industrial age and move directly into the information age, although whether this is the case or not remains to be seen.

Some issues keep IT from growing as fast as it could in developing countries. Excessive government regulation often hampers development of a good telecommunication infrastructure that could better reach all citizens within a country. Political instability, drastic changes in government policies, corruption among government officials, a lack of other infrastructure, such as regular electricity supplies, can all hurt development of telecommunication technologies in a country.

Southeast Asian nations such as Singapore and Malaysia have been promoting themselves as high-speed Internet e-commerce zones that will provide the most technologically advanced support for online business operations in the hope of attracting Western businesses. However, important issues arise regarding the free flow of information from a cultural or political, rather than a technical, perspective. Singapore strictly controls access to most forms of media, even banning some Western newspapers that have criticized the government, and attempts to tightly control access to the Internet. Western companies, especially

The dominance of Western media in developing countries can often hamper development of local entertainment and media.

media companies, may balk at these restrictions on access to information and that may keep them away.

The Globalization of Media

As global media enterprises arise to exploit economies of scale, these media companies frequently produce content that is presented to audiences around the world, oftentimes overwhelming the voices of locally produced content. The most visible examples include music, motion pictures, and news, which are most often produced in the United States but distributed to global audiences, often with little or no significant modification. U.S.–based global media companies battle with other foreign-based multinational media enterprises for market dominance.

Going hand-in-hand with media globalization is cultural imperialism, or the imposition of foreign, usually Western and from the United States, values on local populations. Because of their "exotic" status in the eyes of a non-American audience, even low-budget Hollywood action movies can obtain a status and popularity in foreign countries that they do not enjoy in the United States. The same phenomena can be seen with U.S.–based fast food restaurants such as Burger King or McDonald's, which are often considered status symbols or "nice restaurants" when first appearing in some developing countries.

Critical and cultural communication scholars such as Herbert Schiller and Cees Hamelink have argued that despite the growth of new communication technologies, information and media still tend to rest in the hands of the economic elite, especially the corporate elite. As a result, the wealthy, industrial, and post-industrial nations tend to dominate the international flow of mediated information, while poorer, less-developed nations tend to have relatively little voice. The media of the West, especially the United States, have the strongest media voice and, as a result, exert a form of cultural imperialism over much of the developing world through books, movies, television, advertising, and even the Web, because most Web content is in English. In contrast, U.S. audiences see and hear relatively little content produced elsewhere in the world, especially from the developing nations. Much of the reason is economic. It is expensive to produce, market, and distribute media content in its traditional forms, and Internet access in developing nations, which would greatly reduce distribution costs, is still limited.[2]

Propaganda

An important part of the international communication mix is **propaganda,** or the regular dissemination of a belief, doctrine, cause, or information that reflects the views or interests of the group advocating the belief or doctrine. Many governments around the world publish, broadcast, or webcast propaganda extensively, both in war time and peace.

One of the largest purveyors of propaganda around the world is the U. S. government. The official international propaganda arm of the U.S. government is operated under the U.S. Department of State and is called International Information Programs, formerly the United States Information Agency (USIA).

The mandate of the International Information Programs is to explain and support U.S. foreign policy and promote U.S. interests. With 190 posts in 142 countries, the International Information Programs budget is approximately U.S. $1 billion and employs more than 6000 people worldwide, making it a very large communication organization.

Among International Information Programs operations are a variety of mass communication activities, including Voice of America (VOA), Radio and TV Martí, Worldnet Television, Radio Free Europe/Radio Liberty, and the new Radio Free Asia.

Not everyone would agree that the stories produced and broadcast by VOA and Radio Free Europe, for example, qualify as propaganda. The staffs of these operations are in many cases highly trained and qualified journalists and other communication professionals.

What conflicts may arise for these media professionals between high journalistic standards of conduct and the needs of promoting the U.S. government's views on an issue? Can a suitable balance that satisfies both the information needs of their listeners and viewers and the government's interests be found; and, if so, what would that be?

Weblink
International Information Programs
[usinfo.state.gov/]

Press Freedoms; Press Dangers

Many countries do not enjoy the constitutional or other legal protection of freedom of expression as in the United States. Throughout the world, governments in many countries have routinely placed journalists under arrest for their outspoken reporting on government problems, policies, or abuses.

Government leaders have many means to control journalists and the media other than outright imprisonment or threats of harm. Pressure can be placed on the owners of media organizations to silence journalists within the organization. Advertisers can be convinced to stop advertising in certain media outlets, thereby

propaganda—the regular dissemination of a belief, doctrine, cause, or information that reflects the views or interests of the group advocating the belief or doctrine.

Every year scores of journalists are killed while covering wars or civil unrest, and dozens more are threatened or attacked while doing stories. Italian journalist Maria Grazia Cutuli (right) was one of four journalists killed by armed men in Afghanistan on November 19, 2001.

depriving the media organizations of a major source of income. Access to newsprint or printing presses can be blocked, or newspapers can be gathered and destroyed before reaching a widespread audience. Television or radio signals can be jammed or stations taken over by the military in order to stop broadcasts the government objects to. Some countries force journalists to obtain government-sanctioned licenses in order to practice journalism.

In an effort to strengthen freedom of expression throughout the Americas, members of the Inter American Press Association (IAPA) drafted the 10-part Declaration of Chapultepec in March 1994, a document articulating the principles of freedom of expression. To date, the Declaration has been signed by the heads of state of some 14 countries in the Western Hemisphere.

Among the most important principles in the document are that no people or society can be free without freedom of expression and of the press, that every person has the right to seek and receive information, express opinions, and disseminate them freely; that prior censorship (what U.S. courts have called prior restraint), and restrictions on the circulation of the media or dissemination of their reports directly contradict freedom of the press; and that no news medium nor journalist may be punished for publishing the truth or criticizing or denouncing the government.

Partly as a consequence of not having constitutional or legal protection, working for the media in other parts of the world can be a very hazardous occupation. Every year several dozen journalists are killed throughout the world, and many more are attacked, imprisoned, or injured while reporting. Countries with civil unrest or military actions are especially dangerous for journalists. In Afghanistan during the military actions against the Taliban, some journalists were robbed by brigands in lawless tribal areas or were charged exorbitant rates to obtain basic transportation services. Eight journalists were killed in Afghanistan between October and December 2001, and many others were attacked while covering the war.

Weblink
International Press Institute
[www.freemedia.at]

Media Geography

In many cases, the media within countries of a particular part of the world have much in common not simply because of proximity to each other but also because of regional politics, culture, and economics. We will look at the state of media

Brazil has a vibrant entertainment media system. Luciana Gimenez, the ex-girlfriend of Mick Jagger and mother of his son, records her television show during a press conference by top Brazilian model Gisele Bundchen.

and how communication technologies are being used in six geographic regions of the world, as well as giving thumbnail descriptions of the state of press freedom within those regions. Particularly interesting countries from a mass communication, media use, or technological perspective will be examined as well. Through examining media in other countries and regions around the world, it is hoped that a better understanding of the U.S. media system can be obtained.

The Americas

Although many countries in North, Central, and South America have relatively strong and stable economies and democratic forms of government, with some notable exceptions, it was the most dangerous place in the world to practice journalism in 2001, with 21 journalists killed and dozens of others harassed or intimidated, according to the International Press Institute's annual report on press freedoms worldwide. In Colombia alone 11 journalists were killed, as the civil unrest and drug trafficking there continue.

The terrorist attacks on Sept. 11, 2001, and general slowdown in the U.S. economy even before the attacks also hurt the economies of countries elsewhere in the Western Hemisphere because of the United States' dominance as a trading partner.

Brazil

The largest media market in South America is Brazil, with a country similar in geographic size and population to the United States. Because Portuguese is the main language, Brazil stands apart culturally from much of the rest of Latin America, where Spanish is predominant. Brazil enjoys a relatively strong economy, although there are significant pockets of poverty, and economic development outside of urban areas is uneven.

Brazil has more than 100 daily newspapers, nearly 1700 AM and FM radio stations, and 138 television stations, most of them commercial in nature and privately owned. In September 2002 nearly 14 million Brazilians, or about 8 percent of the population, had Internet access.

The government of Brazil has sometimes encroached on press freedom and in 1999 passed a bill prohibiting various public officials, including police officers, judges, and officers of the tax auditing office, from providing information to the media. Moreover, journalists have sometimes been attacked by military police, and the situation in general has been sometimes dangerous for media professionals.[3]

Despite these trends, the country has a history of an independent press, both print and electronic, although journalists in rural areas often face harassment or attacks from local power brokers or corrupt officials.

Brazil has a moderately sized motion picture and television industry, and many of its cultural products are distributed throughout the Americas. Popular music, especially that inspired by samba and other Brazilian rhythms, is another important Brazilian media export.

Organizacoes Globo of Rio de Janeiro is the largest media company in South America. It publishes the largest newspaper in Brazil and has the most popular television operations, including both broadcast and cable television systems and a wireless pay television system.

Canada

Canadian media are very similar to those of the United States. Most media are privately owned and relatively free from governmental control. Commercial interests feature prominently in the character of mass communication, although Canada's public television system produces a great deal of quality programming, especially for children. Canada has more than 200 newspapers, and commercial broadcasters provide a combination of news, entertainment, and sports programming supported largely by advertising and some pay per view sources.

Economic change has been sweeping through the Canadian media system, with the country's two magnates of print media selling off most of their newspapers since the late 1990s. Multibillionaire Kenneth Thomson, the country's wealthiest man, sold most of his company's Canadian papers as he reinvented his firm into an electronic information provider. Thomson's flagship newspaper, *The Globe and Mail* of Toronto, was merged into a new media company with Bell Canada Enterprises. The number-two Canadian media mogul, Conrad Black, sold most of his company's papers, too. Canada's newest media baron is Israel Asper, a lawyer who created a television and radio group in western Canada and in other international venues such as Australia, New Zealand, and Ireland.

The Torstar Corporation is a newspaper publisher based in Toronto and important media company in Canada. Its flagship paper is the *Toronto Star*, the largest daily circulation (460,000) newspaper in Canada. The company is a leading publisher of romance novels, with its Harlequin Enterprises imprint. Also important is Southam Inc., based in Don Mills, Ontario, a daily newspaper group with some 30 dailies, including the *Calgary Herald* and *The Ottawa Citizen*.

Canada is an information society, with not only a vibrant press but extensive electronic media as well. Canada has nearly 600 radio stations, 80 broadcast television stations, and a well-developed cable television system. More than 17 million Canadians, 53 percent of the population, have Internet access.

Despite its reputation as a relatively free and safe society, Canada is not a perfectly safe haven for journalists and other media professionals. One of the country's leading crime reporters, Michel Auger of *Le Journal de Montreal*, was shot and nearly killed in 2000 for reporting too closely on the drug trade in the province of Quebec. The first ever assassination of a Canadian newspaper editor took place in 2000 as well, in Vancouver, when Tara Singh Hayer, 64, publisher and editor of the *Indo-Canadian Times*, was shot and killed. His paper is the largest and oldest Punjabi weekly in North America. He was targeted for his paper's moderate position on the issue of an independent Sikh homeland in India.

Chile

Once tightly controlled by General Augusto Pinochet's military dictatorship, the Chilean media have enjoyed relative freedom since 1999. Both print and broadcast media, however, are still subject to certain dangerous restrictions, especially the State Security Law, which criminalizes any publication or broadcast that might besmirch the honor of state institutions and symbols. Other South and Central American countries have similar "honor" laws that curtail press freedoms. Self-censorship and a lack of investigative reporting dampen the importance of Chilean media in the emerging democracy. Restrictions affect not just journalism. Chile's Supreme Court recently upheld a 1989 ban on Martin Scorsese's film *The Last Temptation of Christ,* which it called blasphemous. Chilean media have used the Internet to publish information when otherwise subject to court gag orders.

Chile has a fairly well-developed system of electronic broadcast media, with more than 240 AM and FM radio stations and 63 broadcast television stations. More than two dozen newspapers are published, and more than 3 million Chileans, or 20 percent of the population, had Internet access as of December 2001.

Cuba

Cuba's media system stands in stark contrast to those of the rest of the Americas. Because of its long-standing communist dictatorship under Fidel Castro, the mass communication system has operated largely under an authoritarian system. The government strictly controls all the press, including both print and electronic media. Cuban law permits only government-sanctioned journalists and media organizations.

Cuba's weak economy has supported only a limited development of electronic media. The country has 58 television stations and about 235 AM and FM radio stations. Just 120,000 Cubans, or 1 percent of the population, have Internet access, and only a handful of newspapers are published.

Media Spotlight: **Noble's Grupo Clarín**

Grupo Clarín is a leading South American media company, with diverse interests that include newspapers, television, radio, cable television, and satellite broadcasting. The company began with the debut of its flagship newspaper, *Clarín,* in 1945 in Buenos Aires, Argentina.

Clarín today is known for its commitment to excellence in journalism and is the largest circulation Spanish-language daily newspaper in the world, with a circulation of 2 million. The company was founded by Roberto Noble, a past recipient of the Maria Moors Cabot prize, the oldest award for international journalism, and is today headed by his widow, Ernestina Herrera de Noble.

Weblink
Clarín Web site
[www.clarin.com/diario/hoy/index_diario.html]

Clarín is South America's largest newspaper, with over 2 million newspapers.

Independent media professionals can operate only outside the law and provide their stories only to foreign media. The rise of the Internet facilitates this process, but the government considers independent media professionals traitors and frequently subjects them to arrest, seizure of their equipment, and other forms of repression, intimidation, and harassment. A 1999 law places heavy sentences on any person who is perceived to have collaborated with or provided information to foreign media that support U.S. policies.

Among the most important independent voices in Cuba is Cuba Press, an independent news agency operating out of Havana, that specializes in investigative reporting of human rights violations, political prisoners, and other important issues. It was founded in 1991 by Raul Rivero, an award-winning journalist and poet who previously headed the science and culture service of the official Cuban news agency. He left the official journalism post in 1991, declaring it a "fiction about a country that does not exist."

Since founding Cuba Press, Rivero's books have been banned, and he has been arrested and threatened numerous times. He received a variety of international journalism awards, including the Maria Moors Cabot award in 1999 and the Reporters sans Frontières-Fondation de France Prize in 1997, but has been unable to attend the award ceremonies because the Cuban government has indicated that if he leaves the country, he will not be permitted to re-enter and continue his work.

Mexico

Mexico has not enjoyed the robust economy that the United States' other neighbor, Canada, has enjoyed. Despite the North American Free Trade Agreement, economic growth has been limited and unemployment has been high in Mexico. Mexico in 2000 saw the end of seven decades of one-party rule by the Institutional Revolutionary Party and is only now moving toward an openly pluralistic, democratic political system. As a result, Mexico's media system does not enjoy quite the same vitality as the Canadian or U.S. systems. Many journalists have been threatened, harassed, or physically attacked. In 2001, two journalists were killed.

Yet, Mexico has a substantial media system. Newspaper readership is high, and more than 50 newspapers are published. The country has nearly 1400 AM and FM radio stations and more than 230 television stations. Mexican media produce extensive programming that is exported throughout not just Latin America but to the United States and Europe, as well. Mexican soap operas have proved extremely popular in Russia, for example. About 3.5 million Mexicans, or almost 3.5 percent of the population, had Internet access as of December 2001.

Among the most important media companies in Mexico and the Americas is Grupo Televisa, S.A., the oldest Mexican television network and the world's largest Spanish-language media company, with interests in television, publishing, radio, music recording, and professional sports teams. The long-time chairman, president, and CEO was Emilio Azcarraga, who died in 1996. Known as "el tigre," for his hair streaked with a lock of white hair, Azcarraga was a leading figure in the global media business.

Weblink
Grupo Televisa, S.A.
[www.televisa.com]

Asia and the Pacific

From China to India, the economic, political, and culture of Asia ranges widely, and the systems of mass communication reflect this diversity. Although some stars, such as Jackie Chan or Gong Li, are able to attract pan-Asian audiences, for the most part each country has its own unique types of entertainment, media organizations, and news organizations.

The political and cultural differences, combined with restrictive trade policies in a number of areas, including media ownership, have prevented any single Asian media company from owning media in other countries or dominating local media programming. Perhaps the closest to pan-Asian programming is Rupert Murdoch's Hong Kong–based Star TV, the satellite television subsidiary of his News Corp., which is beamed primarily into India and China.

Despite countries such as Japan or Singapore, which are known for being at the forefront of using new communication technologies, Asia has the only two countries in the world that do not have any Internet access: Afghanistan and North Korea.

Political repression also has played an important role in hampering the media. Myanmar continues to suppress journalists, with 18 journalists imprisoned in 2001 and the government censoring words like "democracy" and "corruption." Although there has been much economic liberalization in China, journalists who criticize the government are often arrested or the papers are shut down, especially before sensitive times such as the Communist Party Congress in November 2002. Historical traditions of not openly questioning authority in most Asian countries means most media organizations do not seriously challenge the ruling parties when there are abuses of power. One bright spot is the freedom of the press in Cambodia, widely considered to have the most press freedoms in the region. This is especially important after the years of genocide and warfare endured by the Cambodian people.

China

In China, media are controlled by the state. Media play an important role in both informing the public of important developments in the country and in disseminating official policy on a variety of issues. Media professionals who do not comply with the authorities are subject to disciplinary action, arrest, and imprisonment. Although some private media ownership is permitted, most media, including newspapers, television, and radio, are state-run. However, there have been a growing number of magazines that have been more vocal about criticizing the government on various issues, although some editors and journalists are arrested when the government feels they have gone too far.

The 2001 award by the International Olympics Committee of the summer games to Beijing in 2008 opens a new window to press freedom in China. The Chinese government has announced that foreign press will be allowed total freedom in covering the games. China has enjoyed dramatic economic growth since the mid-1990s when it introduced capitalistic economic policies, and this is propelling the country to be a leading information society.

More than 46 million of China's 1.27 billion people have Internet access—3.6 percent of the population—and 85 million have mobile phones (second only to the United States in terms of the number of mobile phone users, although it is only 7 percent of the population). The Chinese periodically close down thousands of unlicensed Internet cafes in an attempt to keep control of what information Chinese Internet users can access, an almost impossible task. Through informal online networks, dissidents send out news about human rights abuses and other issues that is then widely disseminated on the Internet and made available to other Chinese who access the Internet inside the country. It is interesting to ponder what effects on the Internet more Chinese Internet users will have, as even if only 25 percent of the Chinese population has Internet access that will still be a higher number, in terms of sheer numbers, than the entire U.S. population.

More than 600 AM and FM radio stations operate in China. More than 3240 television stations operate in the country, although 209 are operated by China Central Television. Roughly 30 are regional stations, and about 3000 are local stations.

Foreign media are gradually being permitted greater access to the Chinese market, which is the largest in the world. China has been trying to compete with India as a source of computer programmers and software developers, but the lack of widespread English-language education is likely to keep them behind India in that area.

Hong Kong

Hong Kong was handed back to China by the British in 1997, although it officially operates independently as a special administrative region (SAR). Hong Kong has had an independent, largely privately owned media system based on principles and practices of the West, although there has been increasing suppression of the media by Chinese authorities since 1997, despite the Communist Party's statements that they would not interfere.

Authorities in Beijing have been wary of the territory's independent media. In one case, Hong Kong's public television system, which is funded by and subordinate to Beijing authorities, had its chief executive, who happened to be a woman and one of the few top female media executives in the region, removed from her post for violating a Beijing policy. The policy forbade allowing anyone on television who was from Taiwan's government and supported the notion of Taiwan as an independent state from China.

The tiny island city-state operates 20 AM and FM radio stations and four broadcast television stations. Cable television is well developed and gradually converting to digital format. About 4.5 million people, or almost 60 percent of the population, have Internet access. About a dozen newspapers are published, including some of the most influential media voices in Asia.

Hong Kong–based Sing Tao Holdings Limited publishes a number of important newspapers, including the *Sing Tao Daily*, the oldest Chinese-language newspaper in Hong Kong. South China Morning Post (Holdings) Ltd. is also based in Hong Kong. Its flagship paper is the *South China Morning Post*, an English-language newspaper with a circulation of 100,000. The company has wide-ranging media interests that include music publishing, magazines, and an Internet edition.

W

Weblink
South China Morning Post Online Edition
[http://www.scmp.com/]

India

Historically, Indian media have been vibrant and diverse, with extensive print, electronic, and motion picture industries. Print media have been especially active in their watchdog role as government critic. Many of India's approximately 100 major daily newspapers have been among the most respected in the region and the world. India's motion picture industry is one of the biggest in the world, with Indian films seen widely across the globe. India has produced a successful music recording industry, with its own unique style of popular song and dance. Moreover, the music videos produced for Indian music recordings are popular around much of the world. More than 560 television stations and 220 radio stations broadcast in India, most of them privately owned.

About 7 million people have Internet access in India as of December 2001, a jump of 2 million from the year before. Even so, that is still only 0.67 percent of India's population. Most Indians connect to the Internet through public Internet cafes. Many Indian media organizations have developed substantial online media outlets, reaching both a large Indian expatriate audience as well as others simply interested in India and its rich cultural heritage. In 2002, 2.5 million Indians had mobile phones, although some groups in India are protesting their use by using short messaging as a corruption of traditional Indian culture, even going so far to claim that short messaging on mobile phones have been the cause of numbers of divorces.

Japan

Japan has often been a world leader not only in the development of new communication and media technologies, but in their application and integration into daily life. Japan-based Sony Corporation is one of the largest media and entertainment companies in the world. Much of the newest high-tech gadgetry that reaches the United States has often been on the Japanese market for at least a year before crossing the ocean.

Media Spotlight: Bollywood: Like Hollywood, Only Much, Much Bigger

With 800 films produced each year and 14 million people a day going to movies, India's film industry is the largest in the world in terms of numbers of films produced. The Indian film industry is primarily centered around Bombay (thus the name Bollywood), although there are important regional centers of film throughout the country, such as Bengali cinema, South Malayalam cinema, Telugu cinema, and Tamil cinema.

Most movies are popular, escapist fare, with simple love stories and plots and lots of singing and dancing. However, some directors do make serious documentaries that chronicle some of the social problems India faces or highly artistic films.

As in the West, movie stars are revered by adoring fans, and entertainment news about stars is avidly read by many. Some actors, especially in southern India, have become popular politicians. Music videos and Indian music, much of it from the movies, is popular throughout Asia. Numerous Web sites help fans of Indian entertainment keep up-to-date on the latest releases and news, as well as talk with each other.

Despite the dedication of fans and sheer numbers of movies produced each year, the revenues generated by Bollywood pale in comparison to most Hollywood movies. Even successful movies, such as *Dil To Pagal Hai* (1997), which grossed $12 million and sold 10 million copies of its soundtrack, had less than the total gross in India of the film *Titanic,* which brought in $12.5 million.

Weblink
eBolly
[www.ebolly.com/]

Planet Bollywood
[www.planetbollywood.com/]

India has the world's largest cinema, although in terms of revenues it remains far smaller than Hollywood.

Japan has a vibrant system of entertainment media production, including both cinema and recorded music. Japanese pop stars often become famous throughout Asia. Japan also created the popular Asia-wide pastime of *karaoke* ("empty orchestra" in Japanese), in which people sing popular prerecorded songs.

Print media flourish in Japan, with dozens of daily newspapers published throughout the country. Moreover, Japan has the two largest circulation newspapers in the world, the *Yomiuri Shimbun* with a circulation of more than 14 million, and *Asahi Shimbun,* with a circulation of more than 12 million. The *Yomiuri Shimbun* is a conservative, progovernment newspaper, while the *Asahi Shimbun* is known for its left-wing views and frequent criticisms of the government. Some *Asahi Shimbun* journalists have been attacked and killed by right-wing fanatics in recent years.

Japan has a well-developed system of electronic media, including more than 7000 television stations, nearly 300 radio stations, and cable and satellite television. Moreover, Japan spearheaded the development of high-definition television and has lead the introduction of digital broadcasting. Japan also has some of the largest media companies in Asia and the world. Among these companies are

Japanese tend to adopt new communication technologies faster than people in many other parts of the world.

Sony, Nippon Hoso Kyokai, Nippon Television Network Corporation, the Tokyo Broadcasting System, and Asahi Shimbun Publishing Company.

Sony Corporation is a massive enterprise, with substantial interests in consumer electronics (including the Sony PlayStation home video game system, cameras, and computers) and entertainment. Sony's entertainment interests feature motion picture and television show production, including Columbia TriStar Motion Picture Group. Sony Pictures Entertainment also produces and distributes television programs, such as *Dawson's Creek* and *Jeopardy*. Sony also has substantial interests in recorded music, with record labels Columbia and Epic.

Nippon Hoso Kyokai (NHK), a public television and radio channel, is the largest media company in Asia. Based in Tokyo, NHK delivers 1200 hours of analog and digital noncommercial television programming each week on its five channels, including general, educational, two satellite channels, and Hi-Vision HDT.

Nippon Television Network (NTV) Corporation is also based in Tokyo and is a leading broadcaster in Japan, providing news, sports, and variety shows. NTV began broadcasting digital TV in 2000. Tokyo Broadcasting System (TBS) operates a leading digital news channel, JNN Newsbird, and is expanding its digital satellite broadcastings.

More than 56 million Japanese, or 44 percent of the population, had Internet access as of June 2002, according to Japan's Ministry of Posts and Telecommunications (MPT). DoCoMo, a leading Japanese telecommunications provider, in 2000 introduced the first Internet-enabled telephone, the iMode, and in 2001 introduced in Tokyo the world's first third-generation wireless communications device, the FOMO phone. The next-generation digital device offers broadband Internet services, such as built-in real-time video conferencing (i.e., the phone has a built-in color video camera, and if two people are talking via FOMO devices, they can hear and see each other), as well as traditional voice capabilities.

The Philippines

Despite a free-market economy, a democratic government, and both the president and opposition leader claiming they are the defenders of press freedom, the Philippines was second only to Afghanistan in the numbers of journalists killed

Weblink
Japan Today
[www.japantoday.com/]

in Asia in 2001. Most of the deaths were related to Muslim separatists in the southern Philippines, but Filipino journalists also state that most of the media owners are associated with ruling politicians and thus criticism of the government is often muted in order to protect business interests.

The population is served by 31 television stations and more than 600 AM and FM radio stations but is quite diverse linguistically, with an estimated 70 dialects spoken, although Tagalog is the largest indigenous language.

Internet access doubled between December 2000 and September 2002, with 4.5 million Filipinos now online. Great disparities in wealth, rugged terrain, and the nation's many islands, as well as the Muslim separatist movement in the southern part of the country, make establishing a modern telecommunications system difficult.

South Korea

South Korea has one of the strongest information societies in Asia or anywhere in the world. As a democracy with a robust economy, the nation has seen its media system develop well, although some political groups who disagree with criticisms of themselves in the press have started litigation to silence their critics. More than 200 AM and FM radio stations and 121 television stations are broadcast in South Korea, most of them privately owned. About a dozen daily newspapers serve the country.

Some uncertainty exists regarding the independence of the Yonhap News Agency, the main news agency in the country. The government has authority to appoint the president of the agency through public broadcasters Korean Broadcasting System and Munhwa Broadcasting Corporation.

More than 25 million South Koreans have Internet access as of July 2002, almost 54 percent of the population, and broadband access is among the highest in the world, with more than a third having high-speed connections.

Taiwan

Taiwan has a robust and independent system of mass communication, with a substantially developed electronic and digital communications infrastructure. There are over 500 AM and FM radio stations and 29 television stations on the island state, and Taiwan is a major manufacturer of information technology equipment such as silicon chips. Taiwan's 22 million citizens are served by more than 6000 magazines, 350 newspapers, and 250 news agencies.

Press freedom is expanding as the country's democracy becomes more pluralistic. The government has traditionally controlled the electronic media, especially state-owned television, where a past president's son-in-law was named to head the operation in 2000. Government influence in radio is less evident. The press is constitutionally protected, but government restrictions still pertain, especially with regard to regulations of information pertaining to national secrets.

With 11.6 million Taiwanese online as of July 2001, or almost 52 percent of the population, Taiwan is one of the more wired nations in the world.

Australia and Oceania

Australia dominates the South Pacific region known as Oceania, where many island states exist, such as New Zealand, Fiji, the Solomon Islands, Vanuatu, and

Tonga. In general, the media of Australia, New Zealand, and many of the island nations of Oceania are well developed and independent. Most of the nations in Oceania depend heavily on Australia, New Zealand, and Japan as trading partners, with some states, such as American Samoa, relying on the United States.

Australia enjoys both a robust economy and a vibrant media system. Media operate free of most government controls, and the press is fully able to question government policies and public figures. Commercial broadcasting, with its 600 AM and FM radio stations and 104 television stations, is well developed and is on track toward a digital television system, as per federal legislation passed in 2001.

Complementary to the commercial broadcasting system is the Australian Broadcasting Corporation, a publicly funded broadcaster similar to the British Broadcasting Corporation of the United Kingdom.

The newspaper business in Australia is also growing, with roughly 200 daily newspapers. Free commuter newspapers were launched in 2001 in some major cities, including Sydney and Melbourne. Magazine circulations have been declining, however, although competition is brisk.

Telstra Corporation is a leading telecommunications enterprise and operates an extensive cable television network. Australian media are increasingly concentrated in ownership and leading the way in globalization. Rupert Murdoch's diversified media company, News Corporation Limited, is the prime example. News Corp. publishes dozens of newspapers, including more than 130 Australian papers and many leading international ones, such as *The Times* of London and the *New York Post*. News Corp. also publishes books through companies such as HarperCollins and Avon Books. News Corp. has a majority interest in Fox Entertainment Group, producing and broadcasting extensive television programming through its 33 television stations. Its motion picture companies, such as Twentieth Century Fox, produce motion pictures seen around the world, including *Star Wars* and *Titanic*. News Corp. also is a global leader in digital and satellite-delivered television, with BskyB delivering satellite television in Europe, and Star TV delivering satellite television in Asia.

Approximately 10.6 million Australians had Internet access as of February 2002, 54 percent of the population.

Europe

Made up of more than three dozen diverse countries and cultures, Europe has among the world's most active and free media systems. With the 1993 launch of a single market, the European Union (a group of European countries organized into a unified regional economy) has reinforced the strength of mass communication industries throughout the region. Although some monarchies remain, most countries have well-established democracies and legally protected media systems.

Both print and broadcast media in most countries of Europe operate independently, although governments in many nations operate public broadcasting facilities, and certain restrictions are placed on various electronic media with regard to issues of protecting children, limiting foreign broadcast importations, and encouraging multilanguage transmissions. Satellite television is widely seen throughout Europe, and had been a commercial success long before it got a foothold in the United States. One of the first terrestrial digital television systems was launched in Spain in 1999. Odna Digital offers 14 channels of digital television program content.

The Scandinavian countries of Norway, Sweden, Denmark, and Finland have some of the highest rates of Internet penetration in the world, with 60 percent or more of the population having Internet access. Mobile phone use is also widespread in these countries, and Finland and Sweden, with companies such as Nokia and Ericsson, have often led the way in initiating new wireless communication technologies and products.

Following is a discussion of the media systems in five countries that reflect the character and diversity of Europe's mass media.

Denmark

Like the other Scandinavian countries of northern Europe, Denmark enjoys legally and culturally protected freedom of expression. The economy is healthy, and democracy is pluralistic. Despite having only about 5 million people, Denmark has more than 350 AM and FM radio stations, two dozen television stations, and about 30 newspapers. Nearly 3.4 million Danes, or 63 percent of the population, have Internet access.

Among the leading media concerns in Denmark are the increasing concentration of ownership of media properties, declining newspaper circulation, eroding media credibility, journalistic practices in a commercially dominated marketplace, and uncertainty over the digital future of mass communication.

France

France is something of a paradox regarding press freedom. On the one hand, France has long enjoyed a vibrant system of mass communication with fiercely independent media. Newspapers, magazines, broadcasters, and news services have all produced quality news reporting recognized internationally as excellent. There are more than 3000 AM and FM radio stations and nearly 600 broadcast television stations in France. Dozens of newspapers are published, including world leaders such as *Le Monde* and *Le Figaro*.

Terrestrial broadcast and satellite pay television services are also popular in France. The motion picture and recorded music industries are similarly exceptional in quality and volume. Book publishing has historically been among the most important in any part of the world. Technologically, France has been among the most innovative in the world, with the introduction of Minitel, the first commercially successful system of online communication in 1980, paving the way for today's Internet.

Yet France also has some of the most significant restrictions on press activities in Western Europe. In 2000, the French government passed a law prohibiting photographers and videographers from photographing suspects wearing handcuffs or from taking pictures of crime scenes in which a victim's dignity may be jeopardized.

Rather than relying on the media to exercise independent judgment responsibly, the government has imposed restrictions on the press. The law was inspired by allegations that **paparazzi,** or press photographers seeking photos of celebrities, may have inadvertently contributed to the death of Princess Diana in 1997,

paparazzi—press photographers who attempt to get candid photos of celebrities to sell to various media outlets.

France has imposed more restrictions on media coverage following the death of Princess Diana in a Paris car accident in which her driver was trying to evade paparazzi.

who was killed when the car she was traveling in crashed in a Paris tunnel—some say because her car was being chased by paparazzi in another car.

French authorities have also taken legal action to control the sale of Nazi memorabilia via the Internet, thereby imposing limitations on freedom of expression online. Yahoo! and other online service providers have been subject to legal action in the French courts regarding their members' discussion and sale of Nazi memorabilia. Despite the continuing popularity of Minitel, nearly 17 million French also had Internet access as of May 2002; 28 percent of the population.

France is home to some of the leading media organizations of Europe and the world. Among these firms are Vivendi Universal, Havas Advertising, Hachette Filipacchi Media, and Agence France-Presse, the oldest international news agency in the world.

Germany

Germany's 83 million citizens enjoy a long history of an extensive system of mass communication. There are approximately 200 newspapers, more than 370 broadcast television stations, and more than 800 AM and FM radio stations, most of which are privately owned, although the government operates a public broadcasting system as well. Among the major media companies based in Germany are Bertelsmann, Axel Springer, and KirchGruppe. Over 32 million Germans, or 39 percent of the population, have Internet access.

Freedom of the press is guaranteed in the Basic Law of Germany. As a result, the press has established a reputation for some of the best investigative reporting in Europe. For example, news magazines such as *Der Spiegel* in 2000 aggressively reported on the corporate spying activities of a leading German financial institution, the Dresdner Bank, despite pressure to withhold the report. Similarly, despite economic threats, the *Financial Times Deutschland (FTD)* in 2000 published an article critical of the financial state of Lufthansa, the national German airline.

Russia

With its soviet past still only a dozen or so years behind it, Russia is still somewhat tentative in its creation of a free system of mass communication. Print media, including more than 200 newspapers and magazines, operate more independently than electronic media, although the government has sometimes imposed direct censorship of unpopular political commentary.

Russia has seen an explosion in media since the fall of the Communist government in 1991.

Prime Minister Vladimir Putin, a former KGB colonel, introduced in 2000 a "Doctrine of the Information Security of the Russian Federation," which imposes restrictions on the press's access to government information. The doctrine evokes Cold War imagery by discouraging the publication of information that might "infringe on Russia's sovereignty" and argues in favor of "developing methods to make more effective the participation of the state in shaping the information policy of the state-owned mass media." After Chechen terrorists held more than 700 people hostage for a few days in a Moscow theater in October 2002, Putin proposed further restrictions on press coverage of military activities, supposedly in the interests of national security and in the fight against terrorism.

Many Russian journalists have been killed by oftentimes unknown assailants or under suspicious circumstances. In 1999, for example, the editor of a leading news publication, *Pravo,* died in a mysterious fire in police headquarters after arriving to cover a story.

Yet Russia operates more than 7000 television stations and nearly 900 AM and FM radio stations nationwide. Many are controlled by the state, however, or those that are privately run are owned by powerful businessmen with ties to the government. The largest independent broadcast media enterprise is Media-Most, which stations have offered a more critical perspective on government polices. Media-Most operates the only independent nationwide television station, NTV.

Russia's struggling economy and rampant corruption have undermined efforts of the media to expand. Nevertheless, Internet use has been growing, and by December 2001 more than 18 million Russians, or over 12 percent of the population, had online access.

The United Kingdom

Having given birth in the 16th century to the libertarian theory of the press, the United Kingdom has a long history of a free system of mass communication, although not without limits and not without numerous instances of government attempts to control the media through various taxes on paper, printing presses, or government-granted printing licenses. It was not until 2000 that the government passed a Freedom of Information Act, giving media and the public improved access to public records, a foundation for investigative reporting.

The BBC is a respected news organization with dozens of offices worldwide.

With a powerful tabloid press, the British are accustomed to aggressive reporting on political affairs and public figures, and reports of scandal are relatively commonplace in media, although some public officials and entertainment figures have been able to win large cash settlements from some newspapers that have proved too careless in reporting the truth. Most media are privately owned and operate commercially. Britain's more than 200 newspapers are widely read by its citizenry. About 34 million people, or 54 percent of the population, have Internet access.

Britain also has a vibrant system of production of motion pictures and popular music recording. From the Beatles to the Spice Girls, the United Kingdom has produced some of the world's most popular and influential musical artists.

British cinema has been equally influential, from classic English movie makers such as David Lean or Alfred Hitchcock to contemporary directors such as Ngozi Onwurah.

Television programming production is also lively in the United Kingdom, where many of the most popular shows in the world have been created. The British Broadcasting Corporation, a publicly funded channel, and Britain's commercial networks consistently produce high-quality dramas and series—although soap operas such as *East Enders* or foreign imports such as *Dynasty* or Australia's *Neighbors* have also been very popular with the public.

The United Kingdom is also home to some of the most important global media organizations. Among them are Reuters Group PLC, the British Broadcasting Corporation, Pearson plc, and United News & Media plc.

London-based Reuters Group is the largest provider of financial information in the world. Its staff of nearly 2100 journalists provides financial information to 500,000 subscribers worldwide as well as millions more through its affiliated portal sites, such as Yahoo! The Reuters World Service publishes some 600 news stories a day. Reuters is one of the oldest media companies in the world, having been founded in 1851 by Paul Julius Reuter, a German-born immigrant.

The BBC was established by royal charter and is the leading broadcaster in the United Kingdom, with five national radio networks, two public TV channels, a 24-hour cable news channel, and an online news service, Hoovers.com. The BBC World Service provides radio programming in 40 languages around the world and offers a free Internet service. More than 90 percent of the BBC's funding of more than $4 billion dollars annually comes from license fees citizens of the United Kingdom must pay on their television sets.

Media Spotlight: Central Europe: Emerging from Communism and Chaos

The emerging media voices of Central Europe, the region under Soviet influence for much of the latter half of the 20th century, deserve some attention. The media of this region have undergone a remarkable transformation since the end of the Cold War and are also experiencing important changes in the digital age.

One of the leading analysts of the media of Central Europe is Jerome Aumente, professor and former long-time director of the Journalism Resources Institute in the School of Communication, Information and Library Studies at Rutgers University. Aumente has led media assistance programs in Central and Eastern Europe since 1989.

In 1999 he noted that despite persistent dictatorial opposition, an independent press in Central and Eastern Europe has emerged and bears important lessons for global media assistance elsewhere.

In Poland, for example, "is a media success story with a robust print and electronic press and a growing advertising base in one of Europe's better economies," Aumente observes. In a country of 40 million people, there are nine nationwide dailies, 46 regional dailies, and 120 national weeklies, as well as hundreds of local and specialized periodicals, with almost all print media in private hands. About 25 percent of the population get cable or satellite services, and a private nationwide TV network named Polstat competes strongly against Polish Public TV.[4]

After a devastating war in the late 1990s, the situation for the media is hopeful in Serbia, largely because of the possibilities presented by digital technology best exemplified by the radio station B92. Forced off the air by Serbian President Slobodan Milosevic's government in spring 1999, B92 employed the "OpenNet" Internet Service Provider to send audio reports globally via the Web, which were then fed back into Serbia by international broadcasters. Its bulletins in a Web newsletter format on the computer screen were easily reproduced, and the bulletins were read aloud in town squares and posted on walls and billboards or otherwise copied and distributed.

Although Serbia once again has no functioning independent media outlets, the experiences of B92 and OpenNet have shown how new communications technologies can be used to distribute information outside of government-controlled media.

The third-largest media company in Europe is also based in London. Pearson plc is a global media company with diverse assets including newspaper and book publishing, as well as television production. Its newspapers include the *Financial Times* and *The Economist* (50 percent ownership), as well as publishing groups Les Echos (France) and Recoletos (Spain). Its book divisions include Addison Wesley, Prentice Hall, Allyn & Bacon, and the Penguin Group (including Penguin, Dutton, and Viking). Its Pearson Television produces more than 100 programs, including *Baywatch,* one of the most popular shows in the world.

Weblink

Pearson plc
[http://www.pearson-plc.com]

United News & Media plc is also based in London. Its main area is business services, broadcasting, and consumer publishing. United owns CMP Media, a large publisher of high-technology information and also owns PR Newswire, an important public relations news service. It also owns the U. K. newspapers *The Express* and *Daily Star* and has a 50 percent interest in Internet service provider LineOne.

The Middle East and Africa

The media of the Middle East and Africa, with a few notable exceptions, tend to reflect elements of the authoritarian and development theories of the press.

The World at a Glance . . . and Click

Nowhere can one see that the World Wide Web is a global publishing medium better than by looking at portal sites of online newspapers and magazines from around the world. At these sites, users can choose the regions, countries, and even languages from which to see online news sites. Reading what the local press is writing about certain issues can often provide different and sometimes even contrary perspectives to what most U.S. news consumers see.

Kidon Media provides links to some 1300 European news media outlets online, as well as covering thousands of others in all regions of the world. Online Newspapers.com and ABYZ Newslinks likewise cover thousands of online publications in a variety of languages, although many are in English.

Although local media outlets can of course be biased, it is important to consider what biases news organizations in the United States may be guilty of. Should online news organizations be required to include links to sites that oppose their views, or should they make their views and biases clear in some kind of editorial statement?

Weblink
Kidon Media
[http://www.kidon.com/]

Online Newspapers.com
[http://www.onlinenewspapers.com/]

ABYZ Newslinks
[http://www.abyznewslinks.com/]

Many countries have weak economies struggling to enter the information age, authoritarian forms of government, or are restricted by religious, political, or cultural systems that hamper open access to information. Moreover, some of these countries, especially in Africa, have either unstable political systems or are categorized as nonfunctioning states, in which the civil structure of the nation-state has broken down and the country is ruled by various warlords all struggling for power.

The Middle East

Political and religious differences have long caused conflict in the Middle East, and the issues of terrorism and possible weapons of mass destruction in Iraq have refocused attention sharply on the region. Despite great oil wealth in some countries, wealth is unevenly distributed among citizens, leading to simmering tensions between the ruling elite and the populace. Within the Middle East and North Africa there is a range of restrictions on media, from strict controls in places like Libya to fewer restrictions in countries like Morocco or Egypt.

Media Spotlight: Al-Jazeera: CNN of the Middle East?

Before the terrorist attacks on the World Trade Center and Pentagon on September 11, 2001, the Al-Jazeera satellite news channel was largely unknown outside the Middle East. Al-Jazeera made its name in the international community during the Afghan war following its exclusive footage of Osama bin Laden, which Western networks refused to air out of fear they might contain hidden messages to al Qaeda operatives. During the 2003 war in Iraq, CNN's coverage consisted of battle scenes from "embedded" reporters. Al-Jazeera, which was denied such access by the government of Iraq, focused on the suffering of the Iraqi people. It also angered the Western world by airing footage of dead and captured American soldiers.

Al-Jazeera, which means "the peninsula" in Arabic, was founded in 1996 by Qatar's ruler Sheik Hamad bin Khalifa-Thani, who was dismayed by the lack of press freedom in much of the Middle East. The station prides itself on its independence. Al-Jazeera's coverage of sensitive topics has often led to strained relations between Qatar and other Arab nations, as well as getting Al-Jazeera expelled from those countries. Al-Jazeera is accustomed to criticism from government authorities, as the news organization has outraged almost every Arab government as it tries to follow its motto: "We get both sides of the story."

Al-Jazeera claims at least 45 million viewers in the Arab world and 175,000 cable subscribers in North America. Its Web site, which was knocked out by hackers during the war in Iraq, gets 17 million hits a day, they claim.

"Al-Jazeera is undoubtedly a new trend in Arab media," said Roger Hardy, a Mideast specialist for the BBC World Service in London. "And as far as I can tell, it's the station of choice for Arabs, whether you're a Palestinian in Gaza . . . or you're part of the Arab diaspora in Canada or America."[5]

The Web site includes a program that translates Arabic articles into English and a number of links to various stories about Al-Jazeera itself as well as the stories it covers.

Weblink
Al-Jazeera
[www.cursor.org/aljazeera.htm]

Al-Jazeera has had several important scoops in news coverage in the Middle East.

Egypt is a democracy with an officially free system of mass communication. However, with a struggling economy and militant Islamic groups periodically making attacks within the country, the government in practice shows little support for media freedom. Newspapers, of which there are about 15, must have a government-issued license to publish.

The government operates a Censorship on Foreign Publications Department that vets all foreign media before allowing them to be distributed. In 2000 the department confiscated the March 19 issue of *Cairo Times* (published from Cyprus) for publishing an opinion poll on press freedom. Egypt is a developing nation with a limited system of electronic media. Just 56 AM and FM radio stations and 98 television stations operate nationwide. Internet access is quite limited, with only 600,000 users, or 0.65 percent of the population—a much smaller percentage than other Middle Eastern countries, which typically have between 5 and 10 percent of their populations online.

Israel has a much stronger economy than many other countries in the Middle East, despite an ongoing conflict with its Palestinian residents and its neighbors. For this and other reasons, the media system in Israel is relatively active and free, especially in comparison to other Middle Eastern countries.

Nevertheless, Israel is still a dangerous place for journalists and media professionals in general. Both Palestinian and Israeli authorities have taken steps to prevent negative media coverage of the frequent violent clashes. Reporters have been arrested, harassed, and otherwise intimidated.

Israel operates 38 AM and FM radio stations and 17 television stations and has about a dozen newspapers. Internet use is high, with almost 2 million users as of July 2001, or 17 percent of the population.

Saudi Arabia is ruled by a monarchy and has no written constitution. In this sense, the press operates freely. Yet, the monarchy rules according to Islamic Sharia law and has absolute power over everything in the country, including the media. Moreover, it implemented a press code in 1964, which authorized the government to limit freedom of expression through censorship of any criticism of the Islamic religion, the ruling family, or the government. Saudi authorities in 2000 shut down an Internet cafe for women because the Internet can be used for "immoral reasons," and the government has used filters to block access to any Web sites it deems to have objectionable content, especially those containing sexually explicit content. There are only 60,000 people with Internet access in Saudi Arabia, just 0.35 percent of the population.

Saudi Arabia's dozen newspapers and magazines are privately owned but subject to coverage guidelines imposed by the Ministry of Information, which also has authority to appoint and dismiss editors. Newspapers may publish reports only after they are released by the government-owned news agency, the Saudi Press Agency (SPA). The country's 117 television and 74 AM and FM radio stations are owned by the government and report only official views.

Africa

African countries are often at the bottom of lists when it comes to measures such as economic development, trade revenues, and public health. Yet they are often on the tops of lists in such categories as human rights violations and repressive regimes toward citizens and a free press. Inhospitable terrain extremes ranging from deserts to dense jungles, numerous ethnic and religious tensions between groups, inadequate infrastructure, and legacies of colonial systems still plague many African countries.

Yet, partly because many African nations face such basic development challenges, the continent could be extremely fertile ground to see just how communication and information technologies may allow developing countries to "jump start" their economies and raise their standards of living. Lessons learned in African countries could be applied to other developing countries that have far fewer ethnic and linguistic diversity.

However, there is a long way to go. Most African countries have less than 1 percent of their populations with Internet access, and some can count Internet users in the hundreds or thousands rather than the millions. Even South Africa, by far the most developed country in terms of mass communication in Africa, only has 7 percent of its population with Internet access.

South Africa's media system has enjoyed greater freedom since the formal end of apartheid. Print and electronic media are substantial in the country, establishing it as the leading information society on the continent. About 20 newspapers are published, and more than 360 AM and FM radio stations and 556 television stations operate in the country. South Africa had 3 million people with Internet access as of December 2001.

The official end of apartheid has brought greater diversity to the media, as well. Still, the post-apartheid media reflect significant racial prejudices. Media ownership is still predominantly in white hands, and many publications express mostly white, suburban concerns and fears, says Barney Pityana, chairman of the South African Human Rights Commission.

As elsewhere in the world, the alternative press in South Africa has taken perhaps the greatest advantage of the Web as a publishing medium. The oldest online newspaper in Africa is the Daily Mail and Guardian Online, launched in 1994 by a Johannesburg alternative newspaper. Generating more than 2 million page views a month, the online paper is staffed by 12 full-time journalists. The online site and the newspaper continue a tradition of muckraking journalism, combined with entertainment content.

Weblink
Daily Mail and Guardian Online
[http://www.mg.co.za/]

SUMMARY

To understand the variation in media systems around the world, we have outlined four basic theories of the press, or media, of mass communication. These four theories are the authoritarian theory, the libertarian theory, the social responsibility theory, and the soviet theory. Although few media systems conform exactly to these media theories, they provide a useful comparative framework for examining media form and function internationally.

In addition to these four theoretical perspectives, we have identified three overarching issues that characterize international mass communication. These are the role of media in economic development, globalization and cultural imperialism, and press freedom, the latter which in part has sometimes presented threats to mass communication professionals around the world.

We also have examined the world's main geographic regions in relation to mass communication and information technologies, highlighting especially noteworthy trends in regions or countries and providing thumbnail descriptions of some countries in order to provide a broad overview of the system of international mass communication.

Discussion Questions

1. Write down how many things you do with your mobile phone or laptop computer, such as keeping an address book or calendar, using text messaging, and the like. Then compare the functions you actually use with all the functions that are available. Why do you think you don't use some of these other functions?

2. Create a table with three columns labeled "Government," "Media," and "Public." Then list each of the four theories of international communication on the left side of the table. Write down the pros and cons each theory would have for each of the three sectors in society. Which theory or theories would be best for each sector in terms of giving it the most power? How about in terms of society as a whole?

3. Discuss ways in which cultural imperialism could be slowed or stopped using media technologies or government regulations. What might the effects of these be in the long term?

4. Covering wars or civil unrest for news organizations is a dangerous job, yet journalists are not supposed to carry weapons. Why do you think this is so? Do you agree with this reasoning?

5. How might the Internet world change when more Chinese get online, and what could this do for the current dominance English now enjoys on the Internet?

6. Most people in democratic societies assume that more access to information is better, especially for developing countries that could fall far behind in the move toward information economies. However, what if that information clashes with established cultural or religious norms? Should it be banned or regulated? Why or why not? Can you think of any cases in which you would want information to be banned? How is it similar or different from cases with other countries?

Notes

Chapter 1

[1]Friedman, Thomas L. (2002, May 12). Global Village Idiocy. *New York Times*. Retrieved May 30, 2002, from http://www.nytimes.com.

[2]Shannon, Claude F., and Weaver, Warren (1964). *The Mathematical Theory of Communication* (p. 7). Urbana: The University of Illinois Press.

[3]Schramm, Wilbur (1961). How Communication Works. In Wilbur Schramm (Ed.), *The Process and Effects of Mass Communication* (pp. 5–6). Urbana: The University of Illinois Press. Retrieved January 25, 2002 from http://muextension.missouri.edu/xplor/comm/cm0109.htm.

[4]MacLean, M., and Westley, B. (1950). A Conceptual Model for Communication Research, *Audio-Visual Communication Review*, 3: 3–12.

[5]White, D. M. (1950). The "Gatekeeper": A case study in the selection of news. *Journalism Quarterly*, 27, 383–390.

[6]Riley, John W., Jr., and Riley, Matilda White (1965). Mass Communication and the Social System. In Robert K. Merton, Leonard Brown and Leonard D. Cottrell, Jr. (eds.), *Sociology Today, Volume II* (pp. 537–578). New York: Harper and Row.

[7]Severin, Werner J., and Tankard, James Jr., W. (2001). Introduction to Mass Communication Theory. In *Communication Theories: Origins, Methods, and Uses in the Mass Media, Fifth Edition* (p. 16). New York: Addison Wesley Longman.

[8]Smith, Anthony (1993, October). New Communication Technology and Changing Political Boundaries. Technology Paper, the Freedom Forum Media Studies Center.

[9]Lasswell, Harold D. (1948). The Structure and Function of Communication in Society. In Lyman Bryson (ed.), *The Communication of Ideas* (p. 37). New York: Institute for Religious and Social Studies, Jewish Theological Seminary of America.

[10]Whatis?com. Retrieved May 15, 2002 from http://whatis.techtarget.com/definition/0,,sid9_gci212361,00.html.

[11]Rafaeili, Sheizav. Retrieved May 15, 2002 from http://jcmc.huji.ac.il/vol2/issue4/rafaeli.sudweeks.html#Interactivity.

[12]Manovich, Lev (2001). What New Media Is Not. *The Language of New Media* (p. 55). Cambridge, MA: MIT Press.

[13]Delio, Michelle (2001, Dec. 10). Interior Dept. Sites Still Down. *Wired News*. Retrieved May 15, 2002, from http://www.wired.com/news/politics/0,1283,48980,00.html.

[14]Veronis Suhler Releases 15th Annual *Communications Industry Forecast*. Retrieved May 15, 2002, from http://www.veronissuhler.com/publications/forecast/highlights2001.html.

[15]Grenier, Melinda Patterson (updated 2002, January 16). Record Number of Office Workers Use Webcasts Last Month. *The Wall Street Journal Online*. Retrieved May 15, 2002, from http://online.wsj.com/public/us.

[16]York, Anthony (2001, May 2). Drudge vs. Blumenthal. Salon.com. Retrieved May 16, 2002, from http://dir.salon.com/politics/red/2001/05/02/blue/index.html.

[17]Langfield, Amy (2002, April 3). Democratizing Journalism: Internet sees spike in "personal journalism" after September 11. *Online Journalism Review*. Retrieved May 30, 2002, from http://www.ojr.org/ojr/technology/1017872659.php.

[18]Irwin, Zachary. A Kosovo Primer. Retrieved May 15, 2002 from http://www.psu.edu/ur/NEWS/news/kosovohelp.html.

[19]Jupiter Communications Web survey (1998, November). Retrieved May 15, 2002, from http://www.jup.com/home.jsp. NielsenNetRatings (2000, December). Retrieved May 15, 2002, from http://www.nielsen-netratings.com/hot_off_the_net.jsp.

[20]Grenier, Melinda Patterson (2001, October 23). Traffic to News Outlets Remains Higher after Attacks. *The Wall Street Journal Online*. Retrieved May 15, 2002, from http://online.wsj.com/public/us.

Chapter 2

[1]W. James Potter, *Media Literacy*, 2nd ed. (Thousand Oaks, CA: Sage Publications, 2001) pp. 4–7.

[2]Sherwood Schwartz, "Send help before it's too late," *Parent's Choice* (1984, Winter), p. 2.

[3]"Former 'Survivor' Stillman suing show, claims it was rigged," CNN.com, February 7, 2001. Retrieved 15 May 2002, from http://www.cnn.com/2001/SHOWBIZ/TV/02/07/survivor.stillman/.

[4]Hallmark Channel web site, "About Hallmark Channel." Retrieved 15 May, 2002, from http://www.hallmarkchannel.com/tv/about/index.asp.

[5]"Who Pays for Public Broadcasting?", CPB–Public Broadcasting Web site. Retrieved 18 May, 2002, from http://www.cpb.org/pubcast/#who_pays.

[6]Bill Carter, "Jamie Tarses Resigns from ABC Entertainment," Business Section, *The New York Times*, August 27, 1999. Retrieved 18 May 2002, from http://www.nytimes.com/yr/mo/day/news/financial/abc-tarses.html.

[7]Clifford G. Christians, Mark Fackler, Kim B. Rotzoll, Kathy Brittain McKee, *Media Ethics: Cases and Moral Reasoning*, 6th ed. (Boston: Allyn & Bacon, 2001), pp. 51–53.

[8]Clifford G. Christians, Mark Fackler, Kim B. Rotzoll, Kathy Brittain McKee, *Media Ethics: Cases and Moral Reasoning*, 6th ed. (Boston: Allyn & Bacon, 2001), pp. 41–43.

Chapter 3

[1]Jules Tewlow, "New Study Shows U.S. That Baby Boomers Are Reading More," U.S. Ifra Correspondent, 3 August, 1999.

[2]Heinrich Wilhelm Wallau, *The Gutenberg Society (Mainz, 1902–)*. Transcribed by Bryan R. Johnson from the Catholic Encyclopedia (New York: Encyclopedia Press: 1913).

[3]Jean Peters, "Book Industry Statistics from the R.R. Bowker Company," *Publishing Research Quarterly* 8, Fall 1992: 18.

[4]Audit Bureau of Circulations, 2000; Newspaper Association of America, 2000.

[5]W. R. Simmons & Associates Research Inc. 1970–1977, Simmons Market Research Bureau Inc. 1980–1994, Scarborough Research—Top 50 DMA Market Report, 1995–1998.

[6]Leo Bogart, *Press and Public*, 2nd ed., p. 81 (Mahwah, NJ: Lawrence Erlbaum Associates, 1989).

[7]Audit Bureau of Circulations; Morton Research Newspaper Newsletter; NAA's Facts About Newspapers, 1992 and 1995, and the companies.

[8]Steve Mariotti, Debra DeSalvo, Tony Towle, *The Young Entrepreneur's Guide to Starting and Running a Business* (New York: Three Rivers Press, 2000).

[9]Magazine Publishers of America Web site, http://www.magazine.org/.

Chapter 4

[1]Robert Leggat, "The Beginnings of Photography," retrieved 15 May 2002, from http://www.rleggat.com/photohistory/.

[2]Leggat, ibid.

[3]Smithsonian American Art Museum, "Secrets of the Dark Chamber: The Art of the American Daguerreotype," retrieved 1 June 2002, from http://www.nmaa.si.edu/.

[4]"Smithsonian American Art Museum," retrieved 1 June 2002, from http://www.nmaa.si.edu/; "A Brief History of Daguerreotypy," retrieved 1 June 2002, from http://nmaa-ryder.si.edu/collections/exhibits/secrets/secrets_history.html; "Infoplease.com: Inventions and Discoveries," retrieved 1 June 2002, from http://www.infoplease.com/ipa/A0004637.html.

[5]"Mathew Brady," retrieved 1 June 2002, from http://www.dickinson.edu/~osborne/404_98/whitep.htm.

[6]Dorothy Kunhardt, *Mathew Brady and His World*. (New York: Time-Life, 1977), p. 248.

[7]Elizabeth Valk Long, "The Life and Death of Kevin Carter," *Time*, September 12, 1994. Retrieved 2 June 2002, from http://home-4.tiscali.nl/~t892660/msp/time.htm.

[8]Heinz Richter, "The History of Color Photography," in *F32— The Online Photography Magazine*, retrieved 12 August 2002, from http://www.f32.com/articles/article.asp?artID=128.

[9]John V. Pavlik, *New Media Technology* (Boston: Allyn & Bacon, 1999).

[10]As computer science Prof. Steven Feiner observed during personal communication, 2000.

[11]"Sprocket Holes: The Lumiere Brothers," retrieved 3 June 2002, from http://www.presscard.com/sprocketholes2.html; "Edison Elementary School: Thomas Alva Edison," retrieved 3 June 2002, from http://www.minot.k12.nd.us/mps/edison/edison/edison.html.

[12]Erik Barnouw, *Documentary: A History of the Non-Fiction Film*, 2nd revised ed. (New York: Oxford University Press, 1993).

[13]Viewers can see excerpts of this and other Griffith films online at "DG: Excerpts from D. W. Griffith's Greatest Films," retrieved 3 June 2002, from http://www.uno.edu/~drcom/Griffith/.

[14]Ephraim Katz, *The Film Encyclopedia* (New York: Thomas Y. Crowell Publishers, 1979).

[15]For example, *A Fool There Was*, Fox, 1915; see Eve Golden, *Vamp: The Rise and Fall of Theda Bara*. (West Vestal, NY: Emprise Publishing, 1996).

[16]Gary Johnson, "Images—Sinsational Sinema: Following the Grindhouse Circuit with Eddie Muller," retrieved 5 June 2002, from http://www.imagesjournal.com/issue02/features/grind.htm.

[17]"Czech and Slovak Films," retrieved 5 June 2002, from http://www.utexas.edu/depts/eems/Czech.html; Tim Dirks, "Tarzan and His Mate (1934)," retrieved 5 June 2002, from http://www.filmsite.org/tarz2.html.

[18]"Movie Times: Box Office: Top 100 Grossing Movies Ever" retrieved 5 June 2002, from http://www.the-movie-times.com/thrsdir/Top10ever.html.

[19]"Sony Smashes North American Box Office Record," Reuters, August 18, 2002. Retrieved 18 August 2002 from http://story.news.yahoo.com.

[20]"Hoover's Online" retrieved 15 August 2002, from http://www.hoovers.com/co/capsule/7/0,2163,56367,00.html.

[21]"Hoover's Online" retrieved 15 August 2002, from http://www.hoovers.com/co/capsule/0/0,2163,103440,00.html.

[22]"American Film Institute," retrieved 6 June 2002, from http://www.afionline.org/.

[23]"Hoover's Online" retrieved 15 August 2002, from http://www.hoovers.com/co/capsule/6/0,2163,103206,00.html.

[24]"Hoover's Online" retrieved 15 August 2002, from http://www.hoovers.com/co/capsule/2/0,2163,103362,00.html.

[25]"Hoover's Online" retrieved 15 August 2002, from http://www.hoovers.com/co/capsule/3/0,2163,103363,00.html.

[26]"Hoover's Online" retrieved 15 August 2002, from http://www.hoovers.com/co/capsule/9/0,2163,43679,00.html.

[27]C. H. Sterling and T. R. Haight, *The Mass Media: Aspen Institute Guide to Communication Industry Trends* (New York: Praeger, 1978), p. 352.

[28]"*Titanic* vs. *The Phantom Menace*," retrieved 5 June 2002, from http://www.the-movie-times.com/thrsdir/titanicVSmenace.html.

[29]Barry R. Litman, *The Motion Picture Mega-Industry* (Boston: Allyn & Bacon, 1998), pp. 74–88.

[30]"Curtains Rise Halfway on Digital Cinema," *Business 2.0*, May 29, 2001, pp. 32–33.

[31]"Boeing Puts Digital Movie Systems in 23 Theaters," *Yahoo! News (Reuters)*, May 9, 2002, retrieved 6 June 2002, from http://www.yahoo.com.

[32]"Hollywood Should Use Technology to Creatively Solve License Fight," *The Wall Street Journal Online*, March 18, 2002, retrieved 7 June 2002, from http://www.wsj.com.

Chapter 5

[1]"The Structure of the Recorded Music Industry" in Albert N. Greco (ed.), *The Media and Entertainment Industries* (Boston: Allyn & Bacon, 2000).

[2]Ibid, p. 94.

[3]Biography of Alan Freed, retrieved 18 August 2002, from http://www.alanfreed.com.

[4]"Veronis Suhler Releases 15th Annual *Communications Industry Forecast*" retrieved 18 August 2002, from http://www.veronissuhler.com/publications/forecast/highlights2001.html.

[5]"Hoover's Online," retrieved 12 May 2002, from www.hoovers.com.

[6]Bob Lochte, "The Life and Legend of Nathan B. Stubblefield: A Chronology," retrieved 17 May 2002, from http://campus.murraystate.edu/academic/faculty/bob.lochte/NBSDates.htm.

[7]"ThinkQuest Internet Challenge of Entries," retrieved 17 May 2002, from http://tqd.advanced.org/11646/data/woods.htm; "Welcome to the ThinkQuest Junior of Entries," retrieved 17 May 2002, from http://tqjunior.advanced.org/4091/woods.htm.

[8]Thomas White, "'Battle of the Century': The WJY Story," January 1, 2000, retrieved 18 August 2002, from http://www.ipass.net/~whitetho/WJY.htm.

[9]"NPR" retrieved 18 May 2002, from http://www.npr.org.

[10]"PRI: Public Radio International" retrieved 18 May 2002, from www.pri.org.

[11]Albert N. Greco, "The Structure of the Radio Industry," in *The Media and Entertainment Industries*, ed. Albert N. Greco (Boston: Allyn & Bacon, 2000).

[12]"FCC: Federal Communications Commission," retrieved 18 May 2002, from www.fcc.gov.

[13]"Hoover's Online," retrieved 19 May 2002, from www.hoovers.com.

[14]"Veronis Suhler Releases 15th Annual *Communications Industry Forecast*," retrieved 19 May 2002, from http://www.veronissuhler.com/publications/forecast/highlights2001.html.

[15]"Television Bureau of Advertising Online," retrieved 19 May 2002, from http://www.tvb.org/tvfacts/index.html.

[16]Steve Mariotti, Debra DeSalvo, and Tony Towle, *The Young Entrepreneur's Guide to Starting and Running a Business* (New York: Three Rivers Press, 2000).

[17]"Broadcast Stations as of June 30, 2001," retrieved May 19, 2002, from http://www.fcc.gov/Bureaus/Mass_Media/News_Releases/2001/nrmm0107.txt.

[18]"Television Bureau of Advertising Online: Television Facts," retrieved 20 May 2002, from http://www.tvb.org/tvfacts/index.html.

[19]"National Cable & Telecommunications Associates: Industry Statistics," retrieved 20 May 2002, from www.ncta.com/industry_overview/indStat.cfm?indOverviewID=2.

[20]Nielsen Media Research, 1999; Cable TV Facts, New York: Cable Television Advertising Bureau, 1996: 5.

[21]Retrieved 1 November 2001, from http://www.directv.com.

[22]"Hoover's Online," retrieved 20 May 2002, from www.hoovers.com.

[23]Joseph Treaster, "Adelphia Files for Bankruptcy," retrieved 26 June 2002, from http://www.nytimes.com.

[24]Lawrence K. Grossman, "Making a Mess of Digital TV," *Columbia Journalism Review*, March/April 1999: 53–4.

[25]John Carey, *Winky Dink to Stargazer: Five Decades of Interactive Television* (Dobbs Ferry, NY: Greystone Communication, 1998).

Chapter 6

[1]Nielsen NetRatings, "Monthly Web Usage, June 2002," retrieved 19 August 2002, from http://pm.netratings.com/nnpm/owa/NRpublicreports.usagemonthly.

[2]John Carey, "The First 100 Feet for Households: Consumer Adoption Patterns," paper presented to "The First 100 Feet: Options for Internet and Broadband Access" conference by The Freedom Forum in Arlington, Va. (October 29–30, 1996). Retrieved 20 June 2002, from http://www.ksg.harvard.edu/iip/doeconf/carey.html.

[3]Jon Krakauer, "Into Thin Air," *Outside*, September 1996.

[4]P. Tichenor, C. Olien, and G. Donohue, "Mass media flow and differential growth in knowledge," *Public Opinion Quarterly*, 1970, 34 (2):159–170.

[5]Robert H'obbes' Zakon, "Hobbes' Internet Timeline," version 5.6. Retrieved 20 June 2002, from http://www.zakon.org/robert/internet/timeline/.

[6]Judith Newman, "Inventor of E-Mail, A New Discourse," *Discover*, Vol. 23, No. 7, July 2002.

[7]George T. Hawley, "DSL: Broadband by Phone," *Scientific American*, Oct. 1999: 102–105.

[8]David D. Clark, "High-Speed Data Races Home," *Scientific American*, October 1999: 95.

[9]P. William Bane and Stephen P. Bradley, "The Light at the End of the Pipe," *Scientific American*, Oct. 1999: 110–115.

[10]David D. Clark, "High-Speed Data Races Home," *Scientific American*, Oct. 1999: 95–96.

[11]Doreen Carvajal, "Racing to Convert Books to Bytes." Retrieved 20 June 2002, from http://www.nytimes.com/library/tech/99/12/biztech/articles/09book.html.

[12]Carl Sullivan, "Newspapers Run 9 of Top 20 News Sites," Editor and Publisher Online. Retrieved 19 August 2002, from http://www.editorandpublisher.com/editorandpublisher/headlines/article_display.jsp?vnu_content_id=1608740.

Chapter 7

[1]Marvin R. Bensman, "A History of Radio Program Collecting," retrieved 22 August 2002, from http://www.people.memphis.edu/~mbensman/collectingarticle.html.

[2]James D. Livingston, "100 Years of Magnetic Memories," *Scientific American*, Nov. 1998: 106–111.

[3]"The Sum of All Data," Business 2.0, February 6, 2001, p. 24.

[4]"Thomas: Legislative Information on the Internet," retrieved 22 August 2002, from http://thomas.loc.gov/.

[5]"TiVo, Inc.: Changing the Way You Watch TV," retrieved 22 August 2002, from http://www.tivo.com/flash.asp?page=tivoinc_index.

[6]Comments made to the author at the Gorbachev Foundation Conference on Technology and Democracy, March 6, 1999, Boston, MA, USA.

[7]NEC Research Institute Web site, retrieved 22 August 2002, from http://www.neci.nj.nec.com.

[8]Shih-fu Chang, William Chen, Horace J. Meng, Hari Sundaram, and Di Zhong, "VideoQ: An Automated Content-Based Video Search System Using Visual Cues," 1997 paper, retrieved 22 August 2002, from http://www.acm.org/sigs/sigmm/MM97/papers/sundaram/acmMM97paper.html.

[9]E-mail from Dr. Madeleine (Lyn) Bates, GTE Internetworking/BBN Technologies, 70 Fawcett St., Cambridge, MA 02138 USA. E-mail sent on Tue, 29 Dec 1998, to the author from Lyn Bates.

Chapter 8

[1]Lisa Napoli, "A Gadget That Taught a Nation to Surf: The TV Remote Control," *Cybertimes, The New York Times on the Web,* February 11, 1999. Retrieved 10 January, 2002, from http://www.nytimes.com/library/tech/99/02/circuits/articles/11howw.html.

[2]"Control Data Corporation," *Jones Telecommunications and Multimedia Encyclopedia,* retrieved 12 January 2002, from http://www.digitalcentury.com/encyclo/update/cdc.html.

[3]Mark Fischetti, "Mice and Men," *Scientific American,* October 2001, 86–87.

Chapter 9

[1]David F. Gallagher, "Star of 'I Kiss You' Site Moves from Farce to Folklore," NYTimes.com, July 4, 2002. Retrieved 10 July 2002 from http://www.nytimes.com.

[2]John Borland, "New Age Pirates Rap Eminem CD," ZDNet.com, May 28, 2002. Retrieved 10 July 2002 from http://zdnet.com/2100-1106-923658.html.

[3]The first optical long-distance data network actually was created in 1200 BC. It was the series of beacon fires built over a distance of 400 km to announce the return home of Agamemnon after the Greek victory in the Trojan Wars. It wasn't exactly high-speed, at least by today's standards: It took ten years for the one-bit communication network to transfer the information from Troy to Argos.

[4]Stewart Brand, "Founding Father" *Wired,* March 2001.

[5]"Appeals Court Rules against Napster," ABCNEWS.com February 12, 2001. Retrieved 11 July 2002 from http://abcnews.go.com.

[6]"Morpheus Gets a Tune-up, Delays 2.0," CNET News.com, June 11, 2002. Retrieved 11 July 2002 from http://news.com.com/2100-1023-934581.html.

[7]Andy Oram, ed., *Peer-to-Peer: Harnessing the Power of Disruptive Technologies,* (Cambridge: O'Reilly, March 2001) pp. 95–98.

[8]Retrieved 13 July 2002 from freenet Web site: http://freenetproject.org/cgi-bin/twiki/view/Main/WhatIs.

Chapter 10

[1]Berger Meyer, *The story of the New York Times—1851–1951* (New York: Simon & Schuster, Inc. 1951); Francine Silverman, "The Man Who Saved the *Times:* Aldolph S. Ochs; *New York Times.*" *Editor and Publisher:* June 8, 1006, pp. 16–19.

[2]Michael Schudson, *Discovering the News: A Social History of Newspapers* (New York: Basic Books, 1978), pp. 10–11.

[3]The Write Site, "Tracing the Story of Journalism in the United States." Retrieved July 5, 2002, from http://www.writesite.org/html/tracing.html.

[4]Michael G. Robinson, American Culture Studies, 1890s course, Spring 1996; http://ernie.bgsu.edu/~wgrant/1890s/yellowkid/introducton.html.

[5]Joseph Pulitzer, "The College of Journalism," May 1904, *North American Review.*

[6]George Seldes, "Farewell: Lord of San Simeon," Chapter 17, *Lords of the Press* (New York: Julian Messner, 1938).

[7]"Media Layoffs," I Want Media Web site. Retrieved September 30, 2002, from http://www.iwantmedia.com/layoffs.html.

[8]Seth Schiesel and Felicity Barringer, "News Media Risk Big Losses to Cover War," NYTimes.com. Retrieved September 30, 2002, from http://www.nytimes.com/2001/10/22/business/media/22COST.html.

Chapter 11

[1]Dolf Zillman, "The Coming of Entertainment," in Dolf Zillman and Peter Voderer (eds.), *Media Entertainment: The Psychology of Its Appeal* (Mahwah, NJ: Lawrence Erlbaum Associates, 2000), p. 17.

[2]Dolf Zillman, "The Coming of Entertainment," in Dolf Zillman and Peter Voderer (eds.), *Media Entertainment: The Psychology of Its Appeal* (Mahwah, NJ: Lawrence Erlbaum Associates, 2000), p. 9.

[3]*Les Brown's Encyclopedia of Television,* 3rd edition (Detroit, MI: Gale Research, 1992).

[4]Gary Shubach, "A Critic's View of Adult Film," on DoctorG.com Web site. Retrieved October 25, 2002, at www.doctorg.com/adult_film.htm.

[5]Kagan World Media, 2001.

[6]"Mario Generates $10 Billion in Revenues," from PCGameworld.com Web site. Retrieved October 25, 2002, from http://www.pcgameworld.com/story.php/id/419/.

[7]David Becker, "When Games Stop Being Fun," CNET News.com Web site, April 12, 2002. Retrieved August 22, 2002, from http://news.com.com/2100-1040-881673.html.

Chapter 12

[1]A project of the *Digital Scriptorium, Rare Book, Manuscript, and Special Collections Library,* Duke University. Retrieved 31 October 2002 from http://scriptorium.lib.duke.edu/eaa/timeline.html.

[2]Kathleen Jamieson Hall, *Dirty Politics* (Oxford University Press, New York, 1992), pp. 54–55.

[3]"Internet Advertising Skyrockets: Online Advertising to Reach $33 Billion Worldwide by 2004," *Forrester Research, Inc.* (August 12, 1999). Retrieved 31 October 2002 from http://www.forrester.com.

[4]"*Coke Is It: True or False?* Interview with 'truth in advertising' specialist Ivan Preston," *Stay Free!,* Issue 14, Winter 1998. Retrieved 31 October 2002 from http://ibiblio.org/pub/electronic-publications/stay-free/archives/14/ivanpreston.html.

[5]Daniel J. Boorstin, "From News-Gathering to News-Making: A Flood of Pseudo Events." *The Modern World: The Image* (New York: Vintage, 1961).

[6]Stephen Millies, "The Ludlow Massacre and the Birth of Company Unions." *Workers World,* 26 January 1995. Retrieved 31 October 2002 from http://www.hartford-hwp.com/archives/45b/030.html.

[7]Andrew Marlatt, "Patrick Doesn't Work Here Anymore," *Wired,* December 1999, p. 114.

Chapter 13

[1]Tom Gormley, "'Ruination once again'—Cases in the study of media effects," www.theory.org.uk, 1998. Retrieved 4 November 2002 at http://www.theory.org.uk/effectg.htm.

[2]Garth S. Jowett, Ian C. Jarvie, and Kathryn H. Fuller (eds.), *Children and the Movies: Media Influence and the Payne Fund Controversy* (Cambridge, England: Cambridge University Press, 1996).

[3]P. W. Holaday and G. D. Stoddard, *Getting Ideas from the Movies* (New York: Macmillan, 1933).

[4]Pam Belluck, "A Battlefield of Dreams for Iowa Farmers," *The New York Times,* Aug. 5, 1999: A1.

[5]Garth Jowett et al. "Payne Fund Radio Broadcasting Research, 1928–1935." *Children and the Movies: Media Influence and the Payne Fund Controversy* (Cambridge, England: Cambridge University Press, 1996).

[6]A. L. Eisenberg, *Children and Radio Programs* (New York: Columbia University Press, 1936).

[7]H. Herzog, *Children and Their Leisure Time Listening to the Radio* (New York: Radio Council on Children's Programs, 1941).

[8]George Comstock, Steven Chaffee, Natan Katzman, Maxwell McCombs, and Donald Robers, *Television and Human Behavior* (New York: Columbia University Press, 1978), p. 12.

[9]"A Short Biography of Jean Piaget," Retrieved 4 November 2002 from http://www.piaget.org/biography/biog.html.

[10]Scott Ward, Daniel B. Wackman, and Ellen Wartella, *How Children Learn to Buy* (Thousand Oaks, CA: Sage Publications, 1977).

[11]R. S. Lichter and D. Amundson, *A Day of Television Violence* (Washington, DC: Center for Media and Public Affairs, 1992).

[12]Rolf Wigand Lichter, "Communication and Violent Behavior," *ICA Newsletter,* July 1999:5.

[13]Leonard Eron, University of Illinois at Chicago, Testimony before the Senate Committee on Commerce, Science and Transportation, Subcommittee on Communications, June 12, 1995.

[14]Statistics compiled by TV-Free America, Washington, D.C., 1996.

[15]National Television Violence Study, issued by Mediascope, February 1996.

[16]The UCLA Television Violence Monitoring Report, issued by the UCLA Center for Communications Policy, September 1995.

[17]C. W. Turner and M. R. Fern, *Effects of White Noise and Memory Cues on Verbal Aggression,* presented at meetings of the International Society for Research on Aggression, 1978.

[18]W. Schramm., J. Lyle, and E. B. Parker, *Television in the Lives of Our Children* (Stanford, CA: Stanford University Press, 1961).

[19]Brad J. Bushman, Roy Baumeister, and Angela D. Stack, "Catharsis, Aggression and Persuasive Influence: Self-Fulfilling or Self-Defeating Prophecies?" *Journal of Personality and Social Psychology.* Vol. 76, No. 3 (March 1999).

[20]Carl Hovland, Irving Janis, and Harold H. Kelley, *Communication and Persuasion* (New Haven: Yale University Press, 1953).

[21]David Chandler, "Why Do People Watch Television?" The Media and Communications Studies Site. Retrieved 4 November 2002, from http://www.aber.ac.uk/media /Documents/short/usegrat.html.

[22]Jane Levere, "When, Where and How Young Adults Get Information," New York Times on the Web. December 9, 1999. Retrieved 4 November 2002 from http://www.nytimes .com/library/financial/columns /120999media-adcol.html.

[23]Stuart Elliott, "Women's Group to Present Good, Bad and Ugly Awards," *The New York Times,* Sept. 28, 1999.

[24]*Internet News Takes Off: Event-Driven News Audiences,* Pew Center report, June 8, 1998:9. Retrieved 5 November 2002 from http://people-press.org/reports /display.php3?ReportID=88.

[25]Michael Schrage, "The Relationship Revolution," The Merrill Lynch Forum, 1998.

[26]Melinda Patterson Grenier, "Traffic to Web Sites over Two Days Sets Records," from WSJ.com, Sept. 13, 2001. Retrieved 15 July 2002 from http://www.wsj.com.

[27]Jeffrey Cole, "Surveying the Digital Future: A Longitudinal International Study of the Individual and Social Effects of PC/Internet Technology." Retrieved 5 November 2002, from http://www.webuse.umd .edu/abstracts2001/abstract _2001_cole.htm.

[28]Derek Top, "Arbitron Releases New Streaming Reports," *Streaming Media Newsletter,* received via e-mail, September 22, 2000.

Chapter 14

[1]Everette Dennis, David Grey, Donald Gilmor (eds.), *Justice Hugo Black and the First Amendment: "No Law" Means No Law* (Ames: Iowa State Press, 1978).

[2]Dwight L. Teeter, Jr., and Don R. Le Duc, *Law of Mass Communications* (Westbury, NY: The Foundation Press, 1992).

[3]"Vanessa Leggett Wins First Amendment Award," from Reporters Committee for Freedom of the Press Web site, http://www.rcfp.org. Retrieved 30 April 2002 from http://www .rcfp.org/news/2002/0411thepen. html.

[4]"How Effective Are Shield Laws?" from *Agents of Discovery: A Report on the Incidence of Subpoenas Served on the News Media in 1997,* on the Reporters Committee for Freedom of the Press Web site, http://www.rcfp.org. Retrieved 8 November 2002 from http: //www.rcfp.org/agents/shieldlaws .html.

[5]Reed E. Hundt, FCC Chairman. Transcript of speech given at The Museum of Television and Radio, New York, June 3, 1997. Retrieved 8 November 2002 from http://www.fcc.gov /Speeches/Hundt/spreh729.txt.

[6]"How Effective Are Shield Laws?" Retrieved 8 November 2002 from http://www.rcfp.org /agents/shieldlaws.html.

[7]Linda Greenhouse, "'Virtual' Child Pornography Ban Overturned," April 17, 2002, from New York Times on the Web, http://www.nytimes.com.

[8]Stephen Labaton, "Court Rejects F.C.C. Mandate to Broadcast Political Replies," October 12, 2000, in New York Times on the Web, http://www.nytimes.com. Retrieved 28 April 2002 from http://www.nytimes.com/2000 /10/12/politics/12FAIR.html.

[9]"Few Parents Use V-chip to Block TV Sex and Violence, but More Than Half Use TV Ratings to Pick What Kids Can Watch," July 24, 2001 news release from Kaiser Family Foundation. Retrieved 8 November 2002 from http://www.kff.org/content /2001/3158/V-Chip%20release .htm.

[10]Mark Goodman, "The Radio Act of 1927 as a Product of Progressivism," *Media History Monographs,* Volume 2, Number 2. Retrieved 8 November 2002 from http://www.scripps .ohiou.edu/mediahistory /mhmjour2-2.htm.

[11]Erik Barnouw, *A Tower of Babel: A History of Broadcasting in the United States,* Vol. 1. New York: Oxford University Press, 1966.

[12]Mark Goodman, "The Radio Act of 1927 as a Product of Progressivism," *Media History Monographs,* Volume 2, Number 2. Retrieved 8 November 2002 from http://www.scripps .ohiou.edu/mediahistory /mhmjour2-2.htm.

[13]M. S. Mander, "The Public Debate about Broadcasting in the Twenties: An Interpretive History," *Journal of Broadcasting,* 28(1984), 167–185.

[14]Alan B. Albarran and Gregory G. Pitts, *The Radio Broadcasting Industry,* pp. 27–29. Boston: Allyn & Bacon, 2001.

[15]Eli Noam and Robert Freeman, "The Media Monopoly and Other Myths," *Television Quarterly,* 1998, pp. 18–23.

[16]Matthew Rose, "High Court Supports Free-Lancers in Case on Electronic Databases," *Wall Street Journal,* A3, June 26, 2001.

Chapter 15

[1]Joseph Pulitzer, "The College of Journalism," *The North American Review,* May 1904.

[2]Paul F. Lazarsfeld and Robert K. Merton, "Mass Communication, Popular Taste and Organized Social Action," in Lyman Bryson (ed.), *The Communication of Ideas.* New York: Institute for Religious and Social Studies, 1948, pp. 95–118.

[3]Bernard Cohen, *The Press and Foreign Policy.* Princeton, NJ: Princeton University Press, 1963, p. 13.

[4]Daniel Hallin "Sound bite news: Television coverage of elections 1968–1988." *Journal of Communication,* 42(2), 1992, pp. 5–24. Also see William Shakespeare, *Julius Caesar.* Retrieved 7 November 2002 from http://www.litrix.com /caesar/caesa010.htm.

[5]Daniel Hallin, *We Keep America on Top of the World.* London: Routledge, 1994, p. 137.

[6]Herbert E. Alexander, "Financing Presidential Election Campaigns," *Issues of Democracy,* USIA Electronic Journals, Vol. 1, No. 13, September 1996. Retrieved 7 November 2002 from http: //usinfo.state.gov/journals /itdhr/0996/ijde/alex.htm.

[7]Syzybillo and Hartenbaum, "Political Advertising and the Broadcast Media," *Journal of Advertising,* Vol. 17, 1988.

[8]Larry Sabato, *The Rise of Political Consultants: New Way of Winning Elections.* New York: Basic Books, 1981, pp. 165–166.

[9]Kathleen Hall Jamieson, *Dirty Politics.* New York: Oxford University Press, 1992, pp. 19–20.

[10]Everette E. Dennis, Wendy Zeligson, Martha FitzSimon, John Pavlik, Dirk Smillie, David Stebenne, and Mark Thalhimer, "An Uncertain Season: Reporting in the Postprimary Period," The Freedom Forum Media Studies Center, 1992: 21.

Chapter 16

[1]Frederick S. Siebert, Wilbur Schramm, and Theodore Peterson, *Four Theories of the Press: The Authoritarian, Libertarian, Social Responsibility, and Soviet Communist Concepts of What the Press Should Be and Do.* Champaign: University of Illinois Press, 1956.

[2]H. Schiller, *Who knows: Information in the age of the Fortune 500.* Norwood, NJ: Ablex, 1981. C. Hamelink, *Information imbalance: Core and periphery in questioning the media: A critical introduction.* London: Sage, 1990.

[3]Michael Kudlak, "A Climate of Intimidation," from IPI World Press Freedom Review on IPI Web site at http://www. freemedia.at. Retrieved 9 November 2002 from http://www.freemedia.at/wpfr /world.html.

[4]Jerome Aumente, Dean Mills, Peter Gross, Owen Johnson, Ray Hiebert, and David L. Paletz (eds.), *Eastern European Journalism: Before, during and after Communism.* Waverly, Victoria, Australia: Hampton Press, 1999.

[5]Susan Taylor Martin, "Scrappy Al-Jazeera stands up," September 22, 2002, *St. Petersburg Times.*

Glossary

A

actualities used in radio and television to denote edited audio or video clips of people interviewed.

ad agency commission a percentage amount of the cost of an advertisement taken by the advertising agency that helped create and sell the ad.

advertising an ancient form of human communication generally designed to inform or persuade members of the public with regard to some product or service.

advertorial a type of display advertisement that is created to look like an article within the publication, although most publications have the words "advertisement" or "paid advertisement" in tiny print somewhere near the advertorial.

agenda setting function a role the media play during the course of deciding what topics to cover, which then, by virtue of being covered in the media, become topics of discussion and perceived importance to the public.

AIDA a foundational principle of effective advertising, this refers to attention (sometimes, awareness), interest, desire, and action.

Alien and Sedition Acts a series of four acts passed by the U.S. Congress in 1798 that, among other things, prohibited sedition, or spoken or written criticism of the U.S. government, and imposed penalties of a fine or imprisonment upon conviction. Although they expired in 1801, other sedition acts have been passed periodically, especially during times of war.

amplitude modulation (AM) the original method of radio broadcasting; it refers to the height of the electromagnetic wave being adjusted. AM is generally not as clear as FM and has a shorter range, usually about 100 miles maximum.

analog media originally used in audio recording for media that was analogous to the sound it was recreating. It now refers to all nondigitized media, such as print media, audio and video recordings, photography, and film.

analog-to-digital converter (ADC) a device that electronically changes the continuously variable analog signal into a multilevel digital signal without changing its content.

Armstrong, Edwin Howard inventor of FM radio transmission and Columbia University engineering professor.

aspect ratio the ratio of a screen's height to its width. The incompatible aspect ratios of films and television mean that films either have to be cropped to fit within a television screen or, in order to keep the original aspect ratio, black borders must appear on the top and bottom of the screen.

Associated Press (AP) founded as a not-for-profit members' cooperative in 1848 by a group of six New York newspaper publishers in order to share the costs of gathering news by telegraph. Today 1700 newspapers and 5000 television and radio stations are members of this news-gathering organization.

asynchronous media media that do not require the audience to assemble at a given time in order to use that media. Examples of asynchronous media are printed materials or recorded audio or video.

audience fragmentation along with media differences, message characteristics, and individual characteristics and conditions, this is one of the four basic factors that affect mediated persuasive communication. The growth in media channels over the course of the 20th century essentially splintered the audience for mass communication.

auteur French for *author*, this term is usually used in the context of filmmakers who stamp their vision on the films they make, as opposed to a form of filmmaking in which the director has but one role among many other professionals in the making of a film.

authoritarian theory of the press a theory of how the mass media works in which authoritarian governments exert direct control over the media.

automation a process in which machines or computer programs do the work that was formerly done by humans. In mass communication terms, automation can range from spreadsheet programs that sort data in a variety of ways to Web site search engines and other such programs.

avatar a graphical representation of an Internet user, which can be used in online communities or to otherwise represent oneself on the Web.

B

Baird, John Logie Scottish inventor who created the first mechanically scanned television device in 1923. His 30-line TV had better resolution than the first attempts at electronic televisions.

balance in news coverage, the concept of presenting sides equally or of reporting on a broad range of news events.

banner ad an advertisement across the top of a Web page; the original form of advertising on the Web.

beat a geographic or subject area of coverage by a reporter that he or she specializes in. Common beats in large- or medium-sized newspapers can include education, crime, or state politics.

Bennett, James Gordon founder of the *New York Herald* in 1835. He started many features found in modern newspapers, including a financial page, editorial commentary, and public affairs reporting.

bit short for binary digit, it is the smallest unit of digital information. A bit has a single binary value, either 0 or 1.

blockbuster a big-budget, high-production quality film, often with famous stars, that is very successful at the box office and that is usually produced by one of the large Hollywood studios

Brady, Mathew B. a famous photographer of the nineteenth century who took portraits of many famous people of his day as well as Civil War battlefield photographs.

branding the process of creating in the consumer's mind a clear identity for a particular company's product, logo, or trademark.

broadband a network connection that allows for a large amount of bandwidth to be transmitted, which allows for more information to be sent in a shorter period of time. Although there are no agreed-upon transmission speeds that can define broadband, most experts agree it can include aDSL, DSL, ISDN, cable modem, satellite, and T1 and T3 lines, as well as fiber optic trunk lines.

broadcast originally used in terms of widely spreading numerous seeds in a field as opposed to planting them one by one, it came to be the term used for radio and later transmissions from which a single source sent messages over the airwaves to a wide number of people.

byte the most common base unit used to measure computer storage and information, it consists of eight bits, or some combination of 0s and 1s, to form letters, numbers, and all modes of computer information that are displayed.

C

calotype the first type of photography that created a negative photograph from which positive copies could be made, although it was inferior in picture quality to the daguerreotype.

camera obscura a dark box or room with a small hole in it that allowed an inverted image of an outside scene to be shown on the opposite inner wall.

Cary, Mary Shadd the first African American woman to edit a weekly newspaper. She founded and edited the *Provincial Freeman* in Canada after leaving the United States to avoid being captured and put into slavery under the Fugitive Slave Act.

catharsis in media effects research, the belief that watching violent television content may purge violent feelings from the viewer and thereby have a beneficial effect, rather than a negative one as is commonly thought. Research has failed to confirm the cathartic effect, however.

cathode ray tube (CRT) a device that is still used in most television screens and computer monitors in which electrons are transmitted to a screen for viewing.

censorship the act of prohibiting certain expression or content. Censors usually do not target the whole publication, program, or Web site, but seek to prohibit some part of the content.

Chiariglione, Leonardo former leader of MPEG and now in charge of the Secure Digital Music Initiative, a group created by the recording industry to examine ways to protect copyrights and stop unauthorized copying of music in the digital age.

Children's Television Act created in 1990, it places limits on the amount of commercial content that programming can carry and forces stations to carry certain amounts of educational programming for children 16 and under, among other provisions to help protect children.

Cinematographe an early movie projector and camera technology that allowed for projection of films to a small audience.

circuit switching the original system used for telephony in which circuits connected two people communicating. Once the circuit was connected, or "on," the people on either end of the circuit used the whole circuit exclusively, even if they didn't speak. When they hung up, the circuit was disconnected by an operator and available for others to use.

classified advertising a type of advertising usually found in print media, especially newspapers but also in some magazines and now increasingly online; messages are posted by individuals and organizations to sell specific goods or services.

clear and present danger a restriction on speech when it meets both of the following conditions: 1) It is intended to incite or produce dangerous activity (such as falsely shouting fire in a crowded theater);

and 2) it is likely to succeed in achieving the purported result.

client/server network a model of network computing in which some computers store and send information to other computers on the network (clients). For a number of technical reasons, this has been the primary model used for the Internet.

coaxial cable an insulated and layered conducting wire typically about a half-inch thick; the delivery medium traditionally used for delivering cable television to the home. Coaxial cable provides broadband transmission capabilities for the delivery of full-motion video as well as telephony.

codex a book with individually bound pages; the form that replaced the scroll in the early centuries AD.

cognitive response model a theoretical model explaining how negative political advertising works that proposes the persuasion that occurs during or following a communication is in fact self-persuasion.

collaborative filtering a process carried out by software that records a Web site user's viewing or buying patterns and then compares those with similar patterns by other users to determine some likely areas of common interest. Amazon.com is the most famous example of a company using collaborative filtering to help suggest books and products of interest based on previous activity on the site.

Communications Act of 1934 an Act that established the FCC and gave it power to regulate broadcasting such as in licensing stations, assigning call letters and radio frequencies, and levying fines on stations that did not meet its regulations. The Act was superseded by the Telecommunication Act of 1996.

Community Antenna Television (CATV) also known as cable television, it was developed in 1948 so communities in hilly terrain could still have access to television broadcasts.

content-based systems search and retrieval systems that allow searches based on the attributes of content, such as visual or audio features of a piece of content regardless of the details of what is shown or heard.

contextualization the act of putting online news into a larger context by adding hyperlinks to other news sites on related issues, organizational Web sites, expert or primary sources, and online communities.

convergence the coming together of computing, telecommunications, and media in a digital environment. Convergence and the changes it is bringing are fundamentally changing many aspects of mass media and communication.

convergent media buying purchasing online ads as well as complementary space or time on the parent media company's other media properties, including newspaper, magazine, television, or radio.

cookie information that a Web site puts on a user's local hard drive so that it can recognize when that computer accesses the Web site again. Cookies allow for conveniences like password recognition and personalization.

copyright the exclusive right to use, publish, and distribute a work such as a piece of writing, music, film, or video.

correlation primarily the interpretation of aspects of society as a function of mass communication, and the individual to society, including how journalism, advertising, and public relations shape public opinion through comments or criticism or through propaganda.

cost per thousand (CPM) the standard unit for measuring advertising rates for publications, based on circulation.

critical–cultural studies studies that describe phenomena in words instead of numbers or measures. Ethnographic studies, such as interviews with people to learn about beliefs or trends, are an example of critical–cultural studies. Also called qualitative studies.

cultivation analysis a theory of media effects that states television cultivates audiences to view reality in a manner similar to the world portrayed in television programs. For example, it posits that viewing thousands of murders on television is unlikely to increase the chances that an individual will commit murder but does lead to a belief that the world is a more dangerous place than it actually is.

cultural studies approach a framework in studying theories of communication that shuns the scientific approach used by scholars in the empirical school and that tries to examine the symbolic environment created by mass media and the role it plays in culture and society.

cultural transmission primarily refers to the transference of the dominant culture as a function of mass communication, as well as its subcultures, from one generation to the next or to immigrants. This function includes socialization, which the media perform in helping persons learn society's rules or how to fit into society.

D

Daguerre, Jacques Louis a French scene painter and inventor of the daguerreotype, an early type of photography.

daguerreotype an early type of photography that used a silver-coated copper plate coated with iodine vapor to create a positive image. Although image clarity was extremely good, daguerreotypes did not allow for copies of photographs to be made, unlike another early photography type, the calotype.

Day, Benjamin publisher of the *New York Sun,* he ushered in the era of the penny press when he began offering his paper on the streets for a penny on September 3, 1833.

daypart a segment of time used by radio and television program planners to decide who the primary audience is during that time of day or night.

de Forest, Lee considered the "father" of radio broadcasting technology because of his invention that permitted reliable voice transmissions for both point-to-point and broadcasting.

deep linking a hypertext link to another Web site's inside page or pages rather than its homepage.

developmental learning a theoretical approach, based on psychologist Jean Piaget's research, that posits learning as a progressive process in which a child's intellectual capacity grows through several stages of increasing ability.

Digital Millennium Copyright Act (DMCA) an act of Congress in 1998 that reformed copyright law comprehensively in trying to update copyright laws for the digital age. Key provisions included the circumvention of copyright protection systems, fair use in a digital environment, and Internet service provider (ISP) liability for content sent through their lines.

digital television (DTV) television programming that is created, distributed, and shown using digital means, which offers much sharper pictures and more functionality than traditional analog TV.

digital watermark computer code (usually invisible, but sometimes visible) inserted into any digital content, whether images, graphics, audio, video, or even text documents, that authenticates the source of that content.

digitization the process in which media is made into computer-readable form.

dime novel the first paperback book form, which cost ten cents. This made it accessible even to the poor.

Disney, Walter Elias creator of animated cartoon characters such as Mickey Mouse, Goofy, and Donald Duck and classic cartoons such as *Bambi, Snow White and the Seven Dwarfs,* and *Fantasia.* Founded the Disney media empire.

display advertising a type of advertising in print media that usually consists of illustrations or images and text and that can be anywhere from a small section of a page to a full-page or multipage advertise-ment. Because of their high costs, they are usually bought by large companies or organizations.

E

Edison, Thomas Alva inventor whose inventions include the electric light, the phonograph, and the Kinetoscope. Edison's lab in Menlo Park, New Jersey, had over 60 scientists and produced as many as 400 patent applications a year.

Eisenstein, Sergei a Russian filmmaking pioneer who was the first to use quick edits and crosscutting to help tell stories visually. He also experimented with combining music with scenes for maximum audience effect.

electronic news gathering (ENG) tools such as video cameras and satellite dishes that allow journalists to gather and broadcast news much more quickly than in the past.

electronic program guides (EPG) guides available on television that provide program listings and some simple interactivity such as ordering pay-per-view programs through the television or buying CDs or DVDs of music or shows that are listed.

entertainment a function of mass communication that is performed in part by all three of the other four main functions (surveillance, correlation, cultural transmission) but also involves the generation of content designed specifically and exclusively to entertain.

episodic framing a type of media framing mostly used by television news that portrays a story in terms of concrete events that highlight real issues, such as covering a local crime by focusing on the perpetrator. This is in contrast to thematic framing.

equal-time provision the requirement that broadcasters give equal air time to opposing candidates running for election for commentaries and commercials. It did not apply to candidates appearing in newscasts, as part of documentaries, or in news event coverage. The provision was thrown out by the FCC in October 2000, and its future is unclear as it works its way to a hearing by the Supreme Court.

ethnographic studies taken from methods used in anthropology, a researcher enters a culture or milieu and studies how the population behaves in its natural setting, trying to create as little impact as possible while conducting his or her studies.

expectancy theory a motivational framework that proposes an individual will act in a certain way based on the anticipation that the act will be followed by a given outcome and on the attractiveness of that outcome to the individual.

expert source clearinghouse a company that maintains lists of expert sources in various fields from which journalists can draw when they need an authoritative source to comment on some news story.

F

fairness in news coverage, the concept of covering all relevant sides of an issue and allowing spokespeople representing those various sides a chance to be covered in the same way.

Fairness Doctrine adopted by the FCC in 1949, it required broadcasters to seek out and present all sides of a controversial issue they were covering. It was discarded by the FCC in 1987.

fair use an exception to copyright law that allows someone to use an excerpt of a work without paying for its use. Quotations from works in reviews or their use in commentary or criticism are examples of fair use.

Federal Communication Commission (FCC) the principal communications regulatory body at the federal level in the United States, established in 1934.

Federal Radio Commission (FRC) formed by the Radio Act of 1927, the commission was the precursor to the FCC and created a policy that favored fewer, high-power radio broadcasting stations rather than more numerous, low-power stations. The commission revoked thousands of existing radio licenses as it implemented its policies.

First Amendment amendment to the U.S. Constitution that guarantees that Congress shall make no law restricting freedom of speech, press, or religion.

fourth estate another term for the press, or journalism, in which it acts as a fourth branch of government and one that watches the other branches (executive, legislative, and judicial).

Freedom of Information Act (FOIA) an act that provides legal access to public records maintained by the federal government. States and local jurisdictions also have freedom of information laws that allow public access to state or local records.

frequency modulation (FM) the length of the wave is modulated with FM. It generally has better sound but relies on line-of-sight transmission, meaning that mountains, tall buildings, or other obstructions can block reception.

functionalist paradigm a research paradigm that posits that people have certain needs, especially psychological and social, which they seek to satisfy through media usage.

G

gatekeeping an aspect of communication theory in which experts, or editors, serve as content filters of mass mediated communication

for others in deciding what is more or less important and what an audience sees.

Gates, Bill founder, chairman, and chief software architect of Microsoft Corporation, which produces the Windows operating system and popular software such as Word, Excel, PowerPoint, and Access.

genre a type of story that has recognizable and defined elements, usually with the same types of characters, plot development, and story structure.

global positioning system (GPS) a system of satellites that provide location information anywhere in the world, operating at frequencies between 1227 MHz and 1575 MHz.

gramophone developed by inventor Emil Berliner, it used a flat disc to record sound rather than a cylinder that was used up to that time.

graphical user interface (GUI) a computer interface that shows graphical representations of file structures, applications, and files in the form of folders, icons, and windows.

graphophone an improvement on Thomas Edison's phonograph in recording audio, it used beeswax to record sound rather than tinfoil. Developed by Alexander Graham Bell and inventor Charles Tainter.

Gutenberg Bible one of a handful of surviving Bibles printed by Johannes Gutenberg, considered the first mechanically printed works in Europe.

Gutenberg, Johannes German printer credited with creating the first mechanical printing press in Europe in 1455.

H

Hays Code a code established in 1930 by the movie industry to censor itself regarding showing of nudity or glorifying antisocial acts in movies. Officials for the Hays office had to approve each film that was distributed to a mass audience.

Hearst, William Randolph newspaper publisher and media magnate who owned several major newspapers. His circulation wars and rivalry with Joseph Pulitzer's newspapers helped sparked the term "yellow journalism" because of the sensational, and sometimes false, coverage before and during the Spanish-American War in 1898.

Hertz, Heinrich German scientist who experimented with electromagnetic waves and demonstrated the existence of radio waves. His work set the stage for the development of modern wireless communications.

hierarchy of effects model a theoretical model that proposes how negative political advertising works based on a classification of media effects into three categories: the cognitive (knowledge or intellectual

realm), the affective (emotional or motivational realm), and the conative (behavioral realm).

high-definition television (HDTV) a new form of television with much higher resolution than standard television, as well as a different screen size ratio.

Hutchins Commission a commission that issued an influential report on the press in 1947 called *A Free and Responsible Press* that outlines the responsibilities the press has toward public service and states that if news organizations fail in that responsibility then some other agency should carry them out.

hyperlink a word, graphic, or image that is linked through HTML code to another Web page or media element either within the same Web site or in a different Web site on the World Wide Web.

hypertext text online that is linked to another Web page, Web site, or different part of the same Web page by HTML coding.

hypertext markup language (HTML) the language used to create Web pages and determine how they appear; allows pages to have hypertext links and other interactive features.

hypertext transfer protocol (HTTP) a protocol that enables the standardized transfer of text, audio, and video files, as well as e-mail from one address to another.

hypodermic needle model a model of media effects, also called the "magic bullet" model, largely derived from learning theory and simple stimulus–response models in behavioral psychology, that states media has a profound, direct, and uniform impact on the public.

I

icons small images or graphics that represent an object, function, or command.

indecent speech language or material that, in context, depicts or describes, in terms patently offensive as measured by contemporary community standards for the broadcast medium, sexual or excretory organs or activities.

independent films films made by production companies outside the main Hollywood studios.

independent labels small record production and distribution companies that are not part of the five major label companies. They can include companies producing only one or two albums a year to larger independents such as Disney. The independent labels produce 66 percent of the albums each year but only 20 percent of the sales.

individual characteristics along with media differences, message characteristics, and audience fragmentation, one of four basic factors that affect mediated persuasive com-

munication. Individual characteristics are the various identifiable qualities, such as demographic factors, geographic location, and media habits that account for or shape public tastes, preferences, opinions, knowledge, and behaviors.

institutional/issue one of the two basic types of advertising. It usually tries to improve the image of an organization or persuade people to have a more favorable viewpoint on an issue.

intellectual property (IP) ideas that have commercial value, such as literary or artistic works, patents, business methods, and industrial processes.

interactive television (ITV) television programming that allows viewers to navigate through on-screen programming guides and set reminder times or order products, select parts of a program to view more details, choose camera angles or replays themselves, click on items in the show to purchase, or engage in online discussions with other viewers as part of the program.

interactivity although an exact definition is still being debated, for digital media purposes interactivity can be defined as having three main elements: 1) a dialog that occurs between a human and a computer program, 2) a dialog that occurs simultaneously or nearly so, and 3) an audience that has some measure of control over what media content they see and in what order they see it.

interpersonal communication communication between two or more individuals, usually in a small group, although it can involve communication between a live speaker and an audience.

interpretive reporting a type of reporting that tries to put the facts of a story into a broader context by relying on knowledge and experience the reporter has about the subject.

interstitial ad a type of pop-up ad on the Web that opens a new browser window when a Web site is clicked on, forcing users to close the window to see the Web site they originally wanted to see.

intrapersonal communication communication within an individual.

J

joint operating arrangements (JOAs) legal agreements that permit newspapers in the same market or city to merge their business operations for reasons of economics while maintaining independent editorial operations.

K

Kinetoscope a peephole movie viewer invented by Thomas Edison that allowed one viewer at a time to watch a short film.

L

laugh track a device used in television sitcoms that generates prerecorded laughter, timed to coincide with punch lines of jokes.

libel a type of defamation that is written and published, such as a false attack on a person's character, that damages a person's reputation.

libertarian theory a theory of international mass communication that is rooted in the idea of the individual and his or her rights to publish whatever he or she wants, even material that is critical to the government or of government officials.

limited effects a view that sees media as a minor component in a much larger, and more fundamental, system of societal and institutional influences to which all are subject.

listserv an automated mailing list for e-mail that allows a user to send a message to multiple users on the list and that allows list members to automatically subscribe, unsubscribe, or post messages to all other members in the list, depending on the listserv settings.

listservers also known as listservs, these are automated mailing list administrators that allow for easy subscription, subscription cancellation, and sending of e-mails to subscribers on the e-mail list.

Lumiere brothers Auguste and Louis Lumiere used Edison's Kinetoscope to create the Cinematographe, which was not only portable but allowed projection of movies as well so they could be shown to an audience.

lurker a person on an online discussion board who does not contribute to discussions by posting messages but who simply reads what others write.

M

magnetic recording a type of recording that involves placing tiny iron-based magnetic particles in substrate, such as a plastic film. The particles can be modified, or "written," by magnetizing them in either a north or south pole direction, thereby encoding or storing information.

major labels the five biggest recording arts companies that control much of the music industry, partly through their powerful distribution channels and ability to market music to mass audiences. They are Universal Music Group, BMG Entertainment, Sony Music, EMI, and the Warner Music Group.

Marconi, Guglielmo Italian inventor and creator of radio telegraphy, or wireless transmission, in 1899.

mass communication communication to a large group or groups of people that remain largely unknown to the sender of the message.

massively multiplayer online games (MMOGs) a type of video game played online with tens of thousands of other players who are also online. The format allows for real-time communication and trading items, as well as fighting each other or working together toward common goals.

mass-market paperbacks introduced in 1939 by Pocket Books, these books were small enough to fit in a back pocket, had laminated covers, and cost 25 cents, ushering in the paperback book revolution.

McLuhan, Marshall A communication scholar who wrote *Understanding Media* and *The Gutenberg Galaxy,* among other books. He is perhaps most famous for creating the "global village" metaphor regarding electronic media and his often-misunderstood phrase "the medium is the message."

media differences along with message characteristics, audience fragmentation, and individual characteristics and conditions, one of four basic factors that affect mediated persuasive communication. Media differences are the qualities that distinguish the various media of mass communication, such as print vs. electronic and interactive vs. passive.

media framing the practice of organizing news and information within a central idea or theme to provide some sort of context so the information makes sense as part of a greater whole.

media literacy the process of interacting with media content and critically analyzing it by considering its particular presentation, its underlying political or social messages, and ownership and regulation issues that may affect what media is presented in what form.

media of mass communication any technologically based means of communicating between or among large groups of people distributed widely over space or time.

media oligopoly a marketplace in which media ownership and diversity are severely limited and the actions of any single media group substantially affect its competitors, including the content and price of media products for both consumers and advertisers.

mediated communication communication that involves a process by which a message, or communication, is transmitted via some form, or medium.

Méliès, Georges an early French filmmaker who pioneered the use of special effects in film in order to show imaginative stories.

message characteristics along with media differences, audience fragmentation, and individual characteristics and conditions, one of four basic factors that affect mediated persuasive communication. Message characteristics are the qualities of the communications themselves, such as the level of complexity, credibility, or emotional or informational quality of a message.

Metcalfe's Law the value of a network rises in proportion to the square of the number of people on that network. In other words, the more people who are connected to a network such as the Internet, the more valuable that network becomes.

micropayments small fees, even under a penny, paid for each online transaction, such as downloading a song or text article.

mobilization a function of mass communication in which the media can influence the public, especially regarding political issues or movements.

modem derived from the terms modulate–demodulate; a device that converts digital signals from a computer to analog signals for transmission over a phone line, as well as analog signals being transmitted to digital signals.

morgue an archive of news articles or photographs from a publication and other publications on various topics that can be used as a background reference source for a journalist doing a story.

Morse, Samuel F. B. inventor of the telegraph and the system of clicks used to communicate on it called Morse code. He was also a noted painter and inventor.

MPEG Motion Pictures Experts Group, established in 1988 and responsible for creating the standards for digital and audio compression. Also used for the types of compression, such as MPEG-1, MPEG-4, and so on.

muckrakers a group of journalists in the latter 19th and early 20th centuries who investigated business and political corruption. Their activities were likened to raking up mud, or muck, by Theodore Roosevelt, who meant it as a term of derision.

multicast simultaneously transmitting multiple channels of compressed digital content over the television airwaves.

multimedia a combination of different types of media in one package; thus film or video with sound is a type of multimedia because it combines visual and audio elements. Web pages that combine text, video, animation, audio, or graphics are another type of multimedia.

multipoint, multichannel distribution systems (MMDS) a type of terrestrial wireless service that can transmit as many as 33 analog TV channels over the air via microwave transmission and up to 99 compressed digital channels.

multitasking in a computer environment, doing several activities at once with a variety of programs, such as simultaneously doing word-processing, spreadsheet, and database work, while conducting real-time chat through an instant messenger service.

Murrow, Edward R. a radio and later television journalist and announcer who set the standard for journalistic excellence on television during television's Golden Age.

N

narrowband a network connection that does not provide very much bandwidth, thus receiving and sending information more slowly than broadband connections. Dial-up modems and some of the early wireless connection speeds of 56 kHz or under are considered narrowband.

narrowcasting specialized media channels used to deliver messages to highly targeted audiences that can be defined by interests, demographics, or some other specific focus.

National Television System Committee (NTSC) the standard television protocol for television transmission in the United States and Japan, in which the image consists of 525 horizontal lines per frame scanned left to right and top to bottom. Other parts of the world use either the PAL system or the SECAM systems as television protocols, none of which is compatible with the others.

networked media media that exist in an interconnected series of communication nodes or points.

newsgroup a category for discussion groups within Usenet.

news hole typically used with newspapers, it is the amount of total space available after advertisement space has been blocked out.

Newspaper Preservation Act created in 1970, it is intended to preserve a diversity of editorial opinion in communities where only two competing, or independently owned, daily newspapers exist.

O

objectivity a journalistic principle that says journalists should be impartial and free of bias in their reporting. This principle has come under attack in recent years because of the impossibility of people being completely objective and has largely been replaced by the concepts of fairness and balance.

obscenity one of the forms of speech not protected by the First Amendment and thus subject to censorship. Although the exact definition of the term has been difficult to achieve in various court cases, generally a three-part standard is applied for media: the material must appeal to prurient interests as defined by community standards; the content must show in an offensive manner sexual conduct; and the content on the whole must lack serious artistic, literary, political, or scientific value.

oligopoly an economic structure in which a few very large, very powerful, and very rich owners control an industry or series of related industries.

one-way symmetric public relations a model of public relations used in the press agentry format, in which information about a company is almost exclusively sent by the company via the media to the public.

open source any program in which the programmer allows the source code of the program to be seen by others. This lets others improve upon and modify a program's source code. Most proprietary software programs do not allow the public to see their source code.

opinion poll a poll that is usually conducted by professional polling organizations asking members of the public their opinions on issues or political candidates.

optical fiber a transparent filament, usually made of glass or plastic, that uses light to carry information. This makes transmission of information much faster and with much greater capacity than twisted-pair copper wires or coaxial cable.

optical storage uses light in the form of lasers to store and read data of all types, whether text, audio, or video. Using light is highly efficient and permits storage devices to record vastly greater amounts of data in small spaces and enable faster retrieval of the stored data than do magnetic storage devices.

P

packet switching a type of switching that occurs within a network in which information is divided up into pieces, or packets, and transported as separate packets using the least congested routes. At the end of the route the packets are reassembled in their proper order and delivered over the telephone line or Internet.

paid programming also called "infomercials," these are 30- or 60-minute television shows that seek to sell a product and that usually involve a celebrity spokesperson and testimony from customers about how good the product is.

paparazzi press photographers who attempt to get candid photos of celebrities to sell to various media outlets.

patent law protects the right to produce and sell an invention, rather than a literary or artistic work, which is covered by copyright law.

Payne Fund studies a 12-volume series of media effects research on film conducted between 1928 and 1933 by some of the most prominent psychologists, educators, and sociologists of the day. It helped further the move for the movie industry's self-regulation and laid the foundation for the movie rating system.

payola cash or gifts given to radio disc jockeys by record labels in exchange for greater air play given to the label's artists or most recent songs. The practice is now illegal after several scandals involving payola in the 1950s.

peer-to-peer (P2P) a computer communications model in which all users have equal abilities to store, send, and accept communications from other users.

penny press newspapers that sold for a penny, making them accessible to everyone. They differed from older newspaper forms in that they tried to attract as large an audience as possible and were supported by advertising rather than subscriptions.

performance-based advertising any form of online ad buying in which an advertiser pays for results rather than paying for the size of the publisher's audience, or CPM.

personal information space a virtual "space" online in which a user has stored information about him- or herself, contact information, and material the user may have received from the Internet.

personal video recorders (PVRs) another term for digital video recording and playback devices, including such products as ReplayTV, TiVo, and UltimateTV. Devices like these, which allow many hours of recording and several other features, will fundamentally alter the relationship between the TV viewer and broadcaster.

personalization the ability of media content producers to provide content that is of interest to a specific user based either on criteria the user has selected, such as a ZIP code, or on automated tracking of their Web-viewing habits.

persuasive communication the process of using messages to influence others to adopt a new position, opinion, attitude, or behavior.

phonograph first patented by Thomas Edison in 1877 as a "talking machine," it used a tinfoil cylinder to record voices from telephone conversations. Successive technological improvements in electronics and the type of material the sounds were recorded on made sound quality better.

point-and-click functionality the ability to use a mouse to move a cursor on the screen and to click a mouse button to interact with what is being pointed to, such as opening a folder with files or starting a program by clicking on its icon.

preferred position balancing theory a theory stated by Don Pember that states there must be a balance between speech and other rights, with speech given a preferred position (especially print media) and limitations on freedom of speech usually being illegal.

press agentry the practice of getting publicity for clients by getting them mentioned in media outlets, such as news stories or feature articles, as well as on television or radio.

press freedom model an adaptation of a famous question on media effects first posed by psychologist Harold Lasswell, it provides a guide for understanding the legal framework for restricting media freedom in the United States by asking seven questions.

print on demand (POD) a technology developed in the late 1990s that allows for high-speed printing and binding of a book requested by a customer.

prior restraint situation in which the government prevents or blocks the publication, broadcasting, showing, or distribution of media content, whether in print, over the air, in movie theaters, or online.

product placement the practice of having actual products shown prominently and used in television shows and movies, which advertisers pay for.

product/service one of the two basic types of advertising and the most common. It tells the audience what to do in getting them to buy a product or use a service.

propaganda the regular dissemination of a belief, doctrine, cause, or information that reflects the views or interests of the group advocating the belief or doctrine.

public information campaign media program often funded by the government and designed to achieve some social goal, or what might be called social engineering.

public service announcement (PSA) advertising-like message for which the media donate time or space to organizations with a worthy purpose that ostensibly benefits the public.

puffery exaggerated advertising claims deemed allowable by the FTC because they are unverifiable statements of opinion that cannot be tested.

Pulitzer, Joseph newspaper publisher and owner of the *St. Louis Post-Dispatch*, the *New York Post*, and the *New York World*. After the sensational coverage of the Spanish-American War in 1898, Pulitzer advocated professionalism in journalism and bequeathed money to found the Graduate School of Journalism at Columbia University.

push poll a type of negative political advertising that appears to be a telephone poll but is actually a telemarketing campaign to sway voters by giving them false or misleading information about opposing candidates.

Q

quantitative studies—studies that focus on numbers and measures and experimentation to describe phenomena. Researchers usually have a hypothesis they are trying to prove or disprove through controlled experimentation.

R

Radio Act of 1912 Act that assigned three- and four-letter codes to radio stations and assigned frequencies to the stations, as well as limiting broadcasting to the 360-meter wavelength.

Radio Act of 1927 an act of Congress that replaced the Radio Act of 1912 and created the Federal Radio Commission, precursor to the FCC, and that was intended to help establish some sort of regulation and order over the chaos of the largely unregulated airwaves. It helped establish the principle that the airwaves were a limited public good and that companies using those airwaves had a duty to act responsibly toward the public in terms of the type of material they broadcast.

random access memory usually used for a type of computer memory and abbreviated to RAM, in storage technology terms it is a type of media that allows for readers or viewers to randomly obtain specific pieces of content they are looking for by doing searches, using an index, or taking some other action.

rate card a listing of advertising rates by size, placement, and other characteristics such as whether ads are black-and-white or full-color. Frequency discounts are also usually offered, and the listed rates are usually negotiable, especially for large advertisers.

rating used in broadcast media to explain the numbers of households that watched a particular show.

reliability in media research terms, the extent of how accurate or repeatable a certain result is in an experiment.

royalties the payments artists or copyright holders receive for the works they produce, paid as a percentage of the income from the number of works sold.

S

Sarnoff, David president and chief executive officer of RCA. He helped push the development of television as a mass medium, yet blocked the development of FM radio for years because its adoption would hurt AM listenership and the AM radio receivers that RCA produced and sold.

selective processing a belief in media effects research that media processing by individuals is selective and that they accept information that tends to confirm what they feel they already know to be true.

sensational journalism news that exaggerates or features lurid details and depictions of events in order to get a larger audience.

sequential access memory a type of media in which a reader, viewer, or user must go through the media in the order they received it in order to find specific information they are looking for.

shield laws laws intended to protect journalists from legal challenges to their freedom to report the news.

simplified communications model developed by Wilbur Schramm in 1954 and based on the mathematical theory of communication. It includes a source, who encodes a message, or signal, which is transmitted (via the media or directly via interpersonal communication) to a destination, where the receiver decodes it.

slander a type of defamation that is spoken, as opposed to written (libel), that damages a person's reputation or otherwise harms them.

smart mob a term coined by author Howard Rheingold to define a group of people communicating with each other via text messaging or wireless networks that allow them to coordinate their activities even though they are in different places.

soap opera a type of programming that began on radio and successfully moved to television but that is now threatened with the rise of media types and changes in lifestyles. Soap operas are dramatic story series involving numerous characters and aimed at a daytime audience of homemakers.

social responsibility theory a theory of international mass communication that perhaps best exemplifies the media's role in democratic societies. It says that the media play an important role in informing the public of important information that allows them to make informed decisions, so therefore the media should be largely free of governmental constraints in providing news.

soft news day a day in which not much of importance happens so editors are more likely to add features that may not be of real news value, such as human-interest stories.

sound bite the length of time a news subject is allowed to speak without being edited by a reporter. It also has come to refer to short utterances that are catchy and designed to capture the media's attention.

soviet theory a theory of international mass communication that states the media should be publicly owned and used to further the needs of the working class.

spam unwanted e-mail sent out by advertisers as a mass mailing.

spiral of silence hypothesis states that people are naturally afraid of isolation, realize that if they are in the minority on a issue they are likely to be isolated, and have a kind of sixth sense that helps them gauge when their opinions are contrary to the majority, which makes them refrain from expressing their opinions.

storage technology any type of device or medium in which information can be maintained for later retrieval.

subtext the message beneath the message; the underlying, or implicit, message that is being conveyed by media content.

superstation a local TV station that reaches a national audience by beaming its programming nationwide via satellite to local cable systems, which then transmit the program to local subscribers.

superstitial ad a type of pop-up ad on the Web that opens underneath the Web site that was clicked on and is not apparent until closing browser windows.

surveillance primarily the journalism function of mass communication, which provides information about the processes, issues, events, and other developments in society.

synchronous media media that take place in real time, such as live television or radio and that require the audience to be present when the media is being broadcast or performed.

T

Telecommunications Act of 1996 the first major overhaul of regulations regarding the telecommunications industry since 1934, this legislation was designed to open the telecommunications field to greater competition by deregulating many aspects of the industry.

telephone newspapers a type of news delivery tried between 1876 and 1912. News stories were read on telephone lines at certain times during the day, and subscribers would call in to hear the news.

3D fax a fax that sprays fine plastic particles in layers onto a surface that allows for the construction of a three-dimensional model of the object being faxed.

thematic framing a type of media framing that depicts news events in a general context or as part of larger issues. This contrasts with episodic framing.

third-person effect of communication a media characteristic in which a media message does not affect its intended audience but does affect the behavior of a third party who takes action with the belief that the media message will affect the intended audience.

time shift the recording of an audio or video event, usually by the audience, so they can watch the event at a time other than when it was originally broadcast. Setting a VCR to record a favorite program while out is an example of time-shifting.

transmission control protocol (TCP) a method for computers to have a common language to send messages to each other over a network and communicate.

two-step flow hypothesis a theory about how mass communication affects the public that states that information flows from print or electronic media to opinion leaders and then to less active members of the population.

two-way asymmetric public relations public relations conducted within a framework of two-way information flow between an organization and the public, but with the flow dominated by the organization.

two-way symmetric public relations a model of public relations that emphasizes a system of managing relationships between organizations and their many publics, of which communication through the mass media is one tool to manage the relationship.

U

user interface the junction between a medium of communication and the people who use it.

uses and gratifications research a branch of research on media effects that looks at why people use certain types and looks at what people do with media rather than what media do to them.

V

validity in experimental terms, the measure of how well the results or conclusions can be inferred from the data.

V-chip a computer device that enables parents or any other viewers to program their TV sets to block access to programs containing violent and sexual content based on the program rating.

viral marketing spreading news and information about media content through word-of-mouth, usually via online discussion groups, chats, and e-mails, without utilizing traditional advertising and marketing methods.

voice-over an unseen announcer or narrator talking while other activity takes place either on radio or while a scene is being shown on television.

W

watermark a symbol or mark embedded in a photograph that identifies who owns the copyright for that photograph. With digital media, any piece of content can be watermarked and the watermark, itself digital, can be completely invisible.

weblog (or blog) a type of Web site in which a person posts regular journal or diary entries; the posts are arranged chronologically.

Wells, Ida B. a female African American journalist in the latter 19th century who wrote and fought against racism and the lynching of blacks.

wet collodion process a type of photography invented in 1851 that used glass plates covered in a syrupy chemical called collodion and dipped in silver nitrate solution to make them light sensitive.

Woods, Granville T. inventor of railway telegraphy in 1887, a type of wireless communication that allowed moving trains to communicate with each other and with stations, greatly reducing the number of railway collisions.

Y

yellow journalism a style of journalism practiced especially by publishers Joseph Pulitzer and William Randolph Hearst during the late 1890s in which stories were sensationalized and often partly or wholly made up in order to be more dramatic.

Z

Zenger, John Peter a New York printer and journalist who published *New York Weekly Journal,* a political journal opposed to the colonial governor, William Cosby. He was acquitted by a jury of libel in August 1735, establishing an important precedent in the American colonies for the principle of press freedom.

Zworykin, Vladimir inventor of an improved cathode ray tube he called the "iconoscope" that is the basis for the CRTs still used today in television sets and many computer monitors. He is considered one of the fathers of electronic television.

Index

Photo Credits

Chapter 1: pages 2 and 4, © Newsmakers/Getty Images; page 5, AP/Wide World Photos; page 7, © Bonnie Kamin/PhotoEdit; page 8, Courtesy of Lucent Technologies; page 13 (top), © Abbas/Magnum Photos; page 12, Courtesy of James Carey; page 13 (right), © KJ Historical/CORBIS; page 14 (top), © Jeff Greenberg/PhotoEdit; page 14 (bottom), Everett Collection; page 17, AP/Wide World Photos; page 20, Courtesy of 3D Systems Corporation; page 22, Everett Collection; page 27, AP/Wide World Photos; page 28, AP/Wide World Photos; page 30, © Tony Hopewell/Getty Images/Taxi; page 32, © Newsmakers/Getty Images.

Chapter 2: pages 32 and 34, © Time Inc./Timepix; page 38, © Chuck Savage/CORBIS; page 41, Everett Collection; page 42, © AFP/CORBIS; page 43, Everett Collection; page 48, Everett Collection; page 50, AP/Wide World Photos; page 56, © Reuters NewMedia/CORBIS; page 59, © Bettmann/CORBIS; page 61, © Flip Schulke/CORBIS; page 62, © Time Inc./Timepix.

Chapter 3: pages 64 and 66, Courtesy of M. J. Rose; page 69, ©Newsmakers/Getty Images; page 70, © Bettmann/CORBIS; page 71, The Pierpont Morgan Library/Art Resource, NY; page 72, North Wind Picture Archives; page 73, © Bettmann/CORBIS; page 74 , Courtesy of Marsh Technologies Inc.; page 79, © David Young-Wolff/PhotoEdit; page 80, British Library; page 82, North Wind Picture Archives; page 84, © Hulton/Archive/Getty Images; page 93 (upper right), © Bettmann/CORBIS; page 93 (bottom), North Wind Picture Archives; page 94 (left), Courtesy of EInk Corporation; page 98, AP/Wide World Photos; page 100, Courtesy of M. J. Rose.

Chapter 4: pages 102 and 104, Lucasfilms/Everett Collection; page 106, © James Estrin/Reuters/TimePixl; page 107, Library of Congress; page 108, © CORBIS; page 109, Library of Congress; page 110, © Carter Kevin/CORBIS Sygma; page 111, © Hulton/Archive/Getty Images; page 112, Courtesy of National Oceanographic and Atmosphere Administration; page 113, © Hulton/Archive/Getty Images; page 114, Everett Collection; page 115, Rue des Archives/Everett Collection; page 117, Everett Collection; page 118, Everett Collection; page 122, © Bettmann/CORBIS; page 125, Everett Collection; page 126, Everett Collection; page 127, Everett Collection; page 128, AP/Wide World Photos; page 131, Courtesy of Artisan Entertainment; page 134, Lucasfilms/Everett Collection.

Chapter 5: pages 136 and 138, © CORBIS Sygma; page 140, © Bettmann/CORBIS; page 141 (top) © Bettmann/CORBIS; page 141 (bottom) © Blank Archives/Getty Images; page 146, © Keith Dannemiller/CORBIS Saba; page 149, Everett Collection; page 151, AP/Wide World Photos; page 152, © Bettmann/CORBIS; page 153, © Bettmann/CORBIS; page 155, AP/Wide World Photos; page 159, Courtesy of XM Satellite Radio Inc.; page 161, © Peter Cade/Getty Images/Stone; page 162 (left), © Getty Images; page 162 (top), © Hulton-Deutsch Collection/CORBIS; page 163, © Bettmann/CORBIS; page 164, © Reuters NewMedia Inc./CORBIS; page 173, © Mark Richards/PhotoEdit; page 174, © CORBIS Sygma.

Chapter 6: pages 176 and 178, Copyright Association frères Lumière; page 182, © Getty Images; page 183, AP/Wide World Photos; page 184, Courtesy of the authors; page 186, AP/Wide World Photos; page 187, Courtesy of Mosaic; page 189, © Scott Goodwin Photography; page 192, AP/ Wide World Photos; page 193, Courtesy www.GameZone.com; page 195, AP/Wide World Photos; page 197, Courtesy of Salon.com. Reprinted with Permission; page 199 (top), Courtesy of Project Gutenberg; page 199 (bottom), © Getty Images; page 202, Copyright © 1995–2002 RealNetworks, Inc. All rights reserved. RealNetworks, Real.com, RealAudio, RealVideo, RealSystem, RealPlayer, RealJukebox and RealMedia are trademarks of registered tradmarks of RealNetworks, Inc.; page 205, © Mitch Wojnarowicz/The Image Works; page 216, Copyright Association frères Lumière.

Chapter 7: pages 218 and 220, © Archivo Iconografico, S.A./CORBIS; page 222, © Hulton/Archive/Getty Images; page 223, © Sandro Vannini/CORBIS; page 224, Courtesy of Seagate Technology LLC; page 227, © Austrian Archives/CORBIS; page 228 (top), Everett Collection; page 228 (bottom), © Bettmann/CORBIS; page 230, AP/Wide World Photos; page 231, AP/Wide World Photos; page 232, AP/Wide World Photos; page 234, AP/Wide World Photos; page 236, AP/Wide World Photos; page 238, © Jim West/The Image Works; page 244, © Archivo Iconografico, S.A./CORBIS.

Chapter 8: page 246, Courtesy of Urban Data Solutions; page 249, © Tannen Maury/The Image Works; page 251, © Jacksonville Journal-Courier/The Image Works; page 252 (top), © Michael Newman/PhotoEdit; page 252 (bottom), © Hot Ideas/Index Stock; page 255, AP/Wide World Photos; page 257, Everett Collection; page 259, Star Tree Visualization by Inxight Software, Inc.; page 264, AP/Wide World Photos; page 265, © David Young-Wolff/PhotoEdit; page 266, Everett Collection; page 272, © 1993 Milana Huang, Electronic Visualization Laboratory, University of Illinois at Chicago; page 274, Courtesy of Urban Data Solutions.

Chapter 9: pages 276, 278, © Scott Goodwin Photography; page 280, © Jack Kurtz/The Image Works; page 281, © George DeSota/Newmakers/Getty Images; page 285, © Hulton/Archives/Getty Images; page 286, © Bettmann/CORBIS; page 287, © Bettmann/CORBIS; page 288, © Billy Houstace/Getty Images/Stone; page 290, © Lou Dematteis/The Image Works; page 294, Everett Collection; page 296, Courtesy of Salon.com. Reprinted with Permission; page 297, Courtesy of Dave Winer/Scripting News; page 305, © Scott Goodwin Photography.

Chapter 10: pages 306, 308, © Mark Ludak/The Image Works; page 310, © Scott Goodwin Photography; page 311, © Hulton/Archive Getty Images; page 313, © Bettmann/CORBIS; page 314, © Bettmann/CORBIS; page 315, © Bettmann/CORBIS; page 319, © Getty Images; page 321, © Jeff Greenberg/PhotoEdit; page 324, © Reuters NewMedia Inc./CORBIS; page 327, © Scott Goodwin Photography; page 329, Courtesy of Google; page 331, City of Phoenix General Plan reprinted from ESRI Map Book, Volume 16, and used herein with permission. Copyright © 2001 ESRI. All rights reserved; page 333, Courtesy of NASA Jet Propulsion Laboratory; page 334, Courtesy Steven Feiner, Tobias Höllerer, Columbia University; page 337, AP/Wide World Photos; page 341, Courtesy of NABJ; page 342, © Mark Ludak/The Image Works.

Chapter 11: pages 344 and 346, © Getty Images; page 348, © Getty Images; page 352, The Everett Collection; page 353, The Everett Collection; page 356, The Everett Collection; page 358, AP/Wide World Photos; page 360, AP/Wide World Photos; page 362, The Everett Collection; page 363, The Everett Collection; page 365, EverQuest is a registered trademark of Sony Computer Entertainment America, Inc. in the U.S. and/or other countries. © 1999–2002 Sony Computer Entertainment America, Inc. All rights reserved; page 369, AP/Wide World Photos; page 371, © Reuters NewMedia Inc./CORBIS; page 373, © Bettmann/CORBIS; page 374, The Everett Collection; page 375, The Everett Collection; page 376, © Getty Images.

Chapter 12: pages 378 and 380, © Scott Goodwin Photography; page 378 (inset), © Michael Newman/PhotoEdit; page382 (top), © Rommel Pecson/The Image Works; page 382 (bottom), © Felicia Martinez/PhotoEdit; page 384, © Michelle Bridwell/PhotoEdit; page 386 (top), Collection of The New-York Historical Society, New York City; page 386 (bottom), © Getty Images; page 389, © Paul Conklin/PhotoEdit; page 390, AP/Wide World Photos; page 390 (inset), AFP Photo; page 391, Courtesy of Pepsi Co.; page 392, © Leslie Hugh Stone/The Image Works; page 396, Courtesy of Tony Schwartz; page 399, Reprinted by permission of The Wall Street Journal, © 2002 Dow Jones & Company, Inc. All Rights Reserved Worldwide; Ad, Copyright 2002 GM Corp. All rights reserved; page 400, © David Young-Wolff/PhotoEdit; page 401, AP/Wide World Photos; page 402, © Michael Newman/PhotoEdit; page 404, © Getty Images; page 406 (left), Photo courtesy of The Museum of Public Relations (www.prmuseum.com); page 406 (right), © Bettmann/CORBIS; page 407, AP/Wide World Photos; page 409, Snow Summit Mountain Resort; page 410, © Rachel Epstein/PhotoEdit; page 413, AP/Wide World Photos; page 415, © Scott Goodwin Photography.

Chapter 13: pages 416 and 418, © Robert E. Daemmrich/Getty Images; page 420, © Spencer Grant/PhotoEdit; page 421, © TimePix; page 423, © Archivo Iconografico, S.A./CORBIS; page 424, The Everett Collection; page 425, The Everett Collection; page 427, AP/Wide World Photos; page 428, TM and Copyright © 2000 20th Century Fox Television. All rights reserved. Courtesy: Everett Collection; page 429, © Bettmann/CORBIS; page 431, TM and Copyright © 2001 20th Century Fox Television. All rights reserved. Courtesy: Everett Collection; page 432, The Everett Collection; page 434, AP/Wide World Photos; page 435, The Everett Collection; page 438, The Everett Collection; page 439, © Michael Siluk/The Image Works; page 440, Copyright © 1995–2002 RealNetworks, Inc. All rights reserved. RealNetworks, Real.com, RealAudio, RealVideo, RealSystem, RealPlayer, RealJukebox and RealMedia are trademarks of registered tradmarks of RealNetworks, Inc.; page 441, © Rommel Pecson/The Image Works; page 443, wbur.org is a production of WBUR, Boston's NPR News Station; page 445, Screen shot reprinted by permission from Microsoft Corporation; page 446, © David Young Wolff/PhotoEdit; page 448, © Jon Riley/Index Stock; page 449, © Scott Goodwin Photography; page 450, © Robert E. Daemmrich/Getty Images.

Chapter 14: pages 452 and 456, © Rob Crandall/The Image Works; page 455, © Hulton/Archive/Getty Images; page 457, AP/Wide World Photos; page 458, © Minnesota Historical Society/CORBIS; page 460, AP/Wide World Photos; page 462, © Monika Graff/The Image Works; page 463, AP/Wide World Photos; page 466, © Frank Siteman/PhotoEdit; page 471, The Everett Collection; page 472, AP/Wide World Photos; page 473, © David Young-Wolff/PhotoEdit; page 475, © CORBIS; page 483, Dorling Kindersley Media Library; page 484, © Rob Crandall/ The Image Works.

Chapter 15: pages 486 and 488, AP/Wide World Photos; page 490, © Philadephia Daily News/The Image Works; page 492, © Getty Images; page 493, AP/Wide World Photos; page 495 (left), AP/Wide World Photos; page 495 (right), AP/Wide World Photos; page 497, Courtesy of Annenberg/CPB; page 502, © Hulton/Archive/Getty Images; page 503, © Tannen Maury/The Image Works; page 504, The Advertising Archive Ltd./ © SEPS: Curtis Publishing, Indianapolis, IN All rights reserved; page 505, Courtesy of Howard R. Baer; page 507, © Getty Images; page 508, AP/Wide World Photos.

Chapter 16: pages 510 and 512, © Getty Images; page 514, Library of Congress; page 517, AP/Wide World Photos; page 519, © Cristiano Laruffa/Getty Images; page 520, AFP Photo/Mauricio LIMA; page 523, AP/Wide World Photos; page 527, © Topham/The Image Works; page 528, © Getty Images; page 532, AP/Wide World Photos; page 533, © Scott Goodwin Photography; page 534, AFP Photo; page 537, AP/Wide World Photos; page 540, © Getty Images.